New York

timeoutnewyork.com

Time Out Guides Ltd
Universal House
251 Tottenham Court Road
London W1T 7AB
United Kingdom
Tel: +44 (0)20 7813 3000
Fax: +44 (0)20 7813 6001
Email: guides@timeout.com
www.timeout.com

Published by Time Out Guides Ltd, a wholly owned subsidiary of Time Out Group Ltd.
Time Out and the Time Out logo are trademarks of Time Out Group Ltd.

© Time Out Group Ltd 2013
Previous editions 1990, 1992, 1994, 1996, 1997, 1998, 1999, 2000, 2001, 2002, 2003, 2004, 2005, 2006, 2007, 2008, 2009, 2010, 2011, 2012.

10 9 8 7 6 5 4 3 2 1

This edition first published in Great Britain in 2013 by Ebury Publishing.
A Random House Group Company
20 Vauxhall Bridge Road, London SW1V 2SA

Random House Australia Pty Ltd 20 Alfred Street, Milsons Point, Sydney, New South Wales 2061, Australia

Random House New Zealand Ltd 18 Poland Road, Glenfield, Auckland 10, New Zealand

Random House South Africa (Pty) Ltd Isle of Houghton, Corner Boundary Road & Carse O'Gowrie, Houghton 2198, South Africa

Random House UK Limited Reg. No. 954009

Distributed in the US and Latin America by Publishers Group West (1-510-809-3700)
Distributed in Canada by Publishers Group Canada (1-800-747-8147)

For further distribution details, see www.timeout.com.

ISBN: 978-1-84670-371-3

A CIP catalogue record for this book is available from the British Library.

Printed and bound in Great Britain by Butler Tanner & Dennis, Frome, Somerset.

The Random House Group Limited supports the Forest Stewardship Council® (FSC®), the leading international forest-certification organisation. Our books carrying the FSC label are printed on FSC®-certified paper. FSC is the only forest-certification scheme supported by the leading environmental organisations, including Greenpeace. Our paper procurement policy can be found at www.randomhouse.co.uk/environment

Time Out carbon-offsets its flights with Trees for Cities (www.treesforcities.org).

Contents

Arts & Entertainment 250

Escapes & Excursions 336

In Context 348

Essential Information 370

Maps 396

Introduction

In late October 2012, attention was drawn to the precarious nature of the metropolis's topography when superstorm Sandy unleashed a tidal surge that debilitated lower Manhattan and parts of Brooklyn, Staten Island and Queens. The devastation brought home the extraordinary fact that beneath its carapace of concrete, steel and glass, a slender island, less than 14 miles long and little more than two miles wide, forms the core of America's quintessential big city.

Perhaps it's the awareness of Manhattan's sprawl-resistant nature, bordered as it is by water, that spurs its constant reinvention, as neighbourhoods are 'discovered' and developed, and the city soars ever higher. New York's tallest building, 1 World Trade Center, due to be completed in early 2014, should have reached full height by the time you read this. One of the most dramatic recent changes to the urban scene is the still-evolving World Trade Center site; Ground Zero has been transformed from a gaping hole to a pleasant, tree-shaded plaza with two monumental memorial waterfalls. In fact, there are more quiet spots than ever to stop and take a breather from Gotham's ceaseless activity: new parks have blossomed in Chelsea (the latest phase of the still-evolving High Line; see p82), Brooklyn (see p115) and downtown along the East River (see p54).

Of course, it's not only the cityscape that is in constant flux. Each week, the editors of *Time Out New York* magazine review countless new shows and exhibitions and cover dozens of restaurant, bar and shop openings. In this guide, we've selected the best of what's new while reserving space for the essential classics. Many things in NYC remain reassuringly constant. The leafy, film-set-perfect streets of the West Village retain their quaint character and old-school institutions like the Grand Central Oyster Bar & Restaurant, celebrating its centennial this year, are doing a roaring trade. The iconic panoramas – lower Manhattan's vast harbour views, midtown's skyscraper canyons, the lurid electronic spectacle of Times Square – are as sweeping and thrilling as ever.

As NYC becomes more culturally unified, with major arts venues such as Brooklyn's new Barclays Center opening in the outer boroughs, the city is defying its island origins. These days, Manhattanites – and visitors – think nothing of crossing the river to have dinner and catch a gig in Brooklyn, or see an exhibition and sip cocktails in Queens.

Lisa Ritchie, Editor

About the Guide

GETTING AROUND

The back of the book contains street maps of New York City, as well as a Manhattan bus map and a citywide subway map. The maps start on page 396; on them are marked the locations of hotels (❶), restaurants and cafés (❶), and pubs and bars (❶). The majority of businesses listed in this guide are located in the areas we've mapped; the grid-square references in the listings refer to these maps.

THE ESSENTIALS

For practical information, including visas, disabled access, emergency numbers, lost property, useful websites and local transport, please see the Essential Information section. It begins on page 370.

THE LISTINGS

Addresses, phone numbers, websites, transport information, hours and prices are all included in our listings, as are selected other facilities. All were checked and correct at press time. However, business owners can alter their arrangements at any time, and fluctuating economic conditions can cause prices to change rapidly.

The very best venues in the city, the must-sees and must-dos in every category, have been marked with a red star (★). In the Sights chapters, we've also marked venues with free admission with a FREE symbol.

PHONE NUMBERS

New York has a number of different area codes. Manhattan is covered by 212 and 646, while Brooklyn, Queens, the Bronx and Staten Island are served by 718 and 347. Even if you're dialling from within the area you're calling, you'll need to use the area code, always preceded by 1.

From outside the US, dial your country's international access code (00 from the UK) or a plus symbol, followed by the number as listed in the guide; here, the initial '1' serves as the US country code. So, to reach the Metropolitan Museum of Art, dial +1-212 535 7710. For more on phones, *see p381*.

FEEDBACK

We welcome feedback on this guide, both on the venues we've included and on any other locations that you'd like to see featured in future editions. Please email us at guides@timeout.com.

Time Out Guides

Founded in 1968, Time Out has grown from humble beginnings into the leading resource for anyone wanting to know what's happening in the world's greatest cities. Alongside our influential weeklies in London, New York, Chicago and Dubai, we publish more than 20 magazines in cities as varied as Beijing and Beirut; a range of travel books, with the City Guides now joined by the pocket-sized Shortlist series; and an information-packed website. The company remains proudly independent, still owned by Tony Elliott four decades after he launched *Time Out London*.

Written by local experts and illustrated with original photography, our books also retain their independence. No business has been featured because it has advertised, and all restaurants and bars are visited and reviewed anonymously.

ABOUT THE EDITOR

Manhattan-born **Lisa Ritchie** lived in London for 20 years before returning to her native city. Now Travel & Guides Editor at *Time Out New York*, she has also written for publications including London's *Evening Standard* and *The Times*.

A full list of the book's contributors can be found on page 13.

NATIONAL SEPTEMBER 11 MEMORIAL & MUSEUM

Pay your respects at the 9/11 Memorial (see p50), where two monumental waterfalls have been created in the voids left by the Twin Towers; nearby is the ferry to the Statue of Liberty (see p49).

THE HIGH LINE

The elevated railway line-turned-promenade (see p82) has revitalised a downtown-to-midtown stretch of the far West Side. Stroll from the boutiques of the Meatpacking District through Chelsea's gallery enclave, taking in river and skyline views.

LOWER EAST SIDE

Some of the city's hottest bars, boutiques and galleries have moved into the tenement buildings of the erstwhile immigrant slum (see p63). You can see how 19th-century arrivals lived in the Lower East Side Tenement Museum.

Hudson River

ELEVENTH AVE
WEST SIDE HWY
TENT
NI
ELEVENTH AVE
W 23RD ST
W 14TH ST
EIGHTH AVE
SEVENTH AVE
SIXTH AVE
FIFTH AVE
BROADWAY
PARK AVE SOUTH
LEXINGTON AVE
THIRD AVE
SECOND AVE
FIRST AVE
E 23RD ST
Madison Square
Madison Square Park
GRAMERCY PARK
Gramercy Park
E HOUSTON ST
Tompkins Square
EAST VILLAGE
St Mark's Church in-the-Bowery
New York University
Washington Square
Grace Church
LAFAYETTE
FOURTH AVE
THE BOWERY
LOWER EAST SIDE
E BROADWAY
WILLIAMSBURG BRIDGE
East River Park
HUDSON ST
AVE SOUTH
CHELSEA
Laura Pantaleoni Garden
Penn Station
Penn Plaza Pavilion
Madison Square Garden

Ninth Avenue Post Office
Flatiron Building

CHURCH ST
CENTRE ST
BROADWAY
WALL ST
FRANKLIN D ROOSEVELT DR
PARK ROW
VESEY ST
World Financial Center
World Trade Center
Museum of Jewish Heritage
Battery Park
BATTERY PARK CITY
WEST ST
Trinity Church
St Paul's Church
NY Stock Exchange
City Hall
Coenties Slip
WHITEHALL ST
Ferry to Statue of Liberty
Staten Island Ferry Terminal

BROOKLYN BRIDGE
MANHATTAN BRIDGE
LOWER EAST SIDE

© Copyright Time Out Group 2013

0   0.5 m
0   1 km

FIFTH AVENUE

March down this major artery to midtown (see p86) for some of the city's most iconic attractions, including the Empire State Building and MoMA.

CENTRAL PARK

All of New York congregates in this bucolic 843-acre green haven (see p92), with its picturesque lake and expansive lawns. In summer, the park hosts a slate of free performances and events.

MUSEUM MILE

Dip into the massive Metropolitan Museum of Art for its globe- and period-spanning collection, but don't neglect gems such as the Frick Collection and the Guggenheim on this world-class cultural strip (see p95).

Time Out New York

Editorial
Editor Lisa Ritchie
Listings Editor Julien Sauvalle
Proofreader Ros Sales
Indexer Holly Pick

Editorial Director Sarah Guy
Management Accountant Margaret Wright

Design
Senior Designer Kei Ishimaru
Designer Darryl Bell
Group Commercial Senior Designer Jason Tansley

Picture Desk
Picture Editor Jael Marschner
Picture Researcher Ben Rowe
Freelance Picture Researcher Isidora O'Neill

Advertising
Sales Director St John Betteridge
Advertising Sales Ari Ben, Melissa Keller, Dan Kenefick
Christine Legname, Jessica Rohls, Christy Stewart,
Christiana Zafiriadis

Marketing
Senior Publishing Brand Manager Luthfa Begum
Head of Circulation Dan Collins

Production
Group Production Manager Brendan McKeown
Production Controller Katie Mulhern-Bhudia

Time Out Group
Chairman & Founder Tony Elliott
Chief Executive Officer Aksel Van der Wal
Editor-in-Chief Tim Arthur
UK Chief Commercial Officer David Pepper
Time Out International Ltd MD Cathy Runciman
Group IT Director Simon Chappell
Group Marketing Director Carolyn Sims

Contributors
Introduction Lisa Ritchie. **New York Today** Howard Halle. **Gotham's Greatest Hits** Steve Smith and contributors to *Time Out New York* magazine. **Diary** Lisa Ritchie, Julien Sauvalle and contributors to *Time Out New York* magazine. **Tour New York** Anne P Quigley, Julien Sauvalle (*Running Start* Erin Clements). **Downtown** Lisa Ritchie (*Walk* Carl Williott; *Profile: Statue of Liberty, Last Orders* Richard Koss; *The People's Museum* Rebecca Fishbein). **Midtown** Lisa Ritchie (*Walk* Carl Williott). **Uptown** Lisa Ritchie (*Profile: Metropolitan Museum of Art*, Richard Koss; *Literary NYC* Drew Toal). **Brooklyn** Lee Magill (*Walk* Mike Olsen; *Profile: Brooklyn Bridge* Rebecca Dalzell). **Queens** Lee Magill. **The Bronx** Lee Magill. **Staten Island** Lee Magill. **Restaurants & Cafés** Gabriella Gershenson and contributors to *Time Out New York* magazine. **Bars** contributors to *Time Out New York* magazine (*Cocktail Chronicles* Mari Uyehara). **Shops & Services** Lisa Ritchie and contributors to *Time Out New York* magazine (Gallery-Hopping Guide Howard Halle). **Hotels** Lisa Ritchie. **Children** Lee Magill. **Film & TV** Joshua Rothkopf (*Dinner at the Movies* Chris Schonberger). **Gay & Lesbian** Ethan LaCroix. **Performing Arts** Adam Feldman, Gia Kourlas, Matthew Love, Steve Smith. **Nightlife** Adam Feldman, Sophie Harris, Matthew Love, Hank Shteamer, Bruce Tantum. **Sports & Fitness** Amanda Angel (*Life in the Gutter* Drew Toal). **Escapes & Excursions** Lisa Ritchie, Jennifer M. Wood and contributors to *Time Out New York* magazine. **History** Richard Koss, Kathleen Squires. **Architecture** Eric P Nash. **Essential Information** Lisa Ritchie, Julien Sauvalle.

Maps john@jsgraphics.co.uk, except pages 413-416, used by kind permission of the Metropolitan Transit Authority.

In Focus

New York Today

*In the aftermath of the superstorm,
development surges forward.*

TEXT: HOWARD HALLE

From 9/11 and the 2003 blackout to the Wall Street meltdown of 2008 and Hurricane Irene in 2011, Gotham has endured one catastrophe after another over the past dozen years. But none seemed quite as biblical as the mega-storm named Sandy, which hit New York just before Halloween in 2012. A meteorological convergence of a tropical hurricane, a low-pressure system over the mid-Atlantic states and a blast of Arctic air from Canada, Sandy came ashore with sustained winds of 80 miles per hour. The result: a disaster without modern precedent, one that may even have affected the outcome of the 2012 Presidential race.

The impact was felt from Washington, DC, to Massachusetts, but New York and New Jersey sat in the storm's bullseye, suffering a total of 60 deaths and $71 billion in damage. Within the five boroughs, Sandy provided the added spectacle of Mother Nature bringing the greatest metropolis on earth to its knees. The storm struck at the heart of New York's economic and cultural vitality, and threw the city's class divisions into sharp relief.

APOCALYPSE NOW

Sandy pushed a surge of water across New York Harbor and into the Hudson and East Rivers. New York's vast system of subway tunnels was inundated, as was the Brooklyn Battery Tunnel, a major artery into the city. The 9/11 Memorial, as well as parts of Battery Park City, Tribeca and Chelsea, were flooded; likewise Dumbo and Red Hook in Brooklyn. In the outer boroughs, waves smashed Staten Island, Coney Island, Brooklyn, and the Rockaways in Queens. In Breezy Point, Queens, a fire driven by the winds laid waste to 100 homes. Thousands across the city were left homeless. Hundreds of thousands more lost electricity when Sandy tore into the Consolidated Edison substation on 14th Street near FDR Drive, trapping 19 workers, and setting off an explosion that plunged Manhattan below 42nd Street into darkness. Sardonic residents came up with a new acronym for their neighborhood, SoPo: South of Power.

The city lay paralysed, with the stock market and area airports closed. All 40 of Broadway's theatres were shuttered, generating a loss of $6 million dollars in ticket sales compared to the previous week. In Chelsea, where major galleries were readying their November shows, the waters seeped in to ruin floors, freshly painted walls and works of art unpacked and waiting to be hung; damage was estimated to be in the $40 million range. One of the most iconic pieces of footage of the storm – a video that went viral on the Web – showed the tide in Brooklyn Bridge Park swirling around Jane's Carousel, the merry-go-round ensconced in a jewel-box pavilion designed by French starchitect, Jean Nouvel, which debuted in a revamped section of the park in autumn 2011. Remarkably, the restored vintage amusement-park ride needed only minor repairs. Businesses were hard hit, especially the city's restaurants, including such iconic Coney Island destinations as Nathan's hot dogs and Totonno's pizzeria (opened by the man who helped to bring the pizza to America). Both landmarks remained closed for months following Sandy, highlighting an unfortunate truism about the storm's aftermath: the speed with which services were restored was directly proportional to a neighbourhood's wealth. While the lights came back on within days in places like the Financial District, parts of Queens and Staten Island remained without power and heat for more than a month. Still, the subway reopened within a week, and local politicians comported themselves well.

RISING TIDES, FALLING CRIME

Both New York City Mayor Michael Bloomberg and New Jersey Governor Chris Christie responded to the crisis with alacrity, as did President Obama,

IN FOCUS

Far Rockaway, Queens, after Sandy.

whose performance during the emergency in the days leading up to the 2012 election was credited with sealing his victory over Republican candidate Mitt Romney. That contest was largely fought over the growing gap between the wealthy and everyone else, a disparity symbolised in some quarters by One57, the condominium tower soaring 1,000 feet above Central Park on West 57th Street. New York's tallest residence to date, One57 has been dubbed 'the billionaires boy's club', thanks to apartments priced in the $50-$100 million dollar range. But even there, Sandy prevailed, snapping the arm of a massive construction crane, which dangled dangerously over the traffic 90 storeys below. Another echo of the battle over social justice was the re-emergence of Occupy Wall Street, as a volunteer effort to help with the recovery effort out in shattered Rockaway Beach.

But one thing Sandy heralded went nearly unmentioned during the campaign: global warming. Sandy was the second major storm to strike New York in just over a year, leading political leaders like New York Governor Andrew Cuomo to start seriously talking about climate change. Indeed, research suggests that by the end of the century, rising sea levels could make the five boroughs start to resemble Venice, Italy, if not the legendary city of Atlantis. City Council President Christine Quinn has proposed a $16 billion storm surge barrier as part of a possible plan to safeguard the city. And there have been any number of inventive proposals to stem the tides, from a gated seawall spanning the Verazzano narrows in New York Harbor, to huge inflatable bladders that could plug the entrances to subway tunnels in the event of a storm.

Nevertheless, catastrophe or no, New York continued along the same path of gentrification it's been on for more than a decade, growing ever wealthier – and safer. Gotham's murder rate is on target to hit its lowest point since 1960. And on 29 November, 2012, the city recorded its first day without a single violent crime in recent memory. The truth is, it would probably take a thermonuclear device to stop New York. Much as it did after 9/11, Gotham picked itself up and dusted itself off following Sandy. A lot had been going on before the storm, creating a momentum of its own.

BATTLE OF THE BOROUGHS

Brooklyn maintained its march to evolve into a distinct urban entity, separate from the rest of New York (it actually was an independent city before 1898, when it

New York City Mayor Michael Bloomberg.

High Line

was consolidated as one of the five boroughs of New York City). The Fulton Mall, a strip of fast-food joints, discount clothing stores and purveyors of gold-plated bling, is slowly but surely being transformed into a shopping mecca meant to appeal to more upscale consumers. Shake Shack, the nouveau-burger chain created by restaurateur Danny Meyer, opened a location there in 2011. Nearby, the construction of the City Point mega-development, which will combine retail with residences, proceeds apace, with fashion tenants like Century 21 and Armani AX signing up for space. Elsewhere in the Borough of Kings, the long-delayed, controversy-dogged Atlantic Yards project in downtown Brooklyn came closer to fruition with the opening of the Barclays Center arena.

The brainchild of Cleveland, Ohio-based developer Bruce Ratner, Atlantic Yards is surely the most ambitious undertaking of its kind in the city since the creation of Rockefeller Center. After years of lawsuits, court challenges and near collapse of financing due to the credit crunch, the major sports and entertainment venue, which resembles a rusty flying saucer grounded at the intersection of Flatbush and Atlantic Avenues, was inaugurated with a concert by hip-hop mega-star Jay-Z, who is also an investor in the Brooklyn (formerly New Jersey) Nets basketball team that calls the Barclays Center home. The new arena got another boost when it was announced that the New York

Islanders hockey team would also begin playing there in 2015. Meanwhile, work began on the first of 15 high-rise towers scheduled for the area. Called B2, the tower measures 32 storeys and will be built using an innovative modular construction technique in which whole units will be manufactured off-site, then trucked in and assembled Lego-style. The design is the work of SHoP Architects, who also created the Barclay's Center. Neighbours of Atlantic Yards, of course, have complained about traffic, noise and drunken Nets supporters, but that hasn't stopped local real estate values from jumping, or new restaurants from opening to take advantage of the influx of fans.

WEST SIDE STOREYS

Speaking of irate neighbours, the Greenwich Village Society for Historic Preservation has been railing against another controversial development: a proposed high-rise addition to the Chelsea Market, located along the High Line – the freight train track turned public park running along Manhattan's far West Side – in the fashionable Meatpacking District. Despite arguments that the project would have been out of scale for the neighborhood, the City Council issued its approval to proceed.

Still, you have to wonder just what 'out of scale' means in a part of town in which the main attraction, the aforementioned High Line, draws crowds of tourists that rival those in Times Square. The days

GET THE LATEST
ISSUE OF TIME OUT

DELIVERED RIGHT
TO YOUR IPAD

Download it now in Newsstand

when the far West Side was a forlorn strip populated by tranny hookers, cab company garages and commuters stuck in traffic on their way to the Lincoln Tunnel are long gone. And the numbers of people living there or just traipsing through will only skyrocket when the final leg of the High Line above West 30th Street is completed, connecting Chelsea and vicinity to yet another mega-development under way, Hudson Yards, between Tenth Avenue and the Hudson River. Late in 2012, Mayor Bloomberg presided over groundbreaking for the project's first phase – a pair of angular towers leaning away from one another at a rakish tilt. Designed by Kohn Pedersen Fox Associates, the taller of the two structures will be higher than the Empire State building, and will feature an observation deck jutting out 1,100 feet above street level.

Now in his last term, Bloomberg has been busy. Although the mayor barely eked out re-election after temporarily changing the city charter's two-term limit for political office, the autocratic billionaire – who outlawed smoking not only in indoor public spaces but in parks and plazas – charged ahead with another of his imperious nanny-state decrees: a ban on the sale of sugared soft drinks in cups larger than 16 ounces. The move was ostensibly prompted by the epidemic of obesity among area teenagers, and it's certainly the case that 'supersizing' sodas has contributed to a nationwide problem. Still, the ban struck New Yorkers as nit-picky in the extreme, contributing to an ever-growing sense of Bloomberg exhaustion that will hopefully dissuade the mayor from the temptation to amend the city charter once again and run for a fourth term.

NYC myths busted

Think you know New York? We dispell some common misconceptions.

IN FOCUS

The myth: New Yorkers don't care about each other.
Busted: Would heartless people jump onto the subway tracks to save one another? Construction worker Wesley Autrey is perhaps the most famous subway hero: in 2007, he helped protect the life of a young man who fell on to the tracks at the 137th Street-City College station. And Gothamites don't just haul people out of harm's way – in 2011, Joseph Lozito disarmed a knife attacker on the uptown 3 train between 34th and 42nd Streets.

The myth: Only millionaires can (or do) live in Manhattan.
Busted: The one-percenters may occupy Park Avenue, but there are plenty of island neighbourhoods with down-to-earth rents: the cost of a studio in Harlem hovers around $1,400 per month, although it's twice that in Soho. Middle-classers abound in Washington Heights, where the median annual income is $31,000,

and the median yearly take-home pay for Lower East Side and Chinatown residents is $35,600.

The myth: NYC is a hotbed of crime.
Busted: We've got a lower per capita murder rate (5.6 per cent) than the not-so-scary Charlotte, North Carolina (7.5 per cent) – and that's half of what it is in Indianapolis. We have about as many murders as Chicago, and that city has less than half New York's population.

The myth: New Yorkers are a rude and generally unpleasant bunch.
Busted: We're not wildly cheerful – a 2009 Centers for Disease Control and Prevention study ranked New York State dead last in happiness levels – but there are hints of whimsy and glee among the city's eight million residents. Comedian Mark Malkoff got strangers to piggyback or carry him across Manhattan on a cold December day in 2009, just to prove that his fellow denizens weren't scrooges.

Gotham's Greatest Hits

Load up your playlist with the 40 best NYC songs.

Over the years, New York City has inspired odes to its majesty and danger, its punk vitality and all-embracing spirit. Love it or hate it, if you're a musician based here, sooner or later you're going to write about it. *Time Out New York* music editors and writers sorted through all the tracks they could find that dealt with what it means to live in or visit New York to create a list of the 100 best – we've narrowed it further for this top-40 countdown.

40 Alice Cooper, 'Big Apple Dreamin' (Hippo)' (1973)

Alice Cooper had three smash records by '73, so this song's titular reverie feels more like a Broadway-style fantasy of hitting it big than a real-life dream. What does ring true is the track's pervasive sleaze: Vincent Furnier embodies one of a pair of prostitutes transfixed by the promise of sin dens that 'never close'. Few paeans better capture the city's salacious promise: 'New York is waiting/For you and me, baby/Waiting to swallow us down.'

39 The Rolling Stones, 'Shattered' (1978)

The iconic English rockers had a notorious love-hate relationship with the States, especially NYC. That ambivalence is conveyed nowhere better than in this song, which Mick Jagger reportedly wrote in the back of a yellow cab. It's a sleazy punk track about the grime that was rife in '70s New York: the trash, the greed, the sex, the despair. Shadoobie!

38 The Avett Brothers, 'I and Love and You' (2009)

There is nothing as sweet as returning to New York after a rough time. This song starts out sad: 'Load the car and write the note', but finds its release at its chorus: 'Ah Brooklyn, Brooklyn, take me in! Are you aware the shape I'm in?' Probably the best thing about New York's lived-in shabbiness is the fact that it accepts everyone, frayed edges and all.

37 Bruce Springsteen, 'The Rising' (2002)

The title track from the Boss's chart-topping 2002 LP was the anthem that New York and the nation seemed to need after 9/11. Starting from the perspective of a fireman climbing the stairs inside one of the burning towers, Springsteen waxes bardic and biblical to evoke a sense of everyman resolve and redemption.

36 The Strokes, 'New York City Cops' (2001, UK only)

Julian Casablancas's chronicle of a strange booze- and rock 'n' roll-fuelled night involves a girl named Nina, the desire to get the hell out of New York and a bunch of dumb police officers.

35 The Bee Gees, 'Stayin' Alive' (1977)

Just try to imagine John Travolta's iconic strut down the streets of Brooklyn at the start of *Saturday Night Fever* without hearing this disco classic thumping behind him. As Barry Gibb's falsetto vocals alternate between cockiness ('Got the wings of heaven on my shoes') and desperation ('Life going nowhere, somebody help me'), the song taps into both the pride and the anxiety of urban survival.

34 Tom Waits, 'Downtown Train' (1985)

Rod Stewart's cover version was a hit in 1989, but the throaty grit of Tom Waits's original cut adds layers to his portrait of romantic obsession in a world of grimy anonymity. Is the contemptuous narrator a soulful dreamer? A muttering stalker? Both? You never quite know who might be hanging his or her hopes on the subway strap next to yours.

Bob Dylan. *See p24.*

33 Bob Dylan, 'Talkin' New York' (1962)

If the bumpkinism Dylan affects on this early-career classic was a pose, it was a thoroughly convincing one. After chronicling a 'rockin, reelin', rollin'' subway ride, the wide-eyed hayseed from Hibbing, Minnesota, arrives at the clincher: a phonetic name check of the 'hood that would make him famous, 'Green-which Village'.

32 Ella Fitzgerald, 'Manhattan' (1957)

The Great American Songbook team of Richard Rodgers and Lorenz Hart had its first hit with this adorably clever 1925 ode to urban staycations, which finds gentle romance amid the bustle of city life: the 'balmy breezes' of the subway, the 'sweet pushcarts gently gliding by' on Mott Street. Ella wears the song's wit on her sleeve like a charm bracelet.

31 James Cagney, 'Give My Regards to Broadway' (1942)

A master of infectious pop Americana, George M Cohan wrote this cheerful ditty for the 1904 musical *Little Johnny Jones*. It has been stuck deep in the country's head ever since, boosted by James Cagney's memorable celluloid turn as

Cohan himself in biopic *Yankee Doodle Dandy*. A statue of Cohan has pride of place in Times Square today.

30 Bobby Womack, 'Across 110th Street' (1972)

The genius of this funk-soul marvel lies in the way it captures the Greek-tragedy-calibre pathos of ghetto life. Penned for a blaxploitation film of the same name, the song portrays Harlem as the ultimate crucible: 'You don't know what you'll do until you're put under pressure,' croons Womack, who grew up in Cleveland and clearly knows a thing or two about urban poverty. 'Across 110th Street is a hell of a tester.'

29 Jennifer Lopez, 'Jenny from the Block' (2002)

In this 2002 chart-topper, J Lo insists that even though she's now a superstar, she hasn't forgotten her Bronx roots. Since then she's racked up sales of more than 55 million albums, plus awards for acting ventures. 'Used to have a little, now I have a lot,' she insists. Whether she's still Jenny from the block is questionable; the track's catchiness is not.

28 Suzanne Vega, 'Tom's Diner' (1987)

The original version of Suzanne Vega's stark, unaccompanied melody sounded like antifolk before there was antifolk. A girl sits in a diner, reads the paper, watches customers and drifts occasionally ('I am...thinking of your voice'). Just as the song is specific but endlessly remixable (as 1991's *Tom's Album* attested), so too Tom's Restaurant, a real eaterie in Morningside Heights, could be anywhere.

27 Simon & Garfunkel, 'The Only Living Boy in New York' (1970)

After Art Garfunkel ditched a planned songwriting session for a trip to Mexico, Paul Simon penned this veiled sonic fuck-you to his partner. In it, he sings of a special kind of loneliness known to New Yorkers, who often wonder why it doesn't seem like there's anything to do in the city where the options are limitless.

Ella Fitzgerald

Simon & Garfunkel.

26 Elton John, 'Mona Lisas and Mad Hatters' (1972)

'Now I know that rose trees never grow in New York City,' sings John in the first verse of this disillusioned song from his *Honky Château* album. But despite his anger at the Big Apple's benighted upper classes – inscrutable and crazy as the figures in the title – he soldiers on with the faith that if he goes his own way, '[his] own seeds shall be sown.'

25 Stevie Wonder, 'Living for the City' (1973)

Listen past this track's fist fade to the dramatic interlude at its heart, and you'll hear the tale of a wide-eyed new arrival in NYC stung immediately as a drug mule and tossed in the can for a decade. The anger in Wonder's voice is genuine, fuelled by social injustice and by his collaborators, who forced take after take of the song just to piss him off for effect.

24 Ryan Adams, 'My Blue Manhattan' (2004)

Written long before Mandy Moore sweetened Adams's perennially salty view on life, this piano-driven song about first snowfalls and boning the wrong people is clipped, classic Adams – and totally New York.

23 Lou Reed, 'Halloween Parade' (1989)

In his inimitable offhand style, Lou Reed zooms in on the West Village's annual queer-friendly costume bonanza, delivering vivid reportage and a lament for a generation ravaged by AIDS. Reed never names the disease; instead, he catalogues the characters he misses ('There ain't no Hairy and no Virgin Mary/You won't hear those voices again') and gives himself a pep talk, exhibiting the resilience cultivated by every self-respecting New Yorker.

22 New York Dolls, 'Subway Train' (1973)

Country bluesmen couldn't get their minds off the railroad; in this Stonesy glam classic, David Johansen transposes that sentiment to seedy early-'70s NYC. He's lovesick, you see – smitten with a hooker who has to 'get on back to Daddy' – and he finds solace in riding the subway incessantly and aimlessly. Johnny Thunders' lead guitar blares like a train whistle, completing this quintessential ode to being bummed out in the Big Apple.

21 Nas, 'NY State of Mind' (1994)

This sinister, piano-driven track introduced the world to the studied, Dickensian style of street reportage that would become Nas's trademark, all but transporting listeners to the street corners of his native Queensbridge, while offering one of the rap legend's most famed lines: 'I never sleep 'cause sleep is the cousin of death.'

20 The Ramones, 'Rockaway Beach' (1977)

Penned by Dee Dee Ramone (reportedly the only beachgoing member of this pasty Queens punk band), 'Rockaway Beach' celebrates the South Shore strand known

The Ramones. *See p25.*

as the 'Irish Riviera'. The highest-charting single of the Ramones' career, it peaked at No. 66 on Billboard's Hot 100. For locals during a hot summer, it's No. 1 with a bullet.

19 Billy Joel, 'New York State of Mind' (1976)

'Some folks like to get away, take a holiday from the neighborhood' – but not Billy Joel, whose soulful neostandard extols the comforts of being home in New York, even in a somewhat melancholic mood. 'It comes down to reality, and it's fine with me 'cause I've let it slide,' he sings; the song's jazzy piano and saxophone lines are not carefree so much as stubbornly inured to care.

18 Vampire Weekend, 'M79' (2008)

This gem from VW's breakout debut portrays a crosstown bus ride as an opportunity for bittersweet reverie. The song conjures the world of a bookish, self-absorbed Columbia-ite in just a few choice phrases: 'I'll ride across the park/Backseat on the 79/Wasted days/You've come to pass.'

17 Simon & Garfunkel, 'The 59th Street Bridge Song (Feelin' Groovy)' (1966)

Most of the time, New Yorkers operate under the assumption that feelin' groovy is best achieved by rushing through everything. Here, Simon & Garfunkel tap us on the shoulder and tell us to take in the view, look for some fun and just chill.

'Life, I love you,' Simon croons. We're pretty sure he also means NYC.

16 Joni Mitchell, 'Chelsea Morning' (1969)

Mitchell's tune was eclipsed in commercial success by Judy Collins's version, but the singer's own recording, in which she happily recounts the joys of waking up in her picturesque room in the Chelsea Hotel, grips us hardest. A grey Manhattan morning is dappled in exuberant hippie-commune sunlight after Joni's through with it.

15 LL Cool J, 'Doin' It' (1996)

As far as filth goes, 'Doin' It' sounds every bit as naughty as Khia's 'My Neck, My Back (Lick It)' – just without the explicit lyrics. That's thanks in no small part to lady rapper LeShaun, who murmurs its restless hook ('Doin' it an' doin' it an' doin' it well'). That LL Cool J responds with a firm, manly rejoinder ('I represent Queens, she was raised out in Brooklyn') only adds fuel to the fire.

14 George Benson, 'On Broadway' (1978)

The work of not just one, but two legendary songwriting teams, Mann-Weil and Leiber-Stoller, 'On Broadway' was a Top 10 hit for the Drifters in 1963; myriad covers followed. But it's hard to imagine a version that better captures the song's aspirational moxie – or its six-string braggadocio – than George Benson's smooth-sailing, chart-topping live take.

13 The Velvet Underground, 'I'm Waiting for the Man' (1967)

Like many of the Velvets' songs that focus on New York City's dark underbelly, 'I'm Waiting for the Man' is supposedly based on fact. Legendary downtowner Lou Reed wrote this gritty track about scoring heroin for $26 at a Harlem brownstone – which he claims is a true story, aside from the price he paid.

12 Duke Ellington Orchestra, 'Take the 'A' Train' (1941)

In 1939, Duke Ellington tapped Billy Strayhorn as his new right-hand man and sent for the pianist-composer, then living in Pittsburgh. Ellington's instructions said to hop on the A, bound for Harlem, and Strayhorn was off – both creatively and careerwise. The lyrics, added later, spelled out the sentiment –'Hurry, get on now/It's coming/Listen to those rails a-thrumming' – but Strayhorn's brass-festooned original achieves the same effect: a musical depiction of a rising star getting his shot at the glitzy big time.

11 Wu-Tang Clan, 'C.R.E.A.M.' (1993)

This track – the title of which stands for 'cash rules everything around me', chanted by Method Man in each chorus – helped to forge the Shaolin mythos at the heart of the Wu-Tang empire. Verses spat in turn by Raekwon and Inspectah Deck paint a gritty portrait of urban survival over an eerie piano-and-organ backdrop that circles endlessly and aimlessly.

10 Leonard Cohen, 'Chelsea Hotel No. 2' (1974)

Cohen's disarmingly tender reference to a blow job from Janis Joplin still shocks, but that's not what makes this song such an enduring portrait of NYC bohemia. When he sings, 'Those were the reasons/And that was New York/We were runnin' for the money and the flesh,' he doesn't come off as a perv so much as a sad, old poet, memorialising his own bygone wild days and the ones who didn't make it through theirs.

9 Ryan Adams, 'New York, New York' (2001)

Modern-day balladeer Ryan Adams shot the devastatingly gorgeous video for this New York City hymn of praise against a backdrop that would change forever just four days later, when the Twin Towers were destroyed. The Grammy-nominated single from his excellent *Gold* album remains a fierce declaration of love, as well as a courageous rallying cry from a city recovering from loss and pain.

8 Grandmaster Flash and the Furious Five, 'The Message' (1982)

Hip hop existed before this breakthrough single dropped; still, with unprecedented prominence given to Grandmaster Flash's harrowing narrative over the Furious Five's slow groove, 'The Message' arguably marks the birth of rap as we know it. The clear-eyed and explicit lyrics still pack a punch; in the repeated line 'Don't push me/'Cause I'm close to the edge,' you can sense the desperation of a neighbourhood, a culture and a generation.

7 Leonard Bernstein with the Columbia Symphony Orchestra, Rhapsody in Blue (1959)

George Gershwin was 25 years old when he wrote this genre-bending composition for piano and jazz orchestra in 1924. A sublime collage of melodies and rhythms, the piece conjures the throb and clang of Jazz Age urban life so evocatively that it has become an aural signifier for New York City. It was notably used in the opening montage of Woody Allen's *Manhattan*.

6 Lou Reed, 'Walk on the Wild Side' (1972)

Reed paints a wise, sympathetic portrait of the misfits, hustlers and junkies drawn like flies to New York City, where every outsider can find a sliver of acceptance, if not outright redemption. Even the track's signature sound – tubby acoustic bass tangled with slinky, fretless electric – was a hustle: in a 2005 interview, session player Herbie Flowers (who played both instruments) claimed he was just trying to make twice the cash.

IN FOCUS

5 Billie Holiday, 'Autumn in New York' (1952)

The bruised optimism of Vernon Duke's much-covered 1934 jazz standard found its perfect expression in Billie Holiday's yearning version with pianist Oscar Peterson. Duke's moody music and poetic lyrics ('Glittering crowds and shimmering clouds in canyons of steel') are an invitation to fall in love.

4 LCD Soundsystem, 'New York, I Love You but You're Bringing Me Down' (2007)

The downtempo, half-shrugged first verse turns into a punch-by-punch slugfest by the song's end – the perfect equivalent to any New Yorker's relationship with the city we love to hate and hate to love. And why is it all so infuriating? New York knows we'll never break up with her: 'You're still the one pool where I'd happily drown.'

3 Beastie Boys, 'No Sleep Till Brooklyn' (1986)

Like the Beasties themselves, this *Licensed to Ill* anthem runs on a mixture of local pride and adolescent obnoxiousness. Slayer guitarist Kerry King backs the three MCs as they chronicle the lifestyles of the young, rich and tasteless on the road ('Got limos, arenas, TV shows/Autograph pictures and classy ho's'). They also drop in a reference to 'cold kickin' it live' at MSG, just so you know they've risen to the top of the local heap as well.

2 Frank Sinatra, 'Theme from New York, New York' (1980)

The city's unofficial anthem sees New York through the wide eyes of a small-town striver who's hoping that 'If I can make it there, I'll make it anywhere.' John Kander and Fred Ebb wrote it for Liza Minnelli to sing in the 1977 film, and Frank Sinatra made it famous three years later. Even though it's not quite 'A-number-one, top of the list' in our rankings, it remains the quintessential paean to 'old New York', where brand-new New Yorkers arrive every day.

1 Jay-Z with Alicia Keys, 'Empire State of Mind' (2009)

Of all the world's glitzy capitals, New York is truly the city of dreamers. But from the many knocks, something amazing emerges. When Jay-Z's roll-with-the-punches verse gives way to Alicia Keys's chorus, it's the musical equivalent of the first time you touched down on the JFK tarmac or saw the Statue of Liberty.

For the complete list of 100 best NYC songs (and videos), go to www.timeout.com/newyork/music/100-best-nyc-songs.

Jay-Z.

Diary

The year's best seasonal celebrations and shows.

New Yorkers hardly struggle to find something to celebrate. The venerable city-wide traditions are well known, but don't miss the neighbourhood shindigs: you can soak up the local vibe at quirky annual events such as Brooklyn's **Mermaid Parade** or East Village beatnik bash **Howl!**, and take advantage of free summer concerts and outdoor films in the city's green spaces, such as Bryant, Central and Madison Square Parks. For more festivals and events, check out the other chapters in the Arts & Entertainment section. Specific dates are given for 2013-14 where possible, but before you set out or plan a trip around an event, it's wise to call or check online first as dates, times and locations are subject to change. For the latest listings, consult *Time Out New York* magazine or www.timeout.com/newyork.

MARCH, APRIL

ADAA: The Art Show
Seventh Regiment Armory, 643 Park Avenue, at 67th Street, Upper East Side (1-212 488 5550, www.artdealers.org/artshow). Subway 6 to 68th Street-Hunter College. **Date** 6-10 Mar. **Map** p405 E21.
Whether you're a serious collector or a casual art fan, this vast fair, run by the Art Dealers Association of America, offers the chance to peruse some of the world's most impressive, museum-quality pieces on the market. More than 70 galleries show paintings, drawings, photography, sculpture and multimedia works dating from the 17th century to the present.

Armory Show
Piers 92 & 94, Twelfth Avenue, at 55th Street, Hell's Kitchen (1-212 645 6440, www.thearmory show.com). Subway C, E to 50th Street. **Date** 7-10 Mar. **Map** p405 B22.
This contemporary international art mart debuted in Gramercy Park's 69th Regiment Armory in 1999. Now held on the Hudson River, it has expanded to include 20th-century work.

St Patrick's Day Parade
Fifth Avenue, from 44th to 86th Streets, midtown to uptown (www.nycstpatricksparade. org). **Date** 17 Mar. **Map** p404 E24, p406 E18.
Dating from 1762, this massive march is one of the city's longest-running annual traditions. If you feel like braving huge crowds and potentially nasty weather, you'll see thousands of green-clad merrymakers strutting to the sounds of pipe bands.

Easter Parade
Fifth Avenue, from 49th to 57th Streets, Midtown (1-212 484 1222). Subway E, M to Fifth Avenue-53rd Street. **Date** 31 Mar. **Map** p404 E23-E22.
'Parade' is something of a misnomer for this little festival of creative hat-wearers. Starting at 10am on Easter Sunday, Fifth Avenue becomes a car-free promenade of gussied-up crowds milling around and showing off their extravagant bonnets. Be sure to arrive early to secure a prime viewing spot near St Patrick's Cathedral, at 50th Street.

SOFA New York
Seventh Regiment Armory, 643 Park Avenue, at 67th Street, Upper East Side (1-800 563 7632, www.sofaexpo.com). Subway 6 to 68th Street-Hunter College. **Date** 12-15 Apr. **Map** p405 E21.
Browse this giant show of Sculptural Objects and Functional Art – with fine art, ceramics, sculpture and jewellery – and you might go home with a treasure.

Tribeca Film Festival
Date 17-28 Apr.
See p263.

Sakura Matsuri (Cherry Blossom Festival)
For listings, *see p121* **Brooklyn Botanic Garden**. **Date** late Apr.

The climax to the cherry blossom season, when the BBG's 220 trees are in flower, the annual *sakura matsuri* celebrates both the blooms and Japanese culture with concerts, traditional dance, manga exhibitions and tea ceremonies.

MAY-AUGUST

TD Five Boro Bike Tour
Battery Park to Staten Island (1-212 870 2080, www.bikenewyork.org). Subway A, C, J, Z, 1, 2, 3 to Chambers Street; R to City Hall; 4, 5, 6 to Brooklyn Bridge-City Hall, then bike to Battery Park. **Date** 5 May. **Map** p402 E34.

Thousands of cyclists take over the city for a 42-mile Tour de New York. (Pedestrians and motorists should plan for extra getting-around time on this date.) Advance registration is required if you want to take part. Event organisers suggest using the trains listed above, as some subway exits below Chambers Street may be closed to bike-toting cyclists for safety reasons, and bikes are not allowed at South Ferry (1), Whitehall Street (R) or Bowling Green (4, 5) stations.

Lower East Side Festival of the Arts
Theater for the New City, 155 First Avenue, between 9th & 10th Streets, Lower East Side (1-212 254 1109, www.theaterforthenewcity.net). Subway L to First Avenue; 6 to Astor Place. **Date** 24-26 May. **Map** p403 F28.

This annual celebration of artistic diversity features performances by dozens of theatrical troupes, poetry readings, films and family-friendly programming. It's run by the Theater for the New City company, which has been performing political and community-themed plays in New York since 1971.

Washington Square Outdoor Art Exhibit
Various streets surrounding Washington Square Park, Greenwich Village (1-212 982 6255, www.washingtonsquareoutdoorartexhibit.org). Subway A, B, C, D, E, F, M to W 4th Street; N, R to 8th Street-NYU. **Date** 25-27 May, 1, 2 June; 31 Aug-2 Sept, 7, 8 Sept. **Map** p403 E28/29.

Since 1931, this outdoor exhibit has filled the area around Washington Square with a fine mix of photography, sculpture, paintings and unique crafts. If you miss it in May and June, you'll have another chance to browse in late summer.

Howl! Festival
Various East Village locations (1-212 466 6666, www.howlfestival.com). **Date** 31 May, 1, 2 June. **Map** p403.

A reading of Allen Ginsberg's seminal poem kicks off this three-day arts fest – a grab bag of art events, film screenings, poetry readings, performance art and much more.

Sakura Matsuri (Cherry Blossom Festival). *See p29.*

IN FOCUS

SummerStage

Rumsey Playfield, Central Park, entrance on Fifth Avenue, at 72nd Street, Upper East Side (1-212 360 2777, www.summerstage.org). Subway 6 to 68th Street-Hunter College. **Date** June-Aug. **Map** p405 E20.

Now held in parks across the city, these concerts embody summer for many New Yorkers, and break down the boundaries between artistic mediums. Rockers, orchestras, authors and dance companies take over the mainstage in Central Park at this very popular, mostly free annual series. Show up early or plan to listen from outside the enclosure gates (not a bad option if you bring a blanket and snacks).

Shakespeare in the Park

Date June-Aug.
See p324.

Celebrate Brooklyn!

Prospect Park Bandshell, Prospect Park West, at 9th Street, Park Slope, Brooklyn (1-718 855 7882, www.bricartsmedia.org). Subway F to Seventh Avenue. **Date** June-Aug. **Map** p410 T12.

Non-profit community arts organisation BRIC launched this series of outdoor performances to revitalise Prospect Park, and now the festival is Brooklyn's premier summer culture offering. It includes music, dance, film and spoken word acts, and has showcased the likes of Philip Glass, TV on the Radio, Jimmy Cliff and Lyle Lovett. A $3 donation is requested and there's an admission charge for some shows.

National Puerto Rican Day Parade

Fifth Avenue, from 44th to 79th Streets, midtown to uptown (1-718 401 0404, www.nationalpuertoricandayparade.org). **Date** 9 June. **Map** p404 E24-p405 E19.

Salsa music blares, and scantily clad revellers dance along the route or ride colourful floats at this freewheeling celebration of the city's largest Hispanic community. The party can spill into Central Park, so if you're there you might become part of it.

Egg Rolls & Egg Creams Festival

Eldridge Street Synagogue, 12 Eldridge Street, between Canal & Division Streets, Lower East Side (1-212 219 0903, www.eldridgestreet.org). Subway B, D to Grand Street; F to East Broadway. **Date** 9 June. **Map** p402 F31.

This block party celebrates the convergence of Jewish and Chinese traditions on the Lower East Side, with acrobats, yarmulke makers, Torah scribes, language lessons and, of course, plenty of the titular treats.

Museum Mile Festival

Fifth Avenue, from 82nd to 105th Streets, Upper East Side (1-212 606 2296, www. museummilefestival.org). **Date** 11 June. **Map** p405 E19-p406 E16.

Ten of the city's most prestigious art institutions – including the Guggenheim, the Met and the Museum of the City of New York – open their doors to the public free of charge. Music, dance and children's activities turn this into a 23-block-long celebration.

IN FOCUS

Egg Rolls & Egg Creams Festival.

Mermaid Parade.

★ River to River Festival

Various venues along the West Side & southern waterfronts of Manhattan (1-212 219 9401, www.rivertorivernyc.com). **Date** *16 June-13 July.*
Lower Manhattan organisations present hundreds of free events – from walks to all manner of arts performances – at various waterside venues. Past performers include Patti Smith, Laurie Anderson and the New York City Opera. For the past few years, bookings at South Street Seaport, in particular, have made this one of the coolest concert series in town.

★ Mermaid Parade

Coney Island, Brooklyn (no phone, www.coney island.com). Subway D, F, N, Q to Coney Island-Stillwell Avenue. **Date** *22 June.*
Decked-out mermaids and mermen of all shapes, sizes and ages accompany elaborate, kitschy floats. It's the wackiest summer solstice event you'll see.

Broadway Bares

239 W 52nd Street, between Broadway & Eighth Avenue, Theater District (1-212 840 0770, www. broadwaycares.org, www.broadwaybares.com). Subway C, E, 1 to 50th Street; B, D, E to Seventh Avenue. **Date** *23 June.* **Map** *p404 D23.*
Ingenious and unusual, this annual fundraiser for Broadway Cares/Equity Fights AIDS is your chance to see some of the Great White Way's hottest bodies sans costumes; the burlesque extravaganza is usually held in the Theater District's Roseland Ballroom (*see p289*). Broadway Cares also hosts a show tune-filled Easter Bonnet Competition (22, 23 Apr) as well as theatre-themed events throughout the year.

★ Midsummer Night Swing

Damrosch Park at Lincoln Center Plaza, W 62nd Street, between Columbus and Amsterdam Avenues, Upper West Side (1-212 721 6500, www.midsummernightsswing.org). Subway 1 to 66th Street-Lincoln Center. **Date** 25 June-13 July. **Map** p405 C21.

Lincoln Center's Damrosch Park is turned into a giant dancefloor as bands play salsa, Cajun, swing and other music. Each night's dance party (Tue-Sat, $17) is devoted to a different dance style, and is preceded by lessons. Beginners are, of course, welcome.

★ NYC LGBT Pride March
From Fifth Avenue, at 36th Street, to Christopher Street, midtown to West Village (1-212 807 7433, www.nycpride.org). **Date** 30 June.

Downtown Manhattan becomes a sea of rainbow flags as lesbian, gay, bisexual and transgendered people from the city and beyond parade down Fifth Avenue in commemoration of the 1969 Stonewall Riots. After the march, there's a massive street fair and a dance on the West Side piers.

Warm Up
Date late June-early Sept.
See p278.

Macy's Fourth of July Fireworks
1-212 494 4495, www.macys.com/fireworks. **Date** 4 July.

The city's star Independence Day attraction is also the nation's largest Fourth of July fireworks display. Traditionally launched from barges on the East River, in 2009 the fireworks moved to the Hudson for the first time since the 9/11 attacks, and have remained there for the past four years; call or check the website for details of the 2013 location. The pyrotechnics start at around 9pm, but you'll need to scope out your vantage point much earlier than that. Keep in mind, however, that spectators are packed like sardines at prime public spots, so many choose to keep their distance.

Nathan's Famous Fourth of July International Hot Dog Eating Contest
Outside Nathan's Famous, 1310 Surf Avenue, at Stillwell Avenue, Coney Island, Brooklyn (www.nathansfamous.com). Subway D, F, N, Q to Coney Island-Stillwell Avenue. **Date** 4 July.

Liable to amuse and appal in equal measure, this Fourth of July event, which is organised by the 97-year-old Coney Island hot dog vendor, holds an undeniable fascination. Eaters gather from all over the world for the granddaddy of all pig-out contests.

New York Philharmonic Concerts in the Parks
Date 10-16 July.
See p302 **Everything Under the Sun**.

Harlem Week
Various Harlem locations (1-212 862 8477, www.harlemweek.com). Subway B, C, 2, 3 to 135th Street. **Date** 27 July-24 Aug. **Map** p407.

Get into the groove at this massive culture fest, which began in 1974 as a one-day event celebrating all things Harlem. Harlem Day (18 Aug) is still the centrepiece of the event, but 'Week' is now a misnomer; besides the street fair serving up music, art and food along 135th Street, a wealth of concerts, films, dance performances, fashion and sports events are on tap for more than a month.

Summer Restaurant Week
www.nycgo.com/restaurantweek. **Date** late July/early Aug.

Twice a year, for two weeks or more at a stretch, some of the city's finest restaurants dish out three-course prix-fixe lunches for around $24; some places also offer dinner for $35. For the full list of participating restaurants, visit the website. Not surprisingly, the event is immensely popular, so you'll need to make reservations well in advance.

Lincoln Center Out of Doors
For listings, *see p301* **Lincoln Center**.
Date 24 July-11 Aug.

Free dance, music, theatre, opera and more make up the programme at this family-friendly and ambitious festival organised by the Lincoln Center.

New York International Fringe Festival
Various venues (1-212 279 4488, www.fringenyc.org). **Date** 9-25 Aug.

Wacky and sometimes wonderful, downtown's Fringe Festival – inspired by the Edinburgh original and now in its 17th season – shoehorns hundreds of arts performances into 16 theatre-crammed days.
▶ *See p326 for more information on Off-Off Broadway shows.*

SEPTEMBER, OCTOBER

West Indian-American Day Carnival Parade
Eastern Parkway, from Utica Avenue to Grand Army Plaza, Brooklyn (1-718 467 1797, www.wiadca.com). Subway 2, 3 to Grand Army Plaza; 3, 4 to Crown Heights-Utica Avenue. **Date** 2 Sept. **Map** p410 W11-U11.

The streets come alive with the jubilant clangour of steel-drum bands and the steady throb of calypso and soca music at this colourful cultural celebration. Mas bands – and costumed marchers – dance along the route and thousands move to the beat, while vendors sell Caribbean crafts, clothing and food.

Feast of San Gennaro
Mulberry Street, from Canal to Houston Streets, Little Italy (1-212 768 9320, www.sangennaro.org). Subway B, D, F, M to Broadway-Lafayette Street; J, N, Q, R, Z, 6 to Canal Street. **Date** 12-22 Sept. **Map** p404 F30.

This massive 11-day street fair stretches along the main drag of what's left of Little Italy. Come after

IN FOCUS

ING New York City Marathon. *See p36.*

dark, when sparkling lights arch over Mulberry Street and the smells of frying *zeppole* (custard- or jam-filled fritters) and sausages hang in the sultry air. On the final Saturday in September, a statue of San Gennaro is carried in a Grand Procession outside the Most Precious Blood Church (109 Mulberry Street, between Canal & Hester Streets).

Next Wave Festival

For listings, *see p299* **Brooklyn Academy of Music**. **Date** early Sept-late Jan.

The festival is among the most highly anticipated of the city's autumn culture offerings, as it showcases only the very best in avant-garde music, dance, theatre and opera. Legends like John Cale, Meredith Monk and Steve Reich are among the many luminaries the festival has hosted.

Dumbo Arts Festival

Various locations in Dumbo, Brooklyn (1-718 488 8588, www.dumboartsfestival.com). Subway A, C to High Street; F to York Street. **Date** late Sept. **Map** p411 S9-T9.

Dumbo has been an artists' enclave for decades, and this weekend of art appreciation is hugely popular. Expect gallery shows, open studios, installations, concerts, dance and other arts events.

Atlantic Antic

Atlantic Avenue, from Fourth Avenue to Hicks Street, Brooklyn (1-718 875 8993, www.atlantic ave.org). Subway B, Q, 2, 3, 4, 5 to Atlantic Avenue; D, N, R to Pacific Street. **Date** late Sept. **Map** p410 T10-S10.

Entertainment, ethnic food, children's activities and the inimitable World Cheesecake-Eating Contest pack Atlantic Avenue with wide-eyed punters at this monumental Brooklyn festival.

★ New York Film Festival

Date 27 Sept-13 Oct.
See p263.

★ Open House New York

1-212 991 6470, www.ohny.org. **Date** 12, 13 Oct.

Get an insider's view – literally – of the city that most locals haven't even seen. More than 100 sites of architectural interest that are normally off-limits to the public throw open their doors during a weekend of urban exploration. Lectures and an educational programme are also on offer.

CMJ Music Marathon & Film Festival

Various venues (1-212 235 7027, www.cmj.com). **Date** mid Oct.

The annual *College Music Journal* schmooze-fest draws thousands of fans and music-industry types to one of the best showcases for new rock, indie, hip hop and electronica acts. The Film Festival, which runs in tandem with the music blowout, includes a wide range of feature and short films (many music-related) and pulls in a suitably hip crowd.

★ Village Halloween Parade

Sixth Avenue, from Spring to 16th Streets, Downtown (www.halloween-nyc.com). **Date** 31 Oct. **Map** p403 E30-D27.

The sidewalks at this iconic Village shindig are always packed beyond belief. For the best vantage point, don a costume and watch from inside the parade (the line-up starts at 6.30pm on Sixth Avenue, at Spring Street; the parade kicks off at 7pm).

IN FOCUS

Barking Mad

Check out the wackiest events on the NYC calendar.

AIR SEX WORLD CHAMPIONSHIPS
Late June, $15, www.airsexworld.com
Like an adult air-guitar tournament, this competition lets punters display their skills playing an imaginary…um…instrument. Hosted by comedian Chris Trew, the young, virile and shameless take to the stage to show off their erotic technique. The rules are simple: no nudity, all orgasms must be simulated and there must be an imaginary partner or object involved in your act. A panel of judges (comics, sex professionals) adjudicate the first round, with the audience choosing the eventual winner. New York is but one stop on the Air Sex World Championships' nationwide tour – regional winners throw down in Austin, Texas, at the end of the year.

TOMPKINS SQUARE PARK HALLOWEEN DOG PARADE
Late Oct, www.firstrunfriends.org
To see a plethora of puppies in adorable outfits, head to this canine costume parade, which has been an East Village institution for more than two decades. The getups are remarkably elaborate and conceptual; last year's included Evita, ET and one of the sandworms from *Beetlejuice*. Unsurprisingly in an election year, some costumes had a political bent – including 'Mutt Romney', a pooch in a Little Tykes plastic car festooned with the sign '47% of dogs rely on their masters.' Enterprising owners stand to win prizes if their dog is selected Best in Show.

NO PANTS SUBWAY RIDE
January, www.improveverywhere.com
Improv Everywhere's annual barefaced, bare-legged mission began in January 2002 with a handful of operatives in one car on the downtown 6 train, but it's grown into a well-publicised mass event. Admittedly, it's not the mildly subversive, playful prank it was – it's now a chance for New Yorkers to perform a cheeky feat while supported by thousands of fellow residents. For unsuspecting visitors, it's a surreal spectacle.

IN FOCUS

Tompkins Square Park Halloween Dog Parade.

Macy's Thanksgiving Day Parade & Balloon Inflation.

NOVEMBER-FEBRUARY

New York Comedy Festival
Various venues (www.nycomedyfestival.com).
Date Nov.
This five-day laugh fest features big-name talent (Robin Williams, Ricky Gervais and Bill Maher were among the headliners in 2012) as well as up-and-comers.

ING New York City Marathon
Staten Island side of the Verrazano-Narrows Bridge to Tavern on the Green in Central Park (1-212 423 2249, www.ingnycmarathon.org).
Date early Nov.
Around 40,000 marathoners hotfoot it (or puff, pant and stagger) through all five boroughs over a 26.2-mile course. Scope out a spot somewhere in the middle to get a good view of the passing herd. *Photo p34.*

Radio City Christmas Spectacular
For listings, *see p289* **Radio City Music Hall**.
Date early Nov-late Dec.
High-kicking precision dance troupe the Rockettes and an onstage nativity scene with live animals are the rather kitsch attractions at this (pricey) annual homage to the Yuletide season.

Macy's Thanksgiving Day Parade & Balloon Inflation
Central Park West, at 77th Street, to Macy's, Broadway, at 34th Street, uptown to midtown (1-212 494 4495, www.macys.com/parade).
Date 27, 28 Nov. **Map** p405 D19-404 D25.
At 9am on Thanksgiving Day, the stars of this nationally televised parade are the gigantic balloons, the elaborate floats and good ol' Santa Claus. The evening before, New Yorkers brave the cold night air to watch the rubbery colossi take shape at the inflation area (from 77th to 81st Streets, between Central Park West & Columbus Avenue).

Rockefeller Center Tree-Lighting Ceremony
Rockefeller Center, Fifth Avenue, between 49th & 50th Streets, Midtown West (1-212 332 6868, www.rockefellercenter.com). Subway B, D, F, M to 47th-50th Streets-Rockefeller Center.
Date late Nov. **Map** p404 E23.
Proceedings start at 7pm, but this festive celebration is always mobbed, so get there as early as you can. The actual lighting takes place at the end of the programme; most of the two-hour event is devoted to celebrity performances (Rod Stewart and Mariah Carey were among the recent human luminaries). Then the 30,000 energy-efficient LEDs covering the massive evergreen are switched on to mass oohs and aahs. If you'd rather gouge out your eyeballs with the tree's nine-and-a-half-foot-diameter Swarovski-crystal star than brave the crush, there's plenty of time during the holiday season to view the tree at your leisure.

Unsilent Night
Washington Square Arch, Fifth Avenue, at Waverly Place, to Tompkins Square Park, downtown (www.unsilentnight.com). Subway A, B, C, E, D, F, M to W 4th Street. **Date** mid Dec. **Map** p403 E28-G28.

Phil Kline's musical parade – in which participants play his composition on boomboxes while they walk a designated route – has become a bona fide holiday tradition. His luminous, shimmering wash of bell tones is one of the loveliest communal new music experiences you'll ever witness.

National Chorale Messiah Sing-In
Avery Fisher Hall, Lincoln Center, Columbus Avenue, at 65th Street, Upper West Side (1-212 333 5333, www.lincolncenter.org, www.national chorale.org). Subway 1 to 66th Street-Lincoln Center. **Date** mid Dec. **Map** p405 C21.

Hallelujah! Chase those holiday blues away by joining the National Chorale and hundreds of fellow audience members in a rehearsal and performance of Handel's *Messiah*. No previous singing experience is necessary to take part, and you can buy the score on site, though picking one up early for advance perusal would certainly help novices.

Emerald Nuts Midnight Run
Naumburg Bandshell, middle of Central Park, at 72nd Street (1-212 860 4455, www.nyrr.org). Subway B, C to 72nd Street; 6 to 68th Street-Hunter College. **Date** 31 Dec. **Map** p405 E20.

Rockefeller Center Tree-Lighting Ceremony.

Those who prefer to stay sober can see in the new year with a four-mile jog through the park, organised by the New York Road Runners. There's also a masquerade parade, fireworks, prizes and a (booze-free) toast at the halfway mark.

▶ *For more about running in New York, see p334.*

New Year's Eve in Times Square
Times Square, Theater District (1-212 768 1560, www.timessquarenyc.org). Subway N, Q, R, S, 1, 2, 3, 7 to 42nd Street-Times Square. **Date** 31 Dec. **Map** p404 D24.

Get together with a million others and watch the giant illuminated Waterford Crystal ball – the new, 12ft geodesic sphere, double the size of its predecessors, debuted in 2008 – descend amid a blizzard of confetti and cheering. There are DJs, celebrity guests and flashy entertainment, but also freezing temperatures, densely packed crowds, no public conveniences – and very tight security.

New Year's Day Marathon Benefit Reading
For listings, *see p298* **Poetry Project**. **Date** 1 Jan.
Some big-name bohemians (Philip Glass and Patti Smith were among the 2013 roll-call) step up to the mic during this spoken-word spectacle, organised by the Poetry Project, at St Marks Church in the East Village.

Winter Restaurant Week
For listings, *see p33* **Summer Restaurant Week**. **Date** late Jan/early Feb.
The Winter Restaurant Week provides yet another opportunity to sample delicious gourmet food at highly palatable prices.

Chinese New Year
Around Mott Street, Chinatown (www.betterchinatown.com). Subway J, N, Q, R, Z, 6 to Canal Street. **Date** late Jan-early Feb 2014. **Map** p402 E/F31.
Gung hay fat choy!, the greeting goes. Chinatown bustles with colour and is charged with energy during the two weeks of the Lunar New Year. The firecracker ceremony (31 Jan 2014) and parade (7 Feb 2014) are key events.

IN FOCUS

Explore

Tour New York

Get an introduction to the city or see it in a new light.

Navigating New York may at first appear to be a daunting task: it's big, it's busy and it doesn't stop while you pause to rustle in your bag for your pocket map. Fortunately, there are countless options for exploring the city's attractions, whether your pleasure is cycling, sailing, bonding with fellow sightseers on a tour bus, or simply hoofing it – with or without a chaperone. For additional inspiration, weekly listings for urban outings can be found in *Time Out New York* magazine's This Week in New York section (or look online at www.timeout.com/newyork).

BY BICYCLE

For more on cycling, *see p332 and p374.*

Bike the Big Apple
1-877 865 0078, www.bikethebigapple.com.
Tours vary. **Tickets** (incl bicycle & helmet rental) $80-$99. **Credit** AmEx, Disc, MC, V.
You don't have to be a chamois-clad racer to join these gently paced five- to seven-hour rides. Licensed guides lead cyclists through historic and newly hip neighbourhoods: popular tours include Harlem (the 'Sensational Park and Soul' tour), Chinatown ('From High Finance to Hidden Chinatown'), Williamsburg, and a twilight ride across the Brooklyn Bridge.

Central Park Bike Tours
1-212 541 8759, www.centralparkbiketour.com.
Tours *Apr-Nov* 10am, 11am, 1pm, 4pm daily. *Dec-Mar* by reservation. **Tickets** (incl bicycle rental) $49; $40 reductions. **Credit** AmEx, Disc, MC, V.
Central Park Bike Tours focuses its attentions on – yes! – Central Park. The main two-hour tour visits the John Lennon memorial at Strawberry Fields, Belvedere Castle and the Shakespeare Garden. Film buffs will especially enjoy the 'Central Park Movie Scenes Bike Tour', which passes locations from *When Harry Met Sally…* and *Wall Street*. You can also book your own tailor-made private tour.

BY BOAT

★ Circle Line Cruises
Pier 83, 42nd Street, at the Hudson River, Midtown (1-212 563 3200, www.circleline42.com).

Subway A, C, E to 42nd Street-Port Authority.
Tours vary. **Tickets** $27-$38; $21-$33 reductions. **Credit** AmEx, DC, Disc, MC, V. **Map** p404 B24.
The Circle Line's famed three-hour guided circum-navigation of Manhattan Island ($38; $25-$33 reductions) is a fantastic way to get your bearings and see many of the city's sights as you pass under its iconic bridges. Themed tours include a New Year's Eve cruise, a Fourth of July celebration, an evening 'Harbor Lights' sailing tour (mid Apr-Nov) and an autumn foliage ride to Bear Mountain in the Hudson Valley (mid-late Oct). If you don't have time for the full trip, there's a two-hour 'Liberty' tour that goes around downtown to the Brooklyn Bridge and back.
The separately run **Circle Line Downtown** (Pier 16, South Street Seaport, 1-212 742 1969, www.circlelinedowntown.com) has a more intimate vessel, the *Zephyr*, for tours of lower Manhattan (Apr-Dec, $28), including happy hour cruises on Thursday and Friday nights for over-21s (May-Oct, $30). The two companies' rival speedboats – Circle Line's *Beast* (May-Sept, $27, $21 reductions) and Circle Line Downtown's *Shark* (May-Sept, $24, $17-$22 reductions) – offer fun, adrenalin-inducing and splashy 30-minute rides.

Manhattan by Sail
North Cove, Hudson River, between Liberty & Vesey Streets, Financial District (1-800 544 1224, 1-212 619 0885, www.manhattanbysail.com).
Subway A, C to Chambers Street; E to World Trade Center; 2, 3 to Park Place. **Tours** Mid Apr-mid Oct; times vary. **Tickets** *Shearwater* $45-$50; $25-$38 reductions. *Clipper City* $39; $17-$35 reductions. **Credit** AmEx, DC, Disc, MC, V. **Map** p402 D32.

EXPLORE

Running Start

A sightseeing tour and daily workout rolled into one.

Whether you're a seasoned marathoner or just a jogging junkie, getting your daily endorphin fix can be essential – even while on holiday. You may be reluctant, however, to waste valuable sightseeing time within the confines of a hotel gym or aimlessly hitting the streets. Fortunately, you don't have to.

Michael Gazaleh, founder and president of **City Running Tours** (*see p45*), offers a dozen different routes for fleet-footed visitors to explore New York at their preferred running pace. Personalised routes and hotel pick-ups and drop-offs are available. Groups are kept small – just two or three people, on average – so Gazaleh and the 18 guides he employs are able to customise each tour to fit the participants' athletic abilities and cultural interests, even lengthening or shortening a given itinerary. Worry not: if you want to slow down for a photograph or a closer look at a landmark, your guide will be happy to wait.

Gazaleh, a licensed chiropractor and lifelong exercise enthusiast, says his most popular excursion is the New York run, which starts in Brooklyn Heights, traverses the Brooklyn Bridge, then proceeds through the Financial District, Tribeca, Chinatown,

Soho, the Village, Gramercy Park and Times Square before ending at Central Park.

His personal favourites are the eight-mile Harlem run, which takes in sites in northern Manhattan and the Bronx such as Columbia University and Yankee Stadium, and the ten-mile Brooklyn run, which traverses Green-Wood Cemetery, Prospect Park and the Brooklyn Heights Promenade.

There's also a jaunt through Central Park and a trip through the ethnically rich Lower East Side (where Gazaleh lives). If you don't want to run in a pack, you can opt for a customised individual tour ($75 for the first six miles and $5 for each additional mile), which includes a T-shirt, a souvenir photo, product samples and discount coupons for local athletics shops.

One obvious advantage of Gazaleh's service is the vast amount of territory he covers in a mere one to two hours. 'We can go as far as a bus tour, and we take people on a lot of streets that buses can't,' he notes. He also points out that guides are able to connect with participants on a personal level. 'We're runners, so we have that common interest. And we know that if they go too long without a run, they just don't feel like themselves, so we're able to give them that sense of accomplishment.'

EXPLORE

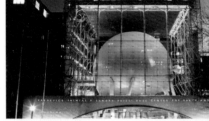

Set sail on the *Shearwater*, an 82ft luxury yacht built in 1929. The Sunday 'Champagne Brunch' ($79) or 'Full Moon' ($45) sail options are lovely ways to take in the skyline. The eight-sail tall ship, *Clipper City*, embarks from Pier 17 at the South Street Seaport.

New York Water Taxi

Pier 17, South Street Seaport, Financial District (1-212 742 1969, www.nywatertaxi.com). **Tours** vary. **Tickets** $28-$35; $16-$25 reductions. **Credit** AmEx, MC, V.

Like their earth-bound counterparts, New York water taxis are bright yellow, speedy and a great way to get around town. Unlike street taxis, they run on a set schedule, and you can hop on and off with a day pass ($28, $16 reductions), enjoying neighbourhood attractions along the way. Offerings include daily Statue of Liberty express tours on the *Zephyr* cruise boat ($28, $17-$24 reductions) and 'Statue by Night' cruises with a free champagne toast for over-21s ($28, $17-$24 reductions), and a weekend wildlife-spotting 'Audubon Eco-Cruise' ($35; $25 reductions) that takes you to uninhabited corners such as South Brother Island, a breeding ground for migratory birds such as the great egret (June-Aug and Jan-Feb; see website for specific days).

★ FREE Staten Island Ferry

Battery Park, South Street, at Whitehall Street, Financial District (1-718 727 2508, www.siferry. com). Subway R to Whitehall Street-South Ferry; 1 to South Ferry; 4, 5 to Bowling Green. **Tickets** free. **Map** p402 E34.

During this commuter barge's 25-minute crossing, you get superb panoramas of lower Manhattan and the Statue of Liberty. Boats leave South Ferry at Battery Park and run 24 hours a day.

BY BUS

Gray Line

777 Eighth Avenue, at 48th Street, Theater District (1-212 445 0848, www.newyorksightseeing.com). Subway A, C, E to 42nd Street-Port Authority; C, E to 50th Street; N, Q, R to 49th Street. **Tours** vary. **Tickets** $39-$115; $39-$99 reductions. **Credit** AmEx, Disc, MC, V. **Map** p404 D23.

Gray Line offers more than 20 bus tours, from a basic two-hour ride (with 40-plus hop-on, hop-off stops) to the guided 'Classic New York' tour, which includes lunch, admission to Top of the Rock or the Empire State Building, and a boat ride to Ellis Island and the Statue of Liberty.

Other locations Times Square Museum & Visitor Center, 1560 Broadway at 46th Street, Times Square.

On-Location Tours

1-212 683 2027, www.screentours.com. **Tours** vary. **Tickets** $24-$48. **Credit** AmEx, MC, V.

Whether you'd prefer to sip cosmos à la Carrie Bradshaw, splurge at Blair and Serena's favourite department store, or visit the Bada Bing, On-Location's well-organised bus trips allow TV fans to simulate the experiences of their favourite characters from *Sex and the City, Gossip Girl* and *The Sopranos*. Or hop aboard the 'New York TV and Movie Sites' tour and visit more than 40 sites from big- and small-screen productions such as *Seinfeld* and *The Godfather*. All tours are led by actors, which gives an insider perspective on filming in New York.

BY HELICOPTER

Liberty Helicopter Tours

Downtown Manhattan Heliport, 6 East River Piers, between Broad Street & Old Slip, Financial District (1-212 967 6464, 1-800 542 9933, www.libertyhelicopter.com). Subway R to Whitehall Street-South Ferry; 1 to South Ferry. **Tours** 9am-6:30pm Mon-Sat; 9am-5pm Sun. **Tickets** $150-$995. **Credit** AmEx, MC, V. **Map** p402 E34.

There'll be no daredevil swooping around the city (Liberty's helicopters provide a fairly smooth flight), but the views are thrilling. Even the popular 15-minute 'Big Apple' tour is long enough to get an adrenalin-pumping look at major sites, including the Statue of Liberty, the National 9/11 Memorial, and the Empire State Building.

ON FOOT

FREE Big Apple Greeter

1-212 669 8159, www.bigapplegreeter.org. **Tours** by arrangement. **Tickets** free (donations appreciatedd).

Set up in 1992, this independent non-profit scheme offers visitors an alternative to the organised tour format. Sign up through the website at least four to six weeks ahead and you'll be paired with a volunteer 'greeter', who'll give you an informal, personal two- to four-hour introduction to one of the city's neighbourhoods (your choice or theirs).

★ Big Onion Walking Tours

1-888 606 9255, www.bigonion.com. **Tours** daily; times vary. **Tickets** $18-$40; $15-$28 reductions. **No credit cards**.

INSIDE TRACK
WHIMSICAL WALKS

For an intimate, idiosyncratic look at New York, join one of **Elastic City**'s conceptual walks (1-347 829 7779, www.elastic-city.com). The artist-devised experiences aim to heighten awareness and form connections with the city. Be ready to tiptoe up Broadway, contemplate gum stains on a sidewalk, or recite lines of poetry to passers-by.

EXPLORE

New York was known as the Big Onion before it became the Big Apple. The tour guides will explain why, and they should know – all guides hold advanced degrees in history (or a related field). Among the offerings is the 'Official *Gangs of New York*' walk and a weekly 'Multi-Ethnic Eating Tour' that explores the history of the Lower East Side, Chinatown and Little Italy with a few samples of cultural cuisine along the way. New to the list is the 'Art and History of the Metropolitan' tour, which intends to demystify the massive art museum by offering tidbits about its history and collection, as well as its impact on the city. Private tours are also available.

★ City Running Tours
1-877 415 0058, www.cityrunningtours.com.
Tours vary. **Tickets** from $25 group tour; $75 individual tour. **Credit** AmEx, MC, V.
See p41 **Running Start**.

Harlem Heritage Tours
1-212 280 7888, www.harlemheritage.com.
Tours vary. **Tickets** $20-$39. **Credit** MC, V.
Now operating more than ten bus and walking tours led by lifelong neighbourhood residents, Harlem Heritage aims to show visitors the soul of the borough. The 'Harlem Civil Rights Multimedia' tour takes participants to landmarks associated with Malcolm X, James Baldwin and Martin Luther King; historical video clips make sites come alive. The 'Harlem Renaissance' tour walks you to the sites of Prohibition-era speakeasies, clubs and one-time residences of artists, writers and musicians. The company also offers a 'Harlem TV and Movie' tour, which highlights numerous film locations in the neighbourhood.

★ Justin Ferate
1-212 223 2777, www.justinsnewyork.com.
Tours vary. **Tickets** $20-$25. **No credit cards**.
This venerated historian wrote the book on Gotham walking tours. No, really – the city commissioned him to write the NYC tour-guide licensing exam, which he designed to educate and assess would-be guides. In addition to a regular roster of tours covering everything from midtown murals to the quaint attractions of the Bronx's City Island, Ferate leads speciality tours – such as one exploring the artwork of historic subway stations around the city – and offers a free 90-minute trek through Grand Central Terminal and its environs every Friday at 12.30pm.

Municipal Art Society Tours
1-212 935 3960, 1-212 439 1049 recorded information, http://mas.org/tours. **Tours** vary.
Tickets from $15. Credit AmEx, MC, V.
The Municipal Art Society (MAS) organises bus and walking tours in New York and further afield. Many – such as 'East Midtown and Post-Modernism' – are led by architects, designers and writers, and reflect the society's focus on contemporary architecture, urban planning and historic preservation. There's also a guided walk through Grand Central Terminal on Wednesdays at 12.30pm (suggested donation $10). Private tours are available by appointment.

★ NoshWalks
1-212 222 2243, www.noshwalks.com.
Tours vary. **Tickets** $45-$54; $20 reductions.
Each culinary outing is led by NoshWalks founder Myra Alperson, who's been writing about New York's food scene for more than a decade. Taking you to corners of the city you'd never visit on your own, Alperson fills you in on the neighbourhood's culinary and cultural history, introducing you to chefs and shopkeepers, street food and snacks along the way. Trips have included South Asian cuisine in Jackson Heights, Queens, and the kosher-Caribbean combo tour in Crown Heights, Brooklyn.

Urban Oyster
1-347 618-8687, urbanoyster.com. **Tours** vary.
Tickets $24-$60. **Credit** AmEx, Disc, MC, V.
Brooklyn-based Urban Oyster partners with local businesses and the Brooklyn Historical Society to give tour-goers insight into the individuals that make the city tick, such as food vendors and brew-masters. On the 'Food Cart' tour ($48), you might meet Fatima, the 23-year owner of a popular midtown halal cart, or visit a third-generation Brooklyn coffee shop on the 'Neighborhood Eats' tour ($55). Beer lovers will savour the 'Brewed in Brooklyn' tour ($60), which illuminates the borough's suds-making legacy with tastings along the way.

EXPLORE

Downtown

The lowdown on lower Manhattan.

The southern tip of Manhattan has always been the city's financial, legal and political powerhouse. It's where New York began as a Dutch colony in the 17th century, and where the 19th-century influx of immigrants injected the city with new energy. Yet with much of it off the Big Apple's orderly grid, downtown doesn't conform to standard.

Here, the landscape shifts from block to block. In the **Financial District**, gleaming towers rub shoulders with 18th-century landmarks; **Tribeca**'s haute dining spots are only a short hop from **Chinatown**'s frenetic food markets; and around the corner from the flashy nightspots of the **Meatpacking District**, affluent locals reside in stately **West Village** brownstones.

The character of these diverse neighbourhoods is constantly changing, but while the counterculture that erupted in **Greenwich Village** and the **Lower East Side** may have been tamed by relentless gentrification and commercial development, iconoclastic art, vibrant nightlife and independent shops still thrive.

Map pp402-403
Hotels pp223-234

Restaurants & cafés pp143-162
Bars pp177-182

THE FINANCIAL DISTRICT
Battery Park

Subway J, Z to Broad Street; R to Whitehall Street-South Ferry; 1 to South Ferry; 4, 5 to Bowling Green.

It's easy to forget that Manhattan is an island – what with all those gargantuan skyscrapers obscuring your view of the water. Until, that is, you reach the southern tip, where salty ocean breezes are reminders of the millions of immigrants who travelled on steamers in search of prosperity, liberty and a new home. This is where they landed, after passing through Ellis Island's immigration and quarantine centres.

On the edge of Battery Park, **Castle Clinton** was one of several forts built to defend New York Harbor against attacks by the British in the War of 1812 (others included Castle Williams on Governors Island, Fort Gibson on Ellis Island and Fort Wood, now the base of the Statue of Liberty). After serving as an aquarium, immigration centre and opera house, the sandstone fort is now a visitors' centre and ticket booth for **Statue of Liberty** and **Ellis Island** tours (although it's preferable to book online; *see p49*), as well as an intimate, open-air setting for concerts. The park is a key venue of the annual **River to River Festival** (*see p32*) – a summertime celebration of downtown culture and the city's largest free arts festival.

Joining the throngs making their way to Lady Liberty, you'll head south-east along the shore, where several ferry terminals jut into the harbour. Among them is the **Whitehall Ferry Terminal**, the boarding place for the famous **Staten Island Ferry** (*see p43*). Constructed in 1907, the terminal was severely damaged by fire in 1991, but was completely rebuilt in 2005. More than 75,000 passengers take the free, 25-minute journey to Staten Island each day; most are commuters but many are tourists, taking advantage of the views of the Manhattan skyline and the Statue of Liberty. Before the Brooklyn Bridge was completed in 1883, the **Battery Maritime Building** (11 South Street, between Broad & Whitehall Streets) served as a terminal for the ferry services between Manhattan and Brooklyn. Now, it's the launch point for a free ferry to tranquil **Governors Island** on summer weekends (*see p48* **Island Getaway**).

Just north of Battery Park you'll find the triangular **Bowling Green**, the city's oldest park and a popular lunchtime spot for Financial District workers; it's also the front lawn of the **Alexander Hamilton US Custom House**, now home to the **National Museum of the American Indian** (*see p49*). On its northern side stands a three-and-a-half-ton bronze sculpture of a bull (symbolising the bull, or rising, share market). The statue was deposited without permission outside the Stock Exchange by guerrilla artist Arturo di Modica in 1989 and has since been moved by the city to its current location on the Green. The bull's enormous balls are often rubbed for good luck by tourists (and perhaps the occasional broker).

Dwarfed by the surrounding architecture, the **Stone Street Historic District** is a small pocket of restored 1830s buildings on the eponymous winding cobblestoned lane, also encompassing South William and Pearl Streets and Coenties Alley. Office workers and tourists frequent its restaurants and bars, including the boisterous **Ulysses** (95 Pearl Street, between Broad Street & Hanover Square, 1-212 482 0400) and **Stone Street Tavern** (52 Stone Street, between Broad Street & Hanover Square, 1-212 785 5658).

Vestiges of the city's past lurk amid the skyscrapers: the rectory of the **Shrine of St Elizabeth Ann Seton** (7 State Street, between Whitehall Street & Battery Park, 1-212 269 6865, www.setonshrine.com), a 1792 Federal building dedicated to the first American-born saint; and the **Fraunces Tavern Museum** (*see p49*), the restored alehouse where George Washington toasted victory over the British. Marking more recent events, the **New York Vietnam Veterans Memorial** (55 Water Street, between Coenties Slip & Hanover Square) stands one block to the east. Erected in 1985 and refreshed with a new plaza in 2001, it features the Walk of Honor – a pathway inscribed with the names of the 1,741 New Yorkers who lost their lives in the conflict – and a monument etched with excerpts from letters, diary entries and poems written during the war. Nearby, in Hanover Square (William Street at Pearl Street), is the **British**

Battery Park.

Island Getaway

The former military HQ is now an arty seasonal sanctuary.

A 172-acre chunk of prime waterside real estate that can never be developed into luxury condos, **Governors Island** (*see p49*) is a secluded anomaly a scant 800 yards from lower Manhattan. The verdant commons and stately red-brick buildings evoke an Ivy League campus by way of a colonial New England village – oddly emptied of its inhabitants.

The peaceful backwater has had a tumultuous history. Initially a seasonal fishing and gathering ground for the Lenape Indians, it was particularly plentiful in nut trees, earning it the name 'Noten Eylant' when the Dutch arrived in the 1620s. In 1674, the British secured it for 'the benefit and accommodation of His Majesty's Governors'. Perhaps the most colourful of these was Edward Hyde, Viscount Cornbury, Governor of New York and New Jersey from 1702 to 1708. A cousin of Queen Anne, he was alleged to be a cross-dresser (a portrait, said to be of Lord Cornbury in drag, is in the collection of the New-York Historical Society; *see p104*).

The island's strategic position cemented its future as a military outpost (by the late 19th century it was the army's headquarters for the entire eastern US), and it still retains a significant chunk of its military-era construction, including Fort Jay, started in 1776, and Castle Williams, completed in 1812. When the army began to outgrow the space, excavated soil from the Lexington Avenue subway line was used to enlarge the island by 103 acres.

The modest patch has been the backdrop for some huge events. In 1909, it launched the first overwater flight, when Wilbur Wright circled the Statue of Liberty before flying back. Such legendary figures as Generals Ulysses S Grant and Douglas MacArthur had stints on the island.

Since Governors Island opened to visitors in 2006, the programme of events, including concerts and major art installations, has increased dramatically. The first phase of the strategy to revitalise the island has been to draw visitors, explains president of the trust of Governors Island, Leslie Koch. The second is the continued investment in the infrastructure and preservation of its 52 historic landmarks.

The third phase is to create 'a world-class set of public spaces and parks'. In 2007, a team of internationally known design firms, led by Rotterdam's West 8, was chosen to develop the plans. Construction began in spring 2012, and by autumn 2013, 30 acres of green space will open to the public. A Hammock Grove of 1,500 trees will offer shady reclining and 14 acres of lawn will include two ball fields. Eventually, new hills constructed from the debris of demolished (non-historic) buildings will provide even more spectacular viewpoints for harbour panoramas.

EXPLORE

Memorial Garden. Completed in 2007, it commemorates the 67 Britons who died in New York on 9/11, and features hand-carved stone from Scotland, plants from Prince Charles's estate and iron bollards from London.

FREE Alexander Hamilton US Custom House/National Museum of the American Indian

1 Bowling Green, between State & Whitehall Streets (1-212 514 3700, www.nmai.si.edu). Subway R to Whitehall Street-South Ferry; 1 to South Ferry; 4, 5 to Bowling Green. **Open** 10am-5pm Mon-Wed, Fri-Sun; 10am-8pm Thur. **Admission** free. **Map** p402 E33.

Cass Gilbert's magnificent Beaux Arts Custom House, completed in 1907, housed the Customs Service until 1973, when the federal government moved it to the newly built World Trade Center complex. Four monumental figures by Lincoln Memorial sculptor Daniel Chester French – representing America, Asia, Europe and Africa – flank the impressive entrance. The panels surrounding the elliptical rotunda dome were designed to feature murals, but this wasn't realised until the 1930s, when local artist Reginald Marsh was commissioned to decorate them under the New Deal's Works Progress Administration; the paintings depict a ship entering New York Harbor.

In 1994, the National Museum of the American Indian's George Gustav Heye Center, a branch of the Smithsonian, moved into the first two floors of the building. On the second level, the life and culture of Native Americans are illuminated in three galleries radiating out from the rotunda. The permanent exhibition, 'Infinity of Nations', displays 700 of the museum's wide-ranging collection of Native American art and objects, from decorated baskets to elaborate ceremonial headdresses, organised by geographical region. Changing exhibitions showcase contemporary artwork. On the ground floor, the Diker Pavilion for Native Arts & Culture is the city's only dedicated showcase for Native American performing arts.

Fraunces Tavern Museum

2nd & 3rd Floors, 54 Pearl Street, at Broad Street (1-212 425 1778, www.frauncestavernmuseum. org). Subway J, Z to Broad Street; 4, 5 to Bowling Green. **Open** noon-5pm daily. **Admission** $7; $4 reductions; free under-6s. **Credit** AmEx, Disc, MC, V. **Map** p402 E33.

True, George Washington slept here, but there's little left of the original 18th-century tavern he favoured during the Revolution. Fire-damaged and rebuilt in the 19th century, it was reconstructed in its current Colonial Revival style in 1907. The museum itself features period rooms, a collection of 800 reproduction regimental flags, paintings devoted to events of the Revolutionary War, and such Washington relics as a lock of his hair. It was

here, after the British had finally been defeated, that Washington took tearful farewell of his troops and vowed to retire from public life. Luckily, he had a change of heart six years later and became the country's first president. You can still raise a pint in the bar, which is now run by Dublin's Porterhouse Brewing Company.

★ FREE Governors Island

1-212 440 2202, www.govisland.com. Subway R to Whitehall Street-South Ferry; 1 to South Ferry; 4, 5 to Bowling Green. Then take ferry from Battery Maritime Building at Slip no.7. **Open** Late May-late Sept (see website for hours and ferry schedule). *See p48* **Island Getaway**.

★ Statue of Liberty & Ellis Island Immigration Museum

Liberty Island & Ellis Island (1-212 363 3200, www.nps.gov/stli, www.nps.gov/elis). Subway R to Whitehall Street-South Ferry; 1 to South Ferry; 4, 5 to Bowling Green. Then take Statue of Liberty ferry (1-201 604 2800, 1-877 523 9849, www. statuecruises.com), departing from gangway 4 or 5 in southernmost Battery Park. **Open** Call or see website for information. **Admission** Call or see website for information. **Credit** AmEx, DC, MC, V.

As this guide went to press, the Statue of Liberty and Ellis Island were closed due to damage caused by Hurricane Sandy, and the National Park Service was unable to provide a reopening date. For up-to-date information, visit the websites.

For the Statue of Liberty, *see p51* **Profile**. A half-mile across the harbour from Liberty Island is the 32-acre Ellis Island, gateway for over 12 million people who entered the country between 1892 and 1954. In the Immigration Museum (a former check-in depot), three floors of photos, interactive displays and exhibits pay tribute to the hopeful souls who made the voyage. Tickets can be purchased online, by phone or at Castle Clinton in Battery Park.

World Trade Center site & Battery Park City

Subway A, C to Broadway-Nassau Street; E to World Trade Center; J, Z, 2, 3, 4, 5 to Fulton Street; R, 1 to Rector Street; 4, 5 to Bowling Green.

The streets around the site of the former World Trade Center have been drawing the bereaved and the curious since that traumatic day in September 2001. The worst attack on US soil took nearly 3,000 lives and left a gaping hole where the Twin Towers had once helped to define the New York skyline. After the site was fenced off, there wasn't much to see for almost a decade. Construction on the new World Trade Center complex – due to include five office buildings, a performing arts centre and a transit hub designed by Santiago Calatrava – has been

EXPLORE

plagued by infighting, missed deadlines and budget overruns, but the National September 11 Memorial opened as planned on the tenth anniversary of the attacks (*see p55* **Rebuilding Ground Zero**). The **National September 11 Museum** won't be completed until late 2013 or early 2014, but before then, visitors can stop by the **9/11 Memorial Preview Site** (*see p52*) to get a sense of how the finished site will look. Until the museum opens, the **9/11 Tribute Center** (*see p52*), established in 2006 by a not-for-profit organisation formed by families of the victims, provides insight into the tragedy through artefacts and a timeline of events. Although still under construction, the development's centrepiece skyscraper, **1 World Trade Center** (the renamed Freedom Tower) has now overtaken the Empire State Building as the city's tallest building; after it's completed in early 2014, it will count media giant Condé Nast, publisher of the *New Yorker*, *Vogue* and other titles, among its tenants. Calatrava's ambitious designs for the PATH/subway transportation hub, due for completion in 2015, were scaled back due to budget constraints.

Just east of the World Trade Center site, bargain hunters can sift through designer duds at discount department store **Century 21** (*see p199*). And west of it, the glass and granite office towers of the **World Financial Center** (from Liberty to Vesey Streets, between the Hudson River & West Street, 1-212 417 7000, www.worldfinancialcenter.com) overlook a marina; the complex's Winter Garden hosts numerous arts events, including June's annual contemporary-classical music festival Bang on a Can Marathon (www.bangonacan.org).

The World Financial Center abuts **Battery Park City**, a 92-acre planned community devised in the 1950s to replace decaying shipping piers with new apartments, green spaces and schools. It's a man-made addition to the island, built on soil and rocks excavated from the original World Trade Center construction site and sediment dredged from New York Harbor. Home to roughly 10,000 people, the neighbourhood was devastated after 9/11, and nearly half of its residents moved away, although the area has been improved with new commercial development drawn by economic incentives. Visitors can enjoy its esplanade, a favoured route for bikers, skaters and joggers, and a string of parks that run north along the Hudson River from Battery Park.

Providing expansive views of the Statue of Liberty and Ellis Island at its southernmost reaches, the stretch is dotted with monuments and sculptures. Close by the marina is the 1997 **Police Memorial** (Liberty Street, at South End Avenue), a granite pool and fountain that symbolically trace the lifespan of a police officer through the use of moving water, with names of the fallen etched into the wall. The **Irish Hunger Memorial** (Vesey Street, at North End Avenue) is here too, paying tribute to those who suffered during the famine from 1845 to 1852. Designed by artist Brian Tolle and landscape architect Gail Wittwer-Laird, the quarter-acre memorial incorporates vegetation, soil and stones from Ireland's various counties, and a reproduction of a 19th-century Irish cottage.

To the north, **Nelson A Rockefeller Park** attracts sun worshippers, kite flyers and soccer players in the warm-weather months. Look out for Tom Otterness's whimsical sculpture installation, *The Real World*. Just east is **Teardrop Park**, a two-acre space designed to evoke the bucolic Hudson River Valley, and to the south are the inventively designed **South Cove**, with its quays and island, and **Robert F Wagner Jr Park**, where an observation deck offers fabulous views of both the harbour and the Verrazano-Narrows Bridge; below it, Louise Bourgeois's *Eyes* gaze over the Hudson from the lawn. The **Museum of Jewish Heritage** (*see below*), Gotham's memorial to the Holocaust, is on the edge of the green. Across the street at the **Skyscraper Museum** (*see p52*), you can learn about the buildings that have created the city's iconic skyline.

Museum of Jewish Heritage: A Living Memorial to the Holocaust

Robert F Wagner Jr Park, 36 Battery Place, at First Place (1-646 437 4200, www.mjhnyc.org). Subway 4, 5 to Bowling Green. **Open** 10am-5.45pm Mon, Tue, Thur, Sun; 10am-8pm Wed; 10am-5pm Fri (until 3pm Nov-mid Mar); 10am-3pm eve of Jewish hols. **Admission** $12; $7-$10 reductions; free under-13s; free 4-8pm Wed. **Credit** AmEx, DC, MC, V. **Map** p402 E34.
This museum explores Jewish life before, during and after the Nazi genocide. The permanent collection includes documentary films, thousands of photos and 800 artefacts, many donated by Holocaust survivors and their families. The Keeping History Center brings the collection to life with interactive displays, including 'Voices of Liberty', a soundscape of émigrés' and refugees' reactions to arrival in the United States – made all the more poignant juxtaposed with the museum's panoramic views of Ellis Island and the Statue of Liberty. Special exhibitions tackle historical events or themes. The Memorial Garden features English artist Andy Goldsworthy's *Garden of Stones*, 18 fire-hollowed boulders embedded with dwarf oak saplings.

National September 11 Memorial & Museum

Enter on Albany Street, at Greenwich Street (1-212 266 5211, www.911memorial.org). Subway A, C, J, Z, 2, 3, 4, 5 to Fulton Street; E to World

Profile Statue of Liberty

The long history of New York's first lady.

Although she no longer greets new arrivals, the **Statue of Liberty** (*see p49*) is still New York's, if not America's, most iconic sight. The sole occupant of Liberty Island, she stands 305 feet from the bottom of her base to the tip of her gold-leaf torch. Up close, you can appreciate how huge she truly is: her nose is four and a half feet long.

Lady Liberty was intended as a gift from France on America's 100th birthday. Frédéric Auguste Bartholdi, the statue's designer, was inspired by the ancient Colossus at Rhodes, although it was said that the face was modelled on that of his mother – and the body on that of his mistress. Bartholdi had initially planned a giant lighthouse-statue to stand sentry at the mouth of the Suez Canal, then under construction.

But when the Egyptians were unreceptive, Bartholdi turned to New York Harbor. And so the proposed *Egypt Bringing Light to Asia* was reborn as *Liberty Enlightening the World*, the current statue's official title, as the French raised millions of francs to fund this expression of friendship for their ally from the Revolutionary War.

Construction began in Paris in 1874, with Gustave Eiffel (of Tower fame) crafting the skeletal iron framework. However, the French desire that she should be completed in time for America's centennial proved ill-fated: only the arm and torch were finished. The celebrated limb was exhibited at the Centennial Exhibition in Philadelphia and then spent six years on show in Madison Square Park; the head, meanwhile, was first displayed at the 1878 Paris Exposition.

In 1884, the statue was finally completed – only to be taken apart into hundreds of pieces to be shipped to New York, where it was placed on its pedestal and unveiled by President Grover Cleveland in 1886. It served as a lighthouse until 1902 and as the welcoming sign for millions of immigrants. These 'tired… poor… huddled masses' were evoked in Emma Lazarus's poem 'The New Colossus', written in 1883 to raise funds for the pedestal and engraved inside the statue in 1903.

After a year-long renovation, the interior of the statue was set to reopen in autumn 2012, allowing visitors to enter the pedestal and crown. But then Hurricane Sandy struck, causing significant damage to the statue's infrastructure. As this guide went to press, the Statue of Liberty remained closed to visitors, and a reopening date had yet to be determined.

EXPLORE

VITAL STATS
There are 345 steps from her base to her top; she weighs 204 tons and has a 35-foot waist.

Trade Center; N, R, 1 to Rector Street. **Open**
Mar-Sept 10am-8pm daily. *Oct-Feb* 10am-6pm
daily (see website for updates and extended
holiday hours). **Map** p402 E32.

Until construction is completed on the World Trade
Center site, visitors must reserve timed entry passes
to the memorial online or at the 9/11 Memorial
Preview Site (20 Vesey Street, at Church Street),
where you can also see an architectural model of the
plans and other displays; there are further exhibits
at the visitor centre (90 West Street, at Albany
Street). *See p55* **Rebuilding Ground Zero**.

Skyscraper Museum

*39 Battery Place, between Little West Street & 1st
Place (1-212 968 1961, www.skyscraper.org).
Subway 4, 5 to Bowling Green.* **Open** noon-6pm
Wed-Sun. **Admission** $5; $2.50 reductions.
Credit AmEx, Disc, MC, V. **Map** p402 E34.

The only institution of its kind in the world, this
modest space explores high-rise buildings as objects
of design, products of technology, real-estate invest-
ments and places of work and residence. A large part
of the single gallery (a mirrored ceiling gives the illusion of height) is devoted to temporary exhibitions –
such as one celebrating the Woolworth Building's
centennial, through July 2013.

A substantial chunk of the permanent collection
relates to the Word Trade Center, including original
models of the Twin Towers and the 1,776ft 1 World
Trade Center, currently under construction on the site.
Other highlights of the display are large-scale photographs of lower Manhattan's skyscrapers from 1956,
1976 and 2004, and a 1931 silent film documenting
the Empire State Building's construction.
► *For more on the history of New York's
skyscrapers, see p367* **Race to the Top**.

9/11 Tribute Center

*120 Liberty Street, between Church & Greenwich
Streets (1-866 737 1184, www.tributewtc.org).
Subway A, C to Broadway-Nassau Street; E to
World Trade Center; J, Z, 2, 3, 4, 5 to Fulton
Street; R, 1 to Rector Street.* **Open** 10am-6pm
Mon-Sat; 10am-5pm Sun. **Admission** $15; free
under-12s. **Credit** AmEx, MC, V. **Map** p402 E32.

Created by a not-for-profit organisation started by
families of 9/11 victims, this centre serves several
functions: a collective memorial; a historical testament of the events and aftermath; and a repository
of morbidly fascinating artefacts from that unthink-
able day. Ground-floor galleries contain a timeline
of the tragedy on panels the same width as the Twin
Towers' windows, along with recovered objects; a
strangely unharmed paper menu from the 106th-
floor Windows on the World restaurant contrasts
sharply with a twisted steel beam from the wreck-
age. The final gallery contains photographs and
names of the dead; tissues are provided. Downstairs,
visitors are invited to write down their own memories or feelings, a selection of which are posted.

Wall Street

*Subway J, Z to Broad Street; R, 1 to Rector
Street; 2, 3, 4, 5 to Wall Street.*

Since the city's earliest days as a fur-trading
post, commerce has been the backbone of its
prosperity. The southern point of Manhattan
quickly evolved into the Financial District
because, in the days before telecommunications,
banks established their headquarters near the
city's active port. Although the neighbourhood
is bisected vertically by the ever-bustling
Broadway, it's the east–west **Wall Street** (or
'the Street' in trader lingo) that's synonymous
with the world's greatest den of capitalism.

The name derives from a defensive wooden
wall built in 1653 to mark the northern limit of
New Amsterdam, and despite its huge
significance, the thoroughfare is less than a mile
long. At its western intersection with Broadway,
you'll find the Gothic Revival spire of **Trinity
Wall Street** (*see p54*). The original church
burned down in 1776, and a second was
demolished in 1839; the current version became
the island's tallest structure when it was
completed in 1846. **St Paul's Chapel** (*see
p54*), the church's older satellite, is one of the
finest Georgian structures in the US.

A block to the east of Trinity, at 26 Wall
Street, is the **Federal Hall National
Memorial** (26 Wall Street, at Nassau Street
(1-212 825 6990, www.nps.gov/feha, closed Sat,
Sun), an august Greek Revival building and
– in a previous incarnation – the site of George
Washington's first inauguration. It was along
this stretch that corporate America made its first
audacious architectural statements; a walk
eastwards offers much evidence of what money
can buy. Structures include the **Bankers Trust
Building** at 14 Wall Street (at Broad Street),
completed in 1912 and crowned by a seven-
storey pyramid modelled on the Mausoleum
of Halicarnassus; **40 Wall Street** (between
Nassau & William Streets), which battled the
Chrysler Building in 1929 for the title of world's
tallest building (the Empire State trounced them

INSIDE TRACK
ABOVE THE FRAY

Slip inside the Financial District office
complex at 55 Water Street, between
Broad Street and Old Slip, and take
the escalator up to the **Elevated Acre**
(www.elevatedacre.com), a hidden open-
air park more than 30 feet (nine metres)
above street level that commands a great
view of the East River and Brooklyn Bridge.

Wall Street.

both in 1931); and the former **Merchants' Exchange** at 55 Wall Street (between Hanover & William Streets), with its stacked rows of Ionic and Corinthian columns, giant doors and a remarkable ballroom. Back around the corner is the **Equitable Building** (120 Broadway, between Cedar & Pine Streets), whose greedy use of vertical space helped to instigate the zoning laws that now govern skyscrapers; stand across the street from the building to get the best view. Nearby is the **Federal Reserve Bank** (*see below*), with its huge gold vault.

The nerve centre of the US economy is the **New York Stock Exchange** (11 Wall Street, between Broad & New Streets). For security reasons, the Exchange is no longer open to the public, but the street outside offers an endless pageant of brokers, traders and their minions. For a lesson on Wall Street's influence over the years, and the recent credit crisis, visit the **Museum of American Finance** (*see right*). A few blocks from the East River end of Wall Street, on Old Slip, is the **New York City Police Museum** (*see p54*).

FREE Federal Reserve Bank

Visitors' entrance: 44 Maiden Lane, between Nassau & William Streets (1-212 720 6130, www. ny.frb.org/aboutthefed/visiting.html). Subway 2, 3, 4, 5 to Wall Street. **Tours** (reservations required)

11.15am, noon, 12.45pm, 1.30pm, 2.15pm, 3pm, 4pm Mon-Fri. **Admission** free. **Map** p402 E33. For security reasons, tours of this important financial institution must be booked well in advance – the easiest way to do this is online, as a calendar feature shows availability – and a photo ID must be presented upon admission. Descend 50ft below street level and you'll find roughly a quarter of the world's monetary gold (more than $100 billion dollars' worth), stored in a gigantic vault that rests on the solid bedrock of Manhattan Island. Visitors learn about the precious metal's history and the role of the New York Fed in its safeguarding.

Museum of American Finance

48 Wall Street, at William Street (1-212 908 4110, www.moaf.org). Subway 2, 3, 4, 5 to Wall Street; R, 1 to Rector Street. **Open** 10am-4pm Tue-Sat. **Admission** $8; $5 reductions; free under-7s. **Credit** AmEx, MC, V. **Map** p402 E33.

Situated in the old headquarters of the Bank of New York, the permanent collection traces the history of Wall Street and America's financial markets. Displays in the stately banking hall include a bearer bond made out to President George Washington and ticker tape from the morning of the stock market crash of 1929. A timeline, 'Tracking the Credit Crisis' helps to clarify the current global predicament, while themed temporary exhibitions bring the world of money to life.

New York City Police Museum

100 Old Slip, between South & Water Streets
(1-212 480 3100, www.nycpolicemuseum.org).
Subway J, Z to Broad Street; 2, 3, 4, 5 to Wall
Street. **Open** 10am-5pm Mon-Sat; noon-5pm Sun.
Admission $8; $5 reductions. **Credit** AmEx,
Disc, MC, V. **Map** p402 F33.

Housed in the former First Precinct, this institution
tracks more than 300 years of New York City policing. Exhibits include vintage uniforms, squad cars
and firearms, alongside more notorious artefacts
such a gun used by one of Al Capone's minions in
the 1928 murder of Frankie Yale. The museum's
ongoing exhibit, 'Policing a Changed City', looks at
the force's evolving role in a post-9/11 New York.

FREE Trinity Wall Street & St Paul's Chapel

Trinity Wall Street *89 Broadway, at Wall Street*
(1-212 602 0800, www.trinitywallstreet.org).
Subway R, 1 to Rector Street; 2, 3, 4, 5 to Wall
Street. **Open** 7am-6pm Mon-Fri; 8am-4pm Sat;
7am-4pm Sun. **Admission** free. **Map** p402 E33.
St Paul's Chapel *209 Broadway, between Fulton*
& Vesey Streets (1-212 233 4164, www.trinity
wallstreet.org). Subway A, C to Broadway-Nassau
Street; J, Z, 2, 3, 4, 5 to Fulton Street. **Open**
10am-6pm Mon-Sat; 7am-6pm Sun. **Admission**
free. **Map** p402 E32.

Trinity Church was the island's tallest structure
when it was completed in 1846 (the original burned
down in 1776; a second was demolished in 1839). A
set of gates north of the church on Broadway allows
access to the adjacent cemetery, where cracked and
faded tombstones mark the final resting places of
dozens of past city dwellers, including such notable
New Yorkers as founding father Alexander
Hamilton (*see p353* **Profile**), business tycoon John
Jacob Astor and steamboat inventor Robert Fulton.
The church museum displays historic diaries, photographs, sermons and burial records.

Six blocks to the north, Trinity's satellite, St Paul's
Chapel, is more important architecturally. The oldest
building in New York still in continuous use (it dates
from 1766), it is one of the nation's most valued
Georgian structures.

▶ *For Trinity's dirt-cheap Concerts at One series,*
see p301 **Inside Track**.

South Street Seaport

Subway A, C to Broadway-Nassau Street;
J, Z, 2, 3, 4, 5 to Fulton Street.

New York's fortunes originally rolled in on the
swells that crashed into its harbour. The city
was perfectly situated for trade with Europe
and, after 1825, goods from the Western
Territories arrived via the Erie Canal and the
Hudson River. By 1892, New York was also
the point of entry for millions of immigrants.

The **South Street Seaport** is the best place to
appreciate this port heritage.

If you enter the Seaport area from Water
Street, the first thing you're likely to spot is the
whitewashed **Titanic Memorial Lighthouse**.
It was originally erected on top of the Seaman's
Church Institute (Coenties Slip & South Street)
in 1913, the year after the great ship sank,
but was moved to its current location at the
intersection of Pearl and Fulton Streets in
1976. Check out the magnificent views of the
Brooklyn Bridge from this bit of the district.

When New York's role as a vital shipping
hub diminished during the 20th century, the
South Street Seaport area fell into disuse, but a
massive redevelopment project in the mid 1980s
saw old buildings converted into restaurants,
bars, chain stores and the **South Street
Seaport Museum** (*see below*). The public
spaces, including pedestrianised sections of both
Fulton and Front Streets, are a favourite with
sightseers and street performers, but it's only
recently that New Yorkers have begun to
rediscover the area, attracted by the arrival of
cool cafés and bars such as **Jack's Stir Brew
Coffee** (*see p144*) and sleek wine bar **Bin No.
220** (220 Front Street, between Beekman Street
& Peck Slip, 1-212 374 9463). Free summer
concerts, held during the River to River Festival
(*see p32*), are another draw.

Pier 17 once supported the famous Fulton
Fish Market, a bustling, early-morning trading
centre dating back to the mid 1800s. However,
in 2006 the market relocated to a larger facility
in the Hunts Point area of the Bronx (*see
p132*). Interest in Pier 17, now occupied by
an unremarkable mall, dwindled after its
redevelopment in the 1980s, although the
recent arrival of **Beekman Beer Garden
Beach Club** (1-212 896 4600, www.beekman
beergarden.com), a seasonal sandy patch
offering ping pong, craft beer and bar food on
the pier's north side, has boosted its appeal. A
proposal to replace the mall with a mixed-use
complex, including shops and a hotel, has been
stalled by local opposition and the recession, but
the plan by SHoP Architects has been approved
by the Landmarks Preservation Commission.
The city has embarked on its East River
Esplanade and Piers Project, which will
landscape this stretch of waterfront – the first
section, just south of the Seaport, opened in
summer 2011. **Pier 15** has been transformed
into a bi-level lounging space, comprising a
lawned viewing deck above a café and,
eventually, a maritime education centre.

South Street Seaport Museum

12 Fulton Street, at South Street (1-212 748
8600, www.southstreetseaportmuseum.org).
Subway A, C to Broadway-Nassau Street; J, Z, 2,

Rebuilding Ground Zero

The new World Trade Center takes shape.

For most of the decade following 9/11, those who made the pilgrimage to Ground Zero were confronted by an impenetrable fence, and although plans for the World Trade Center site's redevelopment were announced in 2003, there wasn't much evidence of progress. Yet, as the tenth anniversary of the attacks loomed, construction surged, and the 9/11 Memorial opened to visitors on 11 September 2011. In spring 2012, the site's centrepiece tower, 1 World Trade Center, surpassed the Empire State Building as the city's tallest skyscraper; it's expected to be reach its full height of 1,776 feet in spring 2013.

The **National September 11 Memorial & Museum** (*see p50*) occupies half of the WTC site's 16 acres. The memorial itself, Reflecting Absence, designed by architects Michael Arad and Peter Walker, comprises two one-acre 'footprints' of the destroyed towers, with 30-foot man-made waterfalls – the country's largest – cascading down their sides. Bronze parapets around the edges are inscribed with the names of those who died. As the title makes clear,

the intention is to convey a powerful sense of loss. Budget overruns have delayed completion of the underground museum, but you can see its pavilion, designed by Snøhetta – the Oslo-based firm behind its home city's New Norwegian National Opera & Ballet building (2008) – between the waterfalls. Its web-like glass atrium houses two steel trident-shaped columns salvaged from the base of the Twin Towers.

Once it opens in late 2013 or early 2014, visitors will be able to descend to the vast spaces of the original foundations alongside a remnant of the Vesey Street staircase known as the 'Survivors' Stairs', as it was used by hundreds escaping the carnage. The collection commemorates the victims of both the 1993 and 2001 attacks on the World Trade Center. Survivors and victims' families have donated items and helped weave personal tales of people who died in the towers. One gallery will be devoted to artists' responses to the events, and items like the East Village's Ladder Company 3 fire truck, which was dispatched to the towers with 11 firefighters who died during the rescue, will be on display.

EXPLORE

South Street Seaport. *See p54.*

3, 4, 5 to Fulton Street. **Open** 10am-6pm daily. **Admission** $10; $6 reductions; free under-9s. **Credit** AmEx, MC, V. **Map** p402 F32.

Founded in 1967, the South Street Seaport Museum now operates under the auspices of the Museum of the City of New York (*see p99*). The Museum Mile institution brought new programming, including *Timescapes*, a 22-minute multimedia presentation that illuminates the history of NYC. In addition to three floors of galleries devoted to changing exhibitions illuminating aspects of the city and its relationship with the sea, the museum also encompasses historic ships and Bowne & Co Stationers (*see p213*).

City Hall Park

Subway J, Z to Chambers Street; R to City Hall; 2, 3 to Park Place; 4, 5, 6 to Brooklyn Bridge-City Hall.

The business of running New York takes place in the grand buildings in and around **City Hall**

Park, an area that formed the budding city's northern boundary in the 1700s. The park itself was renovated just before the millennium, and pretty landscaping and abundant benches make it a popular lunching spot for office workers.

At the park's southern end, a granite 'time wheel' tracks its history. At the northern end of the park, **City Hall** (*see p57*) houses the mayor's office and the chambers of the City Council. When City Hall was completed in 1812, its architects were so confident that the city would grow no further north that they didn't bother to put any marble on its northern side. Nevertheless, the building is a beautiful blend of Federalist form and French Renaissance detail. Overlooking the park from the west is Cass Gilbert's famous **Woolworth Building** (233 Broadway, between Barclay Street & Park Place), the tallest building in the world when it opened in 1913. The neo-Gothic skyscraper's grand spires, gargoyles, vaulted ceilings and church-like interior earned it the moniker 'the Cathedral of Commerce'.

Behind City Hall, on Chambers Street, is the 1872 Old New York County Courthouse; it's popularly known as the **Tweed Courthouse**, a symbol of the runaway corruption of mid 19th-century municipal government. William 'Boss' Tweed (*see p355*), leader of the political machine Tammany Hall, famously pocketed some $10 million of the building's $14 million construction budget. What he didn't steal bought a beautiful edifice, with exquisite Italianate detailing. These days, it houses the city's Department of Education and a New York City public school, but it's also open for tours (1-212 788 2656, www.nyc.gov/designcommission). To the east,

> ### INSIDE TRACK
> ### THE GHOST SUBWAY STATION
>
> If you take the 6 train to its last downtown stop, Brooklyn Bridge-City Hall, ignore the recorded entreaty to get off. Stay aboard while the train makes its U-turn loop before heading uptown and you'll get a glimpse of the original 1904 City Hall Station (out of use since 1945) and its brass chandeliers, vaulted ceilings, tile mosaics and skylights.

other civic offices and services occupy the one million square feet of office space in the 1914 **Manhattan Municipal Building** at 1 Centre Street. This landmark limestone structure, built by McKim Mead & White, also houses New York City's official gift shop (www.nyc.gov/citystore, closed Sat, Sun).

The houses of crime and punishment are located in the **Civic Center**, near Foley Square, once a pond and later the site of the city's most notorious 19th-century slum, Five Points. These days, you'll find the State Supreme Court in the **New York County Courthouse** (60 Centre Street, at Pearl Street), a hexagonal Roman Revival building; the beautiful rotunda is decorated with a mural entitled *Law Through the Ages*. The **United States Courthouse** (40 Centre Street, between Duane & Pearl Streets) is a Corinthian temple crowned with a golden pyramid.

The **Criminal Courts Building & Manhattan Detention Complex** (100 Centre Street, between Leonard & White Streets) is still known as 'the Tombs', a nod to the original 1838 Egyptian Revival building – or, depending on who you ask, its current grimness. There's no denying that the hall's great granite slabs and looming towers are downright lugubrious.

Nearby, the **African Burial Ground** (*see below*) was officially designated a National Monument in 2006.

FREE African Burial Ground

Duane Street, between Broadway & Centre Streets, behind 290 Broadway (1-212 637 2019, www.nps. gov/afbg). Subway J, Z to Chambers Street; R to City Hall; 4, 5, 6 to Brooklyn Bridge-City Hall. **Open** 9am-5pm daily. *Visitor centre* 10am-4pm Tue-Sat. **Admission** free. **Map** p402 E31.

A major archaeological discovery, the African Burial Ground is a small remnant of a 6.6-acre unmarked gravesite where between 10,000 and 20,000 enslaved Africans – men, women and children – were buried. The burial ground, which closed in 1794, was unearthed during the construction of a federal office building in 1991 and later designated a National Monument. In 2007, a stone memorial, designed by architect Rodney Leon, was erected; the tall, curved structure draws heavily on African architecture and contains a spiral path leading to an ancestral chamber. The visitor centre is located on the ground floor of 290 Broadway, south of the building's main entrance.

FREE City Hall

City Hall Park, from Vesey to Chambers Streets, between Broadway & Park Row (1-212 788 2656, www.nyc.gov/designcommission). Subway J, Z to Chambers Street; R to City Hall; 2, 3 to Park Place; 4, 5, 6 to Brooklyn Bridge-City Hall. **Open** *Tours* (individuals) noon Wed, 10am Thur;

City Hall

EXPLORE

(groups) 10.30am Mon-Wed. **Admission** free.
Map p402 E32.

Designed by French émigré Joseph François Mangin and New Yorker John McComb Jr, the fine, Federal-style City Hall was completed in 1812. Tours take in the City Council Chamber and the Governor's Room, which houses a collection of American 19th-century political portraits as well as historic furnishings (notably including George Washington's desk). Individuals can book (at least two days in advance) for the Thursday morning tour; alternatively, sign up before 11.45am on Wednesday at the NYC tourism kiosk at the southern end of City Hall Park on the east side of Broadway, at Barclay Street; the tour is limited to 20 people on a first-come, first-served basis. Group tours should be booked at least a week in advance.

TRIBECA & SOHO

Subway A, C, E, 1 to Canal Street; C, E to Spring Street; N, R to Prince Street; 1 to Franklin Street or Houston Street.

In the 1960s and '70s, artists colonised the former industrial wasteland that was **Tribeca** (the Triangle Below Canal Street), squatting in its abandoned warehouses. Following the example of fellow creatives in neighbouring Soho, they eventually worked with the city to rezone and restore them. The preponderance of large, hulking former industrial buildings gives Tribeca an imposing profile, but fine small-scale cast-iron architecture still stands along White Street and the parallel thoroughfares.

Seeking luxury (and privacy), many celebrities have settled in the area. Robert De Niro is the neighbourhood's best-known resident, founding the **Tribeca Film Center** (375 Greenwich Street, at Franklin Street) with partner Jane Rosenthal in 1988, which contains industry magnet and neighbourhood stalwart **Tribeca Grill** (1-212 941 3900). A few blocks away, De Niro's **Tribeca Cinemas** (54 Varick Street, at Laight Street, 1-212 941 2001, www.tribeca cinemas.com) hosts premieres and glitzy parties, when it isn't serving as a venue for the **Tribeca Film Festival** (*see p29*). In 2008, the actor unveiled the exclusive **Greenwich Hotel** (*see p225*).

Upscale retail and haute eateries cater to the well-heeled locals. Browse luxe basics at the shop/studio of **Nili Lotan** (188 Duane Street, between Greenwich & Hudson Streets, 1-212 219 8794, www.nililotan.com) and **Grown & Sewn** (116 Franklin Street, between Church Street & West Broadway, 1-917 686 2964, www.grownandsewn.com, closed Sun), home of a handcrafted line created by a former Ralph Lauren design director. Top dining options include sushi shrine **Nobu** (105 Hudson Street,

between Franklin & N Moore Streets, 1-212 219 0500, www.noburestaurants.com); modern French restaurant **Corton** (*see p145*); and the evolving empire of celebrity chef David Bouley, including his flagship **Bouley** (163 Duane Street, at Hudson Street, 1-212 964 2525, www.davidbouley.com) and his superb Japanese venture **Brushstroke** (*see p145*).

Now a retail mecca of the highest order, **Soho** (the area South of Houston Street) was once a hardscrabble manufacturing zone with the derisive nickname Hell's Hundred Acres. In the 1960s, it was earmarked for destruction by over-zealous urban planner Robert Moses, but its signature cast-iron warehouses were saved by the artists who inhabited them as cheap live-work spaces. The **King & Queen of Greene Street** (respectively, 72-76 Greene Street, between Broome & Spring Streets, and 28-30 Greene Street, between Canal & Grand Streets) are both fine examples of the area's beloved architectural landmarks. The most celebrated of Soho's cast-iron edifices, however, is the five-storey **Haughwout Building**, at 488-492 Broadway, at Broome Street. Designed in 1857, it featured the world's first hydraulic lift (still in working condition).

After landlords sniffed the potential for profits in converting old loft buildings, Soho morphed into a playground for the young, beautiful and rich. It can still be a pleasure to stroll around the cobblestoned side streets on weekday mornings, and there are some standout shops in the area, but the large chain stores and sidewalk-encroaching street vendors along Broadway create a shopping-mall-at-Christmas crush on weekends. Although many of the galleries that made Soho an art capital in the 1970s and '80s decamped to Chelsea and, more recently, the Lower East Side, some excellent art spaces remain, including the newly expanded **Drawing Center**. Also in the neighbourhood is the **New York City Fire Museum** (for both, *see p59*).

Just west of West Broadway, tenement- and townhouse-lined streets contain remnants of the Italian community that once dominated the area. Elderly men and women stroll along Sullivan Street to **St Anthony of Padua Roman Catholic Church** (no.155, at Houston Street), dedicated in 1888. You'll still find old-school neighbourhood flavour at **Joe's Dairy** (no.156, between Houston & Prince Streets, 1-212 677 8780, closed Mon, Sun) and **Pino's Prime Meat Market** (no.149, 1-212 475 8134, closed Sun). The iconic Vesuvio Bakery is now occupied by **Birdbath Neighborhood Green Bakery** (160 Prince Street, between Thompson Street & West Broadway, 1-646 556 7720, www.buildagreenbakery.com), which has kept the old-fashioned façade intact.

EXPLORE

★ Drawing Center

35 Wooster Street, between Broome & Grand Streets (1-212 219 2166, www.drawingcenter.org). Subway A, C, E, 1 to Canal Street. **Open** noon-6pm Wed-Sun; noon-8pm Thur. **Admission** $5; $3 reductions; free under-12s; free 6-8pm Thur. **Credit** AmEx, Disc, MC, V. **Map** p403 E30.

Established in 1977, this non-profit standout recently reopened after expanding its gallery space by 50%. Now comprising three galleries, the Drawing Center assembles shows of museum-calibre legends such as Philip Guston, James Ensor and Willem de Kooning, but also 'Selections' surveys of newcomers. Art stars such as Kara Walker, Chris Ofili and Julie Mehretu received some of their earliest NYC exposure here.

New York City Fire Museum

278 Spring Street, between Hudson & Varick Streets (1-212 691 1303, www.nycfiremuseum.org). Subway C, E to Spring Street; 1 to Houston Street. **Open** 10am-5pm daily. **Admission** $8; $5 reductions. **Credit** AmEx, Disc, MC, V. **Map** p403 D30.

An active firehouse from 1904 to 1959, this museum is filled with all manner of life-saving gadgetry, from late 18th-century hand-pumped fire engines to present-day equipment.

LITTLE ITALY & NOLITA

Subway B, D, F, M to Broadway-Lafayette Street; J, N, Q, R, Z, 6 to Canal Street; J, Z to Bowery; N, R to Prince Street; 6 to Spring Street.

Abandoning the dismal tenements of the Five Points district (in what is now the Civic Center and part of Chinatown), immigrants from Naples and Sicily began moving to **Little Italy** in the

Last Orders

Dylan Thomas and the fatal glass of scotch – the story behind the legend.

'I've had 18 straight whiskies. I think that's the record,' Welsh poet Dylan Thomas is reputed to have said before dying in November 1953, and the boast has since entered New York bohemian lore. Many believe this heroic feat of alcohol consumption occurred in one sitting at the **White Horse Tavern** (*see p73*), where Thomas was a regular (a portrait of him now hangs in the middle room, above his favourite table in the corner). Bar staff have even been known to recount how he expired on the premises following the fatal 18th dram.

In reality, Thomas left his room at the Chelsea Hotel at 2am on 4 November for a bout of drinking at the White Horse, returning after closing time some two hours later to make that highly unlikely claim of 18 scotches to his mistress. He then slept it off before rising mid-morning and heading back with her to the same bar, where he had two glasses of beer. Returning once more to the Chelsea, Thomas – who was also taking medication for depression – suddenly collapsed, and a doctor was summoned. The poet was admitted the following day to St Vincent's Hospital, where he died on 9 November 1953 at the age of 39. It is alleged that Dylan Thomas's ghost still haunts the White Horse, appearing at the side of his corner table. You would probably have to drink an ungodly amount of whiskey to see it, though – something we can't recommend.

Soho.

1880s. The area once stretched from Canal Street to Houston Street, between Lafayette Street and the Bowery, but these days a strong Italian presence can only truly be observed on the blocks immediately surrounding Mulberry Street. As families prospered in the 1950s, they moved to the outer boroughs and suburbs; the area has long been shrinking in the face of Chinatown expanding from the south and migrating boutiques from **Nolita** (North of Little Italy).

Another telling change in the district: **St Patrick's Old Cathedral** (260-264 Mulberry Street, between Houston & Prince Streets) no longer holds services in Italian, but in English and Spanish. Completed in 1809 and restored after a fire in 1868, this was the city's premier Catholic church until it was demoted upon consecration of the Fifth Avenue cathedral of the same name. But ethnic pride remains: Italian-Americans flood in from across the city during the 11-day **Feast of San Gennaro** (*see p33*).

Touristy cafés and restaurants line Mulberry Street between Broome and Canal Streets, but pockets of the past linger nearby. Long-time residents still buy fresh mozzarella from **DiPalo's Fine Foods** (200 Grand Street, at Mott Street, 1-212 226 1033). Legend has it that the first pizzeria in New York was opened by Gennaro Lombardi on Spring Street in 1905. **Lombardi's** moved down the block in 1994 (32 Spring Street, at Mott Street, 1-212 941 7994), but

still serves its signature clam pies. These days, the area's restaurants are largely undistinguished grills and pasta houses, but two reliable choices are **Il Cortile** (125 Mulberry Street, between Canal & Hester Streets, 1-212 226 6060) and **La Mela** (167 Mulberry Street, between Broome & Grand Streets, 1-212 431 9493). Drop in for dessert at **Caffè Roma** (385 Broome Street, at Mulberry Street, 1-212 226 8413), which opened in 1891.

Of course, Little Italy is also the site of several notorious Mafia landmarks. The brick-fronted store now occupied by a shoe boutique (247 Mulberry Street, between Prince & Spring Streets) was once the Ravenite Social Club, where Mafia kingpin John Gotti made his deals

EXPLORE

until his arrest in 1990. Mobster Joey Gallo was shot and killed in 1972 while celebrating his birthday at Umberto's Clam House, which has since moved around the corner to 132 Mulberry Street, between Grand & Hester Streets (1-212 431 7545).

Nolita became a magnet for pricey boutiques and trendy eateries in the 1990s. Elizabeth, Mott and Mulberry Streets, between Houston and Spring Streets, in particular, are home to hip shops such as vintage clothier **Resurrection** (217 Mott Street, at Spring Street, 1-212 625 1374, www.resurrectionvintage.com), offbeat vintage-inspired jeweller **Erica Weiner** (*see p208*) and hip LA boutique spin-off **Creatures of Comfort** (205 Mulberry Street, between Kenmare & Spring Streets, 1-212 925 1005, www.creaturesofcomfort.us).

An international cast of pretty young things gravitates to eateries such as rustic Italian **Peasant**, global-inspired **Public** (for both, *see p149*) and neo-old-school Italian deli-and-dining room duo **Parm** and **Torrisi Italian Specialties** (*see p148*).

CHINATOWN

Subway J, N, Q, R, Z, 6 to Canal Street.

Take a walk in the area south of Broome Street and east of Broadway, and you'll feel as though you've entered not just a different country but a different continent. You won't hear much English spoken on the streets of **Chinatown**. Mott and Grand Streets are lined with fish-, fruit- and vegetable-stocked stands selling some of the best and most affordable seafood and produce in the city – you'll see buckets of live eels and crabs, square watermelons and piles of hairy rambutans. Street vendors sell satisfying snacks such as pork buns and sweet egg pancakes by the bagful. Canal Street glitters with cheap jewellery and gift shops, but beware furtive vendors of (undoubtedly fake) designer goods.

Some of the neighbourhood's residents eventually decamp to one of the two other Chinatowns in the city (in Sunset Park, Brooklyn, and Flushing, Queens). However, a steady flow of new arrivals keeps this hub full to bursting, with thousands of residents packed into the area surrounding East Canal Street, making this among the largest Chinese communities outside Asia. The busy streets get even wilder during the **Chinese New Year** festivities (*see p37*).

Between Kenmare and Worth Streets, Mott Street is lined with restaurants representing the cuisine of virtually every province of mainland China and Hong Kong; the Bowery, East Broadway and Division Street are just as diverse. Adding to the mix are myriad

Chinatown.

EXPLORE

Indonesian, Malaysian, Thai and Vietnamese eateries and shops.

Cheap eats abound in the area: head for Eldridge Street, where Chinese businesses mingle with old Lower East Side landmarks. At tiny, hole-in-the-wall **Prosperity Dumpling** (46 Eldridge Street, between Canal & Hester Streets, 1-212 343 0683), a plate of pork or veggie versions costs a few bucks, and **Super Taste Restaurant** (*see p151*) serves hand-pulled *la mian* (a Chinese relative of ramen) at around $5 for a bowl.

Explore the Chinese experience on these shores at the stylish **Museum of Chinese**

in America (*see below*), which reopened in 2009 in much larger premises. The **Eastern States Buddhist Temple of America** (64 Mott Street, between Bayard & Canal Streets, 1-212 925 8787), founded in 1962, is one of the country's oldest Chinese Buddhist temples.

Museum of Chinese in America

215 Centre Street, between Grand & Howard Streets (www.mocanyc.org). Subway J, N, Q, R, Z, 6 to Canal Street. **Open** 11am-6pm Tue, Wed, Fri-Sun; 11am-9pm Thur. **Admission** $10; $5 reductions; free under-12s; free Thur. **Credit** AmEx, Disc, MC, V. **Map** p403 E30.

Walk Murder Most Cool

Swap the fashionable scene for crime scenes on downtown's once mean streets.

These days, trendy downtown districts – the East Village, Lower East Side and Nolita/Little Italy – are pretty safe, but they used to be home to a rougher, and in some cases more homicidal, crowd. Start your blood-stained ramble in **Tompkins Square Park** (Avenue A, between 7th & 10th Streets), once the stomping ground of Daniel Rakowitz ('the Butcher of Tompkins

Park'). In 1989, the 28-year-old East Village resident, who walked around carrying a live chicken, chopped up his girlfriend, Monika Beerle, later serving her in a soup to the Tompkins Square homeless population.

Exit the park on Avenue A and head west on East 7th Street, then take a left on to Second Avenue. As you make your way past what used to be the **Binibon Café** (87 Second Avenue, at 5th Street), know that you are in the midst of literary greatness. This is the spot where Norman Mailer's one-time protégé, Jack Henry Abbott, stabbed a waiter to death in the summer of 1981, after being told that the bathroom was unavailable. Only six weeks earlier, Mailer had helped the author, who had penned the critically acclaimed *In the Belly of the Beast*, earn parole for a murder he had committed while serving a sentence in a Utah prison.

Continue south on Second Avenue until you hit East Houston Street, then turn left. Near the **intersection of East Houston and Allen Streets**, in the early hours of a June day in 1993, serial killer Joel Rifkin picked up his last victim, a prostitute whom he killed in the *New York Post* parking lot at 210 South Street. He kept the body in his car until police pulled him over in Long Island. It turned out that Rifkin had been killing women for years – 17 by his count (though not all were found).

Turn right into Allen Street, then right again at Stanton and make your way to Mulberry Street. Now home to fancy boutiques, this was once a mob-dominated patch, with bodies frequently turning up in dumpsters. Turn left on Mulberry and note first the former **headquarters of John**

Designed by prominent Chinese-American architect Maya Lin, MoCA reopened in an airy former machine shop in 2009. Its interior is loosely inspired by a traditional Chinese house, with rooms radiating off a central courtyard and areas defined by screens. The core exhibition traces the development of Chinese communities in the US from the 1850s to the present through objects, images and video. Innovative displays (drawers open to reveal artwork and documents, portraits are presented in a ceiling mobile) cover the development of industries such as laundries and restaurants in New York, Chinese stereotypes in pop culture, and the suspicion and humiliation Chinese-Americans endured during World War II and the McCarthy era. A mocked-up Chinese general store evokes the feel of these multi-purpose spaces, which served as vital community lifelines for men severed from their families under the 1882 Exclusion Act that restricted immigration.

Spring 2013 sees the opening of two fashion exhibitions (17 Apr-29 Sept): 'Fashion Forward' spotlights contemporary Chinese-American designers in NYC, and 'Subversive Glamour' features early-20th-century Shanghai ensembles, predominantly from the China National Silk Museum's collection.

LOWER EAST SIDE

Subway B, D to Grand Street; F to East Broadway; F to Delancey Street or Lower East Side-Second Avenue; J, Z to Bowery or Delancey-Essex Streets.

The **Lower East Side**, a roughly defined area south of Houston Street and west of the East River, is one of the more recent Manhattan neighbourhoods to be radically altered by the forces of gentrification. In the 19th century, tenement buildings were constructed here to house the growing number of German, Irish, Jewish and Italian immigrants – by 1900 it was the most populous neighbourhood in the US. The appalling conditions of these overcrowded, unsanitary slums were captured by photographer and writer Jacob Riis in *How the Other Half Lives* in 1890; its publication spurred activists and prompted the introduction of more humane building codes. The dwellings have since been converted or demolished, but you can see how newcomers once lived by visiting the recreated apartments of the **Lower East Side Tenement Museum** (*see p65*).

The neighbourhood was also the focal point of Jewish culture in New York. Between 1870 and 1920, hundreds of synagogues and religious schools thrived alongside Yiddish newspapers, social-reform societies and kosher bakeries. Vaudeville and classic Yiddish theatre also prospered here – the Marx Brothers, Eddie Cantor and George Gershwin all once lived in the district. Today, the Yiddish theatres are long gone and most of the synagogues founded by Eastern European immigrants in the 19th century have been repurposed or sit empty. But vestiges of Jewish life can be found amid the Chinese businesses spilling over from sprawling Chinatown and the ever-multiplying fashionable boutiques, restaurants and bars. The **Eldridge Street Synagogue** (*see p66*), which has undergone extensive renovation, still has a small but vital congregation. Heading east down Canal Street rewards with a view of the façade of the **Sender Jarmulowsky Bank** (on the corner of Canal & Orchard Streets), which catered to Jewish immigrants until its collapse in 1914; note

Gotti Jr (247 Mulberry Street, between Prince & Spring Streets), where the mafia kingpin used to conduct his 'business' affairs, which included racketeering, more than a dozen murders, gambling, extortion and other unsavoury pastimes. When his youngest son, Frank, was accidently struck by a car driven by his neighbour in the Howard Beach section of Queens where the mob boss lived, Gotti allegedly had the neighbour bumped off and his remains dissolved in acid.

As you walk through Little Italy, feast your eyes on what was **Umberto's Clam House** (129 Mulberry, at Hester Street), where 'Crazy' Joey Gallo – a violent gangster who attempted to poison rivals while serving prison time – was shot dead in April 1972 while celebrating his 43rd birthday. Today, it's home to Ristorante Da Gennaro (1-212 431 3934), where you can enjoy a lovely *cappellini primavera* (provided you're not on anyone's hit list).

Turn briefly right on to Walker Street before going south on Centre Street until you get to White Street, where you'll see a series of ominous-looking buildings known as **the Tombs** (125 White Street, between Centre & Lafayette Streets). Police have processed criminals here for 175 years. Over time, the buildings may have changed (they have been periodically torn down, rebuilt and renamed), but the clientele has not. Convicts were actually hanged from the gallows here – including members of the Daybreak Boys gang in 1853 – until the electric chair was invented and executions were outsourced.

If it's only your feet that are killing you, count yourself lucky.

EXPLORE

Lower East Side.

the reclining classical figures of the sculpture above the door bookending the clock. Further down Canal, at the corner of Ludlow, you'll find the former home of the **Kletzker Brotherly Aid Association**, a lodge for immigrants from Belarus still marked by the Star of David and the year of its opening, 1892.

On the southern edge of Chinatown, the **First Shearith Israel Graveyard** (55-57 St James Place, between James & Oliver Streets) is the burial ground of the country's first Jewish community; some gravestones date from 1683, including those of Spanish and Portuguese Jews who fled the Inquisition. However, the gate is usually locked. The **Forward Building** (175 E Broadway, at Canal Street) was once the headquarters of the *Jewish Daily Forward*, a Yiddish-language paper that had a peak circulation of 275,000 in the 1920s; it's now home to multimillion-dollar condominiums.

Those looking for a taste of the old Jewish Lower East Side should grab a table at **Katz's Delicatessen** (*see p152*). Opened in 1888, this kosher deli continues to serve some of the best pastrami in New York (and was the site of Meg Ryan's famous 'fauxgasm' scene in *When Harry Met Sally…*). A few blocks west, **Yonah Schimmel Knish Bakery** (137 E Houston Street, between First & Second Avenues, 1-212 477 2858) has been doling out its carb-laden goodies since 1910. About 20 varieties are available, but traditional potato, kasha and spinach knishes are the most popular. Lox lovers are devoted to the still family-run **Russ & Daughters** (*see p212*), which has been selling its famous herring, caviar and smoked salmon since 1914. **Essex Market** (www. essexstreetmarket.com), which opened in 1940 as part of La Guardia's plan to get pushcarts off the streets, contains a mix of high-quality vendors selling cheese, coffee, sweets, produce, fish and meat.

By the 1980s, when young artists and musicians began moving into the area, it was a patchwork of Asian, Latino and Jewish enclaves. Hipster bars and music venues sprang up on and around Ludlow Street, creating an annex to the East Village. That scene still survives, but rents have risen dramatically and some stalwarts have closed their doors. Check who's playing at **Arlene's Grocery** (95 Stanton Street, between Ludlow & Orchard Streets, 1-212 358 1633, www.arlenesgrocery.net), the **Bowery** (*see p285*) **Ballroom** or **Cake Shop** (*see p286*).

These days, visual art is the Lower East Side's main cultural draw. In 2007, the **New Museum of Contemporary Art** (*see p66*) decamped here from Chelsea, opening a $50-million building on the Bowery. A narrow glass tower designed by Norman Foster, a block north at 257 Bowery, opened in 2010 as the HQ for established art dealers **Sperone Westwater** (*see p207*), whose high-profile stable includes Bruce Nauman, Susan Rothenberg and William Wegman. Dozens of storefront galleries have opened in the vicinity over the past several years (for our picks, *see pp206-207*).

Although the **Orchard Street** bargain district – a row of shops selling utilitarian goods such as socks, sportswear and luggage, and beloved of hagglers – persists, the strip is at the centre of a proliferation of small indie shops. These include hatter **Victor Osborne** (*see p205*), clothing store-cum-bar the **Dressing Room** (*see p201*), and vintage jewellery trove **Doyle & Doyle** (*see p208*).

More mainstream commercial gloss is encroaching on the area in the form of high-rise hotels and apartment buildings. The National

Trust for Historic Preservation designated the Lower East Side one of America's 11 most endangered historic places in 2008, but as the area continues to change, groups such as the Lower East Side Conservancy are working to preserve its unique character.

★ Lower East Side Tenement Museum
Visitors' centre, 103 Orchard Street, at Delancey Street (1-212 982 8420, www.tenement.org). Subway F to Delancey Street; J, Z to Delancey-Essex Streets. **Open** *Museum shop & ticketing* 10am-6pm daily. **Tours** 10.30am-5pm daily (see website for schedule). **Admission** $22; $17 reductions. **Credit** AmEx, Disc, MC, V. **Map** p403 G30.
This fascinating museum – actually a series of restored tenement apartments at 97 Orchard Street

Lower East Side Tenement Museum.

EXPLORE

– is accessible only by guided tour, which start at the visitors' centre at 103 Orchard Street. Tours often sell out, so it's wise to book ahead.

'Hard Times' visits the homes of an Italian and a German-Jewish clan; 'Sweatshop Workers' explores the apartments of two Eastern European Jewish families as well as a garment shop where many of the locals would have found employment; and 'Irish Outsiders' unfurls the life of the Moore family, who are coping with the loss of their child. Families may want to stop by quarters once occupied by a Sephardic Jewish Greek family and speak to an interpreter in period costume channelling the 14-year-old daughter of the house, Victoria Confino. A new tour, 'Shop Life' explores the diverse retailers that occupied the building's storefronts, including a 19th-century German saloon. From mid March through December, the museum also conducts themed daily walking tours of the Lower East Side ($22-$45).

★ Museum at Eldridge Street (Eldridge Street Synagogue)

12 Eldridge Street, between Canal & Division Streets (1-212 219 0302, www.eldridgestreet.org). Subway F to East Broadway. **Open** 10am-5pm Mon-Thur, Sun; 10am-3pm Fri. **Admission** $10; $6-$8 reductions; free under-5s; free Mon. **Credit** AmEx, Disc, MC, V. **Map** p402 F31.

With an impressive façade that combines Moorish, Gothic and Romanesque elements, the first grand synagogue on the Lower East Side is now surrounded by dumpling shops and Chinese herb stores, but rewind about a century and you would have found delicatessens and *mikvot* (ritual bathhouses). For its first 50 years, the 1887 synagogue had a congregation of thousands and doubled as a mutual-aid society for new arrivals in need of financial assistance, healthcare and employment. But as Jews left the area and the congregation dwindled, the building fell into disrepair.

A 20-year, $18.5-million facelift has restored its splendour; the soaring main sanctuary features hand-stencilled walls and a resplendent stained-glass rose window with Star of David motifs. The renovations were completed in autumn 2010, with the installation of a new stained-glass window designed by artist Kiki Smith and architect Deborah Gans. The admission price includes a guided tour (see website for schedule). Downstairs, touch-screen displays highlight the synagogue's architecture, aspects of worship and local history, including other (extant or long-vanished) Jewish landmarks.

★ New Museum of Contemporary Art

235 Bowery, between Prince & Stanton Streets (1-212 219 1222, www.newmuseum.org). Subway N, R to Prince Street; 6 to Spring Street. **Open** 11am-6pm Wed, Fri-Sun; 11am-9pm Thur. **Admission** $14; $10-$12 reductions; free under-18s; free 7-9pm Thur. **Credit** DC, MC, V. **Map** p403 F29.

Having occupied various sites for 30 years, New York City's only contemporary art museum finally got its own purpose-built space in late 2007, and has since sparked a gallery boom in the area. The museum is dedicated to emerging media and important but under-recognised artists; through June 2013, it is staging the time-capsule exhibition 'NYC 1993', one of the first surveys of '90s art. The seven-floor museum is worth a look for the building alone – a striking, off-centre stack of aluminium-mesh-clad boxes designed by cutting-edge Tokyo architectural firm Sejima + Nishizawa/SANAA. The shop, hidden behind a metal mesh wall in the lobby, has a well-curated selection of art books and limited-edition objects created by exhibitors, and refreshments are provided by an outpost of organic bakery Birdbath. At weekends, don't miss the fabulous views from the minimalist seventh-floor Sky Room, and be sure to stop into the adjacent Studio 231, which features exhibitions and performance by emerging artists from around the world.

EAST VILLAGE

Subway B, D, F, M to Broadway-Lafayette Street; L to First Avenue or Third Avenue; 6 to Astor Place or Bleecker Street.

Originally part of the Lower East Side, the **East Village** developed its distinct identity as a countercultural hotbed in the 1960s. The seeds had been planted as early as the turn of the century, however, when anarchists such as Emma Goldman and Johann Most plotted revolution in a 1st Street salon owned by Julius Schwab. By the dawning of the Age of Aquarius, rock clubs thrived on almost every corner; among them were the now-demolished Fillmore East, on Second Avenue, between 6th and 7th Streets, and the Dom (23 St Marks Place, between Second & Third Avenues), where the Velvet Underground often headlined (the building is now a condo). In the '70s, the neighbourhood took a dive as drugs and crime prevailed – but that didn't stop the influx of artists and punk rockers. In the early '80s, East Village galleries were among the first to display the work of groundbreaking artists Jean-Michel Basquiat and Keith Haring.

The blocks east of Broadway between Houston and 14th Streets may have lost some of their edge, but remnants of their spirited past endure. Although the former tenements are increasingly occupied by young professionals and trust-fund kids, humanity in all its guises converges in the parks, bargain restaurants, indie record stores and grungy watering holes on First and Second Avenues and St Marks Place. For insights into the area's activist legacy, stop by the new **Museum of Reclaimed Space** (*see p67 and p70*).

EXPLORE

The People's Museum

A monument to local activism takes root in the East Village.

While the word 'museum' tends to evoke a sense of permanence, the **Museum of Reclaimed Space** (*see p70*) resides in more ephemeral digs. 'The museum is actually in the most famous squat in New York City right now,' explains co-founder Bill Di Paola. As the founding director of advocacy group Time's Up!, Di Paola has fought for bikers' rights and environmental causes for 25 years; his new project with co-founder and Time's Up volunteer Laurie Mittelmann builds on his experience on picket lines and in rallies to show how activism can spark community change.

Known as C-Squat, the five-floor walk-up has housed activists, down-on-their-luck artists and members of several punk bands (including Leftover Crack, Old Skull and Nausea) from the 1970s through the present. 'People can knock on the door and sleep there, and work there,' says Di Paola. 'They play shows in the basement.'

The fight to establish and maintain spots like C-Squat has been waged in community gardens and abandoned buildings around New York City. Di Paola and Mittelmann spent two years gathering documents from local residents related to events such as the 1988 Tompkins Square Park Riot, which erupted when Community Board 3 tried to impose a 1am closing time on the outdoor space. 'It was an incredible battle about curfew and public spaces, the struggle between corporations and community,' explains Di Paola. Zines from art and activist centre ABC No Rio, an Occupy Wall Street banner and a Time's Up! energy bike that helped power Zuccotti Park during its occupation in 2011 illustrate how city residents, both past and present, created, protected and took back

community spaces. Other pieces commemorate lost causes, such as a map painted on the museum's floor that marks battlegrounds like the 5th Street Squat, which the city knocked down in 1997 with residents' belongings and pets still inside, as well as community gardens. Volunteers will also lead daily tours to places including La Plaza Cultural (www.laplazacultural.com), a once-illegal plot that is now an official community garden, and the Christodora House, a former social services building that became a symbol of gentrification following its conversion in the '80s into a pricey East Village co-op.

Di Paola hopes that highlighting the history of local protests and subsequent victories might inspire a new generation of activists. 'A lot of people like to do the quick fix…especially with the Occupy Wall Street kids,' says Di Paola. 'People can get involved in their community and make proper choices about what they buy. The solution is all around us. We don't really need a revolution. We just need to support things that already work.'

AS A LIVING ARCHIVE OF URBAN ACTIVISM,
the Museum of Reclaimed Urban Space (MoRUS) chronicles the East Village community's history of grassroots action. It

EXPLORE

Providing a sharp contrast to the radical associations of its more recent past, the **Merchant's House Museum** (*see p70*), on East 4th Street, is a perfectly preserved specimen of upper-class domestic life in the 1800s. A short walk north brings you to the East Village's unofficial cultural centre: **St Mark's Church in-the-Bowery** (131 E 10th Street, at Second Avenue, 1-212 674 6377). Built in 1799, the Federal-style church sits on the site of Peter Stuyvesant's farm; the old guy himself, one of New York's first governors, is buried in the adjacent cemetery. Regular services are still held, as are art exhibitions and performances.

From the 1950s to the '70s, **St Marks Place** (E 8th Street, between Lafayette Street & Avenue A) was a hotbed of artists, writers, radicals and musicians, including WH Auden, Abbie Hoffman, Lenny Bruce, Joni Mitchell and GG Allin; the cover of Led Zeppelin's 1975 album *Physical Graffiti* depicts the apartment buildings at nos.96 and 98. St Marks is still fizzing with energy well into the wee hours, but these days, the grungy strip is packed with cheap eateries, shops selling T-shirts, tourist junk and pot paraphernalia, and tattoo parlours – among them the famous **Fun City** (94 St Marks Place, between First Avenue & Avenue A, 1-212 353 8282), whose awning advertises cappuccino and tattoos.

Cutting between Broadway and Fourth Avenue south of East 8th Street, **Astor Place** still attracts young skateboarders and other modern-day street urchins. It is marked by a steel cube that has sat on a traffic island by the entrance to the 6 train since 1968. With a little elbow grease, the cube, whose proper title is *Alamo*, will spin on its axis. This is also the site of the **Cooper Union**; comprising schools of art, architecture and engineering, it bears the distinction of being the only free private college in the United States. It was here, in February 1860, that Abraham Lincoln gave his celebrated Cooper Union Address, which argued for the regulation (though not abolition) of slavery and helped to propel him into the White House. During the 19th century, Astor Place marked the boundary between the slums to the east and some of the city's most fashionable homes. **Colonnade Row** (428-434 Lafayette Street, between Astor Place & E 4th Street) faces the distinguished Astor Public Library building, which theatre legend Joseph Papp rescued from demolition in the 1960s. Today, the old library houses the **Public Theater** (*see p324*), a platform for first-run American plays, and cabaret venue **Joe's Pub** (*see p288*). The Public Theater also stages summer's **Shakespeare in the Park** (*see p324*). Below Astor Place, Third Avenue (one block east of Lafayette Street) becomes the **Bowery**. For decades, the street

languished as a seedy flophouse strip and the home of missionary organisations catering to the down and out. Although the sharp-eyed can find traces of the old flophouses, and the more obvious Gothic Revival headquarters of **Bowery Mission** at no.227 (between Rivington & Stanton Streets), the thoroughfare has been cleaned up and repopulated by high-rise condo buildings, ritzy restaurants, clubs and hotels.

One casualty of this gentrification was the hallowed CBGB, once the unofficial home of US punk, which fostered legends such as the Ramones, Talking Heads and Patti Smith (although, let's face it, the average post-1995 show was pretty lame). The site is now occupied by swanky menswear shop **John Varvatos** (315 Bowery, at Bleecker Street, 1-212 358 0315), which has preserved a section of the club's flyer-plastered wall behind glass.

Elsewhere in the neighbourhood, East 7th Street is a stronghold of New York's Ukrainian community, of which the focal point is the Byzantine **St George's Ukrainian Catholic Church** at no.30. The **Ukrainian Museum** (222 E 6th Street, between Second & Third Avenues, 1-212 228 0110, www.ukrainian museum.org, closed Mon, Tue) houses folk and fine art and photos from that country. One block over, there's often a long line of loud fraternity types waiting at weekends to enter **McSorley's Old Ale House** (*see p180*). Festooned with aged photos, yellowed newspaper articles and dusty memorabilia, the 158-year-old Irish tavern is purportedly the oldest continually operating pub in New York and the spot where Lincoln repaired after giving his Cooper Union Address. Representing a different corner of the globe, **Curry Row** (East 6th Street, between First & Second Avenues) is lined with Indian restaurants that are popular with budget-minded diners.

Alphabet City (which gets its name from its key avenues: A, B, C and D) stretches towards the East River. It was once an edgy Puerto Rican neighbourhood with links to the drug trade, but its demographic has dramatically shifted over the past 20 years. Avenue C is also known as Loisaida Avenue, a rough approximation of 'Lower East Side' when pronounced with a Hispanic accent. Two churches on 4th Street are built in the Spanish colonial style: **San Isidro y San Leandro** (345 E 4th Street, between Avenues C & D) and **Iglesia Pentecostal Camino Damasco** (289 E 4th Street, between Avenues B & C). The **Nuyorican Poets Café** (*see p298*), a clubhouse for espresso-drinking wordsmiths since 1974, is known for its poetry slams, in which performers do lyric battle before a score-keeping audience.

Dating from 1837, **Tompkins Square Park** (from 7th to 10th Streets, between Avenues A

EXPLORE

Greenwich Village.

& B), honours Daniel D Tompkins, governor of New York from 1807 to 1817, and vice-president during the Monroe administration. Over the years, this 10.5-acre park has been a site for demonstrations and rioting. The last major uprising occurred in 1988, when the city evicted squatters from the park and renovated it to suit the influx of affluent residents. Along with dozens of 150-year-old elm trees (some of the oldest in the city), the landscaped green space has basketball courts, playgrounds and dog runs, and remains a place where bongo beaters, guitarists, multi-pierced teenagers, hipsters, local families and vagrants mingle.

North of Tompkins Square, around First Avenue and 11th Street, are remnants of earlier communities: discount fabric dealers, Italian cheese shops, Polish butchers and two great Italian coffee and cannoli houses: **De Robertis** (176 First Avenue, between 10th & 11th Streets, 1-212 674 7137) and **Veniero's Pasticceria & Caffè** (342 E 11th Street, between First & Second Avenues, 1-212 674 7070).

Merchant's House Museum

29 E 4th Street, between Lafayette Street & Bowery (1-212 777 1089, www.merchants house.org). Subway B, D, F, M to Broadway-Lafayette Street; 6 to Bleecker Street. **Open** noon-5pm Mon, Thur-Sun. **Admission** $10; $5 reductions; free under-12s. **Credit** ($20 min requested) AmEx, MC, V. **Map** p403 F29.
Merchant's House Museum, the city's only fully preserved 19th-century family home, is an elegant, late Federal-Greek Revival property kitted out with the same furnishings and decorations it contained when it was inhabited from 1835 by hardware tycoon Seabury Tredwell and his family. Three years after Tredwell's eighth daughter died in 1933, it opened as a museum. You can peruse the house at your own pace, following along with the museum's printed guide, or opt for the 2pm guided tour. Be sure to ascend to the servants' quarters on the recently renovated fourth floor, and note the original bell that summoned the four Irish immigrant maids at the top of the stairs.

Museum of Reclaimed Urban Space

155 Avenue C, between 9th & 10th Streets (1-646 833 7764, www.morusnyc.org). Subway L to First Avenue. **Open** 11am-7pm Tue, Thur-Sun. **Admission** free (donations appreciated). **Map** p403 G28.
See p67 **The People's Museum**.

GREENWICH VILLAGE

Subway A, B, C, D, E, F, M to W 4th Street; L, N, Q, R, 4, 5, 6 to 14th Street-Union Square; N, R to 8th Street-NYU; 1 to Christopher Street-Sheridan Square.

Washington Square Park.

Stretching from Houston Street to 14th Street, between Broadway and Sixth Avenue, **Greenwich Village** has been inspiring bohemians for almost a century. Now that it has become one of the most expensive (and exclusive) neighbourhoods in the city, you need a lot more than a struggling artist's or writer's income to inhabit its leafy streets. However, it's still a fine place for idle wandering, candlelit dining in out-of-the-way restaurants, and hopping between bars and cabaret venues.

Great for people-watching, **Washington Square Park** attracts a disparate cast of characters that takes in hippies, students and hip hop kids. Skateboarders clatter near the base of the Washington Arch, a modestly sized replica of Paris's Arc de Triomphe, built in 1895 to honour George Washington. The park hums with musicians and street artists, but the once-ubiquitous pot dealers have largely disappeared thanks to the NYC Police Department's surveillance cameras. The 9.75-acre Village landmark is in the final stages of a $16-million redesign. When the plans were announced in 2007, community activists protested strongly, fearing it would ruin the park's bohemian flavour. Yet even vehement detractors were pleasantly surprised with the results of the first phase, which included new lawns and flower beds in the western section of the park and restoration and a minor relocation of the 19th-century fountain to align it with the arch.

In the 1830s, the wealthy began building handsome townhouses around the square. A few of those properties are still privately owned and occupied, but many others have become part of the ever-expanding NYU campus. The university also owns the Washington Mews, a row of charming 19th-century former stables that line a tiny cobblestoned alley just to the north of the park between Fifth Avenue and University Place. Several famed literary figures, including Henry James (author of the celebrated novel which took its title from the square), Herman Melville, Edith Wharton, Edgar Allan Poe and Eugene O'Neill, lived on or near the square. In 1871, the local creative community founded the **Salmagundi Club** (47 Fifth Avenue, between 11th & 12th Streets, 1-212 255 7740, www.salmagundi.org), America's oldest artists' club. Now situated north of Washington Square on Fifth Avenue, it has galleries that are open to the public.

Greenwich Village continues to change with the times, for the better and for the worse. In the 1960s, **8th Street** was the closest New York got to San Francisco's hippie Haight Street. Although the strip is now a long procession of piercing parlours, punky boutiques and shoe stores, Jimi Hendrix's **Electric Lady Studios** is still at 52 West 8th Street, between Fifth & Sixth Avenues. Once the dingy but colourful stomping ground of Beat poets and folk and jazz musicians, the well-trafficked section of **Bleecker Street**, between La Guardia Place and Sixth Avenue, is now an overcrowded

EXPLORE

INSIDE TRACK
DYLAN'S VILLAGE

Bob Dylan lived at and owned 94 MacDougal Street (on a row of historic brownstones near Bleecker Street) through much of the 1960s, performing in Washington Square Park and at clubs such as **Café Wha?** and the **Bitter End** (for both, *see below*).

stretch of poster shops, cheap restaurants and music venues for the college crowd. Renowned hangouts such as Le Figaro Café (184 Bleecker Street, at MacDougal Street), Kerouac's favourite, are no more, but a worthy alternative is **Caffe Reggio** (119 MacDougal Street, at W 3rd Street, 1-212 475 9557). The oldest coffeehouse in the village, it opened in 1927, and appealed to Kerouac, native Villager Gregory Corso and other 1950s poets. Nearby, a former literati favourite of the likes of Hemingway and Fitzgerald, **Minetta Tavern** (*see p158*), has been rehabilitated by golden-touch restaurateur Keith McNally.

Although 1960s hotspot **Café Wha?** (115 MacDougal Street, between Bleecker & W 3rd Streets, 1-212 254 3706, www.cafewha.com) is now running on the fumes of its illustrious past, it has a decent house band and a weekly Brazilian party night. Nearby, the **Bitter End** (147 Bleecker Street, between La Guardia Place & Thompson Street, 1-212 673 7030, www.bitterend.com) has proudly championed the singer-songwriter – including a young Bob Dylan – since 1961.

The famed Village Gate jazz club at the corner of Bleecker and Thompson Streets – which staged performances by Miles Davis, Nina Simone and John Cage – closed in 1993. However, in 2008, **Le Poisson Rouge** (*see p289*) opened on the site with a similar mission to present diverse genres under one roof. Up the street on La Guardia Place is the **AIA Center for Architecture** (*see right*), which hosts exhibitions on plans and projects in the city and beyond.

Not far from here, in the triangle formed by Sixth Avenue, Greenwich Avenue and 10th Street, you'll see the Gothic-style **Jefferson Market Library** (a branch of the New York Public Library). The lovely flower-filled garden facing Greenwich Avenue once held the art deco Women's House of Detention, which was torn down in 1974. Mae West did a little time there in 1926, on obscenity charges stemming from her Broadway show *Sex*.

Just behind the library, off 10th Street, lies **Patchin Place**, which was home to some of the leading luminaries of New York's literary pantheon. This cul-de-sac lined with brick houses built during the mid 19th century is off limits to the public, but through the gate you can make out no.4, where the poet and staunch foe of capitalisation ee cummings resided from 1923 to 1962; and no.5, where Djuna Barnes, author of *Nightwood*, lived from 1940 to 1982. Indeed, cummings would reportedly check on the reclusive Barnes by calling 'Are you still alive, Djuna?' though his neighbour's window.

FREE AIA Center for Architecture

536 La Guardia Place, between Bleecker & W 3rd Streets (1-212 683 0023, www.aiany.org). Subway A, B, C, D, E, F, M to W 4th Street. **Open** 9am-8pm Mon-Fri; 11am-5pm Sat. **Admission** free. **Map** p403 E29.

Designed by architect Andrew Berman, this three-storey building is a fitting home for architectural debate: the sweeping, light-filled design is a physical manifestation of AIA's goal of promoting transparency in both its access and programming. Berman cut away large slabs of flooring at the street and basement levels, converting underground spaces into bright, museum-quality galleries. Exhibitions at the center focus on both local and international themes.

WEST VILLAGE & MEATPACKING DISTRICT

Subway A, C, E to 14th Street; L to Eighth Avenue; 1 to Christopher St-Sheridan Square; 1, 2, 3 to 14th Street.

In the early 20th century, the **West Village** was largely a working-class Italian neighbourhood. These days, the highly desirable enclave is home to numerous celebrities (including Brooke Shields, Jennifer Aniston and Sarah Jessica Parker and Matthew Broderick – well, one of their homes, anyway), but a low-key, everyone-knows-everyone feel remains. It may not have the buzzy vibe of the East Village, but it has held on to much of its picturesque charm. The area west of Sixth Avenue to the Hudson River, from 14th Street to Houston Street, possesses the quirky geographical features that moulded the Village's character. Only here could West 10th Street cross West 4th Street, and Waverly Place cross… Waverly Place. The West Village's layout doesn't follow the regular grid pattern but rather the settlers' original horse paths.

Locals and visitors crowd bistros along Seventh Avenue and Hudson Street, and patronise the high-rent shops on this stretch of Bleecker Street, including no fewer than three Marc Jacobs boutiques. Venture on to the side streets for interesting discoveries, such as indie boutique **Castor & Pollux** (*see p200*) on West 10th Street and his-and-hers flagships of rustic-chic label **Rag & Bone** (*see p198*) on Christopher Street. The area's bohemian population may have dwindled years ago, but a few old landmarks remain. Solemnly raise a glass in the **White Horse Tavern** (567 Hudson Street, at 11th Street, 1-212 989 3956), a favourite of such literary luminaries as Ezra Pound, James Baldwin, Norman Mailer and Dylan Thomas, who included it on his last drinking binge before his death in 1953. On and just off Seventh Avenue South are jazz and cabaret clubs, including the **Village Vanguard** (*see p294*).

The West Village is also a longstanding gay neighbourhood, although the young gay scene has mostly migrated north to Chelsea and Hell's Kitchen. The **Stonewall Inn** (*see p271*), on Christopher Street, was the site of the 1969 riots that marked the birth of the modern gay-liberation movement. In **Christopher Park**, which faces the bar, is George Segal's *Gay Pride*, a piece composed of plaster sculptures of two same-sex couples that commemorates the street's role in gay history. Along Christopher Street from Sheridan Square to the Hudson River pier, most of the area's shops, bars and restaurants are out, loud and proud. The Hudson riverfront features grass-covered piers, food vendors and picnic tables.

The north-west corner of the West Village has been known as the **Meatpacking District** since the area was dominated by the wholesale meat industry in the early 20th century. As business waned, gay fetish clubs took root in derelict buildings and, until the 1990s, the area was a haunt for transsexual prostitutes. In recent years, however, following the arrival of pioneering fashion store **Jeffrey New York** (*see p192*), designer boutiques started to move in. Frequent mentions on *Sex and the City,* along with the arrival of swanky hotel **Gansevoort Meatpacking NYC** (*see p231*) and hip eateries such as **Pastis** (9 Ninth Avenue, at Little W 12th Street, 1-212 929 4844, www.pastisny.com) in the noughties, cemented the area's reputation as a consumer playground. Nightclubs, including **Cielo** and **Le Bain** (for both, *see p275*), draw a young crowd after dark.

The 2009 opening of freight-track-turned-park the **High Line** (*see p82* **Profile**) has brought even bigger crowds to the area. Slick style hotel the **Standard** (*see p232*) straddles the elevated park at West 13th Street, and its seasonal Biergarten, nestled beneath it, is a great spot for a pint. Ironically, the arrival of the luxury hotel unintentionally restored some of the area's old raunchy reputation when the *New York Post* reported that naked hotel guests were putting on explicit shows in their glass-fronted rooms for the strollers below.

EXPLORE

Meatpacking District.

Midtown

Iconic sights and cool art cluster in Manhattan's core.

The area from 14th to 59th Streets is iconic New York: jutting skyscrapers, crowded pavements and a yellow river of cabs streaming down the congested avenues. The impression is reinforced by the fact that the city's most recognisable landmarks are located here, from the slender spire of the Empire State Building and the stately lions of the New York Public Library to the bright lights of Times Square. But there's a lot more to midtown than glistening towers and high-octane commerce. It contains the city's most concentrated contemporary gallery district (**Chelsea**), its hottest gay enclaves (Chelsea and **Hell's Kitchen**), some of its swankiest shops (**Fifth Avenue**) and, of course, the majority of its major theatres (along **Broadway**). There are even a few lovely, serene spots where you can retreat from the jostling crowds and traffic. In particular, the city's newest park, the High Line, has boosted the area's green quotient considerably.

Map pp403-405	Restaurants &
Hotels pp234-244	cafés pp162-171
	Bars pp182-185

CHELSEA

Subway A, C, E, 1, 2, 3 to 14th Street;
C, E, 1 to 23rd Street; L to Eighth Avenue;
1 to 18th Street or 28th Street.

Formerly a working-class Irish and Hispanic neighbourhood, the corridor between 14th and 29th Streets west of Sixth Avenue emerged as the nexus of New York's queer life in the 1990s. Owing to rising housing costs and the protean nature of the city's cultural landscape, it's being slowly eclipsed by Hell's Kitchen to the north (just as Chelsea once overtook the West Village), but it's undeniably still a homo hotspot, with numerous bars, restaurants, clothing stores and sex shops catering to the once-ubiquitous 'Chelsea boys'.

The formerly desolate western edge of the neighbourhood has been the focus of the most eagerly embraced project in the city's recent history: the transformation of a disused elevated

freight train track into a lush, landscaped public park, the **High Line** (*see p82* **Profile**).

In the 1980s, many of New York's galleries left Soho for this patch, from West 20th Street to West 29th Street, between Tenth and Eleventh Avenues (*see p206* **Gallery-Hopping Guide**). Today, internationally recognised spaces such as **Mary Boone Gallery**, **Gagosian Gallery** and **Haunch of Venison**, as well as numerous less exalted names, attract swarms of art aficionados. The High Line has brought even more gallery-hoppers to the area as it provides verdant pathway from the boutique- and restaurant-rich Meatpacking District (*see p72*) to the art enclave. Traversing the elevated promenade, you'll pass through the old loading dock of the former Nabisco factory, where the first Oreo cookie was made in 1912. This conglomeration of 18 structures, built between the 1890s and the 1930s, now houses **Chelsea Market** (75 Ninth Avenue, between 15th & 16th Streets, www.chelseamarket.com). The

Insider's Guide to Times Square

Six local-approved things to do pre- or post-show.

1. SNEAK A PEEP AT THE PAST

It's hard to believe 42nd Street was once throbbing with XXX-rated movie theatres, adult bookstores and peep-shows instead of multiplexes, Madame Tussauds and McDonald's. One of the last vestiges of sleaze on the strip, Peep-O-Rama, closed in 2002. Now it's back – in the free **Times Square Museum and Visitor Center** (Seventh Avenue, between 46th & 47th Streets, 1-212 452 5283, www.timessquarenyc.org). The salvaged Peep-O-Rama sign hovers above three original booths, set against the centre's landmarked 1925 interior, formerly the States' first newsreel theatre. Other displays include a model of 1 Times Square (an elegant 1904 structure) without its sheath of billboards, and the 2007 New Year's Eve Ball, which performs a dazzling light show every 20 minutes.

2. RISE ABOVE IT ALL AND ADMIRE THE VIEW

Times Square may have lost most of its grit, but the spectacle is still exhilarating. While scoring cheap tickets to a show, ascend the TKTS ticket booth's **red glass structural steps** in Duffy Square (Broadway, at 47th Street; *see p312*) for an eye-popping panorama of the Great White Way. The glowing staircase was the brainchild of Australians John Choi and Tai Ropiha, who won a globe-spanning competition for a new design in 1999; it debuted in 2008.

3. OGLE FIVE-FIGURE FENDERS

Music Row may have diminished since its mid-century heyday, but would-be guitar heroes can still drool over rare instruments at **Sam Ash Custom Guitars** (156 W 48th Street, between Sixth & Seventh Avenues, 1-212 719 2625). Head through the door at the back labelled 'Guitars of Distinction' for such treasures as a Gibson Les Paul signed by Jeff Beck (yours for $14,999), though you can pick up a custom Fender Stratocaster for a mere $3,000. Who knows, you might find store regular Steve Miller fingering the strings.

4. GET A TASTE OF OLD TIMES SQUARE

'Up until a few years ago, it was a very rough bar: the folks there were five to ten dollars away from being homeless, and the women looked like Tom Waits.' That's how Rich Brooks sums up **Smith's Bar & Restaurant** (701 Eighth Avenue, at 44th Street, 1-212 246 3268, www. smithsbar.com). Yet the comedian, who has been performing in this patch for more than ten years, counts it among his favourite local spots. From the vintage neon sign to the 50-foot mahogany bar, the dive invokes pre-Disney Times Square, and prices for the standard pub grub (burgers, nachos, fish and chips) hover around $10.

5. CAMP IT UP WITH CABARET QUEENS

What good is singing alone in your room when you can sing along with showtunes at **Don't Tell Mama** (343 W 46th Street, between Eighth & Ninth Avenues, 1-212 757 0788, www. donttellmamanyc.com)? The line-up in the cabaret room ($10-$25 plus two-drink minimum) may include pop, jazz and musical-theatre singers, as well as comedians and drag artists. Performers often congregate in the piano bar before and after their numbers.

6. SATISFY LATE-NIGHT CRAVINGS

The Bromberg brothers, the sibling team behind the Blue Ribbon eateries (www.blueribbonrestaurants.com), which built a reputation as after-hours hubs for restaurant workers, supply the snacks at the surprisingly unhyped **R Lounge** in the Renaissance Hotel (714 Seventh Avenue, at 48th Street, 1-212 261 5200, www. rloungetimessquare.com). Try the signature 'Northern fried' chicken wings ($12) – with a Manhattan, of course – while enjoying a ringside view of Times Square.

EXPLORE

ground-floor food arcade offers artisanal bread, wine, baked goods and freshly made ice-cream, among other treats.

Also among the area's notable industrial architecture is the **Starrett-Lehigh Building** (601 W 26th Street, at Eleventh Avenue). The stunning 1929 structure was left in disrepair until the dot-com boom of the late 1990s, when media companies, photographers and designers snatched up its loft-like spaces.

While some of the Hudson River piers, which were once terminals for the world's grand ocean liners, remain in a state of ruin, the four that lie between 17th and 23rd Streets have been transformed into mega sports centre **Chelsea Piers** (see p330).

To get a glimpse of how Chelsea looked back when it was first developed in the 1880s, stroll along **Cushman Row** (406-418 W 20th Street, between Ninth & Tenth Avenues) in the Chelsea Historic District. Just to the north is the block-long **General Theological Seminary of the Episcopal Church** (440 W 21st Street, between Ninth & Tenth Avenues, 1-212 243 5150, www.gts.edu), where the verdant garden courtyard (closed after 3pm & Sun) is a hidden oasis of tranquillity. The seminary's land was part of the estate known as Chelsea, owned by poet Clement Clarke Moore, author of *A Visit from St Nicholas* (more commonly known as *'Twas the Night Before Christmas*).

The nearby **Chelsea Hotel** on West 23rd Street, has been a magnet for creative types since it first opened in 1884; Mark Twain was an early guest. The list of former residents reads like an international *Who's Who* of the artistic elite: Sarah Bernhardt (who slept in a coffin), William Burroughs (who wrote *Naked Lunch* here), Dylan Thomas, Arthur Miller, Quentin Crisp, Leonard Cohen, Bob Dylan, Janis Joplin and Jimi Hendrix, to name a few. In the 1960s, it was the stomping ground of Andy Warhol's coterie of superstars, and the location of his 1966 film *The Chelsea Girls*. The Chelsea gained punk-rock notoriety on 12 October 1978, when Sex Pistol Sid Vicious stabbed girlfriend Nancy Spungen to death in Room 100. It's still home to about 95 permanent residents, working artists among them, but the hotel, which was sold to a developer in spring 2011, was undergoing renovations at the time of writing and not taking reservations for short-term guests; check the website (www.hotelchelsea.com) for updates.

Chelsea provides a variety of impressive cultural offerings. The **Joyce Theater** (see p308) is a renovated art deco cinema that presents better-known contemporary dance troupes, while **New York Live Arts** (see p311) performs at the Bessie Schönberg Theater. A dazzling array of Himalayan art and artefacts is on display at the **Rubin Museum of Art**

(see below). Pioneering arts centre the **Kitchen** (see p311) is also based here.

The weekend flea markets tucked between buildings along 25th Street, between Seventh Avenue and Broadway, have shrunk in recent years (casualties of development), but you'll still find a heady assortment of clothes, furnishings, cameras and knick-knacks at the rummage-worthy **Antiques Garage** (see p218) and the more upmarket **Showplace Antique & Design Center** (see p219).

Not far from here, the Fashion Institute of Technology, on 27th Street, between Seventh and Eighth Avenues, counts Calvin Klein, Nanette Lepore and Michael Kors among its alumni. The school's **Museum at FIT** mounts free exhibitions.

FREE Museum at FIT

Building E, Seventh Avenue, at 27th Street (1-212 217 4558, www.fitnyc.edu/museum). Subway 1 to 28th Street. Open noon-8pm Tue-Fri; 10am-5pm Sat. Admission free. Map p404 D26.

The Fashion Institute of Technology owns one of the largest and most impressive clothing collections in the world, including some 50,000 garments and accessories dating from the fifth century to the present. Under the directorship of fashion historian Dr Valerie Steele, the museum showcases a rotating selection from the permanent collection, as well as temporary exhibitions focusing on individual designers or the role that fashion plays in society. September 2013 sees the debut of its sure-to-be-controversial 'Queer Style', tracing the history of gay and lesbian fashion.

Rubin Museum of Art

150 W 17th Street, at Seventh Avenue (1-212 620 5000, www.rmanyc.org). Subway A, C, E to 14th Street; L to Eighth Avenue; 1 to 18th Street. Open 11am-5pm Mon, Thur; 11am-7pm Wed; 11am-10pm Fri; 11am-6pm Sat, Sun. Admission $10; $5 reductions; free under-13s; free 6-10pm Fri. Credit AmEx, DC, Disc, MC, V. Map p403 D27.

Dedicated to Himalayan art, the Rubin is a very stylish museum – in fact, the six-storey space was once occupied by famed fashion store Barneys. The ground-floor café, where you can sample inexpensive Himalayan dishes, used to be the accessories department, and retail lives on in the colourful gift shop. A dramatic central spiral staircase ascends to the galleries, where rich-toned walls are classy foils for the serene statuary and intricate, multicoloured painted textiles. The second level is dedicated to 'Gateway to Himalayan Art', a yearly rotating display of selections from the permanent collection of more than 2,000 pieces from the second century to the present day. The upper floors are devoted to temporary themed exhibitions.

EXPLORE

INSIDE TRACK MYSTERIES OF THE METRONOME

It's not uncommon to see passers-by perplexed by the **Metronome**, a massive sculptural installation attached to 1 Union Square South that bellows steam and generates a barrage of numbers on a digital read-out. Although they appear strange, they're not random numbers – the 15-digit display is actually a clock indicating the time relative to midnight. There's a detailed explanation at the website of Kristin Jones and Andrew Ginzel, the artists responsible; see www.jonesginzel.com.

FLATIRON DISTRICT & UNION SQUARE

Subway F, M to 14th Street; L, N, Q, R, 4, 5, 6 to 14th Street-Union Square; L to Sixth Avenue; N, R, 6 to 23rd Street or 28th Street.

Taking its name from the distinctive wedge-shaped **Flatiron Building**, this district extends from 14th to 29th Streets, between Sixth and Lexington Avenues. Initially, it was predominantly commercial, home to numerous toy manufacturers and photography studios. It's still not uncommon to see models and actors strolling to and from their shoots. However, in the 1980s, the neighbourhood became more residential, as buyers were drawn to its 19th-century brownstones and early 20th-century industrial architecture. Clusters of restaurants and shops soon followed. By the turn of the millennium, many internet start-ups had moved to the area, earning it the nickname 'Silicon Alley'.

There are two major public spaces in the locale: Madison Square Park and Union Square. Opened in 1847, **Madison Square Park** (from 23rd to 26th Streets, between Fifth & Madison Avenues) is the more stately of the two. In the 19th century, the square was a highly desirable address. Winston Churchill's grandfather resided in a magnificent but since-demolished mansion at Madison Avenue and 26th Street; Edith Wharton also made her home in the neighbourhood and set many of her high-society novels here. By the 1990s, the park had become a decaying no-go zone given over to drug dealers and the homeless, but it got a much-needed makeover in 2001 thanks to the efforts of the Madison Square Park Conservancy (www.madisonsquarepark.org), which has created a programme of cultural events, including Mad Sq Art, a year-round 'gallery without walls', featuring sculptural, video and installation

exhibitions from big-name artists. A further lure is restaurateur Danny Meyer's original **Shake Shack** (*see p173*), which attracts queues in all weathers for its burgers – considered by many New Yorkers to be top of the heap.

The square is surrounded by illustrious buildings. Completed in 1909, the **Metropolitan Life Tower** (1 Madison Avenue, at 24th Street) was modelled on the Campanile in Venice's Piazza San Marco (an allusion as commercial as it was architectural, for Met Life Insurance wished to remind people that it had raised funds for the Campanile after its fall two years earlier). The **Appellate Division Courthouse** (35 E 25th Street, at Madison Avenue) features one of the most beautiful pediments in the city, while Cass Gilbert's **New York Life Insurance Company Building** (51 Madison Avenue, at 26th Street) is capped by a golden pyramid that's one of the skyline's jewels.

The most famous of all Madison Square's edifices, however, lies at the southern end. The **Flatiron Building** (175 Fifth Avenue, between 22nd & 23rd Streets) was the world's first steel-frame skyscraper, a 22-storey Beaux Arts edifice

Flatiron Building

clad conspicuously in white limestone and terracotta. But it's the unique triangular shape (like an arrow pointing northward to indicate the city's progression uptown) that has drawn sightseers since it opened in 1902. Legend has it that a popular 1920s catchphrase originated at this corner of 23rd Street – police would give the '23 skidoo' to ne'er-do-wells trying to peek at ladies' petticoats as the unique wind currents that swirled around the building blew up their dresses. Speaking of rampant libidos, the nearby **Museum of Sex** (*see below*) houses an impressive collection of salacious ephemera.

In the 19th century, the neighbourhood went by the moniker of Ladies' Mile, thanks to the ritzy department stores that lined Broadway and Sixth Avenue. These retail palaces attracted the 'carriage trade', wealthy women who bought the latest imported fashions and household goods. By 1914, most of the department stores had moved north, leaving their proud cast-iron buildings behind. Today, the area is peppered with chain clothing stores, bookshops and tasteful home-furnishing shops such as **ABC Carpet & Home** (*see p219*).

The Flatiron District's other major public space, **Union Square** (from 14th to 17th Streets, between Union Square East & Union Square West) is named after neither the Union of the Civil War nor the labour rallies that once took place here, but simply for the union of Broadway and Bowery Lane (now Fourth Avenue). Even so, it does have its radical roots: from the 1920s until the early '60s, it was a favourite spot for tub-thumping political oratory. Following 9/11, the park was home to candlelit vigils and became a focal point for the city's grief. Formerly grungy, the park is fresh from a rolling renovation project started in the 1980s. It's best known as the home of the **Union Square Greenmarket** (*see right*). The square is flanked by a variety of large businesses, including a **Barnes & Noble** bookstore that hosts an excellent programme of author events.

Museum of Sex

233 Fifth Avenue, at 27th Street (1-212 689 6337, www.museumofsex.com). Subway N, R, 6 to 28th Street. **Open** 10am-8pm Mon-Thur, Sun; 10am-9pm Fri, Sat. **Admission** $17.50; $15.25 reductions. Under-18s not admitted. **Credit** AmEx, MC, V. **Map** p404 E26.

MoSex explores the subject within a cultural context – but that doesn't mean some content won't shock the more buttoned-up visitor. Highlights of the permanent collection range from the tastefully erotic to the outlandish: an 1890s anti-onanism device looks as uncomfortable as the BDSM gear donated by a local dominatrix, there is kinky art courtesy of Picasso and Keith Haring, a display of vintage vibrators and a lifesize silicone Real Doll. Rotating

exhibitions in the three-level space cover such topics as 'The Sex Lives of Animals'. The gift shop stocks books and arty sex toys, while the museum's bar dispenses aphrodisiac cocktails, stimulating soft drinks and light bites.

Union Square Greenmarket

From 16th to 17th Streets, between Union Square East & Union Square West (1-212 788 7476, www.grownyc.org/greenmarket). Subway L, N, Q, R, 4, 5, 6 to 14th Street-Union Square. **Open** 8am-6pm Mon, Wed, Fri, Sat. **Map** p403 E27.

Shop elbow-to-elbow with top chefs for all manner of locally grown produce, handmade breads and baked goods, preserves and cheeses at the city's flagship farmers' market around the periphery of Union Square Park. Between Thanksgiving and Christmas, a holiday market sets up shop. *Photo p80.*

GRAMERCY PARK & MURRAY HILL

Subway L, N, Q, R, 4, 5, 6 to 14th Street-Union Square; L to Sixth Avenue; N, R, 6 to 23rd Street or 28th Street; S, 4, 5, 6, 7 to 42nd Street-Grand Central; 6 to 33rd Street.

A key to **Gramercy Park**, the tranquil, gated square at the bottom of Lexington Avenue, between 20th and 21st Streets, is one of the most sought-after treasures in all the five boroughs. For the most part, only residents of the beautiful surrounding townhouses and apartment buildings have access to the park, which was developed in the 1830s to resemble a London

EXPLORE

INSIDE TRACK
TROUBLE AT THE FACTORY

In 1967, Andy Warhol moved his Factory from Midtown East to the Decker Building, at 33 Union Square West, ostensibly to be nearer to Max's Kansas City club. So-called because the process for creating his famous silkscreens suggested an assembly line, the Factory was also the scene of legendary debauched parties and the set of Warhol's experimental films. On 3 June 1968, Valerie Solanas, the disturbed author of the *SCUM Manifesto* (which advocated killing all males) and *Up Your Ass*, a play Warhol had briefly expressed an interest in producing before misplacing the script, shot Andy three times in the lobby of the Factory. Warhol survived, and Solanas spent three years in a psychiatric ward. More than a decade after both had died, *Up Your Ass* made it to the stage for a brief run in 2000.

Union Square Greenmarket. *See p79.*

square. The park is flanked by two private clubs; members of both also have access to the square. One is the **Players Club** (16 Gramercy Park South, between Park Avenue South & Irving Place, 1-212 475 6116, www.theplayersnyc.org), inspired by London's Garrick Club. It's housed in an 1845 brownstone formerly owned by Edwin Booth, the celebrated 19th-century actor and brother of John Wilkes Booth, Abraham Lincoln's assassin. Next door at no.15 is the Gothic Revival Samuel Tilden House, which houses the **National Arts Club** (1-212 475 3424, www.nationalartsclub.org, closed Sat, Sun & July, Aug). The busts of famous writers (Shakespeare, Dante) along the façade were chosen to reflect Tilden's library, which, along with his fortune, helped to create the New York Public Library. The NAC's galleries are open to non-members, but call before visiting as they may close for private events or between shows.

Leading south from the park to 14th Street, Irving Place is named after author Washington Irving (although he never actually lived here). Near the corner of 15th Street sits **Irving Plaza** (*see p287*), a music venue. At the corner of Park Avenue South and 17th Street is the final base of the once-omnipotent Tammany Hall political machine. Built in 1929, it now houses the New York Film Academy. Popular local hangout **71 Irving Place Coffee & Tea Bar** (*see p167*) is a good place to revive with a cup of New York State-roasted java. A few blocks away from here is the **Theodore Roosevelt Birthplace** (*see p81*), a national historic site.

The largely residential area bordered by 23rd and 30th Streets, Park Avenue and the East River is known as **Kips Bay** after Jacobus Henderson Kip, whose farm covered the area in the 17th century. Third Avenue is the district's main thoroughfare, and a locus of restaurants representing a variety of eastern cuisines, including Afghan, Tibetan and Turkish.

Murray Hill spans 30th to 40th Streets, between Third and Fifth Avenues. Townhouses of the rich and powerful were once clustered around Madison and Park Avenues. It's now populated mostly by upwardly mobiles fresh out of university and only a few streets retain their former elegance. One is **Sniffen Court** (150-158 E 36th Street, between Lexington & Third Avenues), an unspoiled row of 1864 carriage houses located within earshot of the Queens Midtown Tunnel's ceaseless traffic. The **Morgan Library & Museum** (*see below*), also on 36th Street, houses some 500,000 rare books, manuscripts, prints, and objects. Nearby, **Scandinavia House – The Nordic Center in America** (*see p81*) is the centre of Scandie culture in NYC.

★ Morgan Library & Museum

225 Madison Avenue, at 36th Street (1-212 685 0008, www.themorgan.org). Subway 6 to 33rd Street. **Open** 10.30am-5pm Tue-Thur; 10.30am-9pm Fri; 10am-6pm Sat; 11am-6pm Sun. **Admission** $15; $10 reductions; free under-13s; free 7-9pm Fri. **Credit** AmEx, DC, MC, V. **Map** p404 E25.

This Madison Avenue institution began as the private library of financier J Pierpont Morgan, and is his artistic gift to the city. Building on the collection Morgan amassed in his lifetime, the museum houses first-rate works on paper, including drawings by Michelangelo, Rembrandt and Picasso; three Gutenberg Bibles; a copy of *Frankenstein* annotated by Mary Shelley; manuscripts by

Dickens, Poe, Twain, Steinbeck and Wilde; sheet music handwritten by Beethoven and Mozart; and an original edition of Dickens's *A Christmas Carol* that's displayed every Yuletide. A massive renovation and expansion orchestrated by Renzo Piano brought more natural light into the building and doubled the available exhibition space. The final phase restored the original 1906 building, designed by McKim, Mead & White, which reopened in autumn 2010. As a result, visitors can now see Morgan's spectacular library (the East Room), with its 30ft-high book-lined walls and murals designed by Henry Siddons Mowbray (who also painted the ceiling of the newly restored Rotunda).

The 2013 roster of shows includes 'Drawing Surrealism' (through 21 Apr); 'Degas, Miss La La and the Cirque Fernando' (through 12 May); and 'Subliming Vessel: The Drawings of Matthew Barney' (10 May-1 Sept).

Scandinavia House – The Nordic Center in America

58 Park Avenue, at 38th Streets (1-212 879 9779, www.scandinaviahouse.org). Subway S, 4, 5, 6, 7 to 42nd Street-Grand Central. **Open** varies. *Gallery* noon-6pm Tue, Thur-Sat; noon-7pm Wed. **Admission** varies. **Credit** AmEx, MC, V. **Map** p404 E24.

One of the city's top cultural centres, Scandinavia House serves as a link between the US and the five Scandinavian nations, and offers a full schedule of film screenings, lectures and art exhibitions. In April, look out for 'Munch/Warhol and the Multiple Image', which ties in with the 150th anniversary of Nowegian artist Edvard Munch's birth and explores themes later adopted by the Pop artist in a series of prints. An outpost of Smörgas Chef (open 11am-10pm Mon-Sat, 11am-5pm Sun), serves tasty Swedish meatballs, and the shop is a showcase for chic Scandinavian design.

FREE Theodore Roosevelt Birthplace

28 E 20th Street, between Broadway & Park Avenue South (1-212 260 1616, www.nps.gov/thrb). Subway 6 to 23rd Street. **Tours** hourly 10am-4pm, except noon. **Admission** free. **Map** p403 E27.

The brownstone where the 26th President of the United States was born, and where he lived until he was 14 years old, was demolished in 1916. But it was recreated after his death in 1919, complete with authentic period furniture (some from the original house), personal effects and a trophy room. The house can only be explored by guided tour.

HERALD SQUARE & THE GARMENT DISTRICT

Subway A, C, E, 1, 2, 3 to 34th Street-Penn Station; B, D, F, M, N, Q, R to 34th Street-Herald Square.

Seventh Avenue, aka Fashion Avenue, is the main drag of the **Garment District** (roughly from 34th to 40th Streets, between Broadway & Eighth Avenue) and where designers – along with their seamstresses, fitters and assistants – feed America's multi-billion-dollar clothing industry. Many showrooms hold sample sales (*see p190*). Delivery trucks and workers pushing racks of clothes clog streets lined with wholesale trimming, button and fabric shops. The scene is particularly busy on 38th and 39th Streets.

Taking up an entire city block, from 34th Street to 35th Street, between Broadway and Seventh Avenue, is the legendary **Macy's** (*see p193*). With one million square feet of selling space spread across nine floors, it's the biggest and busiest department store in the world. Facing Macy's, at the intersection of Broadway, 34th Street and Sixth Avenue, is **Herald Square**, named after a long-gone newspaper, the *New York Herald*. The lower section is known as **Greeley Square** after editor and reformer Horace Greeley, owner of the *Herald*'s rival, the *New York Tribune* (the two papers merged in 1924). Once seedy, the square now offers bistro chairs and tables that get crowded with shoppers and office lunchers in the warmer months. To the east, the many spas, restaurants and karaoke bars of small enclave **Koreatown** line 32nd Street, between Broadway and Fifth Avenue.

Located not in Madison Square but on Seventh Avenue, between 31st and 33rd Streets, **Madison Square Garden** (*see p327*) is home for the Knicks and Rangers, and has welcomed rock icons from Elvis to Lady Gaga as well as the Barnum & Bailey Circus and other big events. The massive arena is actually the fourth building to bear that name (the first two were appropriately located in the square after which they're named) and opened on Valentine's Day 1968, replacing the grand old Pennsylvania Station razed four years earlier. This brutal act of architectural vandalism spurred the creation of the city's Landmarks Preservation Commission, which has saved countless other edifices from a similar fate.

Beneath Madison Square Garden stands **Penn Station**, a claustrophobic catacomb serving 600,000 Amtrak, Long Island Railroad and New Jersey Transit passengers daily and the busiest train station in America. A proposal to relocate the station across the street to the stately **James A Farley Post Office** (421 Eighth Avenue, between 31st & 33rd Streets), was championed by the late Senator Patrick Moynihan in the early 1990s. The project, which has stalled over the years, finally got the necessary funding and government approval, and Moynihan Station is expected to be completed in 2016.

THE THEATER DISTRICT & HELL'S KITCHEN

Subway A, C, E to 42nd Street-Port Authority; N, Q, R, S, 1, 2, 3, 7 to 42nd Street-Times Square.

Times Square's evolution from a traffic-choked fleshpot to a tourist-friendly theme park has accelerated in the past few years. Not only has 'the Crossroads of the World' gained an elevated viewing platform atop the TKTS discount booth, from which visitors can admire the surrounding light show (*see p75* **Insider's Guide**), but in 2009 Mayor Bloomberg designated stretches of Broadway, from 47th to 42nd Streets and from 35th to 33rd Streets, pedestrian zones complete with seating, in an effort to streamline midtown traffic and create a more pleasant environment for both residents and visitors.

Originally Longacre Square, the junction of Broadway and Seventh Avenue, stretching from 42nd to 47th Streets, was renamed after the *New York Times* moved here in the early 1900s. The first electrified billboard graced the district in 1904, on the side of a bank at 46th and Broadway. The same year, the inaugural New Year's Eve party in Times Square doubled as the *Times*'s housewarming party in its new HQ. Today, about a million people gather here to watch a glittery mirrorball descend every 31 December.

The paper left the building only a decade after it had arrived (it now occupies an $84-million tower on Eighth Avenue, between 40th and 41st Streets). However, it retained ownership of its

---

Profile The High Line

All aboard New York's popular – and still-evolving – new park.

Back in the early days of the 20th century, the West Side had something in common with the Wild West. When freight-bearing trains competed with horses, carts and pedestrians on Tenth Avenue, the thoroughfare was so treacherous it earned the moniker 'Death Avenue'. In an attempt to counteract the carnage, mounted men known as 'West Side Cowboys' would ride in front of the train, waving red flags to warn of its imminent approach. These urban cowboys lost their jobs when the West Side Improvement Project finally raised the railway off street level and put it up on to an overhead trestle – the High Line – in 1934. Originally stretching from 34th Street to Spring Street, the line fell into disuse after World War II as trucks replaced trains. A southern chunk was torn down beginning in the 1960s, and, after the last train ground to a halt in 1980, local property owners lobbied for its destruction. However, thanks to the efforts of railroad enthusiast Peter Obletz and, later, the Friends of the High Line, which was founded by local residents Joshua David and Robert Hammond, the industrial relic was saved. A decade after the group began advocating for its reuse as a public space, the first phase of New York's first elevated public park opened in summer 2009; the second leg followed two years later.

Running from Gansevoort Street in the Meatpacking District, where Renzo Piano's new Whitney Museum of American Art building will be taking shape over the next couple of years, through Chelsea's gallery district to 30th Street, the slender, sinuous green strip has been designed by landscape architects James Corner Field Operations and architects Diller Scofidio + Renfro. In autumn 2012, construction began on the final section, which will open in three phases, starting in 2014. Stretching from 30th to 34th Streets, it skirts the West Side Rail Yards, which are being developed into the long-planned residential and commercial complex, Hudson Yards.

As well as trees, flowers and landscaped greenery, the High Line has several interesting features along the way. Commanding an expansive river view, the 'sun deck' between 14th and 15th Streets features wooden deck chairs that can be

old headquarters until the 1960s, and erected the world's first scrolling electric news 'zipper' in 1928. The readout, now sponsored by Dow Jones, has trumpeted momentus breaking stories from the stock-market crash of 1929 to the death of Osama Bin Laden.

Times Square is also the gateway to the **Theater District**, the zone between 41st Street and 53rd Street, from Sixth Avenue to Ninth Avenue, where extravagant shows are put on six days a week (Monday is the traditional night off). While numerous showhouses stage first-rate productions in the area, only 39 are officially Broadway theatres. The distinction is based on size rather than location or quality – Broadway theatres must have more than 500 seats.

The Theater District's transformation from the cradle of New York's sex industry began in 1984, when the city condemned properties along 42nd Street ('Forty Deuce', or 'the Deuce' for short), between Seventh and Eighth Avenues. A change in zoning laws meant adult-oriented venues must now subsist on X-rated videos rather than live 'dance' shows; the square's sex trade is now relegated to short stretches of Seventh and Eighth Avenues, just north and south of 42nd Street.

The streets to the west of Eighth Avenue are filled with eateries catering to theatregoers, especially the predominantly pricey, tourist-oriented places along **Restaurant Row** (46th Street, between Eighth & Ninth Avenues). Locals tend to walk west to Ninth Avenue – in the 40s and 50s, the Hell's Kitchen strip is tightly packed with inexpensive restaurants serving a variety of ethnic cuisines. Other

rolled along the original tracks, plus a water feature with benches for cooling your feet. The old Nabisco factory that houses Chelsea Market (*see p210*) received deliveries via the line; now the section cutting through the building is devoted to long-term, site-specific art, though befitting the park's art-rich location, there are changing installations dotted along its length. A seasonal open-air café, the Porch, at 15th Street, serves sandwiches and local wine and beer from cult vino spot Terroir (*see p181*); other food vendors set up shop in the park in the warmer months. At 17th Street, steps descend into a sunken amphitheatre with a glassed-over 'window' in the steel structure overlooking the avenue. Further along, look out for the Empire State Building rising above the skyline to the east.

Not all the views from the High Line have been welcome, however. Soon after the park opened, there were reports in the press of naked antics in the glass-fronted rooms of luxury hotel the Standard, which squats over the promenade at West 13th Street – in full view of the strollers below.

The High Line is open from 7am to 10pm daily most of the year; for updates, see www.thehighline.org.

popular options include celebuchef Mario Batali's **Esca** (402 W 43rd Street, at Ninth Avenue, 1-212 564 7272, www.esca-nyc.com, closed lunch Sun) and fondue-and-wine spot **Kashkaval** (*see p168*).

Recording studios, record labels, theatrical agencies and other entertainment and media companies reside in the area's office buildings. The **Brill Building** (1619 Broadway, at 49th Street) has long housed music publishers and producers; such luminaries as Jerry Lieber, Mike Stoller and Carole King wrote and auditioned their hits here. Visiting rock royalty and aspiring musicians alike drool over the selection of new and vintage guitars (and other instruments) on **Music Row** (48th Street, between Sixth & Seventh Avenues). **ABC Television Studios**, at 7 Times Square, at 44th Street and Broadway, entices early risers hoping to catch a glimpse of the *Good Morning America* crew.

Flashy attractions strive to outdo one another in hopes of snaring the tourist throngs. **Madame Tussauds New York**, a Gothamised version of the London-born wax museum chain, sits next to **Ripley's Believe It Or Not! Odditorium** (for both, *see p86*), which returned to the locale in 2007 after a 35-year absence. **Discovery Times Square** (*see right*), an exhibition centre affiliated with the Discovery Channel, stages blockbuster shows. The vast **Toys 'R' Us** (1514 Broadway, at 44th Street, 1-646 366 8800) boasts a 60-foot indoor Ferris wheel and a two-floor Barbie emporium.

For more refined entertainments, head further uptown. Open since 1891, **Carnegie Hall** (*see p301*) has staged legendary shows by the likes of Judy Garland, Miles Davis and Yo-Yo Ma. Nearby is the famous **Carnegie Deli** (854 Seventh Avenue, at 55th Street, 1-212 757 2245), home to five-inch-tall pastrami sandwiches.

West of the Theater District lies **Hell's Kitchen**. The precise origins of the name are unclear, but no doubt arose from its emergence as an Irish-mob-dominated neighbourhood in the 19th-century – *The New York Times* claims that the first known documented reference was in that very paper in 1881, to describe an unsavoury tenement in the locale. In the 1950s, clashes between Irish and recently arrived Puerto Rican factions were dramatised in the musical *West Side Story*. It was a particularly violent incident in 1959, in which two teenagers died, that led to an attempt by local businesses to erase the stigma associated with the area by renaming it Clinton (taken from a park named after one-time mayor DeWitt Clinton). The new name never really took, and gang culture survived until the 1980s.

Today, the area is emerging as New York's hottest queer neighbourhood, with numerous bars (*see p272*) and the city's first gay-oriented

luxury hotel, **The Out NYC**, which contains one of Gotham's few full-on dance clubs (*see p268* **Staying in the Out**). As gentrification takes hold, new apartment blocks are also springing up in the former wasteland near the Hudson River. This area is dominated by the massive, black-glass **Jacob K Javits Convention Center** (Eleventh Avenue, between 34th & 39th Streets), host of a never-ending schedule of large-scale trade shows. A couple of major draws are also here: the **Circle Line Terminal**, at Pier 83, the departure point for the cruise company's three-hour circumnavigation of Manhattan Island (*see p40*), and the **Intrepid Sea, Air & Space Museum** (*see below*), a retired aircraft carrier-cum-naval museum.

Discovery Times Square

226 W 44th Street, between Seventh & Eighth Avenues (1-866 987 9692, www.discoverytsx. com). Subway A, C, E to 42nd Street-Port Authority; N, Q, R, S, 1, 2, 3, 7 to 42nd Street-Times Square. **Open** 10am-8pm Mon-Thur, Sun; 10am-9pm Fri, Sat. **Admission** $27; $19.50-$23.50 reductions; free under-4s. **Credit** AmEx, Disc, MC, V. **Map** p404 D24.
This Discovery Channel-sponsored exhibition centre stages big shows on such crowd-pleasing subjects as King Tut, Pompeii, the *Titanic* and the Harry Potter franchise.

Intrepid Sea, Air & Space Museum

USS Intrepid, Pier 86, Twelfth Avenue & 46th Street (1-877 957 7447, www.intrepidmuseum. org). Subway A, C, E to 42nd Street-Port Authority, then M42 bus to Twelfth Avenue or 15min walk. **Open** *Apr-Oct* 10am-5pm Mon-Fri; 10am-6pm Sat, Sun. *Nov-Mar* 10am-5pm Tue-Sun. **Admission** $24-$30; $12-$26 reductions; free under-3s, active & retired US military. **Credit** AmEx, DC, Disc, MC, V. **Map** p404 B23.
Commissioned in 1943, this 27,000-ton, 898ft aircraft carrier survived torpedoes and kamikaze attacks in World War II, served during Vietnam and the Cuban Missile Crisis, and recovered two space capsules for NASA. The 'Fighting I' was finally decommissioned in 1974, but real-estate mogul Zachary Fisher saved it from the scrap yard by resurrecting it as an educational institution. On its flight deck and portside aircraft elevator are stationed top-notch examples of American military might, including the US Navy F-14 Tomcat (from *Top Gun*), an A-12 Blackbird spy plane and a fully restored Army AH-1G Cobra gunship helicopter. (Foreign powers are represented by a French Entendard IV-M, a Polish MiG-21, and the British Airways Concorde, among others.)

Following a two-year, $8-million makeover, the museum has an Exploreum featuring interactive exhibits, such as a Bell 47 helicopter you can sit in, while a re-created mess room and sleeping quarters

EXPLORE

Walk Mad Men in Midtown

Stroll through the sharp-dressed, hard-drinking world of the retro TV series.

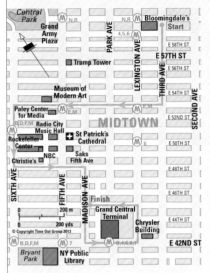

Before you get started, suit up! You can't properly be a Mad Man without a grey flannel suit and a skinny tie, so start at **Bloomingdale's** (1000 Third Avenue, between 59th & 60th Streets; *see p192*). If you suffer from buyer's remorse, the store's return policy is generous – although when smarmy Pete Campbell returned a chip 'n' dip here in season one, it cost him his sense of manhood.

We don't want to encourage you to buy a pack of Lucky Strikes, Don Draper's smoke of choice (emphysema never looked so dapper!), so cross the street to pick up some retro candy cigarettes at sugar superstore **Dylan's Candy Bar** (1011 Third Avenue, at 60th Street, 1-646 735 0078). At little more than a couple of bucks a box, they're a lot cheaper than the real thing. With the 'smoking' comes the drinking, so take a right on Third and stop by **PJ Clarke's** (915 Third Avenue, at 55th Street, 1-212 317 1616), where the younger Sterling Cooperites celebrated Peggy's writing achievement.

The **Museum of Modern Art** (11 W 53rd Street, between Fifth & Sixth Avenues; *see p88*) is just a few blocks away. Browse staples of the early '60s such as Andy Warhol's pop art paintings, which more or

less prove what you've been saying for years: advertising is an art form.

By now it would be wise to stop by the office. In season four, the newly formed Sterling Cooper Draper Pryce moved into Rock Center's five-year-old **Time & Life Building**. Continue west on 53rd Street and take a left on Sixth Avenue to check it out at no.1271, between 50th and 51st Streets. Since the building's lobby has landmark status, it won't have changed much since the '60s. Good thing you wore that suit! Then head south down Sixth before turning left at 48th Street to swing by the fictional firm's original premises, at 405 Madison Avenue (between 47th & 48th Streets).

Continue south and hang a left on 42nd Street to grab dinner at the **Grand Central Oyster Bar** (89 E 42nd Street, at Park Avenue; *see p169*), inside the terminal, where you can recreate one of the series' iconic scenes – Don dupes boss Roger into a clam-eating/vodka-drinking contest before the latter famously vomits in front of clients. The super-fresh bivalves here shouldn't leave you with an upset stomach, but the third round of martinis might.

Exit the terminal on Lexington Avenue and head north, before turning left at 45th Street and back to Madison and the **Roosevelt Hotel** (45 E 45th Street, at Madison Avenue, 1-212 661 9600). This was Don's crash pad after Betty kicked him out before their final split. Even if you're not spending the night, hop into the Madison Club Lounge for more drinks.

Grand Central Oyster Bar & Restaurant. *See p169.*

New York Public Library. *See p88.*

evoke the on-board living conditions of the late 1960s. In summer 2011, the museum became home to the *Enterprise* (OV-101), the first Space Shuttle Orbiter, which was recently retired (entry to the new Space Shuttle Pavilion costs extra).

Madame Tussauds New York
234 W 42nd Street, between Seventh & Eighth Avenues (1-866 841 3505, www.madame tussauds.com/newyork). Subway A, C, E to 42nd Street-Port Authority; N, Q, R, S, 1, 2, 3, 7 to 42nd Street-Times Square. **Open** 10am-8pm Mon-Thur, Sun; 10am-10pm Fri, Sat. **Admission** $39.20; $31.57 reductions; free under-4s. **Credit** AmEx, MC, V. **Map** p404 D24.
With roots in 18th-century Paris and founded in London in 1802, the world's most famous wax museum now draws celebrity-hungry crowds to more than a dozen locations worldwide. At the New York outpost, you can get a stalker's-eye view of paraffin doppelgangers of an array of political, sports, film and pop stars, from Barack Obama and Carmelo Anthony to Denzel Washington and Lady Gaga. A new crop of freshly waxed victims debuts every few months.

Ripley's Believe It or Not! Odditorium
234 W 42nd Street, between Seventh & Eighth Avenues (1-212 398 3133, www.ripleysnewyork. com). Subway A, C, E to 42nd Street-Port Authority; N, Q, R, S, 1, 2, 3, 7 to 42nd Street-Times Square. **Open** 9am-1am daily (last entry midnight). **Admission** $32.61; $24.99 reductions; free under-4s. **Credit** AmEx, DC, Disc, MC, V. **Map** p404 D24.
Times Square might be a little whitewashed these days, but you can get a feel for the old freak show at this repository of the eerie and uncanny. Marvel at such bizarre artefacts as a six-legged cow, the world's largest collection of shrunken heads and a cache of weird art that includes a portrait of President Obama composed of 12,600 gumballs.

Carrying a torch for gritty bygone attractions, Ripley's provides a platform for a new generation of sideshow acts with free weekend performances by the likes of Albert Cadabra, the human blockhead, at the entrance (see website for schedule).

FIFTH AVENUE & AROUND
Subway B, D, F, M, N, Q, R to 34th Street-Herald Square; B, D, F, M to 47-50th Streets-Rockefeller Center; E, M to Fifth Avenue-53rd Street; 7 to Fifth Avenue.

The stretch of Fifth Avenue between Rockefeller Center and Central Park South showcases retail palaces bearing names that were famous long before the concept of branding was developed. Bracketed by **Saks Fifth Avenue** (49th to 50th Streets; *see p193*) and **Bergdorf Goodman** (57th to 58th Streets; *see p190*), tenants include Gucci, Prada and Tiffany & Co (and the parade of big names continues east along 57th Street). Along with Madison Avenue uptown, this is the centre of high-end shopping in New York, and the window displays – particularly during the frenetic Christmas shopping season – are worth a look even if you're not buying.

Fifth Avenue is crowned by Grand Army Plaza at 59th Street, presided over by a gilded statue of General William Tecumseh Sherman. To the west stands the **Plaza** (*see p241*), the famous hotel that was home to fictional moppet Eloise. Stretching north above 59th Street (the parkside stretch is called Central Park South), is **Central Park** (*see p92*).

Fifth Avenue is the main route for the city's many public processions: the **St Patrick's Day Parade** (*see p29*), the **LGBT Pride March** (*see p33*) and many others. Even without floats or marching bands, the sidewalks are generally teeming with gawking tourists, fashion victims and wealthy socialites. The most famous skyscraper in the world also has its entrance on Fifth Avenue: the **Empire State Building** (*see below*), located smack-bang in the centre of midtown.

A pair of impassive stone lions, which were dubbed Patience and Fortitude by Mayor Fiorello La Guardia during the Great Depression, guard the steps of the beautiful Beaux Arts humanities and social sciences branch of the **New York Public Library** (*see p88*) at 42nd Street, now officially named the Stephen A Schwarzman Building. Just behind the library is **Bryant Park**, a well-manicured lawn that hosts a popular outdoor film series in summer (*see p259* **Inside Track**) and an ice-skating rink in winter (*see p333*).

The luxury **Bryant Park Hotel** (*see p242*) occupies the former American Radiator Building on 40th Street. Designed by architect Raymond Hood in the mid 1920s, the structure is faced with near-black brick and trimmed in gold leaf. Alexander Woollcott, Dorothy Parker and her 'vicious circle' held court and traded barbs at the nearby **Algonquin** (*see p242*); the lobby is still a great place to meet for a drink. Just north of the park, on Sixth Avenue, is the always thought-provoking **International Center of Photography** (*see below*).

Step off Fifth Avenue into **Rockefeller Center** (*see p89*) and you'll find yourself in a 'city within a city', an interlacing complex of 19 buildings housing corporate offices, retail space and the popular Rockefeller Plaza. After plans for an expansion of the Metropolitan Opera on the site fell through in 1929, John D Rockefeller Jr set about creating the complex to house radio and television corporations. Designed by Raymond Hood and many other prominent architects, Rock Center grew over the decades, with each new building conforming to the original master plan and art deco design.

On weekday mornings, a (tourist-dominated) crowd gathers at the NBC network's glass-walled, ground-level studio (where the *Today* show is shot), at the south-west corner of Rockefeller Plaza and 49th Street. The complex is also home to art auction house **Christie's** (20 Rockefeller Plaza, 49th Street, between Fifth & Sixth Avenues, 1-212 636 2000, www.christies.com, usually closed Sat, Sun); pop into the lobby to admire a mural by conceptualist Sol LeWitt.

When it opened on Sixth Avenue (at 50th Street) in 1932, **Radio City Music Hall** (*see p289*) was designed as a showcase for high-end variety acts, but the death of vaudeville led to a quick transition into what was then the world's largest movie house. Today, the art deco jewel hosts concerts and a traditional Christmas Spectacular featuring renowned precision dance troupe the Rockettes. Visitors can get a peek backstage, and meet one of the high-kicking dancers, on the Stage Door tour (every 30mins, 11am-3pm daily; $19.25, $15 reductions; see www.stagedoortour.com for details).

Facing Rockefeller Center is the beautiful **St Patrick's Cathedral** (*see p89*). Famous couples from F Scott and Zelda Fitzgerald to Liza Minnelli and David Gest have tied the knot here; funeral services for such notables as Andy Warhol and baseball legend Joe DiMaggio have been held in its confines. A few blocks north is the **Museum of Modern Art** (MoMA) and the **Paley Center for Media** (for both, *see p88*).

★ Empire State Building

350 Fifth Avenue, between 33rd & 34th Streets (1-212 736 3100, www.esbnyc.com). Subway B, D, F, M, N, Q, R to 34th Street-Herald Square. **Open** 8am-2am daily (last lift at 1.15am). **Admission** *86th floor* $25; $19-$22 reductions; free under-5s. *102nd floor* $17 extra. **Credit** AmEx, DC, Disc, MC, V. **Map** p404 E25.

Financed by General Motors executive John J Raskob at the height of New York's skyscraper race, the Empire State sprang up in a mere 14 months, weeks ahead of schedule and $5 million under budget. Since its opening in 1931, it's been immortalised in countless photos and films, from the original *King Kong* to *Sleepless in Seattle*. Following the destruction of the World Trade Center in 2001, the 1,250ft tower resumed its title as New York's tallest building but has since been overtaken by the new 1 World Trade Center. The nocturnal colour scheme of the tower lights – recently upgraded to flashy LEDs – often honours holidays, charities or special events.

The enclosed observatory on the 102nd floor is the city's highest lookout point, but the panoramic deck on the 86th floor, 1,050ft above the street, is roomier. From here, you can enjoy views of all five boroughs and five neighbouring states (when the skies are clear).

International Center of Photography

1133 Sixth Avenue, at 43rd Street (1-212 857 0000, www.icp.org). Subway B, D, F, M to 42nd

EXPLORE

INSIDE TRACK
EMPIRE STATE EXPRESS

If you're visiting the **Empire State Building** (*see above*), allow at least two hours for queueing and viewing. To save time, bypass one of three lines by buying tickets online (the others, for security and entry, are unavailable), and visit late at night, when most sightseers have turned in. Alternatively, springing for an express pass ($47.50) allows you to cut to the front.

Street-Bryant Park; N, Q, R, S, 1, 2, 3, 7 to 42nd Street-Times Square; 7 to Fifth Avenue. **Open** 10am-6pm Tue, Wed, Sat, Sun; 10am-8pm Thur, Fri. **Admission** $14; $10 reductions; free under-12s; pay what you wish 5-8pm Fri. **Credit** AmEx, Disc, MC, V. **Map** p404 D24.

Since 1974, the ICP has served as a pre-eminent library, school and museum devoted to all forms of the photographic image, and photojournalism remains a vital facet of the centre's programme. Spring 2013 ushers in the fourth ICP Triennial (17 May-1 Sept), an international survey of contemporary photography, video, new media and installation art. This will be followed by an exhibition focusing on early-20th-century documentary photographer Lewis Hine (13 Sept-12 Jan 2014).

★ Museum of Modern Art (MoMA)

11 W 53rd Street, between Fifth & Sixth Avenues (1-212 708 9400, www.moma.org). Subway E, M to Fifth Avenue-53rd Street. **Open** 10.30am-5.30pm Mon, Wed, Thur, Sat, Sun; 10.30am-8pm Fri; 10.30am-8.30pm 1st Thur of the mth & every Thur in July, Aug. **Admission** (incl admission to film programmes) $25; $14-$18 reductions; free under-17s; free 4-8pm Fri. **Credit** AmEx, MC, V. **Map** p404 E23.

After a two-year renovation based on a design by Japanese architect Yoshio Taniguchi, MoMA reopened in 2004 with almost double the space to display some of the most impressive artworks from the 19th, 20th and 21st centuries. The museum's permanent collection now encompasses seven curatorial departments: Architecture and Design, Drawings, Film, Media, Painting and Sculpture, Photography, and Prints and Illustrated Books. Highlights include Picasso's *Les Demoiselles d'Avignon*, Van Gogh's *The Starry Night* and Dali's *The Persistence of Memory* (back on view September 2013) as well as masterpieces by Giacometti, Hopper, Matisse, Monet, O'Keefe, Pollock, Rothko, Warhol and many others. Outside, the Philip Johnson-designed Abby Aldrich Rockefeller Sculpture Garden contains works by Calder, Rodin and Moore. The destination museum also contains a destination restaurant: the Modern, which overlooks the garden; if the prices are too steep, dine in the bar, which shares the kitchen. Starting in May 2013, MoMA will be open seven days a week.

Exhibitions for 2013 include 'Bill Brandt: Shadow and Light' (6 Mar-13 Aug); 'Claes Oldenburg: *The Street* and *The Store*' (14 Apr-5 Aug), featuring the Pop art pioneer's early New York works; 'Le Corbusier: An Atlas of Modern Landscapes' (9 June-23 Sept), MoMA's first major show dedicated to the multifaceted artist, architect and designer; 'American Modern' (11 Aug-27 January 2014), featuring pieces from its holdings from the first half of the 20th century; and 'Magritte: The Mystery of the Ordinary 1926-1938' (22 Sept-12 Jan 2014).

► *For MoMA PS1 in Queens, see p126.*

> ### INSIDE TRACK THE '21' CLUB
>
> A former speakeasy during the Prohibition era, the **'21' Club** (21 W 52nd Street, between Fifth & Sixth Avenues, 1-212 582 7200; closed Sun & lunch Mon, Sat) has since gone decidedly legit and acquired a much loftier profile. Presidents (Roosevelt, Kennedy, Nixon) and Hollywood aristocracy (Frank Sinatra, Marilyn Monroe, Elizabeth Taylor) have supped here over the years. The restaurant has also been widely featured on the screen, most notably in *All About Eve, Sweet Smell of Success, Sex and the City, Wall Street*, and *Manhattan Murder Mystery*.

★ FREE New York Public Library

Fifth Avenue, at 42nd Street (1-917 275 6975, www.nypl.org). Subway B, D, F, M to 42nd Street-Bryant Park; 7 to Fifth Avenue. **Open** *Sept-June* 10am-6pm Mon, Thur-Sat; 10am-8pm Tue, Wed; 1-5pm Sun. *July, Aug* 10am-6pm Mon, Thur-Sat; 10am-8pm Tue, Wed (see website for gallery hours). **Admission** free. **Map** p404 E24.

Guarded by the marble lions Patience and Fortitude, this austere Beaux Arts edifice, designed by Carrère and Hastings, was completed in 1911. The building was renamed in honour of philanthropist Stephen A Schwarzman in 2008, but Gothamites still know it as the New York Public Library, although the city-wide library system consists of 91 locations. Free hour-long tours (11am, 2pm Mon-Sat; 2pm Sun, except July & Aug) take in the Rose Main Reading Room on the third floor, which at 297 feet long and 78 feet wide is almost the size of a football field. Specialist departments include the Map Division, containing some 431,000 maps and 16,000 atlases, and the Rare Books Division boasting Walt Whitman's personal copies of the first (1855) and third (1860) editions of *Leaves of Grass*.

The library also stages major exhibitions and events, including the excellent 'Live from the NYPL' series of talks and lectures from big-name authors and thinkers (see website for schedule). *Photo p86.*

Paley Center for Media

25 W 52nd Street, between Fifth & Sixth Avenues (1-212 621 6600, www.paleycenter.org). Subway B, D, F, M to 47-50th Streets-Rockefeller Center; E, M to Fifth Avenue-53rd Street. **Open** noon-6pm Wed, Fri-Sun; noon-8pm Thur. **Admission** $10; $5-$8 reductions. **No credit cards. Map** p404 E23.

Nirvana for telly addicts and pop-culture junkies, the Paley Center (formerly the Museum of Television & Radio) houses an immense archive of almost 150,000 radio and TV shows. Head to the fourth-floor library to search the system for your favourite episode of *Star Trek, Seinfeld*, or rarer fare, and watch it on your assigned console; radio shows are also available. A theatre on the concourse level is the site of frequent screenings, premières and high-profile panel discussions. There's also a small ground-floor gallery for themed exhibitions.

★ Rockefeller Center

From 48th to 51st Streets, between Fifth & Sixth Avenues (Tours & Top of the Rock 1-212 698 2000, NBC Studio Tours 1-212 664 3700, www.rockefellercenter.com). Subway B, D, F, M to 47-50th Streets-Rockefeller Center. **Open** *Tours vary. Observation deck 8am-midnight daily (last lift at 11pm).* **Admission** *Rockefeller Center tours $15 (under-6s not admitted). Observation deck $25; $16-$23 reductions; free under-6s. NBC Studio tours $24; $21 reductions (under-6s not admitted).* **Credit** AmEx, DC, Disc, MC, V. **Map** p404 E23.

Constructed under the aegis of industrialist John D Rockefeller in the 1930s, this art deco city-within-a-city is inhabited by NBC, Simon & Schuster, McGraw-Hill and other media giants, as well as Radio City Music Hall, Christie's auction house, and an underground shopping arcade. Guided tours of the entire complex are available daily, and there's a separate NBC Studio tour (call the number above or see website for details).

The buildings and grounds are embellished with works by several well-known artists; look out for Isamu Noguchi's stainless-steel relief, *News*, above the entrance to 50 Rockefeller Plaza, and José Maria Sert's mural *American Progress* in the lobby of 30 Rockefeller Plaza (also known as the GE Building). But the most breathtaking sights are those seen from the 70th-floor Top of the Rock observation deck (combined tour/observation deck tickets are avail-

able). In the cold-weather months, the Plaza's sunken courtyard – eternally guarded by Paul Manship's bronze statue of Prometheus – transforms into a picturesque, if crowded, ice-skating rink (*see p333*).

FREE St Patrick's Cathedral

Fifth Avenue, between 50th & 51st Streets (1-212 753 2261, www.saintpatrickscathedral. org). Subway B, D, F, M to 47-50th Streets-Rockefeller Center; E, M to Fifth Avenue-53rd Street. **Open** 6.30am-8.45pm daily. **Admission** free. **Map** p404 E23.

The largest Catholic church in America, St Patrick's counts presidents, business leaders and movie stars among its past and present parishioners. The Gothic-style façade features intricate white-marble spires, but equally impressive is the interior, including the Louis Tiffany-designed altar, solid bronze baldachin, and the rose window by stained-glass master Charles Connick. Note that due to crucial restoration work, part of the exterior may be under scaffolding until spring 2014.

► *Further uptown is another awe-inspiring house of worship, the Cathedral Church of St John the Divine; see p106.*

MIDTOWN EAST

Subway E, M to Lexington Avenue-53rd Street; S, 4, 5, 6, 7 to 42nd Street-Grand Central; 6 to 51st Street.

Shopping, dining and entertainment options wane east of Fifth Avenue in the 40s and 50s. However, the area is home to many iconic landmarks and world-class architecture.

EXPLORE

JOHN·D·ROCKEFELLER·JR
1874–1960
FOUNDER·OF·ROCKEFELLER·CENTER

Rockefeller Center.

Terminal Trivia

Six facts that illuminate Grand Central's colourful 100-year history.

THE CEILING IS BACKWARDS

The opulent ceiling mural in the main concourse, by French painter Paul Helleu, depicts the October zodiac in the Mediterranean sky, complete with 2,500 stars (some now lit by LEDs). There's just one problem. According to Daniel Brucker, manager of GCT Tours, an amateur-astronomer commuter wrote to the owning Vanderbilt family to point out the constellations were backwards. Their response? It had been done on purpose to represent God's view of the sky.

CAMPBELL CALLED IT HOME

In the 1920s, the financier John Campbell was granted an office-cum-pied-à-terre in the terminal. 'He had a bond rating firm,' explains Brucker, 'he was a large shareholder in New York Central Railroad stock, and a good friend of the Vanderbilts. Putting it all together, he got New York's largest ground-floor apartment, with marble walls, a working fireplace and a wine cellar.' After Campbell's death, the space was used by railroad police, and the wine cellar was turned into a jail cell. In the late '90s it was restored and converted into a bar.

IT HAS A PHANTOM TRACK

In the 1930s, FDR's private train would arrive via a secret subterranean track. According to Brucker, the train car that carried his Pierce-Arrow limousine is still there. Brucker surmises the disabled president was driven off the train into an extra-large elevator, which brought him into the ballroom of the Waldorf Astoria hotel.

THE WALLS HAVE EARS

The archway just outside the Grand Central Oyster Bar & Restaurant, a fixture of the terminal since it opened, creates an interesting acoustical trick. Stand in one corner and whisper a message to a friend standing diagonally across from you. Because of the unique design of the low ceramic arches, it will sound as if you're next to each other.

IT WAS A LOFTY ART HUB

In early 1920s, a group of artists including John Singer Sargent established art galleries on the top floor. The vast space now houses the state-of-the-art control centre for Metro-North Railroad.

THERE'S A KENNEDY CONNECTION

Because CBS studios were on the third floor from 1939 to 1964, the midcentury's biggest news stories issued from Grand Central – it was here that Walter Cronkite announced the assassination of JFK in 1963. Five years later, when a developer proposed building an office tower above the terminal, Jacqueline Kennedy Onassis was one of Grand Central's strongest supporters. It is now a protected landmark.

EXPLORE

The 1913 **Grand Central Terminal** (*see below*) is the city's most spectacular point of arrival, although these days it only welcomes commuter trains from Connecticut and upstate New York. Looming behind the terminal, the **MetLife Building** (formerly the Pan Am Building) was the world's largest office tower when it opened in the 1960s. On Park Avenue is the famed **Waldorf Astoria New York** (*see p244*), formerly located on Fifth Avenue but rebuilt here in 1931 after the original was demolished to make way for the Empire State Building. Other must-see buildings in the vicinity include **Lever House** (390 Park Avenue, between 53rd & 54th Streets), the **Seagram Building** (375 Park Avenue, between 52nd & 53rd Streets), the slanted-roofed **Citigroup Center** (from 53rd Street to 54th Street, between Lexington & Third Avenues) and the stunning art deco skyscraper that anchors the corner of Lexington Avenue and 51st Street, formerly the **General Electric Building** (and before that, the RCA Victor Building). A Chippendale crown tops the **Sony Building** (550 Madison Avenue, between 55th & 56th Streets), Philip Johnson's postmodern icon.

East 42nd Street has a wealth of architectural distinction, including the Romanesque Revival hall of the former **Bowery Savings Bank** (no.110) and the art deco details of the **Chanin Building** (no.122). Completed in 1930 by architect William Van Alen, the gleaming **Chrysler Building** (at Lexington Avenue) is a pinnacle of art deco architecture, paying homage to the automobile with vast radiator-cap eagles in lieu of traditional gargoyles and a brickwork relief sculpture of racing cars complete with chrome hubcaps. The **Daily News Building** (no.220), another art deco gem designed by Raymond Hood, was immortalised in the *Superman* films. Although the namesake tabloid no longer has its offices here (it moved to 33rd Street in the 1990s), the lobby still houses its giant globe and weather instruments.

To the east lies the literally elevated **Tudor City** (between First & Second Avenues, from E 41st to E 43rd Streets), a pioneering 1925 residential development that resembles high-rise versions of England's Hampton Court Palace. The enclave features a charming park, perfect for a respite from the rush of traffic. At the end of 43rd Street is a terrace overlooking, and stairs leading down to, the **United Nations Headquarters** (*see right*). Not far from here is the **Japan Society** (*see right*).

FREE Grand Central Terminal

From 42nd to 44th Streets, between Vanderbilt & Lexington Avenues (audio tours 1-917 566 0008, www.grandcentralterminal.com). Subway S, 4, 5, 6, 7 to 42nd Street-Grand Central. **Map** p404 E24.

Each day, the world's largest terminal sees more than 750,000 people shuffle through its Beaux Arts threshold. Designed by Warren & Wetmore and Reed & Stern, the gorgeous transport hub opened in 1913 with lashings of Botticino marble and staircases modelled after those of the Paris opera house. After midcentury decline, the terminal underwent extensive restoration between 1996 and 1998 and is now a destination in itself, with shopping and dining options including the Campbell Apartment (1-212 953 0409), the Grand Central Oyster Bar & Restaurant (*see p169*) and the city's newest Apple Store. In February 2013, Grand Central kicked off its centenniel celebrations, and events will take place throughout the year, including a 'parade' of historic trains (11, 12 May). Check the website for information about what's on and self-guided audio tours ($7; $5-$6 reductions). *See also p90* **Terminal Trivia**.
▶ *For trains from Grand Central, see p373.*

Japan Society

333 E 47th Street, between First & Second Avenues (1-212 832 1155, www.japansociety.org). Subway E, M to Lexington Avenue-53rd Street; 6 to 51st Street. **Open** hrs vary. *Gallery* 11am-6pm Tue-Thur; 11am-9pm Fri; 11am-5pm Sat, Sun. **Admission** $15; $12 reductions; free under-16s; free 6-9pm Fri. **Credit** AmEx, Disc, MC, V. **Map** p404 F23.

Founded in 1907, the Japan Society moved into its current home, complete with waterfall and bamboo garden, in 1971. Designed by Junzo Yoshimura, it was the first contemporary Japanese building in New York and is now the city's youngest official landmark. The gallery mounts temporary exhibitions on such diverse subjects as the art of anime, manga, video games and textile design. In 2013, look out for 'Edo Pop: The Graphic Impact of Japanese Prints' (9 Mar-9 June) and an exhibition of recent work by video/multimedia artist Mariko Mori (Oct-Jan 2014).

United Nations Headquarters

Temporary visitors' entrance: First Avenue, at 42nd Street (tours 1-212 963 8687, http://visit. un.org). Subway S, 4, 5, 6, 7 to 42nd Street-Grand Central. **Tours** 10am-4pm Mon-Fri. **Admission** $16; $9-$11 reductions (under-5s not admitted). **Credit** AmEx, Disc, MC, V. **Map** p404 G24.

The UN is undergoing extensive renovations that have left the Secretariat building, designed by Le Corbusier, gleaming – though that structure is off-limits to the public. The 45-minute public tours discuss the history and role of the UN, and, starting in April 2013, will visit the Security Council Chamber (when not in session) in the newly renovated Conference Building. At the same time, the General Assembly Hall will close for construction for at least a year. Although some artworks and objects given by member nations are not on public display during this period, you can now see pieces such as Norman Rockwell's mosaic *The Golden Rule* for the first time in four years.

EXPLORE

Uptown

Head north for high culture and Harlem cool.

In the early 19th century, the largely rural area above 59th Street was a bucolic getaway for locals living in Manhattan's southern neighbourhoods. Today, much of uptown still feels comparatively serene, thanks largely to **Central Park** and the presence of a number of New York's premier cultural institutions.

Although New York's super-rich have made their gilded nests all over town, the air of old money is most palpable on the **Upper East Side**, where exclusive streets are kept clean by hose-wielding liveried doormen while socialites drift in and out of **Madison Avenue**'s designer flagships. The area also plays host to some of the world's finest museums. Across the park, the cultured **Upper West Side** is home to world-class performing-arts complex Lincoln Center. Further north lies **Harlem**, the country's most iconic African-American neighbourhood. A dangerous no-go area for visitors in the 1960s and '70s, it has undergone a remarkable renewal over the last decade and features well-preserved 19th-century architecture and vibrant nightlife.

Map pp405-409	Restaurants &
Hotels pp244-248	cafés pp171-174
	Bars pp186-187

CENTRAL PARK

Numerous subway stations on multiple lines.

In 1858, the newly formed Central Park Commission chose landscape designer Frederick Law Olmsted and architect Calvert Vaux to turn a vast tract of rocky swampland into a rambling oasis of lush greenery. Inspired by the great parks of London and Paris, the Commission imagined a place that would provide city dwellers with respite from the crowded streets. It was a noble thought, but one that required the eviction of 1,600 mostly poor or immigrant inhabitants, including residents of Seneca Village, the city's oldest African-American settlement. Still, clear the area they did: when it was completed in 1873, it became the first man-made public park in the US.

Although it suffered from neglect at various points in the 20th century (most recently in the 1970s and '80s, when it gained a reputation as a dangerous spot after dark), the park has been returned to its green glory thanks largely to the Central Park Conservancy. Since this not-for-profit civic group was formed in 1980, it's been instrumental in the park's restoration and maintenance.

The 1870 Gothic Revival **Dairy** (midpark at 65th Street, 1-212 794 6564, www.centralpark nyc.org, open 10am-5pmdaily) houses one of Central Park Conservancy's five visitor centres and a gift shop; there are additional staffed information booths dotted around the park.

The southern section abounds with family-friendly diversions, including the **Central Park Zoo** (*see p95*), between 63rd & 66th Streets, the **Friedsam Memorial Carousel** (and the **Trump Wollman Rink** (midpark, at 62nd Street; *see p334*), which doubles as a small children's amusement park (*see p256*) in the warmer months.

EXPLORE

Central Park.

Come summer, kites, Frisbees and soccer balls seem to fly every which way across **Sheep Meadow**, the designated quiet zone that begins at 66th Street. Sheep did indeed graze here until 1934, but they've since been replaced by sunbathers improving their tans and scoping out the throngs. **Tavern on the Green** (Central Park West, at 67th Street), the landmark restaurant housed in the former shepherd's residence, closed in 2009 after its long-term owners declared bancruptcy. A new locally focused eatery with plenty of outdoor seating is due to open in late 2013; until then the building serves as a visitor centre and gift shop. East of Sheep Meadow, between 66th and 72nd Streets, is the **Mall**, an elm-lined promenade that attracts street performers and in-line skaters. And just east of the Mall's Naumburg Bandshell is Rumsey Playfield – the main venue of the annual **SummerStage** series (*see p31*), an eclectic roster of free and benefit concerts in the city's parks.

One of the most popular meeting places (and loveliest spots) in the park is north of here, overlooking the lake: the grand **Bethesda Fountain & Terrace**, near the midpoint of the 72nd Street Transverse Road. *Angel of the Waters*, the sculpture in the centre of the fountain, was created by Emma Stebbins, the first woman to be granted a major public art commission in New York. Be sure to admire the Minton-tiled ceiling of the ornate passageway that connects the plaza around the fountain to the Mall – after years of neglect in storage, the tiles, designed by Jacob Wrey Mould, were restored and reinstated in 2007. Mould also designed the intricate carved ornamentation of the stairways leading down to the fountain.

To the west of the fountain, near the West 72nd Street entrance, sits **Strawberry Fields**, which memorialise John Lennon, who lived in, and was shot in front of, the nearby Dakota Building (*see p102*). Also called the International Garden of Peace, it features a mosaic of the word 'imagine' that was donated by the city of Naples. More than 160 species of flowers and plants from all over the world flourish here, strawberries among them. Just north of the fountain is the **Loeb Boathouse** (midpark, at 75th Street, 1-212 517 2233, www.thecentralparkboathouse. com). From here, you can take a rowing boat or a gondola out on the lake, which is crossed by the elegant Bow Bridge. The Loeb houses a restaurant and bar (closed dinner Nov-mid Apr), and lake views make it a lovely place for brunch or drinks.

Further north, the popular **Belvedere Castle** (*see p256*), a restored Victorian folly, sits atop the park's second-highest peak. Besides offering excellent views and a terrific setting for a picnic, it also houses the Henry Luce Nature Observatory. The nearby Delacorte Theater hosts **Shakespeare in the Park** (*see p324*), a summer run of free open-air performances of plays by the Bard and others. Further north still sits the **Great Lawn** (midpark, between 79th & 85th Streets), a sprawling stretch of grass that doubles as a rallying point for political protests and a concert spot for just about any act that can attract six-figure audiences. At other times, it's put to use by seriously competitive soccer, baseball and softball teams. East of the Great

EXPLORE

Lawn, behind the **Metropolitan Museum of Art** (*see p96* **Profile**), is the **Obelisk**, a 69-foot hieroglyphics-covered granite monument dating from around 1500 BC, which was given to the US by the Khedive of Egypt in 1881.

In the mid 1990s, the **Reservoir** (midpark, between 85th & 96th Streets) was renamed in honour of the late Jacqueline Kennedy Onassis, who used to jog around it. Whether you prefer a running or walking pace, a turn here commands great views of the skyscrapers rising above the park on the East and West Sides as well as midtown; in spring, the cherry trees that ring the reservoir path and the bridle path below it make it particularly beautiful.

In the northern section, the exquisite **Conservatory Garden** (entrance on Fifth Avenue, at 105th Street) comprises formal gardens inspired by English, French and Italian styles. At the top of the park, next to the Harlem Meer, the **Charles A Dana Discovery Center** (entrance at Malcolm X Boulevard/Lenox Avenue, at 110th Street, 1-212 860 1370, www.centralparknyc.org, closed Mon Apr-Oct, Mon & Tue Nov-Mar) operates a roster of activities, events and exhibitions. It also lends out fishing rods and bait (for 'catch and release fishing', Apr-Oct); prospective fishermen need to take photo ID.

Central Park Zoo

830 Fifth Avenue, between 63rd & 66th Streets (1-212 439 6500, www.centralparkzoo.org). Subway N, Q, R to Fifth Avenue-59th Street. **Open** *Apr-May, Sept-Oct* 10am-5pm Mon-Fri; 10am-5.30pm Sat, Sun. *June-Aug* 10am-5.30pm daily. *Nov-Mar* 10am-4.30pm daily. **Admission** (under-16s must be accompanied by an adult) $12; $7-$9 reductions; free under-3s. **Credit** AmEx, DC, Disc, MC, V. **Map** p405 E21.

A collection of animals has been kept in Central Park since the 1860s. But in its current form, Central Park Zoo dates only from 1988. Around 130 species inhabit its 6.5-acre corner of the park, polar bears and penguins among them. There is also a habitat dedicated to the endangered snow leopard. The Tisch Children's Zoo houses more than 30 species that enjoy being petted, and the roving characters on the George Delacorte Musical Clock – perched atop a brick arcade between both zoos – delight children every half-hour.

UPPER EAST SIDE

Subway F to Lexington Avenue-63rd Street; 4, 5, 6 to 86th Street; 6 to 68th Street-Hunter College, 77th Street, 96th Street or 103rd Street.

Gorgeous pre-war apartments owned by blue-blooded socialites, soigné restaurants filled with Botoxed ladies-who-lunch, the deluxe

boutiques of international designers… this is the clichéd image of the **Upper East Side**, and you'll see a lot of supporting evidence on Fifth, Madison and Park Avenues.

Encouraged by the opening of Central Park in the late 19th century, the city's more affluent residents began building mansions along Fifth Avenue. By the start of the 20th century, even the superwealthy had warmed to the idea of giving up their large homes for smaller quarters provided they were near the park, which resulted in the construction of many new apartment blocks and hotels. Working-class folk later settled around Second and Third Avenues, following construction of an elevated East Side train line (now defunct), but affluence remains the neighbourhood's dominant characteristic.

Along Fifth, Madison and Park Avenues, from 59th to 90th Streets, you'll see great old mansions, many of which are now foreign consulates, and stretches of restored carriage houses on the side streets. The 1916 limestone structure at 820 Fifth Avenue (at 63rd Street) was one of the earliest luxury apartment buildings on the avenue, and still has just one residence per floor. Wrapping around the corner of Madison Avenue at 45 East 66th Street, another flamboyant survivor (1906-08) features terracotta ornamentation that would befit a Gothic cathedral. (Andy Warhol lived a few doors up at no.57 from 1974 to 1987.) And further north, Stanford White designed 998 Fifth Avenue (at 81st Street) in the image of an Italian Renaissance palazzo.

Philanthropic gestures made by the moneyed classes over the past 130-odd years have helped to create an impressive cluster of art collections, museums and cultural institutions. Indeed, Fifth Avenue from 82nd to 104th Streets is known as **Museum Mile**, and for good reason: it's lined by the **Metropolitan Museum of Art** (*see p96* **Profile**); the Frank Lloyd Wright-designed **Solomon R Guggenheim Museum** (*see p100*); the **Cooper-Hewitt, National Design Museum** (*see p98*), housed in Andrew Carnegie's former mansion; the **Frick Collection** (*see p98*), lodged in the former mansion of Henry Clay Frick; the **Jewish Museum** (*see p99*); the **Museum of the City of New York** (*see p99*); and

EXPLORE

the **National Academy Museum** (1083 Fifth Avenue, at 89th Street, 1-212 369 4880, www.nationalacademy.org, closed Mon, Tue), whose collection includes works by Louise Bourgeois, Jasper Johns and Robert Rauschenberg. **El Museo del Barrio** (*see p98*), technically in Spanish Harlem, used to define the Mile's northern border, but the strip is lengthening: the future home of the **Museum for African Art** (www.africanart.org) is at the corner of 110th Street, though the opening has been delayed by lack of funding.

Other collections are scattered throughout the museum-saturated neighbourhood, including the

Asia Society & Museum (*see p98*), the **China Institute** (*see p98*), the **Neue Galerie** (*see p99*) and the **Whitney Museum of American Art** (*see p100*).

Madison Avenue is New York's world-class shopping strip. Between 57th and 86th Streets, it's packed with top designer names: the usual Euro suspects, such as Gucci, Prada, Chloé and Lanvin, and Americans including Donna Karan, Ralph Lauren and Tom Ford. Fashionable department store **Barneys New York** (*see p190*) is stocked with unusual designer finds and features witty, sometimes audacious, window displays.

Profile Metropolitan Museum of Art

The mother of all Manhattan museums is an essential stop on any itinerary.

Occupying 13 acres of Central Park, the **Metropolitan Museum of Art** (*see p99*), which opened in 1880, is impressive in scale and quality. Despite its vast size, the museum is easy to negotiate, particularly if you come early on a weekday and avoid the crowds. The steep $25 admission price is only a suggestion (a dollar will gain you entrance without reproachful glares), but it does include access to the Met's blockbuster temporary shows, plus, for those with boundless energy, same-day admission to the **Cloisters** (*see p112*) in Inwood. It would take many visits to cover all the Met's gallery space – it's wise to focus on certain collections to save time.

The original 1880 Gothic-Revival building was designed by Calvert Vaux and Jacob Wrey Mould, but is now almost completely hidden by subsequent additions (though you can still glimpse the west façade in the Robert Lehman Wing). A redesign of the museum's four-block-long plaza is expected to be completed in 2014, bringing new fountains and tree-shaded seating.

COLLECTIONS

In the first floor's north wing sits the collection of **Egyptian Art** (all gallery names are given in bold here), and the glass-walled atrium housing the Temple of Dendur,

moved from its original Nile-side setting and now overlooking a reflecting pool. Antiquity is also well represented in the southern wing by the halls housing **Greek and Roman Art**. Look out for the famous 'New York kouros', one of the earliest free-standing marble statues from Greece.

Turning west brings you to the **Arts of Africa, Oceania and the Americas** collection; it was donated by Nelson Rockefeller as a memorial to his son Michael, who disappeared while visiting New Guinea in 1961. A wider-ranging bequest, the two-storey **Robert Lehman Wing**, can be found at the western end of the floor. This eclectic collection is housed in a re-creation of the Lehman family townhouse and features works by Botticelli, Bellini, Ingres and Rembrandt.

Rounding out the highlights is the **American Wing** in the north-west corner. Its grand Engelhard Court has reopened as part of the wing's recent revamp. Now more a sculpture court than an interior garden, the light-filled space is flanked by the façade of Wall Street's Branch Bank of the United States (saved when the building was torn down in 1915) and a stunning loggia designed by Louis Comfort Tiffany for his Long Island estate.

From the Great Hall where you originally entered, a staircase

Just a few blocks from Barneys, on Lexington Avenue, is hugely popular department store **Bloomingdale's** (*see p192*). If you head east on 59th Street, you'll eventually reach the **Ed Koch Queensboro Bridge**, which was recently renamed to honour the former mayor, and links to Queens. At Second Avenue you can catch the overhead tram to **Roosevelt Island**. Suspended on a cable, the tram reaches a height of 250 feet above the East River and the fare is the same as a subway ride – MetroCards are accepted (the subway's F line also stops on the island). The two-mile-long isle between Manhattan and Queens is largely residential.

However, from 1686 to 1921, it went by the name of Blackwell's Island, during which time it was the site of an insane asylum, a smallpox hospital and a prison – notable inmates included Mae West, who served eight days here after being moved from the Women's House of Detention in the Village, and Emma Goldman, the anarchist, feminist and political agitator. In autumn 2012, **Franklin D Roosevelt Four Freedoms Park** (www.fdrfourfreedoms park.org) finally opened on the island's southern tip, 40 years after Mayor John Lindsay and Governor Nelson A Rockefeller announced the memorial. The plans languished until 2005,

leads to the second level. Veer left – pausing for the **Drawings, Prints and Photographs** galleries, which often hold small yet intriguing temporary shows – and you'll come to the galleries housing **19th Century European Paintings and Sculpture**. These contain some of the Met's most popular rooms, particularly the two-room Monet holdings and a colony of Van Goghs that includes his oft-reproduced *Irises*. This Impressionist hall of fame gives way to the post-Impressionist section, which includes Modigliani, Matisse, Picasso and Seurat (look out for his pointillist masterpiece *Circus Sideshow*), as well as American masters of the period such as Sargent and Whistler.

The museum's nearby cache of **Modern Art** includes works by Pollock, de Kooning and Rothko, to name a few.

Retrace your steps eastward, past the 19th- and early 20th-century rooms, and you'll reach the new **Galleries of the Art of the Arab Lands, Turkey, Iran, Central Asia and Later South Asia**. The central western section of this floor is dominated by the **European Paintings** galleries, which hold an amazing reserve of old masters. The Dutch section boasts five Vermeers, the largest collection of the master in the world, and a

haunting Rembrandt self-portrait; the jewel of the French rooms is David's riveting *Death of Socrates*; and the Spanish rooms include works by El Greco and Velázquez's stately *Portrait of Juan de Pareja*.

In the north-east wing of the floor, you'll find the sprawling collection of **Asian Art**. It's easy to lose yourself among the Chinese lacquer, Japanese figurines and Indian sculpture, but do check out the ceiling of the Jain Meeting Hall in the South-east Asian gallery. If you're still on your feet, give them a deserved rest in the Astor Court, a tranquil re-creation of a Ming Dynasty garden – or head up to the Iris & B Gerald Cantor Roof Garden (open late April to early November), which showcases large-scale contemporary sculpture by a different artist each year.

EXPLORE

when an exhibition at Cooper Union revived interest in the project. Commemorating the 32nd President's famous 'four freedoms' speech, the space offers postcard-worthy views of the Manhattan skyline.

Asia Society & Museum

725 Park Avenue, at 70th Street (1-212 288 6400, www.asiasociety.org). Subway 6 to 68th Street-Hunter College. **Open** *July, Aug* 11am-6pm Tue-Sun. *Sept-June* 11am-6pm Tue-Thur, Sat, Sun; 11am-9pm Fri. **Admission** $10; $5-$7 reductions; free under-16s (must be accompanied by an adult). Free 6-9pm Fri. **Credit** AmEx, DC, MC, V. **Map** p405 E20.

The Asia Society sponsors study missions and conferences while promoting public programmes in the US and abroad. The headquarters' striking galleries host exhibitions of art from dozens of countries and time periods (from ancient India and medieval Persia to contemporary Japan); some are assembled from public and private collections, including the permanent Mr and Mrs John D Rockefeller III collection of Asian art. A spacious, atrium-like café, with a pan-Asian menu, and an attractive gift shop, help to make the society a one-stop destination for anyone with even a passing interest in Asian culture.

China Institute

125 E 65th Street, between Park & Lexington Avenues (1-212 744 8181, www.chinainstitute. org). Subway F to Lexington Avenue-63rd Street; 6 to 68th Street-Hunter College. **Open** varies. *Galleries* 10am-5pm Mon, Wed, Fri-Sun; 10am-8pm Tue, Thur. **Admission** $7; $4 reductions; free under-12s. Free to all 6-8pm Tue, Thur. **Credit** AmEx, Disc, MC, V. **Map** p405 E21.

With two small galleries, the China Institute is somewhat overshadowed by the nearby Asia Society. But its rotating exhibitions, which include high-profile collections on loan from Chinese institutions, are compelling. 'Dunhuang: Buddhist Art at the Gateway of the Silk Road' (4 Apr-21 July 2013) illuminates the famous site in north-west China with excavated artworks and a replica of an eighth-century Mogao Grotto, one of a series of manmade caves functioning as Buddhist temples, with statues from an original cave. It will be followed by 'Inspired By Dunhuang' (19 Sept-8 Dec 2013), examining the site's influence on Chinese artists since its rediscovery in the 20th century. The institute also offers lectures, courses and arts events such as concerts and films.

Cooper-Hewitt, National Design Museum

2 E 91st Street, at Fifth Avenue (1-212 849 8400, www.cooperhewitt.org). Subway 4, 5, 6 to 86th Street. Closed until 2014 (see website for off-site exhibitions and updates). **Map** p406 E18.

Founded in 1897 by the Hewitt sisters, granddaughters of industrialist Peter Cooper, the only museum in the US solely dedicated to design (both historic and modern) has been part of the Smithsonian since the 1960s. In 1976, it took up residence in the former home of steel magnate Andrew Carnegie. The museum is currently closed during a major renovation and expansion project, which will more than double its exhibition space. Meanwhile, the Cooper-Hewitt is taking its exhibitions on the road.

El Museo del Barrio

1230 Fifth Avenue, at 104th Street (1-212 831 7272, www.elmuseo.org). Subway 6 to 103rd Street. **Open** 11am-6pm Tue-Sat; 1-5pm Sun. **Admission** *Suggested donation* $9; $5 reductions; free under-12s; free over-65s Wed. Free 3rd Sat each mth. **Credit** AmEx, Disc, MC, V. **Map** p406 E16.

Founded in 1969 by the artist (and former MoMA curator) Rafael Montañez Ortiz, El Museo del Barrio takes its name from its East Harlem locale. Dedicated to the art and culture of Puerto Ricans and Latin Americans all over the US, El Museo reopened in autumn 2009 following a $35-million renovation. The redesigned spaces within the museum's 1921 Beaux Arts building provide a polished, contemporary showcase for the diversity and vibrancy of Hispanic art. The new galleries allow more space for rotating exhibitions from the museum's 6,500-piece holdings – from pre-Columbian artefacts to contemporary installations – as well as around three temporary shows a year. In 2013, the museum mounts 'El Museo's Bienal: The (S) Files' (11 June-1 Sept 2013), showcasing art by emerging Latino and Latin-American artists in New York.

★ Frick Collection

1 E 70th Street, between Fifth & Madison Avenues (1-212 288 0700, www.frick.org). Subway 6 to 68th Street-Hunter College. **Open** 10am-6pm Tue-Sat; 11am-5pm Sun. **Admission** (under-10s not admitted) $18; $10-$15 reductions. Pay what you wish 11am-1pm Sun. **Credit** AmEx, Disc, MC, V. **Map** p405 E20.

Industrialist, robber baron and collector Henry Clay Frick commissioned this opulent mansion with a view to leaving his legacy to the public. Designed by Thomas Hastings of Carrère & Hastings (the firm behind the New York Public Library) and built in 1914, the building was inspired by 18th-century British and French architecture.

In an effort to preserve the feel of a private residence, labelling is minimal, but you can opt for a free audio guide or pay $2 for a booklet. Works spanning the 14th to the 19th centuries include masterpieces by Rembrandt, Vermeer, Whistler, Gainsborough, Holbein and Titian, exquisite period furniture, porcelain and other decorative objects. Aficionados of 18th-century French art will find two rooms especially enchanting: the panels of the Boucher Room (1750-52) depict children engaged in adult occupations; the Fragonard Room contains the artist's

EXPLORE

series *Progress of Love* – four of the paintings were commissioned (and rejected) by Louis XV's mistress Madame du Barry. A new gallery in the enclosed garden portico is devoted to decorative arts and sculpture. The interior Garden Court is a serene spot to rest your feet and turn your art-saturated gaze to a soothing fountain.

The museum also stages temporary exhibitions; 'The Impressionist Line from Degas to Toulouse-Lautrec: Drawings and Prints from the Clark' (12 Mar-16 June 2013) and 'Vermeer, Rembrandt and Hals: Masterpieces from the Mauritshuis' (22 Oct 2013-19 Jan 2014) are bound to be among the highlights of the city's art calendar.
▶ *For the Frick's excellent concert series, see p303.*

Jewish Museum
1109 Fifth Avenue, at 92nd Street (1-212 423 3200, www.thejewishmuseum.org). Subway 4, 5, 6 to 86th Street; 6 to 96th Street. **Open** 11am-5.45pm Mon, Tue, Sat, Sun; 11am-9pm Thur; 11am-4pm Fri. Closed on Jewish holidays. **Admission** $12; $7.50-$10 reductions; free under-12s. Free to all Sat. Pay what you wish 5-9pm Thur. **Credit** AmEx, MC, V. **Map** p405 E18.
The Jewish Museum is housed in a magnificent 1908 French Gothic-style mansion – the former home of the financier, collector and Jewish leader Felix Warburg. Inside, 'Culture and Continuity: The Jewish Journey' traces the evolution of Judaism from antiquity to the present day. The two-floor permanent exhibition comprises thematic displays of 800 of the museum's cache of 26,000 works of art, artefacts and media installations.

The excellent temporary shows appeal to a broad audience: the first American retrospective of Canadian-born artist Jack Goldstein (10 May-29 Sept 2013) will be followed by an exhibition focusing on Marc Chagall's work from the 1930s and '40s (13 Sept 2013-2 Feb 2014), an often overlooked period in the artist's career.
▶ *The Museum of Jewish Heritage: A Living Memorial to the Holocaust (see p50) and the Museum at Eldridge Street (see p66), both Downtown, further explore Jewish culture.*

★ Metropolitan Museum of Art
1000 Fifth Avenue, at 82nd Street (1-212 535 7710, www.metmuseum.org). Subway 4, 5, 6 to 86th Street. **Open** 9.30am-5.30pm Tue-Thur, Sun; 9.30am-9pm Fri, Sat. **Admission** *Suggested donation* (incl same-day admission to the Cloisters) $25; $12-$17 reductions; free under-12s. **Credit** AmEx, Disc, MC, V. **Map** p405 E19.
Scheduled exhibitions at the Met in 2013 include 'Impressionism, Fashion and Modernity' (26 Feb-27 May); 'Photography and the American Civil War' (2 Apr-2 Sept); 'The Civil War and American Art' (28 May-2 Sept) and 'Ken Price Sculpture: A Retrospective' (18 June-22 Sept). For the permanent collection, *see p96* **Profile**.

INSIDE TRACK
NIGHT AT THE MUSEUM

Most of the city's major museums are free or pay what you wish one evening (usually Thursday or Friday) or afternoon of the week. Some enhance the experience with musical and other performances.

▶ *For the Cloisters, which houses the Met's medieval art collection, see p112.*

Museum of the City of New York
1220 Fifth Avenue, between 103rd & 104th Streets (1-212 534 1672, www.mcny.org). Subway 6 to 103rd Street. **Open** 10am-6pm daily. **Admission** *Suggested donation* $10; $6 reductions; $20 family; free under-13s. **Credit** AmEx, DC, Disc, MC, V. **Map** p405 E16.
A great introduction to New York, this institution contains a wealth of city history. 'Timescapes', a 22-minute multimedia presentation that illuminates the history of NYC, is shown free with admission every half hour. About a dozen temporary exhibitions each year spotlight different aspects of the city and its inhabitants, from its early development to contemporary urban life.

As part of a $92 million project to expand and modernise its premises, scheduled for completion in 2015, the museum has reopened its renovated south wing. Holdings include prints, drawings and photos of NYC, decorative arts and furnishings and an extensive collection of toys. The undoubted jewel is the amazing Stettheimer Dollhouse: it was created in the 1920s by Carrie Stettheimer, whose artist friends reinterpreted their masterpieces in miniature to hang on the walls. Look closely and you'll even spy a tiny version of Marcel Duchamp's famous *Nude Descending a Staircase*.
▶ *There's more city history at the New-York Historical Society (see p104), Lower East Side Tenement Museum (see p65) and Ellis Island Immigration Museum (see p49), among others.*

Neue Galerie
1048 Fifth Avenue, at 86th Street (1-212 628 6200, www.neuegalerie.org). Subway 4, 5, 6 to 86th Street. **Open** 11am-6pm Mon, Thur-Sun; 11am-8pm 1st Fri of the mth. **Admission** (under-16s must be accompanied by an adult; under-12s not admitted) $20; $10 reductions. Free to all 6-8pm 1st Fri of the mth. **Credit** AmEx, MC, V. **Map** p405 E18.
The elegant Neue Galerie is devoted entirely to late 19th- and early 20th-century German and Austrian fine and decorative arts. The creation of the late art dealer Serge Sabarsky and cosmetics mogul Ronald S Lauder, it has the largest concentration of works by Gustav Klimt and Egon Schiele outside of Vienna.

EXPLORE

There's also a bookstore, a small design shop and the ultra-refined Café Sabarsky (*see p171*), serving modern Austrian cuisine and ravishing Viennese pastries.

★ Solomon R Guggenheim Museum
1071 Fifth Avenue, between 88th & 89th Streets (1-212 423 3500, www.guggenheim.org). Subway 4, 5, 6 to 86th Street. **Open** 10am-5.45pm Mon-Wed, Fri, Sun; 10am-7.45pm Sat. **Admission** $22; $18 reductions; free under-12s. Pay what you wish 5.45-7.15pm Sat. **Credit** AmEx, DC, Disc, MC, V. **Map** p406 E18.

The Guggenheim is as famous for its landmark building as it is for its impressive collection and daring temporary shows. The dramatic structure, with its winding, cantilevered curves, was designed by Frank Lloyd Wright. His only NYC building, apart from a private house on Staten Island, it caused quite a stir when it debuted 1959. In 1992, the addition of a ten-storey tower provided space for a sculpture gallery (with park views), a café and an auditorium. The museum owns Peggy Guggenheim's trove of Cubist, Surrealist and Abstract Expressionist works, along with the Panza di Biumo Collection of American minimalist and conceptual art from the 1960s and '70s. As well as works by Manet, Picasso, Chagall and Bourgeois, it includes the largest collection of Kandinskys in the US.

Scheduled exhibitions in 2013 include 'Gutai: Splendid Playground' (through 8 May) and shows devoted to the work of light-and-space master James Turrell (21 June-25 Sept) and painter and photographer Christopher Wool (25 Oct 2013-22 Jan 2014).

Whitney Museum of American Art
945 Madison Avenue, at 75th Street (1-212 570 3600, www.whitney.org). Subway 6 to 77th Street. **Open** 11am-6pm Wed, Thur, Sat, Sun; 1-9pm Fri. **Admission** $18; $14 reductions; free under-19s. Pay what you wish 6-9pm Fri. **Credit** AmEx, DC, MC, V. **Map** p405 E20.

Like the Guggenheim, the Whitney is set apart by its unique architecture, but these are the last couple of years the museum will occupy the Marcel Breuer-designed granite cube with its all-seeing upper-storey 'eye'. When sculptor and art patron Gertrude Vanderbilt Whitney opened the museum in 1931, she dedicated it to living American artists. Today, the Whitney holds more than 19,000 pieces by around 2,700 artists, including Willem de Kooning, Edward Hopper, Jasper Johns, Georgia O'Keeffe and Claes Oldenburg. In spring 2011, architect Renzo Piano broke ground on the museum's new nine-storey home at the foot of the High Line (*see p82* **Profile**) in the Meatpacking District. Once it opens in 2015, there will be space for a comprehensive display of the collection for the first time.

In the run-up to the move, the Whitney has been rummaging through its holdings to stage a series of six exhibitions based on its permanent collection, each covering roughly two decades of American art – 2013 will bring us into the 1970s. Still, the Whitney's reputation rests primarily on its

Whitney Museum of American Art.

temporary shows – particularly the Whitney Biennial, the exhibition that everyone loves to hate. Launched in 1932 and held in even-numbered years, it's the most prestigious and controversial assessment of contemporary art in the US.

Yorkville

The atmosphere becomes noticeably less rarefied as you walk east from Central Park, with grand edifices giving way to bland modern apartment blocks and walk-up tenements. Not much remains of the old German and Hungarian immigrant communities that once filled **Yorkville**, the Upper East Side neighbourhood between Third Avenue and the East River, with delicatessens, beer halls and restaurants. However, one such flashback is the 77-year-old **Heidelberg** (1648 Second Avenue, between 85th & 86th Streets, 1-212 628 2332, www. heidelbergrestaurant.com), where dirndl-wearing waitresses serve up steins of Spaten and platters of sausages from the wurst-meisters at butcher shop Schaller & Weber a few doors up (1654 Second Avenue, 1-212 879 3047, closed Sun). Second Avenue in the 70s and 80s throbs with rowdy pick-up bars frequented by preppy, twentysomething crowds. But tasteful new craft-beer spot the **Penrose** (1590 Second Avenue, between 82nd & 83rd Streets, 1-212 203 2751, www.penrosebar.com) has brought a bit of the indie-chic East Village uptown.

The only Federal-style mansion in Manhattan, **Gracie Mansion** (*see p101*) stands at the eastern end of 88th Street. The stately pile has served as New York's official mayoral residence since 1942 – although the current mayor, billionaire Michael Bloomberg, famously eschews this traditional address in favour of his own Beaux Arts mansion at 17 East 79th Street (between Fifth & Madison Avenues). Although Gracie Mansion is fenced off, much of the exterior can be seen from surrounding **Carl Schurz Park**; you can buy provisions for a picnic in this undulating, shady green patch (or on the adjacent East River Promenade) at sprawling Italian gourmet food shop **Agata & Valentina** (1505 First Avenue, at 79th Street, 1-212 452 0690, www.agatavalentina.com).

One block from Gracie Mansion, the **Henderson Place Historic District** (at East End Avenue, between 86th & 87th Streets) contains 24 handsome Queen Anne row houses – commissioned by furrier and noted real-estate developer John C Henderson as servants' quarters – with their original turrets, double stoops and slate roofs.

Looking slightly architecturally incongruous in the area, the large **Islamic Cultural Center** (1711 Third Avenue, at 96th Street, 1-212 722 5234, www.islamicculturalcenter-ny.org), built

in 1990, was the city's first major mosque. There are around 150 mosques and masjids throughout the city, ministering to around 600,000 Muslims.

Gracie Mansion
Carl Schurz Park, 88th Street, at East End Avenue (1-212 570 4751). Subway 4, 5, 6 to 86th Street. **Tours** 10am, 11am, 1pm, 2pm most Wed; reservations required. **Admission** $7; $4 reductions; free students. **No credit cards**. **Map** p406 G18.
This green-shuttered yellow edifice was built in 1799 by wealthy Scottish merchant Archibald Gracie as a country house. Today, the stately house is the focal point of tranquil Carl Schurz Park, named in honour of the German immigrant who became a newspaper editor and US senator. When big-bucks mayor Michael Bloomberg declined to move in after taking up office in 2002, Gracie Mansion's living quarters were opened up to public tours for the first time in 60 years.

UPPER WEST SIDE

Subway A, B, C, D, 1 to 59th Street-Columbus Circle; B, C to 81st Street-Museum of Natural History; 1, 2, 3 to 72nd Street; 1, 2, 3 to 96th Street.

The four-mile-long stretch west of Central Park is culturally rich and cosmopolitan. New Yorkers were drawn here during the late 19th century after the completion of Central Park, the opening of local subway lines and Columbia University's relocation to Morningside Heights. In the 20th century, central Europeans found refuge here, and Puerto Ricans settled along Amsterdam and Columbus Avenues in the 1960s. These days, new real estate and chain stores are reducing eye-level evidence of old immigrant life, and the neighbourhood's intellectual, politically liberal spirit has waned a little as apartment prices have risen. Sections of Riverside Drive and Central Park West still rival the grandeur of the East Side's Fifth and Park Avenues.

The gateway to the Upper West Side is **Columbus Circle**, where Broadway meets 59th Street, Eighth Avenue, Central Park South and Central Park West – a rare rotary in a city of right angles. The architecture around it could make anyone's head spin. At the entrance to Central Park, a 700-ton statue of Christopher Columbus goes almost unnoticed under the **Time Warner Center** across the street, which houses offices, apartments, hotel lodgings and Jazz at Lincoln Center's stunning **Frederick P Rose Hall**. The first seven levels of the enormous glass complex are filled with high-end retailers and gourmet restaurants, such as **Per Se** (*see p172*) and **A Voce Columbus** (*see p171*). In 2008, the **Museum of Arts &**

EXPLORE

American Museum of Natural History. *See p104*.

Design (*see p104* opened its new digs in a landmark building on the south side of the circle, itself the subject of a controversial redesign.

While the Upper East Side is the nexus of the city's museums, the Upper West Side's seat of culture is largely concentrated on **Lincoln Center** (*see p301*), a complex of concert halls and auditoriums built in the early 1960s and the home of the New York Philharmonic, the New York City Ballet, the Metropolitan Opera and a host of other notable arts organisations. The big circular fountain in the central plaza is a popular gathering spot – especially in summer, when amateur dancers converge on it to dance alfresco at **Midsummer Night Swing** (*see p32*).

The centre just completed a major overhaul that included a redesign of public spaces, refurbishment of the various halls and a new visitor centre, the **David Rubenstein Atrium** (between W 62nd & W 63rd Streets, Broadway & Columbus Avenue). Conceived as a contemporary interior garden with lush planted walls, the Atrium sells same-day discounted tickets to Lincoln Center performances and stages free genre-spanning concerts on Thursday nights (see www.lincolncenter.org for details). It's also the starting point for guided tours of the complex (1-212 875 5350, $17, $8-$14 reductions), which, in addition to the hallowed concert halls, contains several notable artworks, including Henry Moore's *Reclining Figure* in the plaza near Lincoln Center Theater, and two massive music-themed paintings by Marc Chagall in the lobby

of the Metropolitan Opera House. Nearby is the **New York Public Library for the Performing Arts** (40 Lincoln Center Plaza, at 65th Street, 1-212 870 1630, www.nypl.org, closed Sun); alongside its extraordinary collection of films, letters, manuscripts, videos and sound recordings, it's also a venue for concerts and lectures.

Around Sherman and Verdi Squares (from 70th to 73rd Streets, where Broadway and Amsterdam Avenue intersect), classic early 20th-century buildings stand cheek-by-jowl with newer, often mundane high-rises. The jewel is the 1904 **Ansonia Hotel** (2109 Broadway, between 73rd & 74th Streets). Over the years, Enrico Caruso, Babe Ruth and Igor Stravinsky have lived in this Beaux Arts masterpiece; it was also the site of the Continental Baths, the gay bathhouse and cabaret where Bette Midler got her start, and Plato's Retreat, a swinging 1970s sex club.

The perpetually crowded 72nd Street subway station on Broadway, which opened in 1904, is notable for its Beaux Arts entrance. The splendidly restored rococo **Beacon Theatre** (*see p285*), originally a 1920s movie palace, is now one of New York City's premier mid-size concert venues.

After Central Park was completed, magnificently tall residential buildings rose up along **Central Park West** to take advantage of the views. The first of these great apartment blocks was the **Dakota** (at 72nd Street), so

named because its location was considered remote when it was built in 1884. The fortress-like building is known as the setting for *Rosemary's Baby* and the site of John Lennon's murder in 1980 (Yoko Ono still lives here); other residents have included Judy Garland, Rudolph Nureyev, Lauren Bacall and Boris Karloff – but not Billy Joel, who was turned away by the co-op board when he tried to buy an apartment. You might recognise **55 Central Park West** (at 66th Street) from the movie *Ghostbusters*. Built in 1930, it was the first art deco building on the block. Heading north on Central Park West, you'll spy the massive twin-towered **San Remo Apartments** (at 74th Street), which also date from 1930. Rita Hayworth, Steven Spielberg, Tiger Woods and U2's Bono have been among the building's many celebrity residents over the years.

A few blocks to the north, the **New-York Historical Society** (*see p105* **Profile**) is the city's oldest museum, founded in 1804. Across the street, at the glorious **American Museum of Natural History** (*see p104*), dinosaur skeletons, a planetarium and an IMAX theatre lure adults and battalions of school groups.

The cluster of classic food stores and restaurants lining the avenues of the district's northern end is where the Upper West Side shops, drinks and eats. To see West Siders in their natural habitat, queue at the perpetually jammed smoked fish counter at gourmet market **Zabar's** (*see p210*). The legendary

(if scruffy) restaurant and delicatessen **Barney Greengrass**, the self-styled 'Sturgeon King' (*see p171*), has specialised in smoked fish, knishes and what may be the city's best chopped liver since 1908.

Designed by Central Park's Frederick Law Olmsted, **Riverside Park** is a sinuous stretch of riverbank that starts at 72nd Street and ends at 158th Street, running between Riverside Drive and the Hudson River. You'll probably see yachts, along with several houseboats, berthed at the **79th Street Boat Basin**. Several sites provide havens for quiet reflection. The **Soldiers' and Sailors' Monument** (89th Street, at Riverside Drive), built in 1902 by French sculptor Paul EM DuBoy, honours Union soldiers who died in the Civil War; and a 1908 memorial (100th Street, at Riverside Drive) pays tribute to fallen firemen. The stretch of park below 72nd Street, called **Riverside Park South**, is a particularly peaceful city retreat, with a pier, and landscaped patches of grass with park benches.

FREE American Folk Art Museum

2 Lincoln Square, Columbus Avenue, at 66th Street (1-212 595 9533, www.folkartmuseum.org). Subway 1 to 66th Street-Lincoln Center. **Open** noon-7.30pm Tue-Sat; noon-6pm Sun. **Admission** free. **Map** p405 C21.

Following a budget crisis that forced the American Folk Art Museum to give up its midtown premises, the institution is going strong in the small original space it had retained as a second location. Its unparalleled holdings of folk art include more than 5,000 works from the late 18th century to the present. Exhibitions explore the work of self-taught and outsider artists, as well as showing traditional folk art such as quilts and needlework, and other decorative objects. You can purchase original handmade pieces in the large gift shop, and the museum regularly hosts free musical performances, inexpensive craft workshops and other events.

EXPLORE

INSIDE TRACK
FROM ROSEBUD TO BUDDHA

At 331 Riverside Drive, between 105th and 106th Street, lies the Beaux Arts-style **New York Buddhist Church**, formerly the home of actress Marion Davies, mistress of William Randolph Hearst. The newspaper magnate purportedly nicknamed her 'Rosebud', which Orson Welles used as the name of the sled in *Citizen Kane*, which was based on Hearst's life. The large statue of the Buddha outside the church originally stood in Hiroshima and survived the atomic bomb.

INSIDE TRACK BOATS & BEER

From late March through October (weather permitting), you can take in the view of the **79th Street Boat Basin** (see p103) with a beer and a burger at the no-reservations **Boat Basin Café** (www.boatbasincafe. com). The patio of this extremely popular spot overlooks the marina, but there's also an adjacent covered rotunda.

★ American Museum of Natural History/Rose Center for Earth & Space

Central Park West, at 79th Street (1-212 769 5100, www.amnh.org). Subway B, C to 81st Street-Museum of Natural History. **Open** 10am-5.45pm daily. **Admission** *Suggested donation* $19; $10.50-$14.50 reductions. **Credit** AmEx, Disc, MC, V. **Map** p405 C19.

Home to the largest collection of dinosaur fossils in the world, the American Museum of Natural History's fourth-floor dino halls have been blowing minds for decades. The thrills begin when you cross the threshold of the Theodore Roosevelt Rotunda, where you meet the skeleton of a towering barosaurus rearing high on its hind legs to protect its young from an attacking allosaurus – an impressive welcome. Roughly 80% of the bones on display were dug out of the ground by Indiana Jones types. But during the museum's mid 1990s renovation, several specimens were remodelled to incorporate discoveries made during the intervening years. The Tyrannosaurus rex, for instance, was once believed to have walked upright, *Godzilla*-style; it now stalks prey with its head lowered and tail raised parallel to the ground.

The rest of the museum is equally dramatic. The Hall of North American Mammals, part of a two-storey memorial to Roosevelt, reopened in autumn 2012 after extensive restoration to its formerly faded 1940s dioramas. The Hall of Human Origins houses a fine display of our old cousins, the Neanderthals. The Hall of Biodiversity examines world ecosystems and environmental preservation, and a life-size model of a blue whale hangs from the cavernous ceiling of the Hall of Ocean Life. In the Hall of Meteorites, the space's focal point is Ahnighito, the largest iron meteor on display anywhere in the world, weighing in at 34 tons.

The spectacular $210-million Rose Center for Earth & Space – dazzling at night – is a giant silvery globe where you can discover the universe via 3-D shows in the Hayden Planetarium and light shows in the Big Bang Theater. An IMAX theatre screens larger-than-life nature programmes.

Temporary exhibitions are thought-provoking for all ages: 'Whales: Giants of the Deep' (23 Mar 2013-5 Jan 2014), on loan from the Museum of New Zealand Te Papa Tongarewa, includes a 58-foot sperm whale, life-size models and inventive interactive displays. *Photos pp102-103.*

★ Museum of Arts & Design

2 Columbus Circle, at Broadway (1-212 299 7777, www.madmuseum.org). Subway A, B, C, D, 1 to 59th Street-Columbus Circle. **Open** 11am-6pm Tue, Wed, Sat, Sun; 11am-9pm Thur, Fri. **Admission** $15; $12 reductions; free under-13s Pay what you wish 6-9pm Thur, Fri. **Credit** AmEx, Disc, MC, V. **Map** p404 C22.

Founded in 1956 as the Museum of Contemporary Crafts, this institution brings together contemporary objects created in a wide range of media – including clay, glass, wood, metal and cloth – with a strong focus on materials and process. In 2008, the museum crafted itself a new home. Originally designed in 1964 by Radio City Music Hall architect Edward Durell Stone to house the Gallery of Modern Art, 2 Columbus Circle was a windowless monolith that had sat empty since 1998. The redesigned ten-storey building now has four floors of exhibition galleries, including the Tiffany & Co Foundation Jewelry Gallery. Curators are able to display more of the 3,000-piece permanent collection, including porcelain ware by Cindy Sherman, stained glass by Judith Schaechter, basalt ceramics by James Turrell and Robert Arneson's ceramic sculpture, *Alice House Wall.*

But the real attractions here are the imaginative temporary shows. 'Against the Grain: Wood in Contemporary Craft and Design' (13 Mar-May 2013) features around 80 artworks and functional objects. In autumn 2013, 'Out of Hand: Materializing the Postdigital' looks at computer-aided production across several design disciplines. You can also watch resident artists create works in studios on the sixth floor, while the ninth-floor American bistro has views over the park.

★ New-York Historical Society

170 Central Park West, between 76th & 77th Streets (1-212 873 3400, www.nyhistory.org). Subway B, C to 81st Street-Museum of Natural History. **Open** 10am-6pm Tue-Thur, Sat; 10am-8pm Fri; 11am-5pm Sun. **Admission** $15; $5-$12 reductions; free under-4s. Pay what you wish 6-8pm Fri. **Credit** AmEx, DC, MC, V. **Map** p405 D20.

Temporary exhibitions in 2013 include 'Audubon's Aviary: Part I of the Complete Flock' (through 19 May); 'WWII & NYC' (through 27 May); 'Swing Time: Reginald Marsh and Thirties New York' (21 June-1 Sept); 'The Armory Show at 100' (11 Oct 2013-23 Feb 2014). For the permanent collection, *see p105* **Profile.**

MORNINGSIDE HEIGHTS

Subway B, C, 1 to 110th Street-Cathedral Parkway; 1 to 116th Street.

Morningside Heights runs from 110th Street (also known west of Central Park as Cathedral Parkway) to 125th Street, between Morningside

Profile New-York Historical Society

The city's oldest museum embraces the 21st century.

Founded in 1804 by merchant John Pintard and a group of prominent New Yorkers that included Mayor Dewitt Clinton, the **New-York Historical Society** is the city's oldest museum. Originally based at City Hall, the institution was set up to preserve colonial and federal documents for posterity. It had subsequent stints in several locations before settling into its stately current home in 1908. The building, designed by York & Sawyer, the architects behind the Federal Reserve Bank of New York, is a fittingly solid structure for safeguarding the city's historical treasures. In November 2011, the museum reopened after a three-year, $65-million renovation that opened up the interior spaces to make the collection more accessible to a 21st-century audience.

Entering from Central Park West, visitors will find themselves in the large Robert H and Clarice Smith New York Gallery of American History, previously a warren of smaller rooms. The space provides an overview of the collection and a broad sweep of New York's place in American history – Revolutionary-era maps are juxtaposed with a piece of the ceiling mural from Keith Haring's Pop Shop (the artist's Soho store, which closed after his death in 1990). An installation, *Liberty/Liberté*, by NYC-based artist Fred Wilson, puts a contemporary spin on objects from the museum's collection, grouping a wrought-iron balustrade from the original Federal Hall with a bust of Washington and artefacts associated with slavery.

Touch-screen monitors illuminate artworks, documents and other objects from the early Federal period, while large-scale, column-mounted HD screens display a continuous slide show of highlights of the museum's holdings, such as original watercolours from Audubon's *Birds of America* and some of its 132 Tiffany lamps. A dozen circular exhibition cases in the floor, resembling manholes, contain items dug up by a group of amateur archaeologists founded by the Society in 1918; these include Lenape Indian arrowheads, a pair of baby shoes that survived the 1904 fire on the *General Slocum* pleasure boat, and an enormous oyster shell.

The updated auditorium screens an 18-minute film tracing the city's development, while downstairs the DiMenna Children's History Museum engages the next generation with 3-D 'pavilions' profiling six city kids, including the orphaned West Indies immigrant Alexander Hamilton (who became a founding father), and a 19th-century 'newsie' (paper seller). The upper floors house changing shows and the Henry Luce III Center for the Study of American Culture, a visible-storage display that spans everything from spectacles and toys to Washington's Valley Forge camp bed.

The Society's name is itself a historical preservation – placing a hyphen between 'New' and 'York' was common in the early 19th century. In fact, according to the Society, the *New York Times,* the paper of record, maintained the convention until 1896.

EXPLORE

Park and the Hudson River. The campus of **Columbia University** exerts a considerable influence over the surrounding neighbourhood, while the Cathedral Church of St John the Divine draws visitors from all over the city.

One of the oldest universities in the US, Columbia was initially chartered in 1754 as King's College (the name changed after the Revolutionary War). It moved to its present location in 1897. If you wander into Columbia's campus entrance at 116th Street, you won't fail to miss the impressive **Low Memorial Building**, modelled on Rome's Pantheon. The former library, completed in 1897, is now an administrative building. The list of illustrious graduates includes Alexander Hamilton, Allen Ginsberg and Barack Obama.

Thanks to the large student population of Columbia and its sister school, Barnard College, the area has an academic feel, with bookshops, inexpensive restaurants and coffeehouses lining Broadway between 110th and 116th Streets. The façade of **Tom's Restaurant** (2880 Broadway, at 112th Street, 1-212 864 6137) will be familiar to *Seinfeld* aficionados, but the interior doesn't resemble Monk's Café, which was created on a studio set for the long-running sitcom. Better fare can be found at **Community Food & Juice** (2893 Broadway, between 112th & 113th Streets, 1-212 665 2800, www.communityrestaurant.com).

The **Cathedral Church of St John the Divine** (*see right*) is the seat of the Episcopal Diocese of New York. Subject to a series of construction delays and misfortunes, the enormous cathedral (larger than Paris's Notre Dame) is on a medieval schedule for completion: according to the church, the hammering and chiselling will continue for a couple more centuries, although it has wrapped up work for the time being. Just behind is the green expanse of **Morningside Park** (from 110th to 123rd Streets, between Morningside Avenue & Morningside Drive), while across the street is the **Hungarian Pastry Shop** (1030 Amsterdam Avenue, between 110th & 111th Streets, 1-212 866 4230), a great place for coffee, dessert and engaging graduate students in esoteric discussions as they procrastinate over their theses.

North of Columbia, **General Grant National Memorial** (aka Grant's Tomb), the mausoleum of former president Ulysses S Grant, is located in Riverside Park. Across the street stands the towering Gothic-style **Riverside Church** (490 Riverside Drive, at 120th Street, 1-212 870 6700, www.the riversidechurchny.org), built in 1930. The tower contains the world's largest carillon: 74 bells, played every Sunday at 10.30am, 12.30pm and 3pm.

★ **Cathedral Church of St John the Divine**
1047 Amsterdam Avenue, at 112th Street (1-212 316 7540, www.stjohndivine.org). Subway B, C, 1 to 110th Street-Cathedral Parkway. **Open** 7am-6pm daily. **Admission** *Suggested donation $10. Tours $6-$20; $5-$15 reductions.* **Credit** Disc, MC, V. **Map** p406 C15.

Construction of this massive house of worship, affectionately nicknamed 'St John the Unfinished', began in 1892 in Romanesque style, was put on hold for a Gothic Revival redesign in 1911, then ground to a halt in 1941, when the US entered World War II. It resumed in earnest in 1979, but a fire in 2001 that destroyed the church's gift shop and damaged two 17th-century Italian tapestries further delayed completion. It's still missing a tower and a north transept, among other things, but the nave has been restored and the entire interior reopened and rededicated. No further work is planned… for now. In addition to Sunday services, the cathedral hosts concerts and tours (the Vertical Tour, which takes you the top of the building, is a revelation). It bills itself as a place for all people – and it certainly means it. Annual events include both winter and summer solstice celebrations, the Blessing of the Animals during the Feast of St Francis, which draws pets and their people from all over the city, and even a Blessing of the Bicycles every spring.

FREE General Grant National Memorial
Riverside Drive, at 122nd Street (1-212 666 1640, www.nps.gov/gegr). Subway 1 to 125th Street. **Open** *Visitor centre 9am-5pm Mon, Thur-Sun.* **Admission** free. **Map** p407 B14.

Although he was born in Ohio, Civil War hero and 18th president Ulysses S Grant lived in New York for the last five years of his life, and wanted to be buried in the city. More commonly referred to as Grant's Tomb, the neoclassical granite and marble mausoleum was completed in 1897; his wife, Julia, is also laid to rest here. The tomb is open for self-guided tours on the hour from 10am to 4pm; if you arrive between slots, the visitor centre offers exhibits and free talks by National Park Service rangers at 11.15am, 1.15pm and 3.15pm.

HARLEM

In the mythical melting pot that New Yorkers often cite to define their city, **Harlem** has long been an integral yet uneasy ingredient. During the Jazz Age, America's most iconic black neighbourhood lured whites to its celebrated nightclubs, only to deter downtowners in the 1960s and '70s with the urban decay and crime of which it became emblematic. Duke Ellington's famous invitation to 'Take the A Train' uptown had lost its appeal, and many visitors (and many native New Yorkers) decline it even today.

Harlem

The loss is theirs. Although the area isn't spilling over with sights, it has exuberant gospel choirs in historic churches, soul food restaurants serving down-home and upscale fare, markets selling African clothes, and a rejuvenated bar and jazz scene.

Few of the city's arteries pulsate like the main drag of 125th Street, where street preachers and mix-tape hawkers vie for the attentions of the human parade. Harlem's buildings maintain the city's eclectic architectural heritage, as a stroll along broad avenues such as Adam Clayton Powell Jr Boulevard (Seventh Avenue) or down the side streets off Convent Avenue readily attest.

The village of Harlem, named by Dutch colonists after their native Haarlem, was annexed by the City of New York in 1873. The extension of the elevated subway two decades later brought eager developers who overbuilt in the suddenly accessible suburb. The consequent housing glut led to cheap rents, and Jewish, Italian and Irish immigrants escaping the tenements of the Lower East Side snapped them up.

Around the turn of the 20th century, blacks joined the procession into Harlem, their ranks swelled by the great migration from the Deep South. By 1914, the black population of Harlem had risen well above 50,000; by the 1920s, Harlem was predominately black and the country's most populous African-American community. This prominence soon attracted some of black America's greatest artists: writers such as Langston Hughes and Zora Neale Hurston and musicians including Duke Ellington, Louis Armstrong and Cab Calloway,

an unprecedented cultural gathering known as the Harlem Renaissance. White New York took notice, venturing uptown – where the enforcement of Prohibition was lax – to enjoy the Cotton Club, Connie's Inn, Smalls Paradise and the Savoy Ballroom, which supplied the beat for the city that never sleeps.

The Depression killed the Harlem Renaissance; it deeply wounded Harlem. By the 1960s, the community had been ravaged by middle-class flight and municipal neglect. Businesses closed, racial tensions ran high, and the looting during the 1977 blackout was among

INSIDE TRACK
CASTRO COMES TO HARLEM

Although it no longer accepts guests, the Theresa Towers (2090 Adam Clayton Powell Jr Boulevard, at 125th Street) was Harlem's most illustrious hotel until closing in 1966. Known as the 'Waldorf of Harlem', the **Hotel Theresa** was home away from home to Louis Armstrong, Josephine Baker and Joe Louis, whose fans thronged outside following a victorious bout in 1941. In 1960, Fidel Castro, in New York to address the United Nations, moved the Cuban delegation to the Theresa after a falling out with the Hotel Shelburne downtown. Nehru and Krushchev visited Castro at the Theresa, as did Malcolm X, who conducted meetings of his Organization of Afro-American Unity there.

Literary NYC

See five iconic sites through the eyes of great New York writers.

Bethesda Fountain.

THE BETHESDA FOUNTAIN
Angels in America by Tony Kushner
Though endlessly witty, sexy and brainy, Kushner's Pulitzer-winning pair of plays portrays a New York City in a way that's nothing like the candy-coloured depictions in other mainstream AIDS-related dramas. Kushner's protagonist Prior Walter – who was visited by angels and watched his lover leave him while his body was racked by the AIDS virus – comes to his favourite place, the Bethesda Fountain (*see p93*), at the play's conclusion. There, the iconic *Angel of the Waters* inspires Walter's final benediction: 'More life'. You'll certainly see life in all its guises at Central Park's prime meeting spot.

THE MUSEUM OF NATURAL HISTORY
The Catcher in the Rye by JD Salinger
The young and disaffected narrator of *The Catcher in the Rye* wanders to a number of recognisable New York City places in his escape from the phonies at Pencey Prep, but perhaps none of them have changed as little over the years as the Museum of Natural History (*see p104*). 'They were always

showing Columbus discovering America, having one helluva time getting old Ferdinand and Isabella to lend him the dough to buy ships with, and then the sailors mutinying on him and all.' The lower reaches of the museum are probably full of some of the same artefacts that were collecting dust in Holden Caulfield's time; the 'fuck you' graffiti he encounters might just still be visible.

THE PLAZA
The Great Gatsby by F Scott Fitzgerald
The Plaza (*see p241*), which opened in 1907, is the site of the dissolution of literature's most famous bad romance: new-money poster boy Jay Gatsby and his all-consuming siren, Daisy Buchanan. It's here that the callow Daisy shows her true colours, siding with her emotionally abusive husband, Tom, rather than her slightly less emotionally abusive beau. But at least they enjoy top-notch room service and a nice view of the park before everyone's day gets ruined by vehicular manslaughter.

WASHINGTON SQUARE PARK
Washington Square by Henry James
Catherine Sloper, the dim-witted heroine of Henry James's novel, finds herself at odds with her father over a shady suitor. The father, correctly suspecting that the amorous Morris Townsend is nothing more than a money-grubbing jackanapes, repeatedly warns Catherine that it would be folly to marry such a rake. Things don't really work out… In today's Washington Square Park (*see p71*), you can still meet many cads, grifters and shady figures possibly involved in the low-level narcotics trade. Catherine's story is a cautionary tale: Don't take any wooden nickels.

The Plaza.

the worst the city had seen. However, as New York's economic standing improved in the mid '90s, investment began slowly spilling into the area, spawning new businesses and the phalanxes of renovated brownstones that beckon the middle class (white and black). This moneyed influx's co-existence with Harlem's long-standing residents can be tense, but it is seldom volatile.

Harlem rises up from the top of Central Park at 110th Street and extends north as far as 155th Street, though the neighbourhood's southern boundary on the West Side is marked by 125th Street. East Harlem begins on 96th Street and peters out around 125th Street before it's cut off by the Harlem River. Visitors using the common sense they would use elsewhere have nothing to fear and will be amply rewarded by one of New York's most distinctive neighbourhoods.

West Harlem

Subway 2, 3 to 125th Street or 135th Street; A, B, C, D to 125th Street

Harlem's main artery, **125th Street** (also known as Martin Luther King Jr Boulevard), beats loudest in **West Harlem** and most soulfully at the celebrated **Apollo Theater** (*see p285*), which hosts occasional concerts, a syndicated TV show and the classic Amateur Night every Wednesday – James Brown, Ella Fitzgerald, Michael Jackson and Lauryn Hill are among the starry alumni. A block east on 125th is the highly regarded **Studio Museum in Harlem** (*see p110*).

Although new boutiques, restaurants and cafés are scattered around the neighbourhood, especially on Frederick Douglass Boulevard (Eighth Avenue) between 110th and 125th Streets, the recession has slowed Harlem's renewal in other areas, particularly as you head east and north. Yet because redevelopers shunned Harlem for so long, it has managed to retain many of the buildings that went up around the turn of the century. Of particular interest, the **Mount Morris Historic District** (from 119th to 124th Streets, between Malcolm X Boulevard/Lenox Avenue & Mount Morris Park West) contains charming brownstones and a collection of religious buildings in a variety of architectural styles.

Most tourists wind up at **Sylvia's** (328 Malcolm X Boulevard/Lenox Avenue, between 126th & 127th Streets, 1-212 996 0660, www.sylviasrestaurant.com), Harlem's best-known soul-food specialist, or **Amy Ruth's** (113 W 116th Street between Malcolm X Boulevard/Lenox Avenue and Adam Clayton Powell Jr Boulevard/Seventh Avenue, 1-212 280 8779, www.amyruthsharlem.com), where each dish is named after a prominent African-American. But Harlemites (and visitors in the know)

head for **Red Rooster** (*see p174*), a gourmet Scandinavian-soulfood hotspot that opened at the end of 2010. The section of West 116th Street between St Nicholas Avenue and Morningside Park is known as **Little Senegal**, a strip of West African shops and restaurants; we recommend **Africa Kine** (256 W 116th Street, between Frederick Douglass & Adam Clayton Powell Jr Boulevards, 1-212 666 9400). Continue east along 116th Street West, past the domed **Masjid Malcolm Shabazz** (no.102, 1-212 662 2200), the mosque of Malcolm X's ministry, to the **Malcolm Shabazz Harlem Market** (no.52, 1-212 987 8131), an outdoor bazaar that buzzes with vendors, most from West Africa, selling clothes, jewellery and other goods from covered stalls.

No visit to Harlem is complete without a visit to one of the nightspots devoted to the jazz that made the neighbourhood world renowned. The **Lenox Lounge** (*see p186*) is where Billie Holiday sang, John Coltrane played, the young Malcolm X hustled and James Baldwin held court. **Showman's Bar** (375 W 125th Street, between St Nicholas & Morningside Avenues, 1-212 864 8941, closed Sun), is another must for jazz-lovers.

Further north is **Strivers' Row**, also known as the St Nicholas Historic District. On 138th and 139th Streets, between Adam Clayton Powell Jr Boulevard (Seventh Avenue) and Frederick Douglass Boulevard (Eighth Avenue), these harmonious blocks of brick townhouses were developed in 1891 by David H King Jr and designed by three different architects, one of which was Stanford White. The enclave is so well preserved that the alleyway sign advising you to 'walk your horses' is still visible.

Harlem's rich history is stored in the archives of the nearby **Schomburg Center for Research in Black Culture** (*see p110*). This branch of the New York Public Library contains more than five million documents, artefacts, films and prints relating to the cultures of peoples of African descent, with a strong emphasis on the African-American experience. A few blocks south, the **Abyssinian Baptist Church** (*see below*) is celebrated for its history, political activism and rousing gospel choir. For more secular inspiration, drop by the **Shrine** (2271 Adam Clayton Powell Jr Boulevard, between 133rd & 134th Streets; *see p186*) for imaginative cocktails and an ever-changing array of musical acts.

FREE Abyssinian Baptist Church

132 Odell Clark Place (138th Street), between Malcolm X Boulevard (Lenox Avenue) & Adam Clayton Powell Jr Boulevard (Seventh Avenue) (1-212 862 7474, www.abyssinian.org). Subway 2, 3 to 135th Street. **Services** 7pm Wed; 11am Sun. **Admission** free. **Map** p407 E11.

From the staid gingerbread Gothic exterior, you'd never suspect the energy that charges the Abyssinian when the gospel choir rocks the church every Sunday at 11am and Wednesday at 7pm (get there early, and don't wear shorts or flip-flops). A cauldron of community activism since its Ethiopian elders moved it uptown in the 1920s, the church was under the leadership of legendary civil rights crusader Adam Clayton Powell Jr in the 1930s (there's a modest exhibit about him inside). Today, the pulpit belongs to the Rev Dr Calvin Butts, who carries on the flame.

FREE Schomburg Center for Research in Black Culture

515 Malcolm X Boulevard (Lenox Avenue), between 135th & 136th Streets (1-212 491 2200, www.nypl.org). Subway 2, 3 to 135th Street. **Open** *General Research & Reference Division* noon-8pm Tue-Thur; 10am-6pm Fri, Sat. *Other departments* times vary. **Admission** free. **Map** p407 D12.

Part of the New York Public Library, this institution holds an extraordinary trove of vintage literature and historical memorabilia relating to black culture and the African diaspora, much of which was amassed by notable bibliophile Arturo Alfonso Schomburg, who was curator from 1932 until his death in 1938. (It was posthumously renamed in his honour.) Note that parts of the collection can only be viewed on certain days by appointment; call or refer to detailed hours by department on the NYPL's website. The centre also hosts occasional exhibits, jazz concerts, films, lectures and tours.

Studio Museum in Harlem

144 W 125th Street, between Adam Clayton Powell Jr Boulevard (Seventh Avenue) & Malcolm X Boulevard (Lenox Avenue) (1-212 864 4500, www.studiomuseum.org). Subway 2, 3 to 125th Street. **Open** noon-9pm Thur, Fri; 10am-6pm Sat; noon-6pm Sun. **Admission** *Suggested donation* $7; $3 reductions; free under-12s. Free to all Sun. **No credit cards. Map** p407 D13.

The first black fine arts museum in the United States when it opened in 1968, the Studio Museum is an important player in the art scene of the African diaspora. Under the leadership of director and chief curator Thelma Golden (formerly of the Whitney), the stripped-down, three-level space presents shows in a variety of media by black artists from around the world. The museum supports emerging visual artists of African descent through its coveted artist-in-residence programme.

East Harlem

Subway 6 to 110th Street or 116th Street.

East of Fifth Avenue is **East Harlem**, commonly called Spanish Harlem but also known to its primarily Puerto Rican residents as El Barrio. North of 96th Street and east of Madison Avenue,

El Barrio moves to a different beat. Its main east–west cross street, East 116th Street, shows signs of a recent influx of Mexican immigrants. A slight touch of East Village-style bohemia can be detected in such places as **Camaradas El Barrio** (2241 First Avenue, at 115th Street, 1-212 348 2703, www.camaradaselbarrio.com), a Puerto Rican tapas bar whose wooden benches, exposed brick and modest gallery create a casual hangout for kicking back over a pitcher of sangria or taking in a salsa or jazz show. The modest **Graffiti Hall of Fame** (106th Street, between Madison & Park Avenues) celebrates old- and new-school taggers in a schoolyard. Be sure to check out the recently revamped **El Museo del Barrio** (*see p98*), which has an impressive collection of Latin-American art and a lively programme of cultural events.

Hamilton Heights

Subway A, B, C, D, 1 to 145th Street.

Named after Alexander Hamilton, who owned an estate and a farm here, **Hamilton Heights** extends from 125th Street to the Trinity Cemetery at 155th Street, between Riverside Drive and St Nicholas Avenue. Hamilton's 1802 Federal-style house, the **Grange**, now a national memorial, recently reopened to visitors after being moved from 287 Convent Avenue around the corner to St Nicholas Park.

The former factory neighbourhood developed after the West Side elevated train was built in the early 20th century. Today, it's notable for the elegant turn-of-the-20th-century row houses in the **Hamilton Heights Historic District**, centred on the side streets off scenic **Convent Avenue** between 140th and 145th Streets – just beyond the Gothic Revival-style campus of the **City College of New York** (Convent Avenue, from 135th to 140th Streets). Its main building, Shepard Hall (on Convent Avenue, at 138th Street), is striking for its combination of white terracotta interlaid with black stone that was removed to create the site for the college.

FREE Hamilton Grange National Memorial

St Nicholas Park, 414 W 141st Street, near Convent Avenue (1-646 548 2310, www.nps.gov/hagr) **Open** *Visitor centre* 9am-5pm Wed-Sun. *Tours* 11am, noon, 1pm, 2pm, 4pm. **Admission** free. **Map** p407 C11.

The Federal-style estate of America's first Secretary of the Treasury was completed two years before he was shot in a duel with Vice President Aaron Burr (*see p353* **Profile**). Rooms, accessed via park ranger-led tours, include Hamilton's study and the parlour, with his daughter's pianoforte. A short film about the founding father's life is shown in the visitor centre.

WASHINGTON HEIGHTS & INWOOD

Subway 1 to 157th Street; A, C, 1 to 168th Street-Washington Heights; A to 190th Street.

The area from West 155th Street to Dyckman (200th) Street is called **Washington Heights**; venture north of that and you're in Inwood, Manhattan's northernmost neighbourhood, where the Harlem and Hudson Rivers converge. An ever-growing number of artists and young families are relocating to these parts, attracted by the spacious pre-war buildings, big parks, hilly streets and (comparatively) low rents.

Washington Heights' main attraction is the **Morris-Jumel Mansion** (*see p112*), a stunning Palladian-style mansion that served as a swanky headquarters for George Washington during the autumn of 1776. But the small and often overlooked **Hispanic Society of America** (*see p112*), featuring a surprising collection of masterworks, is the real gem here.

Since the 1920s, waves of immigrants have settled in Washington Heights. In the post-World War II era, many German-Jewish refugees (among them Henry Kissinger, Dr Ruth Westheimer and Max Frankel, a former executive editor of the *New York Times*) moved to the western edge of the district. Broadway once housed a small Greek

The Cloisters. *See p112.*

EXPLORE

population – opera singer Maria Callas lived here in her youth. But in the last few decades, the southern and eastern parts of the area have become predominantly Spanish-speaking due to a large population of Dominican settlers.

A trek along Fort Washington Avenue, from about 173rd Street to **Fort Tryon Park**, puts you in the heart of what is now called **Hudson Heights** – the posh area of Washington Heights. Start at the **George Washington Bridge**, the city's only bridge across the Hudson River. A pedestrian walkway (also a popular route for cyclists) allows for dazzling Manhattan views. Under the bridge on the New York side is a diminutive lighthouse. To see it up close, look for the footpath on the west side of the interchange on the Henry Hudson Parkway at about 170th Street. If you need to refuel, stop off at the lovely **New Leaf Café** (1 Margaret Corbin Drive, near Park Drive, 1-212 568 5323, closed Mon) within the Frederick Law Olmsted-designed Fort Tryon Park.

At the northern edge of the park is the **Cloisters** (*see below*), a museum built in 1938 using segments of five medieval cloisters shipped from Europe by the Rockefeller clan. It houses the Metropolitan Museum of Art's permanent medieval art collection.

Inwood stretches from Dyckman Street up to 218th Street, the last residential block in Manhattan. Dyckman buzzes with street life from river to river, but, north of that, the island narrows considerably and the parks along the western shoreline culminate in the seclusion of **Inwood Hill Park**, another Frederick Law Olmsted legacy. Some believe that this is the location of the legendary 1626 transaction between Peter Minuit and the Native American Lenapes for the purchase of a strip of land called Manahatta – a plaque at the south-west corner of the ballpark near 214th Street marks the purported spot. The 196-acre refuge contains the island's last swathes of virgin forest and salt marsh. Today, with a bit of imagination, you can hike over the hilly terrain, liberally scattered with massive glacier-deposited boulders (called erratics), and picture Manhattan as it was before development. In recent years, the city's Parks Department has used the densely wooded area as a fledging spot for newly hatched bald eagles.

★ The Cloisters

Fort Tryon Park, Fort Washington Avenue, at Margaret Corbin Plaza (1-212 923 3700, www.metmuseum.org). Subway A to 190th Street, then M4 bus or follow Margaret Corbin Drive north, for about the length of 5 city blocks, to the museum. **Open** *Mar-Oct* 9.30am-5.15pm Tue-Sun. *Nov-Feb* 9.30am-4.45pm Tue-Sun. **Admission** *Suggested donation* (incl admission to Metropolitan Museum of Art on the same day)

$25; $12-$17 reductions; free under-12s. **Credit** AmEx, DC, Disc, MC, V. **Map** p409 B3.

Set in a lovely park overlooking the Hudson River, the Cloisters houses the Met's medieval art and architecture collections. A path winds through the peaceful grounds to a castle that seems to have survived from the Middle Ages. It was built a mere 75 years ago, using pieces of five medieval French cloisters. The collection is an inspired trove of Romanesque, Gothic and Baroque treasures brought from Europe and assembled in a manner that somehow manages not to clash. Be sure to check out the famous Unicorn Tapestries (c1500), the 12th-century Fuentidueña Chapel and the Annunciation triptych by Robert Campin. *Photos p111.*

FREE Hispanic Society of America

Audubon Terrace, Broadway, between 155th & 156th Streets (1-212 926 2234, www.hispanic society.org). Subway 1 to 157th Street. **Open** 10am-4.30pm Tue-Sat; 1-4pm Sun. **Admission** free. **Map** p408 B9.

Though few people who pass this way seem aware of it, the Hispanic Society boasts the largest assemblage of Spanish art and manuscripts outside Spain. Goya's masterful *Duchess of Alba* greets you as you enter, while several haunting El Greco portraits can be found on the second floor. The collection is dominated by religious artefacts, including 16th-century tombs from the monastery of San Francisco in Cuéllar, Spain. Also among its holdings are decorative art objects and thousands of black and white photographs that document life in Spain and Latin America from the mid 19th century to the present. Among the highlights is Valencian painter Joaquín Sorolla y Bastida's *Vision of Spain*, comprising 14 monumental oils commissioned by the Society in 1911.

Morris-Jumel Mansion

65 Jumel Terrace, between 160th & 162nd Streets (1-212 923 8008, www.morrisjumel.org). Subway C to 163rd Street-Amsterdam Avenue. **Open** 10am-4pm Wed-Sun. **Admission** $5; $4 reductions; free under-12s. **Credit** AmEx, MC, V. **Map** p408 C8.

Constructed in 1765, Manhattan's only surviving pre-Revolutionary manse was originally the heart of a 130-acre estate that stretched from river to river (on the grounds, a stone marker points south with the legend 'New York, 11 miles'). George Washington planned the Battle of Harlem Heights here in 1776, after the British colonel Roger Morris moved out. The handsome 18th-century Palladian-style villa offers fantastic views. Its former driveway is now Sylvan Terrace, which has the longest continuous stretch (one block in total) of old wooden houses in all of Manhattan.

▶ *Other 18th-century buildings that are open to visitors include the Fraunces Tavern Museum (see p49) and the Van Cortlandt House Museum (see p136).*

Brooklyn

No longer a bridge too far, Kings County is synonymous with cool.

Years ago, most tourists who found themselves in Brooklyn were likely to have missed the last subway stop in Manhattan. Recently, however, the second borough has become a destination in its own right. 'Brooklyn' has become shorthand for a particular brand of indie cool. New bars and restaurants continue to proliferate, the music scene is thriving, and it's a standard destination on the tour-bus itinerary.

Settled by the Dutch in the early 17th century, Breukelen took its name from the Dutch town. It was America's third largest municipality until its amalgamation with the four other boroughs that created New York City in 1898. Its many brownstones are a testament to a large and wealthy merchant class that made its money from the shipping trade. By the end of the 19th century, Brooklyn had become so

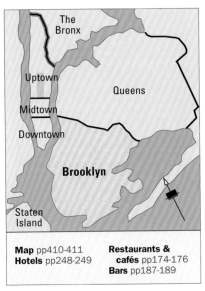

Map pp410-411	**Restaurants &**
Hotels pp248-249	**cafés** pp174-176
	Bars pp187-189

prosperous, and its view of itself so grandiloquent, it built copies of the Arc de Triomphe (in Grand Army Plaza) and the Champs-Elysées (Eastern Parkway), and a greensward (Prospect Park) to rival Central Park.

EXPLORE

BROOKLYN HEIGHTS & DUMBO

Brooklyn Heights – Subway A, C, F to Jay Street-Borough Hall; A, C, G to Hoyt-Schermerhorn; M, R to Court Street; 2, 3, 4, 5 to Borough Hall. Dumbo – Subway to A, C to High Street; F to York Street.

Home to well-to-do families, bankers and lawyers lured by its proximity to Wall Street, **Brooklyn Heights** is where you'll find the idyllic leafy, brownstone-lined streets of Brooklyn legend. Thanks to the area's historic district status, it has many Greek Revival and Italianate row houses dating from the 1820s. Take a stroll down the gorgeous tree-lined streets – try Cranberry, Hicks, Pierrepont and Willow – to see the area at its best.

Given its serenity and easy access to Manhattan, it's not surprising that Brooklyn

Heights has been home to numerous illustrious (and struggling) writers. Walt Whitman printed the first edition of *Leaves of Grass* at 98 Cranberry Street (in a building since demolished); Truman Capote wrote *Breakfast at Tiffany's* at 70 Willow Street; and Thomas Wolfe penned *Of Times and the River* at 5 Montague Terrace. Seven Middagh Street was something of a writers' commune, where Carson McCullers, Paul and Jane Bowles, WH Auden and Richard Wright resided at various times.

Henry and Montague Streets are the prime strips for shops, restaurants and bars. At the end of Montague, the **Brooklyn Heights Promenade** offers spectacular waterfront views of lower Manhattan, New York Harbor and the nearby **Brooklyn Bridge** (*see p116*), a marvel of 19th-century engineering that became the borough's iconic landmark. For those interested in history of the underground variety, the **New**

Walk Tombs with a View

Pay your respects to the great and the good at Brooklyn's landmark cemetery.

A century ago, Brooklyn's **Green-Wood Cemetery** (*see p121*) vied with Niagara Falls as New York State's greatest tourist attraction. Established in 1838, it's filled with Victorian mausoleums, cherubs and gargoyles. In fact, these winding paths, rolling hills and natural ponds served as the model for Central Park. It remains a beautiful place to spend a few hours, paying your respects to the celebrated and the notorious – among them Jean-Michel Basquiat, Leonard Bernstein and Louis Comfort Tiffany – who lie at rest in this 428-acre outdoor museum.

Start your walk at the Gothic main gate (Fifth Avenue at 25th Street, Sunset Park). The spectacular, soaring arches are carved from New Jersey brownstone. That chirping you hear comes from monk parakeets that

escaped a shipment to JFK in the 1960s and have nested here ever since.

Bear right and walk down **Landscape Avenue** to the chapel. Built in 1911, it was designed by Warren & Wetmore, the firm that also built Grand Central Terminal. Outside, with the creepy Receiving Tomb on your left (this was where bodies were stored when the ground was frozen too hard to dig), head to the corner of Lake Avenue. Graves here belong to Clifton and William Prentiss, brothers who fought on opposite sides of the Civil War. They were both mortally wounded on the same day in 1865 (and both were treated by a nurse named Walt Whitman).

Follow the pond on Waterside Path to **Valley Avenue**. The monument with the jug on top is the grave of John Eberhard Faber

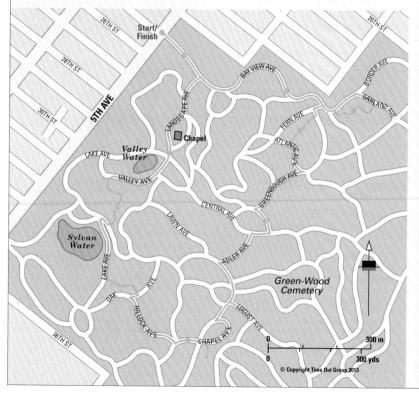

(who first put erasers on pencils). Make a left up Hill Side Path. The grave with the carved figure staring up at scenes from the deceased's life belongs to John Matthews, inventor of the soda fountain.

Cut across the grass and follow **Bluff Side Path** to the stairs down to Sylvan Water. Turn left on Lake, stopping by the tomb of Leonard Jerome, namesake of the Bronx's Jerome Avenue and grandfather of Winston Churchill. Make a left on **Ravine Path**. Up the steep incline, stop at the headstone marked 'Aloi' for a nice view of the Statue of Liberty. At the end of the path, go right on Oak Avenue (turn around – that green bust is the grave of newspaperman Horace Greeley) and take the first left on to Hillock Avenue.

Make a left on **Landscape Avenue** and you'll find Bill 'the Butcher' Poole (think *Gangs of New York*), behind the huge tree on your left. Otherwise, head up Chapel Avenue and turn right on Thorn Path to the grave of Samuel Morse, inventor of the telegraph. Double back and make a right on **Chapel Avenue**. Walk around the Steinway family mausoleum and bear right. Make a right on Locust Avenue and see disgraced power-monger Boss Tweed's grave (left side), or stay on Chapel past Forest and Vista Avenues and make a right on Alder Avenue.

Next, make a right on Central Avenue and then a left on Sycamore Avenue. Then turn on Greenbough Avenue (you'll pass Henry Raymond, the founder of the *New York Times*), left on Atlantic Avenue and right on Warrior Path. Take the path to the end and climb the staircase to the **Civil War Soldiers' Monument**. The bench behind it has sweet views and it's also the site of the first and largest major battle of the Revolutionary War.

Follow Battle Path to the end, turn left on Garland Avenue. When you're even with the big tree, turn right. You're looking at the grave of Dodgers owner Charles Ebbets and, up the hill behind, the highest point in Brooklyn. Go straight on Garland, left on Border Avenue and right down Battle Avenue to the corner of Bay View Avenue. You'll pass the obelisk honouring the victims of the 1876 Brooklyn Theatre fire on your way back to the main gate.

York Transit Museum (*see p118*) is a must. There are more remnants of bygone Brooklyn at the **Brooklyn Historical Society** (*see p118*) which, when completed in 1881, was the first structure in New York to feature local terracotta on its façade. The grand **Borough Hall** (209 Joralemon Street, at Court Street), the seat of local government, stands as a monument to Brooklyn's past as an independent municipality. Completed in 1851 but only later crowned with a Victorian cupola, the Greek Revival edifice was renovated in the late 1980s. The building is linked to the **New York State Supreme Court** (360 Adams Street, between Joralemon Street & Tech Place) by **Cadman Plaza** (from Prospect Street to Tech Place, between Cadman Plaza East & Cadman Plaza West).

At the turn of the 19th century, **Dumbo** (Down Under the Manhattan Bridge Overpass) was a thriving industrial district; all kinds of manufacturers, including Brillo and Benjamin Moore, were based here, leaving behind a fine collection of factory buildings and warehouses; the most famous of these, the Eskimo Pie Building (100 Bridge Street, at York Street), with its embellished facade, was actually built for the Thomson Meter Company in 1908-09.

In the 1970s and '80s, these warehouses were colonised by artists seeking cheap live/work spaces, but playing out a familiar New York migration pattern, the area is now bursting with million-dollar apartments and high-end design shops. The spectacular views – taking in the Statue of Liberty, the lower Manhattan skyline and the Brooklyn and Manhattan Bridges – remain the same. The best vantage point is below the Brooklyn Bridge at the **Fulton Ferry Landing**, which juts out over the East River at Old Fulton and Water Streets. It was here that General George Washington and his troops beat a hasty retreat by boat from the Battle of Brooklyn in 1776. It's now a stop on the East River Ferry service (*see p374*), which links Dumbo to six points in Manhattan, Brooklyn and Queens. Along the same pier is the **Brooklyn Ice Cream Factory** (Fulton Ferry Landing, 1 Water Street, 1-718 246 3963, closed Mon Dec-Mar), located in a 1920s fireboat house. Next door, docked at the pier, is one of the borough's great cultural jewels: **Bargemusic** (*see p303*), a 100-foot steel barge that was built in 1899 but has staged chamber music concerts for the last 36 years.

On both sides of the landing, **Brooklyn Bridge Park** (riverside, from the Manhattan Bridge to Atlantic Avenue) has been undergoing a rolling redesign that includes lawns, freshwater gardens, a water fowl-attracting salt marsh and the Granite Prospect, a set of stairs fashioned out of salvaged granite facing the Manhattan skyline. But the undoubted

EXPLORE

INSIDE TRACK
DUMBO ART PARTY

Each month, around 25 Dumbo galleries remain open late – some hosting special events – for the **1st Thursday Gallery Walk** (www.dumboculture411.com). On the night, you can pick up a map at 111 Front Street (between Adams & Washington Streets), which houses many of the galleries.

centrepiece is the long-awaited vintage merry-go-round known as **Jane's Carousel**, which made its park debut in 2011 in a Jean Nouvel-designed pavilion in the section of park alongside the post-Civil War coffee warehouses, Empire Stores (between Main Street and the Brooklyn Bridge; *see p257* **Horsing Around**). Miraculously, it survived the 14-foot tidal surge of 2012's superstorm Sandy.

The artists who flocked to the area en masse in the 1970s and '80s maintain a presence in the local galleries, most of which support the work of emerging talent. Among them are non-profit **Smack Mellon** (92 Plymouth Street, at Washington Street, 1-718 834 8761, http://smackmellon.org, closed Mon, Tue) and the **Dumbo Arts Center** (Suite 212, 111 Front Street, between Adams & Washington Streets, 1-718 694 0831, www.dumboartscenter.org, closed Mon, Tue), which mounts shows and sponsors the **Dumbo Arts Festival** (*see p34*), held in the autumn. If you're in the neighbourhood in spring 2013, look out for Tom Fruin's *Watertower*, which perches on the roof of 20 Jay Street through June. The Brookyn artist used salvaged Plexiglas from throughout the city to create the tower, giving the familiar NYC skyline feature the look of medieval stained glass.

Dumbo is also becoming a performing arts hotspot. You can catch anything from puppet theatre to Lou Reed in concert at **St Ann's Warehouse** (*see p324*). Another artsy venue, which has even more diverse programming – think burlesque, camp variety and contemporary classical – is the **Galapagos Art Space** (*see p286*), which relocated a few years ago from its Williamsburg birthplace to a gleaming, LEED-certified green space.

If you crave an authentic New York pizza, join the throngs lining up for a coal-fired pie at the famous **Grimaldi's** (19 Old Fulton Street, between Front & Water Streets, 1-718 858 4300). The fortress-like structure across the street, the Eagle Warehouse & Storage (28 Old Fulton Street at Elizabeth Place), was completed in 1894 on the site of the old *Brooklyn Daily Eagle* offices (and subsequently converted into condos). The

paper was edited by Brooklyn resident Walt Whitman between 1846 and 1848, before he was fired for his lefty political leanings.

Two new restaurants have expanded Dumbo's culinary cred: **Gran Electrica** (5 Front Street, between Dock and Old Fulton Streets, 1-718 852 2789, www.granelectrica.com), a market-driven Mexican spot, and **Governor** (15 Main Street, at Plymouth Street, 1-718 858 4756), a farm-to-table restaurant whose seasonal menu reflects the chef's interest in foraging and pickling techniques.

Water Street has been evolving into Sugar Row: **Jacques Torres Chocolate** (*see p212*) purveys premium made-on-site chocolates. Cross the street for exquisite French pastries and espresso at **Almondine** (85 Water Street, between Main & Dock Streets, 1-718 797 5026). At **One Girl Cookies** on the end of the strip (33 Main Street, at Water Street, 1-347-338-1268, www.onegirlcookies.com), you can pair your tea cookies or whoopie pies with Stumptown coffee – or a craft beer or glass of wine.

While a good chunk of the retail is furniture shops catering to the loft-dwelling locals, Dumbo has a brace of destination stores for books and records. Also serving as a gallery and performance space, the **Powerhouse Arena** (37 Main Street, at Water Street; *see p298*) is the cavernous retail arm of Powerhouse Books, which produces sumptuous coffee-table tomes on such diverse subjects as rock stars, celebrity dogs and the Brooklyn Navy Yard. **Halcyon** (57 Pearl Street, at Water Street, 1-718 260 9299), one of the city's few surviving DJ-oriented music boutiques, has been in business for more than a decade.

Head east on Water or Front Street to discover one of Brooklyn's forgotten neighbourhoods. Once a rough and bawdy patch dotted with bars and brothels frequented by sailors and dockworkers, **Vinegar Hill**, between Bridge Street and the Navy Yard, earned the moniker 'Hell's Half Acre' in the 19th century. Only fragments of the enclave remain (parts of it were designated a historic district in the late 1990s). Today, it's considerably quieter. Although inhabited, the isolated strips of early-19th-century row houses and defunct storefronts on Bridge, Hudson and Plymouth Streets, and a stretch of Front, have a ghost-town quality, heightened by their juxtaposition with a Con Edison generating station. For refreshment, seek out the enclave's cosy, tavern-like **Vinegar Hill House** (*see p175*) or its satellite wine bar/café, Hillside.

★ FREE **Brooklyn Bridge**

Subway A, C to High Street; J to Chambers Street; 4, 5, 6 to Brooklyn Bridge-City Hall. **Map** p411 S8. *See p117* **Profile**.

Profile Brooklyn Bridge

Love and death on New York's most iconic span.

The Brooklyn Bridge was built in response to the harsh winter of 1867 when the East River froze over, severing connection between Manhattan and what was then the nation's third most populous city. When it opened in 1883, the 5,989ft-long structure was the world's longest bridge, and the first in the world to use steel suspension cables.

Construction began on the Brooklyn side. To lay the foundation on bedrock 44 feet below, workers in airtight containers chipped away at the riverbed. More than 100 were paralysed with the bends, caused by the change in air pressure when they surfaced. When the Manhattan side was built, chief engineer Washington Roebling got the bends too. (He wasn't the only family casualty; his dad, bridge designer John, died in 1869 after his foot was crushed by a docking ferry.) Washington spent the next decade watching the bridge's progress through a telescope and relaying directions through his wife, Emily. Fearing more deaths on the Manhattan tower, he stopped construction before it reached the 100-foot-deep bedrock. To this day, the tower rests on sand and hardpan.

Every day, 6,600 people walk or bike across the bridge's wide, wood-planked promenade, taking in views of New York Harbor, the Statue of Liberty and the skyscrapers of lower Manhattan. Crowds have always been part of the scene here. Six days after the bridge debuted, a stampede on a stairway crushed 12 people to death and injured 35. A scream apparently sparked hysteria that the structure was collapsing, and people surged down the steps.

A lot of people propose on the bridge. Look out for padlocks scattered on the fence: couples attach them and throw the keys in the river as a symbol of everlasting love – until Department of Transportation workers cut them off, that is.

A plaque on the Brooklyn tower honours Emily Roebling: 'Back of every great work we can find the self-sacrificing devotion of a woman.' According to Seth Kamil of Big Onion Walking Tours (*see p43*), Emily became quite the powerhouse, eventually making some of her own decisions about the bridge, which she carried out without her husband's approval.

In 2006, workers found a Cold War bunker in an arched structure under the entrance ramp on the Manhattan side. The emergency stash inside included medical supplies and cans of crackers; one container was labelled 'To be opened after attack by the enemy'.

EXPLORE

▶ *You can also walk or bike into Brooklyn across the Manhattan or Williamsburg Bridges.*

Brooklyn Historical Society

128 Pierrepont Street, at Clinton Street, Brooklyn Heights (1-718 222 4111, www.brooklynhistory. org). Subway A, C, F to Jay Street-Borough Hall. **Open** noon-5pm Wed-Sat. **Admission** $6; $4 reductions; free under-12s. **Credit** AmEx, MC, V. **Map** p411 S9.

Founded in 1863, the BHS resides in a landmark four-storey Queen Anne-style building and presents ongoing and temporary exhibits, including the long-term 'Inventing Brooklyn: People, Places, Progress', an overview of the borough's evolution. A major photo and research library – featuring historic maps and newspapers, notable family histories and archives from the area's abolitionist movement – is accessible by appointment only.

New York Transit Museum

Corner of Boerum Place & Schermerhorn Street, Brooklyn Heights (1-718 694 1600, www.mta. info/mta/museum). Subway A, C, G to Hoyt-Schermerhorn; 2, 3, 4, 5 to Borough Hall. **Open** 10am-4pm Tue-Fri; noon-5pm Sat, Sun. **Admission** $6; $4 reductions; free under-3s; free seniors Wed. **Credit** AmEx, DC, MC, V. **Map** p411 S10.

Housed in a historic 1936 IND subway station, this is the largest museum in the United States devoted to urban public transportation history. Exhibits explore the social and practical impact of public transportation on the development of greater New York; among the highlights is an engrossing walk-through display charting the construction of the city's century-old subway system, when fearless 'sandhogs' were engaged in dangerous tunnelling. A line-up of turnstiles shows their evolution from the 1894 'ticket chopper' to the current Automatic Fare Card model. But the best part is down another level to a real platform where you can board an exceptional collection of vintage subway and El ('Elevated') cars, some complete with vintage ads. **Other locations** New York Transit Museum Gallery Annex & Store, Grand Central Terminal, adjacent to stationmaster's office, main concourse (1-212 878 0106; *see p91*).

INSIDE TRACK CAFFEINE FIX

If you need a jolt of java in Dumbo, the **Brooklyn Roasting Co** (25 Jay Street, between John & Plymouth Streets, 1-718 522 2664, www.brooklynroasting.com), supplier of Fairtrade, organic beans to many of Brooklyn's best cafés, has an on-site café where coffee starts at a wallet-friendly $1.50 for an 8oz cup.

BOERUM HILL, CARROLL GARDENS & COBBLE HILL

Subway A, C, F to Jay Street; F, G to Bergen Street, Carroll Street; M, N, R, 2, 3, 4, 5, to Court Street-Borough Hall.

A convenient if annoying real estate agents' contraction for these blurred-boundaried 'hoods, BoCoCa is a prime example of gentrification at work. Gone are the bodegas and cheap shoe shops along the stretch of Smith Street that runs from Atlantic Avenue to the Carroll Street subway stop; it's now known as the area's Restaurant Row. Among the strip's hottest spots are the classic bistro **Bar Tabac** (no.128, at Dean Street, Boerum Hill, 1-718 923 0918); new American favourite **The Grocery** (no.288, between Sackett & Union Streets, Carroll Gardens, 1-718 596 3335, www. thegroceryrestaurant.com, closed Mon, Sun); and **Saul** (no.140, between Bergen & Dean Streets, Carroll Gardens, 1-718 935 9844, www.saulrestaurant.com). Check out the stylish women's clothing at **Bird** (no.220, at Butler Street, Cobble Hill, 1-718 797 3774, www.shopbird.com) and **Dear Fieldbinder** (no.198, between Sackett & Warren Streets, Carroll Gardens, 1-718 852 3620, www. dearfieldbinder.com).

Head east on Boerum Hill's **Atlantic Avenue** for a slew of antique and modern furniture stores. Among the best are **City Foundry**, an industrial-chic furniture store (no.365, between Bond & Hoyt Streets, 1-718 923 1786) and **Darr** (no.369, between Bond & Hoyt Streets, 1-718-797-9733), a favourite among stylists and set designers for its taxidermy, industrial cabinets and tamer goods such as horn tableware. The same owners also operate top-notch, neo-rustic menswear emporium **Hollander & Lexer** across the street (no.358, 1-718 797 9190). Browse women's haute designer fashion at the minimalist **Eva Gentry** (no.389, between Bond & Hoyt Streets, 1-718 260 9033) and its more affordable sister store **Eva Gentry Consignment** (no.371, between Hoyt & Bond Streets, 1-718 522 3522).

The mile-long stretch of Atlantic Avenue between Henry and Nevins Streets was once crowded with Middle Eastern restaurants and markets, but gentrification has also taken its toll here. One stalwart is the **Sahadi Importing Company** (no.187, between Clinton & Court Streets, Cobble Hill, 1-718 624 4550, closed Sun), a neighbourhood institution that sells olives, spices, cheeses, nuts and other gourmet treats.

West of Boerum Hill, **Cobble Hill** has a palpable small-town feel. Here, **Court Street** is dotted with cafés and shops, such as local favourite **Book Court** (no.163, between Pacific

& Dean Streets, 1-718 875 3677). Be sure to stop by **Café Pedlar** (no.210, at Warren Street, 1-718 855 7129), for expertly pulled espresso drinks and house-made baked goods from the folks behind Frankies 457 (*see below*). Walk over the Brooklyn-Queens Expressway to Cobble Hill's industrial waterfront and the corner building housing Mexican bistro **Alma** (187 Columbia Street, at DeGraw Street, 1-718 643 5400, www.almarestaurant.com). The rooftop dining area (closed Mon-Wed Nov-Mar) has great views of the East River and lower Manhattan.

Further south, you'll cross into the still predominantly Italian-American **Carroll Gardens**. Pick up a prosciutto loaf from **Caputo Bakery** (329 Court Street, between Sackett & Union Streets, 1-718 875 6871) or an aged *soppressata* salami from **G Esposito & Sons** (357 Court Street, between President & Union Streets, 1-718 875 6863); then relax in **Carroll Park** (from President to Carroll Streets, between Court & Smith Streets) and watch the old-timers play *bocce* (lawn bowls). Alternatively, a cluster of excellent eateries on Court Street includes casual trattoria **Frankies 457** (no.457, between Lucquer Street & 4th Place, 1-718 403 0033, www.frankiesspuntino. com), its Germanic spin-off **Prime Meats** (no.465, 1-718 254 0327, www.frankspm.com) and seasonal American bistro **Buttermilk Channel** (no.524, at Huntington Street, 1-718 852 8490, www.buttermilkchannelnyc.com).

RED HOOK

Subway F, G to Smith-9th Streets, then B61 bus.

To the south-west of Carroll Gardens, beyond the Brooklyn-Queens Expressway, the formerly rough-and-tumble industrial locale of **Red Hook** has long avoided urban renewal. In recent years, however, the arrival of gourmet mega-grocer Fairway and Swedish furniture superstore IKEA have served notice that gentrification is slowly moving in.

Luckily for its protective residents, the Hook still feels secluded, tucked away on a peninsula. While the area continues to evolve, its time-warp charm is still evident, and its decaying piers make a moody backdrop for massive cranes, empty warehouses and trucks clattering over cobblestone streets. The lack of public transport has thus far prevented it from becoming the next Williamsburg. From the Smith-9th Streets subway stop, it's either a half-hour walk south or a transfer to the B61 bus, although the **New York Water Taxi** (*see p43*) has improved the situation with its IKEA express shuttle from downtown Manhattan.

Urban adventurers are rewarded if they make a trip out here. The area offers singular views of the Statue of Liberty and New York Harbor from **Valentino Pier**, and has an eclectic selection of artists' studios, bars and eateries. Retro bar and grill **Hope & Anchor** (347 Van Brunt Street, at Wolcott Street, 1-718 237 0276) opened a decade ago, when the stretch was still a culinary wasteland. Similarly pioneering was the **Good Fork** (391 Van Brunt Street, near Coffey Street, 1-718 643 6636, www.goodfork.com, closed Mon), now a local institution, which blends traditional Korean flavours into its trendy American cooking. More recently, the area received a major culinary boost with the arrival of **Pok Pok NY** (*see p175*), a convincing replica of a Chiang Mai dive. Long-standing dive **Sunny's Bar** (253 Conover Street, between Beard & Reed Streets, 1-718 625 8211) remains keeper of the 'hood's gritty waterfront vibe.

A scattering of quirky local shops includes **Metal & Thread** (398 Van Brunt Street, between Coffey & Dikeman Streets, 1-718 414 9651, www.metalthread.com, closed Tue), which artfully juxtaposes a mix of locally made and vintage items, and the fastidiously curated antique jewellery shop **Erie Basin** (388 Van Brunt Street, at Dikeman Street, 1-718 554 6147, www.eriebasin.com, closed Mon, Tue, Sun).

To check out the work of local artists, look for the word 'Gallery' hand-scrawled on the doors of the **Kentler International Drawing Space** (353 Van Brunt Street, between Wolcott & Dikeman Streets, 1-718 875 2098, www.kentlergallery.org, closed Mon-Wed), or, at weekends, visit the **Brooklyn Waterfront Artists Coalition**'s 25,000-square-foot exhibition space (499 Van Brunt Street, at Beard Street Pier, 1-718 596 2507, www.bwac.org) in a Civil War-era warehouse on the pier just south of Fairway. BWAC hosts large group shows in the spring and autumn.

PARK SLOPE & PROSPECT HEIGHTS

Park Slope – Subway F to 7th Avenue, 15th Street-Prospect Park; F, G to Fourth Ave-9th Street; R to Union Street. Prospect Heights – Subway B, Q, Franklin Avenue S to Prospect

EXPLORE

**INSIDE TRACK
THE TRUCK STOPS HERE**

At weekends from May through October, Latin American food trucks descend on the corner of Bay and Clinton Streets, adjacent to the **Red Hook Ballfields** (www.redhook foodvendors.com), to serve up some of the best street food in the city, including Ecuadoran *ceviche*, Salvadoran *papusas*, and Mexican tacos and *huaraches*. Originally catering to soccer players, the vendors now attract foodies from all over.

Park; 2, 3 to Eastern Parkway-Brooklyn Museum or Grand Army Plaza; M, R to 25th Street.

Bustling with lively children, baby strollers and the parents who cart them around, **Park Slope** houses hip, young families in Victorian brownstones and feeds them organically from the nation's oldest working food co-operative (only open to members). The neighbourhood's intellectual, progressive-minded and lefty political heritage is palpable; local residents include Hollywood actors (Maggie Gyllenhaal and Peter Sarsgaard, John Turturro and Steve Buscemi, among others) and famous authors (Paul Auster and Jonathan Safran Foer).

Fifth Avenue is the prime locale for restaurants and hip bars. Locals flock to the always-packed Venetian mainstay **Al di là** (*see p174*) and late-night favourite **Blue Ribbon Brooklyn** (no.280, between Garfield Place & 1st Street, 1-718 840 0404), the Brooklyn outpost of an acclaimed New York mini-chain (www.blueribbonrestaurants.com). Interesting shops can be found all along Fifth Avenue too, including urban gear depot **Brooklyn Industries** (no.206, at Union Street, 1-718 789 2764, www.brooklynindustries.com) and **Cog & Pearl** (no.190, at Sackett Street, 1-718 623 8200, www.cogandpearl.com), offering artist-made items including jewellery, fine art, home accessories and greeting cards. Stop by the wonderful purveyor of capes, X-ray goggles and gallon tins of Immortality, **Brooklyn Superhero Supply Company** (no. 372, between 5th & 6th Streets, 1-718 499 9884) – its secret identity is a non-profit kids' writing centre, concealed in the back.

Park Slope's lesbian community is one of the Big Apple's strongest. You can explore Sapphic lore at the **Lesbian Herstory Archives** (*see p266*), then do field research at **Ginger's Bar** (*see p273*). Park Slope's gay gents frequent **Excelsior** (*see p273*), a low-key bar with a vibrant jukebox and lush back garden. And

whether you're straight or gay, you'll want to head off the beaten path to clubby bar **Union Hall** (*see p188*), which has its own indoor bocce courts and a live music space downstairs.

The western edge of Prospect Park is a section of the landmarked **Park Slope Historic District**. Brownstones and several fine examples of Romanesque Revival and Queen Anne residences grace these streets. Particularly charming are the brick edifices that line Carroll Street, Montgomery Place and Berkeley Place. Fans of writer-director Noah Baumbach, who grew up in these parts, may recognise the locale from 2005 hit *The Squid and the Whale*, much of which was set here.

Central Park may be bigger and far more famous, but **Prospect Park** (main entrance at Grand Army Plaza, Prospect Heights, 1-718 965 8999, www.prospectpark.org) has a more rustic quality. By taking a short stroll into its lush green expanse, you may forget you're in the midst of a bustling metropolis. This masterpiece, which designers Frederick Law Olmsted and Calvert Vaux said was more in line with their vision than Central Park, is a great spot for birdwatching, especially with a little guidance from the **Prospect Park Audubon Center at the Boathouse** (park entrance on Ocean Avenue, at Lincoln Road, 1-718 287 3400, closed Mon-Wed Apr-mid Dec, Mon-Fri mid Jan-Mar). The centre offers an excellent seasonal tour of Prospect Park Lake on the electric boat *Independence*. Alternatively, you can pretend you've left the city altogether by hiking along the paths of the **Ravine District** (park entrances on Prospect Park West, at 3rd, 9th & 15th Streets), a landscape of dense woods, waterfalls and stone bridges in the park's centre.

The rolling green park was created with equestrians in mind; you can saddle a horse at the nearby **Kensington Stables** (*see p333*) or hop on a bike and pedal alongside Rollerbladers and runners. Children enjoy riding the hand-carved horses at the antique carousel (Flatbush Avenue, at Empire Boulevard) and seeing real animals in the **Prospect Park Zoo** (park entrance on Flatbush Avenue, near Ocean Avenue, Prospect Heights, 1-718 399 7339). A 15-minute walk from Prospect Park is the verdant necropolis of **Green-Wood Cemetery** (*see p121*).

Near the main entrance to Prospect Park sits the massive Civil War memorial arch at **Grand Army Plaza** (intersection of Flatbush Avenue, Eastern Parkway & Prospect Park West) and the central branch of the **Brooklyn Public Library** (10 Grand Army Plaza, Prospect Heights, 1-718 230 2100). The library's central Brooklyn Collection includes thousands of artefacts and photos tracing the borough's history. Around the corner are the tranquil **Brooklyn Botanic Garden** and the **Brooklyn Museum** (for both, *see below*), which has a renowned Egyptian collection and a section devoted to feminist art among its many attractions.

To the north, is the borough's biggest and most prominent new development, the 22-acre Atlantic Yards complex, on the edge of downtown Brooklyn, which encompasses more than 6,000 (yet-to-be-built) apartments and the Barclays Center, a major concert venue and the new home of the New Jersey Nets. Despite nine years of local opposition, contentious legal battles and the recession, the venue was christened by Jay-Z in September 2012.

Brooklyn Botanic Garden

1000 Washington Avenue, at Eastern Parkway, Prospect Heights (1-718 623 7200, www.bbg.org). Subway B, Q, Franklin Avenue S to Prospect Park; 2, 3 to Eastern Parkway-Brooklyn Museum. **Open** *Mar-Oct* 8am-6pm Tue-Fri; 10am-6pm Sat, Sun. *Nov-Feb* 8am-4.30pm Tue-Fri; 10am-4.30pm Sat, Sun. **Admission** $10; $5 reductions; free under-12s. Free Tue; 10am-noon Sat. **Credit** DC, MC, V. **Map** p411 U11.

This 52-acre haven of luscious greenery was founded in 1910. In spring, when Sakura Matsuri (*see p29*), the annual Cherry Blossom Festival, takes place, prize buds and Japanese culture are in full bloom, but the serene Japanese Hill-and-Pond Garden is worth a visit in any season. The cool new visitor centre has a roof covered in 45,000 plants.

★ Brooklyn Museum

200 Eastern Parkway, at Washington Avenue, Prospect Heights (1-718 638 5000, www.brooklyn museum.org). Subway 2, 3 to Eastern Parkway-Brooklyn Museum. **Open** 11am-6pm Wed; 11am-10pm Thur; 11am-6pm Fri-Sun; 11am-11pm 1st Sat of mth (except Sept). **Admission** Suggested donation $12; $8 reductions; free under-12s. Free 5-11pm 1st Sat of mth (except Sept). **Credit** AmEx, MC, V. **Map** p411 U11.

While most visitors tend to overlook the Brooklyn Museum, getting their artistic fix from Manhattan's more illustrious collections, the borough's premier institution is one of the city's cultural gems. It presents a tranquil alternative to Manhattan's bigger-name spaces and it's rarely crowded.

Among the museum's many assets are the third-floor Egyptian galleries (the entire collection is one of the finest outside Egypt and numbers more than 8,000 objects). Highlights include the resplendent cartonnage of the priest Nespanetjerenpere; a rare terracotta female figure from 3500-3400 BC; and the Mummy Chamber, an installation of 170 objects related to the post-mortem practice, including human and animal mummies. Also on this level, master-works by Cézanne, Monet and Degas, part of an impressive European art collection, are displayed in

the museum's skylighted Beaux-Arts Court. The Elizabeth A Sackler Center for Feminist Art on the fourth floor is dominated by American artist Judy Chicago's monumental mixed-media installation, *The Dinner Party* (1974-79); its centrepiece is a massive, triangular 'table' with 39 place settings, each representing important women down the ages. The fifth floor is devoted to American works, including Albert Bierstadt's immense *A Storm in the Rocky Mountains, Mt Rosalie*, and the Visible Storage-Study Center, where paintings, furniture and other objects are intriguingly juxtaposed.

It's always worth checking the varied schedule of temporary shows; a 2013 highlight is a major exhibition of John Singer Sargent watercolours (5 Apr-28 July).

★ FREE Green-Wood Cemetery

Fifth Avenue, at 25th Street, Sunset Park (1-718 768 7300, www.green-wood.com). Subway M, R to 25th Street. **Open** varies by season; usually 8am-5pm daily. **Admission** free. **Map** p411 S13.
See p114 **Walk**.

WILLIAMSBURG & BUSHWICK

Williamsburg – Subway G to Metropolitan Avenue; J, M, Z to Marcy Avenue; L to Bedford Avenue or Lorimer Street. Bushwick – Subway L to Jefferson Street or Morgan Avenue.

With a thriving music scene and an abundance of laid-back bars, small galleries and independent shops, **Williamsburg** – or 'Billyburg' as it's affectionately known – channels the East Village (just one stop away on the L train) in its heyday. But the area teeters on the brink of (or, some argue, has already fallen into) hipster cliché. Long before the trendsetters invaded, Williamsburg's waterfront location made it ideal for industry. When the Erie Canal linked the Atlantic Ocean to the Great Lakes in 1825, the area became a bustling port. Companies such as Pfizer and Domino Sugar started here, but businesses had begun to abandon the area's huge industrial spaces by the late 20th century. The Domino refinery closed in 2004, though its signature sign is still a local landmark.

Bedford Avenue is the neighbourhood's main thoroughfare. By day, the epicentre of the strip is the **Bedford MiniMall** (no.218, between North 4th & North 5th Streets) – you won't find a Gap or Starbucks here, but you will be able to contemplate a beer selection that will make your head spin at **Spuyten Duyvil Grocery** (1-718 384 1520, closed Mon), browse an exceptionally edited selection of books and magazines at **Spoonbill & Sugartown, Booksellers** (1-718 387-7322, www.spoonbillbooks.com) and drink some of the

EXPLORE

best iced coffee around at the **Verb Café** (1-718 599 0977). The area has a constantly shifting array of cafés and eateries; inexpensive options include organic haven **Ella Café** (177 Bedford Avenue, between North 7th & North 8th Streets, 1-718 218 8079) and daytime-only **Egg**, which serves breakfast until 6pm (135 North 5th Street, at Bedford Avenue, 1-718 302 5151, www.pigandegg.com). South of the Williamsburg Bridge on Broadway, **Marlow & Sons** (*see p175*) was a pioneer in the kind of rustic aesthetic and farm-to-table fare that's become the knee-jerk norm in Kings County. Nearby, New York institution **Peter Luger** (*see p175*) grills what most carnivores consider to be the best steak in the city. For our pick of the neighbourhood's many bars, *see pp187-189*.

You'll find chic shops dotted around the area, including innovative home-design emporium **The Future Perfect** (*see p220*) and **In God We Trust** (*see p201*), which combines local-appropriate clothes for both genders with witty accessories and gifts. The 'hood also has more than 25 art galleries, which stay open late on the second Friday of every month. Pick up the free gallery guide *Wagmag* at local shops and cafés or visit www.wagmag.org for listings. However, as artists are priced out of the area, more experimental spaces have taken root in the warehouses of Bushwick to the west.

Billyburg is famously band central. Local rock bands and touring indie darlings play at **Music Hall of Williamsburg**, **Pete's Candy Store** and **Knitting Factory Brooklyn** (for all, *see pp288-289*).

Those with a nostalgic bent will enjoy quirky repository of NYC ephemera, **City Reliquary** (*see right*). Another local gem is the **Brooklyn Brewery** (79 North 11th Street, between Berry Street & Wythe Avenue, 1-718 486 7422, www.brooklynbrewery.com), housed in a former ironworks. Visit during the happy 'hour' (Fridays 6-11pm) for $4 drafts or take a tour on weekends (hourly 1-5pm Sat; 1-4pm Sun).

After condo development took hold in the neighbourhood, boutique hotels weren't far behind. The new **Wythe Hotel** (*see p248*), which houses popular local restaurant **Reynards**, successfully embodies the 'Burg's elusive hip factor.

With Williamsburg approaching hipster saturation point and rents rising accordingly, neighbouring **Bushwick** has caught on as a cheap(er) place for digs, attracting an arty crowd to its industrial spaces. In late spring (1, 2 June in 2013), the annual **Bushwick Open Studios** (www.artsinbushwick.org) gives you a glimpse inside more than 500 artists' work spaces, but you'll also see plenty of street art in the vicinity of the Morgan Avenue subway stop. Bounded by Bushwick Avenue to the

north-west and Broadway to the south-west, this traditionally Latino neighbourhood has begun to sprout coffee shops and vintage stores over the last few years, not to mention restaurants, such as intimate faux-rustic hotspot **Northeast Kingdom** (18 Wyckoff Avenue, at Troutman Street, 1-718 386 3864, www.north-east kingdom.com) and acclaimed locavore eaterie **Roberta's** (*see p175*). Afterwards, slake your thirst in one of the vinyl car-seat booths at the **Wreck Room** (940 Flushing Avenue, at Evergreen Avenue, 1-718 418 6347).

City Reliquary

370 Metropolitan Avenue, at Havemeyer Street (1-718 782 4842, www.cityreliquary.org). Subway G to Metropolitan Avenue; L to Lorimer Street. **Open** noon-6pm Thur-Sun. **Admission** *Suggested donation* $5. **Credit** ($10 min) AmEx, MC, V. **Map** p411 U8.

This not-for-profit mini-museum of New York history reopened in 2012 after a renovation that coincided with its ten-year anniversary. Peruse Gotham ephemera such as memorabilia from both NYC World's Fairs, a vintage barber-shop diorama furnished with a chair from Barber Hall of Famer Antonio Nobile's Bay Ridge, Brooklyn, shop, and a transplanted Chinatown newsstand. A new gift shop sells locally made wares like borough-themed pillows and quilts covered in street maps.

FORT GREENE

Subway B, Q, R to DeKalb Avenue; B, D, N, Q, R, 2, 3, 4, 5 to Atlantic Avenue-Barclays Center; C to Lafayette Avenue; G to Fulton Street or Clinton-Washington Avenues.

With its stately Victorian brownstones and other grand buildings, Fort Greene has undergone a major revival over the past two decades. It has long been a centre of African-American life and business – Spike Lee, Branford Marsalis and Chris Rock have all lived here. **Fort Greene Park** (from Myrtle to DeKalb Avenues, between St Edwards Street & Washington Park) was conceived in 1846 at the behest of poet Walt Whitman (then editor of the *Brooklyn Daily Eagle*); its masterplan was fully realised by Olmsted and Vaux in 1867.

At the centre of the park stands the Prison Ship Martyrs Monument, erected in 1909 (from a design by Stanford White) in memory of 11,000 American prisoners who died on squalid British ships that were anchored nearby during the Revolutionary War.

Despite its name, the 34-floor **Williamsburgh Savings Bank**, located at the corner of Atlantic and Flatbush Avenues, is in Fort Greene, not Williamsburg. The 512-foot-high structure was long the tallest in the borough and, with its

Williamsburg.

four-sided clocktower, one of the most recognisable features of the Brooklyn skyline. The 1927 building has now been renamed One Hanson Place, and converted into (what else?) luxury condominiums.

Every Saturday, meandering Brooklynites – and a slew of other New Yorkers – hit the **Brooklyn Flea** (*see p211* **Market Forces**) in the yard of a public high school on Lafayette Avenue between Clermont & Vanderbilt Avenues. The combination of antiques, vintage clothes, indie crafts and food has proved so popular it's sparked several spin-offs and other markets in the borough.

Though originally founded in Brooklyn Heights, the **Brooklyn Academy of Music** (*see p299*) moved to its current site on Fort Greene's southern border in 1901. America's oldest operating performing arts centre, BAM was the home of the Metropolitan Opera until 1921; today, it's known for ambitious cultural performances of all varieties that draw big audiences from throughout the metropolitan area. Almost as famous is the cheesecake at nearby **Junior's Restaurant** (386 Flatbush Avenue, at DeKalb Avenue,1-718 852 5257).

In addition to some funky shops, a slew of restaurants can be found on or near **DeKalb Avenue**, including South African **Madiba Restaurant** (no.195, between Carlton Avenue & Adelphi Street, 1-718 855 9190, www. madibarestaurant.com); lively bistro **Chez**

Oskar (no.211, at Adelphi Street, 1-718 852 6250, www.chezoskar.com); and French-accented fave **iCi** (no.246, at Vanderbilt Avenue, 1-718 789 2778, www.icirestaurant.com).

CONEY ISLAND & BRIGHTON BEACH

Subway B, Q to Brighton Beach; D, F, N, Q to Coney Island-Stillwell Avenue; F to Neptune Avenue; F, Q to West 8th Street-NY Aquarium.

Combining old-time fairground attractions, new amusement park rides and traditional seaside pleasures against a gritty urban backdrop, Coney Island is a strange hybrid in the early stages of a revitalisation plan that also includes improvements to the surrounding residential neighbourhood (*see p124* **New Thrills at the Old Fairground**).

Nostalgic visitors will enjoy a stroll along the three-mile-long boardwalk, lined with corny carnival games, souvenir shops and a seasonal outpost of **Nathan's Famous** hot dog stand – the main location is at 1310 Surf Avenue, at Stillwell Avenue (1-718 946 2202). Both spots serve the sizzling, juicy dogs that made its name in 1916, and **Nathan's Famous Fourth of July Hot Dog Eating Contest** (*see p33*) always draws a crowd. The iconic 1941 Parachute Jump has been restored and is illuminated by night. Other (still operational) holdouts from the past include the **Cyclone**, a whiplash-inducing rollercoaster opened in 1927, and the 1918 **Wonder Wheel** – both protected landmarks. Non-profit arts organisation Coney Island USA keeps the torch burning for 20th-century-style attractions at its **Coney Island Museum** with the seasonal Sideshows by the Seashore, as well as kitsch summer spectacle the **Mermaid Parade** (*see p32*). The local baseball team, **Brooklyn Cyclones** (*see p328*), play at the seaside **MCU Park**.

Walk left along the boardwalk from Coney Island and you'll reach **Brighton Beach**, New York's Little Odessa. Groups of Russian expats (the display of big hair and garish fashion can be jaw-dropping) crowd semi-outdoor eateries such as **Tatiana** (3152 Brighton 6th Street, at the Boardwalk, 1-718 891 5151) – at night, it morphs into a glitzy club. A better, if less picturesquely placed, bet is **Primorski** (282 Brighton Beach Avenue, between Brighton 2nd & Brighton 3rd Streets, 1-718 891 3111), north of the seafront.

Coney Island Museum

1208 Surf Avenue, at 12th Street, Coney Island, Brooklyn (1-718 372 5159, www.coneyisland.com). Subway D, F, N, Q to Coney Island-Stillwell Avenue. **Open** *Museum* noon-6pm Sat, Sun. *Shows* vary. **Admission** *Museum* $5. *Shows* $5-$15. **Credit** AmEx, Disc, MC, V.

Housed in a landmarked 1917 building, the Coney Island Museum acts as both a repository of the seaside district's past and the focus of its current alternative culture. Closed for renovation at time of writing, the museum is due to reopen in spring 2013. Between early May and the middle of September, Sideshows by the Seashore showcases the talents of such legendary freaks as human pincushion Scott Baker (aka the Twisted Shockmeister), snake charmer Serpentina and fire eater Insectavora, while Burlesque at the Beach slinks on to the stage on summer Thursday and Friday nights (see website for the schedule). In October, the entire venue morphs into Creepshow at the Freakshow – a Halloween-themed extravaganza.

New Thrills at the Old Fairground

Coney Island rides again.

In its heyday, from the turn of the century until World War II, **Coney Island** was New York City's playground, drawing millions each year to its seaside amusement parks Dreamland, Luna Park and Steeplechase Park. The first two were destroyed by fire (Dreamland in 1911 and Luna Park in 1944) and not rebuilt, while Steeplechase Park staggered on until 1964. Astroland was built in 1962 in the euphoria of the World's Fair, went up in flames in 1975 and was rebuilt, only to shutter in 2008.

A few years before, a developer had bought about half the area's entertainment district with a view to transforming it into a glitzy, Las Vegas-style resort, with hotels and condos, as well as restaurants, shops and rides. But a standoff with municipal planners halted progress. Then, in 2009, the city agreed to buy almost seven acres near the boardwalk that would form the core of a 27-acre amusement district. A new incarnation of Luna Park (www.luna parknyc.com) opened in summer 2010, with such adrenaline-pumping attractions as the Air Race, which simulates the movement of a fighter aircraft, and the Brooklyn Flyer, which spins riders nearly 100 feet above ground. A year later, the thrill quotient was bumped up with the Scream Zone, featuring the first large-scale rollercoasters to debut since the 1927

Cyclone. The Steeplechase is modelled after the original Coney Island ride of the same name; riders sit atop horses with their legs locked in place, but where the previous version was propelled by gravity, this electric twister takes you from zero to 40mph in less than two seconds. More attractions, including the Boardwalk Flight, a 110-foot free-fall ride, were added for the 2012 season.

The latest component of the city's Coney Island Revitalization Plan is a 57,000-square-foot addition to the New York Aquarium. The building, which will house a new 'Ocean Wonders: Sharks!' exhibition and have such cool design features as a 1,101-foot-long 'shimmer' wall that will wrap the exterior, is set to open in 2015. While there's no fast track to the complete revitalisation of the area, the 'poor man's Riviera' is looking a lot less down at heel.

Queens

The fabled ethnic food destination is also the city's film industry hub.

Queens has not traditionally been on most visitors' must-see list – though many pass through the borough if they fly into JFK or La Guardia airports. Now, however, cultural institutions, such as the Museum of Modern Art-affiliated MoMA PS1 and the revamped Museum of the Moving Image, are drawing both out-of-towners and Manhattanites across the Ed Koch Queensboro Bridge.

Queens is also an increasingly popular gastronomic destination. The city's largest borough is the country's most diverse urban area, with almost half its 2.3 million residents hailing from nearly 150 nations. Not for nothing is the elevated 7 subway line that serves these parts nicknamed the 'International Express'. **Astoria** is home to Greek tavernas and Brazilian *churrascarias*; **Jackson Heights** provides Indian, Thai and South American eateries; and **Flushing** boasts the city's second largest Chinatown.

Map p412	**Restaurants &**
Hotels p249	**cafés** p176
	Bars p189

EXPLORE

LONG ISLAND CITY

Subway E, M to Court Square-23rd Street; G to 21st Street; 7 to Vernon Boulevard-Jackson Avenue or 45th Road-Court House Square.

Just across the East River from Manhattan, Long Island City has been touted as the 'next Williamsburg' (the hipster Brooklyn enclave; *see p121*) for so long that several other 'hoods have since claimed and passed on the mantle. In truth, LIC's proximity to midtown and the proliferation of modern apartment towers on the waterfront have proved more of a draw to upwardly mobile professionals and young families than cutting-edge cool hunters. Nevertheless, the neighbourhood has one of the city's most adventurous museums and several interesting galleries and performance spaces. It's also an active player in the city's film industry. *Broadway Danny Rose* (1984) and *Do the Right Thing* (1989) are among the

movies shot at **Silvercup Studios** (42-22 22nd Street, between 43rd & 44th Avenues, www. silvercupstudios.com), a former bread factory in an industrial section by the Ed Koch Queensboro Bridge. The studios have also been home to some of the most iconic New York-set (and New Jersey-set) TV shows: *Sex and the City* (the series and both movies), *The Sopranos* and *Girls*.

Fronting the main stretch of residential riverside development, **Gantry Plaza State Park** (48th Avenue, at Center Boulevard) commands an impressive panorama of midtown Manhattan. The 12-acre park takes its name from the hulking industrial gantries that still stand watch over the piers and were used to haul cargo from rail barges. Wavy deckchairs offer direct views of the United Nations across the East River. While Vernon Avenue is the neighbourhood's prime restaurant, retail and bar hub, the **Waterfront Crabhouse** (2-03 Borden Avenue, at 2nd Street, 1-718 729 4862), an old-time saloon and seafood restaurant in an

1880s brick building, evokes an earlier time with a jumble of bric-a-brac dangling from the dining room ceiling. **Testaccio** (47-30 Vernon Boulevard, between 47th Road & 48th Avenue, 1-718 937 2900) has won praise for its modern Roman cuisine. For liquid refreshments, **Communitea** (47-02 Vernon Boulevard, at 47th Avenue, 1-718 729 7708) offers more than 40 loose-leaf teas (and locally roasted coffee). If you want something stronger, sleuth out the discreet entrance to comfortable cocktail den **Dutch Kills** (27-24 Jackson Avenue; see p189).

The neighbourhood's cultural jewel is the progressive art institution **MoMA PS1** (see right). In summer months, the courtyard of the museum becomes a dance-music hub with its Saturday-afternoon **Warm Up** parties (see p277). Diagonally opposite on Jackson Avenue is the city's most spectacular display of street art: the exterior of **5Pointz Aerosol Art Center** (www.5ptz.com), an old warehouse on Jackson Avenue between Crane and Davis Streets, is completely covered in more than 350 vivid murals by graffiti artists from around the world. Admire it while you can because the landlord has plans to develop new apartment blocks on the site. In complete contrast, a well-preserved block of 19th-century houses constitutes the **Hunter's Point Historic District** (45th Avenue, between 21st & 23rd Streets). With several artists' studio complexes lodged in Long Island City, a nascent art scene has taken hold. **SculptureCenter** (see right), housed in a dramatic converted industrial space, is a great place to see new work, while the **Fisher Landau Center** (38-27 30th Street, between 38th and 39th Avenues, 1-718 937 0727) showcases the 1,500-piece contemporary art collection of Emily Fisher Landau. For details of open-studio events in the neighbourhood, check out www.licartists.org.

It was only a matter of time before Long Island City's rampant residential development spread to hotels – the **Z NYC Hotel** (see p249) has been designed so that every room faces the river.

★ MoMA PS1

22-25 Jackson Avenue, at 46th Avenue (1-718 784 2084, www.momaps1.org). Subway E, M to Court Square-23rd Street; G to 21st Street; 7 to 45th Road-Court House Square. **Open** noon-6pm Mon, Thur-Sun. **Admission** *Suggested donation* $10; $5 reductions. **Credit** AmEx, DC, MC, V. **Map** p412 V5.

In a distinctive Romanesque Revival building, MoMA PS1 mounts cutting-edge shows and hosts an acclaimed international studio programme. Be sure to peek into the stairwells, as artwork turns up in unexpected corners of the former public school. The contemporary art centre became an affiliate of MoMA in 1999, and the two institutions sometimes stage collaborative exhibitions. The museum's DJed summer Warm Up parties (see p277) are an unmissable fixture of the city's dance-music scene, and its new eaterie M Wells Dinette (see p176) is a foodie destination.

★ SculptureCenter

44-19 Purves Street, at Jackson Avenue (1-718 361 1750, www.sculpture-center.org). Subway E, M to Court Square-23rd Street; G to Long Island City-Court Square; 7 to 45th Road-Court House Square. **Open** 11am-6pm Mon, Thur-Sun. **Admission** *Suggested donation* $5. **Map** p412 V5.

One of the best places in New York City to see sculpture by blossoming and mid-career artists, this non-profit space – housed inside an impressive former trolley-repair shop that was redesigned by acclaimed architect Maya Lin in 2002 – is known for its very broad definition of the discipline.

ASTORIA

Subway R, M to Steinway Street; N, Q to Broadway, 30th Avenue, 36th Avenue or Astoria-Ditmars Boulevard.

A lively, traditionally Greek and Italian neighbourhood, Astoria has over the last few decades seen an influx of Brazilians, Bangladeshis, Eastern Europeans, Colombians and Egyptians; they've been joined by post-grads sharing row-house digs. A 15-minute downhill hike from Broadway subway station towards Manhattan brings you to the **Noguchi Museum** (see p127), which was created by the visionary sculptor. Nearby lies the **Socrates Sculpture Park** (Broadway, at Vernon Boulevard, www.socratessculpturepark.org), a riverfront art space in an industrial setting with great views of Manhattan.

Gantry Plaza State Park.
See p125.

In the early days of cinema, Astoria was a major celluloid star. Taking advantage of its proximity to talent-laden Broadway, Famous Players-Lasky (later Paramount Pictures) opened its first studios in the neighbourhood in 1920. Portions of Valentino's blockbuster *The Sheikh* (1921) were filmed there, and the studio produced the Marx Brothers' *Animal Crackers* (1930) and *The Cocoanuts* (1929) before Paramount moved its operations west. After years of neglect, the studios were declared a National Historic Landmark in 1976, and, in 1982, developer George S Kaufman bought the site and created **Kaufman Astoria Studios** (34-12 36th Street, between 34th & 35th Avenues, www.kaufmanastoria.com). Scenes for numerous films, including *The Taking of Pelham 1 2 3* (2009) and *Wall Street: Money Never Sleeps* (2010) were shot there, and the studios are also home to long-running kids' TV show *Sesame Street*. The recently expanded **Museum of the Moving Image** (*see p128*) is across the street.

Still New York's Greek-American stronghold, Astoria is well known for Hellenic eateries specialising in impeccably grilled seafood. **Elias Corner** (24-02 31st Street, at 24th Street, 1-718 932 1510) serves meze and a catch of the day in a breezy garden setting, while **Athens Café** (32-07 30th Avenue, between 32nd & 33rd Streets, 1-718 626 2164) is the neighbourhood's social nexus and a terrific place to stop for Greek coffee and pastries. One of the city's last central European beer gardens, **Bohemian Hall & Beer Garden** (29-19 24th Avenue, at 29th Street; *see p189*) offers Czech-style dining and drinking. Arrive early on warm weekends to nab a picnic table in the expansive, linden tree-shaded yard. Cocktail aficionados and local hipsters flock to gastropub **Sweet Afton** (30-09 34th Street, between 30th & 31st Avenues, 1-718 777 2570).

You can puff on a shisha – a (legal) hookah pipe – with thick Turkish coffee in the cafés of 'Little Egypt' along Steinway Street, between 28th Avenue and Astoria Boulevard. At the end of the N and Q subway lines (Astoria-Ditmars Boulevard), walk west to Astoria Park (from Astoria Park South to Ditmars Boulevard, between Shore Boulevard & 19th Street) for its dramatic views of two bridges: the Robert F Kennedy Bridge (formerly the Triborough), Robert Moses's automotive labyrinth connecting Queens, the Bronx and Manhattan; and the 1916 Hell Gate Bridge, a steel single-arch tour de force and template for the Sydney Harbour Bridge. On the area's north-east fringes, you can take a tour (by appointment) of the still-thriving red-brick 1871 piano factory **Steinway & Sons** (1 Steinway Place, between 19th Avenue & 38th Street, 1-718 721 2600).

★ Noguchi Museum

9-01 33rd Road, between Vernon Boulevard & 10th Street (1-718 204 7088, www.noguchi.org). Subway N, Q to Broadway, then 15min walk or Q104 bus to 11th Street; 7 to Vernon Boulevard-Jackson Avenue, then Q103 bus to 10th Street. **Open** 10am-5pm Wed-Fri; 11am-6pm Sat, Sun. **Admission** $10; $5 reductions; free under-12s; pay what you wish 1st Fri of the mth. No pushchairs/strollers. **Credit** AmEx, MC, V. **Map** p412 V3.

When Japanese-American sculptor and designer Isamu Noguchi (1904-88) opened his Queens museum in 1985, he became the first living artist in the US to establish such an institution. The Noguchi Museum occupies a former photo-engraving plant across the street from the studio he had occupied since the 1960s, which allowed him to be close to stone and metal suppliers along Vernon Boulevard. Noguchi designed the entire building to be a meditative oasis amid its gritty, industrial setting. Ten galleries – spread over two floors – and an outdoor space are populated with his sculptures, as well as drawn, painted and collaged studies, architectural models, and stage and furniture designs. A shuttle service from Manhattan is available on Sundays (call or see the website for more information).

EXPLORE

Museum of the Moving Image

35th Avenue, at 36th Street (1-718 777 6888, www.movingimage.us). Subway R, M to Steinway Street; N, Q to 36th Avenue. **Open** *Galleries* 10.30am-5pm Tue-Thur; 10.30am-8pm Fri; 10.30am-7pm Sat, Sun. **Admission** $12; $6-$9 reductions; free 4-8pm Fri. **Credit** AmEx, MC, V. **Map** p412 W4.
See p129 **Profile.**

JACKSON HEIGHTS

Subway E, F, M, R to Jackson Heights-Roosevelt Avenue; 7 to 74th Street-Broadway.

Dizzying even by Queens standards, Jackson Heights' multiculturalism gives it an energy all its own. Little India greets you with a cluster of small shops on 74th Street between 37th Road and 37th Avenue, selling Indian music, Bollywood DVDs, saris and glitzy jewellery. But the main appeal for visitors is culinary. The unofficial HQ of the Indian expat community, **Jackson Diner** (*see p176*) serves sumptuous curries. For more intimate dining, try **Talk of the Town** (37-21 72nd Street, between Broadway and 37th Avenue, 1-718 533 9131), whose speciality is Bombay-style 'sizzlers', sautéed meat or fish glazed with a soy-chilli sauce. Along with adjoining Elmhurst, Jackson Heights has also welcomed waves of Latin American immigrants. Mexicans, Colombians and Argentinians are old-school in these parts: get a taste of Buenos Aires at the exuberant, *fútbol*-themed **Boca Junior Argentinian Steakhouse** (81-08 Queens Boulevard, at

51st Avenue, Elmhurst, 1-718 429 2077), or stop by **Taqueria Coatzingo** (76-05 Roosevelt Avenue, between 76th & 77th Streets, 1-718 424 1977) for meaty tacos (*al pastor*, slow-roasted goat and tongue) with a definite edge over the other holes-in-the-wall under the elevated 7 train. The Thai contingent is reflected in several fine eateries: **Arunee Thai Cuisine** (37-68 79th Street, between Roosevelt & 37th Avenues, 1-718 205 5559) doesn't hold back with the spices – or the Thai music videos.

The neighbourhood claims a roughly 30-square-block landmark district of mock Tudor and neo-Gothic-style co-op apartment buildings with tree-dotted lawns and park-like courtyards. There are good examples of these 1920s beauties on 70th Street, between 34th Avenue and Northern Boulevard, and on 34th Avenue, between 76th and 77th Streets, and between 80th and 81st Streets.

FLUSHING

Subway 7 to Flushing-Main Street, 103rd Street-Corona Plaza, 111th Street or Mets-Willets Point.

Egalitarian Dutchmen staked their claim to 'Vlissingen' in the 1600s and were shortly joined by pacifist Friends, or Quakers, seeking religious freedom in the New World. These religious settlers promulgated the Flushing Remonstrance, a groundbreaking 1657 edict extending 'the law of love, peace and liberty' to Jews and Muslims. It's now regarded as a forerunner of the United States Constitution's First Amendment. The plain wooden **Old Quaker Meeting House** (137-16 Northern Boulevard, between Main & Union Streets), built in 1694, creates a startling juxtaposition to the prosperous Chinatown that rings its weathered wooden walls. The neighbourhood has hundreds of temples and churches used by immigrants from Korea, China and South Asia. **St George's Church** (135-32 38th Avenue, between Main & Prince Streets, 1-718 359 1171), an Episcopalian church with a striking steeple, chartered by King George III, was once a dominant site, but now competes for attention with restaurants and shops. The interior is worth a brief visit if only to see the two examples of Queens-made Tiffany stained glass and to hear church services in Caribbean-accented English, Chinese and Spanish. Ambitious explorers will want to make the jaunt south to the **Hindu Temple Society** (45-57 Bowne Street, between Holly & 45th Avenues, 1-718 460 8484), a Ganesh temple whose ornate exterior was hand-carved in India.

Most visitors, however, come for the restaurants and dumpling stalls of Flushing's sprawling **Chinatown**, which has a more

Flushing.

EXPLORE

Profile Museum of the Moving Image

The state-of-the-art institution proves Queens is where the action is.

The **Museum of the Moving Image** reopened in 2011 after a major renovation that doubled its size and sealed its reputation as one of the world's finest museums dedicated to TV, film and video. The collection and screening facilities are housed in one of the buildings of the Astoria Studios complex, which was the New York production headquarters of Paramount Pictures before talkies moved the industry to Hollywood. Architect Thomas Leeser's sleek new design integrates moving pictures into the space itself. As visitors pass through the mirrored, screen-like entrance into the lobby, they'll encounter a panoramic video installation of constantly changing work.

The museum's film curator, David Schwartz, compares walking into its new 267-seat theatre to 'entering a spaceship and going on a voyage'; the effect is achieved with vibrant blue wraparound panels, a steep seating rake and flawless acoustics (no subway rumbles here), allowing for a completely immersive experience. Every conceivable format can be screened here, from high-definition 3-D pictures to silent classics (there's a mini orchestra pit for accompaniment).

Meanwhile, a smaller, 68-seat screening room allows for more intimate showings of indie and experimental films.

The upgraded core exhibition, 'Behind the Screen', which explores all the nuances of the movie and TV programme-making process, is now spread over the second and third floors. Not only can you see artefacts from more than 1,000 productions (including the super-creepy stunt doll used in *The Exorcist*, with full head-rotating capabilities, and the famous diner booth from *Seinfeld*), it's now packed with interactive displays. You can insert sound effects into film scenes, record your voice into a part of *The Wizard of Oz*, or even make a short animated film and email it to yourself. Learn about live video editing in the TV control room, where 14 different camera feeds from a Mets game show how a director splices the pieces together.

Astoria Studios has certainly come a long way from the days of the silent movie.

---

affluent demographic than its Manhattan counterpart – case in point is the gleaming **New World Mall** (136-20 Roosevelt Avenue, at Main Street, www.newworldmallny.com) and its opulent third-floor dim sum palace, **Grand Restaurant** (1-718 321 8258). Downstairs, at the spacious **JMart** supermarket, peruse such exotic produce as the formidably prickled durian and the notoriously elusive mangosteen, or gawk at buckets full of live eels and frogs. **Fu Run** (40-09 Prince Street, between Roosevelt Avenue & 40th Road, 1-718 321 1363) has been gaining acclaim for its Northern-style cuisine, while the popular **Xi'an Famous Foods** (Golden Shopping Mall, 41-28 Main Street, at 41st Road, no phone, www.xianfoods.com) even scored Anthony Bourdain's seal of approval. Tucked on a side street, **Szechuan Gourmet** (135-15 37th Avenue, between Main & Prince Streets, 1-718 888 9388) serves mainland Chinese cuisine that bears little resemblance to Americanised 'Szechuan' fare. For authentic Hunan specialities head south along Main Street to the **Hunan Kitchen of Grand Sichuan** (42-47 Main Street, at Franklin Avenue, 1-718 888 0553).

Flushing Town Hall (137-35 Northern Boulevard, at Linden Place, 1-718 463 7700, www.flushingtownhall.org), built during the Civil War in the highly fanciful Romanesque Revival style, showcases local arts groups, and hosts jazz and chamber music concerts. The most visited site in Queens is rambling **Flushing Meadows-Corona Park** (*see right*), where the 1939-40 and 1964-65 World's Fairs were held. Larger than Central Park, it's home to the **Queens Zoo** (1-718 271 1500, www.queenszoo.com); **Queens Theatre in the Park**, an indoor amphitheatre designed by Philip Johnson; the **New York Hall of Science** (*see p253*), an acclaimed interactive museum; the **Queens Botanical Garden**, a 39-acre cavalcade of greenery; and the **Queens Museum of Art** (*see right*). Also here are **Citi Field**, the home of the Mets baseball team (*see p328*), and the **USTA (United States Tennis Association) National Tennis Center**. The US Open (*see p330*) raises an almighty racket at summer's end, but the general public can play here the other 11 months of the year.

FREE Flushing Meadows-Corona Park

From 111th Street to Van Wyck Expressway, between Flushing Bay & Grand Central Parkway (1-718 760 6565, www.nycgovparks.org). Subway 7 to Mets-Willets Point.

Most Manhattanites only venture to these parts to catch a Mets game or tennis at the US Open, but visitors will also be enticed by the 1964-65 World's Fair sculptures, particularly the iconic 140ft Unisphere, a mammoth steel globe that was the symbol of the fair (and site of the apocalyptic battle scene between humans and aliens in the first *Men in Black* movie). Also visible are the remnants of the New York State Pavilion, designed for the fair by Philip Johnson. Measuring 350ft by 250ft, this now-eerie plaza is bordered by 16 100ft steel columns.

Louis Armstrong House

34-56 107th Street, between 34th & 37th Avenues, Corona (1-718 478 8274, www.louisarmstrong house.org). Subway 7 to 103rd Street-Corona Plaza. **Open** 10am-5pm Tue-Fri; noon-5pm Sat, Sun. *Tours* hourly (last tour 4pm). **Admission** $10; $7 reductions; free under-4s. **Credit** ($15 min) MC, V.

Pilgrims to the two-storey house where the great 'Satchmo' lived from 1943 until his death in 1971 will find a shrine to the revolutionary trumpet player – as well as his wife's passion for wallpaper. Her decorative attentions extended to the interiors of cupboards, closets and even bathroom cabinets. The 40-minute tour is enhanced by audiotapes of Louis that give much insight into the tranquil domesticity he sought in the then suburban neighbourhood.

Queens Museum of Art

New York City Building, park entrance on 49th Avenue, at 111th Street, Flushing Meadows-Corona Park (1-718 592 9700, www.queens museum.org). Subway 7 to 111th Street, then walk south on 111th Street, turning left on to 49th Avenue; continue into the park & over Grand Central Parkway Bridge. **Open** noon-6pm Wed-Sun. **Admission** *Suggested donation* $5; $2.50 reductions. **Credit** MC, V.

Housed in a building constructed for the 1939 World's Fair (and which hosted the United Nations for four years after its founding in 1946), the QMA holds one of the city's most amazing sights: the Panorama of the City of New York, a 9,335sq ft, 895,000-building scale model – one inch equals 100ft – of all five boroughs. Commissioned by Robert Moses for the 1964 World's Fair, it has received periodic updates, and a recently upgraded lighting system mimics the arc of the sun as it passes over NYC. Yet one part of the Panorama remains decidedly untouched – the Twin Towers still stand proudly. The museum's contemporary exhibits have grown bolder and more inventive in recent years, garnering increasing acclaim. An expansion project to double the museum's size will provide more space for changing exhibitions when completed by the end of 2013.

The Bronx

There's more to the boogie-down borough than gritty cityscapes.

The only NYC borough that's physically attached to the mainland of America, the Bronx seems remote to most visitors – and, indeed, many New Yorkers. Part of this perceived distance is due to the holdover of the **South Bronx**'s global reputation for urban strife in the 1970s, which means the borough's two best-known visitor attractions, **Yankee Stadium** and the **Bronx Zoo**, are generally covered in quick trips in and out. This is a shame, for the Bronx also glistens with the art deco gems of the **Grand Concourse**, cooks up a storm with its own Little Italy in **Belmont**, enchants nature-deprived urbanites with its world-class **New York Botanical Garden** and takes pride in an up-and-coming art scene.

THE BRONX IN BRIEF

The Bronx was settled in the 1630s by the family of Jonas Bronck, a Swedish farmer who had a 500-acre homestead in what is now the south-eastern Morrisania section. The area became known as 'the Broncks' farm – although the spelling was altered, the name stuck. Originally part of Westchester County, it was incorporated with the other boroughs into New York City in 1898.

Like Queens and Brooklyn, the Bronx in the early 20th century drew much of its population from the ever-expanding pools of Irish, German, Italian and Eastern European Jewish immigrants who flocked to the area for its cheap rents and open spaces.

After World War II, as the borough became ever more urbanised and transport links improved, the descendants of the European immigrants moved out to the suburbs of Long Island and Westchester, and fresh waves of newcomers, hailing from the Caribbean, Latin America, Africa, the Balkans and Russia, took their places. From the late 1940s until the early '70s, the Bronx probably witnessed more upheaval than the other areas of the New York combined, bearing the brunt of city planner

Robert Moses's drastic revamping of the city. Thousands of residents saw their old tenements razed to make room for the Whitestone and Throgs Neck Bridges, the east–west Cross Bronx Expressway and the north–south Bruckner Boulevard extension of the New England Thruway.

Many areas fell into neglect, a condition exacerbated by the economic and social downturns that plagued the entire city in the 1960s and '70s. The local community felt cut off, forgotten and left to rot, and with good reason. The Bronx became a symbol of urban decay. It's only during the last decade that the

INSIDE TRACK
THE BRONX CULTURE TROLLEY

To check out the South Bronx's burgeoning art scene, hop on the free **Bronx Culture Trolley** (www.bronxarts.org), which stops at about a dozen venues on the first Wednesday of each month, except September and January, and also selected Saturdays in spring and summer; see website for details.

area has really started to come alive once more. Visitors should note that although some parts of the Bronx are gentrifying, others, such as the northern swathe of the Grand Concourse, are still rough around the edges and might make less intrepid urban explorers uncomfortable.

THE SOUTH BRONX

Subway 4 to 161st Street-Yankee Stadium; 6 to Hunts Point Avenue or 138th Street-Third Avenue.

In the 1960s and '70s, the **South Bronx** was so ravaged by post-war 'white flight' and community displacement from the construction of the Cross Bronx Expressway that the neighbourhood became virtually synonymous with urban blight. Crime was rampant and arson became widespread, as landlords discovered that renovating decayed property was far less lucrative than simply burning it down to collect insurance. During a World Series game at Yankee Stadium in 1977, TV cameras caught a building on fire just blocks away. 'Ladies and gentlemen,' commentator Howard Cosell told the world, 'the Bronx is burning.'

These days, the South Bronx is rising from the ashes. In 2006, Mayor Bloomberg announced the South Bronx Initiative, aiming to revitalise the area, while eco-sensitive outfits such as Sustainable South Bronx (www.ssbx.org) are converting vacant lots into green spaces such as **Barretto Point Park** (between Tiffany & Barretto Streets) and **Hunts Point Riverside Park** (at the foot of Lafayette Avenue on the Bronx River). In 2005, Hunts Point became the new home to the city's **Fulton Fish Market** (1-718 378 2356, www.newfultonfishmarket.com), which moved from the site it had occupied for 180 years near South Street Seaport to a 400,000-square foot modern facility that is the largest consortium of seafood retailers in America.

Unsurprisingly, the rejuvenated area has also seen an influx of young professional refugees from overpriced Manhattan and Brooklyn: new condos are sprouting up, old warehouses are

being redeveloped, once-crumbling tenements are being refurbished and, inevitably, chain stores are moving in. Young families have been snapping up the renovated townhouses on Alexander Avenue and furnishing them from the thoroughfare's antiques stores, while industrial lofts on Bruckner Boulevard have become homes to creatives. Yet despite developers' hopes for 'SoBro', the area has not quite turned into the Next Big Thing. Yet.

Hunts Point is also becoming a creative live-work hub. In 1994, a group of artists and community leaders converted an industrial building into the **Point** (940 Garrison Avenue, at Manida Street, 1-718 542 4139, www.the point.org, closed Sun), an arts-based community development centre with a much-used performance space and gallery, studios for dance, theatre and photography, an environmental advocacy group, and lively summer and after-school workshops for neighbourhood children. The Point also leads walking tours (call for reservations) that explore the history of locally born music, such as mambo and hip hop. The nearby **Bronx Academy of Arts & Dance** (BAAD; 2nd floor, 841 Barretto Street, between Garrison & Lafayette Avenues, 1-718 842 5223, www.bronxacademyofartsanddance.org) provides a platform for dance, theatre and visual arts events; it's the venue for festivals such as Out Like That!, which celebrates works by lesbian, gay, bisexual and transgender artists, and BAAD Ass Women, a showcase for the work of female artists. BAAD shares its 1909 building – once the HQ of the American Banknote Company, which printed currency, stamps and other financial documents – with several artists' studios.

Another artistic South Bronx hotbed is simmering further south-west in **Mott Haven**. Here, **Longwood Art Gallery @ Hostos** (450 Grand Concourse, at 149th Street, 1-718 518 6728, www.bronxarts.org/lag.asp), the creation of the Bronx Council on the Arts, mounts top-notch exhibits in a variety of media. Most cultural crawls end up at **Bruckner Bar & Grill** (1 Bruckner Boulevard, at Third Avenue, 1-718 665 2001), which features an eclectic menu, art exhibitions that change bi-monthly in its gallery and occasional poetry readings.

Of course, the vast majority of visitors to the South Bronx are just stopping long enough to take in a baseball game at **Yankee Stadium** (*see p328*), at 161st Street and River Avenue. Some of baseball's most famous legends made history on its diamond, from Babe Ruth to Derek Jeter. In April 2009, the Yankees vacated the fabled 'House that Ruth Built' and moved into their new $1.3-billion stadium across the street – and went on to win their first World Series in seven years. **Monument Park**, an open-air

---

INSIDE TRACK
HIP HOP HISTORY

DJ **Kool Herc's old digs** at 1520 Sedgwick Avenue in the West Bronx is the acknowledged birthplace of hip hop, but the area in and around the **Bronx River Houses** (174th Street, between Bronx River & Harrod Avenue) is where Afrika Bambaataa and his Universal Zulu Nation developed it into a phenomenon.

Bronx Museum of the Arts.

museum behind centre field that celebrates the exploits of past Yankee heroes, can be visited as part of a tour ($20 adults, $15 reductions; 1-646 977 8687), along with the New York Yankees Museum, the dugout, and – when the Yankees are on the road – the clubhouse.

THE GRAND CONCOURSE

Subway B, D to 167th Street; B, D, 4 to Kingsbridge Road; 4 to 161st Street-Yankee Stadium.

A few blocks east of Yankee Stadium runs the four-and-a-half-mile **Grand Concourse**, which begins at 138th Street in the South Bronx and ends at Mosholu Parkway just shy of **Van Cortlandt Park** (*see p136*). Once the most prestigious drag in the Bronx, the Grand Boulevard and Concourse (to give the artery's grandiose official title) is still a must for lovers of art deco. Engineer Louis Risse designed the boulevard in 1892, modelling it on Paris's Champs-Elysées and it opened to traffic in 1909. Following the arrival of a new subway line nearly a decade later, rapid development along the Concourse began in the deco style so popular in the 1920s and '30s.

Starting at 161st Street and heading south, look for the permanent street plaques that make up the **Bronx Walk of Fame**, honouring famous Bronxites from Stanley Kubrick and Tony Orlando to Colin Powell and hip hop 'godfather' Afrika Bambaataa. Heading north, the buildings date mostly from the 1920s to the early '40s, and constitute the country's largest concentration of art deco housing outside Miami Beach. Erected in 1937 at the corner of 161st Street, **888 Grand Concourse** has a large concave entrance of gilded mosaic and is topped by a curvy metallic marquee. Inside, the mirrored

lobby's central fountain and sunburst-patterned floor could rival those of any hotel on Miami's Ocean Drive. On the south side of **Joyce Kilmer Park**, at 161st Street, is the elegant white-marble fountain of Lorelei, built in 1893 in Germany in homage to Heinrich Heine, who wrote the poem of the same name. This was intended as the original entrance to the Concourse before it was extended south. The grandest building on the Concourse is the landmark **Andrew Freedman Home**, a 1924 French-inspired limestone palazzo between McClennan and 166th Streets. Freedman, a millionaire subway contractor, left the bulk of his $7 million fortune with instructions to build a poorhouse for the rich – that is, those who had lost their fortunes and were suffering an impecunious old age. In 2012, it was reborn as a '20s-inspired B&B (1-718 588 8200, www.freedmanontheconcourse.com; $130-$150) and a venue for arts events and exhibitions, while the Family Preservation Center (FPC), a community-based social service agency, occupies the lower level. Across the street, the **Bronx Museum of the Arts** (*see below*), established in 1971 in a former synagogue, stages socially conscious, contemporary exhibitions.

A few blocks north, at **1150 Grand Concourse**, at McClellan Place, is a 1937 art deco apartment block commonly referred to as the 'fish building' because of the colourful marine-themed mosaic flanking its doors; pause inside the restored lobby for a glimpse of its two large murals depicting pastoral scenes, which are in sharp contrast with their surroundings. Near the intersection of Fordham Road, keep an eye out for the Italian rococo exterior of the **Paradise Theater** (2403 Grand Concourse, at 187th Street, www.paradisetheater.net), once the largest cinema in the city. To see the elaborate murals, fountains and grand staircase of the interior, which was restored in 2005, you'll need to buy a ticket for one of the concerts staged here. Just north is the ten-storey **Emigrant Savings Bank**, at 2526 Grand Concourse, worth ducking into for a glimpse of five striking murals by the artist Angelo Manganti, depicting scenes of the Bronx's past, including Jonas Bronck buying land from the Indians.

Further north to Kingsbridge Road lies the **Edgar Allan Poe Cottage** (*see p134*), a small wooden farmhouse where the writer lived from 1846 to 1849. Moved to the Grand Concourse from its original spot on Fordham Road in 1913, the museum has period furniture and details about Poe and his work.

★ Bronx Museum of the Arts
1040 Grand Concourse, at 165th Street (1-718 681 6000, www.bronxmuseum.org). Subway B, D

EXPLORE

Bronx Zoo

to 167th Street; 4 to 161st Street-Yankee Stadium.
Open 11am-6pm Thur, Sat, Sun; 11am-8pm Fri.
Admission $5; $3 reductions; free through 2013.
Credit AmEx, DC, Disc, MC, V.
Founded in 1971 and featuring more than 800 works,
this multicultural art museum shines a spotlight on
20th- and 21st-century artists who are either Bronx-
based or of African, Asian or Latino ancestry. In
2013, the museum presents 'Bronx Lab: Style Wars',
an interactive series of exhibits highlighting locally
relevant art forms; the first installment looks at
South Bronx graffiti works by artists such as
Rigoberto Torres, KOS and Keith Haring (through
June 2). In celebration of the museum's 40th anniversary, admission is free through 2013.

Edgar Allan Poe Cottage

*2640 Grand Concourse, at Kingsbridge Road
(1-718 881 8900, www.bronxhistoricalsociety.
org/poecottage). Subway B, D, 4 to Kingsbridge
Road.* **Open** 10am-4pm Sat; 1-5pm Sun.
Admission $5; $3 reductions. **No credit cards**.
Pay homage to Poe in the house where he spent the
last three years of his life and wrote such literary
marvels as *Annabel Lee* and *The Bells*. After a major
renovation, the cottage has been restored with period
furnishings, including the author's rocking chair,
and a new visitors' centre complete with a sloping
shingle roof designed to resemble the wings of the
bird from the poet's famous *The Raven*.

BELMONT & BRONX PARK

*Subway B, D, 4 to Fordham Road, then
Bx12 bus to Arthur Avenue.*

Settled in the late 19th century by Italian
immigrants hired to landscape nearby Bronx
Zoo, close-knit Belmont is centred on Arthur
Avenue, lined with delis, bakeries, restaurants
and stores selling T-shirts proclaiming the
locale to be New York's 'real Little Italy'. Still
celebrating Mass in Italian, neo-classical **Our
Lady of Mt Carmel Church** (627 E 187th
Street, at Hughes Avenue, 1-718 295 3770) has
been serving the community for more than a

century. Aspects of Italian-American history
and culture are highlighted in the modest,
changing exhibits at the **Enrico Fermi
Cultural Center** (in the Belmont Branch
Library, 610 E 186th Street, between Arthur &
Hughes Avenues, 1-718 933 6410, closed Sun).
    Food, however, is the main reason to visit.
Arthur Avenue Retail Market (2344 Arthur
Avenue, between Crescent Avenue & E 186th
Street, closed Sun) is a covered market built in
the 1940s when Mayor Fiorello La Guardia
campaigned to get the pushcarts off the street.
Inside, you'll find **Mike's Deli** (1-718 295
5033), where you can try the trademark Yankee
Stadium Big Boy hero sandwich, filled with
prosciutto, soppressata, mozzarella, capicola,
mortadella, peppers and lettuce. For a full meal,
try old-school, red-sauce joints such as **Mario's**
(2342 Arthur Avenue, between Crescent Avenue
& E 186th Street, 1-718 584 1188, closed Mon),
featured in several *Sopranos* episodes and
Mario Puzo's novel *The Godfather*; or
Dominick's (2335 Arthur Avenue, between
Crescent Avenue & E 186th Street, 1-718 733
2807, closed Tue), where there are no menus
(your waiter will guide you course by course
through your meal). For something a bit more
21st-century, try **Zero Otto Nove** (2357
Arthur Avenue, between 184th & 186th Streets,
1-718 220 1027, www.roberto089.com), a
trattoria serving buzzed-about brick oven pizza;
the spot was opened by the owners of the no-
frills but charming **Roberto's** (603 Crescent
Avenue, between Hughes & Arthur Avenue,
1-718 733 9503, closed Sun).
    Belmont is within easy walking distance of
Bronx Park, home to two of the borough's
most celebrated attractions. Make your way
east along 187th Street, then south along

INSIDE TRACK
FERRAGOSTO FESTIVAL

While the 11-day San Gennaro Festival in
Manhattan's Little Italy draws the hordes,
Belmont's version, the more intimate
Ferragosto, on the second Sunday in
September, is undoubtedly more
authentic. The vendors who gather at
187th Street and Arthur Avenue to serve
Italian delicacies are largely extensions
of local restaurant kitchens.

EXPLORE

Southern Boulevard, and you'll come to the **Bronx Zoo** (*see below*). Opened in 1899 by Theodore Roosevelt, it's the largest urban zoo in the US at 265 acres. A 15-minute walk north of the zoo – and still in Bronx Park – brings you to the serene 250 acres of the **New York Botanical Garden** (*see below*), which offers respite from cars and concrete in the form of 50 different gardens.

Bronx Zoo/Wildlife Conservation Society

Bronx River Parkway, at Fordham Road (1-718 367 1010, www.bronxzoo.com). Subway 2, 5 to to E Tremont/W Farms Square, then walk 2 blocks to the zoo's Asia entrance; or Metro-North (Harlem Line local) from Grand Central Terminal to Fordham, then take the Bx9 bus to 183rd Street and Southern Boulevard. **Open** *Apr-Oct* 10am-5pm Mon-Fri; 10am-5.30pm Sat, Sun. *Nov-Mar* 10am-4.30pm daily. **Admission** $16.95; $11.95-$14.95 reductions; pay what you wish Wed. Some rides & exhibitions cost extra. **Credit** AmEx, DC, Disc, MC, V.

The Bronx Zoo shuns cages in favour of indoor and outdoor environments that mimic natural habitats. There are more than 60,000 creatures and more than 600 species here (including invertebrates and fish). Monkeys, leopards and tapirs live inside the lush, steamy Jungle World, a re-creation of an Asian rainforest inside a 37,000sq ft building, while lions, giraffes, zebras and other animals roam the African Plains. The super-popular Congo Gorilla Forest has turned 6.5 acres into a dramatic Central African rainforest habitat. A glass-enclosed tunnel winds through the forest, allowing visitors to get close to the dozens of primate families in residence, including majestic western lowland gorillas. Tiger Mountain is populated by Siberian tigers, while the Himalayan Highlands features snow leopards and red pandas. Madagascar! is an exhibit focused on the species-rich island off the coast of East Africa.
▶ *For other zoos, see p95, p121 and p130.*

★ New York Botanical Garden

Bronx River Parkway, at Fordham Road (1-718 817 8700, www.nybg.org). Subway B, D to Bedford Park Boulevard, then take the Bx26 bus to Garden gate; or Metro-North (Harlem Line local) from Grand Central Terminal to Botanical Garden. **Open** *Jan, Feb* 10am-5pm Tue-Sun. *Mar-Dec* 10am-6pm Tue-Sun. **Admission** $20-$25; $10-$18 reductions; free (grounds only) Wed, 10-11am Sat. **Credit** AmEx, DC, Disc, MC, V.

The serene 250 acres of the New York Botanical Garden comprise 50 gardens and plant collections, including the Rockefeller Rose Garden, the Everett Children's Adventure Garden and the last 50 original acres of the forest that once covered all of New York City, now called the Thain Family Forest. In spring, the gardens are frothy with pastel blossoms, as clusters of lilac, cherry, magnolia and crab apple trees burst into bloom. Autumn brings vivid foliage in the oak and maple groves. The Azalea Garden, which features around 3,000 vivid azaleas and rhododendrons, opened in spring 2011. On a rainy day, stay warm and sheltered inside the Enid A Haupt Conservatory, a striking glass-walled greenhouse – the nation's largest – built in 1902. It contains the World of Plants, a series of environmental galleries

EXPLORE

New York Botanical Garden.

that take you on an eco-tour through 11 distinct habitats, from tropical rainforests to deserts and a palm tree oasis, as well as seasonal exhibits.

RIVERDALE & VAN CORTLANDT PARK

Subway D to Norwood-205th Street;
1 to 242nd Street-Van Cortlandt Park.

Riverdale, along the north-west coast of the Bronx, reflects the borough's suburban past; its huge homes perch on narrow, winding streets that meander toward the Hudson river. The only one you can actually visit is **Wave Hill House** (*see right*), an 1843 stone mansion set on a former private estate that is now both a cultural and environmental centre. The nearby, 1,146-acre **Van Cortlandt Park** (entrance on Broadway, at 242nd Street) occasionally hosts cricket teams largely made up of West Indians and Indians. You can hike through a 100-year-old forest, play golf on the nation's first municipal course or rent horses at stables in the park.

The oldest building in the Bronx is **Van Cortlandt House Museum** (*see below*), a 1749 Georgian building that was commandeered by both sides during the Revolutionary War. Abutting the park is **Woodlawn Cemetery**, the resting place for such notable souls as Herman Melville, Duke Ellington, Miles Davis, FW Woolworth and Fiorello La Guardia. To help you pay your respects, maps are available at the entrance at Webster Avenue and E 233rd Street. About five blocks south on Bainbridge Avenue, history buffs will also enjoy the **Museum of Bronx History** (*see below*), set in a lovely 1758 stone farmhouse.

Museum of Bronx History

Valentine-Varian House, 3266 Bainbridge Avenue, between Van Cortlandt Avenue & 208th Street (1-718 881 8900, www.bronxhistorical society.org/vvhouse.html). Subway D to Norwood-205th Street. **Open** 10am-4pm Sat; 1-5pm Sun. **Admission** $5; $3 reductions. **No credit cards**.
Operated by the Bronx County Historical Society, the museum displays its collection of documents and photos in the Valentine-Varian House, a Federal-style fieldstone residence built in 1758.
▶ *The society also offers historical tours of the Bronx neighbourhoods.*

Van Cortlandt House Museum

Van Cortlandt Park, entrance on Broadway, at 246th Street (1-718 543 3344, www.vancortlandt house.org). Subway 1 to 242nd Street-Van Cortlandt Park. **Open** 10am-3pm Tue-Fri; 11am-4pm Sat, Sun. **Admission** $5; $3 reductions; free under-12s. Free Wed. **Credit** ($11 minimum) MC, V.

A one-time wheat plantation that has since been turned into a colonial museum, Van Cortlandt House was alternately used as headquarters by George Washington and British General Sir William Howe during the Revolutionary War.

Wave Hill House

W 249th Street, at Independence Avenue (1-718 549 3200, www.wavehill.org). Metro-North (Hudson Line local) from Grand Central Terminal to Riverdale. **Open** *Mid Apr-mid Oct* 9am-5.30pm Tue-Sun. *Mid Oct-mid Apr* 9am-4.30pm Tue-Sun. **Admission** $8; $2-$4 reductions; free under-6s; free 9am-noon Sat; all day Tue Jan-Apr, July, Aug, Nov, Dec; 9am-noon Tue May, June, Sept, Oct. **Credit** AmEx, Disc, MC, V.
Laze around in these 28 lush acres overlooking the Hudson River at Wave Hill, a Georgian Revival house that was home to Mark Twain, Teddy Roosevelt and conductor Arturo Toscanini. It's now a spectacular nature preserve and conservation centre with cultivated gardens and woodlands commanding excellent views of the river. The small in-house art gallery shows nature-themed exhibits, and the property is a venue for concerts and other events.

PELHAM BAY PARK

Subway 6 to Pelham Bay Park.

Pelham Bay Park, in the borough's north-eastern corner, is NYC's largest park. Take a car or a bike if you want to explore the 2,765 acres; pick up a map at the Ranger Nature Center, near the entrance on Bruckner Boulevard at Wilkinson Avenue. The **Bartow-Pell Mansion Museum** (*see below*), in the park's south-eastern quarter, overlooks Long Island Sound. The park's 13 miles of coastline skirt the Hutchinson river to the west and the Long Island Sound and Eastchester Bay to the east. In summer, locals hit sandy **Orchard Beach**; set up in the 1930s, this 'Riviera of New York' is that rare beast – a Robert Moses creation not universally lamented.

Bartow-Pell Mansion Museum

895 Shore Road North, at Pelham Bay Park (1-718 885 1461, www.bartowpellmansionmuseum. org). Subway 6 to Pelham Bay Park, then Bee-Line bus 45 (ask driver to stop at Bartow-Pell Mansion). **Open** noon-4pm Wed, Sat, Sun. **Admission** $5; $3 reductions; free under-6s. **Credit** MC, V.
Operating as a museum since 1946, this stunning estate dates from 1654, when Thomas Pell bought the land from the Siwonay Indians. It was Robert Bartow, publisher and Pell descendant, who added the 1842 Greek Revival stone mansion, which faces a reflecting pool ringed by gardens.
▶ *Just east of Pelham Bay Park lies City Island (see p340), a rustic fishing village with a New England feel.*

EXPLORE

Staten Island

The ferry crossing is just the beginning.

With a largely suburban vibe, abundant parkland and beaches, New York's smallest borough feels removed from the rest of the city. And physically it is. To visitors, Staten Island is best known for its ferry – the locals' sole public-transport link with Manhattan happens to pass by Lady Liberty. But the devastation wrought by Hurricane Sandy in autumn 2012 – the borough suffered more than half the city's total fatalities – trained the media spotlight on the island. At time of writing, its South Shore communities were still struggling to get on their feet again. But the worldwide attention – combined with Mayor Bloomberg's pre-storm announcement of plans to build a $500 million retail and hotel complex on the northern shore in 2014, anchored by the world's tallest Ferris wheel – suggests a more prosperous future.

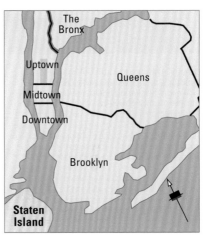

ISLAND LIFE

In its early days, Staten Island was an isolated community, until Henry Hudson sailed in and christened it *Staaten Eylandt* (Dutch for 'State's Island', in reference to Holland's Staaten-Generaal, or parliament) in 1609. Early settlers were driven out by Native Americans, the island's first inhabitants, but the Dutch took hold in 1661, establishing shipping and manufacturing enclaves on the northern shore, and farms and hamlets in the south. It became one of the five boroughs in 1898, but remained a backwater until 1964, when the Verrazano-Narrows Bridge joined the island to Bay Ridge in Brooklyn. Many say that's when small-town Staten Island truly vanished.

Still, many quaint aspects remain – not least the free **Staten Island Ferry**, which links the southern tip of Manhattan with the island's St George terminal (where you can catch the buses noted in this chapter). When you alight, in the St George neighbourhood, head right along the new **Esplanade**, with its stirring views of lower Manhattan across the harbour, to pay your respects at *Postcards*, a memorial to the

274 Staten Islanders lost on 9/11. The fibreglass wings of the sculpture frame the spot where the Twin Towers used to stand.

Across the street from the terminal look for the distinctive clocktower of **Borough Hall** (10 Richmond Terrace); step inside for a peek at the Works Progress Administration murals depicting local history. Exiting the building, turn left to reach the small, 140-year-old **Staten Island Museum** (75 Stuyvesant Place, at Wall Street, 1-718 727 1135, www.statenisland museum.org), devoted to local history, art and natural science.

Walk up Hyatt Street behind Borough Hall for a glimpse of the Spanish baroque-styled lobby of the restored 1920s vaudeville venue **St George Theatre** (35 Hyatt Street, between St Marks & Stuyvesant Places, 1-718 442 2900, www.stgeorgetheatre.com), which stages family-friendly fare and gigs by stars such as Tony Bennett, Liza Minnelli and Judy Collins.

If you turn right on to St Marks Place, you will come upon the landmark **St George Historic District**. Covering portions of St Marks and Carroll Places, and Westervelt and Hamilton Avenues, the district features

Staten Island Ferry. *See p137.*

about 80 Queen Anne and Colonial Revival buildings, some from the early 1830s.

Worthwhile eating and drinking options in the area include **Enoteca Maria** (27 Hyatt Street, between Central Avenue & St Marks Place, 1-718 447 2777, www.enotecamaria.com, closed lunch & Mon, Tue), where rotating grandma-chefs from Italy prepare a nightly changing menu; **Beso** (11 Schuyler Street, between Richmond Terrace & Stuyvesant Place, 1-718 816 8162, www.besonyc.com), an intimate Spanish tapas restaurant; and, for light fare like soup and sandwiches, nearby **Every Thing Goes Book Cafe** (208 Bay Street, 1-718 447 8256, www.etgstores.com, closed Mon, Sun), one of four local businesses run by a local hippie commune.

A short bus ride west along Richmond Terrace is the **Snug Harbor Cultural Center**, set in the 83-acre grounds of a former sailors' home. The **Staten Island Zoo**, adjacent to Clove Lakes Park, has a rainforest and one of the East Coast's largest reptile collections.

To explore the island further, take the buses and the single-line Staten Island Railroad that depart from St George for destinations along the eastern half of the island. A 15-minute bus ride along Hylan Boulevard lies **Alice Austen House**, former home of the Victorian photographer. At the east end of Bay Street, **Fort Wadsworth** is one of the oldest military sites in the nation. From here, you can take in views of both the Verrazano Bridge and Downtown Manhattan from one of NYC's highest points. Further along the eastern coast runs the two-mile **FDR Boardwalk**: the fourth longest in the world, it runs by South Beach, a sandy strip popular for picnicking, fishing, beach volleyball and swimming. Note that this spot was hard-hit by the storm, so check the nycgovparks.org website before heading out.

For more spiritual calm, head to the centre of the island, to the **Jacques Marchais Museum of Tibetan Art**, a reproduction of a Himalayan mountain temple. Nearby, guides in period garb offer tours of **Historic Richmond Town**, the island's one-time county seat. A stone's throw away is the 2,800-acre **Greenbelt** network of parks.

Opportunities for good, clean fun abound on the island's south-eastern coast (a 40-minute ride on the S78 bus), where you can swim, picnic and fish at **Wolfe's Pond Park** (Cornelia Avenue, at Hylan Boulevard, 1-718 984 8266). As this area was significantly damaged by the hurricane too, check nycgov parks.org for any closures. To the west, **Sandy Ground Historical Society** (1538 Woodrow Road, at Lynbrook Avenue, 1-718 317 5796, open 1-4pm Tue-Thur, Sun) documents the history of America's first settlement of free blacks. Further south, **Conference House**, site of a failed attempt at peace between the Americans and British in 1776, is now a museum of colonial life.

Alice Austen House

2 Hylan Boulevard, between Bay & Edgewater Streets (1-718 816 4506, www.aliceausten.org). S51 bus to Hylan Boulevard. **Open** *Mar-Dec* 11am-5pm Tue-Sun. **Admission** *Suggested donation* $3. **Credit** AmEx, MC, V.
The beautiful photographs of Alice Austen (1866-1952) are the highlight at this 17th-century cottage – it contains no fewer than 3,000 of her glass negative images. The restored house (called Clear Comfort) and grounds often host concerts and events, and offer breathtaking harbour views.

Conference House (Billopp House)

7455 Hylan Boulevard, at Craig Avenue (1-718 984 6046, www.conferencehouse.org). S78 bus to Craig Avenue & Hylan Boulevard. **Open** *Apr-mid Dec* 1-4pm Fri-Sun. **Admission** free, excl tour groups.
In 1776, Britain's Lord Howe parlayed with John Adams and Benjamin Franklin in this 17th-century house, the only surviving pre-Revolutionary manor in the city, while trying to forestall the American Revolution. Tours point out 18th-century furnishings, decor and daily objects such as quill pens and cookware. The lovely grounds command a terrific view over Raritan Bay, and provide a picturesque setting for free concerts and events.

EXPLORE

FREE Fort Wadsworth

*210 New York Avenue, on the east end of Bay Street
(1-718 354 4500, www.nyharborparks.org). S51 bus
to Fort Wadsworth.* **Open** *dawn-dusk daily. Visitors'
centre* 10am-4.30pm Wed-Sun. **Admission** free.
Explore the fortifications that guarded NYC for
almost 200 years at Ford Wadsworth, which was
occupied by a blockhouse as far back as the 17th century. Park ranger-led tours are offered at weekends.

FREE Greenbelt

Greenbelt Nature Center *700 Rockland Avenue,
at Brielle Avenue (1-718 351 3450, www.sigreen
belt.org). S62 bus to Bradley Avenue, then S57
bus to Brielle & Rockland Avenue.* **Open** *Apr-Oct*
10am-5pm Tue-Sun. *Nov-Mar* 11am-5pm Wed-
Sun. **Admission** free.
High Rock Park *200 Nevada Avenue, at Rockland
Avenue. S62 bus to Manor Road, then S54 bus to
Nevada Avenue.* **Open** *dawn-dusk daily.*
The Greenbelt Nature Center is the best starting
point to explore more than 35 miles of trails in this
network of parks (pick up a map or download one
from the website). A mile away, at the 90-acre High
Rock Park, visitors can hike the mile-long Swamp
Trail, climb Todt Hill or explore trails through
forests, meadows and wetlands. Be sure to check the
website for any hurricane-related closures.

Historic Richmond Town

*441 Clarke Avenue, between Richmond Road &
Arthur Kill Road (1-718 351 1611, www.historic
richmondtown.org). S74 bus to St Patrick's Place.*
Open *July, Aug* 11am-5pm Wed-Sun. *Sept-June*
1-5pm Wed-Sun. **Admission** $8; $5-$6 reductions.
Credit AmEx, Disc, MC, V.
This colonial-era 'living museum' includes residences, public buildings and the oldest schoolhouse
in the nation; it dates from 1695. Tours and activities,
from pumpkin picking to quilting, are offered.

Jacques Marchais
Museum of Tibetan Art

*338 Lighthouse Avenue, off Richmond Road
(1-718 987 3500, www.tibetanmuseum.org). S74
bus to Lighthouse Avenue.* **Open** *Apr-Nov* 1-5pm
Wed-Sun. *Dec-Mar* 1-5pm Fri-Sun. **Admission**
$6; $4 reductions; free under-6s. **Credit** AmEx,
Disc, MC, V.

INSIDE TRACK
THE STATEN ISLAND RAILWAY

Although it isn't connected to any of the
city's other subway lines, the **Staten
Island Railway** (SIR) does accept the
MetroCard. The railway has one line,
which runs from St George to Tottenville
on the southern tip of the island.

This tiny museum contains a formidable Buddhist
altar, tranquil meditation gardens and an extensive
collection of Tibetan art and artefacts: sculptures,
paintings, ritual objects and historic photos. A
Tibetan festival is held in spring and autumn.

★ Snug Harbor Cultural Center

*1000 Richmond Terrace, between Snug Harbor
Road & Tysen Avenue (1-718 448 2500,
www.snug-harbor.org). S40 bus to the north gate
(request stop).* **Open** *Grounds dawn-dusk daily.*
Stately Greek Revival structures form the nucleus
of this former sailors' retirement home. Dating from
1833, the centre has been restored and converted into
an arts complex that includes one of the city's oldest
concert halls. In addition to the listings below, the
Staten Island Children's Museum (1-718 273
2060, www.statenislandkids.org, closed Mon) and
Art Lab (1-718 447 8667, www.artlab.info), a non-
profit art school, are also based here.
Newhouse Center for Contemporary Art
1-718 425 3524, www.snug-harbor.org/newhouse.
Open noon-5pm Wed-Sun. **Admission** $3;
$2 reductions; free under-13s. **No credit cards.**
Staten Island's premier venue for contemporary art
holds several annual exhibitions from leading international sculptors, painters and mixed-media artists.
Noble Maritime Collection *1-718 447 6490,
www.noblemaritime.org.* **Open** 1-5pm Thur-Sun.
Admission Pay what you wish.
This museum is dedicated to the artist-seaman John
A Noble, who had a 'floating studio' moored in the
Kill van Kull, the waterway between Staten Island
and New Jersey, for 40 years. As well as his
maritime-themed paintings, Noble's houseboat is on
display, restored to its appearance when the artist was
featured in *National Geographic* magazine in 1954.
Well worth a look is the recreated dormitory room of
the former Sailors' Snug Harbor, circa 1900, upstairs.
Staten Island Botanical Garden *1-718 448
2500, www.snug-harbor.org.* **Open** 10am-5pm
Tue-Sun. **Admission** *Chinese Scholar's Garden*
$5; $4 reductions; free under-13s. *Grounds & other
gardens* free. **Credit** AmEx, DC, MC, V.
Stroll through more than 20 themed gardens, including the traditional Chinese Scholar's Garden, with
its pavilions, meandering paths and delicate foot-
bridges, and, in spring and summer, the medieval-
style children's Secret Garden, complete with a
38ft-high castle and a maze.

Staten Island Zoo

*614 Broadway, between Glenwood Place &
Colonial Court (1-718 442 3101, www.staten
islandzoo.org). S48 bus to Broadway.* **Open**
10am-4.45pm daily. **Admission** $8; $5-$6
reductions; pay what you wish 2-4.45pm Wed.
Credit AmEx, DC, Disc, MC, V.
The home of 'Staten Island Chuck', NYC's very own
furry Groundhog Day forecaster, also holds a large
reptile and amphibian collection.

EXPLORE

Consume

Restaurants & Cafés

Variety is the dominant spice in NYC's mind-bogglingly diverse food scene.

New Yorkers have a seemingly insatiable appetite for novel tastes and different dining experiences. The sheer number and variety of restaurants in the city – there are approximately 24,000, ranging from high-end food palaces to neighbourhood holes-in-the-wall – mean that even long-time residents need never eat at the same place twice. Fierce competition for your cash ensures restaurateurs are always thinking of creative ways to appeal to your taste buds – and diners are benefiting from special deals and more solicitous service.

THE LOCAL SCENE

Chef-watching is a favourite local pastime, even among those who don't consider themselves avid foodies. Despite the bleak economy, New York's top toques continue to churn out new eateries. Together with business partner Will Guidara, chef Daniel Humm of Eleven Madison Park has garnered rave reviews for his show-stopping cuisine at opulent hotel dining room the **NoMad** (*see p166*). On the flip side, haute cuisine superstar Jean Georges Vongerichten brought his food down to earth with the more affordable, green-centric **ABC Kitchen** (*see p164*) within a furniture store. Other high-profile chefs have branched out into new culinary territory: David Bouley brought a Japanese element to his Tribeca empire with **Brushstroke** (*see p145*), importing young chef Isao Yamada to oversee the kitchen, while Daniel Boulud looks beyond the Med to North African and Middle Eastern influences at **Boulud Sud** (*see p172*). Andrew Carmellini, a haute-cuisine vet who made his name cooking family-style Italian at **Locanda Verde** (*see p147*) is a toque to watch. At the **Dutch** (*see p145*) he channelled his experiences road-tripping across the States into an exuberant menu that highlights NYC institutions like the oyster bar while delivering impulsive comfort

food from across the country (hot fried chicken, a cracker-domed rabbit pot pie). Meanwhile, Justin Smillie, a veteran of Barbuto, has made **Il Buco Alimentari e Vini** (*see p155*) a breakout success with his fresh take on Italian cooking.

New Yorkers are slaves to fashion, and if a restaurant is hot, chances are they'll want in. Perhaps the most illustrious entrant to the list of impossible-to-get-into places – even five years after it opened – is **Momofuku Ko**. This 12-seat spot, from pork bun wunderkind David Chang, requires diners to snare reservations online – a new day opens for booking each morning – at www.momofuku.com. Suffice to say that it's one of the most sought-after tables (or, in this case, chef's counters) in town, but, luckily, Chang has three other fine options: Momofuku Ssäm Bar, Momofuku Noodle Bar and Má Pêche (for all, *see p156*). The past year has seen a surge in progressive Asian cooking, with the arrival of two restaurants with roots in San Francisco, California, and Portland, Oregon, respectively: **Mission Chinese Food** (*see p152*), and **Pok Pok NY** (*see p175*), a Thai restaurant from chef Andy Ricker. Despite the laid-back vibe at both, the no-reservation policy means seats are hard to score. Meanwhile, restaurateur Ed Schoenfeld and chef Joe Ng bring farm-to-table zeal to the ancient art of dim sum at **RedFarm** (*see p162*).

Foodies watching their pennies should head for the **East Village**, which has a knack for sprouting reasonably priced eateries that draw cult followings. And no discussion of New York dining is complete without mention of **Brooklyn**. The farm-to-table movement has

> ❶ Blue numbers given in this chapter correspond to the location of each restaurant and café as marked on the street maps. See pp402-412.

firmly taken root in the borough, whose denizens are known for their DIY spirit and devotion to local purveyors. Enjoy urban-rustic menus and salvaged-wood furnished environments at the cosy **Vinegar Hill House** (*see p175*), in the quiet neighbourhood of the same name; or the locavore hub **Roberta's** (*see p175*) in Bushwick, which recently added a fine-dining annexe, **Blanca**, tucked behind the main restaurant.

Elsewhere in the city, there are numerous cheek-by-jowl Asian eateries in **Chinatown**, while **Koreatown**, the stretch of West 32nd Street between Fifth Avenue and Broadway, is lined with Korean barbecue joints and other eateries. Further afield, **Harlem** offers soul food and African cooking, and the proverbial melting pot that is **Queens** counts Greek (in Astoria) and Indian (in Jackson Heights) among its globe-spanning cuisines.

The essentials

Snagging reservations for popular places can be difficult, so it's wise to call as far ahead as possible, although the majority of places will only require a few days' notice (or less). However, there's also a trend for hotspots not to take reservations except for large parties, which can translate into a long wait for a table. Most restaurants fill up between 7pm and 9pm; if you don't mind eating early (5pm) or late (after 10pm), your chances of getting into a sought-after spot will improve greatly. Alternatively, you can try to nab a reservation by calling at 5pm on the day you want to dine and hoping for a last-minute cancellation. Dress codes are

---

THE BEST NYC INSTITUTIONS

For simply delicious burgers
Corner Bistro. See p159.

For bivalves & beer
**Grand Central Oyster Bar
& Restaurant**. See p169.

For an honest steak
Peter Luger. See p175.

---

rarely enforced, but some old-school fancy dining rooms require men to don a jacket and tie. If in doubt, call ahead and ask, but remember that you can never really overdress in this town.

Note that prices given for main courses in this chapter are averages. We've used the **$** symbol to indicate operations offering particularly good value: restaurants with main courses averaging less than $15, plus cafés and sandwich stops.

DOWNTOWN
Financial District

Adrienne's Pizzabar
54 Stone Street, between Coenties Alley & Mill Street (1-212 248 3838, www.adriennespizzabar.com). Subway R to Whitehall Street-South Ferry; 2, 3 to Wall Street. **Open** 11.30am-midnight Mon-Sat; 11.30am-10pm Sun. **Average pizza** $19. **Credit** AmEx, DC, Disc, MC, V. **Map** p402 E33 ❶ Pizza

CONSUME

North End Grill. *See p144.*

Brushstroke.

CONSUME

Good, non-chain eateries are scarce in the Financial District, but this bright, modern pizzeria on quaint Stone Street provides a pleasant break from the crowded thoroughfares – there are outside tables from April through November. The kitchen prepares nicely charred pies with delectable toppings such as the rich *quattro formaggi*. If you're in a hurry, you can eat at the 12-seat bar, or opt for the sleek, wood-accented dining room to savour small plates and main courses such as baked sea scallops and ravioli al formaggio.

$ Jack's Stir Brew Coffee

222 Front Street, between Beekman Street & Peck Slip (1-212 227 7631, www.jacksstirbrew.com). Subway A, C to Broadway-Nassau Street; J, Z, 2, 3, 4, 5 to Fulton Street. **Open** *Apr-Sept* 7am-7pm Mon-Sat; 8am-7pm Sun. *Oct-Mar* 7am-6pm Mon-Sat; 8am-6pm Sun. **Coffee** $2.50. **Credit** $5 min) AmEx, Disc, MC, V. **Map** p402 F32 ❷ **Café**
Java fiends convene at this award-winning caffeine spot that offers organic, shade-grown beans and a homey vibe. Coffee is served by espresso artisans with a knack for oddball concoctions, such as the super-silky Mountie latte, infused with maple syrup. **Other locations** 138 W 10th Street, between Greenwich Avenue & Waverly Place, West Village (1-212 929 0821).

North End Grill

104 North End Avenue, at Murray Street (1-646 747 1600, www.northendgrillnyc.com). Subway A, C to Chambers Street; E to World Trade Center; 2, 3 to Park Place. **Open** 11.30am-2pm, 5.30-10pm Mon-Thur; 11.30am-2pm, 5.30-11pm Fri; 11am-2pm, 5.30-11pm Sat; 11am-2.30pm, 5.30-9pm Sun. **Main courses** $30. **Credit** AmEx, DC, Disc, MC, V. **Map** p402 D32 ❸ **American**
Danny Meyer brings his Midas touch to Battery Park City for this instant classic. The place has all the hallmarks of a Meyer joint: effortless, affable service; a warm, buzzy space with top-notch acoustics; and cooking that's easy and accessible. Former Tabla toque Floyd Cardoz leaves his stamp on the seasonal menu, devoting an entire section to eggs and adding generous doses of fire and spice. We were impressed by a starter of evanescent cod throats meunière and excellent composed plates such as wood-fired lamb loin shingled on a bed of stewed chickpeas seasoned with mint. *Photo p143.*

Tribeca & Soho

Balthazar

80 Spring Street, between Broadway & Crosby Street (1-212 965 1414, www.balthazarny.com). Subway N, R to Prince Street; 6 to Spring Street. **Open** 7.30-11.30am, noon-5pm, 6pm-midnight Mon-Thur; 7.30-11.15am, noon-5pm, 6pm-1am Fri; 8am-4pm, 6pm-1am Sat; 8am-4pm, 5.30pm-midnight Sun. **Main courses** $29. **Credit** AmEx, DC, MC, V. **Map** p403 E30 ❹ **French**

The Dutch.

At dinner, this iconic eatery is perennially packed with rail-thin lookers dressed to the nines. But it's not only fashionable – the kitchen rarely makes a false step and the service is surprisingly friendly. The $145 three-tiered seafood platter casts an impressive shadow, and the roast chicken with garlic mashed potatoes for two is *délicieux*.

★ Brushstroke

30 Hudson Street, at Duane Street (1-212 791 3771, www.davidbouley.com). Subway 1, 2, 3 to Chambers Street. **Open** 5.30-10pm Mon-Sat. **Tasting menus** $85-$135. **Credit** AmEx, Disc, MC, V. **Map** p402 E31 ❺ **Japanese**

Prominent local chef David Bouley's name may be behind this venture, but he's not in the kitchen. Instead, he has handed the reins to talented import Isao Yamada, who turns out some of the most accomplished Japanese food in the city. The ever-changing seasonal menu, which rotates through 5,000 dishes that Yamada spent years testing, is best experienced as an intricate multicourse feast inspired by the Japanese *kaiseki*. (A small à la carte selection is also available.) A meal might start with muted petals of raw *kombu*-wrapped sea bass, before building slowly towards a subtle climax. In keeping with the basic tenets of this culinary art form, the savoury procession concludes with a rice dish – top-notch *chirashi* or seafood and rice cooked in a clay casserole – and delicate sweets such as creamy soy-milk panna cotta.

Corton

239 West Broadway, between Walker & White Streets (1-212 219 2777, www.cortonnyc.com). Subway A, C, E to Canal Street; 1 to Franklin Street. **Open** 5.30-10.30pm Tue-Sat. **Tasting menus** $115-$155. **Credit** AmEx, DC, Disc, MC, V. **Map** p402 E31 ❻ **French**

When it opened in 2008, Corton was given the highest possible star rating by *Time Out New York*'s critics. A meal here is an extraordinary experience. Veteran restaurateur Drew Nieporent's white-on-white sanctuary focuses all attention on chef Paul Liebrandt's finely wrought food. The presentations, in the style of the most esteemed modern kitchens of Europe, are Photoshop flawless: sweet bay scallops, for example, anchored a visual masterpiece featuring wisps of radish, marcona almonds and sea urchin.

★ The Dutch

131 Sullivan Street, at Prince Street (1-212 677 6200, www.thedutchnyc.com). Subway C, E to Spring Street. **Open** 11.30am-3pm, 5.30pm-midnight Mon-Thur; 11.30am-3pm, 5.30pm-1am Fri; 10am-3pm, 5.30pm-1am Sat; 10am-3pm, 5.30pm-midnight Sun. **Main courses** $30. **Credit** AmEx, Disc, MC, V. **Map** p403 E29 ❼ **American**

Andrew Carmellini, Josh Pickard and Luke Ostrom – the white-hot team behind Italian hit Locanda Verde (*see p147*) – turned to good ol' American eats for their sophomore effort. The Dutch boasts late-night hours and a freewheeling menu, completing Carmellini's progression from haute golden boy (Café Boulud, Lespinasse) to champion of lusty plates and raucous settings. Carmellini plays off the country's diverse influences with a broad spectrum of dishes. Rabbit pot pie, dry-aged steaks and peel 'n' eat prawns all get their due. Guests can drop by the airy oak bar or adjacent oyster room to order

CONSUME

GET INSPIRED
GET TICKETS
GET GOING

"Tomas Saraceno on the Roof: Cloud City"

Our apps do it all

Download them today at
timeout.com/newyork/time-out-apps

from the full menu or sip cocktails such as the Concord Sling (corn whiskey, grape purée and lime).

Jack's Wife Freda

224 Lafayette Street, between Kenmare & Spring Streets (1-212 510 8550, www.jacks wifefreda.com). Subway 6 to Spring Street. **Open** 10am-midnight Mon-Sat; 10am-10pm Sun. **Main courses** $20. **Credit** AmEx, MC, V. **Map** p403 E30 ❽ **Café**

Keith McNally protégé Dean Jankelowitz is behind this café. The 40-seat spot – sporting dark-green leather banquettes, brass railings and marble counters – serves homey fare, like Jankelowitz's grandmother's matzo ball soup made with duck fat or a skirt steak sandwich served alongside hand-cut fries.

Landmarc Tribeca

179 West Broadway, between Leonard & Worth Streets (1-212 343 3883, www.landmarc-restaurant.com). Subway 1 to Franklin Street. **Open** 11am-midnight daily. **Main courses** $30. **Credit** AmEx, DC, Disc, MC, V. **Map** p402 E31 ❾ **Eclectic**

This downtown dining destination quickly distinguished itself among its Tribeca competitors by serving heady bistro dishes (bone marrow, crispy sweetbreads) until midnight, and stocking the wine list with reasonably priced half bottles. Chef-owner Marc Murphy focuses on the tried and trusted: *frisée aux lardons*, boeuf bourguignon and several types of mussels. Metal beams and exposed brick add an unfinished edge to the elegant bi-level space. Those who have little restraint when it comes to sweets will appreciate the dessert menu: miniature portions cost just $4 a pop and a tasting of six goes for $16. **Other locations** 3rd Floor, Time Warner Center, 10 Columbus Circle, at Broadway, Upper West Side (1-212 823 6123).

Locanda Verde

377 Greenwich Street, at North Moore Street (1-212 925 3797, www.locandaverdenyc.com). Subway 1 to Franklin Street. **Open** 8-11am, 11.30am-3pm, 5.30-11pm Mon-Fri; 8am-3pm, 5.30-11pm Sat, Sun. **Main courses** $25. **Credit** AmEx, MC, V. **Map** p402 D31 ❿ **Italian**

This buzzy eatery in Robert De Niro's Greenwich Hotel is co-owned by the actor and Daniel Boulud protegé Andrew Carmellini. The bold family-style fare is best enjoyed as a bacchanalian banquet. Steak *tartara* piedmontese with hazelnuts, truffles and crispy *guanciale* (pork jowel bacon) won't last long in the middle of the table. Nor will the chef's ravioli – as delicate as silk and oozing pungent robiola. Locanda is the rare Italian restaurant with desserts worth saving room for, courtesy of ace pastry chef Karen DeMasco – try La Fantasia di Caramello, a decadent combination of caramel ice-cream and pear sorbet, roasted pear, pretzels and coffee caramel.

INSIDE TRACK QUICK TIP

Tipping etiquette can be a nightmare if you don't know what you're doing. However, things are simple here. Few restaurants add service to the bill for parties under six; it's customary to give between 15 and 20 per cent. The easiest way to figure out the amount is to double the sales tax. Bartenders also get tipped – $1 a drink should ensure friendly pours.

★ Osteria Morini

218 Lafayette Street, between Broome & Spring Streets (1-212 965 8777, www.osteriamorini.com). Subway 6 to Spring Street. **Open** 11.30am-11pm daily. **Main courses** $25. **Credit** AmEx, MC, V. **Map** p403 E30 ⓫ **Italian**

Michael White is one of New York's most prolific and successful Italian-American chefs, and this terrific downtown homage to a classic Bolognese tavern is his most accessible restaurant. The toque spent seven years cooking in Italy's Emilia-Romagna region, and his connection to the area surfaces in the rustic food. Handmade pastas – frail ricotta gnocchi in tomato cream, fat tortelli bundles oozing an absurdly rich mix of braised meats – are fantastic, while superb meats include porchetta with crisp, crackling skin and potatoes bathed in pan drippings.

Little Italy & Nolita

$ Café Habana

17 Prince Street at Elizabeth Street (1-212 625 2001, www.ecoeatery.com). Subway N, R to Prince Street; 6 to Spring Street. **Open** 9am-midnight daily. **Main courses** $12. **Credit** AmEx, MC, V. **Map** p403 F29 ⓬ **Cuban**

Trendy Nolita types storm this chrome corner fixture for a taste of the addictive grilled corn: golden ears doused in fresh mayo, chargrilled, and generously sprinkled with chilli powder and grated cotija cheese. Staples include a Cuban sandwich of roasted pork, ham, melted swiss and sliced pickles, and crisp beer-battered catfish with spicy mayo. At the takeaway annexe next door, you can get that corn-on-a-stick to go. There's also a sprawling seasonal branch in Brooklyn, Habana Outpost (open Apr-Oct). **Other locations** 757 Fulton Street, at South Portland Avenue, Fort Greene, Brooklyn (1-718 858 9500).

Ed's Lobster Bar

222 Lafayette Street, between Kenmare & Spring Streets (1-212 343 3236, www.lobster barnyc.com). Subway B, D, F, M to Broadway-Lafayette Street. **Open** noon-3pm, 5-11pm

CONSUME

INSIDE TRACK DIY BARBECUE

Many of the Asian barbecue joints in **Koreatown**, the block-long strip of 32nd Street between Broadway and Fifth Avenue, give you the option of cooking your own meat on a gas grill built into the table – although you can also ask the server to do it for you.

Mon-Thur; noon-3pm, 5pm-midnight Fri; noon-midnight Sat; noon-9pm Sun. **Main courses** $28. **Credit** AmEx, DC, MC, V. **Map** p403 E30 ⓭ Seafood

If you secure a place at the 25-seat marble seafood bar or one of the few tables in the whitewashed eaterie, expect superlative raw-bar eats, delicately fried clams and lobster served every which way: steamed, grilled, broiled, chilled, stuffed into a pie and – the crowd favourite – the lobster roll. Here, it's a buttered bun stuffed with premium chunks of meat and just a light coating of mayo.

$ La Esquina

106 Kenmare Street, between Cleveland Place & Lafayette Street (1-646 613 7100, www.esquina nyc.com). Subway 6 to Spring Street. **Open** *Taqueria* 8am-5am Mon-Fri; noon-5am Sat, Sun. *Café* noon-midnight Mon-Fri; 11am-midnight Sat, Sun. *Restaurant* 6pm-2am daily. **Tacos** $3.50. **Main courses** $20. **Credit** AmEx, DC, MC, V. **Map** p403 E30 ⓮ Mexican

This cabbie-pit-stop-turned-taco-stand comprises three dining and drinking areas: first, a street-level *taqueria*, serving a short-order menu of fish tacos and Mexican *tortas*. Around the corner is a 30-seat café, its shelves stocked with books and old vinyl. Lastly, there's a dungeonesque restaurant and lounge accessible through a back door of the *taqueria* (to enter, you have to confirm that you have a reservation). It's worth the hassle: a world of Mexican murals, fine tequilas, *huitlacoche* (Mexican truffle) *quesadillas* and crab *tostadas* awaits.

Other locations Café de la Esquina at Wythe Diner, 225 Wythe Avenue, between Metropolitan Avenue & North 3rd Street, Williamsburg, Brooklyn (1-718 393 5500).

$ Parm & Torrisi Italian Specialties

Parm *248 Mulberry Street, between Prince & Spring Streets (1-212 993 7189, www. parmnyc.com).* **Open** 11am-11pm Mon-Wed, Sun; 11am-midnight Thur-Sat. **Sandwiches** $9.
Torrisi Italian Specialties *250 Mulberry Street, between Prince & Spring Streets (1-212 965 0955, www.torrisinyc.com).* **Open** 5.30-11pm Mon-Thur; noon-2pm, 5.30-11pm Fri-Sun. **Prix fixe** $65.
Subway N, R to Prince Street; 6 to Spring Street. **Credit** AmEx, Disc, MC, V. **Map** p403 F29 ⓯ Italian

Young guns Mario Carbone and Rich Torrisi, two fine-dining vets, brought a cool-kid sheen to red-sauce plates in 2010, when they debuted Torrisi Italian Specialties, a deli by day and haute eaterie by night. People lined up for their buzzworthy sandwiches (outstanding herb-rubbed roasted turkey,

La Esquina.

Parm.

CONSUME

classic cold cuts or chicken parmesan) and hard-to score dinner seats, packing the joint until it outgrew the space. The pair smartly split the operations, devoting their original flagship to tasting menus and transplanting the sandwich offerings to fetching diner digs next door.

Peasant
194 Elizabeth Street, between Prince & Spring Streets (1-212 965 9511, www.peasantnyc.com). Subway B, D, F, M to Broadway-Lafayette Street; 6 to Bleecker Street. **Open** 6-11pm Tue-Thur; 6-11.30pm Fri, Sat; 6pm-10.30pm Sun. **Main courses** $26. **Credit** AmEx, DC, MC, V. **Map** p403 E29 ⑯ *Italian*
The dining room at Peasant, one of downtown's most celebrated Italian restaurants, is equal parts rustic and urban chic. Cement floors and metal chairs give the place an unfinished edge, while the gaping brick oven and lengthy wooden bar provide the tell-tale old-world notes. Dishes that emerge from the fire are particularly good, including gooey, speck-wrapped *bocconcini* (mozzarella).

Public
210 Elizabeth Street, between Prince & Spring Streets (1-212 343 7011, www.public-nyc.com). Subway N, R to Prince Street; 6 to Spring Street. **Open** 6pm-1am Mon-Thur; 6pm-2am Fri; 10.30am-3.30pm, 6pm-2am Sat; 10.30am-3.30pm, 6pm-midnight Sun. **Main courses** $25. **Credit** AmEx, MC, V. **Map** p403 E29 ⑰ *Eclectic*
This sceney restaurant in a former bakery is moodily lit and industrially chic. The mastermind behind the globally inspired cuisine is British-trained Brad Farmerie, whose travels have left a cosmopolitan

mark on his culinary concoctions. Reflecting pan-Pacific, Middle Eastern and South-east Asian influences, the clipboard menu offers creative dishes such as grilled kangaroo on coriander falafel, or snail and oxtail ravioli, all paired with interesting wines.

Chinatown

$ Dim Sum Go Go
5 East Broadway, at Catherine Street (1-212 732 0797). Subway F to East Broadway. **Open** 10am-10pm daily. **Dumplings** $4/3-4. **Credit** AmEx, DC, Disc, MC, V. **Map** p402 F31 ⑱ *Chinese*
A red and white colour scheme spruces up this Chinatown dim sum restaurant, where dumplings (more than 24 types) are the focus. A neophyte-friendly menu is divided into categories that include 'fried', 'baked' and 'steamed'. To avoid tough decisions, order the dim sum platter, whose artful array of ten items includes juicy steamed duck and mushroom dumplings, and the offbeat, slightly sweet pan-fried dumplings filled with pumpkin. Prices are a tad higher than at your average dim sum emporium.

Peking Duck House
28 Mott Street, between Mosco & Pell Streets (1-212 227 1810, www.pekingduckhousenyc.com). Subway J, N, Q, R, Z, 6 to Canal Street. **Open** 11.30am-10.30pm Mon-Thur, Sun; 11.30am-11.30pm Fri, Sat. **Main courses** $20. **Credit** AmEx, MC, V. **Map** p402 F31 ⑲ *Chinese*
Unlike some establishments, Peking Duck House doesn't require you to order the namesake speciality in advance; a chef will slice the aromatic, crisp-skinned, succulent meat at your table. Select the 'three-way' and your duck will yield the main course,

Follow That Truck!

With the advent of Twitter, mobile food vendors are on a roll.

From the pushcart *knish* sellers of the 19th-century Lower East Side to today's ubiquitous hot dog stands, mobile food vendors are an NYC tradition. Now that Twitter facilitates real-time tracking, the food truck craze has gone into overdrive, spawning brick-and-mortar offshoots and festivals where vendors are the main attraction. Yet despite their popularity, a recent court ruling reinforcing a 1950s law prohibiting hawking from metered parking spaces has been driving vendors out of their usual spots, especially in midtown. Still, our favourite trucks and carts manage to keep on trucking…

BIG GAY ICE CREAM TRUCK

Doug Quint had been making his way in New York as a freelance bassoonist, when a friend Facebook-messaged him about driving a soft-serve ice-cream truck. A vision was born, and together with partner Bryan Petroff, the cone-slinger has brought inspired toppings such as Trix cereal and wasabi pea dust to traditional soft serve. Although the truck only operates from May to October, the pair are opening their second, non-mobile shop in spring 2013 (*see p153*).
Signature eats The Salty Pimp (vanilla ice-cream, dulce de leche, sea salt, chocolate dip; $5); the Bea Arthur (vanilla ice-cream, dulce de leche, crushed Nilla wafers; $4).
Track it at www.biggayicecream.com, @biggayicecream.

CALEXICO

The brothers behind this Cal-Mex taco operation – Dave, Jesse and Brian Vendley – are practically mobile-eats royalty. Their original Soho cart has been heavily trafficked since opening in 2006. By 2008, they had a Vendy Award to their name, and their first brick-and-mortar offshoot, Calexico Carne Asada in Red Hook, was crowned 'Best New Mexican' in the *Time Out New York* Food & Drink Awards (they now have a second Brooklyn restaurant). You can find the carts in Soho and the Flatiron District most days, and in Brooklyn Bridge Park in summer.
Signature eats Calexico carne asada burrito ($9); chipotle pork taco ($3).
Track it at www.calexicocart.com, @celexiocartnyc.

DESSERTTRUCK

Helmed by a trio of Le Cirque alums (Jerome Chang, Susana Garcia and Vincent Jaoura), this confectionery on wheels now has a static Lower East Side location, DessertTruck Works (6 Clinton Street, between E Houston & Stanton Streets, 1-212 228 0701).
Signature eats Goat's cheese cake with rosemary caramel and seasonal fruit ($6.25); chocolate bread pudding with bacon custard sauce ($6.25).
Track it at www.desserttruck.com, @desserttruck.

CONSUME

TREATS TRUCK

Baking queen Kim Ima used to make goodies for her colleagues in the theatre business (she worked as an actor and director) before she let the rest of New York in on the action. Now, all her classic sweets are baked in Red Hook before they take to the streets.

Signature eats Oatmeal jammy ($1.25); cran-almond crispy square ($3); sugar-dot iced cookie (50¢).

Track it at 1-212 691 5226, www.treatstruck.com, @thetreatstruck.

WAFELS & DINGES

Belgian expat Thomas DeGeest and his crew operate four carts and one fully fledged truck, which hit more than 20 locations around the city every week. The carts dispense Liège *wafels*, which are chewy and gently caramelised from pearl sugar in the dough, while the truck also offers the Brussels variety, the crispier, yeast-leavened rectangles known stateside as Belgian waffles.

Signature eats Liège *wafel* ($5) with one of the many *dinges* (first topping free, each additional $1), such as gingerbread-like spekuloos spread paired with Nutella.

Track it at 1-866 429 7329, www.wafelsanddinges.com, @waffletruck.

Big Gay Ice Cream Truck.

a vegetable stir-fry with leftover bits of meat, and a cabbage soup made with the remaining bone.
Other locations 236 E 53rd Street, between Second & Third Avenues, Midtown East (1-212 759 8260).

Ping's

22 Mott Street, between Mosco & Pell Streets (1-212 602 9988, www.pingsnyc.com). Subway J, N, Q, R, Z, 6 to Canal Street. **Open** 10.30am-11pm Mon-Fri; 9am-11pm Sat, Sun. **Main courses** $25. **Credit** MC, V. **Map** p402 F31 ⑳ **Chinese**
The bank of fish tanks near the entrance suggests the speciality. Go for something you haven't tried: bite-sized pieces of boneless smelt deep-fried to a golden yellow and served with a mix of Szechuan peppercorns and salt to boost the mild flavour. Big steamed oysters benefit from a splash of Ping's celebrated house-made XO sauce – a spicy condiment made of dried shrimp, scallops and garlic. The sliced sautéed conch is set off by snappy snow peas and a tangy fermented shrimp sauce. Those exotic flavours, plus touches like tablecloths, justify prices that are a notch above the Chinatown norm.

$ Super Taste Restaurant

26 Eldridge Street, at Canal Street (1-212 625 1198). Subway F to East Broadway. **Open** 10.30am-10.30pm daily. **Main courses** $6. **No credit cards. Map** p403 F30 ㉑ **Chinese**
In a sea of cheap Chinatown noodle bars, Super Taste stands out. Watch the cook hand pull your Lanzhou-style *la mian*, the Chinese relative of Japanese ramen, which is served in a soup with a choice of toppings that vary from beef tendon to eel – at little more than a fiver for a bowl.

Lower East Side

Clinton Street Baking Company

4 Clinton Street, between E Houston & Stanton Streets (1-646 602 6263, www.clintonstreet baking.com). Subway F to Second Avenue; J, M, Z to Delancey-Essex Streets. **Open** 8am-4pm, 6-11pm Mon-Fri; 9am-4pm, 6-11pm Sat; 9am-6pm Sun. **Main courses** $15. **Credit** (evenings only) AmEx, DC, Disc, MC, V. **Map** p403 G29 ㉒ **Café**
The warm buttermilk biscuits and fluffy plate-size pancakes at this pioneering little eaterie are reason enough to face the brunch-time crowds. If you want to avoid the onslaught, the homey place is just as reliable for both lunch and dinner. Try the $15 beer and burger special (6-8pm Mon-Thur): 8oz of Black Angus topped with swiss cheese and caramelised onions, served with a beer.

Les Enfants Terribles

37 Canal Street, at Ludlow Street (1-212 777 7518, www.lesenfantsterriblesnyc.com). Subway F to East Broadway. **Open** 5.30pm-midnight

CONSUME

Katz's Delicatessen.

Mon-Fri; 11am-midnight Sat, Sun. **Main courses** $20. **Credit** AmEx, MC, V. **Map** p403 G30

㉓ French-African

Worn-in brown leather banquettes and a sepia-toned colour scheme foster a bohemian vibe at this lively hangout. The menu claims French-African influences but the best items come straight from the bistro, such as steak frites, the meat dripping with juices and served with a side of aggressively seasoned fries.

Freemans

2 Freeman Alley, off Rivington Street, between Bowery & Chrystie Street (1-212 420 0012, www.freemansrestaurant.com). Subway F to Lower East Side-Second Avenue; J, Z to Bowery. **Open** 11am-4pm, 6-11.30pm Mon-Fri; 10am-4pm, 6-11.30pm Sat, Sun. **Main courses** $23. **Credit** AmEx, DC, Disc, MC, V. **Map** p403 F29 **㉔**

American creative

Located at the end of a graffiti-marked alley, Freemans, with its colonial tavern meets hunting lodge style, is an enduring hit with retro-loving New Yorkers. Garage-sale oil paintings and moose antlers serve as backdrops to a curved zinc bar, while the menu recalls a simpler time – devils on horseback (prunes stuffed with stilton cheese and wrapped in bacon); rum-soaked ribs, the meat falling off the bone with a gentle nudge of the fork; and stiff cocktails that'll get you good and sauced.

★ Katz's Delicatessen

205 E Houston Street, at Ludlow Street (1-212 254 2246, www.katzdeli.com). Subway F to Lower East Side-Second Avenue. **Open** 8am-10.45pm Mon-Wed; 8am-2.45am Thur; 24hrs Fri (from 8am), Sat; closes 10.45pm Sun. **Sandwiches** $16. **Credit** AmEx, Disc, MC, V. **Map** p403 F29 **㉕ American**

A visit to Gotham isn't complete without a stop at a quintessential New York deli, and this Lower East Side survivor is the real deal. You might get a kick out of the famous faces plastered to the panelled walls, or the spot where Meg Ryan faked it in *When Harry Met Sally...*, but the real stars of this cavernous cafeteria are the thick-cut pastrami sandwiches and crisp-skinned all-beef hot dogs – the latter a mere $3.45.

▶ *See p64 for more local kosher nosh.*

$ Mission Chinese Food

154 Orchard Street, between Rivington & Stanton Streets (1-212 529 8800, www.missionchinese food.com). Subway F to Lower East Side-Second Avenue. **Open** noon-3pm, 5.30pm-midnight daily. **Main courses** $13. **Credit** AmEx, Disc, MC, V. **Map** p403 F29 **㉖ Chinese**

Anthony Myint and Daniel Bowien shook up the San Francisco dining scene with their eclectic Asian soul food. In 2012, Bowien opened this Lower East Side outpost, decorated with a hanging yellow dragon and plastic flowers in throwaway vases. His cooking features intensely personal spins on a host of Szechuan and Chinese-American classics. The *ma po* tofu spotlights pork shoulder slow-cooked for six hours under seaweed sheets to ramp up the umami, and new dimensions of tongue-numbing heat. Rather than the usual chicken, the kung pao comes with excellent house-smoked pastrami.

Schiller's Liquor Bar

131 Rivington Street, at Norfolk Street (1-212 260 4555, www.schillersny.com). Subway F to Delancey Street; J, Z to Delancey-Essex Streets. **Open** 11am-1am Mon-Thur; 11am-3am Fri; 10am-3am Sat; 10am-1am Sun. **Main courses** $19. **Credit** AmEx, DC, MC, V. **Map** p403 G29 **㉗ Eclectic**

At this artfully reconstructed faux-vintage hangout, the menu is a mix of French bistro (steak frites), British pub (fish and chips) and good ol' American (cheeseburger), while the wine menu famously hawks a down-to-earth hierarchy: Good, Decent, Cheap. As at Keith McNally's other establishments, folks pack in for the scene, triple-parking at the curved central bar for elaborate cocktails and star sightings.

East Village

Back Forty

190 Avenue B, between 11th & 12th Streets (1-212 388 1990, www.backfortynyc.com). Subway L to First Avenue. **Open** 6-11pm Mon-Thur; 6pm-midnight Fri; 11am-3.30pm, 6pm-midnight Sat; 11am-3.30pm, 6-10pm Sun. **Main courses** $15. **Credit** AmEx, DC, MC, V. **Map** p403 G28 **American**

Peter Hoffman (the pioneering chef who launched the market-driven restaurant Savoy, now occupied by his second Back Forty location) is behind this East Village seasonal-eats tavern. Pared-down farmhouse chic prevails in the decor and on the menu. House specialities include juicy grass-fed burgers, stout floats made with beer from New York-area breweries, and golden pork-jowl nuggets. The spacious back garden, open in warmer months, is a bonus.

Other locations 70 Prince Street, at Crosby Street, Soho (1-212 219 8570).

$ Big Gay Ice Cream Shop

125 E 7th Street, between First Avenue & Avenue A (1-212 533 9333, www.biggayicecream.com). Subway L to First Avenue. **Open** 1pm-midnight daily. **Ice-cream** $5. **Credit** AmEx, Disc, MC, V. **Map** p403 F28 **Ice-cream**

Ice-cream truckers Doug Quint and Bryan Petroff now offer their quirky soft-serve creations in this small shop, decorated with a giant unicorn mural bedazzled with 6,000 Swarovski crystals. Toppings run from Trix cereal to cayenne pepper and the menu also includes sweet treats from flea-market friends including La Newyorkina (ice pops) and Melt Bakery (ice-cream sandwiches). A second location is due to open in spring 2013 (61 Grove Street, between Bleecker Street & Seventh Avenue South, West Village).

► *For more about Big Gay Ice Cream, see p150 Follow That Truck!*

$ Caracas Arepa Bar

93½ E 7th Street, between First Avenue & Avenue A (1-212 228 5062, www.caracasarepabar.com). Subway F to Lower East Side-Second Avenue; 6 to Astor Place. **Open** noon-11pm daily. **Arepas** $7. **Credit** AmEx, DC, Disc, MC, V. **Map** p403 F28 **Venezuelan**

This endearing spot, with flower-patterned, vinyl-covered tables and bare-brick walls, zaps you straight to Caracas. Each *arepa* is made from scratch daily; the pitta-like pockets are stuffed with a choice of 18 fillings, such as the classic beef with black beans, cheese and plaintain, or chicken and avocado. Top off your snack with a *cocada*, a thick and creamy milkshake made with freshly grated coconut and cinnamon.

Other locations 291 Grand Street, between Havemeyer & Roebling Streets, Williamsburg, Brooklyn (1-718 218 6050).

$ Crif Dogs

113 St Marks Place, between First Avenue & Avenue A (1-212 614 2728, www.crifdogs.com). Subway L to First Avenue; 6 to Astor Place.

Schiller's Liquor Bar.

CONSUME

CONSUME

Open noon-2am Mon-Thur, Sun; noon-4am Fri, Sat. **Hot dogs** $4. **Credit** AmEx, MC, V. **Map** p403 F28 ➌ **American**

You'll recognise this place by the giant hot dog outside, bearing the come-on 'Eat me'. Crif offers the best Jersey-style dogs this side of the Hudson: handmade smoked pork tube-steaks that are deep-fried until they're bursting out of their skins. While they're served in various guises, including the Spicy Redneck (bacon-wrapped and covered in chilli, coleslaw and jalapeños) and the Chihuahua (baconwrapped with sour cream and avocado), the classic with mustard and kraut is the most popular. If you're wondering why there are so many people hanging around near the public phone booth at night, it's because there's a trendy cocktail bar, PDT (*see p180*), concealed behind it.

Other locations 555 Driggs Avenue, at North 7th Street, Williamsburg, Brooklyn (1-718 302 3200).

DBGB Kitchen & Bar

299 Bowery, at E Houston Street (1-212 933 5300, www.danielnyc.com). Subway B, D, F, M to Broadway-Lafayette Street; 6 to Bleecker Street. **Open** noon-11pm Mon; noon-midnight Tue-Thur; noon-1am Fri; 11am-1am Sat; 11am-11pm Sun. **Main courses** $21. **Credit** AmEx, MC, V. **Map** p403 F29 ➋ **French**

This big, buzzy brasserie – chef Daniel Boulud's most populist venture – stands out for its kitchensink scope. More than a dozen kinds of sausage, from Thai-accented to Tunisienne, are served alongside burgers, different pieces of offal and haute bistro fare. The best way to get your head around the schizophrenic enterprise is to bring a large group and try to sample as much of the range as possible, including ice-cream sundaes or sumptuous cakes for dessert.

▶ *For more of Daniel Boulud's output, see p171 and p172.*

Dirt Candy

430 E 9th Street, between First Avenue & Avenue A (1-212 228 7732, www.dirtcandy nyc.com). Subway L to First Avenue; 6 to Astor Place. **Open** 5.30-11pm Tue-Sat. **Main courses** $18. **Credit** AmEx, Disc, MC, V. **Map** p403 F28 ➌ **Vegetarian**

The shiny, futuristic environment here makes the place look more like a chic nail salon than a restaurant. Chef-owner Amanda Cohen has created an unlikely space to execute her less-likely ambition: to make people crave vegetables. And she mostly succeeds. Elaborate dishes might include a pungent portobello mousse accompanied by shiitake mushrooms and fennel-peach compote or stone-ground grits served with corn cream, pickled shiitake mushrooms, *huitlacoche* (Mexican truffle) and a tempura poached egg. With vegan-friendly options for desserts, Cohen has created a menu that's suitable for omnivores.

▶ *Another excellent veggie option is Pure Food & Wine, see p167.*

Il Buco Alimentari & Vineria

53 Great Jones Street, between Bowery and Lafayette Street (1-212 837 2622, www.ilbuco vineria.com). Subway B, D, F, M to Broadway-Lafayette Street; 6 to Bleecker Street. **Open** 7am-midnight Mon-Thur; 7am-1am Fri; 9am-1am Sat; 9am-11pm Sun. **Main courses** $24. **Credit** AmEx, MC, V. **Map** p403 F29 ❸ **Italian**

Il Buco has been a mainstay of the downtown dining scene since the '90s and a pioneer in the sort of rustic Italian food now consuming the city. Owner Donna Leonard took her sweet time (18 years, to be exact) to unveil her first offshoot, Il Buco Alimentari & Vineria. It was worth the wait: the new hybrid bakery, food shop, café and trattoria is as confident as its decades-old sibling with sure-footed service, the familial bustle of a neighborhood pillar, and heady aromas of wood-fired short ribs and salt-crusted fish drifting from an open kitchen.

Other locations Il Buco 47 Bond Street, between Bowery & Lafayette Street, East Village (1-212 533 1932).

Ippudo NY

65 Fourth Avenue, between 9th & 10th Streets (1-212 388 0088, www.ippudony.com). Subway 6 to Astor Place. **Open** 11am-3.30pm, 5-11.30pm Mon-Thur; 11am-3.30pm, 5pm-12.30am Fri, Sat; 11am-10.30pm Sun. **Ramen** $15. **Credit** AmEx, MC, V. **Map** p403 F28 ❸ **Japanese**

This sleek outpost of a Japanese ramen chain is packed mostly with Nippon natives who queue up for a taste of 'Ramen King' Shigemi Kawahara's *tonkotsu* – a pork-based broth. About half a dozen varieties include the Akamaru Modern, a smooth, buttery soup topped with scallions, cabbage, a slice of roasted pork and pleasantly elastic noodles. Avoid non-soup dishes such as the oily fried-chicken nuggets coated in a sweet batter. Long live the Ramen King – just don't ask him to move beyond his speciality.

Kyo Ya

94 E 7th Street, between First Avenue & Avenue A (1-212 982 4140). Subway 6 to Astor Place. **Open** 5.30-11.30pm Mon-Sat; 5.30-10.30pm Sun. **Main courses** $27. **Credit** AmEx, Disc, MC, V. **Map** p403 F28 ❸ **Japanese**

The city's most ambitious Japanese speakeasy is marked only by an 'Open' sign, but in-the-know diners still find their way inside. The food, presented

CONSUME

Il Buco Alimentari & Vineria.

CONSUME

on beautiful handmade plates, is gorgeous: maitake mushrooms are fried in the lightest tempura batter and delivered on a polished stone bed. Sushi is pressed with a hot iron on to sticky vinegared rice. The few desserts – including an extra-silky crème caramel – are just as ethereal as the savoury food.

★ Momofuku Ssäm Bar

207 Second Avenue, at 13th Street (1-212 254 3500, www.momofuku.com). Subway L to First or Third Avenue; L, N, Q, R, 4, 5, 6 to 14th Street-Union Square. **Open** 11.30am-3.30pm, 5pm-midnight Mon-Thur, Sun; 11.30am-3.30pm, 5pm-1am Fri, Sat. **Main courses** $20. **Credit** AmEx, MC, V. **Map** p403 F27 ❸ **Korean**

At chef David Chang's second modern Korean restaurant, waiters hustle to noisy rock music in the 50-seat space, which feels expansive compared with its Noodle Bar predecessor's crowded counter dining. Try the wonderfully fatty pork-belly steamed bun with hoisin sauce and cucumbers, or one of the ham platters. But you'll need to come with a crowd to sample the house speciality, *bo ssäm* (a slow-roasted hog butt that is consumed wrapped in lettuce leaves, with a dozen oysters and other accompaniments); it serves six to eight people and must be ordered in advance. David Chang has further expanded his E Vill empire with a bar, Booker and Dax (*see p179*) at this location and a sweet annexe, Milk Bar (one of several in the city), across the street.

Other locations Má Pêche 15 West 56th Street, between Fifth & Sixth Avenues, Midtown West (1-212 757 5878); **Momofuku Ko** 163 First Avenue, at 10th Street, East Village (1-212 500 0831); **Momofuku Noodle Bar** 171 First Avenue, between 10th & 11th Streets, East Village (1-212 777 7773); **Milk Bar** throughout the city.

Northern Spy Food Co

511 E 12th Street, between Avenues A & B (1-212 228 5100, www.northernspyfoodco.com). Subway L to First Avenue. **Open** 10am-4pm, 5.30-11pm Mon-Fri; 10am-3.30pm, 5.30-11pm Sat, Sun. **Main courses** $15. **Credit** AmEx, MC, V. **Map** p403 G28 ❸ **American**

Named after an apple indigenous to the North-east, Northern Spy serves locally sourced meals at reasonable prices. The frequently changing menu is based almost entirely on what's in season. The food isn't fancy, but it satisfies. A 'chicken and egg' sandwich memorably combined pan-crisped dark meat, zingy chimichurri, arugula and a poached egg. Toothsome daily cut pork shared the plate with rich pork jus, black-eyed peas and collard greens.

★ $ Porchetta

110 E 7th Street, between First Avenue & Avenue A (1-212 777 2151, www.porchetta nyc.com). Subway F to Lower East Side-Second Avenue; L to First Avenue; 6 to Astor Place. **Open** 11.30am-10pm Mon-Thur, Sun;

11.30am-11pm Fri, Sat. **Sandwiches** $10. **Credit** MC, V. **Map** p403 F28 ❸ **Café**

This small, subway-tiled space has a narrow focus: central Italy's classic boneless roasted pork. The meat – available as a sandwich or a platter – is amazingly moist and tender, having been slowly roasted with rendered pork fat, seasoned with fennel pollen, herbs and spices, and flecked with brittle shards of skin. The other menu items (a mozzarella sandwich, humdrum sides) seem incidental; the pig is the point.

Veselka

144 Second Avenue, at 9th Street (1-212 228 9682, www.veselka.com). Subway L to Third Avenue; 6 to Astor Place. **Open** 24hrs daily. **Main courses** $15. **Credit** AmEx, DC, Disc, MC, V. **Map** p403 F28 ❹ **Eastern European**

When you need food to soak up the mess of drinks you've consumed in the East Village in the early hours, it's worth remembering Veselka: a relatively inexpensive Eastern European restaurant with plenty of seats that's open 24 hours a day. Hearty appetites can get a platter of classic Ukrainian grub: goulash, *kielbasa*, beef stroganoff or *bigos* stew. For dessert, try the *kutya* (traditional Ukrainian pudding made with berries, walnuts, poppy seeds and honey).

Other locations 9 E 1st Street, between Bowery & Second Avenue (1-212 387 7000).

Greenwich Village

Babbo

110 Waverly Place, between MacDougal Street & Sixth Avenue (1-212 777 0303, www.babbo nyc.com). Subway A, B, C, D, E, F, M to

Momofuku Ssäm Bar.

W 4th Street. **Open** 5.30-11.15pm Mon; 11.30am-2pm, 5.30-11.15pm Tue-Sat; 5-11pm Sun. **Main courses** $28. **Credit** AmEx, Disc, MC, V. **Map** p403 E28 **Italian**
See p160 **Diffusion Dining.**

Blue Hill
75 Washington Place, between Washington Square West & Sixth Avenue (1-212 539 1776, www.bluehillfarm.com). Subway A, B, C, D, E, F, M to W 4th Street. **Open** 5-11pm Mon-Sat; 5-10pm Sun. **Main courses** $35. **Credit** AmEx, DC, MC, V. **Map** p403 E28 **American**
More than a mere crusader for sustainability, Dan Barber is also one of the most talented cooks in town, building his menu around whatever's at its peak on the family farm in Great Barrington, Massachusetts, and the not-for-profit Stone Barns Center for Food and Agriculture in Westchester, NY (home to a sibling restaurant), among other suppliers. The evening may begin with a sophisticated seasonal spin on a pig-liver terrine and move on to a sweet slow-roasted parsnip 'steak' with creamed spinach and beet ketchup.

Kin Shop
469 Sixth Avenue, between 11th & 12th Streets (1-212 675 4295, www.kinshopnyc.com). Subway F, M to 14th Street; L to Sixth Avenue. **Open** 11.30am-3pm, 5.30-11pm Mon-Thur; 11.30am-3pm, 5.30-11.30pm Fri, Sat; 11.30am-2pm, 5-10pm Sun. **Main courses** $23. **Credit** AmEx, MC, V. **Map** p403 D28 **Thai**
Top Chef champ Harold Dieterle channels his Southeast Asian travels into the menu at this eatery, which serves classic Thai street food alongside more upmarket Thai-inspired dishes. Although the traditional fare seems extraneous, Dieterle's auteur creations are often inspired. A salad of fried oysters, slivered celery and crispy pork belly is bright and refreshing, while a cheffy riff on massaman curry features long-braised goat neck with a silky sauce infused with coconut milk, duck fat and purple yams. Pair the spicy grub with thoughtful drinks (such as the herbaceous Kin & Tonic) to help tame the flame.

Lupa
170 Thompson Street, between Bleecker & W Houston Streets (1-212 982 5089, www.lupa restaurant.com). Subway A, B, C, D, E, F, M to W 4th Street. **Open** noon-midnight daily. **Main courses** $20. **Credit** AmEx, DC, Disc, MC, V. **Map** p403 E29 **Italian**
No mere 'poor man's Babbo' (Mario Batali's other and pricier restaurant around the corner), this convivial trattoria offers communal dining, reasonably priced wines and hit-the-spot comfort foods. Come for classic Roman fare such as punchy *orecchiette* with greens and sausage, or gumdrop-shaped ricotta gnocchi.
▶ *For a comparison with Babbo, see p160 Diffusion Dining.*

Perla
24 Minetta Lane, between Sixth Avenue & MacDougal Street (1-212 933 1824, www.perla nyc.com). Subway A, B, C, D, E, F, M to W 4th Street. **Open** 4.30-11pm Mon, Sun; 4.30pm-midnight Tue, Wed; 4.30pm-1am Thur-Sat. **Main courses** $27. **Credit** AmEx, MC, V. **Map** p403 E29 **Italian**

CONSUME

For his latest Village hit, restaurateur Gabriel Stulman has teamed up with talented young chef Michael Toscano. The toque has wasted no time in embracing the spotlight here, turning out bold, playful food to match the electric vibe. Settle in for a procession of small plates that tease freshness and excitement from humble Italian classics. You might start with cool pieces of lobster served with robiolina and a sprinkle of caviar, then move on to handmade pastas like translucent brown-buttered tortelli with Technicolor ricotta-beet filling. The generous entrées have self-confident swagger, all big, bold proteins under an assertive sear.

Minetta Tavern

113 MacDougal Street, between Bleecker & 3rd Streets (1-212 475 3850, www.minettatavern ny.com). Subway A, B, C, D, E, F, M to W 4th Street. **Open** 5.30pm-1am Mon, Tue; noon-2.30pm, 5.30pm-1am Wed-Fri; 11am-3pm, 5.30pm-1am Sat, Sun. **Main courses** $25. **Credit** AmEx, Disc, MC, V. **Map** p403 E29 **46 Eclectic**

Thanks to restaurateur extraordinaire Keith McNally's spot-on restoration, this former literati hangout, once frequented by Hemingway and Fitzgerald, is as buzzy now as it must have been in its mid 20th-century heyday. The big-flavoured bistro fare is as much of a draw as the scene, and includes classics such as roasted bone marrow, trout meunière topped with crabmeat, and an airy Grand Marnier soufflé for dessert. But the most illustrious thing on the menu is the Black Label burger. You might find the $26 price tag a little hard to swallow,

but the superbly tender sandwich – essentially chopped steak in a bun smothered in caramelised onions – is worth every penny.

▶ *For less expensive but equally acclaimed burgers, see Corner Bistro (p159) and Shake Shack (p173).*

$ Num Pang Sandwich Shop

21 E 12th Street, between Fifth Avenue & University Place (1-212 255 3271, www. numpangnyc.com). Subway L, N, Q, R, 4, 5, 6 to 14th Street-Union Square. **Open** 11am-10pm Mon-Sat; noon-9pm Sun. **Sandwiches** $8. **No credit cards. Map** p403 E28 **47 Cambodian**

At this small shop, the rotating varieties of *num pang* (Cambodia's answer to the Vietnamese *banh mi*) include pulled duroc pork with spiced honey, peppercorn catfish, and hoisin veal meatballs, all stuffed into crusty baguettes. There's counter seating upstairs, or get it to go and eat in nearby Washington Square Park.

Other locations 140 E 41st Street, between Lexington & Third Avenues, Midtown East (1-212 867 8889).

West Village & Meatpacking District

Barbuto

775 Washington Street, at 12th Street (1-212 924 9700, www.barbutonyc.com). Subway A, C, E to 14th Street; L to Eighth Avenue. **Open** noon-11pm Mon-Wed; noon-midnight Thur-Sat;

Minetta Tavern.

Buvette.

noon-10pm Sun. **Main courses** $22. **Credit** AmEx, Disc, MC, V. **Map** p403 C28 ④ **Italian**
The earthy, season-driven cooking in this raw, cement-floored space is top-notch: for example, marvellously light calamares in lemon-garlic sauce, or seasonally changing gnocchi that might incorporate squash and pumpkin seed pesto. In the summer, the garage doors go up and the crowd of stylists, assistants, yuppies and West Village whatevers mob the corner until last orders.

Buvette
42 Grove Street, between Bedford & Bleecker Streets (1-212 255 3590, www.ilovebuvette.com). Subway 1 to Christopher Street-Sheridan Square. **Open** 8am-2am Mon-Fri; 10am-2am Sat, Sun. **Main courses** $15. **Credit** AmEx, MC, V. **Map** p403 D29 ④ **French**
Chef Jody Williams has filled every nook of tiny, Gallic-themed Buvette with old picnic baskets, teapots and silver trays, among other vintage ephemera. The food is just as thoughtfully curated – Williams' immaculate renditions of coq au vin, goose-fat rillettes or intense, lacquered wedges of tarte Tatin arrive on tiny plates, in petite jars or in miniature casseroles, her time-warp flavours recalling an era when there were still classic bistros on every corner.

$ Corner Bistro
331 W 4th Street, at Jane Street (1-212 242 9502). Subway A, C, E to 14th Street; L to Eighth Avenue. **Open** 11.30am-4am Mon-Sat; noon-4am Sun. **Burgers** $6.50. **No credit cards. Map** p403 D28 ⑤ **American**
There's only one reason to come to this legendary pub: it serves what some New Yorkers say are the city's best burgers – plus the beer is just $3 a mug. The patties are no-frills and served on a flimsy paper plate. To get one, you may have to queue for a good hour, especially on weekend nights; if the wait is too long for a table, try to slip into a space at the bar.

Other locations 47-18 Vernon Boulevard, at 47th Road, Long Island City, Queens (1-718 606 6500).
▶ For other top-ranking burgers, see Minetta Tavern (see *p158*) and Shake Shake (*p173*).

EN Japanese Brasserie
435 Hudson Street, at Leroy Street (1-212 647 9196, www.enjb.com). Subway 1 to Houston Street. **Open** noon-2.30pm, 5.30-10.30pm Mon-Thur; noon-2.30pm, 5.30-11.30pm Fri; 11am-2.30pm, 5.30-11.30pm Sat; 11am-2.30pm, 5.30-10.30pm Sun. **Main courses** $15. **Credit** AmEx, MC, V. **Map** p403 D29 ⑤ **Japanese**
The owners of this popular spot aim to evoke a sense of Japanese living in the multi-level space. On the ground floor are *tatami*-style rooms; on the mezzanine are recreations of a living room, dining room and library of a Japanese home from the Meiji era. But the spacious main dining room is where the action is. Highlights of chef Abe Hiroki's menu include freshly made scooped tofu served with a soy-dashi mix; miso-marinated, broiled Alaskan black cod; and Berkshire pork belly braised in sansho miso. Try the saké and shochu flights (or wonderful cocktails) for an authentic Asian buzz.

Fatty Crab
643 Hudson Street, between Gansevoort & Horatio Streets (1-212 352 3592, www.fatty crab.com). Subway A, C, E to 14th St; L to Eighth Avenue. **Open** noon-midnight daily. **Main courses** $19. **Credit** AmEx, Disc, MC, V. **Map** p403 C28 ⑤ **Malaysian**
This Malaysian-inspired eaterie reflects chef Zak Pelaccio's cunning take on South-east Asian cuisine: Who knew you could squeeze *sambal* mayo and pork belly between slices of Pepperidge Farm bread for a killer tea sandwich? The classic Malaysian chilli crab makes an appearance, but expect to pay quite a bit more for it: 'market price' can mean $40 for a single Dungeness swimming in an admittedly

CONSUME

excellent tomato chilli sauce. Far better bang for your buck is the short rib *rendang*, an unbelievably tender chunk of meat braised in coconut and kaffir lime. This packed spot takes no reservations, but turnover is quick – hard wooden chairs squeezed behind tiny tables in the single red-walled room don't encourage tarrying.

Fedora
239 W 4th Street, between Charles & 10th Streets (1-646 449 9336, www.fedoranyc.com). Subway A, B, C, D, E, F, M to W 4th Street; 1 to Christopher Street-Sheridan Square. **Open** 5.30pm-11pm Mon, Sun; 5.30-2am Tue-Sat. **Main courses** $25. **Credit** AmEx, MC, V. **Map** p403 D28 ❸ **Eclectic**
This French-Canadian knockout is part of restaurateur Gabriel Stulman's West Village mini-empire (his other local eateries are Joseph Leonard, Jeffrey's

Grocery and Perla; *see p157*). Mehdi Brunet-Benkritly produces some of the most exciting toe-to-tongue cooking in town, plying epicurean hipsters with Quebecois party food that's eccentric, excessive and fun – crisp duck breast with hazelnuts, for example, or scallops with bacon, tomatoes and polenta.

★ Kesté Pizza & Vino
271 Bleecker Street, between Cornelia & Jones Streets (1-212 243 1500, www.kestepizzeria.com). Subway 1 to Christopher Street-Sheridan Square. **Open** noon-3.30pm, 5-11pm Mon-Thur; noon-11.30pm Fri, Sat; noon-10.30pm Sun. **Pizzas** $15. **Credit** AmEx, DC, MC, V. **Map** p403 D29 ❸ **Pizza**
If anyone can claim to be an expert on Neapolitan pizza, it's Kesté's Roberto Caporuscio: as president of the US branch of the Associazione Pizzaiuoli Napoletani, he's the top dog for the training and

---

Diffusion Dining

Top chefs offer more-affordable spin-offs from their famous flagships.

DBGB Kitchen & Bar.

MARIO BATALI
Hunger for... Babbo (*see p156*).
Good luck getting a table at Mario Batali's flagship operation. The celebrity chef's restaurant is one of NYC's toughest tables to score. Would you feel better if we said it wasn't worth the effort? On our most recent visit, the sauce coating our goose liver ravioli was reduced almost to the point of being burnt, and other dishes, while serviceable, did not live up to the hype.

Then try... Lupa (*see p157*).
Batali's convivial West Village trattoria offers communal spaces, reasonably priced wines and hit-the-spot comfort foods. Come for classic Roman fare including punchy *orecchiette* with greens and sausage, and gumdrop-shaped ricotta gnocchi. A favourite for late-night diners, it offers such specials as three courses for $29 (including a glass of wine; 10pm-midnight Mon-Thur, Sun).

DANIEL BOULUD
Hunger for... Daniel (*see p171*).
When it reopened in 2009 after a subtle revamp, fine-dining king Daniel Boulud's flagship achieved perfect ratings from the *New York Times* and *Time Out New York* magazine. The prix fixe dinner – $108 for three courses – is served in a hushed two-tiered dining room. Choose a classic Boulud dish, such as the black truffle and scallops in puff pastry. Or visit the less formal lounge for à la carte options.

Then try... DBGB Kitchen & Bar
(*see p154*).
In a continuous attempt to soften his upscale image, Daniel Boulud opened this Bowery meat mecca, known for its international sausages (made by the charcutiers at Bar Boulud), copious beers on tap and indulgent burgers and sundaes. The industrial interior doesn't hide the fact that this is a gourmand's take on casual food. The Beaujolaise sausage, refined yet deeply porky, is among the best in the city.

CONSUME

certification of *pizzaioli*. At his intimate, 46-seat space, it's all about the crust – blistered, salty and elastic, it could easily be eaten plain. Add ace toppings such as sweet-tart San Marzano tomato sauce, milky mozzarella and fresh basil, and you have one of New York's finest pies.

▶ *Robert Caporuscio also had a hand in the latest pedigree pizza place, Don Antonio by Starita (p168).*

$ Moustache

90 Bedford Street, between Barrow & Grove Streets (1-212 229 2220, www.moustache pitza.com). Subway 1 to Christopher Street-Sheridan Square. **Open** noon–midnight daily.
Main courses $13. **No credit cards.**
Map p403 D29 ⑤ **Middle Eastern**
Located on a leafy, brownstone-lined street, this beloved cheap-eats haven serves some of the city's best Middle Eastern food. The small, exposed-brick dining room packs in a neighbourhood crowd nightly and, as it doesn't take reservations, it's not unusual to see a queue outside. It's worth the wait, however; the freshly baked pittas, still puffed up with hot air when served, are perfect for scooping up smoky baba ganoush. More elaborate offerings include *ouzi*: rice, chicken, vegetables and raisins cooked in filo.
Other locations 265 E 10th Street, between First Avenue & Avenue A, East Village (1-212 228 2022); 1621 Lexington Avenue, at 102 Street, East Harlem (1-212 828 0030).

★ Pearl Oyster Bar

18 Cornelia Street, between Bleecker & 4th Streets (1-212 691 8211, www.pearloysterbar.com). Subway A, B, C, D, E, F, M to W 4th Street.

ABC Kitchen.

THOMAS KELLER
Hunger for... Per Se (*see p172*).
When superchef Thomas Keller's Per Se arrived in 2005, it quickly became one of Manhattan's most lauded (and toughest to reserve) haute-cuisine experiences. The $295 tasting menu ($185 for lunch) can bring delights such as Keller's signature oysters-and-caviar starter, as well as dazzling iterations of such classics as poached lobster and calotte de boeuf.

Then try... Bouchon Bakery (*see p172*).
Keller's café, in the same mall as his fine-dining room, lacks ambience, and the soups, tartines and salads are a bit basic. Prices are more palatable, with sandwiches such as a dry-cured ham and emmenthaler baguette for around a tenner. Focus on the bakery: French classics and Keller's takes on American ones – Oreo cookies and Nutter Butters – are the real highlights.

JEAN-GEORGES VONGERICHTEN
Hunger for... Jean Georges (*see p172*).
There may be trendier fine-dining temples in town, but globe-trotting chef Jean-Georges Vongerichten's flagship still delivers on its culinary promises 16 years after its debut. For flawless food, a sense of occasion and Central Park-side location, the eaterie is unmatched (except by its neighbour, Per Se).

Then try... ABC Kitchen (*see p164*).
Vongerichten, together with chef Dan Kluger, brings a winning mix of healthy and decadent cuisine (sumptuous salads and meat that could convert a vegetarian) to this eaterie within a landmark furniture store. The seasonal food is as easy on the palate as the environment, and won't do your wallet as much damage as his flagship.

CONSUME

'sNice

The high-end ingredients and whimsical plating at Ed Schoenfeld's interpretive Chinese restaurant have helped pack the narrow contemporary dining room since opening night. Chef Joe Ng is known for his dim sum artistry: pork and shrimp *shumai* come skewered over shot glasses of warm carrot soup – designed to be eaten and gulped in rapid succession; other nouveau creations include pastrami-stuffed egg rolls and miso-glazed filet mignon in crispy tartlet shells.

The Spotted Pig
314 W 11th Street, at Greenwich Street (1-212 620 0393, www.thespottedpig.com). Subway A, C, E to 14th Street; L to Eighth Avenue. **Open** noon-3pm, 5.30pm-2am Mon-Fri; 11am-3pm, 5.30pm-2am Sat, Sun. **Main courses** $21. **Credit** AmEx, DC, Disc, MC, V. **Map** p403 D28 ⑤⑨ **Eclectic**
With a creaky interior that recalls an ancient pub, this Anglo-Italian hybrid from Ken Friedman and chef April Bloomfield (*see p165* **Profile**) is still hopping nine years after opening. The gastropub doesn't take reservations and a wait can always be expected. The burger is a must-order: a secret blend of ground beef grilled rare (unless otherwise specified) and covered with gobs of pungent roquefort. It arrives with a tower of crispy shoestring fries tossed with rosemary. The indulgent desserts, like the flourless chocolate cake, are worth loosening your belt for.

$ Sweet Revenge
62 Carmine Street, between Bedford Street & Seventh Avenue (1-212 242 2240, www. sweetrevengenyc.com). Subway A, B, C, D, E, F, M to W 4th Street; 1 to Christopher Street-Sheridan Square. **Open** 7am-11pm Mon-Thur; 7am-12.30am Fri; 10.30am-12.30am Sat; 10.30am-10pm Sun. **Cupcakes** $3.50. **Credit** Disc, MC, V. **Map** p403 D29 ⑥⓪ **Café**
Baker Marlo Scott steamrollered over the Magnolia Bakery-model cupcake's innocent charms: at her café/bar, she pairs her confections with wine or beer; where there were pastel swirls of frosting, there are now anarchic spikes of peanut butter, cream cheese and milk-chocolate icing. In the process, she saved the ubiquitous treat from becoming a cloying cliché. Gourmet sandwiches and other plates mean it's not strictly for sweet-tooths.

MIDTOWN
Chelsea

Co
230 Ninth Avenue, at 24th Street (1-212 243 1105, www.co-pane.com). Subway C, E to 23rd Street. **Open** 5-11pm Mon; 11.30am-11pm Tue-Sat; 11am-10pm Sun. **Pizzas** $17. **Credit** AmEx, MC, V. **Map** p404 C26 ⑥① **Pizza**
This unassuming pizzeria was the restaurant debut of Jim Lahey, whose Sullivan Street Bakery supplies bread to many top restaurants. Lahey's crust is so

Open noon-2.30pm, 6-11pm Mon-Fri; 6-11pm Sat. **Main courses** $24. **Credit** MC, V. **Map** p403 D29 ⑤⑥ **Seafood**
There's a good reason this convivial, no-reservations, New England-style fish joint always has a queue – the food is outstanding. Signature dishes include the lobster roll (sweet, lemon-scented meat laced with mayonnaise on a butter-enriched bun) and a contemporary take on bouillabaisse: a briny lobster broth packed with mussels, cod, scallops and clams, topped with an aïoli-smothered croûton.

$ 'sNice
45 Eighth Avenue, at 4th & Jane Streets (1-212 645 0310, www.snicecafe.com). Subway A, C, E to 14th Street; L to Eighth Avenue. **Open** 7.30am-10pm daily. **Sandwiches/salads** $8.75. **Credit** ($15 min) AmEx, Disc, MC, V. **Map** p403 D28 ⑤⑦ **Café/Vegetarian**
If you're looking for a laid-back place to read the papers, do a little laptopping, and enjoy cheap, simple and satisfying veggie fare, then 'sNice is nice indeed. Far roomier than it appears from its windows, the bare-brick café has what may well be the largest menu in the city, scrawled on the wall, giving carefully wrought descriptions of each sandwich and salad. **Other locations** 150 Sullivan Street, between W Houston & Prince Streets, Soho (1-212 253 5405); 315 Fifth Avenue, at 3rd Street, Park Slope, Brooklyn (1-718 788 2121).

RedFarm
529 Hudson Street, between Charles & 10th Streets (1-212 792 9700, www.redfarmnyc.com). Subway 1 to Christopher Street-Sheridan Square. **Open** 5-11.45pm Mon-Fri; 11am-2.30pm, 5-11.45pm Sat; 11am-2.30pm, 5-11pm Sun. **Main courses** $20. **Credit** AmEx, Disc, MC, V. Map p403 D28 ⑤⑧ **Chinese**

CONSUME

good, in fact, it doesn't need any toppings (try the Pizza Pianca, sprinkled with sea salt and olive oil). The most compelling individual-sized pies come from non-traditional sources, such as the ham and cheese, essentially a croque-monsieur in pizza form.

Cookshop
156 Tenth Avenue, at 20th Street (1-212 924 4440, www.cookshopny.com). Subway C, E to 23rd Street. **Open** 8-11am, 11.30am-4pm, 5.30-11.30pm Mon-Fri; 10.30am-4pm, 5.30-11.30pm Sat; 10.30am-4pm, 5.30-10pm Sun. **Main courses** $24. **Credit** AmEx, DC, MC, V. **Map** p403 C27 **American creative**

Chef Marc Meyer and his wife/co-owner Vicki Freeman want Cookshop to be a platform for sustainable ingredients from independent farmers. True to the restaurant's mission, the ingredients are consistently top-notch, and the menu changes daily. While organic ingredients alone don't guarantee a great meal, Meyer knows how to let the natural flavours speak for themselves, and Cookshop scores points for getting the house-made ice-cream to taste as good as Ben & Jerry's.

Tía Pol
205 Tenth Avenue, between 22nd & 23rd Streets (1-212 675 8805, www.tiapol.com). Subway C, E to 23rd Street. **Open** 5.30-11pm Mon; noon-3pm, 5.30-11pm Tue-Thur; noon-3pm, 5.30pm-midnight Fri; 11am-3pm, 5.30pm-midnight Sat; 11am-3pm, 5.30-10.30pm Sun. **Tapas** $9. **Credit** AmEx, Disc, MC, V. **Map** p404 C26 **Spanish**

Reaching crowd capacity at this tapas spot isn't hard: it's as slender as the white asparagus that garnishes some of its dishes. Seating is on high stools, with spillover at the bustling bar, where diners stand cheek by jowl while guzzling fruity sangria. The memorable menu is one part classical, two parts wholly original: munch on superb renditions from the tapas canon – springy squid *en su tinta* (in its own ink); patatas bravas topped with spicy aïoli – and then delve into more eclectic treats, such as chorizo with sherry or crunchy fried chickpeas.

Tipsy Parson
156 Ninth Avenue, between 19th & 20th Streets (1-212 620 4545, www.tipsyparson.com). Subway C, E to 23rd Street. **Open** 11.30am-11pm Mon-Thur; 11.30am-midnight Fri; 10am-midnight Sat; 10am-10pm Sun. **Main courses** $25. **Credit** AmEx, MC, V. **Map** p403 C27 **American regional**

Julie Wallach's Chelsea restaurant channels the experience of dining at home – if home happens to be a charming cottage in the country stocked with grandmotherly knick-knacks, that is. The nostalgic food is grounded firmly in the Deep South. A tasty down-home twist on a burger comes topped with Grafton cheddar (grits and bacon optional), accompanied by batter-fried pickles. Macaroni and cheese features a complex medley of cheddar, gruyère and grana padano, with crumbled corn bread and fresh *cavatelli*. For dessert, try the namesake Tipsy Parson – a boozy trifle served in a stemmed parfait glass.

CONSUME

RedFarm.

Flatiron District & Union Square

★ ABC Kitchen

ABC Carpet & Home, 35 E 18th Street, between Broadway & Park Avenue South (1-212 475 5829, www.abckitchennyc.com). Subway L, N, Q, R, 4, 5, 6 to 14th Street-Union Square. **Open** noon-3pm, 5.30-10.30pm Mon-Wed; noon-3pm, 5.30-11pm Thur, Fri; 11am-3pm, 5.30-11.30pm Sat; 11am-3pm, 5.30-10pm Sun. **Main courses** $20. **Credit** AmEx, Disc, MC, V. **Map** p403 E27 ⓺⓹ **Eclectic**

The haute green cooking at Jean-Georges Vongerichten's artfully decorated restaurant inside a landmark Flatiron furniture store is based on the most gorgeous ingredients from up and down the East Coast. Local, seasonal bounty finds its way into such dishes as a salad of cumin-and-citrus-laced roasted carrots with avocado and crunchy sunflower, pumpkin and sesame seeds, or kasha bowtie pasta with veal meatballs. A sundae of salted caramel ice-cream, candied peanuts and popcorn with chocolate sauce reworks the kids' treat to thrill a grownup palate. ABC delivers one message overall: food that's good for the planet needn't be any less opulent, flavourful or stunning to look at.

★ The Breslin Bar & Dining Room

Ace Hotel, 16 W 29th Street, at Broadway (1-212 679 1939, www.thebreslin.com). Subway N, R to 28th Street. **Open** 7am-midnight daily. **Main courses** $29. **Credit** AmEx, DC, Disc, MC, V. **Map** p404 E26 ⓺⓺ **Eclectic**

The third project from restaurant savant Ken Friedman and Anglo chef April Bloomfield (*see p165* **Profile**), the Breslin broke gluttonous new ground. Expect a wait at this no-reservations hotspot – quell your appetite at the bar with an order of scrumpets (fried strips of lamb belly). The overall ethos might well be described as late-period Henry VIII: groaning boards of house-made terrines feature thick slices of guinea hen, rabbit and pork. The pig's foot for two – half a leg, really – could feed the full Tudor court. Desserts include amped-up childhood treats like ice-cream sundaes.

$ The Cannibal

113 E 29th Street, between Park and Lexington Avenues (1-212 686 5480, www.thecannibal nyc.com). Subway 6 to 28th Street. **Open** 11am-11.30pm daily. **Small plates** $11. **Credit** AmEx, Disc, MC, V. **Map** p404 E25 ⓺⓻ **American creative**

Run by restaurateur Christian Pappanicholas and connected to his Belgian-American eatery, Resto, the Cannibal is an unusual retail-restaurant hybrid – a beer store and a butcher shop but also a laid-back place to eat and drink. The meat counter supplies whole beasts for Resto's large-format feasts, but the carnivore's paradise is otherwise autonomous, with its own chef, Preston Clark (formerly of Jean Georges), and beer master, Julian Kurland. The food is best ordered in rounds, pairing beer and bites –

wispy shavings of Kentucky ham, pâtés, sausages and tartares – as you work your way through some of the 400-plus selections on the drinks list.

$ City Bakery

3 W 18th Street, between Fifth & Sixth Avenues (1-212 366 1414, www.thecitybakery.com). Subway L, N, Q, R, 4, 5, 6 to 14th Street-Union Square. **Open** 7.30am-7pm Mon-Fri; 8am-7pm Sat; 10am-6pm Sun. **Salad bar** $14/lb. **Credit** AmEx, Disc, MC, V. **Map** p403 E27 ⓺⓼ **Café**

Pastry genius Maury Rubin's loft-size City Bakery is jammed with shoppers loading up on creative baked goods such as pretzel croissants and unusual salad bar choices (grilled pineapple with ancho chilli, or beansprouts with smoked tofu, for example). There's also a small selection of soups, pizzas and hot dishes. But never mind all that: the thick, incredibly rich hot chocolate with fat house-made marshmallows is justly famed, and the moist 'melted' chocolate-chip cookies are divinely decadent.

Eataly

200 Fifth Avenue, between 23rd & 24th Streets (1-212 229 2560, www.eataly.com). Subway F, M, N, R to 23rd Street. **Open** 8am-11pm daily. **Main courses** $20. **Credit** AmEx, Disc, MC, V. **Map** p404 E26 ⓺⓽ **Italian**

This massive food and drink complex, from Mario Batali and Joe and Lidia Bastianich, sprawls across 42,500sq ft in the Flatiron District. A spin-off of an operation by the same name just outside Turin, Italy, the store houses five full-service restaurants and a rooftop beer garden, plus a rotisserie dispensing the city's best flame-roasted chickens. The meat-centric white-tablecloth joint Manzo serves a gorgeous tartare of Montana-raised Piedmontese-breed beef.

▶ *For a review of the beer garden Birreria, see p178; for details of the retail side, see p210.*

Hill Country

30 W 26th Street, between Broadway & Sixth Avenue (1-212 255 4544, www.hillcountryny.com). Subway N, R to 28th Street. **Open** noon-10pm Mon-Wed, Sun; noon-11pm Thur-Sat. **Main courses** $18. **Credit** AmEx, DC, MC, V. **Map** p404 E26 ⓻⓪ **Barbecue**

The guys behind Hill Country are about as Texan as Mayor Bloomberg in a stetson, but the cooking is an authentic, world-class take on the restaurant's namesake region. Dishes feature sausages imported from barbecue stalwart Kreuz Market of Lockhart, Texas, and two options for brisket: go for the 'moist' (read: fatty) version for full flavour. Beef shoulder emerges from the smoker in 20lb slabs, and showstealing tips-on pork ribs are hefty, with just enough fat to imbue proper flavour. Desserts, such as jelly-filled cupcakes with peanut butter frosting, live out some kind of *Leave It to Beaver* fantasy, though June Cleaver wouldn't approve of the two dozen tequilas and bourbons on offer.

Profile April Bloomfield

How a Midlands lass made it in Manhattan.

Less than a decade ago, April Bloomfield had never been to New York City. The Birmingham, England-reared chef was working at the famed River Café in London, where her talent and discipline made her revered among fellow cooks. Little did she know that she would soon be the toast of Manhattan and one of the most prominent female chefs in the United States. Her life changed when the UK culinary sensation Jamie Oliver recommended Bloomfield to Ken Friedman, a music industry veteran who wanted to make his first foray into the restaurant world. Friedman was looking for a female cook who could bring something new to the New York City dining vernacular.

The result was the **Spotted Pig**, which holds the distinction of being New York City's first gastropub. Since it opened in 2004, the well-worn pub, with pig-themed bric-a-brac, mismatched furniture and a tap reserved for room temperature cask ale, has been widely imitated for its casual vibe and hearty cooking. Bloomfield's rustic, nose-to-tail style precipitated the trend in New York restaurants for macho foods that include unusual cuts of meat, copious amounts of fat, or both. Her mastery at amping up the latter, along with acid and salt, to deliver the full force of a dish's flavour, is her signature. Near-iconic menu items such as ricotta *gnudi*, cheese dumplings in a sage-infused butter sauce, or her no-frills hamburger, simply topped with crumbled roquefort, exemplify her bold cooking style.

With Bloomfield at the helm, the Spotted Pig performed an unusual coup. Not only did it rise to prominence as a hotspot, thanks in part to Friedman's music industry cachet (Jay-Z is a partner), it also garnered the respect of the culinary world. The chef has won Michelin stars for her cooking, and a James Beard nomination.

Bloomfield is now a 50-50 partner in the Spotted Pig with Friedman. Together, they have gone on to open a string of successful restaurants, including the **Breslin Bar & Dining Room**, a raucous gourmet tavern in the Ace Hotel, serving an evolved iteration of the Spotted Pig's British-inflected cuisine, and the **John Dory Oyster Bar**, the second coming of their short-lived seafood restaurant, which fizzled out off the beaten track on Tenth Avenue but is thriving at the Ace.

The partnership continues to grow – the duo opened a *taqueria* and cocktail bar, **Salvation Taco**, at Pod 39 Hotel in autumn 2012. Rumour has it they're also eyeing a place on the Lower East Side, and nurture a long-term dream of starting a farm to supply all of their kitchens. This year, Bloomfield came out with her first cookbook – aptly titled *A Girl and Her Pig*.

CONSUME

THREE TO TASTE
Gnudi at **The Spotted Pig**. *See p162.*

Lamb burger at **The Breslin Bar & Dining Room**. *See p164.*

Oyster pan roast at the **John Dory Oyster Bar**. *See p166.*

John Dory Oyster Bar

Ace, 1196 Broadway, at 29th Street (1-212 792 9000, www.thejohndory.com). Subway N, R to 28th Street. **Open** noon-midnight daily. **Small plates** $14. **Credit** AmEx, MC, V. **Map** p404 E26 ❼ **Seafood**

April Bloomfield and Ken Friedman's original John Dory in the Meatpacking District was an ambitious, pricey endeavour, but its reincarnation in the Ace Hotel is an understated success. Tall stools face a raw bar stocked with a rotating mix of East and West Coast oysters, all expertly handled and impeccably sourced. True to form, the rest of Bloomfield's tapas-style seafood dishes are intensely flavoured – meaty lobster rolls in a pink dill and celery sauce, for example, or Mediterranean mussels stuffed with saffron aioli.

★ The NoMad

1170 Broadway, at 28th Street (1-347 472 5660, www.thenomadhotel.com). Subway N, R to 28th Street. **Open** 7am-10.30pm Mon-Thur; 7am-11pm Fri, Sat; 7am-10pm Sun. **Main courses** $32. **Credit** AmEx, Disc, MC, V. **Map** p404 E26 ❼ **American**

The sophomore effort from chef Daniel Humm and front-of-house partner Will Guidara, who've been in cahoots at Eleven Madison Park since 2006, the NoMad features plush armchairs around well-spaced tables and a stylish return to three-course dining. The food, like the space, exudes unbuttoned decadence: a bone-marrow gratin stars in one over-the-top starter, served on the bone with shallots, anchovy, toasted croutons and a side of parsley and frisée. And while there are plenty of rich-man roasted chickens for two in New York, the amber-hued bird here – with a foie gras, brioche and black truffle stuffing under the skin – is surely the new gold standard, well worth its $79 price tag.

Union Square Café

21 E 16th Street, between Fifth Avenue & Union Square West (1-212 243 4020, www.unionsquarecafe.com). Subway L, N, Q, R, 4, 5, 6 to 14th Street-Union Square. **Open** noon-2.30pm, 5.30-9.30pm Mon-Thur; noon-2.30pm, 5.30-10.30pm Fri; 11am-2.30pm, 5.30-11pm Sat; 11am-2.30pm, 5.30-9.30pm Sun. **Main courses** $31. **Credit** AmEx, Disc, MC, V. **Map** p403 E27 ❼ **American creative**

Prolific restaurateur Danny Meyer's first New York restaurant – a pioneer in Greenmarket cooking – remains one of the city's most relaxed fine dining establishments. Novelty is not what keeps this place packed year after year: the art collection and floor-to-ceiling murals haven't changed since the 1980s. The menu still features a few signature standbys such as the eponymous burger and the grilled lamb chops Scotta Dita, with a gruyère and potato gratin, but current chef Carmen Quagliata has made his own mark with lusty Italian additions, such as outstanding house-made pastas.

INSIDE TRACK
CHEAP THEATRELAND EATS

The area surrounding Times Square is notoriously thin on decent pre- or post-theatre options. Locals skip the expensive, largely tourist-targeted places on Restaurant Row (46th Street, between Eighth & Ninth Avenues) and head for the multi-ethnic cheap-eats line-up on **Ninth Avenue** in the 40s and 50s.

▶ *For information about the nearby Union Square Greenmarket, see p210.*

Gramercy Park & Murray Hill

Artisanal

2 Park Avenue, at 32nd Street (1-212 725 8585, www.artisanalbistro.com). Subway 6 to 33rd Street. **Open** 11.30am-10pm Mon-Wed; 11.30am-11pm Thur, Fri; 10.30am-11pm Sat; 10.30am-9pm Sun. **Main courses** $24. **Credit** AmEx, DC, Disc, MC, V. **Map** p404 E25 ❼ **French**

As New York's bistros veer towards uniformity, Terrance Brennan's high-ceilinged deco gem makes its mark with an all-out homage to fromage. Skip the appetisers and open with fondue, which comes in three varieties. Familiar bistro fare awaits, with such dishes as steak frites, mussels, and chicken baked 'under a brick', but the curd gets the last word with the cheese and wine pairings. These selections of three cheeses – chosen by region, style or theme (for example, each one produced in a monastery) – are matched with three wines (or beers or even sakés) for a sumptuous and intriguing finale.

Casa Mono

52 Irving Place, at 17th Street (1-212 253 2773, www.casamononyc.com). Subway L to Third Avenue; N, Q, R, 4, 5, 6 to 14th Street-Union Square. **Open** noon-midnight daily. **Small plates** $15. **Credit** AmEx, MC, V. **Map** p403 F27 ❼ **Spanish**

Offal-loving chef-partners Mario Batali and Andy Nusser broke new ground in NYC with their adventurous Spanish fare: oxtail-stuffed piquillo peppers, fried sweetbreads, foie gras with *cinco cebollas* (five types of onion), or the fried duck egg, a delicately flavoured breakfast-meets-dinner dish topping a mound of sautéed fingerling potatoes and salt-cured tuna loin. For a cheaper option, the attached Bar Jamón (125 E 17th Street; open 5pm-2am Mon-Fri; noon-2am Sat, Sun) offers tapas, treasured Ibérico hams and Spanish cheeses.

Maialino

Gramercy Park Hotel, 2 Lexington Avenue, between E 21st & E 22nd Streets (1-212 777 2410,

www.maialinonyc.com). Subway 6 to 23rd Street.
Open 7.30am-10.30pm Mon-Thur; 7.30am-11pm
Fri; 10am-11pm Sat; 10am-10.30pm Sun. **Main
courses** $26. **Credit** AmEx, DC, Disc,
MC, V. **Map** p404 F26 ⑰ **Italian**
Danny Meyer's first full-fledged foray into Italian
cuisine is a dedicated homage to the neighbourhood
trattorias that kept him well fed as a 20-year-old tour
guide in Rome (the name is a corruption of his nickname when he was working in the Eternal City:
'Meyerino'). Salumi and bakery stations between the
front bar and the wood-beamed dining room – hog
jowls and sausages dangling near shelves stacked
with crusty loaves of bread – mimic a market off the
Appian Way. Chef Nick Anderer's menu offers
exceptional facsimiles of dishes specific to Rome,
such as carbonara, braised tripe and suckling pig.

Pure Food & Wine
*54 Irving Place, between 17th & 18th Streets
(1-212 477 1010, www.purefoodandwine.com).
Subway L, N, Q, R, 4, 5, 6 to 14th Street-Union
Square.* **Open** noon-4pm, 5.30-11pm daily.
Main courses $23. **Credit** AmEx, DC, Disc,
MC, V. **Map** p403 F27 ⑰ **Vegetarian**
The dishes delivered to your table – whether out on
the leafy patio or inside the ambient dining room –
are minor miracles, not only because they look gorgeous and taste terrific, but because they come from
a kitchen that lacks a stove. Everything at Pure is
raw and vegan – from the pear ravioli appetiser to
the lasagne (with creamy macadamia nut and pumpkin seed 'ricotta'). Wines, most of which are organic,
are top-notch, as are the desserts, including a classic
vegan ice-cream sundae.

$ 71 Irving Place Coffee & Tea Bar
*71 Irving Place, between 18th & 19th Streets
(1-212 995 5252, www.irvingfarm.com). Subway
L, N, Q, R, 4, 5, 6 to 14th Street-Union Square.*
Open 7am-10pm Mon-Fri; 8am-10pm Sat.
Coffee $2.50. **Credit** AmEx, DC, Disc, MC, V.
Map p403 E27 ⑰ **Café**
Irving Farm's beans are roasted in a 100-year-old
carriage house in the Hudson Valley; fittingly, its
Gramercy Park café, which occupies the ground
floor of a stately brownstone, also has a rustic edge.
Breakfast (granola, oatmeal, waffles, bagels), sand-
wiches and salads accompany the excellent java.
Other locations 224 West 79th Street, between
Amsterdam Avenue & Broadway, Upper West
Side (1-212 874 7979).

Herald Square & Garment District

Gaonnuri
*39th Floor, 1250 Broadway, at 32nd Street (1-
212 971 9045). Subway B, D, F, M, N, Q, R to
34th Street-Herald Square.* **Open** noon-midnight
Mon-Sat. **Main courses** $15. **Credit** AmEx, MC,
V. **Map** p404 E25 ⑲ **Korean**

Located on the 39th floor of a Koreatown tower, this
sleek dining room offers a twinkling skyline view
through its wraparound windows. The cooking is
spectacular too. The kitchen – run by Tae Goo Kang,
a Korean who's cooked Japanese at Nobu 57 and
French at the Modern – highlights grade-A ingredients and upscale presentations. Along with an oversized *pajun*, the ubiquitous seafood-scallion
pancake, you can get a sampler of fluffy miniatures,
delicately flavoured with beef, fish or vegetables.
Tabletop barbecue, centerpiece of a typical Korean
night on the town, is the focus here too. The unusually large roster of proteins includes thick duck
breast pieces, big tiger shrimp, tender boneless short
ribs (*kalbi*) and shaved fatty brisket.

$ Mandoo Bar
*2 W 32nd Street, between Fifth Avenue &
Broadway (1-212 279 3075). Subway B, D, F,
M, N, Q, R to 34th Street-Herald Square.* **Open**
11am-11pm daily. **Dumplings** $11/8-10. **Credit**
AmEx, MC, V. **Map** p404 E25 ⑳ **Korean**
If the staff filling and crimping dough squares in the
front window don't give it away, we will – this wood-
wrapped industrial-style spot elevates *mandoo*
(Korean dumplings) above mere appetiser status. Six
varieties of the tasty morsels are filled with such
delights as subtly piquant kimchi, juicy pork, succulent shrimp and vegetables. Try them minia-
turised, as in the 'baby mandoo', swimming in a
soothing beef broth or atop soupy ramen noodles.

Theater District & Hell's Kitchen

Aureole
*135 W 42nd Street, between Broadway &
Sixth Avenue (1-212 319 1660, www.charlie
palmer.com). Subway B, D, F, M to 42nd Street-
Bryant Park; N, Q, R, S 1, 2, 3, 7 to 42nd Street-
Times Square; 7 to Fifth Avenue.* **Open**
11.45am-2.15pm, 5-10pm Mon-Thur; 11.45am-
2.15pm, 5-11.30 Fri; 5-11.30pm Sat; 5-10pm Sun.
Main courses $30. **Three-course prix fixe**
$39 (lunch), $55-$89 (dinner). **Credit** AmEx, Disc,
MC, V. **Map** p404 D24 ㉛ **American**
In 2009, chef Charlie Palmer's NYC classic moved
from an Upper East Side townhouse to a spiffy modern tower with high ceilings, tall windows and a
showcase wine vault. The complex food (which
Palmer dubs 'progressive American') strikes a fine
balance between big-ticket opulence, homespun
inclinations and globe-spanning flavours. The latter
is unmistakable in starters such as ruby red shrimp
with coconut, lemon grass and Asian pear, and
Wagyu beef carpaccio, while main courses include
a roasted veal ribeye with almonds, accompanied by
brussels sprouts, potato croquette and truffle jus.

$ Café Edison
*Hotel Edison, 228 W 47th Street, between
Broadway & Eighth Avenues (1-212 354 0368).*

CONSUME

Subway N, Q, R to 49th Street; 1 to 50th Street.
Open 6am-9.30pm Mon-Sat; 6am-7.30pm Sun.
Main courses $11. **No credit cards.**
Map p404 D23 ㉒ **American**
This old-school no-frills eaterie draws tourists, theatregoers, actors and just about everyone else in search of deli staples such as cheese blintzes and giant open-faced Reubens. The matzo ball soup is so restorative, you can almost feel it bolstering your immune system.

Don Antonio by Starita

309 W 50th Street, between Eighth & Ninth Avenues (1-646 719 1043, www.donantonio pizza.com). Subway C, E to 50th Street. **Open** 11.30am-11pm Mon-Thur; 11.30am-1am Fri, Sat; 11.30am-10.30pm Sun. **Pizzas** $15. **Credit** AmEx, MC, V. **Map** p404 D23 ㉝ **Italian/Pizza**
Pizza aficionados have been busy colonising this pedigreed recent arrival, a collaboration between Kesté's (*see p160*) talented Roberto Caporuscio and his decorated Naples mentor, Antonio Starita. Start with tasty bites like the *frittatine* (a deep-fried spaghetti cake oozing *prosciutto cotto* and béchamel sauce). The main event should be the habit-forming Montanara Starita, which gets a quick dip in the deep fryer before hitting the oven to develop its puffy, golden crust. Topped with tomato sauce, basil and intensely smoky buffalo mozzarella, it's a worthy new addition to the pantheon of classic New York pies.

Kashkaval

856 Ninth Avenue, between 55th & 56th Streets (1-212 581 8282, www.kashkavalfoods.com). Subway C, E to 50th Street. **Open** 11am-midnight daily. **Main courses** $14. **Credit** AmEx, DC, Disc, MC, V. **Map** p405 C22 ㉞ **Mediterranean**
This charming cheese-shop-cum-wine bar evokes fondue's peasant origins, with deep cast-iron pots and generous baskets of crusty bread – steer clear of the bland and rubbery kashkaval (a Balkan sheep's-milk cheese) and order the gooey and surprisingly mild gorgonzola. Or choose from the selection of tangy Mediterranean spreads – vinegary artichoke dip, hot-

---

**INSIDE TRACK
PRIX FIXE TRICKS**

To make your money stretch further, consider timing your visit to coincide with **Restaurant Week** (*see p33*), held twice a year, in January/February and July/August, when you can dine at notable restaurants around town for around $25 and $35 for a three-course lunch and dinner, respectively. Prix fixe lunches – often more affordable than dinner – are also a great way to experience some of the city's fine-dining establishments.

---

pink beet *skordalia* – and the impressive roster of charcuterie. End the meal with the bittersweet dark-chocolate fondue, a guaranteed crowd-pleaser served with fruit and mini marshmallows.

Midtown West

Bar Room at the Modern

9 W 53rd Street, between Fifth & Sixth Avenues (1-212 333 1220, www.themodernnyc.com). Subway E, M to Fifth Avenue-53rd Street. **Open** 11.30am-3pm, 5-10.30pm Mon-Thur; 11.30am-3pm, 5-11pm Fri, Sat; 11.30am-3pm, 5-9.30pm Sun. **Main courses** $22. **Credit** AmEx, DC, Disc, MC, V. **Map** p405 E22 ㉟ **American creative**
Those who can't afford to drop a pay cheque at award-winning chef Gabriel Kreuther's formal MoMA dining room, the Modern, can still dine in the equally stunning and less pricey bar at the front. The Alsatian-inspired menu is constructed of around 30 small and medium-sized plates (for example, liverwurst with pickled vegetables; slow-poached egg with lobster, eggplant caviar and sea urchin froth; and dry-aged steak with spätzle and beluga lentils), which can be mixed and shared. Desserts come courtesy of pastry chef Marc Aumont, and the wine list is extensive, to say the least.
▶ *For the Museum of Modern Art, see p88.*

Benoit

60 W 55th Street, between Fifth & Sixth Avenues (1-646 943 7373, www.benoitny.com). Subway E, M to Fifth Avenue-53rd Street; F to 57th Street. **Open** 11.45am-11pm Mon-Sat; 11.30am-11pm Sun. **Main courses** $26. **Credit** AmEx, DC, Disc, MC, V. **Map** p405 E22 ㊱ **French**
See p170 **Bargain Brunches.**

Marea

240 Central Park South, between Seventh Avenue & Broadway (1-212 582 5100, www.marea-nyc.com). Subway A, B, C, D, 1 to 59th Street-Columbus Circle. **Open** noon-2.30pm, 5.30-11pm Mon-Thur; noon-2.30pm, 5-11.30pm Fri; 5-11.30pm Sat; 5-10.30pm Sun. **Main courses** $35. **Credit** AmEx, MC, V. **Map** p405 D22 ㊲ **Italian/Seafood**
Chef Michael White's shrine to the Italian coastline seems torn between its high and low ambitions. You might find lofty items such as an unorthodox starter of cool lobster with creamy burrata, while basic platters of raw oysters seem better suited to a fish shack. Seafood-focused pastas – fusilli with braised octopus and bone marrow, or tortelli filled with langoustine, dandelion and butternut squash, for example – are the meal's highlight.

Russian Tea Room

150 W 57th Street, between Sixth & Seventh Avenues (1-212 581 7100, www.russian tearoomnyc.com). Subway F, N, Q, R to

57th Street. **Open** 11.30am-11.30pm Mon-Fri; 11am-11pm Sat, Sun. **Main courses** $40. **Credit** AmEx, DC, MC, V. **Map** p405 D22 ⊕ **Russian**
This refurbished 1920s icon has never looked better. Nostalgia buffs will be happy to hear that nothing's happened to the gilded-bird friezes or the famously tacky crystal-bear aquarium, although the food has not been frozen in time. Chef Marc Taxiera has at once modernised the menu – adding signature novelties such as sliders (mini burgers) – and brought back waylaid classics such as beef stroganoff and chicken kiev. In truth, however, the main reason to make for this tourist magnet is to luxuriate in the opulent setting.

Midtown East

Grand Central Oyster Bar & Restaurant
Grand Central Terminal, Lower Concourse, 42nd Street, at Park Avenue (1-212 490 6650, www.oysterbarny.com). Subway S, 4, 5, 6, 7 to 42nd Street-Grand Central. **Open** 11.30am-9.30pm Mon-Fri; noon-9.30pm Sat. **Main courses** $25. **Credit** AmEx, DC, Disc, MC, V. **Map** p404 E24 ⊕ **Seafood**
The legendary Grand Central Oyster Bar, located in the epic and gorgeous hub that shares its name, just celebrated its 100th anniversary. The surly countermen at the mile-long bar (the best seats in the house) are part of the charm. Avoid the more complicated fish concoctions and play it safe with a reliably awe-inspiring platter of iced, just-shucked oysters (there can be a whopping 30 varieties, including many from nearby Long Island).
▶ For more on the iconic transport hub, see p91.

The Monkey Bar
Hotel Elysée, 60 E 54th Street, between Madison & Park Avenues (1-212 288 1010, www.monkey barnewyork.com). Subway E, M to Lexington Avenue-53rd Street; 6 to 51st Street. **Open** 11.30am-11pm Mon-Fri; 5.30-11pm Sat. **Main courses** $30. **Credit** AmEx, Disc, MC, V. **Map** p405 E22 ⊕ **American**
After the repeal of Prohibition in 1933, this one-time piano bar in the swank Hotel Elysée (*see p243*) became a boozy clubhouse for glitzy artistic types, including the likes of Tallulah Bankhead, Dorothy Parker and Tennessee Williams. Recently, publishing tycoon Graydon Carter assembled a dream team here, including chef Damon Wise, cocktail doyenne Julie Reiner and downtown restaurateur Ken Friedman, to bring new buzz to the historic space. Perched at the bar with a pitch-perfect Vieux Carré or ensconced in a red leather booth with a plate of caviar-crowned smoked fettuccine, you'll find yourself seduced by that rare alchemy of old New York luxury and new-school flair. The only question remaining is how long the star-power magic can last.

CONSUME

Don Antonio by Starita.

Bargain Brunches

Fuel up with an affordable weekend meal in three conveniently placed spots.

CONSUME

Allswell.

Allswell

Why we love it The dinner menu at chef Nate Smith's neighbourly tavern (*see p174*) changes daily, but brunch offerings stay truer to the spot's small-town-diner vibe, with a mostly constant menu of reliable favourites (plus a few specials).

Why it's a deal Most dishes fall into the $8-$13 range. Standbys include eggs any style with bacon or sausage and French toast with seasonal fruit, though fried eggs make a worthy topping for dishes like avocado on toasted red chilli bread or beet-and-corned-beef 'red flannel' hash.

Benoit

Why we love it At Alain Ducasse's upscale French bistro (*see p168*), you'll feel suitably pampered as you sip champagne beneath the dining room's stately sconces and mirrors.

Why it's a deal The dessert bar (per item $4, all-you-can-eat $16) at Benoit's Sunday-only brunch offers a dozen seasonal pastries and tarts, including a cloudlike, orange-blossom-scented tarte Tropézienne. Don't be afraid to make multiple trips to the beautiful buffet – having sweets for breakfast feels downright sophisticated in these elegant environs.

Jack's Wife Freda

Why we love it Brunch purists may balk at the globe-trotting offerings at this airy Soho café (*see p147*), but for the rest of us, the multiculti dishes are a welcome departure from standard bacon-and-eggs fare.

Why it's a deal Most of the creative brunch options clock in at $10 or less. We especially like the green *shakshuka*, a take on a traditional Middle Eastern baked-egg dish that's lavished with a salsa-like concoction of green tomatoes, tomatillos, garlic, cumin and serrano chillies, served with challah toast to mop it all up.

Jack's Wife Freda.

Quality Meats
*57 W 58th Street, between Fifth & Sixth Avenues
(1-212 371 7777, www.qualitymeatsnyc.com).
Subway F, N, Q, R to 57th Street; N, Q, R to
Fifth Avenue-59th Street.* **Open** 11.30am-3pm,
5-10pm Mon-Wed; 11.30am-3pm, 5-11.30pm Thur-
Sat; 5-10pm Sun. **Main courses** $35. **Credit**
AmEx, DC, Disc, MC, V. **Map** p405 D22 ➒
Steakhouse
Michael Stillman – son of the founder of landmark
steakhouse Smith & Wollensky – is behind this
highly stylised industrial theme park complete with
meat-hook light fixtures, wooden butcher blocks,
white tiles and exposed brick. Lespinasse-trained
chef Craig Koketsu nails the steaks (including a $110
double-rib steak) and breathes new life into traditional side dishes. Pudding-like corn crème brûlée
and the airy 'gnocchi & cheese', a clever take on mac
and cheese, are terrific. High-concept desserts are
best exemplified by the outstanding coffee-and-
doughnuts ice-cream crammed with chunks of the
fritters and crowned with a miniature doughnut.

UPTOWN
Upper East Side

★ Café Sabarsky
*Neue Galerie, 1048 Fifth Avenue, at 86th Street
(1-212 288 0665, www.cafesabarsky.com). Subway
4, 5, 6 to 86th Street.* **Open** 9am-6pm Mon, Wed;
9am-9pm Thur-Sun. **Main courses** $22. **Credit**
AmEx, DC, Disc, MC, V. **Map** p406 E18 ➒
Austrian/Café
Purveyor of indulgent pastries and whipped cream-
topped *einspänner* coffee for Neue Galerie patrons
by day, this sophisticated, high-ceilinged room
becomes an upscale restaurant four nights a week.
Appetisers are most adventurous – the creaminess
of the spätzle is a perfect base for sweetcorn, tarragon and wild mushrooms – while main course specials, such as the wiener schnitzel tartly garnished
with lingonberries, are capable yet ultimately feel
like the calm before the *Sturm und Drang* of dessert.
Try the *klimttorte*, which masterfully alternates layers of hazelnut cake with chocolate.

Daniel
*60 E 65th Street, between Madison & Park
Avenues (1-212 288 0033, www.danielnyc.com).
Subway F to Lexington Avenue-63rd Street;
6 to 68th Street-Hunter College.* **Open** 5.30-11pm
Mon-Sat. **Three-course prix fixe** $108. **Credit**
AmEx, MC, V. **Map** p405 E21 ➒ **French**
The cuisine at Daniel Boulud's elegant fine-dining
flagship, designed by Adam Tihany, is rooted in
French technique with au courant flourishes like
fusion elements and an emphasis on local produce.
Although the menu changes seasonally, it always
includes a few signature dishes – Boulud's black
truffle and scallops in puff pastry remains a classic,

and the duo of beef is a sumptuous pairing of Black
Angus short ribs and seared Wagyu tenderloin.
Other locations Café Boulud 20 E 76th
Street, between Fifth & Madison Avenues,
Upper East Side (1-212 772 2600); **Bar Boulud**
1900 Broadway, at 64th Street, Upper West Side
(1-212 595 0303); **DB Bistro Moderne** 55 West
44th Street, between Fifth & Sixth Avenues,
Midtown West (1-212 391 2400).
▶ *For Boulud's Bowery brasserie DBGB,
see p154; for Boulud Sud, see p172.*

Park Avenue Summer
*100 E 63rd Street, between Park & Lexington
Avenues (1-212 644 1900, www.parkavenyc.com).
Subway F to Lexington Avenue-63rd Street.*
Open 11.30am-3pm, 5.30-10pm Mon-Thur;
11.30am-3pm, 5.30-11pm Fri; 11am-3pm, 5.30-
11pm Sat; 11am-3pm, 5-9pm Sun. **Main courses**
$34. **Credit** AmEx, DC, Disc, MC, V. **Map** p405
E21 ➒ **American creative**
Design firm AvroKO and chef Craig Koketsu conceived this ode to seasonal dining: the design, the staff
uniforms and the very name (yes, it's Park Avenue
Autumn, Winter and Spring too) rotates along with
the menu. 'Summer' means sunny wall panels and
flowers to go with the warm-weather foods.
Appetisers showcase produce (baby beet salad, corn
soup) and seafood (peekytoe crab salad, fluke
sashimi), often mixing both with winning results,
while pastry chef Richard Leach, a James Beard
Award winner, dazzles with his sweet confections.

Upper West Side

A Voce Columbus
*3rd Floor, 10 Columbus Circle, at Broadway
(1-212 823 2523, www.avocerestaurant.com).
Subway A, B, C, D, 1 to 59th Street-Columbus
Circle.* **Open** 11.30am-2.30pm, 5-10pm Mon-Wed;
11.30am-2.30pm, 5-11.30pm Thur, Fri; 11am-3pm,
5-11.30pm Sat; 11am-3pm, 5-10pm Sun. **Main
courses** $27. **Credit** AmEx, Disc, MC, V.
Map p405 D22 ➒ **Italian**
Want views over Columbus Circle and the park
without paying Per Se prices? A Voce's sleek
uptown outpost also has a solid menu and impeccable service. Brick-flattened chicken, infused with
roasted garlic, lemon and dried Calabrian chillies
and served with Tuscan kale, enormous white
beans and potatoes, is a comfort-food triumph. The
owner's art collection, including a massive Frank
Stella mixed- media piece that hangs near the host
stand, is a feast for the eyes.
Other locations 41 Madison Avenue, at 26th
Street, Flatiron District (1-212 545 8555).

★ Barney Greengrass
*541 Amsterdam Avenue, between 86th & 87th
Streets (1-212 724 4707, www.barneygreengrass.
com). Subway B, C, 1 to 86th Street.* **Open**

8.30am-4pm Tue-Fri; 8.30am-5pm Sat, Sun. **Main courses** $15. **No credit cards. Map** p406 C18 ⓪ **American**

Despite decor that Jewish mothers might call 'schmutzy', this legendary deli is a madhouse at breakfast and brunch. Enormous egg platters come with the usual choice of smoked fish (such as sturgeon or Nova Scotia salmon). Prices are on the high side, but portions are large, and that goes for the sandwiches too. Or try the less costly items: matzoball soup, creamy egg salad or cold pink borscht served in a glass.

$ Bouchon Bakery

3rd Floor, Time Warner Center, 10 Columbus Circle, at Broadway (1-212 823 9366, www. bouchonbakery.com). Subway A, B, C, D, 1 to 59th Street-Columbus Circle. **Open** 8am-9pm Mon-Sat; 8am-7pm Sun. **Pastries** $9. **Credit** AmEx, DC, MC, V. **Map** p405 D22 ⓪ **Café** *See p160* **Diffusion Dining**.
Other locations 1 Rockefeller Plaza, at 49th Street, Midtown West (1-212 782 3890).

Boulud Sud

20 W 64th Street, between Broadway & Central Park West (1-212 595 1313, www.danielnyc.com). Subway 1 to 66th Street-Lincoln Center. **Open** 12.30-2.30pm, 5-11pm Mon-Fri; noon-3pm, 5-11pm Sat; noon-3pm, 5-10pm Sun. **Main courses** $28. **Credit** AmEx, DC, MC, V. **Map** p405 C21 ⓪ **Mediterranean**

At his most international restaurant yet, superchef Daniel Boulud highlights the new French cuisine of melting-pot cities like Marseille and Nice. With his executive chef, Aaron Chambers (Café Boulud), he casts a wide net – looking to Israel and Egypt, Turkey and Greece. Budget-minded diners can build a full tapas meal from shareable snacks like octopus *à la plancha*, with marcona almonds and arugula. Heartier dishes combine Gallic finesse with polyglot flavours: sweet-spicy chicken tagine and a fragrant bowl of harira lamb soup borrow from the Moroccan pantry. Tunisian-born Ghaya Oliveira's audacious desserts – such as grapefruit *givré* stuffed with sorbet, sesame mousse and rose-scented nuggets of Turkish delight – take the exotic mix to even loftier heights.

Celeste

502 Amsterdam Avenue, between 84th & 85th Streets (1-212 874-4559). Subway 1 to 86th Street. **Open** 5-11pm Mon-Thur; 5-11.30pm Fri; noon-3.30pm, 5-11.30pm Sat; noon-3.30pm, 5-10.30pm Sun. **Main courses** $15. **No credit cards. Map** p406 C18 ⓪ **Italian**

This highly popular spot, offering authentic fare in a rustic setting, doesn't take reservations so a wait is to be expected. Once you're in, start with *carciofi fritti*: fried artichokes that are so light, they're evanescent. Three house-made pastas are prepared

daily – the tagliatelle with shrimp, cabbage and pecorino stands out. Those who can manage a few more bites are advised to try the *pastiera*, a grain-and-ricotta cake flavoured with candied fruit and orange-blossom water.

Jean Georges

Trump International Hotel & Tower, 1 Central Park West, at Columbus Circle (1-212 299 3900, www.jean-georgesrestaurant.com). Subway A, B, C, D, 1 to 59th Street-Columbus Circle. **Open** noon-2.30pm, 5.30-11pm Mon-Thur; noon-2.30pm, 5.15-11pm Fri; 5.15-11pm Sat. **Three-course prix fixe** $118. **Seven-course prix fixe** $168. **Credit** AmEx, DC, MC, V. **Map** p405 D22 ⓪ **French**

Unlike many of its vaunted peers, the flagship of celebrated chef Jean-Georges Vongerichten has not become a shadow of itself: the top-rated food is still breathtaking. Velvety foie gras terrine with spiced fig jam is coated in a thin brûlée shell; other signature dishes include ginger-marinated yellowfin tuna ribbons with avocado and spicy radish. Pastry chef Joseph Murphy's inventive seasonal quartets, comprising four mini desserts, are always a delight. The more casual on-site Nougatine café is less expensive, but still provides a taste of its big brother.

Ouest

2315 Broadway, between 83rd & 84th Streets (1-212 580 8700, www.ouestny.com). Subway 1 to 86th Street. **Open** 5.30-9pm Mon, Tue; 5.30-10pm Wed, Thur; 5.30-11pm Fri, Sat; 11am-2pm, 5.30-9pm Sun **Main courses** $28. **Credit** AmEx, DC, Disc, MC, V. **Map** p406 C19 ⓪ **American creative**

A prototypical local clientele calls chef Tom Valenti's uptown stalwart – one of the neighbourhood's most celebrated restaurants – its local canteen. And why not? The friendly servers ferry pitch-perfect cocktails and rich, Italian-inflected cuisine from the open kitchen to immensely comfortable round red booths. Valenti adds some unexpected flourishes to the soothing formula: salmon gravadlax is served with a chickpea pancake topped with caviar and potent mustard oil, while the house-smoked sturgeon presides over frisée, lardons and a poached egg.

★ Per Se

4th Floor, Time Warner Center, 10 Columbus Circle, at Broadway (1-212 823 9335, www.per seny.com). Subway A, B, C, D, 1 to 59th Street-Columbus Circle. **Open** 5.30-10pm Mon-Thur; 11.30am-1.30pm, 5.30-10.30pm Fri-Sun. **Main courses** (in lounge) $36. **Five-course prix fixe** $185 (Fri-Sun lunch only). **Nine-course tasting menu** $295. **Credit** AmEx, MC, V. **Map** p405 D22 ⓪ **French**

Expectations are high at Per Se – and that goes both ways. You're expected to wear the right clothes

CONSUME

(jackets are required for men), pay a non-negotiable service charge, and pretend you aren't eating in a shopping mall. The restaurant, in turn, is expected to deliver one hell of a tasting menu for $295. And it does. Dish after dish is flawless, beginning with Thomas Keller's signature Oysters and Pearls (a sabayon of pearl tapioca with oysters and caviar). Other hits include a buttery poached lobster and house-made sorbets; an all-vegetable version is also available. If you can afford it, it's worth every penny, but avoid the à la carte option in the lounge, which offers miserly portions at high prices, making it less of a deal than the celebrated tasting menu in the formal dining room.

★ $ Shake Shack
366 Columbus Avenue, at 77th Street (1-646 747 8770, www.shakeshacknyc.com). Subway B, C to 81st Street-Museum of Natural History; 1 to 79th Street. **Open** 10.45am-11pm daily. **Burgers** $6.25. **Credit** AmEx, Disc, MC, V. **Map** p405 C19 ⓾03
American
The spacious offspring of Danny Meyer's wildly popular Madison Square Park concession stand is now one of several locations across the city. Shake Shack gets several local critics' votes for New York's best burger. Sirloin and brisket are ground daily for the patties, and the franks are served Chicago-style on poppy seed buns with a 'salad' of toppings and a dash of celery salt. Frozen-custard shakes hit the spot, and there's beer and wine if you want something stronger. **Other locations** throughout the city.

Harlem

Charles' Country Panfried Chicken
2841 Frederick Douglass Boulevard (Eighth Avenue), between 151st & 152nd Streets (1-212 281 1800). Subway B, D to 155th Street. **Open** 11am-1am Mon-Thur; 11am-2am Fri, Sat; 11am-9pm Sun. **Main courses** $11. **Credit** AmEx, Disc, MC, V. **Map** p408 D10 ⓾04
American regional
Fried chicken has made quite the comeback, and the guru of moist flesh and crackly skin, Charles Gabriel, has also made a triumphant return to Harlem with his resurrected restaurant. In addition to the poultry, you can feast on barbecued ribs, mac and cheese, yams and other Southern favourites.
► *For more Harlem soul food recommendations, see p109.*

Boulud Sud.

CONSUME

CONSUME

Roberta's.

Red Rooster Harlem

310 Malcolm X Boulevard (Lenox Avenue),
between 125th & 126th Streets (1-212 792
9001, www.redroosterharlem.com). Subway
2, 3 to 125th Street. **Open** 11.30am-3pm,
5.30-10.30pm Mon-Thur; 11.30am-3pm, 5.30-
11.30pm Fri; 10am-3pm, 5-11.30pm Sat; 10am-
3pm, 5-10pm Sun. **Main courses** $26. **Credit**
AmEx, Disc, MC, V. **Map** p407 D13 ⑩⑤
American

With its hobnobbing bar scrum, potent cocktails
and lively jazz, this buzzy eaterie serves as a worthy clubhouse for the new Harlem. Superstar chef
Marcus Samuelsson is at his most populist here,
drawing on a 'We Are the World' mix of Southern-
fried, East African, Scandinavian and French
flavours to feed the crowd. Harlem politicos mix at
the teardrop bar with downtown fashionistas,
everyone happily swilling fine cocktails and gorg-
ing on rib-sticking food: chicken liver-enriched
dirty rice topped with plump barbecued shrimp;
crispy fried chicken with hot sauce, mace gravy
and a smoky spice shake; and homey desserts. It
all adds up to a place that has earned its status as
a local hub.

BROOKLYN

Al di là

248 Fifth Avenue, at Carroll Street, Park Slope
(1-718 783 4565, www.aldilatrattoria.com).
Subway R to Union Street. **Open** noon-3pm,
6-10.30pm Mon-Thur; noon-3pm, 6-11pm Fri;
11am-3.30pm, 5.30-11pm Sat; 11am-3.30pm, 5-
10pm Sun. **Main courses** $16. **Credit** MC, V.
Map p410 T11 ⑩⑥ **Italian**

A fixture on the Slope's Fifth Avenue for more than
a decade, this convivial, no-reservations restaurant
is still wildly popular. Affable owner Emiliano
Coppa orchestrates the inevitable wait with
panache. Coppa's wife, co-owner and chef, Anna
Klinger, produces northern Italian dishes with a
Venetian slant. It would be hard to better her
braised rabbit with black olives atop polenta, and
even simple pastas, such as the own-made tagliatelle al ragù, are superb.
Other locations Al di là vino 607 Carroll
Street, at Fifth Avenue, Park Slope, Brooklyn
(1-718 783 4565).

Allswell

124 Bedford Avenue, at North 10th Street,
Williamsburg (1-347 799 2743, http://allswell
nyc.com). Subway L to Bedford Avenue. **Open**
10am-2am daily. **Main courses** $22. **Credit** MC,
V. **Map** p411 U7 ⑩⑦ **American**
See p170 **Bargain Brunches**.

★ Chef's Table at Brooklyn Fare

200 Schermerhorn Street, at Hoyt Street,
Downtown Brooklyn (1-718 243 0050,
www.brooklynfare.com/chefs-table). Subway
A, C, G to Hoyt-Schermerhorn; B, N, Q, R
to DeKalb Ave; 2, 3 to Hoyt St; 2, 3, 4, 5 to
Nevins Street. **Open** *Seatings* 7pm & 7.45pm
Mon-Thur; 6.30pm, 7.45pm & 10pm Fri, Sat.
Prix fixe $225. **Credit** AmEx, MC, V.
Map p410 T10 ⑩⑧ **Eclectic**
Scoring a place at chef César Ramirez's 18-seat
restaurant within the Brooklyn Fare supermarket
takes determination: reservations are only taken on
Mondays at 10.30am, six weeks before your desired

booking. But the luxurious 20-course set dinner is among New York's best small-plate cuisine, and the dinner-party vibe is convivial: diners perch on stools around a prep table. The menu changes weekly, but might include such delicacies as a Kumamoto oyster reclining on crème fraîche and yuzu gelée or halibut served in a miraculous broth of dashi and summer truffles.

Fette Sau

354 Metropolitan Avenue, between Havemeyer & Roebling Streets, Williamsburg (1-718 963 3404, www.fettesaubbq.com). Subway L to Lorimer Street; G to Metropolitan Avenue. **Open** 5-11pm Mon-Fri; noon-11pm Sat, Sun. **Main courses** $16. **Credit** AmEx, Disc, MC, V. **Map** p411 U8 ⓭ **Barbecue**

Communal picnic tables and gallon-size glass jugs of beer foster a casual party vibe at this cavernous former auto body shop. It ain't called 'Fat Pig' for nothing: load up on glistening cuts of beef and pork sold by the pound at the deli-style barbecue counter, then mosey over to the bar to choose your poison – connoisseurs of the hard stuff will appreciate the 100-plus list of bourbon and other whiskies.

Marlow & Sons

81 Broadway, between Berry Street & Whythe Avenue, Williamsburg (1-718 384 1441, www.marlowandsons.com). Subway J, M, Z to Marcy Avenue. **Open** 8am-midnight daily. **Main courses** $23. **Credit** AmEx, MC, V. **Map** p411 U8 ⓭ **American creative**

This popular place serves as an old-time oyster bar, quaint general store and daytime café. Seated in the charming front-room vibe, diners survey the gourmet olive oils and honeys while wolfing down market-fresh salads, succulent brick chicken and the creative crostini of the moment (such as goat's cheese with flash-fried strawberries). In the back room, an oyster shucker cracks open the catch of the day, while the bartender mixes the kind of potent drinks that helped to make the owners' earlier ventures (including next-door Diner, a tricked-out 1920s dining car) successes.

★ Peter Luger

178 Broadway, at Driggs Avenue, Williamsburg (1-718 387 7400, www.peterluger.com). Subway J, M, Z to Marcy Avenue. **Open** 11.45am-9.45pm Mon-Thur; 11.45am-10.45pm Fri, Sat; 12.45-9.45pm Sun. **Steak for two** $94.50. **No credit cards. Map** p411 U8 ⓭ **Steakhouse**

At Luger's old-school steakhouse, the choice is limited, but the porterhouse is justly famed. Choose from various sizes, from a small single steak to 'steak for four'. Although a slew of Luger copycats have prospered in the last several years, none has captured the elusive charm of this stucco-walled, beer hall-style eaterie, with worn wooden floors and tables, and waiters in waistcoats and bow ties.

★ Pok Pok NY

127 Columbia Street, between DeGraw & Kane Streets, Red Hook (1-718 923 9322, www.pokpokny.com). Subway F, G to Bergen Street. **Open** 5.30-10.30pm daily. **Main courses** $14. **Credit** MC, V. **Map** p410 S10 ⓬ **Thai**

James Beard Award-winning chef Andy Ricker's Red Hook restaurant replicates the indigenous dives of Chiang Mai – a tented dining room out back is festooned with dangling plants, colourful oilcloths on the tables and secondhand seats. But what separates Pok Pok from other cultish Thai restaurants is the curatorial role of its minutiae-mad chef. Ricker highlights a host of surprisingly mild northern-Thai dishes, including a delicious sweet-and-sour Burmese-inflected pork curry, *kaeng hung leh*. His *khao soi*, the beloved meal-in-a-bowl from Chiang Mai – chicken noodle soup delicately spiced with yellow curry and topped with fried noodles for crunch – is accompanied here with raw shallots and pickled mustard greens.

★ Roberta's

261 Moore Street, between Bogart & White Streets, Bushwick (1-718 417 1118, www.robertaspizza.com). Subway L to Morgan Avenue. **Open** 11am-midnight Mon-Fri; 10am-midnight Sat, Sun. **Average pizza** $15. **Credit** AmEx, Disc, MC, V. **Map** p411 W8 ⓭ **Italian**

Buzzing with urban-farming fundraisers and food-world luminaries fresh off interviews at the indie Heritage Radio station, this sprawling hangout has become the unofficial meeting place for Brooklyn's sustainable-food movement. Opened in 2008 by a trio of friends, Roberta's has its own on-site garden, a food-focused internet-radio station and a kitchen that turns out excellent, locally sourced dishes, such as delicate romaine with walnuts, pecorino and mint or linguine carbonara made with lamb pancetta. It also doesn't hurt that the pizzas – like the Cheeses Christ, topped with mozzarella, taleggio, parmesan, black pepper and cream – are among Brooklyn's finest. The team recently opened Blanca, a sleek spot in the back garden, to showcase chef Carlo Mirarchi's acclaimed evening-only tasting menu (6-10pm Wed-Sat, $180).

Vinegar Hill House

72 Hudson Avenue, between Front & Water Streets, Dumbo (1-718 522 1018,

THE BEST MEMORABLE MEALS

For flawless fine dining
Per Se. *See p172.*

For a ceremonial Japanese feast
Brushstroke. *See p145.*

For modern opulence
The NoMad. *See p166.*

CONSUME

www.vinegarhillhouse.com). Subway A, C to High Street; F to York Street. **Open** 6-11pm Mon-Thur; 11am-3.30pm, 6-11.30pm Fri, Sat; 11am-3.30pm, 5.30-11pm Sun. **Main courses** $25. **Credit** AmEx, Disc, MC, V. **Map** p411 T9
⑭ American

As it's hidden in a residential street in the forgotten namesake neighbourhood (now essentially part of Dumbo), tracking down Vinegar Hill House engenders a treasure-hunt thrill. Co-owner Jean Adamson, who was at Lower East Side success story Freemans before opening Vinegar Hill House in 2008, relinquished the kitchen to chef Brian Leth (Allen & Delancey, Prune) a couple of years later. But the daily-changing menu still focuses on seasonal comfort foods. The cosy, tavern-like spot has a limited reservation policy (see website for details), but waiting in the secluded garden with drinks is a pleasure. You can also try the tiny next-door wine-bar-cum-café offshoot, Hillside.

▶ *For a review of Freemans, see p152.*

QUEENS

$ Jackson Diner

37-47 74th Street, between 37th Avenue & 37th Road, Jackson Heights (1-718 672 1232, www.jacksondiner.com). Subway E, F, M, R to Jackson Heights-Roosevelt Avenue; 7 to 74th Street-Broadway. **Open** 11.30am-10pm Mon-Thur, Sun; 11.30am-10.30pm Fri, Sat. **Main courses** $13. **Credit** AmEx, DC, Disc, MC, V. **Map** p412 Y5 **⑮ Indian**

Harried waiters and Formica-topped tables complete the diner experience at this weekend meet-and-eat headquarters for New York's Indian expat community. Watch Hindi soaps on Zee TV while enjoying *samosa chat* topped with chickpeas, yoghurt, onion, tomato, and a sweet-spicy mix of tamarind and mint chutneys. Specials such as *murgh tikka makhanwala*, tender pieces of marinated chicken simmered in curry and cream, are fiery and flavourful – ask for mild if you're not immune to potent chillies.

▶ *For more on Little India, see p128.*

M Wells Dinette

22-25 Jackson Avenue, at 46th Avenue, Long Island City (1-718 786 1800). Subway E, M to Court Square-23rd Street; G to 21st Street; 7 to 45th Road-Court House Square. **Open** noon-6pm Mon, Thur, Fri; 10am-6pm Sat, Sun. **Main courses** $15. **Credit** AmEx, Disc, MC, V. **Map** p412 V5 **⑯ Eclectic**

M Wells, the irreverent Queens diner that closed in August 2011, was roundly cheered by the city's critics for playing with its food (foie gras on meatloaf, tripe cut in the shape of noodles). So it's fitting that husband-and-wife team Hugue Dufour and Sarah Obraitis, have resurrected their brand in a former elementary-school space at MoMA PS1. At

this museum cafeteria, Dufour puts his trademark cockeyed spin on Asian plates – *bibimbap* with maple syrup and oysters – as well as classic French dishes like the rich escargot-and-marrow tart sprinkled with parsley leaves. In a nod to the space's educational past, the menu is scrawled on a blackboard and school-desk-styled communal tables are filled with pencils and playing cards.

$ The Queens Kickshaw

40-17 Broadway, between Steinway & 41st Streets, Astoria (1-718 777 0913, www.thequeenskickshaw.com). Subway M, R to Steinway Street. **Open** 7.30am-1am Mon-Fri; 9am-1am Sat, Sun. **Sandwiches** $10. **Credit** AmEx, Disc, MC, V. **Map** p412 X4 **⑰ Café**

Serious java draws caffeine fiends to this airy café, which also specialises in grilled cheese sandwiches. While the pedigreed beans – from Tarrytown, New York's Coffee Labs Roasters – are brewed with Hario V60 drip cones and a La Marzocco Strada espresso machine, there's no coffee-snob attitude here. Of the fancy grilled cheese choices, the simplest riffs are best: one weekend-morning offering features soft egg folded with ricotta, a gruyère crisp and maple hot sauce between two thick, buttery slices of brioche.

★ $ Sripraphai

64-13 39th Avenue, between 64th & 65th Streets, Woodside (1-718 899 9599, www.sripraphai restaurant.com). Subway 7 to 61st Street-Woodside. **Open** 11.30am-9.30pm Mon, Tue, Thur-Sun. **Main courses** $10. **No credit cards**. **Map** p412 Y5 **⑱ Thai**

Woodside's destination eatery offers distinctive, traditional dishes such as catfish salad or green curry with beef: a thick, piquant broth filled out with roasted Thai eggplant. The dining areas, which sprawl over two levels and a garden (open in summer), are packed with Manhattanites who can be seen eyeing the plates enjoyed by the Thai regulars, mentally filing away what to order the next time.

$ Zenon Taverna

34-10 31st Avenue, at 34th Street, Astoria (1-718 956 0133, www.zenontaverna.com). Subway N, Q to Broadway. **Open** noon-11pm daily. **Main courses** $14. **No credit cards**. **Map** p412 W4 **⑲ Greek**

The faux-stone entryway and murals of ancient ruins don't detract from the Mediterranean charm of this humble place that's been serving Greek and Cypriot food for more than 20 years. Specials rotate daily, embracing all the classics – stuffed vine leaves, *keftedes* (Cypriot meatballs), *spanakopita* (spinach pie) – and less ubiquitous dishes such as rabbit stew and plump *loukaniko* (pork sausages). Filling sweets, such as *galaktopoureko* (syrupy layers of filo baked with custard cream), merit a taste, if your stomach isn't already bursting.

Bars

Choose your poison, neighbourhood and vibe.

Sophisticated wine bars, subterranean dives, faux speakeasies, rooftop havens, elegant cocktail lounges, gastropubs, old-school taverns, artisanal beer gardens – choosing from NYC's wealth of watering holes can make your head spin before your first sip. One tactic is to start with a location: Tribeca, Soho, the Lower East Side and the East Village are among the hottest bar-hopping 'hoods, but in recent years, Brooklyn – particularly Williamsburg – has evolved into a major drinking destination. These days, Manhattanites are just as likely to cross the river for a night out as are residents of the second borough.

The bar scene is always evolving, but a number of great classics remain. Stop into **McSorley's Old Ale House** in the East Village or **Bemelmans Bar** on the Upper East Side for a glimpse of the city's tippling past.

DOWNTOWN
Tribeca & Soho

★ Pegu Club
2nd Floor, 77 W Houston Street, at West Broadway (1-212 473 7348, www.peguclub.com). Subway B, D, F, M to Broadway-Lafayette Street; N, R to Prince Street. **Open** 5pm-2am Mon-Thur, Sun; 5pm-4am Fri, Sat. **Credit** AmEx, Disc, MC, V. **Map** p403 E29 ❶
Audrey Saunders, the drinks maven who turned Bemelmans Bar (*see p186*) into one of the city's most respected cocktail lounges, is behind this sleek liquid destination. The place has just the right element of secrecy without any awkward faux-speakeasy trickery. Tucked away on the second floor, this sophisticated spot was inspired by a British officers' club in Burma. The cocktail list features classics culled from decades-old booze bibles. Gin is the key ingredient; these are serious drinks for grown-up tastes.

Silver Lining
75 Murray Street, between West Broadway & Greenwich Street (1-212 513 1234, www.silverliningbar.com). Subway A, C, 1, 2, 3 to Chambers Street. **Open** 5pm-1am Mon-Thur, Sun; 5pm-2am Fri, Sat. **Credit** AmEx, MC, V. **Map** p402 E32 ❷
New York is packed with venues offering craft cocktails and ones that spotlight live jazz. But enjoying these two noble pursuits in the same place has been

nigh impossible. At this well-heeled Tribeca drinkery, the sound of piano keys and shaking jiggers find a common stage inside a majestic 154-year-old townhouse. Little Branch vets Joseph Schwartz and Vito Dieterle, along with bar guru Sasha Petraske, have transported their studied classic cocktails to Tribeca, and Dieterle – who moonlights on the tenor sax – curates the talent.

Lower East Side

Back Room
102 Norfolk Street, between Delancey & Rivington Streets (1-212 228 5098). Subway F to Delancey Street; J, Z to Delancey-Essex Streets. **Open** 7.30pm-3am Mon-Thur, Sun; 7.30pm-4am Fri, Sat. **Credit** AmEx, MC, V. **Map** p403 G30 ❸
For access to this ersatz speakeasy, look for a sign that reads 'The Lower East Side Toy Company'. Pass through the gate, walk down an alleyway, up a metal staircase and open an unmarked door to find a convincing replica of a 1920s watering hole. Cocktails are poured into teacups, and bottled beer is brown-bagged before being served. Patrons must be 25 or older on Fridays and Saturdays. The dress

> ❶ Green numbers given in this chapter correspond to the location of each bar on the street maps. *See pp402-412.*

Back to the Beer Garden

The traditional outdoor hops haven gets a 21st-century revamp.

Bohemian Hall & Beer Garden.

In pre-Prohibition New York, beer gardens were a popular import, brought to the city by European (especially German) immigrants – Astoria's **Bohemian Hall & Beer Garden** (*see p188*) is an original survivor, established in 1910. Recently, as the craze for clandestine neo-speakeasy-style bars has started to wane, there's been a revival in these sprawling, and far more welcoming, outdoor suds spots.

The **Garden at Studio Square** (*see p189*) in Queens is a contemporary interpretation of the classic. The grand cobblestoned courtyard is lined with communal picnic tables and has three mod fire pits to keep out evening chills, plus an indoor bar. The 20-strong list includes European classics (German wheat beer Franziskaner Hefe-Weiss) and American microbrews (Blue Point Toasted Lager, Bear Republic's piney Racer 5 IPA). Basic pub grub is supplemented by sausages (kielbasas and brats), and the party-hearty ambience is fueled by DJs and bands.

Tucked under the city's elevated rail track-turned-park, the High Line, the seasonal, industrial-chic, brick-floored **Standard Biergarten** at the Standard hotel (*see p232*) is at its prettiest at night, when the bar is back-lit by flickering light. As well as bottled beers, wine and cocktails, there

are three Bavarian brews on draft: a Bitburger pils, a wheat beer from Munich and a dark beer from eastern Germany. Bar food includes wursts from venerable Yorkville purveyor Schaller & Weber and massive pretzels, served by beer-hall maidens in full costume. **Birreria**, the massive rooftop beer garden above the blockbuster Eataly complex (*see p164*), offers an Italian twist on the theme. Hops-heads will geek out over the three proprietary cask-conditioned ales brewed on the premises – the collaborative effort of craft-brew pioneers Sam Calagione (founder of Delaware's Dogfish Head), Teo Musso (Piedmont's Birra Baladin) and Leonardo Di Vincenzo (Rome's Birra del Borgo). But you don't have to be a beer nerd to appreciate the 14th-storey views of the Flatiron and Empire State Buildings while sipping on the unpasteurised, unfiltered suds. Drinkers can also choose from nine Italian and American draft microbrews, nearly 30 bottled beers and a selection of wines on tap. There's serious grub as well – hearty Alps-inspired dishes, such as grilled meats, pork shoulder with sauerkraut and house-made sausages.

The Garden at Studio Square.

code is casual, but note that in a departure from the Jazz Age sensibility, real fur is banned in the bar.

Loreley

7 Rivington Street, between Bowery & Chrystie Street (1-212 253 7077, www.loreleynyc.com). Subway J, Z to Bowery. **Open** noon-1am Mon, Tue, Sun; noon-2am Wed; noon-3am Thur; noon-4am Fri, Sat. **Credit** AmEx, DC, Disc, MC, V. **Map** p403 F30 ❹

Perhaps bar owner Michael Momm, aka DJ Foosh, wanted a place where he could spin to his heart's content. Maybe he missed the *biergartens* of his youth in Cologne. Whatever. Just rejoice that he opened Loreley. Twelve draughts and eight bottled varieties of Germany's finest brews are available, along with wines from the country's Loreley region and a full roster of spirits. Try one of five German-named speciality cocktails, such as the Zimtschnitte with Captain Morgan, Cointreau, cinnamon and fresh orange.

Painkiller

49 Essex Street, between Grand & Hester Streets (no phone, www.pk-ny.com). Subway B, D to Grand Street; F to Delancey Street; J, Z to Delancey-Essex Streets. **Open** 6pm-2am Mon-Thur, Sun; 6pm-4am Fri, Sat. **Credit** AmEx, MC, V. **Map** p403 G30 ❺

This (tastefully restrained) tiki-style bar is a refreshing sign that a new age of mixology has arrived – one in which bitters and paper umbrellas can peacefully coexist. Painkiller takes a studied approach to tropical drinks, offering tiki archetypes (frozens, swizzles, zombie punches) tailored to your preferences. A passion fruit-spiked piña colada arrives as a thick, fruity slush served in a hollowed-out pineapple. A classic mai tai balances the acid notes of lime with the round sweetness of aged rum and the bitter edge of house-made curaçao.

Spitzer's Corner

101 Rivington Street, at Ludlow Street (1-212 228 0027, www.spitzerscorner.com). Subway F to Delancey Street; J, Z to Delancey-Essex Streets. **Open** 12pm-4am Mon-Fri; 10am-4am Sat, Sun. **Credit** AmEx, MC, V. **Map** p403 G29 ❻

Referencing the Lower East Side's pickle-making heritage, the walls at this rustic gastropub are made from salvaged wooden barrels. The formidable beer list – 40 rotating draughts – includes Bear Republic's fragrant Racer 5 IPA. Mull over your selection, with the help of appetising tasting notes, at one of the wide communal tables. The gastro end of things is manifest in the menu of quality pub grub, such as pan-seared sea scallops or a lamb burger.

East Village

★ Booker and Dax

207 Second Avenue, at 13th Street (entrance on 13th Street) (1-212 254 3500, www. momofuku.com). Subway L to Third Ave;

INSIDE TRACK
WHERE THERE'S SMOKE

Despite the strict city-wide smoking ban, you can still indulge your habit in places that could prove a percentage of their income came from selling tobacco products when the ban was enforced. Among them are **Circa Tabac** (32 Watts Street, between Sixth Avenue & Thompson Street, Soho, 1-212 941 1781, www.circatabac.com) and **Hudson Bar & Books** (636 Hudson Street, at Horatio Street, West Village, 1-212 229 2642, www.barandbooks.cz), whose Upper East Side sister location, **Lexington Bar & Books** (1020 Lexington Avenue, at 73rd Street, 1-212 717 3902), is also smoke-friendly.

L, N, Q, R, 4, 5, 6 to 14th Street-Union Square. **Open** 6pm-2am Mon-Thur, Sun; 6pm-3am Fri, Sat. **Credit** AmEx, Disc, MC, V. **Map** p403 F28 ❼

This tech-forward cocktail joint, housed in the former Momofuku Milk Bar space next to Ssäm Bar (*see p156*), showcases the boozy tinkerings of wizardly Dave Arnold, the French Culinary Institute's director of culinary technology. Glasses are chilled with a pour of liquid nitrogen, and winter warmers, like the Friend of the Devil (Campari, sweet vermouth, rye, Pernod, bitters), are scorched with a Red Hot Poker, a rod with a built-in 1,500-degree heater created by Arnold. He also showcases new techniques for creating fizzy drinks, like the Gin and Juice, made with Tanqueray gin and grapefruit juice that is clarified in a centrifuge, then carbonated in a CO_2-pressurised cocktail shaker.

Bourgeois Pig

111 E 7th Street, between First Avenue & Avenue A (1-212 475 2246, www.bourgeois pigny.com). Subway F to Lower East Side-Second Avenue; 6 to Astor Place. **Open** 6pm-2am daily. **Credit** AmEx, MC, V. **Map** p403 F28 ❽

Ornate mirrors and antique chairs give this small, red-lit wine and fondue joint a decidedly decadent feel. The wine list is well chosen, and although the hard stuff is verboten here, mixed concoctions based on wine, champagne or beer – such as the thick Le Marin Port Flip, featuring tawny port, espresso chocolate, egg yolk and cream – cater to cocktail aficionados.

Death & Company

433 E 6th Street, between First Avenue & Avenue A (1-212 388 0882, www.deathand company.com). Subway F to Lower East Side-Second Avenue; 6 to Astor Place. **Open** 6pm-2am Mon-Thur, Sun; 6pm-3am Fri, Sat. **Credit** AmEx, MC, V. **Map** p403 F28 ❾

The Wayland.

The nattily attired mixologists are deadly serious about drinks at this pseudo speakeasy with gothic flair (don't be intimidated by the imposing wooden door). Black walls and cushy booths combine with chandeliers to set a luxuriously sombre mood. The inventive cocktails are matched by top-notch food, including goat's cheese profiteroles.

Elsa

217 E 3rd Street, between Avenues B & C (1-917 882 7395). Subway F to Lower East Side-Second Avenue. **Open** 6pm-2am Mon-Thur, Sun; 6pm-4am Fri, Sat. **Credit** AmEx, MC, V. **Map** p403 G29 ⑩

At this stylish *boîte*, named for the iconoclastic 1930s clothing designer Elsa Schiaparelli, nods to couture include framed fashion sketches and three tap lines that flow through a vintage sewing machine. Perch on a white wooden banquette to enjoy speciality cocktails such as the Earhart (rye, St Germain, lemon and cloves).

★ Jimmy's No. 43

43 E 7th Street, between Second & Third Avenues (1-212 982 3006, www.jimmysno43.com). Subway F to Lower East Side-Second Avenue; 6 to Astor Place. **Open** noon-2am Mon-Thur; noon-4am Fri, Sat; 11.30am-2am Sun. **Credit** AmEx, MC, V ($20 min). **Map** p403 F28 ⑪

You could easily miss this worthy subterranean spot if it weren't for the sign painted on a doorway over an inconspicuous set of stairs. Descend them and you'll encounter burnt-yellow walls displaying taxidermy, mismatched wood tables and medieval-style arched passageways that lead to different rooms. Beer is a big attraction here, with 14 quality selections on tap (23 in the bottle), many of which also make it into the slow-food dishes filled with organic ingredients.

★ Mayahuel

304 E 6th Street, between First & Second Avenues (1-212 253 5888, www.mayahuelny. com). Subway F to Lower East Side-Second Avenue; 6 to Astor Place. **Open** 6pm-2am daily. **Credit** AmEx, MC, V. **Map** p403 F28 ⑫

Barkeep Phil Ward focuses on tequila and its cousin, mescal, at this haute cantina. His inventive cocktail menu features the Cinder, a smoky, spicy mix of reposado and jalapeño tequilas, mezcal, lime, angostura bitters and smoked salt. The Slynx cocktail is a liquid campfire of aged tequila, applejack, bitters and a smoky rinse of mescal. The craftsmanship in the drinks is equalled in the bar menu, which features juicy pork bellies.

★ McSorley's Old Ale House

15 E 7th Street, between Second & Third Avenues (1-212 473 9148, www.mcsorleysnewyork.com). Subway F to Lower East Side-Second Avenue. **Open** 11am-1am Mon-Sat; 1pm-1am Sun. **No credit cards**. **Map** p403 F28 ⑬

Ladies should probably leave the Blahniks at home. In traditional Irish-pub fashion, McSorley's floor has been thoroughly scattered with sawdust to take care of the spills and other messes that often accompany large quantities of cheap beer. Established in 1854, McSorley's became an institution by remaining steadfastly authentic and providing only two choices to its customers: McSorley's Dark Ale and McSorley's Light Ale. Both beverages have a lot more character than Pabst Blue Ribbon, though at these prices, it won't be long before you stop noticing.

★ PDT

113 St Marks Place, between First Avenue & Avenue A (1-212 614 0386). Subway L to First Avenue; 6 to Astor Place. **Open** 6pm-2am Mon-Thur, Sun; 6pm-4am Fri, Sat. **Credit** AmEx, MC, V. **Map** p403 F28 ⑭

Word has got out about 'Please Don't Tell', the faux speakeasy inside gourmet hot dog joint Crif Dogs (*see p154*), so it's a good idea to reserve a booth in advance. Once you arrive, you'll notice people lingering outside an old wooden phonebooth near the front. Slip inside, pick up the receiver and the host opens a secret panel to the dark, narrow space. The serious cocktails surpass the gimmicky entry: try the house old-fashioned, made with bacon-infused bourbon, which leaves a smoky aftertaste.

Summit Bar

133 Avenue C, between 8th & 9th Streets (no phone, www.thesummitbar.net). Subway L to First Avenue; 6 to Astor Place. **Open** 5.30pm-3am Mon, Sun; 5.30pm-4am Tue-Sat. **Credit** AmEx, MC, V. **Map** p403 G28 ⑮

In a rebuttal to the clandestine posturing that has defined the city's cocktail revival, no secret buzzer is needed to enter this democratic lounge. Opened by Greg Seider, the mixologist who designed

Minetta Tavern's cocktails, it is a handsome space with blue velvet banquettes, a black granite bar and chandeliers turned low. The drinks are presented in two categories: 'Classic' features spot-on standards, including an old-fashioned owing its peppery kick to Rittenhouse Rye, and a whiskey sour bright with fresh lemon juice; while 'Alchemist' highlights Seider's creative impulses.

Terroir

413 E 12th Street, between First Avenue & Avenue A (1-646 602 1300, www.wineis terroir.com). Subway L to First Avenue; L, N, Q, R, 4, 5, 6 to 14th Street-Union Square. **Open** 5pm-2am Mon-Sat; 5pm-midnight Sun. **Credit** AmEx, MC, V. **Map** p403 F28 ⑯

The surroundings are stripped-back basic at this wine-bar offspring of nearby restaurant Hearth – the focus is squarely on the drinks. Co-owner and oeno-evangelist Paul Grieco preaches the powers of *terroir* – grapes that express a sense of place – and the knowledgeable waitstaff deftly help patrons to navigate about 45 by-the-glass options. Pair the stellar sips with the restaurant-calibre small plates. **Other locations** 24 Harrison Street, between Greenwich & Hudson Streets, Tribeca (1-212 625 9463); 439 Third Avenue, between 30th & 31st Streets, Murray Hill (1-212 481 1920); 284 Fifth Avenue at 1st Street, Park Slope, Brooklyn (1-718 832 9463).

The Wayland

700 E 9th Street, at Avenue C (1-212 777 7022, www. thewaylandnyc.com). Subway L to First Avenue. **Open** 6pm-4am daily. **Credit** AmEx, DC, Disc, MC, V. **Map** p403 F28 ⑰

THE BEST BAR SNACKS

For gourmet pairings
Ardesia. *See p185.*

For top-chef canapés
Bar Pleiades. *See p186.*

For dive-bar eats
The Commodore. *See p188.*

For cheese with everything
Earl's Beer & Cheese. *See p186.*

East Village boozers have been stumbling further down the alphabet for years now, but it's taken Avenue C time to develop the critical mass necessary to attract a late-night buzz. At this fun-loving newcomer, solicitous staff, a young and attractive crowd, and the likelihood of a spontaneous sing-along around the piano all contribute to a convivial vibe that makes you want to call for another round. An old-fashioned riff called I Hear Banjos ($12) –made with moonshine, apple-spice bitters and Laird's bonded applejack – comes with a ceremonious puff of applewood smoke, captured in an overturned glass that's placed over the drink.

Greenwich Village

Corkbuzz Wine Studio

13 E 13th Street, between Fifth Avenue & University Place (1-646 873 6071, www.cork buzz.com). Subway L, N, Q, R, 4, 5, 6 to 14th

Corkbuzz Wine Studio

Street-Union Square. **Open** 5pm-midnight Mon-Wed; 5pm-1am Thur, Fri; 4pm-1am Sat; 4pm-midnight Sun. **Credit** AmEx, Disc, MC, V. **Map** p403 F27 ⑬

This intriguing and elegant hybrid, owned by the world's youngest master sommelier, Laura Maniec, comprises a restaurant, wine bar and educational centre. Before you drink anything, chat with one of the staffers, who preach the Maniec gospel to patrons as they navigate 35 by-the-glass options and around 250 bottles.

Vol de Nuit Bar
(aka Belgian Beer Lounge)

148 W 4th Street, between Sixth Avenue & MacDougal Street (1-212 982 3388, www.volde nuitbar.com). Subway A, B, C, D, E, F, M to W 4th Street. **Open** 4pm-midnight daily. **Credit** AmEx, DC, Disc, MC, V. **Map** p403 E29 ⑲

Duck through an unmarked doorway on a busy stretch of West 4th Street and find yourself in a red-walled Belgian bar that serves brews exclusively from the motherland. Clusters of European grad students knock back glasses of De Konick and La Chouffe – just two of 13 beers on tap and 22 by the bottle. Moules and frites are the only eats (Mon-Sat).

West Village & Meatpacking District

Blind Tiger Ale House

281 Bleecker Street, at Jones Street (1-212 462 4682, www.blindtigeralehouse.com). Subway A, B, C, D, E, F, M to W 4th Street; 1 to Christopher Sreet-Sheridan Square. **Open** 11.30am-4am daily. **Credit** AmEx, Disc, MC, V. **Map** p403 E29 ⑳

Brew geeks descend upon this hops heaven for boutique ales and 28 daily rotating, hard-to-find drafts (like Dale's Pale Ale and Allagash's Belgian-style Dubbel). The clubby room features windows that open onto bustling Bleecker Street. Late afternoons and early evenings are ideal for serious sippers enjoying plates of Murray's Cheese, while the after-dark set veers dangerously close to Phi Kappa territory.

★ Employees Only

510 Hudson Street, between Christopher & W 10th Streets (1-212 242 3021, www.employees onlynyc.com). Subway 1 to Christopher Street-Sheridan Square. **Open** 6pm-4am daily. **Credit** AmEx, MC, V. **Map** p403 D29 ㉑

This Prohibition-themed bar cultivates an exclusive vibe, but there's no cover and no trouble at the door. Pass by the palm reader in the window (it's a front) and you'll find an amber-lit art deco interior where formality continues to flourish: servers wear custom-designed frocks and bartenders don waitstaff whites. The real stars are cocktails such as the West Side, a lethal mix of lemon vodka, lemon juice, mint and club soda.

Gottino

52 Greenwich Avenue, between Charles & Perry Streets (1-212 633 2590, www.ilmiogottino.com). Subway 1 to Christopher Street-Sheridan Square. **Open** 8am-2am Mon-Fri; 10am-2am Sat, Sun. **Credit** AmEx, Disc, MC, V. **Map** p403 D28 ㉒

Jockey for a seat at this narrow enoteca, marked by a long marble bar, a piddling five tables and a menu of choice Italian nibbles to go with the all-Italian wine list. The least expensive glass goes for $9, and there are only a few bottles under $40, so bargain-seekers might want to start with a prosecco cocktail instead. Then attack the menu. Thick-cut *cacciatorini* (cured pork sausage) luxuriates in a shallow pool of olive oil infused with oregano and garlic, while in another wee dish, eye-poppingly tangy white anchovies keep company with celery, parsley and preserved lemon.

Highlands

150 W 10th Street, between Greenwich Avenue & Waverly Place (1-212 229-2670, www.highlands-nyc.com). Subway A, B, C, D, E, F, M to W 4th Street. **Open** 5.30pm-2am Mon-Thur; 5.30pm-3am Fri, Sat; 4pm-midnight Sun. **Credit** AmEx, MC, V. **Map** p403 D28 ㉓

This buzzing bar marks the overdue arrival of a stylish Scottish tavern in New York City. The look is urban drawing room: furnishings include stag heads, and the charming staff sport tartan ties. Scotch is the thing – sip from a collection of 100 whiskies, or try one of the cocktails, which provide a perfect introduction to the spirit. The citrusy Blood and Sand features 12-year-old Glenlivet, cherry Heering, orange juice and bitters. It's worth bringing an appetite for the gastropub fare, too: lamb sausage rolls with harissa aïoli make for a top-flight drinking snack.

MIDTOWN
Chelsea

Half King

505 W 23rd Street, between Tenth & Eleventh Avenues (1-212 462 4300, www.thehalfking. com). Subway C, E to 23rd Street. **Open** 11am-4am Mon-Fri; 9am-4am Sat, Sun. **Credit** AmEx, MC, V. **Map** p404 C26 ㉔

Don't let their blasé appearance fool you – the creative types gathered at the Half King's yellow pine bar are probably as excited as you are to catch a glimpse of the part-owner, author Sebastian Junger. While you're waiting, order one of the 15 draught beers – including several local brews – or a seasonal cocktail.

The Tippler

Chelsea Market, 425 W 15th Street, between Ninth & Tenth Avenues (1-212 206-0000, www.thetippler.com). Subway A, C, E to 14th

Cocktail Chronicles

Five tipples that transformed the way New Yorkers drink.

BENTON'S OLD-FASHIONED

'Fat washing' was hardly a part of the bar lexicon in 2007, when IT-guy-turned-bartender Don Lee started at PDT. The sci-nerd technique of infusing the flavour of a fat-laden ingredient into a liquid wasn't new, though. Eben Freeman, who learned it from pastry chef Sam Mason, had toyed with it at molecular gastronomy eaterie wd~50. But the process wasn't generally known until the Benton's old-fashioned caught on. New York's pork obsession was just spiking when Lee combined Benton's bacon with Kentucky bourbon, and the pairing proved to be a hit.

Try it at PDT (*see p180*).

Pegu Club.

THE BRONX

Though once popular, the Bronx cocktail was among the many victims of Prohibition. The original recipe, created at the Waldorf-Astoria hotel in the early 1900s, was a twist on the perfect martini (gin with equal parts French and Italian vermouths), adding orange peel and two dashes of orange bitters. But when the ban on alcohol drove distilling underground and available spirits became nearly undrinkable, large doses of orange juice were added to cover up the offending bathtub gin. While the drinks industry eventually recovered, the Bronx never regained its prominence.

Try it at The Liberty (*see p185*).

COSMOPOLITAN

Carrie Bradshaw may have inspired legions to jump on the cosmo bandwagon in the 1990s, but the vodka, cran and citrus combo was originally popularised by two serious New York bartending heavyweights.

While its creation myth is a little hazy (Miami bartender Cheryl Cook has declared that she invented the pink libation), Toby Cecchini is credited with replacing Rose's lime juice with fresh juice at Passerby, and Dale DeGroff fashioned a refined version garnished with a flamed orange peel at the Rainbow Room.

Try it at Employees Only (*see p182*).

GIN-GIN MULE

The far-reaching influence of New York's reigning queen of mixology, Audrey Saunders, is hard to measure (her storied cocktail lounge, the Pegu Club, begat many of today's standard-bearers, including Death & Company, PDT and Mayahuel). But the impact of her Gin-Gin Mule, first served at the Beacon Restaurant & Bar in 2000, is clear: the vivacious elixir was one of the first popular cocktails to reflect a culinary approach behind the bar. Instead of the commercial stuff, she mixed homemade ginger beer with Tanqueray gin, fresh mint and lime juice – a turn that inspired a movement towards from-scratch ingredients.

Try it at Pegu Club (*see p177*).

MANHATTAN

High-rolling Wall Street suits still finish their days with this strapping potion, just as JP Morgan did after trading closed every day (according to David Wondrich in his book *Esquire Drinks*). Though the manhattan's origins are debatable – one story points to the Manhattan Club, while another pegs a Broadway saloon keeper as its creator – most historians agree that it was the first drink to combine spirits with the newly popular vermouth, sometime in the late 1800s.

Try it at Flatiron Lounge (*see p184*).

Flatiron Lounge.

CONSUME

Ginny's Supper Club. See p186.

Street; L to Eighth Avenue. **Open** 5pm-2am Mon-Wed, Sun; 5pm-4am Thur-Sat. **Credit** AmEx, MC, V. **Map** p403 C27 ⓛ
Even at its most packed, there's still a fair amount of room to manoeuvre in this expansive lounge, which means you won't have too much trouble finding a space at the long marble bar. The menu includes a number of affordable draft and bottled beers, plus wines from around the world, but you'd be remiss not to try at least one of the sophisticated speciality cocktails, such as the Gin & Chronic (Plymouth gin, hops, spiced lime, tonic).

Flatiron District & Union Square

Flatiron Lounge
37 W 19th Street, between Fifth & Sixth Avenues (1-212 727 7741, www.flatironlounge.com). Subway F, M, N, R to 23rd Street. **Open** 4pm-2am Mon-Wed; 4pm-3am Thur; 4pm-4am Fri; 5pm-4am Sat; 5pm-2am Sun. **Credit** AmEx, MC, V. **Map** p403 E27 ⓜ
Red leather booths, mahogany tables and globe-shaped lamps amp up the vintage vibe at this art deco space. Julie Reiner's notable mixology skills have made the bar a destination for creative libations like the Sun Also Sets (pisco, silver tequila and blood orange shrub). The 30ft bar, built in 1927, stays packed well into the wee hours.

★ Raines Law Room
48 W 17th Street, between Fifth & Sixth Avenues (no phone, www.raineslawroom.com). Subway F, M to 14th Street; L to Sixth Avenue. **Open** 5pm-2am Mon-Thur; 5pm-3am Fri, Sat; 7pm-1am Sun. **Credit** AmEx, MC, V. **Map** p403 E27 ⓝ
There's no bar to belly up to at this louche lounge. In deference to its name (which refers to an 1896

law designed to curb liquor consumption), drinks are prepared in a half-hidden back room known as 'the kitchen'. While this reduces the noise level in the plush, upholstered space, it robs you of the opportunity to watch the barkeep at work. The cocktail list includes classics, and variations thereof. The Gold Rush, a honey- and lemon-laced bourbon drink, tastes like a delectable, alcoholic cold remedy, while the Old Cuban (rum, champagne, mint and bitters) smacks of a mojito with something to celebrate.

Rye House
11 W 17th Street, between Fifth & Sixth Avenues (1-212 255 7260, www.ryehouse nyc.com). Subway F, M to 14th Street; L to Sixth Avenue. **Open** noon-2am Mon-Fri; 11am-2am Sat, Sun. **Credit** AmEx, MC, V. **Map** p403 E27 ⓞ
As the name suggests, American spirits are the emphasis at this dark, sultry bar. As well as bourbons and ryes, there are gins, vodkas and rums, all distilled in the States. Check out the smoky bacon-infused bourbon, a popular take on a Kentucky favourite. While the focus is clearly on drinking, there's excellent upscale pub grub, such as truffle grilled cheese or house-smoked pork cheeks.

230 Fifth
230 Fifth Avenue, between 26th & 27th Streets (1-212 725 4300, www.230-fifth.com). Subway N, R to 28th Street. **Open** 4pm-4am Mon-Fri; 10am-4am Sat, Sun. **Credit** AmEx, Disc, MC, V. **Map** p404 E26 ⓟ
The 14,000sq ft roof garden dazzles with truly spectacular views, including a close-up of the Empire State Building, but the glitzy indoor lounge – with ceiling-height windows, wraparound sofas and bold lighting – shouldn't be overlooked. While the

sprawling outdoor space gets mobbed on sultry nights, it's less crowded in the cooler months when heaters, fleece robes and hot ciders are provided.

Gramercy Park & Murray Hill

Middle Branch
154 E 33rd Street, between Lexington & Third Avenues (1-212 213 1350). Subway 6 to 33rd Street. **Open** 5pm-2am daily. **No credit cards.** **Map** p404 F25 ③⓪
In 2000, visionary barman Sasha Petraske paved the way for the modern cocktail bar with members-only Milk & Honey (134 Eldridge Street, between Broome & Delancey Streets, www.mlkhny.com); since then, he and his acolytes have spread the liquid gospel with a rapidly expanding web of stand-out watering holes. His latest bar, Middle Branch – run by longtime Little Branch lieutenants Lucinda Sterling and Benjamin Schwartz – plants a flag for artisanal cocktails in post-frat epicentre Murray Hill. This is no sly speakeasy, hidden from the masses with a windowless facade and an unmarked ingress: the bi-level drinkery, sporting French doors that offer a glimpse inside, practically beckons passersby. As at Petraske's other highfalutin' joints, the razor-sharp focus is on classic cocktails and riffs (all $12), built with hand-cut ice and superior spirits.
Other locations Little Branch 20 Seventh Avenue South, at Leroy Street, West Village (1-212 929 4360).

Herald Square & the Garment District

The Liberty
29 W 35th Street, between Fifth & Sixth Avenues (1-212 967 4000, www.theliberty nyc.com). Subway B, D, F, M, N, Q, R to 34th Street-Herald Square. **Open** noon-2am Mon-Wed; noon-4am Thur-Sat; noon-midnight Sun. **Credit** AmEx, DC, Disc, MC, V. **Map** p404 E25 ③①
This clubby 4,000sq ft behemoth boasts a 34-foot-long black granite bar, weekend DJs and a wide-ranging bar menu. Not only is the interior inspired by spaces in iconic structures such as the Chrysler Building's defunct Cloud Club, it serves classic NYC cocktails including the Bronx, the Brooklyn, the Queens – oh, and the Manhattan, of course.

Theater District & Hell's Kitchen

★ Ardesia
510 W 52nd Street, between Tenth & Eleventh Avenues (1-212 247 9191, www.ardesia-ny.com). Subway C, E to 50th Street. **Open** 5pm-midnight Mon-Wed, 5pm-2am Thur-Sat, 2pm-2am Sat; 2-11pm Sun. **Credit** AmEx, Disc, MC, V. **Map** p404 C23 ③②

Le Bernardin vet Mandy Oser's iron-and-marble gem offers superior wines in a relaxed setting. The 75-strong collection of international bottles is a smart balance of Old and New World options that pair beautifully with the varied selection of small plates that accompany your choices. A grüner velt-liner – a dry, oaky white from the Knoll winery in Wachau, Austria – had enough backbone to stand up to a duck *banh mi* layered with house-made pâté and duck prosciutto. A blended red from Spain's Cellar Can Blau, meanwhile, was a spicy, velvety match for coriander-rich home-made mortadella. One for the serious oenophile.

Pony Bar
637 Tenth Avenue, at 45th Street (1-212 586 2707, www.theponybar.com). Subway C, E to 50th Street. **Open** 3pm-4am Mon-Fri; noon-4am Sat, Sun. **Credit** AmEx, Disc, MC, V. **Map** p404 C24 ③③
Hell's Kitchen has long been a dead zone for civilised bars, but this sunny paean to American microbrews is an oasis. Choose from a constantly changing selection of two cask ales and 20 beers on tap ; daily selections are artfully listed on signboards according to provenance and potency. The expert curation, combined with low prices (all beers cost $5), suggest that the drought may finally be easing.
Other locations 1444 First Avenue, at 75th Street, Upper East Side (1-212 288 0090).

Rum House
228 W 47th Street, between Seventh & Eighth Avenues (1-646 490 6924). Subway N, Q, R to 49th Street. **Open** 11am-4am daily. **Credit** AmEx, Disc, MC, V. **Map** p404 D23 ③④
In 2009, this rakish, 1970s-vintage piano bar in the Edison Hotel looked destined to go the way of the Times Square peep show. But the team behind Tribeca mixology den Ward III has ushered in a second act, introducing some key upgrades (including serious cocktails) while maintaining the charmingly offbeat flavor of the place. Sip dark spirit-heavy tipples, such as a funky old-fashioned riff that showcases the rich, tropical complexity of Banks 5 Island Rum, while listening to a pianist or jazz trio most nights of the week.

THE BEST CLASSIC INTERIORS

An uptown institution
Bemelmans Bar. *See p186.*

An Irish original
McSorley's Old Ale House. *See p180.*

A gorgeous fake
Raines Law Room. *See p184.*

CONSUME

UPTOWN
Upper East Side

★ Bar Pleiades
*The Surrey, 20 E 76th Street, between Fifth &
Madison Avenues (1-212 772 2600, www.daniel
nyc.com). Subway 6 to 77th Street.* **Open** noon-
midnight Mon-Thur, Sun; noon-1am Fri, Sat.
Credit AmEx, MC, V. **Map** p405 E20 ㉟
Designed as a nod to Coco Chanel, Daniel Boulud's
bar is framed in black lacquered panels that recall
an elegant make-up compact. The luxe setting and
moneyed crowd might seem a little stiff, but the seasonally rotating cocktails are so exquisitely executed
you won't mind sharing your banquette with a suit.
Light eats are provided by Café Boulud next door
(about $15 a plate).

Bemelmans Bar
*The Carlyle, 35 E 76th Street, at Madison
Avenue (1-212 744 1600, www.thecarlyle.com).
Subway 6 to 77th Street.* **Open** 11am-midnight
Mon; 11am-12.30am Tue-Thur; 11am-1am Fri, Sat;
11am-midnight Sun.* **Credit** AmEx, Disc, MC, V.
Map p405 E20 ㊱
The Plaza may have Eloise, but the Carlyle has its
own children's book connection – the wonderful
1947 murals of Central Park by *Madeline* creator
Ludwig Bemelmans in this, the quintessential classy
New York bar. A jazz trio adds to the atmosphere
every night (a cover charge of $15-$30 applies from
9.30pm when it takes up residence).

Earl's Beer & Cheese
*1259 Park Avenue, between 97th & 98th Street
(1-212 289 1581, www.earlsny.com). Subway 6 to
96th Street.* **Open** 4pm-midnight Mon-Wed;
11am- midnight Thur, Sun; 11am-2am Fri, Sat.
Credit AmEx, MC, V. **Map** p406 E17 ㊲
Tucked into the no-man's land between the Upper
East Side and Spanish Harlem, this craft-beer cubby
hole has the sort of community-hub vibe that makes
you want to settle in and become part of the furniture. The well-priced suds (including rotating craft
brews and cheap cans of Genny Light) and slapdash
set-up appeal to a neighbourhood crowd, but it's
Momofuku Ssäm Bar alum Corey Cova's madcap
bar menu that makes it destination-worthy. Try the
NY State Cheddar – a grilled cheese featuring an

**INSIDE TRACK
PROVE YOURSELF**

Don't forget to carry photo ID, such as a
driver's licence or passport, at all times.
Even those who look well over the legal
drinking age of 21 may well get 'carded'
when trying to order drinks at the bar.

---

unstoppable combo of braised pork belly, fried egg
and house-made kimchi. The crew has since opened
a cocktail bar, the Guthrie Inn, next door (at the same
address, 1-212 423 9900) and a wine bar, ABV (1504
Lexington Avenue, at 97th Street, 1-212 722 8959,
www.abvny.com), a block east.

Upper West Side

Ding Dong Lounge
*929 Columbus Avenue, between 105th Street &
106th Street (Duke Ellington Boulevard) (1-212
663 2600, www.dingdonglounge.com). Subway
B, C to 103rd Street.* **Open** 4pm-4am daily.
Credit MC, V. **Map** p406 C16 ㊳
Goth chandeliers and kick-ass music mark this
dark dive as punk – with broadened horizons. The
tap pulls, dispensing Stella Artois, Guinness and
Bass, are sawn-off guitar necks, and the walls are
covered with vintage concert posters (from Dylan
to the Damned). The affable local clientele and
mood-lit conversation nooks make it surprisingly
accessible (even without a working knowledge of
Dee Dee Ramone).

Harlem

Ginny's Supper Club
*310 Malcolm X Boulevard (Lenox Avenue),
between 125th & 126th Streets (1-212 421
3821, www.redroosterharlem.com). Subway
2, 3 to 125th Street.* **Open** 7pm-midnight
Tue-Sat. **Credit** AmEx, DC, Disc, MC, V.
Map p407 D13 ㊵
Red Rooster's sprawling new basement lounge is modelled after the Harlem speakeasies of the '20s. With its
own menu, cocktails from star mixologist Eben
Klemm and a steady lineup of live music, the venue
seems to have caught fire overnight. *Photo p184.*

Lenox Lounge
*288 Malcolm X Boulevard (Lenox Avenue),
between 124th & 125th Streets (1-212 427
0253, www.lenoxlounge.com). Subway 2, 3
to 125th Street.* **Open** Call for information.
Credit AmEx, DC, MC, V. **Map** p407 D13 ㊶
The storied art deco bar and jazz club, where Miles
Davis, Billie Holiday and John Coltrane played,
changed hands as this guide went to press. The new
owner, a managing partner of Nobu, plans to reopen
it in 2013, but whether the place will retain its name
and character is uncertain.

Shrine
*2271 Adam Clayton Powell Jr Boulevard
(Seventh Avenue), between 133rd & 134th
Streets (1-212 690 7807, www.shrinenyc.com).
Subway B, C, 2, 3 to 135th Street.* **Open** 4pm-
4am daily. **No credit cards. Map** p407 D12 ㊸
Playfully adapting a sign left over from the previ-
ous tenants (the Black United Foundation), the

Donna. *See p188.*

Shrine advertises itself as a 'Black United Fun Plaza'. The interior is tricked out with African art and vintage album covers, and actual vinyl adorns the ceiling. Harlemites and downtowners pack into the Shrine for nightly concerts, which might feature indie rock, jazz, reggae or DJ sets. The cocktail menu aspires to similar diversity: drinks range from a smooth mango mojito to signature tipples such as a snappy Afro Trip (a lime and ginger concoction enhanced by Jamaican or Brazilian rum), and a sweet vodka- and Bailey's-driven Muslim Jew.

BROOKLYN

Abilene

442 Court Street, at 3rd Place, Carroll Gardens (1-718 522 6900, www.abilene barbrooklyn.com). Subway F, G to Carroll Street. **Open** 11am-4am daily. **Credit** AmEx, Disc, MC, V. **Map** p410 S11 ⓰
Leah Allen, a Carroll Gardens artist, has decorated her watering hole with various thrift store scores,

a rescued church pew, a 27ft-long bar and painted grass-like patterns. The spot is laid-back and dimly lit. Chatting up the friendly bartenders is easy, as is getting an impromptu game of Scrabble going. Take advantage of happy 'hour' (11am-7pm Mon-Fri; 4-7pm Sat, Sun), when pint-sized cocktails are just $7.

Clover Club

210 Smith Street, between Baltic & Butler Streets, Cobble Hill (1-718 855 7939, www.cloverclub ny.com). Subway F, G to Bergen Street. **Open** 5pm-2am Mon; noon-2am Tue-Fri; 10.30am-4am Sat; 10.30am-1am Sun. **Credit** AmEx, Disc, MC, V. **Map** p410 S10 ⓰
This Victorian-styled cocktail parlour from mixology maven Julie Reiner (Flatiron Lounge) is among Brooklyn's recent spate of serious drinking establishments. Classic cocktails are the Club's signature drink: sours, fizzes, mules, punches and cobblers all get their latter-day due at the 19th-century mahogany bar. Highbrow snacks (fried oysters, steak tartare) and tipples, such as the

---

THE BEST NICHE TIPPLES

For mad-scientist mixology
Booker and Dax. *See p179.*

For new twists on tequila
Mayahuel. *See p180.*

For the 'green fairy'
Maison Premiere. *See right.*

For educated oenophiles
Corkbuzz Wine Studio. *See p181.*

---

eponymous Clover Club (with gin, raspberry syrup, egg whites, dry vermouth and lemon juice) or the Improved Whisky Cocktail with rye and house-made bitters, should absolve you of the folly of your appletini days.

The Commodore

366 Metropolitan Avenue, at Havemeyer Street, Williamsburg (1-718 218 7632). Subway J, M, Z to Marcy Avenue; L to Bedford Avenue. **Open** 4pm-midnight Mon-Thur, Sun; 4pm-1am Fri, Sat. **Credit** AmEx, MC, V. **Map** p411 U8 ❹
With its old arcade games, Schlitz in a can and stereo pumping out the *Knight Rider* theme song, this Williamsburg gastrodive offers some of the city's best cheap-ass bar eats. The 'hot fish' sandwich, for one, is a fresh, flaky, cayenne-rubbed catfish fillet poking out of both sides of a butter-griddled sesame-seed roll. You'll be thankful it's available after a few rounds of the Commodore's house drink – a slushy, frozen piña colada.

★ Donna

27 Broadway at Dunham Place, Williamsburg (1-646 568 6622, www.donnabklyn.com). Subway J, M to Marcy Avenue. **Open** 5pm-2am Mon-Thur; 5pm-4am Fri; 4pm-4am Sat; 4pm-2am Sun. **Credit** AmEx, Disc, MC, V. **Map** p411 U8 ❹
This breezy, rum-soaked drinkery secreted away near the Williamsburg waterfront feels worlds away from the industrial streets outside. The interior is a fever-dream vision of Central America that takes its inspiration from Spanish-colonial cathedrals, Art Nouveau parlor rooms and the sailor's flophouse that existed on this site in the 1800s. Rum anchors the cocktail list: the OJ-splashed Brancolada elevates that tiki warhorse, the piña colada, with herbal and minty Branca Menta – with sophisticated and dangerously easygoing results. If you're making an evening of it, you can keep yourself moored with tapas-style snacks. *Photos p187.*

Floyd, NY

131 Atlantic Avenue, between Clinton & Henry Streets, Cobble Hill (1-718 858 5810, www.floyd

ny.com). Subway R to Court Street; 2, 3, 4, 5 to Borough Hall. **Open** 5pm-4am Mon-Fri; 11am-4am Sat, Sun. **Credit** AmEx, MC, V. **Map** p410 S10 ❹
Floyd, NY is modelled on the taverns in Floyd, Iowa, which was owner Pam Carden's hometown. She and her husband have added country-style elements, such as a jukebox stocked with Hank Williams and the Bad Livers; vintage signs; a salvaged 1870s bar; and nice bartenders. It looks like a joint that's been around for ages – not the renovated liquor store that it actually is. Schlitz beer and Kentucky beer cheese complete the theme. The indoor bocce court is a little incongruous, but works nonetheless.

Maison Premiere

298 Bedford Avenue, between Grand & South 1st Streets, Williamsburg (1-347 335 0446, www.maisonpremiere.com). Subway L to Bedford Avenue. **Open** 4pm-4am Mon-Fri; noon-4am Sat, Sun. **Credit** AmEx, MC, V. **Map** p411 U8 ❹
The majority of NYC's New Orleans-inspired watering holes choose debauched Bourbon Street as their muse, but this gorgeous salon embraces the romance found in the Crescent City's historic haunts. Belly up to the oval, marble-topped bar and get familiar with the twin pleasures of oysters and absinthe: two French Quarter staples with plenty of appeal in Brooklyn. The mythical anise-flavored liqueur appears in 19 international varieties, in addition to a trim list of cerebral cocktails. In warm weather, a small garden maintains the romance with creeping vines and an outdoor oyster bar.

★ Spuyten Duyvil

359 Metropolitan Avenue, at Havermeyer Street, Williamsburg (1-718 963 4140, www.spuytenduyvilnyc.com). Subway L to Bedford Avenue; G to Metropolitan Avenue. **Open** 5pm-2am Mon-Thur; 5pm-4am Fri; 1pm-4am Sat; 1pm-2am Sun. **Credit** AmEx, Disc, MC, V. **Map** p411 U8 ❹
Don't arrive thirsty. It takes at least ten minutes to choose from roughly 150 quaffs, a list that impresses even microbrew mavens. Most selections are middle-European regionals, and bartenders are eager to explain the differences among them. The cosy interior is chock-full of flea market finds, most of which are for sale. There's also a tasty bar menu of smoked meats, pâtés, cheeses and terrines.

Union Hall

702 Union Street, between Fifth & Sixth Avenues, Park Slope (1-718 638 4400, www.unionhallny.com). Subway R to Union Street. **Open** 4pm-4am Mon-Fri; noon-4am Sat, Sun. **Credit** AmEx, MC, V. **Map** p412 T11 ❹
Upstairs at Union Hall, couples chomp on mini burgers and sip microbrews in the gentlemen's club anteroom (decorated with Soviet-era globes, paintings of fez-capped men, fireplaces) – before battling

CONSUME

it out on the clay bocce courts. Downstairs, in the taxidermy-filled basement, the stage hosts bands, comedians and off-beat events.

Union Pool
484 Union Avenue, at Meeker Avenue, Williamsburg (1-718 609 0484, www.union-pool.com). Subway L to Lorimer Street; G to Metropolitan Avenue. **Open** 5pm-4am Mon-Fri; 1pm-4am Sat, Sun. **Credit** AmEx, Disc, MC, V. **Map** p412 V8 ⑩

This former pool-supply outlet now supplies booze to scruffy Williamsburgers, who pack the tin-walled main room's half-moon booths and snap saucy photo-kiosk pics. Bands strum away on the adjacent stage, while the spacious courtyard and outdoor bar is popular during the warmer months. Arrive early to kick back $3 PBRs, $6 Jamesons or two-for-$5 Budweisers. Happy hour is 5-9pm nightly.

▶ *For more on the entertainment at Union Hall and Union Pool, see p290.*

QUEENS

★ Bohemian Hall & Beer Garden
29-19 24th Avenue, between 29th & 30th Streets, Astoria (1-718 274 4925, www.bohemianhall.com). Subway N, Q to Astoria Boulevard. **Open** 5pm-1am Mon-Thur; 5pm-2am Fri; noon-3am Sat, Sun. **Credit** AmEx, MC, V. **Map** p412 X3 ⑤

This authentic Czech beer garden features plenty of mingle-friendly picnic tables, where you can sample cheap, robust platters of sausage and 14 mainly European drafts. Though the huge, tree-canopied garden is open year-round (in winter, the area is tented and heated), summer is prime time to visit.

Dutch Kills
27-24 Jackson Avenue, at Dutch Kills Street, Long Island City (1-718 383 2724, www.dutch killsbar.com). Subway E, R to Queens Plaza. **Open** 5pm-2am daily. **Credit** AmEx, MC, V. **Map** p412 V5 ㊳

What separates Dutch Kills from other mixology temples modelled after vintage saloons is the abundance of elbow room. Settle into one of the deep, dark-wood booths in the front, or perch at the bar. Cocktails are mostly classic, with prices slightly lower than in similar establishments in Manhattan.

The Garden at Studio Square
35-33 36th Street, between 35th & 36th Avenues, Astoria (1-718 383 1001, www.studiosquarenyc. com). Subway M, R to 36th Street; N, Q to 36th Avenue. **Open** noon-3am Mon-Thur; noon-4am Fri-Sun. **No credit cards. Map** p412 W4 ㊴
See p178 **Back to the Beer Garden.**

Sweet Afton
30-09 34th Street, at 30th Avenue, Astoria (1-718 777 2570, www.sweetaftonbar.com). Subway N, Q to 30th Avenue. **Open** 4pm-3.30am Mon-Thur; 3pm-3.30am Fri; 11am-3.30am Sat, Sun. **Credit** AmEx, V. **Map** p412 X3 ㊵

This Queens gastropub combines an industrial feel – lots of concrete and massive beams – with the dim, dark-wood cosiness of an Irish pub. The bar's smartly curated array of reasonably priced suds includes strong selections from craft breweries like Kelso, Six Point and Captain Lawrence, but the unpretentious bartender will just as happily crack open a cheap everyman ale such as Amstel or Miller. The satisfying food menu is highlighted by the beer-battered McClure's pickles – an epic bar snack.

Maison Premiere.

CONSUME

Shops & Services

The ultimate consumer playground.

Although American shopping culture has taken a hit from the recession, you'd never know it in the crowded stores of the country's retail capital. As well as the famous department stores and global flagships, Gotham retains a large number of unusual, independently run businesses. Whatever you're looking for – big-name fashion or one-off items from local artisans, cut-price CDs or rare vinyl, fresh-from-the-studio home design or market bric-a-brac – you won't be disappointed. The only pitfall is exhaustion if you attempt to cover too much ground at once. We recommend taking it

slowly and arranging your retail excursions by neighbourhood; for a guide, *see p191* **Where to Shop**.

THE SHOPPING SCENE

New York is fertile bargain-hunting territory. The traditional post-season sales (which usually start just after Christmas and in early to mid June) have given way to frequent markdowns throughout the year: look for sale racks in boutiques, chain and department stores. The twice-a-year Barneys Warehouse Sale (*see right*) is an important fixture on the bargain hound's calendar, but as the city is the centre of the American fashion industry, every week sees a spate of designer sample sales. The best are listed in the Shopping & Style section of *Time Out New York* magazine and www.timeout.com/newyork. **Racked** (www.ny.racked.com), **Top Button** (www.topbutton.com) and **Clothing Line** (1-212 947 8748, www.clothingline.com), which holds sales for a variety of labels – from J Crew and Theory to Tory Burch and Rag & Bone, at its Garment District showroom (Second Floor, 261 W 36th Street, between Seventh & Eighth Avenues) – are also good resources. *See also p197* **Inside Track**.

While many shops in the city keep late hours most nights of the week, Thursday is generally the unofficial shop-after-work night, when most places remain open until at least 8pm. Stores downtown generally stay open an hour or so later than those uptown. Note that some of the shops listed in this chapter have more than one location; we have detailed up to three other branches below the review. For the bigger

chains, check individual shop websites or consult the business pages in the telephone book for more addresses across the city. Sales tax in the city is 8.875 per cent, though there are exemptions. For details, *see p380*.

General

DEPARTMENT STORES

★ Barneys New York
660 Madison Avenue, at 61st Street, Upper East Side (1-212 826 8900, www.barneys.com). Subway N, Q, R to Fifth Avenue-59th Street; 4, 5, 6 to 59th Street. **Open** 10am-8pm Mon-Fri; 10am-7pm Sat; 11am-6pm Sun. **Credit** AmEx, DC, MC, V. **Map** p405 E22.

Barneys has a reputation for spotlighting less ubiquitous designer labels than other upmarket department stores, and has its own quirky-classic line. Its Co-op boutiques (see website for locations) carry threads from hip, casual labels and the latest hot denim lines. Every February and August, the Chelsea Co-op hosts the Barneys Warehouse Sale, when prices are slashed by 50-80%.
Other locations Co-ops throughout the city.

Bergdorf Goodman
754 Fifth Avenue, between 57th & 58th Streets, Midtown (1-212 753 7300, www.bergdorfgoodman.com). Subway E, M to Fifth Avenue-53rd Street; N, Q, R to Fifth Avenue-59th Street. **Open** 10am-8pm Mon-Fri;

CONSUME

Where to Shop

New York's best shopping neighbourhoods in brief.

SOHO
Although it's been heavily commercialised, especially the main thoroughfares, this once edgy, arty enclave still has some idiosyncratic survivors and numerous top-notch shops. Urban fashion abounds on Lafayette Street, while Broome Street is a burgeoning enclave for chic home design.

NOLITA
This area has been colonised by indie designers, especially along Mott and Mulberry Streets.

LOWER EAST SIDE
Once the centre of the rag trade, this old Jewish neighbourhood was associated with bargain outlets and bagels. Now a bar- and boutique-rich patch, it's especially good for vintage, streetwear and local designers. Orchard, Ludlow and Rivington Streets have the highest concentration of retail.

WEST VILLAGE & MEATPACKING DISTRICT
On the other side of the island, the once-desolate wholesale meat market stretching south from 14th Street has become a high-end consumer playground, its warehouses now populated by fashion boutiques. The western strip of Bleecker Street is lined with a further cache of designer shops.

Soho

EAST VILLAGE
Although the shops are more scattered here than in the LES, you'll find a highly browsable mix of vintage clothing, streetwear, records, stylish homewares and children's goods.

FIFTH AVENUE & UPPER EAST SIDE
Most of the city's famous department stores can be found on Fifth Avenue between 49th and 59th Streets, in the company of big-name designer flagships and chain stores. The exceptions are Bloomingdale's and Barneys, which are both on the Upper East Side. Here, Madison Avenue has long been synonymous with the *crème de la crème* of international fashion.

BROOKLYN
Williamsburg, one subway stop from Manhattan, abounds with hip retail and an excellent flea market (*see p211* **Market Forces**). As well as the main drag, Bedford Avenue, North 6th and Grand Streets are happy hunting grounds for vintage clothes, arty homewares and record stores. Also good are Cobble Hill, Carroll Gardens and Boerum Hill (especially on Court and Smith Streets, and Atlantic Avenue).

Madison Avenue

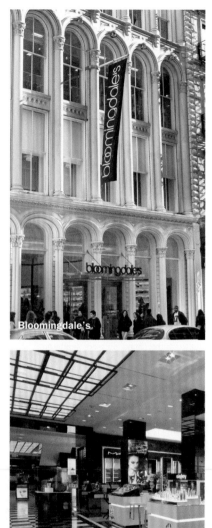

10am-7pm Sat; 11am-6pm Sun. **Credit** AmEx, DC, MC, V. **Map** p405 E22.

Synonymous with understated luxury, Bergdorf's is known for designer clothes (the fifth floor is dedicated to younger, trend-driven labels) and accessories. Also be sure to seek out Kentshire's wonderful cache of vintage jewellery on the ground floor. Descend to the basement for the wide-ranging beauty department. The men's store is across the street at 745 Fifth Avenue.

Bloomingdale's

1000 Third Avenue, at 59th Street, Upper East Side (1-212 705 2000, www.bloomingdales.com). Subway N, Q, R to Lexington Avenue-59th Street; 4, 5, 6 to 59th Street. **Open** 10am-8.30pm Mon, Tue; 10am-10pm Wed-Sat; 10am-9pm Sun. **Credit** AmEx, DC, MC, V. **Map** p405 F22.

Ranking among the city's top tourist attractions, Bloomie's is a gigantic, glitzy department store stocked with everything from handbags to beauty products, home furnishings to designer duds. The beauty hall, complete with an outpost of globe-spanning apothecary Space NK, recently got a glam makeover. The hipper, compact Soho outpost concentrates on young fashion and accessories, denim and cosmetics. **Other locations** 504 Broadway, between Broome & Spring Streets, Soho (1-212 729 5900).

Henri Bendel

712 Fifth Avenue, at 56th Street, Midtown East (1-212 247 1100, www.henribendel.com). Subway E, M to Fifth Avenue-53rd Street; N, Q, R to Fifth Avenue-59th Street. **Open** 10am-8pm Mon-Sat; noon-7pm Sun. **Credit** AmEx, DC, Disc, MC, V. **Map** p405 E22.

While Bendel's merchandise (a mix of jewellery, fashion accessories, cosmetics and fragrances) is comparable to that of other upscale stores, it somehow seems more desirable when viewed in its opulent premises, a conglomeration of three 19th-century townhouses – and those darling brown-and-white striped shopping bags don't hurt, either. Bendel's is also the home of celebrity hairdresser Frédéric Fekkai's flagship salon.

Jeffrey New York

449 W 14th Street, at Tenth Avenue, Meatpacking District (1-212 206 1272, www.jeffreynewyork.com). Subway A, C, E to 14th Street; L to Eighth Avenue. **Open** 10am-8pm Mon-Wed, Fri; 10am-9pm Thur; 10am-7pm Sat; 12.30-6pm Sun. **Credit** AmEx, DC, MC, V. **Map** p403 C27.

Jeffrey Kalinsky, a former Barneys shoe buyer, was a Meatpacking District pioneer when he opened his namesake store in 1999. Designer clothing abounds here – by Yves Saint Laurent, L'Wren Scott, Céline and young British star Christopher Kane, among others. But the centrepiece is without doubt the shoe salon, which features the work of Manolo Blahnik, Prada and Christian Louboutin, as well as newer names to watch.

Macy's

151 W 34th Street, between Broadway & Seventh Avenue, Garment District (1-212 695 4400, www.macys.com). Subway B, D, F, M, N, Q, R to 34th Street-Herald Square; 1, 2, 3 to 34th Street-Penn Station. **Open** 9am-9.30pm Mon-Thur; 8am-11pm Fri; 7am-11pm Sat; 11am-8.30pm Sun. **Credit** AmEx, DC, Disc, MC, V. **Map** p404 D25.
It may not be as glamorous as New York's other famous stores, but for sheer breadth of stock, the 34th Street behemoth is hard to beat. While mid-price fashion for all ages, big beauty names and housewares have traditionally been the store's bread and butter, at press time a $400 million redesign of the ground floor was poised to be unveiled, with new luxury boutiques including Gucci and Burberry.
▶ *There's a Ben & Jerry's outpost here.*

Saks Fifth Avenue

611 Fifth Avenue, between 49th & 50th Streets, Midtown East (1-212 753 4000, www.saksfifthavenue.com). Subway E, M to Fifth Avenue-53rd Street. **Open** 10am-8pm Mon-Sat; 11am-7pm Sun. **Credit** AmEx, DC, Disc, MC, V. **Map** p404 E23.
Although Saks maintains a presence in 25 American states, the Fifth Avenue location is the original, established in 1924 by New York retailers Horace Saks and Bernard Gimbel. The store features all the big names in fashion, from Armani to Yves Saint Laurent, including an expansive shoe salon that shares the eighth floor with a shop-cum-café from deluxe chocolatier Charbonnel et Walker. The opulent beauty hall is fun to peruse, and customer service is excellent, though retiring types might find it too aggressive.

MALLS

Shops at Columbus Circle

Time Warner Center, 10 Columbus Circle, at 59th Street, Upper West Side (1-212 823 6300, www.shopsatcolumbuscircle.com). Subway A, B, C, D, 1 to 59th Street-Columbus Circle. **Open** 10am-9pm Mon-Sat; 11am-7pm Sun (hours vary for some shops, bars and restaurants). **Credit** varies. **Map** p405 D22.
Classier than your average mall, the retail contingent of the 2.8 million-sq-ft Time Warner Center features upscale stores such as Coach, Cole Haan and LK Bennett for accessories and shoes, London shirt-maker Thomas Pink, Bose home entertainment, the fancy kitchenware purveyor Williams-Sonoma, as well as shopping centre staples J Crew, Aveda, and organic grocer Whole Foods. Some of the city's top restaurants (including Thomas Keller's gourmet destination Per Se, *p173*, and his café Bouchon Bakery, *p172*) have made it a dining destination that transcends the stigma of eating at the mall.
▶ *The mall's Metropolitan Museum of Art kiosk is good for gifts, and the Museum of Arts & Design next door also has a gift shop; see p104.*

CONSUME

Macy's

Specialist

BOOKS & MAGAZINES

New York's biggest bookstore chain is **Barnes & Noble** (www.barnesandnoble.com). While the stock varies little from branch to branch, several, including its Union Square flagship, feature readings by authors. **Shakespeare & Co** (www.shakeandco.com) is an independent alternative with four stores.

General

Book Culture

536 W 112th Street, between Amsterdam Avenue & Broadway, Morningside Heights (1-212 865 1588, www.bookculture.com). Subway 1 to 110th Street-Cathedral Parkway. **Open** 9am-10pm Mon-Fri; 10am-8pm Sat; 11am-7pm Sun. **Credit** AmEx, DC, Disc, MC, V. **Map** p406 C15.

Ostensibly catering to the Columbia University community, two-storey Book Culture lures bibliophiles with its stellar fiction and scholarly stock, as well as various discount tables. **Other locations** 2915 Broadway, at 114th Street, Morningside Heights (1-646 403 3000).

McNally Jackson

52 Prince Street, between Lafayette & Mulberry Streets, Nolita (1-212 274 1160, www.mcnallyjackson.com). Subway N, R to Prince Street; 6 to Spring Street. **Open** 10am-10pm Mon-Sat; 10am-9pm Sun. **Credit** AmEx, DC, Disc, MC, V. **Map** p403 F29.

The New York offshoot of Canada's fine independent McNally Robinson, McNally Jackson stocks a distinctly international selection of novels and non-fiction titles. A wide range of writers – which have included Keith Gessen, Garrison Keillor and Francine Prose – read in its comfortable downstairs space.

192 Books

192 Tenth Avenue, between 21st & 22nd Streets, Chelsea (1-212 255 4022, www.192books.com). Subway C, E to 23rd Street. daily. **Credit** AmEx, MC, V. **Map** p404 C26.

In an era when many an indie bookshop has closed, this youngster, open since 2003, is proving that quirky boutique booksellers can make it after all. Owned and 'curated' by art dealer Paula Cooper and her husband, editor Jack Macrae, 192 offers a strong selection of art books and literature, as well as tomes on gardening, history, politics, design and music. The phenomenal reading series brings in top authors such as Joan Acocella, Ben Ratliff and Joan Didion.

St Mark's Bookshop

31 Third Avenue, between 8th & 9th Streets, East Village (1-212 260 7853, www.stmarksbookshop.

com). Subway N, R to 8th Street-NYU; 6 to Astor Place. **Open** 10am-midnight Mon-Sat; 11am-midnight Sun. **Credit** AmEx, DC, Disc, MC, V. **Map** p403 F28.

Students, academics and arty types gravitate to this esteemed East Village bookseller, which maintains strong inventories on cultural theory, graphic design, poetry and film, as well as numerous avant-garde journals and 'zines. The fiction section is one of the finest in the city.

Specialist

Books of Wonder

18 W 18th Street, between Fifth & Sixth Avenues, Flatiron District (1-212 989 3270, www.booksofwonder.com). Subway F, M to 14th Street; L to Sixth Avenue; 1 to 18th Street. **Open** 11am-7pm Mon-Sat; 11am-6pm Sun. **Credit** AmEx, Disc, MC, V. **Map** p403 E27.

The only independent children's bookstore in the city features titles new and old (rare and out-of-print editions), plus a special collection of Oz books. The store also always has a good stock of signed books, and the on-site bakery makes a visit more of a treat.

Forbidden Planet

840 Broadway, at 13th Street, Greenwich Village (1-212 475 6161, www.fpnyc.com). Subway L, N, Q, R, 4, 5, 6 to 14th Street-Union Square. **Open** 10am-10pm Mon, Tue, Sun; 9am-midnight Wed-Sat. **Credit** AmEx, Disc, MC, V. **Map** p403 E27.

Embracing both pop culture and the cult underground, the Planet takes comics seriously. You'll also find graphic novels, manga, action figures, DVDs and more.

Idlewild

12 W 19th Street, between Fifth & Sixth Avenues, Flatiron District (1-212 414 8888, www.idlewildbooks.com). Subway F, M to 14th Street; L to Sixth Avenue. **Open** noon-7.30pm Mon-Thur; noon-6pm Fri, Sat; noon-5pm Sun. **Credit** AmEx, Disc, MC, V. **Map** p403 E27.

Opened by a former United Nations press officer, Idlewild stocks travel guides to more than 100 countries and all 50 US states, which are grouped with related works of fiction and non-fiction. The shop also has a large selection of works in French, Spanish and Italian and holds classes in those languages, plus Arabic.

▶ *JFK was known as Idlewild Airport before it was renamed to honour the assassinated president in 1963.*

Printed Matter

195 Tenth Avenue, between 21st & 22nd Streets, Chelsea (1-212 925 0325, www.printedmatter.org). Subway C, E to 23rd Street. **Open** 11am-7pm Mon-Wed, Sat; 11am-8pm Thur, Fri. **Credit** AmEx, Disc, MC, V. **Map** p404 C26.

CONSUME

Printed Matter. *See p195.*

This non-profit organisation is devoted to artists' books – from David Shrigley's deceptively naive illustrations to provocative photographic self-portraits by Matthias Herrmann – and operates a public reading room as well as a shop. Works by unknown and emerging artists share shelf space with those by veterans such as Yoko Ono and Edward Ruscha.

Used & antiquarian

★ Housing Works Bookstore Café
126 Crosby Street, between Houston & Prince Streets, Soho (1-212 334 3324, www.housing worksbookstore.org). Subway B, D, F, M to Broadway-Lafayette Street; N, R to Prince Street; 6 to Bleecker Street. **Open** 10am-9pm Mon-Fri; 10am-5pm Sat, Sun. **Credit** AmEx, MC, V. **Map** p403 E29.
This endearing two-level space – which stocks literary fiction, non-fiction, rare books and collectibles – is a peaceful spot to relax over coffee or wine. All proceeds go to providing support services for people living with HIV/AIDS. The emerging and the lustrious mingle at the mic at the store's frequent readings.

Strand Book Store
828 Broadway, at 12th Street, East Village (1-212 473 1452, www.strandbooks.com). Subway L, N, Q, R, 4, 5, 6 to 14th Street-Union Square. **Open** 9.30am-10.30pm Mon-Sat; 11am-10.30pm Sun. **Credit** AmEx, DC, Disc, MC, V. **Map** p403 E28.
Boasting 18 miles of books, the Strand has a mammoth collection of more than two million discount volumes (both new and used), and the store is made all the more daunting by its chaotic, towering shelves and sometimes crotchety staff. If you spend enough time here you can find just about anything, from that out-of-print Victorian book on manners to the kitschiest of sci-fi pulp. The rare book room upstairs closes at 6.15pm.
► *There's a seasonal Strand kiosk on the edge of Central Park at Fifth Avenue and 60th Street (Apr-Dec 10am-dusk, weather permitting).*

CHILDREN
Fashion

Babesta Threads
66 West Broadway, between Murray & Warren Streets, Tribeca (1-212 608 4522, www. babesta.com). Subway 1, 2, 3 to Chambers Street. **Open** 11am-7pm Mon-Fri; noon-6pm Sat, Sun. **Credit** AmEx, Disc, MC, V. **Map** p402 E32.
Husband-and-wife team Aslan and Jenn Cattaui fill their cosy store with the stuff kids love – Rowdy Sprout concert tees, Uglydolls and vintage wear that'll make parents envious. The shop focuses on the under-six set, but there are also pieces for children aged up to 12 from popular lines such as Mini Rodini.

Egg
72 Jay Street, between Front & Water Streets, Dumbo, Brooklyn (1-718 422 7811, www.egg-baby.com). Subway A, C to High Street; F to York Street. **Open** 10am-6pm Mon-Sat; 11am-5pm Sun. **Credit** AmEx, MC, V. **Map** p411 T9.

Set in the old HQ of the Grand Union Tea Company, designer Susan Lazar's flagship has a retro garment-factory vibe. Among her seasonally changing creations for babies and kids up to six, you might find peacoats for girls and boys, cute denim dresses and striped infant bodysuits. Lazar uses organic cotton whenever possible; some items, inspired by the craftsmanship she encountered on her travels in South America, are made in Peru.

Other locations 124 Hudson Street, between Ericsson Place & N Moore Streets, Tribeca (1-212 470 0421).

Toys

★ FAO Schwarz

767 Fifth Avenue, at 58th Street, Midtown (1-212 644 9400, www.fao.com). Subway N, Q, R to Lexington Avenue-59th Street; 4, 5, 6 to 59th Street. **Open** 10am-7pm Mon-Thur; 10am-8pm Fri-Sun. **Credit** AmEx, Disc, MC, V. **Map** p405 E22.
Although it's now owned by the ubiquitous Toys 'R' Us company, this three-storey emporium is still the ultimate NYC toy box. Most people head straight to the 22ft-long piano that Tom Hanks famously tinkled in *Big*. Children will marvel at the giant stuffed animals, the detailed and imaginative Lego figures and the revolving Barbie fashion catwalk.

Mary Arnold Toys

1010 Lexington Avenue, between 72nd & 73rd Streets, Upper East Side (1-212 744 8510, www.maryarnoldtoys.com). Subway 6 to 77th Street. **Open** 9am-6pm Mon-Fri; 10am-5.30pm Sat; 10am-5pm Sun. **Credit** AmEx, DC, Disc, MC, V. **Map** p405 E20.
This charming speciality toy shop carries such hard-to-find playthings as racing-car sets. Also head here for Madame Alexander dolls, Jellycat animals and other kid (and grown-up) classics.

ELECTRONICS & PHOTOGRAPHY

iPod junkies can get their fix 24/7 at the **Apple Store**'s Fifth Avenue, open-all-hours flagship (no.767, between 58th & 59th Streets, 1-212 336 1440, www.apple.com), which is marked by a dramatic 32-foot glass entrance. There are further branches at 103 Prince Street, between Greene & Mercer Streets, in Soho; 401 W 14th Street, at Ninth Avenue, in the Meatpacking District; 1981 Broadway, at 67th Street, on the Upper West Side; and inside Grand Central Terminal, Midtown East. All are equipped with Genius Bars, offering technical help for Mac users as well as repairs. Well-regarded Apple specialist **Tekserve** (119 W 23rd Street, between Sixth & Seventh Avenues, Chelsea, 1-212 929 3645, www.tekserve.com) is another

trusted resource. Brendan McElroy offers repairs to Macs, iPhones and PCs at **Dr Brendan Mac Repair** (8 St Marks Place, between Second & Third Avenues, East Village, 1-855 227 5372, www.drbrendan.com); there's also an outlet in Chelsea and in Park Slope, Brooklyn, and he does house calls. Rates start at $50 for phone fixes and $125 for simple computer repairs.

Mobile phones can be hired from **Jojo Talk** (1-212 659 2200, www.jojotalk.com), which delivers at no cost to any address in the city within two hours. The minimum rental charge is $9.99 per day plus tax. However, if you don't need a sophisticated gadget, it's probably cheaper to buy a basic phone (for as little as $15) and a pay-as-you-go card from one of the ubiquitous main service providers. For more on mobile phones, *see p382*.

B&H

420 Ninth Avenue, at 34th Street, Garment District (1-212 444 5040, www.bhphotovideo. com). Subway A, C, E to 34th Street-Penn Station. **Open** 9am-7pm Mon-Thur; 9am-1pm Fri; 10am-6pm Sun. **Credit** AmEx, Disc, MC, V. **Map** p404 C25.
In this huge, busy store, goods are transported from the stock room via an overhead conveyor belt. It's the place to come to for the latest and rarest photo, video and audio equipment at the lowest prices. Note that due to the largely Hasidic Jewish staff, the store is closed on Saturdays and other Jewish holidays.

J&R Music & Computer World

23 Park Row, at Beekman Street, Financial District (1-212 238 9000, www.jr.com). Subway A, C to Broadway-Nassau Street. **Open** 10am-7pm Mon-Wed; 10am-7.30pm Thur, Fri; 11am-7pm Sat, Sun. **Credit** AmEx, Disc, MC, V. **Map** p402 E32.
Established in 1971, this block-long electronics emporium is still family run. As well as a plethora of electronic and electrical goods – from MP3 players and TVs to kitchen appliances – there's an extensive CD section.

INSIDE TRACK
STRIP FOR BARGAINS

Sample sales are usually held in designers' shops, showrooms or rented loft spaces, and shoppers can get seriously competitive for prime goods. Many lack changing rooms, and some don't accept credit cards, so bring a courageous spirit and plenty of cash, and remember to wear appropriate undergarments to avoid embarrassment.

CONSUME

FASHION
Designer

We've listed some of the hottest independent designers below, but if you're looking for the big international names, head for Madison Avenue, between 59th and 79th Streets, or Fifth Avenue from 49th to 57th Streets (and the parade of luxe labels continues east on 57th Street). There are also abundant designer stores in Soho and the Meatpacking District and on Bleecker Street in the West Village.

Christian Siriano
252 Elizabeth Street, between E Houston & Prince Streets, Nolita (1-212 775 8494, www.christianvsiriano.com). Subway B, D, F, M to Broadway-Lafayette Street. **Open** 11.30am-7pm Mon-Sat; noon-6pm Sun. **Credit** AmEx, Disc, MC, V. **Map** p403 F29.
This 1,000sq ft flagship boutique was personally designed by the hotshot *Project Runway* season-four winner, with the glam evening wear that propelled him to success – such as sheer feathered dresses – displayed on mannequins throughout the shop. If you don't have a red-carpet event on your calendar, there are plenty of reasonably priced separates and accessories to paw through, along with his current Payless footwear collection (starting at just $50).

★ Fivestory
18 E 69th Street, between Fifth & Madison Avenues (1-212 288 1338, www.fivestoryny.com). Subway 6 to 68th Street-Hunter College. **Open** 10am-6pm Mon-Wed; 10am-7pm Thur, Fri; noon-6pm Sat, Sun. **Credit** AmEx, DC, Disc, MC, V **Map** p405 E21.
At just 26 (with a little help from her fashion-industry insider dad), Claire Distenfeld opened this glamorous, grown-up boutique, which sprawls over two floors of – yes – a five-storey townhouse. The sophisticated is stocked with clothing, shoes and accessories for men, women and children, plus select home items. The emphasis is on less-ubiquitous American and European labels, including New York-based Lyn Devon and Thakoon, and Peter Pilotto, created by two alums of Antwerp's Royal Academy of Fine Arts.

Lisa Perry
988 Madison Avenue, at 77th Street, Upper East Side (1-212 334 1956, www.lisaperrystyle.com). Subway 6 to 77th Street. **Open** 10am-6pm Mon-Sat; noon-5pm Sun. **Credit** AmEx, MC, V. **Map** p405 E19.
Upon graduation from FIT in 1981, designer Lisa Perry launched her line of retro women's threads inspired by her massive personal collection of 1960s and '70s fashion. Ultrabright pieces, such as her signature colour-blocked minidresses, pop against the

stark white walls of her Madison Avenue flagship. You'll also find the designer's cheerful accessories, such as candy-coloured duffel bags, and her mod home collection, which includes place mats and throw pillows.

Phillip Lim
115 Mercer Street, between Prince & Spring Streets, Soho (1-212 334 1160, www.31philliplim.com). Subway N, R to Prince Street; 6 to Spring Street. **Open** 11am-7pm Mon-Sat; noon-6pm Sun. **Credit** AmEx, MC, V. **Map** p403 E29.
Since Phillip Lim debuted his collection in 2005, he has amassed a devoted international following for his simple yet strong silhouettes and beautifully constructed tailoring with a twist. His boutique gathers together his award-winning womens- and menswear, plus accessories and a children's line, under one roof.

★ Rag & Bone
100 & 104 Christopher Street, between Bedford & Bleecker Streets, West Village (1-212 727 2999 men, 1-212 727 2990 women, www.rag-bone.com). Subway 1 to Christopher Street-Sheridan Square. **Open** 11am-8pm Mon-Sat; noon-7pm Sun. **Credit** AmEx, MC, V. **Map** p403 D28.
Born out of its founders' growing frustrations with mass-produced jeans, what began as a denim line in

Fivestory

2002 has expanded to cover clothing for both men and women. The emphasis is on craftsmanship, and the designs, in substantial, luxurious fabrics such as cashmere and tweed, nod towards tradition (riding jackets, granddad-style cardigans) while exuding an utterly contemporary vibe. This aesthetic is reflected in its elegant, industrial-edged his 'n' hers stores. **Other locations** 119 Mercer Street, between Prince & Spring Streets, Soho (1-212 219 2204); 73 E Houston Street, at Elizabeth Street, Nolita (1-212 777 2210); 909 Madison Avenue, at 73rd Street, Upper East Side (1-212 249 3331); 182 Columbus Avenue, between 68th & 69th Streets, Upper West Side (1-212 362 7138).

Thecast

71 Orchard Street, between Broome & Grand Streets, Lower East Side (1-212 228 2020, www.thecast.com). Subway F to Lower East Side-Second Avenue. **Open** noon-8pm Mon-Sat; noon-6pm Sun. **Credit** AmEx, DC, Disc, MC, V. **Map** p403 F30.

Owner Chuck Guarino traded his (literally) underground location for a weathered sliver of a storefront on Orchard Street, but the shop maintains the neogothic vibe with signature ghoulish knick-knacks, such as a human skull (bought on eBay). At the core of the unabashedly masculine collection is the trinity of well-cut denim, superior leather jackets based on classic motorcycle styles, and the artful T-shirts that

launched the label in 2004. The ladies have their own line, Bitch Club, covering similar ground.

Discount

AvaMaria

107 Crosby Street, between E Houston & Prince Streets, Soho (1-212 966-0909, www. virketyne.com). Subway B, D, F, M to Broadway-Lafayette Street. **Open** 11am-7pm Mon-Fri; 11am-7.30pm Sat; noon-6pm Sun. **Credit** AmEx, MC, V. **Map** p403 E29.

Former competitive ballroom dancer and costume designer Katherine Virketiene opened AvaMaria with a dual purview. In addition to reasonably priced clothing by emerging designers, the small space is a goldmine of never-been-worn deadstock, including threads by Miu Miu, Alberta Ferretti and Stella McCartney, and shoes by Manolo Blahnik, Brian Atwood and Jimmy Choo – all slashed by 15-80%.

★ Century 21

22 Cortlandt Street, between Broadway & Church Street, Financial District (1-212 227 9092, www.c21stores.com). Subway A, C to Broadway-Nassau Street; E to World Trade Center; J, Z, 2, 3, 4, 5 to Fulton Street; R to Cortlandt Street. **Open** 7.45am-9pm Mon-Wed; 7.45am-9.30pm Thur, Fri; 10am-9pm Sat; 11am-8pm Sun. **Credit** AmEx, Disc, MC, V. **Map** p402 E32.

A Gucci men's suit for $300? A Marc Jacobs cashmere sweater for less than $200? Stella McCartney sunglasses for a scant $40? No, you're not dreaming – you're shopping at Century 21. You may have to rummage to unearth a treasure, but with savings of up to 65% off regular prices, it's often worth it. **Other locations** 1972 Broadway, between 66th & 67th Streets, Upper West Side (1-212 518 2121); 472 86th Street, between Fourth & Fifth Avenues, Bay Ridge, Brooklyn (1-718 748 3266).

Loehmann's
101 Seventh Avenue, at 16th Street, Chelsea (1-212 352 0856, www.loehmanns.com). Subway A, C, E to 14th Street; L to Eighth Avenue; 1 to 18th Street. **Open** 9am-10pm Mon-Sat; 11am-8pm Sun. **Credit** AmEx, Disc, MC, V. **Map** p403 D27.
Although this venerable discount emporium is often crowded and cramped, its five floors offer major markdowns on current and off-season clothes, shoes and accessories. Make a beeline upstairs for the 'Back Room' to find big names such as Valentino, Prada and Armani.
Other locations 2101 Broadway, between 73rd & 74th Streets, Upper West Side (1-212 882 9990); 2807 E 21st Street, at Shore Parkway, Sheepshead Bay, Brooklyn (1-718 368 1256).

General

National chains **J Crew**, **Banana Republic** and **Gap**, offering good-value basics for both sexes, are all over town; ubiquitous European behemoths include **Zara** and **H&M**, plus British fashion giant **Topshop/Topman**
(478 Broadway, at Broome Street, Soho, 1-212 966 9555, www.topshop.com). Hip girls' chains **Intermix** (www.intermixonline.com) and **Scoop** (www.scoopnyc.com) combine lofty labels with denim and the latest accessories at locations throughout the city.

(3x1)
15 Mercer Street, between Canal & Grand Streets (1-212 391 6969, www.3x1.us). Subway A, C, E, J, N, Q, R, Z, 6, 1 to Canal Street. **Open** 11am-7pm Mon-Sat; noon-6pm Sun. **Credit** AmEx, DC, Disc, MC, V. **Map** p403 E30.
Denim obsessives who are always looking for the next 'it' jeans have another place to splurge: (3x1) creates entirely limited-edition styles sewn in the store. Designer Scott Morrison, who previously launched Paper Denim & Cloth and Earnest Sewn, fills the large, gallery-like space with a variety of jeans for men and women (prices start at $235) and other denim pieces such as shorts or miniskirts. Watch the construction process take place in a glass-walled design studio, positioned in the middle of the boutique. You can even go bespoke and design your own jeans from scratch (starting at $1,200).

Castor & Pollux
238 W 10th Street, between Bleecker & Hudson Streets, West Village (1-212 645 6572, www.castorandpolluxstore.com). Subway A, B, C, D, E, F, M to W 4th Street; 1 to Christopher Street-Sheridan Square. **Open** noon-7pm Tue-Sat; 1-6pm Sun. **Credit** AmEx, MC, V. **Map** p403 D28.
This small Brooklyn-born boutique showcases a diverse cross-section of clothing and accessories in

a stylish yet relaxed setting. Owner Kerrilynn Pamer mixes European labels such as Ter et Bantine with New York names like Gary Graham, Apiece Apart and Alasdair, former stylist April Johnson's easy-to-wear staples in elegant fabrics. Pamer's own jewellery line, launched with simple brass bracelets, has become a cult hit.

DQM

7 E 3rd Street, between Bowery & Second Avenue, East Village (1-212 505 7551, www.dqmnewyork.com). Subway F to Lower East Side-Second Avenue. **Open** 11.30am-7.30pm Mon-Sat; 11.30am-6.30pm Sun. **Credit** AmEx, Disc, MC, V. **Map** p403 F29.

Dave Ortiz – formerly of urban-threads label Zoo York – and professional skateboarder Chris Keefe stock a range of top-shelf streetwear in their wittily designed shop, complete with butcher-block counter. As well as a line-up of the latest sneaks by Adidas, Nike and Vans, DQM sells its own-label T-shirts, chinos and button-downs.

Other locations Vans DQM General, 93 Grand Street, at Greene Street, Soho (1-212 226 7776).

Dear: Rivington

95 Rivington Street, between Ludlow & Orchard Streets, East Village (1-212 673 3494, www. dearrivington.com). Subway F to Delancey Street; J, Z to Delancey-Essex Streets. **Open** noon-7pm daily. **Credit** AmEx, DC, Disc, MC, V. **Map** p403 G29.

The glass storefront is a stage for Moon Rhee and Hey Ja Do's art installation-like displays; inside the white bi-level space, head downstairs for their own Victorian-inspired line and select pieces by avant-garde Japanese labels such as Comme des Garçons and Yohji Yamamoto. Upstairs is a fascinating archive of vintage homewares, objects and contemporary art, including framed antique silhouettes, old globes and tins.

The Dressing Room

75A Orchard Street, between Broome & Grand Streets, Lower East Side (1-212 966 7330, www.thedressingroomnyc.com). Subway B, D to Grand Street; F to Delancey Street. **Open** 1pm-midnight Tue, Wed; 1pm-2am Thur-Sat; 1-8pm Sun. **Credit** AmEx, MC, V. **Map** p403 F30.

At first glance, the Dressing Room may look like any Lower East side lounge, thanks to a handsome wood bar, but this co-op cum watering hole rewards the curious. The adjoining room displays designs by indie labels alongside select vintage pieces, and there's a second-hand clothing exchange downstairs.

Honey in the Rough

161 Rivington Street, between Clinton & Suffolk Streets, Lower East Side (1-212 228 6415, www.honeyintherough.com). Subway F to Delancey Street; J, Z to Delancey-Essex Streets. **Open** noon-8pm Mon-Sat; noon-7pm Sun. **Credit** AmEx, DC, Disc, MC, V. **Map** p403 G29.

Looking for something sweet and charming? Hit this cosy, ultra-femme boutique. Owner Ashley Hanosh fills the well-worn spot with an excellent line-up of local indie labels, including Samantha Pleet, Whit and Nomia, alongside carefully selected accessories, some of which are exclusive to the shop.

The Hoodie Shop

181 Orchard Street, between E Houston & Stanton Streets (1-646 559 2716, www. thehoodieshop.com). Subway 1 to Houston Street. **Open** noon-9pm Mon-Sat; noon-7pm Sun. **Credit** AmEx, Disc, MC, V. **Map** p403 F29.

More than 50 different brands of hooded apparel for both men and women are showcased in this 1970s-inspired boutique, from retro zip-ups to army-print utility jackets. The shop has a DJ booth and movie screen for late-night shopping parties and other in-store events.

In God We Trust

265 Lafayette Street, between Prince & Spring Streets, Soho (1-212 966 9010, www.ingodwe trustnyc.com). Subway N, R to Prince Street; 6 to Spring Street. **Open** noon-8pm Mon-Sat; noon-7pm Sun. **Credit** AmEx, MC, V. **Map** p403 F29.

Designer Shana Tabor's cosy antique-furnished stores cater to that appealing vintage-intellectual aesthetic, offering locally crafted collections for men and women. The store's line of well-priced, cheeky accessories is a highlight – for example, gold heart-shaped pendants engraved with blunt sayings like 'Talk to the hand', rifle-shaped tie bars, and a wide selection of retro sunglasses for only $20 a pair.

Other locations 129 Bedford Avenue, between North 9th & 10th Streets, Williamsburg, Brooklyn (1-718 384 0700); 70 Greenpoint Avenue, between Milton & Franklin Streets, Greenpoint, Brooklyn (1-718 389 3545).

CONSUME

Patricia Field

CONSUME

Nepenthes New York
307 W 38th Street, between Eighth & Ninth Avenues, Garment District (1-212 643 9540, www.nepenthesny.com). Subway A, C, E, 1, 2, 3 to 34th Street-Penn Station. **Open** noon-7pm Mon-Sat; noon-5pm Sun. **Credit** AmEx, Disc, MC, V. **Map** p404 C24.

Well-dressed dudes with an eye on the Japanese style scene will already be familiar with this Tokyo fashion retailer. Now that its first US location has opened in the Garment District, Nepenthes's followers can finally get the store's urban rustic threads on their home turf. The narrow, high-ceilinged space holds an eclectic mix of well-designed, expertly crafted menswear, including pieces from house label Engineered Garments, such as plaid flannel shirts and workwear-inspired jackets. There is also a small selection of its women's line, FWK.

Odin
199 Lafayette Street, between Broome & Kenmare Streets, Soho (1-212 966 0026, www.odinnewyork.com). Subway 6 to Spring Street. **Open** 11am-8pm Mon-Sat; noon-7pm Sun. **Credit** AmEx, MC, V. **Map** p403 E30.

The Norse god Odin is often portrayed sporting an eye patch and an array of shabby robes to complement his dour, bearded visage. That may have been fashionable in medieval Scandinavia, but to make it in NYC, he'd have to pick up some Engineered Garments, Rag & Bone or Our Legacy gear from this upscale men's boutique bearing his name. Also look out for White Mountaineering, a Japanese brand that combines high-function fabrics with a fashionable aesthetic.

Other locations 328 E 11th Street, between First & Second Avenues, East Village (1-212-475 0666); 106 Greenwich Avenue, between Jane & W 13th Streets, West Village (1-212 243 4724)

★ Opening Ceremony
35 Howard Street, between Broadway & Lafayette Street, Soho (1-212 219 2688, www.opening ceremony.us). Subway J, N, Q, R, Z, 6 to Canal Street. **Open** 11am-8pm Mon-Sat; noon-7pm Sun. **Credit** AmEx, MC, V. **Map** p403 E30.

The name references the Olympic Games; each year the store assembles hip US designers (Band of Outsiders, Alexander Wang, Patrik Ervell, Rodarte) and pits them against the competition from abroad in its chandelier-lit warehouse-size space. The spotlight is on Korea through 2013, when OC is the exclusive US stockist for Goen.J, Kaal E Suktae, Reike Nen and Mvio. The store has been so popular it recently expanded upwards, adding another floor that houses a book and music shop; next door is its Part Deux annex focusing on menswear.
► *There's an additional OC outpost at the Ace Hotel, see p237.*

Patricia Field
306 Bowery, between Bleecker & E Houston Streets, East Village (1-212 966 4066, www.patriciafield.com). Subway 6 to Bleecker Street. **Open** 11am-8pm Mon-Thur; 11am-9pm Fri, Sat; 11am-7pm Sun. **Credit** AmEx, DC, Disc, MC, V. **Map** p403 F29.

The iconic redheaded designer and stylist has moved her flamboyant boutique two doors down into a space that's nearly double the size, combining

Field's former apartment with a vacated store behind it – her old bedroom is now a full-service hair salon. Funky ladies' threads include House of Field neon sleeveless tops and Highest Heel lipstick-heeled pumps, while daring guys will find Keith Haring for House of Field denim shirts and Joy Rich plaid and star-print button downs. Stock up on whimsical accessories such as polka-dot shades, ice-cream-sandwich-shaped iPhone cases and camera-shaped rings.

Reed Space

151 Orchard Street, between Rivington & Stanton Streets, Lower East Side (1-212 253 0588, www.thereedspace.com). Subway F to Delancey Street; J, Z to Delancey-Essex Streets. **Open** 1-7pm Mon-Fri; noon-7pm Sat, Sun. **Credit** AmEx, Disc, MC, V. **Map** p403 F29.
Reed Space is the brainchild of Jeff Ng (AKA Jeff Staple), who has worked on product design and branding with the likes of Nike and Timberland. It stocks local and international urban menswear brands (10.Deep, Undefeated), footwear (including exclusive Staple collaborations), and hard-to-get accessories, such as Japanese Head Porter nylon bags and pouches. Art books and culture mags are shelved on an eye-popping installation of four stacked rows of white chairs fixed to one wall.

Treasure & Bond

350 West Broadway, between Broome & Grand Streets, Soho (1-646 669 9049, www.treasure andbond.com). Subway A, C, E, J, N, Q, R, Z, 6 to Canal Street. **Open** 10am-8pm Mon-Sat; 11-7pm Sun. **Credit** AmEx, Disc, MC, V.

Following the arrival of its discount outpost, Nordstrom Rack in Union Square (60 E 14th Street, between Broadway & Fourth Avenue, 1-212 220 2080, www.nordstromrack.com), West Coast department store giant Nordstrom opened this high-end philanthropic boutique, which donates its profits to select charities that benefit the youth of New York City. The store, which incorporates reclaimed and repurposed materials, stocks around 150 local, national and international fashion, accessories and home-decor luxury brands. Discover glamorous Satya Twena handmade hats, innovative jewellery by Parsons graduate Bliss Lau, delicious-smelling Lafco New York candles and the Vintage Frames Company authentic retro glasses, which are a favourite among celebs such as Lady Gaga.

Used & vintage

Buffalo Exchange

332 E 11th Street, between First & Second Avenues, East Village (1-212 260 9340, www.buffaloexchange.com). Subway L to First Avenue. **Open** 11am-8pm Mon-Sat; on-7pm Sun. **Credit** DC, Disc, MC, V. **Map** p403 F28.
This popular buy-sell-trade clothing shop spans all sartorial tastes, from Forever 21 to Marc Jacobs. You could score a pair of 7 for All Mankind jeans for $25, current-season Manolo Blahniks for $250 or a Burberry men's wool coat for $135.
Other locations 114 W 26th Street, at Sixth Avenue, Chelsea (1-212 675 3535); 504 Driggs Avenue, at North 9th Street, Williamsburg, Brooklyn (1-718 384 6901).

CONSUME

Edith Machinist

104 Rivington Street, between Essex & Ludlow Streets, Lower East Side (1-212 979 9992, www.edithmachinist.com). Subway F to Delancey Street; J, Z to Delancey-Essex Streets. **Open** *1-8pm Mon-Fri; noon-8pm Sat; noon-7pm Sun.* **Credit** *AmEx, DC, Disc, MC, V.* **Map** *p403 G29.*

An impeccable assemblage of leather bags, shoes and boots is the main draw here, but you'll also find a whittled-down collection of clothes, including a small men's section. The store is closed some Mondays, so call before visiting.

INA

15 Bleecker Street, between Bowery & Lafayette Street, Greenwich Village (1-212 228 8511, www.inanyc.com). Subway 6 to Bleecker Street; B, D, F, M to Broadway-Lafayette Street. **Open** *noon-8pm Mon-Sat; noon-7pm Sun.* **Credit** *AmEx, DC, MC, V.* **Map** *p403 F29.*

For more than 20 years, INA has been a leading light of the designer-resale scene. A string of five consignment shops offers immaculate, bang-on-trend items (Christian Louboutin and Manolo Blahnik shoes, Louis Vuitton and Marc Jacobs bags, clothing by Alexander McQueen and Marni) at a fraction of their original prices. This branch caters to both sexes; others are for men or women only (check the website for details of locations).

Other locations throughout the city.

New & Almost New

171 Mott Street, between Broome & Grand Streets, Nolita (1-212 226 6677, www.newandalmostnew.com). Subway B, D to Grand Street; J, Z to Bowery; 6 to Spring Street. **Open** *1-5pm Mon, Sun; noon-6.30pm Tue-Sat.* **Credit** *AmEx, Disc, MC, V.* **Map** *p403 F30.*

Germophobe label-lovers, rejoice: 40% of the merchandise at this resale shop is brand new. Owner Maggie Chan hand-selects every piece, ensuring its quality and authenticity. Among the items hanging on the colour-coded racks are lofty labels such as Prada, Chanel and Hermès (prices range from $15 up to around $600).

What Goes Around Comes Around

351 West Broadway, between Broome & Grand Streets, Soho (1-212 343 1225, www.whatgoesaroundnyc.com). Subway A, C, E, 1 to Canal Street. **Open** *11am-8pm Mon-Sat; noon-7pm Sun.* **Credit** *AmEx, DC, Disc, MC, V.* **Map** *p403 E30.*

A favourite among the city's fashion cognoscenti, this downtown vintage destination sells highly curated stock alongside its own retro label. Style mavens particularly recommend it for 1960s, '70s and '80s rock T-shirts, pristine Alaïa clothing and vintage fur coats.

FASHION ACCESSORIES & SERVICES

Cleaning & repairs

There are numerous dry-cleaners and shoe-repair shops in most of New York's neighbourhoods, but if you don't want to take any chances with special items during your stay, the following are among the very best in the city.

Leather Spa

10 W 55th Street, between Fifth & Sixth Avenues, Midtown (1-212 262 4823, www.leatherspa.com). Subway E, M to Fifth Avenue-53rd Street. **Open** *8am-7pm Mon-Fri; 10am-6pm Sat.* **Credit** *AmEx, Disc, MC, V.* **Map** *p405 E22.*

The crème de la crème of cobblers can rejuvenate even the most faded footwear and handbags – at a price. As well as standard repairs (from $14 for a women's reheel), a cleaning and reconditioning service is offered (from $35-$45).

▶ *For those on the move, Leather Spa also has drop-off spots at the Plaza Hotel and Grand Central Terminal.*

Meurice Garment Care

31 University Place, between 8th & 9th Streets, Greenwich Village (1-212 475 2778, www.garmentcare.com). Subway N, R to 8th Street-NYU. **Open** *7.30am-6pm Mon-Fri; 9am-6pm Sat; 10am-3pm Sun.* **Credit** *AmEx, MC, V.* **Map** *p403 E28.*

This longstanding family-run dry cleaners prides itself on attention to detail. Knitwear is cleaned using a hydrocarbon process, which substitutes a gentler petroleum-based solvent for the traditional perchloroethylene, and very delicate fabrics, including vintage items and shearlings, are hand-cleaned. Be prepared to pay for this superior service; dry cleaning starts at about $15 for a skirt.

Other locations 245 E 57th Street, between Second & Third Avenues, Midtown (1-212 759 9057).

Clothing hire

New York Vintage

117 W 25th Street, between Sixth & Seventh Avenues, Flatiron District (1-212 647 1107, www.newyorkvintage.com). Subway F, M, 1 to 23rd Street. **Open** noon-7pm Mon-Fri; 10am-5pm Sat. **Credit** AmEx, MC, V. **Map** p404 D26.

Vogue photographs featuring the store's antique garb line the walls at this living-history reservoir, where everything from 19th-century walking suits to neon Vivienne Westwood platforms is neatly arranged by era. Walk-ins are welcome at the shop/rental agency, but if you're looking to rent a special item, it's worth calling ahead to peruse the appointment-only showroom upstairs. There, you'll find a priceless ostrich-hemmed 1920s gold lamé gown by designer Charles Frederick Worth, a 1960s chain-link Paco Rabanne vest and Josephine Baker's rhinestone-encrusted 1920s bra (which has been rented by Lady Gaga). Pricing depends on the item and length of rental; there is a minimum fee of $200.

Hats

★ JJ Hat Center

310 Fifth Avenue, at 32nd Street, Flatiron District (1-212 239 4368, www.jjhatcenter.com). Subway B, D, F, M, N, Q, R to 34th Street-Herald Square. **Open** 9am-6pm Mon-Fri; 9.30am-5.30pm Sat; noon-5pm Sun. **Credit** AmEx, DC, Disc, MC, V. **Map** p404 E25.

Trad hats may be back in fashion, but this venerable shop, in business since 1911, is oblivious to passing trends. Dapper gents sporting the shop's wares will help you choose from more than 2,000 fedoras, pork pies, caps and other styles on display in the splendid, chandelier-illuminated, wood-panelled showroom. Prices start at $35 for a wool-blend cap.

Other locations 440 East 9th Street, between 1st Avenue & Avenue A, East Village (1-212 260 0408).

Victor Osborne

160 Orchard Street, between Rivington & Stanton Streets, Lower East Side (1-212 677 6254, www.victorosborne.com). Subway F to Lower East Side-Second Avenue. **Open** noon-7pm Tue-Sun. **Credit** AmEx, Disc, MC, V. **Map** p403 F29.

Victor Osborne, who moved his shop-atelier from Williamsburg, Brooklyn, to the Lower East Side in 2009, displays an ample selection of handmade hats for men and women. The look for non-custom hats is stylishly understated, encompassing patterned fabric hats, vintage-inspired cloches and smart fedoras, which range in price from $100 for caps to around the $200 mark for a structured felt style.

Jewellery

Alexis Bittar

465 Broome Street, between Greene & Mercer Streets, Soho (1-212 625 8340, www.alexisbittar.com). Subway N, R to Prince Street; 6 to Spring Street. **Open** 11am-7pm Mon-Sat; noon-6pm Sun. **Credit** AmEx, MC, V. **Map** p403 E30.

The jewellery designer who started out selling his designs from a humble Soho street stall now has

CONSUME

JJ Hat Center

Gallery-Hopping Guide

Hit these essential stops in the city's three main art 'hoods.

Although commercial galleries are found throughout the city, several areas have a high concentration of art spaces, making them conducive to easy culture crawls. In the converted industrial spaces of **Chelsea**'s far west side, you'll find group shows by up-and-comers, blockbuster exhibitions from art-world celebrities and a slew of provocative work. However, over the past several years, the **Lower East Side** has seen a steady migration of young dealers, aided by the relocation of the New Museum of Contemporary Art to the Bowery. In midtown, the old-guard **57th Street** crew turns out a continuous series of blue-chip shows.

Note that galleries are generally closed or operate on an appointment-only basis on Mondays, except in summer when many keep different hours and close on weekends. Some may shut up shop for two weeks or a month at a stretch in July or August, so call before visiting. The highlights below are a fraction of the galleries in each area, and many have other locations. Check gallery websites or timeout.com/newyork for current exhibitions.

CHELSEA

Subway A, C, E to 14th Street; C, E to 23rd Street; L to Eighth Avenue.
Map pp403-404 C26, C27.

Cheim & Read

547 W 25th Street, between Tenth & Eleventh Avenues (1-212 242 7727, www.cheimread.com). **Open** 10am-6pm Tue-Sat
The international artists here include such superstars as Diane Arbus and Jenny Holzer.

David Zwirner

519, 525 & 533 W 19th Street, between Tenth & Eleventh Avenues (1-212 727 2070, www.davidzwirner.com).
Open 10am-6pm Tue-Sat.
Zwirner mixes museum-quality shows of historical figures with a head-turning array of contemporary artists.

Gagosian Gallery

555 W 24th Street, between Tenth & Eleventh Avenues (1-212 741 1111, www.gagosian.com). **Open** 10am-6pm Tue-Sat.

Larry Gagosian's mammoth (20,000sq ft) contribution to 24th Street's galleries opened in 1999.

Gladstone Gallery

515 W 24th Street, between Tenth & Eleventh Avenues (1-212 206 9300, www.gladstonegallery.com). **Open** 10am-6pm Tue-Sat.
Gladstone is strictly blue-chip, with an emphasis on daring conceptual art.

Haunch of Venison

550 W 21st Street, between Tenth & Eleventh Avenues (1-212 259 0000, www.haunchofvenison.com). **Open** 10am-6pm Tue-Sat.
The London-born mega-gallery showcases a roster of blue-chip talent, such as Isca Greenfield-Sanders and Eve Sussman.

Luhring Augustine

531 W 24th Street, between Tenth & Eleventh Avenues (1-212 206 9100, www.luhringaugustine.com). **Open** 10am-6pm Tue-Sat.
An impressive index of artists includes Rachel Whiteread and Pipilotti Rist.

Mary Boone Gallery

541 W 24th Street, between Tenth & Eleventh Avenues (1-212 752 2929, www.maryboonegallery.com). **Open** 10am-6pm Tue-Sat.
Boone made her name in the '80s representing Julian Schnabel and Jean-Michel Basquiat, among others, and continues to produce hit shows featuring young artists.

Gladstone Gallery

CONSUME

Mary Boone Gallery

Matthew Marks Gallery
*523 W 24th Street, between Tenth &
Eleventh Avenues (1-212 243 0200,
www.matthewmarks.com).* **Open** 10am-
6pm Tue-Sat.
Opened in 1994, The Matthew Marks
gallery was a driving force behind Chelsea's
transformation into an art destination.

Tanya Bonakdar Gallery
*521 W 21st Street, between Tenth &
Eleventh Avenues (1-212 414 4144,
www.tanyabonakdargallery.com).*
Open 10am-6pm Tue-Sat
This elegant space reps such powerhouse
names as New York City *Waterfalls*
maestro Olafur Eliasson.

Yossi Milo
*245 Tenth Avenue, between West 24th &
West 25th Streets (1-212 414 0370, www.
yossimilo.com).* **Open** 10am-6pm Tue-Sat.
Yossi Milo's impressive roster of camera
talent encompasses emerging artists as
well as more established photographers.

LOWER EAST SIDE
*Subway F to East Broadway or Delancey
Street; F to Lower East Side-Second
Avenue; J, Z to Delancey-Essex Streets.*
Map p403 F29, F30, G30.

Eleven Rivington
*11 Rivington Street, between Bowery
& Chrystie Street (1-212 982 1930,
www.elevenrivington.com).* **Open** noon-
6pm Wed-Sun.
The offshoot of 57th Street's Greenberg
Van Doren Gallery offers an impeccable
midtown vibe in small-storefront form.

Miguel Abreu Gallery
*36 Orchard Street, between Canal &
Hester Streets (1-212 995 1774,
www.miguelabreugallery.com).* **Open** 11am-
6.30pm Wed-Sun.
A filmmaker as well as founding member
of the legendary Threadwaxing alternative
space in Soho (now closed), Miguel Abreu
represents conceptually inspired artists.

Rachel Uffner Gallery
*47 Orchard Street, between Grand
& Hester Sreets (1-212 274 0064,
www.racheluffnergallery.com).*
Open 11am-6pm Wed-Sun.
Uffner, who cut her teeth at Christies,
showcases a small but eclectic stable.

Sperone Westwater
*257 Bowery, between E Houston & Stanton
Streets (1-212-999-7337, www.sperone
westwater.com).* **Open** 10am-6pm Tue-Sat.
Started in 1975, this gallery is housed in a
purpose-built showcase designed by
starchitect Lord Norman Foster.

57TH STREET & AROUND
*Subway E, M to Fifth Avenue-53rd Street;
F to 57th Street; N, Q, R to Fifth Avenue-
59th Street.* **Map** p405 E22.

Marian Goodman Gallery
*4th Floor, 24 W 57th Street, between
Fifth & Sixth Avenues (1-212 977 7160,
www.mariangoodman.com).* **Open** 10am-
6pm Mon-Sat.
This well-known space offers a host of
world-renowned names.

The Pace Gallery
*2nd Floor, 32 E 57th Street, between
Madison & Park Avenues (1-212 421
3292, www.pacegallery.com).* **Open**
9.30am-6pm Tue-Fri; 10am-6pm Sat.
For some of the 20th century's most
significant art stalwarts, head to this
institution. Also at this location is the
Pace Prints division and Pace/MacGill,
which specialises in photography.

Peter Blum
*20 West 57th Street, between Fifth & Sixth
Avenues (1-212 244 6055, www.peterblum
gallery.com).* **Open** 10am-6pm Tue-Fri;
11am-6pm Sat.
This gallery, which recently relocated from
Soho, is manned by a dealer with an
impeccable eye and wide-ranging tastes.

CONSUME

three shops to show off his art-object designs, including his trademark sculptural Lucite cuffs and oversized crystal-encrusted earrings. All are handcrafted in his Brooklyn atelier.

Other locations 353 Bleecker Street, between Charles & 10th Streets, West Village (1-212 727 1093); 1100 Madison Avenue, between 82nd & 83rd Streets, Upper East Side (1-212 249 3581).

Doyle & Doyle

189 Orchard Street, between Houston & Stanton Streets, Lower East Side (1-212 677 9991, www.doyledoyle.com). Subway F to Lower East Side-Second Avenue. **Open** 1-7pm Tue, Wed, Fri; 1-8pm Thur; noon-7pm Sat, Sun. **Credit** AmEx, MC, V. **Map** p403 F29.

Whether your taste is art deco or nouveau, Victorian or Edwardian, gemologist sisters Pam and Elizabeth Doyle, who specialise in vintage and antique jewellery, will have that one-of-a-kind item you're looking for, including engagement and eternity rings. The pieces artfully displayed within wall-mounted wooden framed cases are just a fraction of what's in stock.

★ Erica Weiner

173 Elizabeth Street, between Kenmare & Spring Streets, Nolita (1-212 334 6383, www.ericaweiner.com). Subway C, E to Spring Street. **Open** noon-8pm daily **Credit** AmEx, MC, V. **Map** p403 F30.

Seamstress-turned-jewellery-designer Erica Weiner sells her own bronze, brass, silver and gold creations – many under $100 – alongside vintage and reworked baubles. Old wooden cabinets and stacked crates showcase rings and charm-laden necklaces, such as those bearing a tiny dangling harmonica and steel penknife. Other favourites include brass ginkgo-leaf earrings, and moveable-type letter necklaces for your favourite wordsmith.

Lingerie & underwear

Bloomingdale's has an encyclopaedic lingerie department, and **Victoria's Secret** (www. victoriassecret.com) is the choice of the masses for inexpensive yet pretty unmentionables.

Bra Smyth

905 Madison Avenue, between 72nd & 73rd Streets, Upper East Side (1-212 772 9400, www.brasmyth.com). Subway 6 to 77th Street. **Open** 10am-6.30pm Mon-Sat; noon-5pm Sun. **Credit** AmEx, Disc, MC, V. **Map** p405 E20.

This shop stocks sizes to suit all cleavages, and the employees are so experienced that they can guess your bust measurements the second you walk in the door (they're usually right). On-site seamstresses can alter your purchase for a customised fit.

Other locations 2177 Broadway, at 77th Street, Upper West Side (1-212 721 5111).

★ Kiki de Montparnasse

79 Greene Street, between Broome & Spring Streets, Soho (1-212 965 8150, www.kikidm.com). Subway N, R to Prince Street; 6 to Spring Street. **Open** 11am-7pm Mon, Sun; 11am-8pm Tue-Sat. **Credit** AmEx, Disc, MC, V. **Map** p403 E30.

This erotic luxury boutique channels the spirit of its namesake, a 1920s sexual icon and Man Ray muse, with a posh array of tastefully provocative contemporary lingerie in satin and French lace, including such novelties as cotton tank tops with built-in garters and knickers embroidered with saucy legends. Bedroom accoutrements, such as molten crystal 'dilettos' and bespoke 'intimacy kits', give new meaning to the term 'satisfied customer'.

Luggage

Flight 001

96 Greenwich Avenue, between Jane & 12th Streets, Meatpacking District (1-212 989 0001, www.flight001.com). Subway A, C, E to 14th Street; L to Eighth Avenue. **Open** 11am-8pm Mon-Sat; noon-6pm Sun. **Credit** AmEx, DC, Disc, MC, V. **Map** p403 D28.

As well as a tasteful selection of luggage by the likes of Lipault, Rimowa and Hideo Wakamatsu, this one-stop shop carries everything for the chic jet-setter, including fun travel products such as novelty patterned eye masks and emergency totes that squash down to tennis ball size, plus 'essentials' such as expanding hand-towel tablets and single-use packets of Woolite.

Other location 132 Smith Street, between Bergen & Dean Streets, Boerum Hill, Brooklyn (1-718 243 0001).

Shoes

Surprisingly, New York is short on trendy multi-brand shoe stores, although there are some large family footwear emporiums, such as **Harry's Shoes** on the Upper West Side (2299 Broadway, at 83rd Street, 1-212 874 2035, www.harrys-shoes.com), which sells mid-priced brands like UGG, Frye, Converse and Clarks. **Bergdorf Goodman**, **Barneys** and **Saks Fifth Avenue** all have excellent designer collections.

★ Alife Rivington Club

158 Rivington Street, between Clinton & Suffolk Streets, Lower East Side (1-212 432 7200, www.alifenyc.com). Subway F to Delancey Street; J, Z to Delancey-Essex Streets. **Open** noon-7pm Mon-Sat; noon-6pm Sun. **Credit** AmEx, MC, V. **Map** p403 G29.

Whether you're looking for a simple white trainer or a trendy graphic style, you'll want to gain entry to this 'club', which stocks a wide range of major brands including Nike, Adidas and New Balance,

along with less mainstream names including its own label. Sneaker freaks salivate over retro styles such as Warrior Footwear (which originated in China in the 1930s), and the Nike Air Jordan 1.

Moo Shoes

78 Orchard Street, between Broome & Grand Streets, Lower East Side (1-212 254 6512, www.mooshoes.com). Subway F to Delancey Street; J, Z to Delancey-Essex Streets. **Open** 11.30am-7.30pm Mon-Sat; noon-6pm Sun. **Credit** AmEx, Disc, MC, V. **Map** p403 G30.

Cruelty-free footwear is far more fashionable than it once was (Stella McCartney's non-leather line is a case in point). Moo stocks a variety of brands for men and women, such as Vegetarian Shoes and Novacas, plus styles from independent designers such as Elizabeth Olsen, whose arty line of high heels and handbags is anything but hippyish.

FOOD & DRINK

Bakeries

Amy's Bread

672 Ninth Avenue, between 46th & 47th Streets, Hell's Kitchen (1-212 977 2670, www.amysbread. com). Subway C, E to 50th Street; N, Q, R to 49th Street. **Open** 7.30am-11pm Mon-Fri; 8am-11pm Sat; 8am-8pm Sun. **Credit** AmEx, Disc, MC, V. **Map** p404 C23.

Whether you want sweet (double-chocolate pecan Chubbie cookies) or savoury (hefty French sourdough *boules*), Amy's never disappoints. Breakfast and snacks such as the grilled cheese sandwich, (made with New York State cheddar, are also served. **Other locations** Chelsea Market, 75 Ninth Avenue, between 15th & 16th Streets, Chelsea (1-212 462 4338); 250 Bleecker Street, at Leroy Street, West Village (1-212 675 7802).

Billy's Bakery

184 Ninth Avenue, between 21st & 22nd Streets, Chelsea (1-212 647 9956, www.billysbakerynyc.com). Subway C, E to 23rd Street. **Open** 9.30am-11pm Mon-Thur; 9.30am-midnight Fri, Sat; 9.30am-10pm Sun. **Credit** AmEx, Disc, MC, V. **Map** p404 C26.

Amid super-sweet retro delights such as coconut cream pie, cupcakes, Hello Dollies (indulgent graham cracker treats) and Famous Chocolate Icebox Cake, you'll find friendly service in a setting that will remind you of grandma's kitchen – or, at least, it will if your grandmother was Betty Crocker. **Other locations** 75 Franklin Street, between Broadway & Church Street, Tribeca (1-212 647 9958).

Levain Bakery

167 W 74th Street, between Columbus & Amsterdam Avenues, Upper West Side (1-212

Eataly. *See p210.*

CONSUME

874 6080, www.levainbakery.com). Subway 1 to 79th Street. **Open** 8am-7pm Mon-Sat; 9am-7pm Sun. **Credit** AmEx, MC, V. **Map** p405 C20.

Forget the Big Apple – a Big Cookie is much tastier. Levain's are a full 6oz, and the massive mounds stay gooey in the middle. The lush, brownie-like double-chocolate variety, made with extra-dark French cocoa and semi-sweet chocolate chips, is a truly decadent treat.

Other locations 2167 Frederick Douglass Boulevard (Eighth Avenue), between 116th & 117th Streets, Harlem (1-646 455 0952).

Drinks

Astor Wines & Spirits

399 Lafayette Street, at 4th Street, East Village (1-212 674 7500, www.astorwines.com). Subway N, R to 8th Street-NYU; 6 to Astor Place. **Open** 9am-9pm Mon-Sat; noon-6pm Sun. **Credit** AmEx, DC, Disc, MC, V. **Map** p403 F28.

High-ceilinged, wide-aisled Astor Wines is a terrific place to browse for wines of every price range, vineyard and year – which makes it a favourite hunting ground for the city's top sommeliers. Sakés and spirits are also well represented.

Porto Rico Importing Co

201 Bleecker Street, at Sixth Avenue, Greenwich Village (1-212 477 5421, www.portorico.com). Subway A, B, C, D, E, F, M to W 4th Street. **Open** 8am-9pm Mon-Fri; 9am-9pm Sat; noon-7pm Sun. **Credit** AmEx, Disc, MC, V. **Map** p403 E29.

This small, family-run store, established in 1907, has earned a large following for its terrific range of coffee beans, including its own prepared blends. Prices are reasonable, and the selection of teas also warrants exploration.

Other locations 40½ St Marks Place, between First & Second Avenues, East Village (1-212 533 1982); Essex Market, 120 Essex Street, between Delancey & Rivington Streets, Lower East Side (1-212 677 1210); 636 Grand Street, between Manhattan Avenue & Leonard Street, Williamsburg, Brooklyn (1-718 782 1200).

General

New York City now has seven branches of natural food giant **Whole Foods Market** (www.wholefoodsmarket.com), a reliable bet for ready-prepared meals as well as organic produce, baked goods and toiletries. **Fairway** (www.fairwaymarket.com), which has locations on the Upper West and East Sides, Harlem and in Red Hook, Brooklyn, is another superior local supermarket. Longtime Soho gourmet grocer **Dean & DeLuca** (www.deanand deluca.com) operates several stores and cafés throughout the city.

Eataly

200 Fifth Avenue, between 23rd & 24th Streets, Flatiron District (1-212 229 2560, www.eataly. com). Subway F, M, N, R to 23rd Street. **Open** 8am-11pm daily. **Credit** AmEx Disc, MC, V. **Map** p404 E26.

Going big can be a blessing or a curse in this town, but celebrity chef Mario Batali got it right. His massive shrine to Italian cuisine is a haven for foodies, encompassing five proper eateries and a beer garden. Adjacent retail areas offer gourmet provisions, including artisanal breads baked on the premises, fresh mozzarella, *salumi* and a vast array of olive oils. *Photos p209.*

▶ *For details of the restaurants, see p164; for the on-site beer garden, see p178.*

Zabar's

2245 Broadway, at 80th Street, Upper West Side (1-212 787 2000, www.zabars.com). Subway 1 to 79th Street. **Open** 8am-7.30pm Mon-Fri; 8am-8pm Sat; 8am-6pm Sun. **Credit** AmEx, MC, V. **Map** p405 C19.

Zabar's is more than just a market – it's a genuine New York City landmark. It began in 1934 as a tiny storefront specialising in Jewish 'appetising' delicacies and has gradually expanded to take over half a block of prime Upper West Side real estate. What never ceases to surprise, however, is its reasonable prices – even for high-end foods. Besides the famous smoked fish and rafts of delicacies, Zabar's has fabulous bread, cheese, olives and coffee, and an entire floor dedicated to gadgets and homewares.

Markets

More than 50 open-air **Greenmarkets**, run by non-profit organisation GrowNYC, operate in various locations on different days. The largest and best known is at **Union Square**, where small producers of cheese, flowers, herbs, fruits and vegetables hawk their goods on Monday, Wednesday, Friday and Saturday (8am-6pm). Arrive early, before the prime stuff sells out. For other venues, contact GrowNYC (1-212 788 7476, www.grownyc.org/greenmarket).

The indoor **Chelsea Market** (75 Ninth Avenue, at 16th Street, www.chelseamarket. com, open 7am-9pm Mon-Sat; 8am-8pm Sun) is a one-stop gastronomic destination. It has a number of high-quality stores selling flowers, fish, fruit, baked goods, meat and wine.

Specialist

★ Bond Street Chocolates

63 E 4th Street, between Bowery & Second Avenue, East Village (1-212 677 5103, www. bondstchocolate.com). Subway 6 to Bleecker Street. **Open** noon-8pm Tue-Sat; 1-6pm Sun. **Credit** Disc, MC, V. **Map** p403 F29.

CONSUME

Market Forces

Flea fever is sweeping the city.

Brooklyn Flea

CONSUME

Rummaging in the city's outdoor antique markets, often combined with brunch, has long been a favourite New York weekend pastime, but the past few years have seen the emergence of a more sophisticated breed of flea, offering high-quality crafts and gourmet food alongside vintage clothing, furniture and bric-a-brac. Markets – especially in Brooklyn – are multiplying.

It all started with the **Brooklyn Flea** (www.brooklynflea.com), launched in 2008 by Jonathan Butler, founder of Brooklyn real-estate blog Brownstoner.com, and Eric Demby, former PR man for the Brooklyn borough president, who had the foresight to identify Brooklyn as being ripe for a destination market. The original location in the yard of Bishop Loughlin Memorial High School (176 Lafayette Avenue, between Clermont & Vanderbilt Avenues, Fort Greene) is open from April through mid November on Saturdays from 10am to 5pm, and includes around 150 vendors. The mix

Smorgasburg

of vintage clothing, records, furnishings, locally designed fashion and crafts includes Kate Durkin's appealingly simple, illustrative animal pillows, old Brooklyn neighbourhood maps at Intaglio Antique Prints & Maps, and gothic-tinged jewellery (with skull and dagger motifs) by Erica Bradbury of Species by the Thousands.

A second location runs on Sundays in Williamsburg, along the waterfront between North 6th and 7th Streets, which is also the site of a nosh-only Saturday spin-off, **Smorgasburg**. The Flea food has been so popular that it now has a presence at Central Park's SummerStage, and the partners recently struck a deal with retailer Whole Foods, which will stock vendors' grub at the Bowery location. In winter, the Brooklyn Flea moves indoors, occupying a majestic old bank (Skylight One Hanson, at Ashland Place, Fort Greene) on Saturday and Sunday through March.

From May through October, **Hester Street Fair** (Hester Street, at Essex Street, www.hesterstreetfair.com, 10am-6pm Sat), located on the site of a former Lower East Side pushcart market, also has some great gourmet purveyors among its 65 vendors – you can sample everything from locally made ice-cream to tacos as you browse. Organised by MTV News correspondent SuChin Pak, it features vintage fashions and accessories from the likes of Summer Mizer, Top Shelf Premium Vintage and Dealer's Choice. Look out for Uurmi Indian-inspired, digitally printed scarves, Drive By Press wood-block-printed T-shirts and Filthy Farmgirl handmade soaps.

Former pastry chef Lynda Stern's East Village spot is a grown-up's candy store, with quirky chocolate confections in shapes ranging from gilded Buddhas (and other religious figures) to skulls, and flavours from elderflower to bourbon and absinthe.

Jacques Torres Chocolate

350 Hudson Street, between Charlton & King Streets, entrance on King Street, Soho (1-212 414 2462, www.mrchocolate.com). Subway 1 to Houston Street. **Open** 9am-7pm Mon-Sat; 10am-6pm Sun. **Credit** AmEx, Disc, MC, V. **Map** p403 D29.

Walk into Jacques Torres's glass-walled shop and café, and you'll be surrounded by a Willy Wonka-esque factory that turns raw cocoa beans into luscious chocolate goodies before your eyes. As well as selling the usual assortments, truffles and bars (plus more unusual delicacies such as chocolate-covered cornflakes and Cheerios), the shop serves deliciously rich hot chocolate, steamed to order. **Other locations** throughout the city.

Murray's Cheese

254 Bleecker Street, between Sixth & Seventh Avenues, Greenwich Village (1-212 243 3289, www.murrayscheese.com). Subway A, B, C, D, E, F, M to W 4th Street. **Open** 8am-8pm Mon-Sat; 10am-7pm Sun. **Credit** AmEx, MC, V. **Map** p403 D29.

For the last word in curd, New Yorkers have been flocking to Murray's since 1940 to sniff out the best international and domestic cheeses. The helpful staff will guide you through hundreds of stinky, runny, washed rind and aged comestibles.

▶ *Murray's also has an outpost in Grand Central Terminal, plus a Cheese Bar at 264 Bleecker Street, serving spreads and other cheesy fare.*

★ Russ & Daughters

179 E Houston Street, between Allen & Orchard Streets, Lower East Side (1-212 475 4880, www.russanddaughters.com). Subway F to Lower East Side-Second Avenue. **Open** 8am-8pm Mon-Fri; 9am-7pm Sat; 8am-5.30pm Sun. **Credit** AmEx, Disc, MC, V. **Map** p403 F29.

Magpie

The daughters in the name have given way to great-grandchildren, but this Lower East Side survivor (est. 1914) is still run by the same family. Specialising in smoked and cured fish and caviar, it sells over ten varieties of smoked salmon, eight types of herring (pickled, salt-cured, smoked and so on) and many other Jewish-inflected Eastern European delectables. Bagels are available to take away; the Super Heebster is filled with fluffy white-fish salad, horseradish cream cheese and wasabi-flavoured flying-fish roe.

GIFTS & SOUVENIRS

★ Bowne & Co Stationers

South Street Seaport Museum, 211 Water Street, at Fulton Street, Financial District (1-212 748 8651). Open 11am-7pm daily. **Credit** AmEx, MC, V. **Map** p402 F32.

South Street Seaport Museum's re-creation of an 1870s-era print shop, Bowne & Co Stationers, doesn't just look the part: the 19th-century platen presses – hand-set using antique type and powered by a trea-dle – turn out beautiful art prints and cards. The shop also stocks journals and other gifts.

By Brooklyn

261 Smith Street, between DeGraw & Douglass Streets, Carroll Gardens, Brooklyn (1-718 643 0606, www.bybrooklyn.com). Subway F, G to Carroll Street. **Open** 11.30am-8pm Mon-Fri; 11am-8pm Sat; 11am-7pm Sun. **Credit** AmEx, Disc, MC, V. **Map** p410 E14.

Owner Gaia DiLoreto's modern-day general store offers an array of New York-made goods, including pickles, soaps, T-shirts, jewellery, paper goods and books by Brooklyn authors. Look out for Punch ceramic homeware, Lingua Nigra hammered-gold-coin earrings and necklaces, and Lola Falk colour-block handbags.

★ Kiosk

95 Spring Street, between Broadway & Mercer Street, Soho (1-212 226 8601, http://kioskkiosk.com). Subway 6 to Spring Street. **Open** noon-7pm Mon-Sat. **Credit** AmEx, MC, V. **Map** p403 E30.

Don't be put off by the unprepossessing, graffiti-covered stairway that leads up to this gem of a shop. Alisa Grifo has collected an array of inexpensive items – mostly simple and functional but with a strong design aesthetic – from around the world, such as cool Japanese can openers, colourful net bags from Germany and Shaker onion baskets handmade in New Hampshire. It's a great spot for picking up inexpensive, unusual gifts.

Magpie

488 Amsterdam Avenue, between 83rd & 84th Streets, Upper West Side (1-646 998 3002,

www.magpienewyork.com). Subway 1 to 86th Street. **Open** 11am-7pm Mon-Sat; noon-6pm Sun. **Credit** AmEx, Disc, MC, V. **Map** p405 C19.

Sylvia Parker worked as a buyer at the American Folk Art Museum gift shop before opening this eco-friendly boutique. The funky space, which is deco-rated with no-fume paints and bamboo shelves, is packed with locally made, handcrafted, sustainable and fair-trade items. Unique finds include vintage hankies and quilts, handmade Moroccan tote bags and recycled-resin cuff bracelets.

Sustainable NYC

139 Avenue A, between 9th Street & St Marks Place, East Village (1-212 254 5400, www.sustainable-nyc.com). Subway L to First Avenue; 6 to Astor Place. **Open** 8am-10pm Mon-Fri; 9am-10pm Sat, Sun. **Credit** AmEx, Disc, MC, V. **Map** p403 G28.

This gift-centric shop houses a wealth of eco-minded goods within its green walls: organic shampoos and beauty products; Fairtrade chocolate; frames, jewellery, clutch bags and other gifts made from recy-cled metals and materials such as computer keys; and sun-powered BlackBerry chargers. The on-site café serves Fairtrade coffee from Dumbo's Brooklyn Roasting Co and locally made treats.

HEALTH & BEAUTY
Complementary medicine

Continuum Center for Health & Healing

2nd Floor, 245 Fifth Avenue, at 28th Street, Flatiron District (www.healthandhealingny.org). Subway N, R to 28th Street. **Open** 8.30am-6pm Mon, Tue, Thur; 8.30am-7pm Wed; 8.30am-5pm Fri; some Sats (call for info). **Credit** AmEx, DC, Disc, MC, V. **Map** p404 E26.

Affiliated with Beth Israel Medical Center, Continuum is headed by integrative medicine expert Dr Woodson Merrell. Treatment takes the patient's entire lifestyle into account, looking at diet, exercise and stress management. In addition to primary care and other services such as women's health, the center offers acupuncture, physical therapy and mind-body therapies such as reiki. Phone numbers are by department; see website for details.

Hairdressers & barbers

The styling superstars at top salons such as **Frédéric Fekkai** (1-212 753 9500, www.fredericfekkai.com, 4th Floor, Henri Bendel; *see p192*), **John Barrett Salon** (1-212 872 2700, www.johnbarrett.com, 9th Floor, Bergdorf Goodman; *see p190*) and **Sally Hershberger Downtown** (2nd Floor, 423-425 W 14th Street, between Ninth & Tenth Avenues, 1-212 206 8700, www.sallyhershberger.com, closed Sun) are top-notch, but they tend to charge hair-raising prices.

Astor Place Hairstylist

2 Astor Place, at Broadway, East Village (1-212 475 9854). Subway N, R to 8th Street-NYU; 6 to Astor Place. **Open** 8am-8pm Mon, Sat; 7am-9.30pm Tue-Fri; 9am-6pm Sun. **No credit cards.** **Map** p403 E28.

The army of barbers here does everything from neat trims to more complicated and creative shaved designs. You can't make an appointment: just take a number and wait outside with the crowd. Sunday mornings are usually quieter. Cuts start at $16.

Birds & Fellas

75 E 7th Street, between First & Second Avenues, East Village (1-212 533 1592, www.birdsandfellas.com). Subway L to First Avenue; 6 to Astor Place. **Open** noon-8pm Mon-Fri; 11am-7pm Sat, Sun. **Credit** MC, V. **Map** p403 F28.

This East Village salon, which favours fun over fussiness, has moved from its original small digs to a new spot a few blocks away. The off-white walls are a calming backdrop for the communal-table waiting area (the salon offers free Wi-Fi and a smartphone-charging station), eight styling chairs and two shampoo stations. Clients can choose a drink from the complimentary beverage bar (soda, coffee, wine and even seasonal cocktails) to sip while they get cuts ($49 for men; $64 for women) that include a complimentary head massage.

Blow

342 W 14th Street, between Eighth & Ninth Avenues, Meatpacking District (1-212 989 6282, www.blowny.com). Subway A, C, E to 14th Street. **Open** 8am-8pm Mon-Fri; 10am-8pm Sat; noon-6pm Sun. **Credit** AmEx, MC, V. **Map** p403 C27.

Launched as a scissor-free 'blow-dry bar', this award-winning salon now offers cuts, colour and select beauty services as well as expertly executed blow-drying ($40-$60, depending on length and texture). For curling- or flat-irons, add $10-$20.

Fix Beauty Bar

847 Lexington Ave between 64th and 65th Streets, 2nd floor, Upper East Side (1-212 744 0800, www.fixbeautybar.com). Subway F to Lexington Avenue-63rd Street. **Open** 9am-8pm Mon-Wed; 9am-9pm Thur-Sat. **Credit** AmEx, DC, Disc, MC, V. **Map** p405 E21.

Writer Karol Markowicz and Michelle Breskin, whose background is in real estate and finance, are taking the blow-dry bar phenomenon one step further, offering busy New Yorkers manicures ($15) and pedicures ($35) to accompany the affordable flat-rate blow-dries ($40) at their chic lavender-and-grey salon. Hairstyles are named after celebrities with instantly recognisable tresses, such as the Jen (sleek and pin-straight), the Taylor (soft, styled curls) and the Kim (full, dramatic waves).

Paul Molé Barber Shop

1034 Lexington Avenue, at 74th Street, Upper East Side (1-212 535 8461, www.paulmole.com). Subway 6 to 76th Street. **Open** 6am-8pm Mon-Fri; 6am-5.30pm Sat; 8am-4pm Sun. Appointments from 7.30am. **No credit cards.** **Map** p405 E20.

Best known for its precise shaves, this nostalgic barbers' has been grooming men since 1913 (John Steinbeck used to come here to be debearded). As well as its signature Deluxe Open Razor Shave ($35), you can get a haircut (from $34) and other services such as a scalp massage ($10).

Whittemore House

45 Grove Street, between Bleecker & Bedford Streets, West Village (1-212 242 8880, www.whittemorehousesalon.com). Subway 1 to Christopher Street-Sheridan Square. **Open** 10am-8pm Tue, Wed; noon-9pm Thur, Fri; 10am-6pm Sat. **Credit** AmEx, DC, Disc, MC, V. **Map** p403 D28.

Victoria Hunter and Larry Raspanti, who each spent more than 15 years dressing tresses at Bumble & Bumble, opened this salon in the garden level of an 1830s mansion (one of the three oldest buildings in the city). The antithesis of streamlined minimalism, the decor features artfully aged woods, faux-decayed stencilled walls and big, comfy boudoir chairs. Cuts (starting at $115) and natural-looking colour, achieved through the house hair-painting technique (from $225), come courtesy of some of New York's best stylists.

★ Woodley & Bunny

196 North 10th Street, at Driggs Avenue, Williamsburg, Brooklyn (1-718 218 6588, www.woodleyandbunny.com). Subway L to Bedford Avenue; G to Nassau Avenue. **Open** 10am-9pm Mon-Fri; 9am-8pm Sat; 10am-7pm Sun. **Credit** DC, Disc, MC, V. **Map** p411 U7.

With a prime Williamsburg location, Woodley & Bunny is the place to get the most cutting-edge crop (from $86 for women, from $66 for men) or colour,

Woodley & Bunny

but there's a welcome emphasis on individuality at this laid-back beauty spot. Part salon, part apothecary, it also offers beauty treatments such as mini facials and eyebrow tweezing.

Opticians

A former flea market stall, **Fabulous Fanny's** (335 E 9th Street, between First & Second Avenues, East Village, 1-212 533 0637, www.fabulousfannys.com) has been a premier source of period frames for two decades, with more than 30,000 pairs of spectacles on offer, some dating back to the 1700s.

Morgenthal Frederics
399 W Broadway, at Spring Street, Soho (1-212 966 0099, www.morgenthalfrederics.com). Subway C, E to Spring Street. **Open** 11am-8pm Mon-Fri; 11am-7pm Sat; noon-6pm Sun. **Credit** AmEx, Disc, MC, V. **Map** p403 E30.
The house-designed, handmade frames displayed in Morgenthal Frederics' David Rockwell-designed shops exude quality and subtly nostalgic style. Frames start from around $300 for plastic, but the buffalo horn and gold ranges are more expensive; you can even have a pair accented with tiny diamonds if you have $45,000 to spare!
Other locations throughout the city.

Selima Optique
59 Wooster Street, at Broome Street, Soho (1-212 343 9490, www.selimaoptique.com). Subway C, E, 6 to Spring Street. **Open** 11am-8pm Mon-Sat; noon-7pm Sun. **Credit** AmEx, MC, V. **Map** p403 E30.

Eyewear designer Selima Salaun's spacious flagship stocks her full range of frames alongside other brands and vintage eyewear. Nostalgic styles, including square and curvy cat-eye 1950s-inspired shapes and 1970s-vibe large rounded frames, come in a variety of eye-catching colour combinations. You can have your prescription filled on-site (an optician is available for appointments on Tuesdays and Fridays, noon-6pm).
Other locations 7 Bond Street, between Broadway & Lafayette Street, East Village (1-212 677 8487); 357 Bleecker Street, between Charles & W 10th Streets, West Village (1-212 352 1640); 899 Madison Avenue, between 72nd & 73rd Streets, Upper East Side (1-212 988 6690).

Pharmacies

The fact that there's a **Duane Reade** pharmacy on almost every corner of Manhattan is lamented among chain-deriding locals; however, it is convenient if you need an aspirin pronto. Several branches, including the one at 250 W 57th Street, at Broadway (1-212 265 2101, www.duanereade.com), are open 24 hours. Competitor **Rite Aid** (with one of several 24-hour branches at 301 W 50th Street, at Eighth Avenue, 1-212 247 8736, www.riteaid.com) is also widespread.

CO Bigelow Chemists
414 Sixth Avenue, between 8th & 9th Streets, Greenwich Village (1-212 473 7324, www. bigelowchemists.com). Subway A, B, C, D, F, M to W 4th Street; 1 to Christopher Street. **Open** 7.30am-9pm Mon-Fri; 9am-7pm Sat;

CONSUME

9.30am-5.30pm Sun. **Credit** AmEx, Disc, MC, V. **Map** p403 D28.

Established in 1838, Bigelow is the oldest apothecary in America. Its appealingly old-school line of toiletries include such tried-and-trusted favourites as Mentha Lip Shine, Barber Cologne Elixirs and Lemon Body Cream. The spacious, chandelier-lit store is packed with natural and homeopathic remedies, organic skincare products and drugstore essentials – and the staff still fill prescriptions.

Perfumeries

Aedes de Venustas

9 Christopher Street, at Sixth Avenue, West Village (1-212 206 8674, www.aedes.com). Subway A, B, C, D, F, M to W 4th Street; 1 to Christopher Street. **Open** noon-8pm Mon-Sat; 1-7pm Sun. **Credit** AmEx, Disc, MC, V. **Map** p403 D28.

Decked out like a 19th-century boudoir, this perfume collector's palace devotes itself to ultra-sophisticated fragrances and high-end skincare lines, such as Diptyque, Santa Maria Novella and its own glamorously packaged range of fragrances, candles and room sprays. Hard-to-find scents, such as Eau d'Italie's Umbrian wood-accented sprays and Serge Lutens perfumes, line the walls.

Bond No.9

9 Bond Street, between Broadway & Lafayette Street, East Village (1-212 228 1732, www.bondno9.com). Subway B, D, F, M to Broadway-Lafayette Street; 6 to Bleecker Street. **Open** 11am-8pm Mon-Fri; 10am-7pm Sat; noon-6pm Sun. **Credit** AmEx, DC, MC, V. **Map** p403 E29.

The collection of scents here pays olfactory homage to New York City. Choose from 59 'neighbourhoods' and 'sensibilities', including Wall Street, Park Avenue, Eau de Noho, the High Line – even Chinatown (but don't worry, it smells of peach blossoms, gardenia and patchouli, not fish stands). The arty bottles and neat, colourful packaging are particularly gift friendly.

Other locations throughout the city.

CB I Hate Perfume

93 Wythe Avenue, between North 10th & North 11th Streets, Williamsburg, Brooklyn (1-718 384 6890, www.cbihateperfume.com). Subway L to Bedford Avenue. **Open** noon-6pm Tue-Sat. **Credit** AmEx, DC, Disc, MC, V. **Map** p411 U7.

Contrary to his shop's name, Christopher Brosius doesn't actually hate what he sells; he just despises the concept of mass-produced fragrances. Although there's currently a hold on bespoke collaborations due to high demand, you can choose from 40 evocative, ready-made fragrances, such as Gathering Apples or At the Beach 1966.

Kiehl's

109 Third Avenue, between 13th & 14th Streets, East Village (1-212 677 3171, www.kiehls.com). Subway L to Third Avenue; N, Q, R, 4, 5, 6 to 14th Street-Union Square. **Open** 10am-8pm Mon-Sat; 11am-6pm Sun. **Credit** AmEx, DC, Disc, MC, V. **Map** p403 F27.

The apothecary founded on this East Village site in 1851 has morphed into a major, world-renowned skincare brand widely sold in upscale department stores. Although it was acquired by cosmetics giant

Obsessive Compulsive Cosmetics

Cornelia Spa at the Surrey

L'Oréal in 2000, the products, in their minimal-frills packaging, are still good value and produce great results. The lip balms and thick-as-custard Creme de Corps are cult classics. The recently refurbished flagship includes historical displays. The Upper East Side location (157 E 64th Street, between Lexington & Third Avenues, 1-917 432 2503), which was launched to coincide with the company's 160th anniversary, houses the first Kiehl's spa. Treatments incorporate ingredients such as squalane and beta-carotene, also found in its products.
Other locations throughout the city.

Obsessive Compulsive Cosmetics

174 Ludlow Street, between E Houston & Stanton Streets (1-212 675 2404, www.occmakeup.com). Subway F to Lower East Side-Second Avenue. **Open** 11am-7pm Mon-Sat; noon-6pm Sun. **Credit** AmEx, Disc, MC, V. **Map** p403 G29.
Creator David Klasfeld founded OCC in the kitchen of his Lower East Side apartment in 2004. The makeup artist has since expanded his 100% vegan and cruelty-free cosmetics line from just two shades of lip balm to an extensive assortment of bang-for-your-buck beauty products. In the downtown flagship, you can browse more than 30 shades of nail polish and nearly 40 loose eye-shadow powders, among other products, but we especially like the Lip Tars, which glide on like a gloss but have the matte finish and saturated pigmentation of a lipstick.

Spas & salons

Many of the city's luxury hotels are equipped with indulgent spas: we especially recommend the serene sanctuaries at the **Plaza** (*see p217*

Caudalie Vinothérapie Spa), the **Surrey** and **Waldorf Astoria New York** (for both, *see p244*).
   There are cheap nail bars on practically every corner in many parts of the city; many also offer treatments such as massage and facials. Widespread chain **Spa Belles** (www.spabelles.com) is a good bet.

Caudalie Vinothérapie Spa

4th Floor, 1 W 58th Street, at Fifth Avenue, Midtown (1-212 265 3182, www.caudalie-usa.com). Subway N, R to Fifth Avenue-59th Street. **Open** 9am-7pm Tue-Sat; 10am-5pm Sun. **Credit** AmEx. MC, V. **Map** p405 E22.
The first Vinothérapie outpost in the US, and the first not attached to a European vineyard, this original spa harnesses the antioxidant power of grapes and vine leaves. The 8,000sq ft facility in the Plaza (*see p241*) offers such treatments as a Red Vine bath ($75) in one of its cherrywood 'barrel' tubs. In the wine lounge, relax with artisanal tipples from its French vineyard, cheeses and foie gras.

Cornelia Spa at the Surrey

2nd Floor, 20 E 76th Street, between Fifth & Madison Avenues, Upper East Side (1-646 842 6551, www.corneliaspaatthesurrey.com). Subway 6 to 77th Street. **Open** 10am-8pm Mon-Fri; 9am-7pm Sat; 10am-7pm Sun. **Credit** AmEx, Disc, MC, V. **Map** p405 E20.
Husband and wife Rick Aidekman and Ellen Sackoff have reopened this popular boutique spa, which closed in 2009, in a smaller hotel setting. The intimate yet luxurious oasis is designed to make you feel like you're lounging in your own living space

CONSUME

CONSUME

Mantiques Modern

(treatment rooms include a full-size armoire in which to store your stuff), while a 'botanical tasting bar' serves savoury and sweet treats to complement your service, such as cooling sorbet and champagne by the glass. Splurge on the Reparative Caviar and Oxygen Quench facial ($325), or a signature massage ($175), which combines deep-tissue, Swedish and shiatsu techniques.

★ Great Jones Spa

29 Great Jones Street, at Lafayette Street, East Village (1-212 505 3185, www.greatjonesspa. com). Subway 6 to Astor Place. **Open** 9.30am-10.30pm daily. **Credit** AmEx, Disc, MC, V. **Map** p403 F29.
Based on the theory that water brings health, Great Jones is outfitted with a popular water lounge complete with subterranean pools, saunas, steam rooms and a three-and-a-half-storey waterfall. Access to the 15,000sq ft paradise is complimentary with services over $100 – treat yourself to a divinely scented body scrub, a massage or one of the many indulgent packages. Alternatively, a three-hour pass costs $50.

Juvenex

5th Floor, 25 W 32nd Street, between Fifth Avenue & Broadway, Garment District (1-646 733 1330, www.juvenexspa.com). Subway B, D, F, M, N, Q, R to 34th Street-Herald Square. **Open** 24hrs daily. **Credit** AmEx, Disc, MC, V. **Map** p404 E25.
This huge, bustling Koreatown relaxation hub may be slightly rough around the edges (frayed towels, dingy sandals), but it retains appeal for its bathhouse meets Epcot feel (igloo saunas, tiled 'soaking ponds', and a slatted bridge), and 24-hour availabil-

ity (note that it's women only 8am-5pm). The Basic Purification Program – including soak and sauna, face, body and hair cleansing, and a salt scrub – is great value at $115.

Tattoos & piercings

NY Adorned

47 Second Avenue, between 2nd & 3rd Streets, East Village (1-212 473 0007, www.nyadorned. com). Subway F to Second Avenue. **Open** 1-9pm Mon-Thur, Sun; 1-10pm Fri, Sat. **Credit** AmEx, MC, V (for piercings only). **Map** p403 F29.
Proprietor Lori Leven hires world-class tattoo artists to wield needles at this elegant parlour inspired by Far East boudoirs. The army of permanent and visiting tattooists can accommodate any request, from Japanese-style pieces to classic Americana. Those with low pain thresholds can go for gentler henna decoration or body jewellery.

HOUSE & HOME
Antiques

Antiques Garage

112 W 25th Street, between Sixth & Seventh Avenues, Chelsea (1-212 243 5343, www.annex markets.com). Subway F, M to 23rd Street. **Open** 9am-5pm Sat, Sun. **No credit cards**. **Map** p404 D26.
Designers (and the occasional celebrity) hunt regularly at this flea market in a vacant parking garage. Strengths include old prints, vintage clothing and household paraphernalia. The weekend outdoor Hell's Kitchen Flea Market, run by the same people,

features a mix of vintage clothing and textiles, furniture and bric-a-brac.

Other locations 39th Street, between Ninth & Tenth Avenues, Hell's Kitchen.

★ Mantiques Modern

146 W 22nd Street, between Sixth & Seventh Avenues, Chelsea (1-212 206 1494, www. mantiquesmodern.com). Subway 1 to 23rd Street. **Open** 10.30am-6.30pm Mon-Fri; 11am-7pm Sat, Sun. **Credit** AmEx, Disc, MC, V. **Map** p404 D26.
Walking into this two-level shop is a little like stumbling upon the private collection of some mad professor. Specialising in industrial and modernist furnishings and art from the 1880s to the 1980s, Mantiques Modern is a fantastic repository of beautiful and bizarre items, from kinetic sculptures and early 20th-century wooden artists' mannequins to a Russian World War II telescope and a rattlesnake frozen in a slab of Lucite. Pieces by famous designers such as Hermès sit side by side with natural curiosities, and skulls (in metal or Lucite), crabs, animal horns and robots are all recurring themes.

Showplace Antique & Design Center

40 W 25th Street, between Fifth & Sixth Avenues, Flatiron District (1-212 633 6063, www.nyshowplace.com). Subway F, M to 23rd Street. **Open** 10am-6pm Mon-Fri; 8.30am-5.30pm Sat, Sun. **Credit** varies. **Map** p404 E26.
Set over four expansive floors, this indoor market houses more than 200 high-quality dealers selling everything from Greek and Roman antiquities to vintage radios. Among the highlights are Joe Sundlie's spot-on-trend vintage pieces from Lanvin and Alaïa,

and Mood Indigo – arguably the best source in the city for collectable bar accessories and dinnerware. The array of Bakelite jewellery and table accessories, Fiestaware, and novelty cocktail glasses is dazzling, and it's a wonderful repository of art deco cigarette cases, lighters and New York memorabilia.

General

★ ABC Carpet & Home

888 Broadway, at 19th Street, Flatiron District (1-212 473 3000, www.abchome.com). Subway L, N, Q, R, 4, 5, 6 to 14th Street-Union Square. **Open** 10am-7pm Mon-Wed, Fri, Sat; 10am-8pm Thur; 11am-6.30pm Sun. **Credit** AmEx, Disc, MC, V. **Map** p403 E27.
Most of ABC's 35,000-strong carpet range is housed in the store across the street at no.881 – except the rarest rugs, which reside on the sixth floor of the main store. Browse everything from organic soap to hand-beaded lampshades on the bazaar-style ground floor. On the upper floors, furniture spans every style, from slick European minimalism to antique oriental and mid-century modern. The massive Bronx warehouse outlet offers discounted furnishings, but prices are still steep.
Other locations ABC Carpet & Home Warehouse, 1055 Bronx River Avenue, between Bruckner Boulevard & Westchester Avenue, Bronx (1-718 842 8772).

Domus

413 W 44th Street, between Ninth & Tenth Avenues, Hell's Kitchen (1-212 581 8099, www.domusnewyork.com). Subway A, C, E to

CONSUME

The Future Perfect. *See p220.*

CONSUME

42nd Street-Port Authority. **Open** noon-8pm
Tue-Sat; noon-6pm Sun. **Credit** AmEx, MC, V.
Map p404 C24.
Scouring the globe for unusual design products is
nothing new, but owners Luisa Cerutti and Nicki
Lindheimer take the concept a step further; each year
they visit a far-flung part of the world to forge links
with and support co-operatives and individual
craftspeople. The beautiful results, such as vivid
baskets woven from telephone wire by South
African Zulu tribespeople, reflect a fine attention to
detail and a sense of place. It's a great spot to find
reasonably priced gifts, from handmade Thai soaps
to Italian throws.

Fishs Eddy

*889 Broadway, at 19th Street, Flatiron District
(1-212 420 9020, www.fishseddy.com). Subway
N, R to 23rd Street.* **Open** 10am-9pm Mon; 9am-
9pm Tue-Fri, Sat; 10am-8pm Sun. **Credit** AmEx,
DC, Disc, MC, V. **Map** p403 E27.
Penny-pinchers frequent this barn-like space for
sturdy dishware and glasses – surplus stock or recy-
cled from restaurants, ocean liners and hotels (plain
white side plates are a mere 99¢). But there are plenty
of affordable, freshly minted kitchen goods too. Add
spice to mealtime with glasses adorned with male or
female pole-dancers, plates printed with the
Brooklyn or Manhattan skyline and Floor Plan dinnerware – from $8 for a 'studio' side plate, NYC real
estate has never been so cheap!

The Future Perfect

*55 Great Jones Street, between Bowery &
Lafayette Street, East Village (1-212 473 2500,
www.thefutureperfect.com). Subway 6 to Bleecker
Street.* **Open** 10am-7pm Mon-Fri; noon-7pm Sat;
noon-6pm Sun. **Credit** AmEx, Disc, MC, V.
Map p403 E29.
Championing avant-garde interior design, this inno-
vative store showcases international and local talent
– it's the exclusive US stockist of Dutch designer Piet
Hein Eek's furniture and pottery. Look out for Kiel
Mead's quirky gold and silver jewellery and colour-
ful driftwood wall hooks, crafted from wood found
on New York State beaches. *Photo p219.*
Other locations 115 North 6th Street, between
Berry Street & Bedford Avenue, Williamsburg,
Brooklyn (1-718 599 6278).

Modern Anthology

*68 Jay Street, between Front & Water Streets,
Dumbo, Brooklyn (1-718 522 3020, www.modern
anthology.com). Subway A, C to High Street; F to
York Street.* **Open** 11am-8pm Mon-Sat; noon-6pm
Sun. **Credit** AmEx, MC, V. **Map** p411 T9.
Owners Becka Citron and John Marsala – the creative force behind the DIY Network's *Man Caves*
series – have created a one-stop lifestyle shop where
dudes can find items that toe the line between
vintage and contemporary: check out pillows made

from fabric route signs from British buses from the
1930s to '50s, and playful lamps crafted from toy
trucks. And what hip bachelor pad is complete without a stack of vintage issues of *Playboy* and barware?

MUSIC & ENTERTAINMENT
CDs & records

Academy Annex

*96 North 6th Street, between Berry Street &
Wythe Avenue, Williamsburg, Brooklyn (1-718
218 8200, www.academyannex.com). Subway L to
Bedford Avenue.* **Open** noon-9pm daily. **Credit**
AmEx, Disc, MC, V. **Map** p411 U7.
Located just up the street from the Music Hall of
Williamsburg, Academy Records' Brooklyn outpost
finds its true niche in acts not yet sufficiently well
known to play at the largeish neighbouring venue.
The Annex actively stocks local music, proclaiming
on its website, 'If you run a local label, or are in a
band with material released on vinyl, we'd love to
carry it.' From Woodsist to the Social Registry, the
labels that make up the current New York scene are
all well represented.

Downtown Music Gallery

*13 Monroe Street, between Catherine & Market
Streets, Chinatown (1-212 473 0043, www.
downtownmusicgallery.com). Subway J, Z to
Chambers Street; 4, 5, 6 to Brooklyn Bridge-City
Hall.* **Open** noon-6pm Mon-Thur; noon-7pm Fri;
noon-8pm Sat, Sun. **Credit** ($100 min) AmEx,
Disc, MC, V. **Map** p402 F31.
Many landmarks of the so-called downtown music
scene have shuttered, but as long as DMG persists,
the community will have a sturdy anchor. The shop
stocks the city's finest selection of avant-garde jazz,
contemporary classical, progressive rock and related
styles. An entire CD display devoted to John Zorn's
Tzadik imprint illustrates the store's die-hard devotion. The high credit-card minimum is to encourage
customers to pay with cash. The store stages free
performances most Sunday evenings.

★ Other Music

*15 E 4th Street, between Broadway & Lafayette
Street, East Village (1-212 477 8150, www.other
music.com). Subway B, D, F, M to Broadway-
Lafayette Street; 6 to Bleecker Street.* **Open** 11am-
9pm Mon-Fri; noon-8pm Sat; noon-7pm Sun.
Credit AmEx, DC, Disc, MC, V. **Map** p403 E29.
Other Music opened in the shadow of Tower Records
in the mid 1990s, a pocket of resistance to chain-store
tedium. All these years later, the Goliath across the
street is gone, but tiny Other Music carries on.
Whereas the shop's mish-mash of indie rock, experimental music and stray slabs of rock's past once
seemed adventurous, the curatorial foundation has
proved prescient amid the emergence of mixed-genre
venues in the city.

Modern Anthology

Musical instruments

Sam Ash Music

*156 W 48th Street, between Sixth & Seventh
Avenues, Theater District (1-212 719 2299, www.
samashmusic.com). Subway B, D, F, M to 47th-
50th Streets-Rockefeller Center; N, Q, R to 49th
Street.* **Open** 10am-8pm Mon-Sat; noon-6pm Sun.
Credit AmEx, DC, Disc, MC, V. **Map** p404 D23.
This octogenarian musical instrument emporium
dominates its midtown block with three contiguous
shops. New, vintage and custom guitars of all varieties are available, along with amps, DJ equipment,
drums, keyboards, recording equipment, turntables
and an array of sheet music.
Other locations 113-25 Queens Boulevard, at
76th Road, Forest Hills, Queens (1-718 793 7983).

SPORTS & FITNESS

Blades

*659 Broadway, between Bleecker & Bond Streets,
Greenwich Village (1-212 477 7350, www.blades.
com). Subway B, D, F, M to Broadway-Lafayette
Street; 6 to Bleecker Street.* **Open** 10am-9pm Mon-
Sat; 11am-7pm Sun. **Credit** AmEx, Disc, MC, V.
Map p403 E29.
The requisite clothing and accessories are sold here,
alongside in-line skates, skateboards and snow-
boards. The Upper West Side branch rents out in-
line skates for a roll in Central Park.
Other locations 156 W 72nd Street, between
Broadway & Columbus Avenue, Upper West Side
(1-212 787 3911).

Paragon Sporting Goods

*867 Broadway, at 18th Street, Flatiron District
(1-212 255 8036, www.paragonsports.com).
Subway L, N, Q, R, 4, 5, 6 to 14th Street-Union
Square.* **Open** 10am-8.30pm Mon-Fri; 10am-8pm
Sat; 11am-7pm Sun. **Credit** AmEx, DC, Disc, MC,
V. **Map** p403 E27.
Three floors of equipment and clothing for almost
every activity, from the everyday (a slew of gym
gear, trainers and sunglasses) to the more niche (bad-
minton, kayaking) make this a prime one-stop
sports-gear spot.

TICKETS

It's cheaper to buy tickets for performances
directly from the venue, but many don't offer
this option, especially for booking online. The
main booking agencies for concerts and other
events are **Ticketmaster** (1-800 745 3000,
www.ticketmaster.com) and **TicketWeb** (1-866
468 7619, www.ticketweb.com). **Telecharge**
(1-212 239 6200, www.telecharge.com) focuses
on Broadway and Off Broadway shows.

TRAVELLERS' NEEDS

Got carried away in the shops? **XS Baggage**
(1-866 656 6977, www.xsbaggage.com) will ship
a single suitcase or multiple boxes to almost
anywhere in the world, by air or sea. **Flight
001** (*see p208*) sells all manner of travel aids
and accessories. For mobile phone hire and
computer repairs, *see p197*.

CONSUME

Hotels

The city may never sleep, but you'll still want to get a room.

Accommodation is more expensive in New York City than the rest of the country and, while the average room rate dipped sharply in the wake of the financial crisis, remaining under $200 a night in summer 2009, reports from industry research specialist STR show it has been creeping up steadily since then – in autumn 2012 it was nearing $300. New construction has continued, albeit more slowly, throughout the recent economic slump, and hotel occupancy figures are strong (an average of 83 per cent, according to STR). By publication of this guide, the city will have more than 92,000 hotel rooms, according to the official tourist authority. But whether this will create a surplus that will benefit bargain-hunting travellers is anyone's guess.

STAYING IN NEW YORK

Growth areas include the Financial District, which is getting a new lease of life as the World Trade Center site redevelopment nears completion. In summer 2010, upscale chain **W Hotels** (*see p239*) debuted its flashy new property, which includes residences as well as a hotel, directly opposite the WTC, and stylish Hilton offshoot **Conrad New York** (*see p223*) took up a riverside spot in Battery Park City in spring 2012. Hell's Kitchen is popular with a trend-seeking gay clientele – the city's first gay 'urban resort', **The Out NYC** (*see p267*), opened in 2012 – and anyone who wants to be near the Theater Distict. The British team behind capsule hotel brand **Yotel** recently introduced a super-size variation on the concept in the neighbourhood (*see p241*). Hip mini chain **Ace Hotel** (*see p236*) colonised an area at the northern edge of the Flatiron District, which is emerging as a hotel (and restaurant) hotspot – the long-awaited **NoMad Hotel** (*see p237*), from the same developer, debuted in spring 2012 with a restaurant helmed by high-profile chef Daniel Humm. There is now more boutique choice in desirable areas like Nolita, Chelsea and Greenwich Village with the arrival of the **Nolitan** (*see p229*), **Hôtel Americano** (*see p234*) and the **Jade Hotel** (*see p231*). It's also worth looking to the outer boroughs for competitively priced accommodation – Brooklyn, especially, is an increasingly desirable place to stay. Even the Bronx is tipped to get a boutique hotel in mid 2013, a conversion of the borough's former Beaux Arts opera house.

PRICES AND INFORMATION

Rates can vary wildly within a single property, according to room type and season, and the prices quoted here – obtained from the hotels – reflect that disparity. Unless indicated, the rates given are for a double-occupancy room, from the cheapest in low season to the most expensive in high season. While they're not guaranteed, they offer a good indication of the hotel's average rack rates – what you would pay if you walked in off the street and asked for a room.

Special deals are often available, and you can frequently shave more off the price by booking on the hotel's website. Locally based discount agency **Quikbook** (www.quikbook.com) often has a good selection of the properties listed in this chapter on their website. For a budget option with a more personal touch, consider a B&B. Artist-run agency **City Sonnet** (1-212 614 3034, www.citysonnet.com) deals in downtown locations. Expect to pay at least $135 for a double room in a private home. For gay-oriented hotels and B&Bs, *see pp266-267*.

> ❶ Red numbers given in this chapter correspond to the location of each hotel on the street maps. See pp402-412.

Downtown

FINANCIAL DISTRICT
Expensive

★ Andaz Wall Street
*75 Wall Street, between Water Street & Pearl
Street, New York, NY 10005 (1-212 590 1234,
www.wallstreetandaz.com). Subway 2, 3, 4, 5 to
Wall Street.* **Rates** $325-$575 double. **Rooms** 253.
Credit AmEx, DC, Disc, MC, V. **Map** p402 F33 ❶
Although it's a subsidiary brand of global giant
Hyatt, Andaz prides itself in giving each property a
local flavour. Following launches in London and LA,
the first New York outpost occupies the first 13
floors of a former Barclays Bank building, outfitted
by David Rockwell. The vibe inside is anything but
corporate: upon entering the spacious, bamboo-
panelled lobby-lounge, where a barista brews
espresso from New York-based Roasting Plant,
you're greeted by a free-range 'host', who acts as
combination check-in clerk and concierge. The chic,
loft-style rooms (starting at 350sq ft) are equally
casual and user-friendly. A long, blond-wood unit
doubles as desk, entertainment console and dressing
table (the TV has a vanity mirror on the back);
remote-controlled blackout blinds descend to cover
the seven-foot windows; and non-alcoholic drinks
and snacks are free. The local-centric restaurant
(Wall & Water), bar and spa are welcome attributes
in an area with little action at weekends (note that
the gym and spa were closed for refurbishment at
time of writing).
*Bar. Concierge. Disabled-adapted rooms. Gym.
Internet (wireless, free). No-smoking rooms.
Restaurant. Room service. Spa. TV: pay movies.*
Other locations 485 Fifth Avenue, at
41st Street, Murray Hill (1-212 601 1234,
www.5thavenue.andaz.com).

Conrad New York
*102 North End Avenue, at Vesey Street (1-212
945 0100, www.conradnewyork.com). Subway A,
C, 1, 2, 3 to Chambers Street; E to World Trade
Center; R to Cortlandt Street; 2, 3 to Park Place.*
Rates $$249-$4,999 suite. **Rooms** 88. **Credit**
AmEx, DC, Disc, MC, V. **Map** p402 D31 ❷
This sophisticated Hilton offshoot fronts Battery
Park City's riverside Nelson A Rockefeller Park.
West-facing guest quarters have views of the
Hudson, but there's also plenty to see within the art-
rich, all-suite property. Sol LeWitt's vivid 100ft by
80ft painting *Loopy Doopy (Blue and Purple)* graces
the dramatic 15-storey, glass-ceilinged, marble-
floored lobby, and coolly understated suites are
adorned with pieces by the likes of Elizabeth Peyton
and Mary Heilmann. Nespresso machines and mar-
ble bathrooms with Aromatherapy Associates prod-
ucts are indulgent touches. Above the rooftop bar

Conrad New York.

The First Class Of Tourist Class.

10% Off Special*

(open May-Oct), with views of the Statue of Liberty, is a vegetable patch providing fresh produce for the North End Grill (*see p144*) next door.

Bar. Business Centre. Concierge. Disabled-adapted rooms. Gym. Internet (wireless, $15/day). Parking ($65/day). Restaurant. No smoking. Room service. TV: DVD/pay movies.

TRIBECA & SOHO

Deluxe

★ Crosby Street Hotel

79 Crosby Street, between Prince & Spring Streets, New York, NY 10012 (1-212 226 6400, www.firmdalehotels.com). Subway N, R to Prince Street; 6 to Spring Street. **Rates** $525-$755 double. **Rooms** 86. **Credit** AmEx, DC, Disc, MC, V. **Map** p403 E30 ❸

In 2009, Britain's hospitality power couple, Tim and Kit Kemp, brought their super-successful Firmdale formula across the Atlantic with the 11-storey, warehouse-style Crosby Street Hotel – their first outside London. Design director Kit Kemp's signature style – a fresh, contemporary take on classic English decor characterised by an often audacious mix of patterns, bold colours and judiciously chosen antiques – is instantly recognisable. Like its British cousins, Crosby Street has a carefully selected art collection, including a giant head by Jaume Plensa and life-size dog sculptures by Justine Smith in the lobby (a canine theme, a noticeable NYC obsession, pervades the property). Other Firmdale imports include a guests-only drawing room as well as a public restaurant and bar, a slick, 100-seat screening room and a verdant garden. The latter was inspired the bath products' exclusive scent, created by cult London perfumer Lyn Harris.

Bar. Concierge. Disabled-adapted rooms. Gym. Internet (wireless, free). No-smoking floors. Parking ($55-$65). Restaurant. Room service. TV: DVD/pay movies.

★ Greenwich Hotel

377 Greenwich Street, between Franklin & North Moore Streets, New York, NY 10013 (1-212 941 8900, www.thegreenwichhotel.com). Subway 1 to Franklin Street. **Rates** $525-$775 double. **Rooms** 88. **Credit** AmEx, DC, Disc, MC, V. **Map** p402 D31 ❹

'Deluxe guest house' might be a more fitting description of Robert De Niro's latest property, which has the vibe of a large villa located somewhere between Marrakesh and Milan. Rooms are spare and comfortable, appointed with down-filled leather settees, kilims and oriental rugs, and furnished with small libraries of art books. Exquisite Moroccan tile or carrara marble envelops the bathrooms, which have walk-in showers, while the main spaces feature wood-plank floors (beautiful to look at, but unfortunate for those staying under heavy-footed guests).

Many rooms overlook the charming courtyard – just off the drawing room, where guests lounge in over-stuffed chairs – while suites have perks such as fireplaces. The centrepiece of the subterranean Eastern-inspired Shibui Spa is the low-lit pool, set within the frame of a 250-year-old Kyoto farmhouse. Guests get priority reservations to the hotel's hot restaurant, Locanda Verde (*see p147*).

Bar. Concierge. Disabled-adapted rooms. Internet (wireless, free). No-smoking floors. Pool (indoor). Restaurant. Room service. Spa. TV: DVD/pay movies.

▶ *For more on Robert De Niro's Tribeca empire, see p58.*

The Mercer

147 Mercer Street, at Prince Street, New York, NY 10012 (1-212 966 6060, 1-888 918 6060, www.mercerhotel.com). Subway N, R to Prince Street. **Rates** $525-$975 double. **Rooms** 75. **Credit** AmEx, DC, Disc, MC, V. **Map** p403 E29 ❺

Opened in 2001 by trendsetting hotelier André Balazs, Soho's first luxury boutique hotel still has ample attractions that appeal to a celeb-heavy clientele. The lobby, appointed with oversized white couches and chairs, and shelves lined with colourful books, acts as a bar, library and lounge. The loft-like rooms are large by NYC standards and feature furniture by Christian Liagre, enormous washrooms and Face Stockholm products. The restaurant, the Mercer Kitchen, serves Jean-Georges Vongerichten's stylish version of casual American cuisine.

Bars (2). Concierge. Disabled-adapted rooms. Internet (wireless, free). No-smoking rooms. Parking ($55-$65). Restaurant. Room service. TV: DVD/pay movies.

Expensive

Duane Street Hotel

130 Duane Street, at Church Street, New York, NY 10013 (1-212 964 4600, www.duanestreet hotel.com). Subway A, C, 1, 2, 3 to Chambers Street. **Rates** $229-$729 double. **Rooms** 45. **Credit** AmEx, DC, Disc, MC, V. **Map** p402 E31 ❻

In a city with a high tolerance for hype, the Duane Street Hotel stands out by its quiet dedication to doing the simple things well. Opened on a quiet Tribeca street in 2007, the boutique property takes its cues from its well-heeled residential neighbourhood, offering loft-inspired rooms with 11ft ceilings, oversized windows and hardwood floors, and affable, unobtrusive staff. The somewhat spare modern rooms have just been given a striking monochrome redesign. Complimentary passes to the nearby swanky Equinox gym cement the value-for-money package – a rare commodity in this part of town.

Bar. Business centre. Concierge. Disabled-adapted rooms. Internet (wireless, free). No smoking. Parking ($55-$65/day). Restaurant. Room service. TV.

CONSUME

The James New York

27 Grand Street, at Thompson Street, New York, NY 10013 (1-212 465 2000, 1-888 526 3778, www.jameshotels.com). Subway A, C, E to Canal Street. **Rates** $329-$859 double. **Rooms** 114. **Credit** AmEx, DC, Disc, MC, V. **Map** p403 D30 ❼
Hotel art displays are usually limited to some eye-catching lobby installations or forgettable in-room prints. Not so at the James, which maintains a substantial showcase of local talent. The corridor of each guest floor is dedicated to the work of an individual artist, selected by a house curator and complete with museum-style notes – which makes waiting for the elevator a lot less tedious. The Chicago-based owners have given the property a distinctly Gotham vibe – even the doorstaff sport rakish uniforms (designed by Andrew Buckler) that look straight out of *Gangs of New York*. Although compact, bedrooms make the most of the available space with high ceilings, wall-spanning windows and glassed-off bathrooms (modesty is preserved by an artist- embellished, remote-controlled screen). Natural materials (wooden floors, linen duvet covers) warm up the clean contemporary lines, beds are piled with eco-friendly pillows, and bathroom products are courtesy of Intelligent Nutrients, the organic line created by Aveda founder Horst Rechelbacher. While the attractions of Soho and Tribeca beckon, the hotel also offers tempting facilities: a seasonal three-level 'urban garden', which houses an outdoor bar and eaterie (one of two restaurants on site), and a rooftop bar that opens on to the (admittedly tiny) pool.
Bars (3). Business centre. Concierge. Disabled-adapted rooms. Gym. No smoking. Internet (wireless, free). Pool. Restaurants (2). Room service. TV: pay movies.

Mondrian SoHo

9 Crosby Street, between Grand & Howard Streets, New York, NY 10013 (1-212 389 1000, www.mondriansoho.com). Subway J, N, Q, R, Z, 6 to Canal Street. **Rates** $329-$659 double. **Rooms** 270. **Credit** AmEx, DC, Disc, MC, V. **Map** p402 E30 ❽
Designed by Benjamin Noriega Ortiz, who created cool cribs for Lenny Kravitz and gave the Mondrian Los Angeles a glamorous makeover in 2008, Mondrian SoHo has a distinctly un-Gotham vibe. An ivy-covered passageway leads to the 26-storey glass tower, set back from Crosby Street. Inspired by Jean Cocteau's *La Belle et la Bête*, Ortiz has created a fanciful interior in which lobby coffee tables have talons and floor lamps are shaded with petite parasols. Trippy, saturated-blue hallways lead to rooms that combine white minimalism with classic elements such as china blue arabesque-print upholstery and marble-topped vanity sinks that perch outside the bathroom. Floor-to-ceiling windows give rooms on higher floors spectacular vistas, especially in the suites, where double banks of glass provide a panoramic sweep. Going one better than Wi-Fi,

every room is equipped with an in-room iPad that also connects to hotel services. The Italian restaurant, Isola Trattoria & Crudo Bar, offers seating in an adjacent greenhouse, fitted out with crystal chandeliers, ferns and ficus trees, while the dimly lit, cushion-strewn bar, Mister H, looks like a 1930s Shanghai opium den by way of *Casablanca*.
Bar. Disabled-adapted rooms. Gym. Internet (in-room iPad, free; wireless, $10/day). No smoking. Parking ($55-$65/day) Restaurant. Room service. TV: pay movies.

60 Thompson

60 Thompson Street, between Broome & Spring Streets, New York, NY 10012 (1-212 431 0400, 1-877 431 0400, www.thompsonhotels.com). Subway C, E to Spring Street. **Rates** $349-$769 double. **Rooms** 100. **Credit** AmEx, DC, Disc, MC, V. **Map** p403 E30 ❾
The first property of the boutique chain Thompson Hotels remains one of its best. Despite its inauspicious kick-off date of 10 September 2001, this stylish spot has been luring film, fashion and media elites since it opened. Its expansive, somewhat masculine second-floor lobby, done up in dark wood, leather and tasteful shades of beige, brown, cream and grey, sets the tone for the rooms, from the modest doubles to the spectacular duplex, the Thompson Loft, which is often booked for photo shoots. Indulgent details include Sferra linens and REN products. British designer Tara Bernerd, who created the classy contemporary interiors for the group's new London hotel, Belgraves, is behind a redesign planned for spring and summer 2013. A60, the exclusive guests-only rooftop bar, offers magnificent city views and a Moroccan-inspired decor. The hotel's acclaimed restaurant, Kittichai, serves creative Thai cuisine beside a pool filled with floating orchids; in warmer months, request a table on the pavement terrace. For other Thompson hotels in New York City, visit www. thompsonhotels.com.
Bars (2). Concierge. Disabled-adapted rooms. Gym. Internet (wireless, $15/day). No-smoking floors. Parking ($60-$70/day). Restaurant. Room service. TV: DVD/pay movies.
Other locations throughout the city.

SoHo Grand Hotel

310 West Broadway, between Canal & Grand Streets, New York, NY 10013 (1-212 965 3000, 1-800 965 3000, www.sohogrand.com). Subway A, C, E, 1 to Canal Street. **Rates** $329-$759 double. **Rooms** 363. **Credit** AmEx, DC, Disc, MC, V. **Map** p403 E30 ❿
The SoHo Grand, which pioneered the downtown hotel migration in 1996, is fresh from a revamp. The original designer, Bill Sofield, whose subtly sexy, sophisticated style is favoured by Tom Ford, recently introduced new custom pieces to the elegant brown-and-beige guest rooms, including travel trunk-inspired minibars and natty hounds-

CONSUME

Bowery House.

tooth tuxedo chairs. Bathrooms feature charming wallpaper by the late illustrator Saul Steinberg (whose work was a longtime staple of the *New Yorker*) and Kiehl's products. Endearingly, you can request a goldfish for the duration of your stay. Guests can also borrow old-fashioned bicycles in the warmer months to explore the city; after your exertions, claim a lounger in the hotel's seasonal outdoor bar-eaterie the Yard, or hole up with a cocktail by the fireplace in the Club Room, a glamorous year-round lounge. The Soho Grand's Tribeca sibling hotel is reopening after a major redesign in spring 2013.

Bars (3). Concierge. Disabled-adapted rooms. Gym. Internet (wireless, free). No smoking. Parking ($55/day). Restaurants (3). Room service. TV: DVD/pay movies.

Other locations Tribeca Grand Hotel, 2 Sixth Avenue, between Walker & White Streets, Tribeca, New York, NY 10013 (1-212 519 6600, www.tribecagrand.com).

Moderate

Cosmopolitan

95 West Broadway, at Chambers Street, New York, NY 10007 (1-212 566 1900, 1-888 895 9400, www.cosmohotel.com). Subway A, C, 1, 2, 3 to Chambers Street. **Rates** $189-$425 double. **Rooms** 126. **Credit** AmEx, DC, Disc, MC, V. **Map** p402 E31 ⓫

Despite the name, you won't find the legendary pink cocktail at this well-maintained hotel in two adjacent 1850s buildings, let alone a bar in which to drink it (though there is a café). Another handy facility is a business centre with two Macs that guests can use free of charge. Open continuously since the mid 19th century, the hotel remains a tourist favourite for its address, clean rooms and reasonable rates. A wide range of configurations is available, including a suite with two queen beds and a sofa bed, ideal for families.

Business centre. Concierge. Disabled-adapted

rooms. Internet (wireless, free). No smoking.
Parking ($45/day) Room service. TV: pay movies.

LITTLE ITALY & NOLITA
Expensive

The Nolitan
30 Kenmare Street, at Elizabeth Street,
New York, NY 10012 (1-212 925 2555,
www.nolitanhotel.com). Subway J, Z to Bowery;
6 to Spring Street. **Rates** $369-$645 double.
Rooms 55. **Credit** AmEx, DC, Disc, MC, V.
Map p403 F30 ⑫
To make like a Nolitan, check in to this boutique
hotel. The rooms feature floor-to-ceiling windows,
custom-made walnut beds, wooden floors and toiletries from Prince Street spa Red Flower. The
emphasis on keeping it local is reflected in numerous
guest perks: the luxuriously laid-back property lends
out bikes and skateboards and lays on free local
calls, access to an upscale Equinox gym and discounts at neighbourhood boutiques. The lobby's ceiling-height bookshelf is stocked with tomes from
nearby Phaidon Books. Admire views of Nolita and
beyond from the 2,400sq ft roof deck, complete with
fire pit, or your private perch – more than half the
guest quarters have balconies. Standard checkout is
2pm, so you can enjoy a leisurely last morning.
Bar. Concierge. Disabled-adapted rooms. Internet
(wireless, free). No smoking. Parking ($50/day).
Restaurant. Room service. TV: DVD/pay movies.

Budget

Bowery House
220 Bowery, between Prince & Spring Streets,
New York, NY 10012 (1-212 837 2373,
www.theboweryhouse.com). Subway J, Z to Bowery.
Rates $89-$129 double. **Rooms** 75. **Credit**
AmEx, MC, V. **Map** p403 F29 ⑬
Two young real-estate developers have transformed
a 1927 Bowery flophouse into a stylish take on a hostel. History buffs will get a kick out of the original
wainscotted corridors leading to cubicles (singles are
a cosy 35sq ft, and not all have windows) with lat-
ticework ceilings to allow air circulation. It might
not be the best bet for light sleepers, but the place is
hopping with pretty young things attracted to the
hip aesthetic and the location (across the street from
the New Museum and close to Soho and the Lower
East Side). Quarters are decorated with vintage
prints and historical photographs, and illluminated
by lightbulbs encased in 1930s and '40s mason jars;
towels and robes are courtesy of Ralph Lauren. The
immaculate (gender-segregated) communal bathrooms have rain showerheads and products from
local spa Red Flower, while the guest lounge is outfitted with chesterfield sofas, chandeliers, a huge
LCD TV and an assortment of international style
mags. There's also a 3,000sq ft roof terrace, and an

eatery serving eclectic small plates. To keep out the
riff-raff and the rowdy, guests must be over 21 and
reserve with a credit card.
Internet (wireless, free). TV (shared & Prince
Room only).

Sohotel
341 Broome Street, between Elizabeth Street &
Bowery, New York, NY 10013 (1-212 226 1482,
www.thesohotel.com). Subway J, Z to Bowery; 6 to
Spring Street. **Rates** $109-$269 double. **Rooms**
96. **Credit** AmEx, DC, Disc, MC, V. **Map** p403
F30 ⑭
Thanks to new exterior coloured-light effects, this formerly modest hotel at the nexus of Chinatown, Little
Italy and Nolita piques the curiosity of passers-by.
A recent overhaul has given the late 18th-century
building's small rooms a quirky punch, with a
mustard-and-blue colour scheme, flatscreen TVs and
exposed-brick walls. Charming touches such as ceiling fans, bathroom products from venerable NYC
apothecary CO Bigelow, hardwood floors and skylights in some quarters place the Sohotel a rung above
similarly priced establishments. Complimentary
morning tea and coffee is served in the lobby, and the
hotel staff, well aware that the place lacks a lift, are
eager to lend a helping hand on your way in and out.
Sohotel's many Regency Plus rooms ($159-$399),
which can accommodate four to five guests, are the
best bargain. Guests get a 10% discount at the on-site
craft-brew emporium, Randolph Beer.
Internet (wireless in lobby only, free). No smoking.
TV.

LOWER EAST SIDE
Expensive

Hotel on Rivington
107 Rivington Street, between Essex & Ludlow
Streets, New York, NY 10002 (1-212 475 2600,
www.hotelonrivington.com). Subway F to Delancey
Street; J, Z to Delancey-Essex Streets. **Rates** $229-
$595 double. **Rooms** 110. **Credit** AmEx, DC,
Disc, MC, V. **Map** p403 G29 ⑮
When the Hotel on Rivington opened in 2005, its
ultra-modern glass-covered façade was a novelty on
the largely low-rise Lower East Side. Now, with condos popping up on nearly every block, the building
(designed by NYC firm Grzywinski & Pons) seems
less out of place, but it remains one of the few luxury

CONSUME

hotels in the neighbourhood. Rooms are super-sleek and minimalist, with black and white decorative touches, Frette bed linen and robes, and floor-to-ceiling windows (even in the shower stalls) that offer views of Manhattan and beyond. A stylish crowd congregates in the hotel's two restaurants, Co-op Food & Drink, which serves sushi and modern American fare, and Viktor & Spoils, a contemporary taqueria and tequila bar.

Bars (2). Business centre. Concierge. Disabled-adapted rooms. Gym. Internet (wireless, free). No-smoking floors. Parking ($65/day). Restaurants (2). TV: pay movies.

Moderate

Off Soho Suites Hotel

11 Rivington Street, between Bowery & Chrystie Street, New York, NY 10002 (1-212 979 9808, 1-800 633 7646, www.offsoho.com). Subway B, D to Grand Street; F to Lower East Side-Second Avenue; J, Z to Bowery. **Rates** *$179-$299.* **Rooms** *38.* **Credit** *AmEx, DC, Disc, MC, V.* **Map** *p403 F30* ⓰

These no-frills suites have become all the more popular in recent years due to the Lower East Side's burgeoning bar and restaurant scene. The rates are a decent value for the now-thriving location, especially as all have a sitting area and access to a kitchenette. Economy options have two twin beds and a shared kitchen or, if you're travelling in a group, book a deluxe suite – with a queen bed, plus a sleeper sofa in the living area, it can accommodate four. There's also a handy coin-operated laundry in the basement.

Concierge. Disabled-adapted rooms. Gym. Internet (wireless, free). No smoking.
▶ *For more on the Lower East Side's bar scene, see p177; for restaurants, including Katz's 'When Harry Met Sally' Delicatessen, see p151.*

EAST VILLAGE

Expensive

Bowery Hotel

335 Bowery, at 3rd Street, New York, NY 10003 (1-212 505 9100, www.theboweryhotel.com). Subway B, D, F, M to Broadway-Lafayette Street; 6 to Bleecker Street. **Rates** *$325-$725 double.* **Rooms** *135.* **Credit** *AmEx, DC, Disc, MC, V.* **Map** *p403 F29* ⓱

This fanciful boutique hotel from prominent duo Eric Goode and Sean MacPherson is the capstone in the gentrification of the Bowery. Shunning minimalism, they created plush rooms that pair old-world touches (oriental rugs, wood-beamed ceilings, marble washstands) with modern amenities (Wi-Fi, flatscreen TVs, a DVD library). Tall windows offer views of historic tenements, and the property includes an antique-looking trattoria, Gemma.

Bar. Concierge. Disabled-adapted rooms. Internet (wireless, free). No-smoking rooms. Restaurant. Room service. TV: DVD.
▶ *For the hoteliers' flamboyant take on a boarding house, the Jane, see p234.*

Budget

East Village Bed & Coffee

110 Avenue C, between 7th & 8th Streets, New York, NY 10009 (1-917 816 0071, www.bedandcoffee.com). Subway F to Lower East Side-Second Avenue; L to First Avenue. **Rates** *$130-$155 double.* **Rooms** *9.* **Credit** *AmEx, DC, Disc, MC, V.* **Map** *p403 G28* ⓲

Popular with European travellers, this East Village B&B (minus the breakfast) embodies quirky downtown culture. Each of the nine guest rooms has a unique theme: for example, the Black and White Room or the Treehouse (not as outlandish as it sounds: it has an ivory and olive colour scheme, animal-print linens and a whitewashed brick wall). Owner Anne Edris encourages guests to mingle in the communal areas, which include fully equipped kitchens and three loft-like living rooms (bathrooms are also shared). When the weather's nice, sip your complimentary morning java in the private garden.

Internet (wireless, free). No smoking indoors.

Hotel 17

225 E 17th Street, between Second & Third Avenues, New York, NY 10003 (1-212 475 2845, www.hotel17ny.com). Subway L to Third Avenue; L, N, Q, R, 4, 5, 6 to 14th Street-Union Square. **Rates** *$99-$160 double.* **Rooms** *125.* **Credit** *Disc, MC, V.* **Map** *p403 F27* ⓳

Shabby chic is the best way to describe this East Village hotel a few blocks from Union Square. Past the minuscule but well-appointed lobby, the rooms are a study in contrast, as antique dressers are paired with paisley bedspreads and mismatched vintage wallpaper. Bathrooms are generally shared between two to four rooms, but they're kept immaculately clean. Over the years, the building has been featured in numerous fashion mag layouts and films

---

THE BEST CHEAP DIGS

For a deluxe sleeping compartment
The Jane. *See p234.*

For flophouse chic
Bowery House. *See p229.*

For a designer dorm
New York Loft Hostel. *See p248.*

For an eye-popping art house
Carlton Arms Hotel. *See p238.*

– including Woody Allen's *Manhattan Murder Mystery* – and has put up Madonna, and, more recently, transsexual downtown diva Amanda Lepore. Who knows who you might bump into on your way to the loo?
Concierge. Internet (wireless, free). No-smoking floors. TV.

GREENWICH VILLAGE

Expensive

The Jade Hotel
52 W 13th Street, between Fifth & Sixth Avenues, New York, NY 10011 (1-212 375 1300, www.thejadenyc.com). Subway F, M, 1, 2, 3 to 14th Street; L to Sixth Avenue; L, N, Q, R, 4, 5, 6 to 14th Street-Union Square. **Rates** $269-$599. **Rooms** 113. **Credit** AmEx, DC, Disc, MC, V. **Map** p403 E27 ②⓪
See p232 **Modern classics**.
Bar. Disabled-adapted rooms. Gym. Internet (wireless, free). No-smoking floors. Restaurant. Room service. TV.

Moderate

Washington Square Hotel
103 Waverly Place, between MacDougal Street & Sixth Avenue, New York, NY 10011 (1-212 777 9515, 1-800 222 0418, www.washingtonsquarehotel.com). Subway A, B, C, D, E, F, M to W 4th Street. **Rates** $200-$450 double. **Rooms** 152. **Credit** AmEx, DC, MC, V. **Map** p403 E28 ②①
A haven for writers and artists for decades, the 110-year-old Washington Square Hotel is suited to those seeking a quiet refuge in this storied neighborhood. After a recent hotel-wide redecoration, rooms are done up in spare art deco furnishings and an odd but pleasant colour scheme of mauve and beige. The North Square restaurant and lounge – an unsung secret with an eclectic menu – is popular with locals and NYU profs. Rates include continental breakfast. Get a south-facing room for a glimpse of the park.
Bars (2). Gym. Internet (wireless, free). No smoking. Restaurant.

Budget

Larchmont Hotel
27 W 11th Street, between Fifth & Sixth Avenues, New York, NY 10011 (1-212 989 9333, www.larchmonthotel.com). Subway F, M to 14th Street; L to Sixth Avenue. **Rates** $119-$145 double. **Rooms** 66. **Credit** AmEx, DC, Disc, MC, V. **Map** p403 E28 ②②
Housed in a 1910 Beaux Arts building, the attractive, affordable Larchmont is great value for this area. The basic decor has been spruced up with new IKEA furniture and flatscreen TVs, but with

prices this reasonable, you can accept less than glossy-mag style. All the bathrooms are shared, but rooms come with a washbasin, toiletries, bathrobe and slippers. Continental breakfast is included in the rate.
Internet (wireless, free). No smoking. TV.

WEST VILLAGE & MEATPACKING DISTRICT

Expensive

Gansevoort Meatpacking NYC
18 Ninth Avenue, at 13th Street, New York, NY 10014 (1-212 206 6700, www.hotel gansevoort.com). Subway A, C, E to 14th Street; L to Eighth Avenue. **Rates** $345-$525 double. **Rooms** 186. **Credit** AmEx, DC, Disc, MC, V. **Map** p403 C28 ②③
A Meatpacking District pioneer, the Gansevoort is now known for its tri-level rooftop pool-lounge-playgrounds at two NYC locations. The lobby features four 18ft light boxes that change colour throughout the evening, while the rooms have just received a glam makeover that brought fuchsia, plum and metallic accents and Studio 54-inspired photography that plays on the hotel's reputation as a party hub. But the real draw is floor-to-ceiling windows offering incredible views of the Meatpacking District and beyond; unfortunately, the glass is not quite thick enough to keep out noise from the street (even on the eighth floor) and rooms can be draughty in winter. Still, the mini balconies, plush feather beds atop excellent mattresses and Cutler toiletries in the marble bathrooms counterbalance these minor gripes. Spending some time on the roof is a must in any season: the garden has a heated pool (with underwater music) that is enclosed in winter, a bar (Plunge) and, of course, a 360-degree panorama.
Bars (2). Business centre. Disabled-adapted rooms. Gym. Internet (wireless, free). No-smoking floors. Parking ($40/day). Pool (indoor/outdoor). Restaurant. Room service. Spa. TV: DVD/ pay movies.
Other locations 420 Park Avenue South, at 29th Street, enter on 29th Street, Flatiron District (1-212 317 2900, www.gansevoortpark.com).

Soho House
29-35 Ninth Avenue, at W 13th Street, New York, NY 10014 (1-212 627 9800, www. sohohouseny.com). Subway A, C, E to 14th Street; L to Eighth Avenue. **Rates** $400-$1,100 double. **Rooms** 30. **Credit** AmEx, MC, V. **Map** p403 C27 ②④
From its origins as a private members' club in London, Soho House has expanded its empire beyond NYC to LA, Miami, Berlin and Toronto. Designed as a place for creative types to relax, socialise and work, the converted warehouse space

CONSUME

is split into six levels, housing a spa, a library, a screening room, a restaurant and bar – complete with a wood-burning fireplace – and a rooftop pool. You don't have to be a member to stay here, but membership perks apply. The rooms offer the kind of understated luxury you'd actually like to live with: plush rugs on wooden floors, antique chandeliers hanging from wood-beamed ceilings and, in some cases, elaborately carved beds. Showers are stocked with the house spa's divine-smelling Cowshed toiletries, and a selection of things you may have forgotten to pack (hairbrush, dental kit) are available to buy, as well as some cheeky extras (love dice, condoms).

Bar. Concierge. Disabled-adapted rooms. Internet (wireless, free). No smoking. Parking ($45/day).

Pool (outdoor). Restaurant. Room service. Spa. TV: DVD.

The Standard

848 Washington Street, at 13th Street, New York, NY 10014 (1-212 645 4646, www.standardhotels.com). Subway A, C, E to 14th Street; L to Eighth Avenue. **Rates** $295-$1,100 double. **Rooms** 337. **Credit** AmEx, DC, Disc, MC, V. **Map** p403 C27 ㉕

André Balazs's lauded West Coast mini-chain arrived in New York in early 2009. Straddling the High Line, the retro 18-storey structure has been configured to give each room an exhilarating view, either of the river or a midtown cityscape. Quarters are compact, but the combination of floor-to-ceiling

Modern classics

Some of the newest hotels look decidedly old-fashioned.

A magnificent limestone Beaux Arts edifice topped with a copper cupola, the **NoMad Hotel** (*see p237*) looks like a venerable institution that's been putting up affluent travellers for decades. In the opulent lobby, meticulously restored elaborate ceiling mouldings and mosaic-tile floors evoke the belle époque. Yet the NoMad isn't a century-old landmark hotel; a 1903 former office building was given the air of a grande dame with Art Nouveau light fixtures, found in Paris's Marché aux Puces St-Ouen de Clignancourt and painstakingly reproduced period furniture. 'The first time I saw the building, it reminded me of something very Parisian and Haussmann-esque,' says owner Andrew Zobler, and this first impression largely informed the style of the hotel. Zobler enlisted Jacques Garcia, known for designing celebrated rue Saint-

Honoré A-list crash pad Hôtel Costes, to create the opulent interiors.

After seeing a photo in a design book of Garcia's old Paris flat, Zobler encouraged him to bring the same lived-in bohemian style to the hotel's guest quarters. Vintage Heriz rugs soften the weathered maple floor, salvaged from a 1905 factory, and in keeping with the residential aesthetic, the wall concealing the loo and shower cubicle is dressed up as a damask 'screen'. Many rooms feature old-fashioned claw-foot bathtubs, and the exclusive argan-oil products were supplied by provençal perfumer Côté Bastide. Each room has its own travel-themed art collection, amassed from French antique shops.

A vintage aesthetic informed the design of the neighbouring **Ace Hotel** (*see p236*), also developed by Zobler. Designers

The NoMad Hotel.

windows, curving tambour wood panelling (think old-fashioned roll-top desks) and 'peekaboo' bathrooms (with Japanese-style tubs or huge showerheads and Kiss My Face products) give a sense of space. Eating and drinking options include a chop house, a beer garden and an exclusive top-floor bar with a massive jacuzzi and 180-degree views. *Bars (4). Concierge. Disabled-adapted rooms. Gym. Internet (wireless, free). No smoking. Parking ($55-$70/day). Restaurants (2). Room service. TV: pay movies.*
► *For more about the High Line, see p82.* **Profile.**
Other locations 25 Cooper Square, between 5th & 6th Streets, New York, NY 10003 (1-212 475 5700).

Moderate

Abingdon Guest House

21 Eighth Avenue, between Jane & 12th Streets, New York, NY 10014 (1-212 243 5384, www.abingdonguesthouse.com). Subway A, C, E to 14th Street; L to Eighth Avenue. Rates $159-$250 double. **Rooms** 9. **Credit** AmEx, DC, Disc, MC, V. **Map** p403 D28 ㉖

A charming option in a charming neighbourhood on the Meatpacking District's borders: rooms in the Abingdon's two converted townhouses are done up in bold colours, plush fabrics and antique furnishings, and sport homespun details such as original 1950s pine floors, hooked rugs, and four-poster or sleigh beds. Although all rooms have private baths,

Jade Hotel.

Stephen Alesch and Robin Standefer of Roman & Williams combined custom-made furnishings with pieces from different periods to interesting effect. In the lobby, where 1970s seating mingles with industrial salvage, the bar is housed in a panelled library salvaged from a Madison Avenue apartment.

With its Georgian-style portico decorated with carved stone friezes, decorative brickwork and a 50ft copper-clad bay window detail, the **Jade Hotel** (*see p231*) is indistinguishable from the prewar apartment buildings in its Greenwich Village locale. But the sensitively conceived 18-storey structure was built from scratch. The retro appearance carries on in the lobby, where a fireplace, tin ceiling and bookshelves stocked with tomes written by illustrious one-time Village residents such as Walt Whitman and Jack Kerouac greet guests. The bar and restaurant, the

Grapevine, takes its name from a defunct local speakeasy and evokes snug glamour through distressed mirrors and plush red velvet banquettes. The rooms, designed by Andres Escobar in an art deco style, feature marble-inlaid Macassar ebony desks inspired by a piece by early 20th-century master furniture-maker Emile-Jacques Ruhlmann, chrome period lamps and champagne satin poufs – to preserve the period illusion, the TV is secreted behind a decorative cabinet. The classic black-and-white tiled bathrooms (stocked with toiletries from venerable Village pharmacy CO Bigelow) and the fact that there are only five to seven rooms per floor evoke the feel of a residential building. Some rooms have private terraces, floor-to-ceiling windows or cosy window seats, and many offer amazing views – of 1 World Trade Center rising to the south or the Empire State and Chrysler Buildings to the north.

CONSUME

they may not be inside the room. The Ambassador has a kitchenette, while the Garden Room has a small private courtyard.
Internet (wireless, free). No smoking.

★ The Jane

113 Jane Street, at West Street, New York, NY 10014 (1-212 924 6700, www.thejanenyc.com). Subway A, C, E to 14th Street; L to Eighth Avenue. **Rates** $225-$325 double. **Rooms** 208. **Credit** AmEx, DC, Disc, MC, V. **Map** p403 D28 ㉗

Opened in 1907 as the American Seaman's Friend Society Sailors Home, the 14-storey landmark was a residential hotel when hoteliers Eric Goode and Sean MacPherson of the Bowery and the Maritime took it over. The wood-panelled, 50sq ft rooms ($99-$115) were inspired by vintage train sleeper compartments: there's a single bed with built-in storage and brass hooks for hanging up your clothes – but also iPod docks and wall-mounted flatscreen TVs. If entering the hotel feels like stepping on to a film set, there's good reason. Inspiration came from various celluloid sources, including *Barton Fink*'s Hotel Earle for the lobby. The 'ballroom', decorated with mismatched chairs, oriental rugs and a fireplace topped with a stuffed ram, evokes an eccentric mansion.

Bar. Disabled-adapted rooms. Internet (wireless, free). No-smoking rooms. Restaurant. Room service. TV: DVD.

Midtown

CHELSEA

Expensive

Dream Downtown

355 W 16th Street, between Eighth & Ninth Avenues, New York, NY 10011 (1-212 229 2559, www.dreamdowntown.com). Subway A, C, E to 14th Street; L to Eighth Avenue. **Rates** from $395. **Rooms** 316. **Credit** AmEx, DC, Disc, MC, V. **Map** p403 D27 ㉘

Be sure to pack your totem: staying at the latest property from hotel wunderkind Vikram Chatwal may make you wonder if you're in a dream within a Dream. The expansive, tree-shaded lobby, furnished with curvy, metallic-lizard banquettes, and presided over by a DJ nightly, provides an overhead view of swimmers doing laps in the glass-bottomed pool on the terrace above. Housed in the former annex of the New York Maritime Union (now the adjacent Maritime Hotel, *see p235*), the surreal building is riddled with round windows. In the upper-floor rooms, these frame elements of the Manhattan skyline, such as the Empire State Building, in intriguing ways and are picked up by circular mirrors and wallpaper motifs. Quarters combine classic elements (white chesterfield chairs or sofas, Tivoli radios, Turkish

rugs) with futuristic touches like shiny steel bathtubs in some rooms. The hotel recreates a 'beach club' experience on its pool deck with a sandy patch and suites that lead directly on to the pool area from ivy-concealed private spaces. To complete the indulgent vibe, guests can even book massages or other spa treatments in one of the outdoor cabanas. Also channelling the feel of a luxury resort, the rooftop PH-D (short for Penthouse Dream) bar-nightclub has a lushly planted terrace running the entire length of the building and overlooking the pool.

Bars (4). Concierge. Disabled-adapted rooms. Gym. No smoking. Internet (wireless, free). Pool. Restaurants (2). Room service. TV: pay movies.

Eventi

851 Sixth Avenue, between 29th & 30th Streets, New York NY 10001 (1-212 564 4567, www.eventihotel.com). Subway B, D, F, M, N, Q, R to 34th Street-Herald Square; N, R to 28th Street. **Rates** $279-$599 double. **Rooms** 292. **Credit** AmEx, DC, Disc, MC, V. **Map** p404 D25 ㉙

This modern 23-floor hotel takes a playful approach to interior design, planting unexpected features in the lobby – a large-scale reproduction of 19th-century British artist Thomas Benjamin Kennington's *Autumn* peeks out tantalisingly from behind velvet drapes, for instance. Managed by Kimpton, which is known for its informal, friendly ethos, flamboyant decor and nice perks like free wine and cheese gatherings in the evening, accommodation is surprisingly luxurious. The spacious rooms (which feel even more open thanks to floor-to-ceiling outlooks) have either a king-size bed or two queens, outfitted with dapper gray fabric headboards and Frette linens. Cool marble bathrooms are stocked with swanky Etro products. For an on-site bite, choose between the sprawling, indoor-outdoor farm-to-table eaterie Humphrey or Brighton, a boardwalk-style food court with a fish shack, burger joint and pizzeria. There's also a spa.

Bar. Business centre. Concierge. Disabled-adapted rooms. Gym. Internet (wireless, $10/day). No smoking. Parking ($50/day). Restaurant. Room service. Spa. TV: DVD/pay movies.

Hôtel Americano

518 W 27th Street, between Tenth & Eleventh Avenues, New York, NY 10001 (1-212 216 0000, www.hotel-americano.com). Subway C, E to 23rd Street. **Rates** $265-$650 double. **Rooms** 56. **Credit** AmEx, DC, Disc, MC, V. **Map** p404 C26 ㉚

You won't find any Talavera tiles in Grupo Habita's first property outside Mexico. Mexican architect Enrique Norten's sleek, mesh-encased structure stands alongside the High Line (*see p82* **Profile**). The decor evokes classic midcentury American style, interpreted by a European (Colette designer Arnaud Montigny). The minimalist rooms have Japanese-style platform beds, iPads and, in one of several subtle nods to US culture, super-soft denim bathrobes.

CONSUME

After a day of gallery-hopping, get an even more elevated view of the neighbourhood from the rooftop bar and grill, where a petite pool does double duty as a hot tub in winter. There's also an airy ground-floor eaterie and two subterranean bars. *Photos p236.* *Bars (3). Concierge. Disabled-adapted rooms. No smoking. Internet (wireless, free). Pool. Restaurants (2). Room service. TV.*
▶ *For our picks of the many galleries in Chelsea, see p206.*

Maritime Hotel
363 W 16th Street, between Eighth & Ninth Avenues, New York, NY 10011 (1-212 242 4300, www.themaritimehotel.com). Subway A, C, E to 14th Street; L to Eighth Avenue. **Rates** $255-$435 double. **Rooms** 126. **Credit** AmEx, DC, Disc, MC, V. **Map** p403 C27 ③①

Steve Zissou would feel at home at this nautically themed hotel (the former headquarters of the New York Maritime Union), which is outfitted with self-consciously hip details befitting a Wes Anderson film. Standard rooms are modelled on cruise cabins; lined with teak panelling and sporting a single porthole window, they're small but well appointed (CO Bigelow products in the bathroom, a Kiki de Montparnasse 'pleasure kit' in the minibar, a well-curated DVD collection available by phone). The hotel's busy Italian restaurant, La Bottega, also supplies room service, and the adjoining bar hosts a crowd of models and mortals, who throng the umbrella-lined patio in warmer weather.
Bars (4). Concierge. Disabled-adapted rooms. Gym. Internet (wireless, free). No-smoking floors. Restaurant. Room service. TV: DVD/ pay movies.

Dream Downtown.

Moderate

The Inn on 23rd

131 W 23rd Street, between Sixth & Seventh Avenues, New York, NY 10011 (1-212 463 0330, www.innon23rd.com). Subway F, M, 1 to 23rd Street. **Rates** $239-$399 double. **Rooms** 13. **Credit** AmEx, Disc, MC, V. **Map** p404 D26 ☷

This renovated 19th-century townhouse offers the charm of a traditional B&B with enhanced amenities (a lift, pillow-top mattresses, private bathrooms, white-noise machines). Owners and innkeepers Annette and Barry Fisherman have styled each of the bedrooms with a unique theme, such as Maritime, Bamboo and 1940s. One of its best attributes is the 'library', a cosy jumble of tables and chairs open 24/7 to guests for coffee and tea; there are also wine and cheese receptions on Friday and Saturday evenings. Another nice perk: guests receive 25% off the bill at the Guilty Goose, the owners' modern American brasserie on the ground floor. *Concierge. Disabled-adapted rooms. Internet (high-speed, wireless, free). No smoking. Restaurant. TV: DVD (on request).*

Budget

Chelsea Lodge

318 W 20th Street, between Eighth & Ninth Avenues, New York, NY 10011 (1-212 243 4499, www.chelsealodge.com). Subway C, E to 23rd Street. **Rates** $144-$169 double. **Rooms** 26. **Credit** AmEx, DC, Disc, MC, V. **Map** p403 D27 ☷

Situated in a landmark brownstone blocks from the Chelsea gallery district, Chelsea Lodge is a long way from any arcadian idylls. Yet the rustic name is reflected in the mishmash of Americana that adorns the pine panelling of the inn's public spaces, such as rough-hewn duck decoys, cut-out roosters and early 20th-century photos. While all of the mostly tiny rooms come with TVs, showers and seasonal air-conditioning, most share toilets, so it's not for everyone. Still, the low prices and undeniable charm mean that it can fill up quickly. For more privacy, book one of the four suites (from $229) down the block at 334 West 20th Street: all are former studio apartments with kitchenettes, and those at the back have direct access to a private courtyard. *No smoking. TV.*

FLATIRON DISTRICT & UNION SQUARE

Expensive

★ Ace Hotel New York

20 W 29th Street, at Broadway, New York, NY 10012 (1-212 679 2222, www.acehotel.com). Subway N, R to 28th Street. **Rates** $359-$509 double. **Rooms** 265. **Credit** AmEx, Disc, MC, V. **Map** p404 E26 ☷

Hotel Americano. *See p234.*

Bourgeois hipsters tired of crashing on couches will appreciate the New York outpost of the cool chainlet that was founded in Seattle by a pair of DJs. The musical influence is clear: many of the rooms in the 1904 building have playful amenities such as functioning turntables, stacks of vinyl and gleaming Gibson guitars. And while you'll pay a hefty amount for the sprawling loft spaces, there are more reasonable options for those on a smaller budget. The respectable 'medium' rooms are fitted with vintage furniture and original art; even cheaper are the snug bunk-bed set-ups. Should you find the latter lodging stifling, repair to the buzzing hotel lobby, where DJs or other music-makers are on duty every night; have a drink at the bar, sheltered within a panelled library salvaged from a Madison Avenue apartment, or sip coffee from the Stumptown café – the first in the city from the artisan Oregon roasters. Guests can also score a table at chef April Bloomfield's massively popular restaurants, the Breslin Bar & Dining Room (*see p164*) and the John Dory Oyster Bar (*see p166*). There's even an outpost of one of the city's hippest boutiques, Opening Ceremony, in case you find you haven't a thing to wear.
Bars (3). Business centre. Concierge. Disabled-adapted rooms. Gym. Internet (wireless, free). No-smoking floors. Parking ($55-$65/day). Restaurants (2). Room service. TV: pay movies.

★ The NoMad Hotel

1170 Broadway, at 28th Street, New York, NY 10001 (1-212 796 1500, www.thenomad hotel.com). Subway N, R to 28th Street. **Rates** $395-$595 double. **Rooms** 168. **Credit** AmEx, DC, Disc, MC, V. **Map** p404 E26 ③
See p232 **Modern classics.**
Bars (2). Concierge. Disabled-adapted rooms. Internet (wireless, free). Gym. No smoking. Parking. Restaurant. Room service. TV: pay movies.

GRAMERCY PARK & MURRAY HILL

Deluxe

Gramercy Park Hotel

2 Lexington Avenue, at 21st Street, New York, NY 10010 (1-212 920 3300, www.gramercy parkhotel.com). Subway 6 to 23rd Street. **Rates** $675-$725 double. **Rooms** 192. **Credit** AmEx, DC, Disc, MC, V. **Map** p404 F26 ③
New Yorkers held their collective breath when hotelier Ian Schrager announced he was revamping the Gramercy Park Hotel, a 1924 gem that had hosted everyone from Humphrey Bogart to David Bowie. They needn't have worried: the redesigned lobby, unveiled in 2006, retains the boho spirit with its stuccoed walls, red banquettes, an enormous Venetian chandelier and working fireplace designed by Julian Schnabel, and artwork by Jean-Michel

Basquiat, Andy Warhol, Richard Prince and Damien Hirst. The eclectic elegance continues in the spacious rooms, with a jewel-toned colour palette, tapestry-covered chairs, hand-tufted rugs, mahogany drinks cabinets and iPads. Have brunch on the 18th-floor Gramercy Terrace, which features a retractable roof, get a facial at the in-house spa, or sip cocktails at the Schnabel-designed Rose and Jade bars. Danny Meyer's trattoria, Maialino (*see p166*), recently bumped up the attractions.
Bars (2). Concierge. Disabled-adapted rooms. Gym. Internet (wireless, $16/day). No-smoking floors. Parking ($65-$75/day). Restaurants (2). Room service. Spa. TV: DVD/pay movies.

Expensive

Morgans

237 Madison Avenue, between 37th & 38th Streets, New York, NY 10016 (1-212 686 0300, 1-800 334 3408, www.morganshotel.com). Subway S, 4, 5, 6, 7 to 42nd Street-Grand Central. **Rates** $309-$419 double. **Rooms** 113. **Credit** AmEx, DC, Disc, MC, V. **Map** p404 E24 ③
New York's original boutique hotel, Morgans opened in 1984. Some 25 years later, the hotel's designer, octogenerian French tastemaker Andrée Putman, returned to officiate over a revamp that has softened its stark monochrome appearance. Unfussy bedrooms, cast in a calming palette of silver, grey, cream and white, are hung with original Robert Mapplethorpe prints; window seats piled with linen cushions encourage quiet reflection. The bathrooms, with classic black and white tiles, offer products from NYC's Malin + Goetz. The guests' living room, stocked with coffee and tea, is equally understated.
Bar. Business centre. Concierge. Disabled-adapted rooms. Internet (wireless, $10/day). No smoking. Room service. TV: pay movies.

Moderate

Marcel at Gramercy

201 E 24th Street, at Third Avenue, New York, NY 10010 (1-212 696 3800, www.themarcelat gramercy.com). Subway 6 to 23rd Street. **Rates** $199-$399 double. **Rooms** 135. **Credit** AmEx, Disc, MC, V. **Map** p404 F26 ③
Revamped in early 2008, this fashionable hotel has a hip aesthetic that extends from the lobby, with its marble concierge desk, sprawling leather banquette

CONSUME

and in-house library, to the medium-sized rooms, which offer a sleek black and pewter palette, rainhead showers and Egyptian-cotton linens. If you fancy a nightcap, retreat to the subterranean Polar lounge, an Arctic-themed nightspot with 'ice' tables and private party 'caves'.

Bar. Business centre. Concierge. Disabled-adapted rooms. Internet (wireless, $10/day). No-smoking floors. Room service. TV: DVD (on request).

Budget

★ Carlton Arms Hotel

160 E 25th Street, at Third Avenue, New York, NY 10010 (1-212 679 0680, www.carlton arms.com). Subway 6 to 23rd Street. **Rates** $110-$130 double. **Rooms** 54. **Credit** MC, V. **Map** p404 F26 ③

The Carlton Arms Art Project started in the late 1970s, when a small group of creative types brought fresh paint and new ideas to a run-down shelter. Today, the site is a bohemian backpackers' paradise and a live-in gallery – every room, bathroom and hallway is festooned with outré artwork. Themed quarters include the Money Room and a tribute to a traditional English cottage. Roughly half of the quarters have shared bathrooms. The place gets booked up early, so reserve well in advance.

Internet (wireless, shared monitor free).

The Pod Hotel

145 E 39th Street, between Lexington & Third Avenues, New York, NY 10016 (1-212 865 5700, www.thepodhotel.com). Subway S, 4, 5, 6, 7 to 42nd Street-Grand Central. **Rates** $119-$235 double. **Rooms** 366. **Credit** AmEx, DC, MC, V. **Map** p404 F24 ④

The city's second Pod occupies a 1918 residential hotel for single men – the space that was once the gentlemen's sitting room is being reinvented as the Great Room, opening in early 2013, which will feature a fireplace, projection wall and ping-pong table. As the name suggests, rooms are snug, but not oppressively so; some have queen-size beds with room underneath to stash your luggage; others feature stainless-steel bunk beds with individual TVs and bedside shelves inspired by airplane storage. However, you should probably know your roommate well since the utilitarian, subway-tiled bathrooms are partitioned off with sliding frosted-glass doors. Travel-friendly, soft-packaged Fix products by NYC spa Red Flower match the functional aesthetic. Restaurant dream team April Bloomfield (*see p165* **Profile**) and Ken Friedman is behind the on-site taqueria and bar, Salvation Taco, and the roof terrace has a full-frontal Empire State Building view.

Bar. Concierge. Disabled-adapted rooms. Internet (wireless, free). No smoking. Restaurant. TV.
Other locations 230 E 51st Street, at Third Avenue (1-212 355 0300).

HERALD SQUARE & GARMENT DISTRICT
Moderate

★ Hotel Metro

45 W 35th Street, between Fifth & Sixth Avenues, New York, NY 10001 (1-212 947 2500, 1-800 356 3870, www.hotelmetronyc.com). Subway B, D, F, M, N, Q, R to 34th Street-Herald Square. **Rates** $190-$475 double. **Rooms** 181. **Credit** AmEx, DC, MC, V. **Map** p404 E25 ④

It may not be trendy, but the Metro is that rare thing: a solid, good-value hotel that is extremely well maintained. Every two years, the owners start renovating the rooms, floor by floor, starting at the top; by the time they're finished it's almost time to start again. So even 'old' rooms are virtually new. The stylishly contemporary quarters feature marble-topped furniture and beige leather-effect headboards; premier rooms have luxurious rain showers. Unusually for New York, the hotel offers 18 family rooms, consisting of two adjoining bedrooms (one with two beds and a table) and a door that closes. Also rare – a generous continental breakfast buffet is offered in the guests' lounge (or take it in the homey adjoining library), outfitted with several large TVs. The rooftop bar (which is open from April to October) has views of the Empire State Building.

Bar. Business centre. Concierge. Disabled-adapted rooms. Gym. Internet (wireless, free). No-smoking floors. Restaurant. Room service. TV: pay movies.

THEATER DISTRICT & HELL'S KITCHEN
Deluxe

The Chatwal New York

130 W 44th Street, between Sixth Avenue & Broadway, New York, NY 10036 (1-212 764 6200, www.thechatwalny.com). Subway N, Q, R, S, 1, 2, 3 to 42nd Street-Times Square. **Rates** $795-$920 double. **Rooms** 76. **Credit** AmEx, DC, Disc, MC, V. **Map** p404 D24 ④

In a city awash with faux deco and incongruous nods to the style, the Chatwal New York opened in August 2010 in a Stanford White building whose interior art deco restoration is pitch perfect. Hotelier Sant Chatwal entrusted the design of this 1905 Beaux Arts building (formerly the clubhouse for the Lamb's Club), America's first professional theatre organisation) to Thierry Despont, who worked on the centennial restoration of the Statue of Liberty and the interiors of the J Paul Getty Museum in Los Angeles. The result is one of the most glamorous hotels in the Theater District, if not the city. The gracious lobby is adorned with murals recalling the hotel's New York roots and theatrical pedigree – past members of the Lamb's Club include Oscar Hammerstein, Charlie Chaplin, John Wayne and Fred Astaire. The theatrical past is further evoked by black and white photographs in the hotel's restaurant, helmed by Geoffrey Zakarian, which takes its name from the club. The elegant rooms feature vintage Broadway posters as well as hand-tufted Shifman mattresses, 400-thread count Frette linens and custom Asprey toiletries; select rooms have spacious terraces. *Bar. Business centre. Concierge. Disabled-adapted rooms. Gym. Internet (wireless, free). No-smoking floors. Pool. Restaurant. Room service. Spa. TV: pay movies.*

Expensive

The London NYC

151 W 54th Street, between Sixth & Seventh Avenues, New York, NY 10019 (1-866 690 2029, www.thelondonnyc.com). Subway B, D, E to Seventh Avenue. **Rates** $299-$899 suite. **Rooms** 561. **Credit** AmEx, DC, Disc, MC, V. **Map** p405 D22 ⓭
This 54-storey high-rise was completely overhauled by David Collins (designer of some of London's most fashionable bars and restaurants) and reopened as the London NYC in early 2007. The designer's sleek, contemporary-British style pervades the rooms, with attractive signature touches such as limed oak parquet flooring, embossed leather travel trunks at the foot of the beds, hand-woven throws and inventive coffee tables that adjust to dining-table height. But space is perhaps the biggest luxury: the 350-500sq ft London Suites (the starting-priced accommodation) are either open-plan or divided with mirrored French doors, and bathrooms feature double rain showerheads. Upper-floor Vista Suites command city views. The London is, appropriately, the site of two eateries from Britain's best-known celebrity chef, the eponymous Gordon Ramsay at the London and the less formal (and less expensive) Maze. The chef also oversees the room service menu.
Bar. Business centre. Concierge. Disabled-adapted rooms. Gym. Internet (wireless, free). No-smoking floors. Parking ($55-$65/day). Restaurants (2). Room service. TV: DVD/pay movies.

**THE BEST
INDULGENT BOLT-HOLES**

For nouveau opulence
The NoMad Hotel. *See p237.*

For a surreal escape
Dream Downtown. *See p234.*

For celebrity-chef room service
The London NYC. *See above.*

For the dreamiest bed
The Surrey. *See p244.*

W New York-Times Square

1567 Broadway, at 47th Street, New York, NY 10036 (1-212 930 7400, 1-888 627 8680, www.whotels.com). Subway N, Q, R to 49th Street; 1 to 50th Street. **Rates** $314-$699. **Rooms** 509. **Credit** AmEx, DC, Disc, MC, V. **Map** p404 D23 ⓮
The sleek and modern aesthetic of the W brand is on full display at the entrance to this 50-storey tower – featuring a dimly lit, glassed-in waterfall ceiling – and even more so once you reach the hushed and dramatic seventh-floor lobby and lounge. The attention to atmospheric detail fades a bit in the rooms, though, due to a drab taupe colour scheme punctuated by works of art and hot-pink Lucite bedstand cubes. Squint, though, and you'll feel cool amid the minimalism, especially thanks to all sorts of clever in-room lighting options and a well-designed bathroom stocked with Bliss products. And the wonderfully comfortable beds and sparkling Times Square views go quite a long way. Service is friendly and polished, and there's a hip in-house fish restaurant, Blue Fin.
Bar. Business centre. Concierge. Disabled-adapted rooms. Gym. Internet (wireless, $15/day). No-smoking floors. Parking ($55/day). Restaurant. Room service. TV: DVD, pay movies.
Other locations throughout the city.

Moderate

Distrikt Hotel

342 W 40th Street, between Eighth & Ninth Avenues, New York, NY 10018 (1-212 706 6100, www.distrikthotel.com). Subway A, C, E to 42nd Street-Port Authority. **Rates** $199-$509 double. **Rooms** 155. **Credit** AmEx, DC, Disc, MC, V. **Map** p404 C24 ⓯
Although it's on an unlovely street alongside Port Authority, this hotel has much to recommend it. Distrikt's subtle Manhattan theme is conceptual. Each of the 31 guest floors is named after one of the city's beloved 'hoods (Harlem, Soho, Chelsea and so on) and a backlit photo collage created by local artist Chris Rubino adorns the hallways; smaller framed versions liven up the rooms, which are otherwise coolly neutral, with luxury features such as Frette linens and marble in the bathrooms. Request a higher floor for Hudson River or Times Square views – the rates rise accordingly. A 14ft 'living wall' representing Central Park anchors the lobby, but what really impresses are the three big iMacs equipped with free Wi-Fi for guest use.
Bar. Business Centre. Concierge. Disabled-adapted rooms. No smoking. Internet (wireless, free). Restaurant. Room service. TV.

★ 414 Hotel

414 W 46th Street, between Ninth & Tenth Avenues, New York, NY 10036 (1-212 399 0006, www.414hotel.com). Subway A, C, E to 42nd Street-Port Authority. **Rates** $169-$299

double. **Rooms** 22. **Credit** AmEx, DC, MC, V.
Map p404 C23 ⓯

This reasonably priced hotel truly deserves the 'boutique' tag. Nearly everything about it is exquisite yet unshowy, from its power-blasted brick exterior to the modern colour scheme in the rooms that pairs pale walls with grey headboards and red accents. Rooms are equipped with fridges, flatscreen TVs and iPod docks, the bathrooms are immaculate, and a working gas fireplace in the lobby is a welcoming touch. The 414 is twice as big as it looks, as it consists of two townhouses separated by a leafy courtyard – in the warmer months, this is a lovely spot to eat your complimentary breakfast of fresh croissants and bagels. The location in a residential yet central neighbourhood makes it even more of a find.
Concierge. Internet (wireless, shared terminal, free). No smoking. TV.

Hotel Edison

228 W 47th Street, at Broadway, New York, NY 10036 (1-212 840 5000, 1-800 637 7070, www.edisonhotelnyc.com). Subway N, Q, R to 49th Street; 1 to 50th Street. **Rates** $99-$400 double. **Rooms** 800. **Credit** AmEx, DC, Disc, MC, V. **Map** p404 D23 ⓱

This 1931 art deco hotel retains enough original touches – such as gorgeous elevator doors and brass door handles – to evoke old New York. Its affordable rates and proximity to Broadway's theatres seal it as the ideal Gotham hotel for many guests. The no-frills rooms are standard in size, and clean, if also devoid of personality. For more upscale

accommodation, the newly renovated Signature Collection quarters on the 19th and 20th floors feature 32in flatscreen TVs, upgraded bedding, free Wi-Fi and Times Square or river views from some suites. Café Edison, a classic diner just off the lobby, is a long-time fave of Broadway actors – Neil Simon was so smitten that he put it in one of his plays.
Bar. Business centre. Concierge. Disabled-adapted rooms. Gym. Internet (wireless, cost varies depending plan selected). No smoking. Parking ($45-$60/day). Restaurants (2). TV: pay movies.

Stay

157 W 47th Street, between Sixth & Seventh Avenues, 1-212 766 3700, 1-866 950 7829, www.stayhotelny.com). Subway N, Q, R to 49th Street; 1 to 50th Street. **Rates** $159-$340 double. **Rooms** 210. **Credit** AmEx, DC, Disc, MC, V. **Map** p405 D23 ⓳

Hotel mastermind Vikram Chatwal now has a portfolio of five NYC properties – the others are Dream, Dream Downtown (*see p234*), Night, and Time. Stay, which opened in autumn 2008, is the most accessible, but it has several of his signature theatrical lobby flourishes: a huge, tubular tropical fish tank, trippy light effects and snowy seating. In contrast, rooms are sleek but non-statement, decorated in dark wood with copper accents; the Bose Wave radio/iPod docks are a nice detail. Also fitting in with the group's formula, Stay has a striking bar/restaurant/ nightclub, the Aspen Social Club, which replicates a slightly surreal log hunting lodge with aged leather seating and an eye-popping antler-themed light installation in the dining area.

Yotel New York.

Bar. Business centre. Concierge. Disabled-adapted rooms. Internet (wireless in lobby only, free; high-speed, $10/day). No smoking. Parking ($30). Restaurant. Room service. TV: pay movies.
▶ *For Vikram Chatwal's other NYC properties, visit www.vikramchatwalhotels.com.*

★ Yotel New York

570 Tenth Avenue, at 42nd Street, New York, NY 10036 (1-646 449 7700, www.yotel.com). Subway A, C, E to 42nd Street-Port Authority. **Rates** *$149-$399 double.* **Rooms** *669.* **Credit** *AmEx, DC, Disc, MC, V.* **Map** *p404 C24* ⓭

The British team behind this futuristic hotel is known for luxury airport-based capsule accommodation that giveS long-haul travellers just enough space to get horizontal between flights. Yotel New York has ditched the 75sq ft cubbies in favour of 'premium cabins' more than twice the size. Adaptable furnishings (such as motorised beds that fold up futon-style) maximise space, and the bathroom has streamlined luxuries such as a heated towel rail and monsoon shower. If you want to unload excess baggage, the 20ft tall robot (or Yobot, in the hotel's playful lingo) will stash it for you in a lobby locker. In contrast with the compact quarters, the sprawling public spaces include a wraparound terrace so large it's serviced by two bars. The hotel's eaterie, Dohyo (named after its central Sumo-style platform), serves international tapas devised by modern Mexican-fusion master Richard Sandoval. If the property recalls the retro jet-set world of *Catch Me if You Can*, there's good reason: David Rockwell, who co-designed the hotel with the UK's Softroom,

also created the sets for the Broadway adaptation of the 2002 film. There are also ironic nods to swingin' London in this transatlantic design collaboration, including groovy coloured ceiling lights in the lounge and rotating round beds in the VIP suites. Some first-class 'cabins' even have private terraces with hot tubs. Yeah, baby!
Bars (4). Business centre. Disabled-adapted rooms. Gym. Internet (wireless, shared terminal, free) Restaurant.

FIFTH AVENUE & AROUND

Deluxe

The Plaza

768 Fifth Avenue, at Central Park South, New York, NY 10019 (1-212 759 3000, 1-888 850 0909, www.theplaza.com). Subway N, Q, R to Fifth Avenue-59th Street. **Rates** *$825-$1,425 double.* **Rooms** *282.* **Credit** *AmEx, DC, Disc, MC, V.* **Map** *p405 E22* ⓮

The closest thing to a palace in New York, this 1907 French Renaissance-style landmark reopened in spring 2008 after a two-year, $400-million renovation. Although 152 rooms were converted into private condo units, guests can still check into one of 282 elegantly appointed quarters with Louis XV-inspired furnishings and white-glove butler service. The opulent vibe extends to the bathrooms, which feature mosaic baths, 24-carat gold-plated sink fittings and even chandeliers – perhaps to make the foreign royals feel at home. Embracing the 21st century, the hotel recently equipped every room with

an iPad. The property's legendary public spaces – the Palm Court restaurant, the restored Oak Room and Oak Bar, and Grand Ballroom (the setting for Truman Capote's famed Black and White Ball in 1966) – have been designated as landmarks and preserved for the public; however at the time of writing they were only open for private events. There's also an upscale food hall conceived by celebrity chef Todd English, which includes both old and new cult NYC purveyors, such as William Greenberg Desserts and No. 7 Sub. The on-site Caudalie Vinothérapie Spa is the French grape-based skincare line's first US outpost.
Bars (3). Business centre. Concierge. Disabled-adapted rooms. Gym. Internet (wireless, $15/day). No-smoking rooms. Parking ($65/day). Restaurants (3). Room service. Spa. TV: DVD/pay movies.

Expensive

Algonquin Hotel

59 W 44th Street, between Fifth & Sixth Avenues, New York, NY 10036 (1-212 840 6800, www.algonquinhotel.com). Subway B, D, F, M to 42nd Street-Bryant Park; 7 to Fifth Avenue. **Rates** $249-$899 double. **Rooms** 181. **Credit** AmEx, DC, Disc, MC, V. **Map** p404 E24 51

Alexander Woollcott and Dorothy Parker swapped bon mots in the famous Round Table Room of this 1902 landmark – and you'll still find writer types holding court in the sprawling lobby. The Algonquin certainly trades on its literary past (quotes from Parker and other Round Table members adorn the door to each guest room and vintage *New Yorker* covers hang in the hallways), but a major 2012 renovation has spruced up the grande dame. Backlit vintage photographs of NYC in the rooms are nods to old New York but the sleek quarters could be in any corporate hotel, with faux leather headboards, Frette linens, iHome clock radios and slate-floored bathrooms. Although it's now part of the Marriott-affiliated Autograph Collection, the hotel retains some of its quirky identity in the public spaces – in the lobby bar and restaurant, original panelling and some decorative fixtures remain and the hotel cat (always called Matilda or Hamlet depending on sex) still slumbers behind the check-in desk. Sadly, the iconic cabaret venue, the Oak Room, has closed, and the Blue Bar has been glitzed up with coloured lighting, but it retains the original Al Hirschfeld Broadway-themed drawings, donated by the late habitué's gallery.
Bars (2). Business centre. Concierge. Disabled-adapted rooms. Gym. Internet (wireless, free). No smoking. Parking ($35/day). Restaurant. Room service. TV: pay movies.

Bryant Park Hotel

40 W 40th Street, between Fifth & Sixth Avenues, New York, NY 10018 (1-212 869 0100, www.bryantparkhotel.com). Subway B, D, F, M to 42nd Street-Bryant Park; 7 to Fifth Avenue. **Rates** $235-$625 double. **Rooms** 128. **Credit** AmEx, DC, MC, V. **Map** p404 E24 52

When the shows and the shoots are finished, the fashion and film folk flock to this luxe landing pad (it's particularly busy during Fashion Week). In its days as the American Radiator Building, the hotel was immortalised by Georgia O'Keefe. Although the exterior (which you can appreciate up-close in one of several balconied rooms) is gothic art deco, the inside is all clean-lined and contemporary, with soft lighting, blanched hardwood floors, Tibetan rugs and soothing conveniences such as sleep-aiding sound machines and Bose Wave radios. A section of the room service menu is devoted to vibrators and other forms of adult recreation, but don't worry, you can also order in from the house restaurant, slick sushi destination Koi.
Bar. Concierge. Disabled-adapted rooms. Gym. Internet (wireless, free). No smoking. Parking (free-$45/day). Restaurant. Room service. TV: DVD/pay movies.

MIDTOWN EAST

Deluxe

Four Seasons

57 E 57th Street, between Madison & Park Avenues, New York, NY 10022 (1-212 758 5700, www.fourseasons.com). Subway N, Q, R to Lexington Avenue-59th Street; 4, 5, 6 to 59th Street. **Rates** $695-$1,295 double. **Rooms** 368. **Credit** AmEx, DC, Disc, MC, V. **Map** p405 E22 53

The New York arm of the global luxury chain, housed in IM Pei's 52-floor tower, is synonymous with dependable luxury. Whether you're staying in a suite or a deluxe room (at around 600sq ft, it's the most popular accommodation), expect modern, neutral interiors (blond-wood panelling, white high-thread count linens) and sumptuous, user-friendly design throughout: there's room in the walk-in closet to have a seat and take off your shoes, a TV in the toilet, and the bathtub fills in 60 seconds. If you pay a premium for the park view, you'll be treated to an unsurpassed urban vista. There are no surprises, but that's one of the reasons to stay here.
Bars (3). Business centre. Concierge. Disabled-adapted rooms. Gym. Internet (wireless, $18/day). No-smoking floors. Parking ($60/day). Restaurant. Room service. Spa. TV: DVD/pay movies.

Expensive

The Benjamin

125 E 50th Street, at Lexington Avenue, New York, NY 10022 (1-212 715-2500, www.thebenjamin.com). Subway E, M to Lexington

Avenue-53rd Street; 6 to 51st Street. **Rates**
$299-$699 double. **Rooms** 209. **Credit** AmEx,
DC, Disc, MC, V. **Map** p404 E23 ❷
All rooms in this pet-friendly hotel have kitchenettes with microwaves and sinks (some suites
have full-size fridges), so it's a hit with families as
well as business travellers. The decor, in restful
shades of beige and cream, is unfussy, with the
emphasis on comfort: choose from a menu of 12
pillows that includes buckwheat-filled, Swedish
memory foam and anti-snoring. You can even consult the sleep concierge, who will arrange for milk
and cookies or a white-noise machine to help you
nod off. Amenities include a spa and hair salon, a
good-size gym and a chic, David Rockwell-designed
bistro, the National Bar & Dining Rooms, from Iron
Chef Geoffrey Zakarian.
*Bar. Business centre. Concierge. Disabled-adapted
rooms. Gym. Internet (wireless, high speed,
$14/day). No-smoking floors. Parking ($55-$65/
day). Restaurant. Room Service. Spa. TV: DVD/
pay movies.*

Hotel Elysée

*60 E 54th Street, between Madison & Park
Avenues, New York, NY 10022 (1-212 753
1066, www.elyseehotel.com). Subway E, M to
Fifth Avenue-53rd Street; 6 to 51st Street.*
Rates $224-$589 double. **Rooms** 100. **Credit**
AmEx, DC, Disc, MC, V. **Map** p405 E22 ❺
Since 1926, this discreet but opulent hotel has
attracted luminaries from legendary Russian
pianist Vladimir Horowitz (whose grand piano
resides in the premier suite) to (a discreetly
unnamed) modern superstar who stayed for three
months preparing to go on tour. You may bump into
one on the way from your antique-appointed room
to the complimentary wine and cheese served every
weekday evening in the sedate second-floor lounge,
or in the exclusive Monkey Bar (*see p169*), *Vanity
Fair* editor Graydon Carter's restaurant that shares
the building. Ask reception to reserve a table and
your chances of eating among the power set rise
from zilch to good – a few tables are set aside for
guests every night.
*Bar. Business centre. Concierge. Disabled-adapted
rooms. Internet (wireless, free). No smoking.
Restaurant. TV: DVD.*

Library Hotel

*299 Madison Avenue, at 41st Street, New York,
NY 10017 (1-212 983 4500, www.library
hotel.com). Subway S, 4, 5, 6, 7 to 42nd Street-
Grand Central; 7 to Fifth Avenue.* **Rates** $249-
$599 double. **Rooms** 60. **Credit** AmEx, DC,
MC, V. **Map** p404 E24 ❻
This bookish boutique hotel is organised on the
principles of the Dewey decimal system – each of
its ten floors is allocated a category, such as
Literature, the Arts, and General Knowledge, and
each elegantly understated guest room contains a

INSIDE TRACK
BEST FRIENDS WELCOME

New York hotels are increasingly pet-
friendly. The **Benjamin** (*see p242*), **Eventi**
(*see p234*), **SoHo Grand Hotel** (*see p227*)
and the **Surrey** (*see p244*) are among many
that offer special beds, meals and treats –
the Benjamin even has plush dog robes.

collection of books and artwork pertaining to a
subject within that category. The popular Love
room (interestingly, filed under Philosophy) has a
king-size bed, an ivy-clad balcony overlooking the
New York Public Library and reading matter ranging from Ovid's *The Art of Love* to Dr Ruth
Westheimer's *The Art of Arousal* (the veteran sex-
pert is honorary curator of the room's book collection). Nightly receptions dish out wine and cheese,
while upstairs in the rooftop bar, creative libations
are inspired by Ernest Hemingway and Harper Lee.
A massive DVD library is on hand for those who
can't face reading another word.
*Bar. Business centre. Concierge. Disabled-adapted
rooms. Internet (wireless, free). No smoking.
Restaurant. Room service. TV: DVD/pay movies.*

The New York Palace

*455 Madison Avenue, between 50th & 51st
Streets, New York, NY 10022 (1-212 888 7000,
www.newyorkpalace.com). Subway E, M to Fifth
Avenue-53rd Street.* **Rates** $325-$1,300 double.
Rooms 893. **Credit** AmEx, DC, Disc, MC, V.
Map p404 E23 ❺⑦
Modernity literally meets tradition here: a sleek
55-storey tower cantilevers over the landmark 19th-
century Villard Houses. The connected mansions,
which were built as a residence for railroad magnate
Henry Villard, exude Gilded Age splendour, from
the sweeping grand staircase to the marble-
bedecked lobby. Most of the accommodation, however, conveys more contemporary restraint, with
unremarkable, if comfortable, neutral decor.
Westward-facing rooms overlook Rockefeller
Center, with a bird's-eye view of St Patrick's
Cathedral. The Tower Suites, which occupy the
hotel's top 14 floors, have a separate check-in,
dedicated concierge and are undergoing a redesign
in spring 2013 that will introduce luxurious details
like rain shower heads and custom-made rosewood
headboards. In the summer, James Beard Award-
winning chef Michel Richard will debut his first
NYC restaurant in the hotel. In warmer weather, you
can sip cocktails in the charming courtyard bar,
the Palace Gate.
*Bars (2). Business centre. Concierge. Disabled-
adapted rooms. Gym. Internet (wireless, $16/day).
No smoking. Parking ($50/day). Restaurants (2).
Room service. Spa. TV: DVD/pay movies.*

CONSUME

Waldorf Astoria New York

301 Park Avenue, at 50th Street, New York,
NY 10022 (1-212 355 3000, 1-800 925 3673,
www.waldorfnewyork.com). Subway E, M to
Lexington Avenue-53rd Street; 6 to 51st Street.
Rates $319-$899 double. **Rooms** 1,413. **Credit**
AmEx, DC, Disc, MC, V. **Map** p404 E23 ⓺⓼

As you click across the sparkling marble floor of
this 1931 hotel's grandiose lobby, gracious staff will
treat you like Princess Grace (a former guest). It's
worth visiting this art deco historic landmark just
for the history (it's been the hotel of choice for
numerous United States presidents; a temporary
home to Marilyn Monroe in 1955; and, of course, it's
where the Waldorf salad was invented). However,
you might find your room doesn't quite live up to
its gilded past: on a recent stay, our traditionally
decorated room had lost a bit of its shine. A luxurious bathroom with water pressure to rival Niagara
almost compensated, and total indulgence can be
yours in the glamorous 19th-floor Guerlain spa,
which has hydrotherapy suites, an iPad-equipped
wellness lounge serving light dishes – and spectacular city views.
Bars (3). Business centre. Concierge. Disabled-
adapted rooms. Gym. Internet (wireless, high
speed, $15/day). No-smoking floors. Parking
($57/day). Restaurants (3). Room service. Spa.
TV: pay movies.

Uptown

UPPER EAST SIDE

Deluxe

The Pierre

2 E 61st Street, at Fifth Avenue, New York,
NY 10065 (1-212 838 8000, www.tajhotels.com/
thepierre). Subway N, Q, R to Fifth Avenue-
59th Street. **Rates** $895-$1,600 double.
Rooms 189. **Credit** AmEx, DC, Disc, MC, V.
Map p405 E22 ⓹⓽

The 1930 landmark overlooking Central Park
became part of the posh Indian Taj Hotels, Resorts
and Palaces in 2005, setting in motion a $100-million
overhaul – but it retains delightfully old-fashioned
elements such as elevator operators and original
fireplaces in some suites. In contrast to the glitzy
public spaces, including the mural-clad Rotunda and
the Grand Ballroom, the classic rooms are understated, dressed in a neutral colour palette and
immaculate upholstery, with modern gadgets
including Bose radio/iPod docks. The sumptuous
Turkish marble bathrooms are generously stocked
with Molton Brown bath products. The Asian influence is reflected in silk bedspreads from Bangalore
and contemporary Indian art, but the hotel restaurant is a swanky new Italian spot designed by Adam
Tihany, Sirio.

CONSUME

THE BEST HOTEL PERKS

For minibar freebies
Andaz Wall Street. *See p223.*

For cult toiletries
Crosby Street Hotel. *See p225.*

For an in-room pet
SoHo Grand Hotel. *See p227.*

For a hot table
Ace Hotel New York. *See p236.*

Bars (2). Business centre. Concierge. Disabled-
adapted rooms. Gym. Internet (wireless, free in
public spaces; wireless, high speed $13/day in
rooms). No-smoking floors. Parking ($60-$70/day.
Restaurant. Room service. TV: DVD/pay movies.

★ The Surrey

20 E 76th Street, between Fifth & Madison
Avenues, New York, NY 10021 (1-212 288
3700, 1-800 978 7739, www.thesurreyhotel.com).
Subway 6 to 77th Street. **Rates** $495-$699 double.
Rooms 189. **Credit** AmEx, DC, Disc, MC, V.
Map p405 E20 ⓺⓪

A stylish addition to an area thin on unstuffy accommodation, the Surrey, in a solid pre-war Beaux Arts
building given a $60-million overhaul, pitches at
both traditionalists and the trend-driven. Flanked
by top chef Daniel Boulud's Café Boulud and his chic
cocktail destination, Bar Pleiades (*see p186*), it's also
a strong lure for gastronomes on a spree (Boulud's
restaurant also supplies the room service). Those
seeking a pampering break will appreciate the new
Cornelia spa (*see p217*), and guests can lounge on
the 17th-floor roof garden (open Apr-Sept). The
coolly elegant limestone and marble lobby showcases contemporary art by American conceptualist
Jenny Holzer and South African William Kentridge.
Rooms are dressed in a refined palette of cream, grey
and beige, with luxurious white marble bathrooms
featuring products by Italian perfumer Laura
Tonatto. But the centrepiece is undoubtedly the
incredibly comfortable DUX by Duxiana bed,
swathed in luxurious Sferra linens. Coupled with the
hotel's quiet location, it almost guarantees your best
sleep ever.
Bar. Business centre. Concierge. Disabled-adapted
rooms. Gym. Internet (wireless, $15/day). No
smoking. Parking ($55/day). Restaurant. Room
service. Spa. TV: pay movies.

Expensive

Hotel Wales

1295 Madison Avenue, at 92nd Street, New
York, NY 10128 (1-212 876 6000, www.hotel

walesnyc.com). Subway 4, 5, 6 to 86th Street; 6 to 96th Street. **Rates** $225-$525 double. **Rooms** 89. **Credit** AmEx, DC, Disc, MC, V. **Map** p406 E18 ⑤①

Purpose-built as a hotel in the early 1900s, the ten-storey Wales is a comfortable, convenient choice for a culture jaunt due to its proximity to Museum Mile. Tucked in the quietly affluent Carnegie Hill neighbourhood just above Madison Avenue's prime retail stretch, it's also well placed for a posh shopping spree. Standard double rooms are small, but high ceilings, large windows and an unfussy contemporary-classic style prevents them from seeming cramped; about half of the accommodation consists of suites. All quarters have recently been redecorated with designer wallpaper, sleek new bathrooms and HD TVs. Higher-floor rooms on the east side have Central Park views, but all guests can enjoy them on the large roof terrace. Two on-site restaurants (Italian spot Paola's and mini-chain Sarabeth's) provide meals and snacks.
Business centre. Concierge. Disabled-adapted rooms. Gym. Internet (wireless, high-speed, $13/day). No smoking. Parking ($52/day). Restaurants (2). Room service. TV.

UPPER WEST SIDE
Expensive

Country Inn the City
270 W 77th Street, between Broadway & West End Avenue, New York, NY 10024 (1-212 580 4183, www.countryinnthecity.com). Subway 1 to 79th Street. **Rates** $230-$350 double. **Rooms** 4. **No credit cards. Map** p405 C19 ⑥②

The name of this charming B&B on the West Side is pretty accurate. Spacious studios with kitchenettes, four-poster beds and flagons of brandy make this intimate inn a special retreat in the middle of the metropolis. Register on the website to be notified of last-minute specials.
Internet (wireless, free). No smoking.

Moderate

Hotel Belleclaire
250 W 77th Street, at Broadway, New York, NY 10024 (1-212 362 7700, www.hotelbelle claire.com). Subway 1 to 79th Street. **Rates** $159-$569 double. **Rooms** 200. **Credit** AmEx, DC, Disc, MC, V. **Map** p405 C19 ⑥③

Housed in a landmark building a short walk from Lincoln Center, Central Park and the Museum of Natural History, the sleek Hotel Belleclaire is a steal for savvy travellers. Comfort-centric details include hypo-allergenic comforters, Frette linens and padded headboards Each room is equipped with an iPod docking station, HD TV and a refrigerator – perfect for chilling your protein shake while you're hitting the 24-hour fitness centre.

Bar. Business centre. Concierge. Disabled-adapted rooms. Gym. Internet (wireless, free). No smoking. Room service. TV: pay movies.

On the Ave Hotel
222 W 77th Street, between Broadway & Amsterdam Avenue, New York, NY 10024 (1-212 362 1100, 1-800 509 7598, www. ontheave-nyc.com). Subway 1 to 79th Street. **Rates** $129-$699 double. **Rooms** 282. **Credit** AmEx, DC, Disc, MC, V. **Map** p405 C19 ⑥④

Given the affluent area, it's hardly surprising that On the Ave's rooms are stylish, with industrial-style bathroom sinks, HD TVs, ergonomic Herman Miller chairs, plus down comforters and Egyptian-cotton sheets. On the upper floors, Panoramic Deluxe rooms and penthouse suites command fantastic private-balcony views of Central Park or the Hudson River, but all guests have access to terraces on the 14th and 16th floors to admire the cityscape. Although there's no shortage of excellent restaurants in the district, On the Ave will soon house the new location of acclaimed modern Chinese spot RedFarm (*see p162*).
Bar. Business centre. Concierge. Disabled-adapted rooms. Gym. Internet (wireless, $14/day). No smoking. Parking ($55/day). Restaurants (3). TV.

Budget

Broadway Hotel & Hostel
230 W 101 Street, at Broadway, New York, NY 10024 (1-212 865 7710, www.broadway hotelnyc.com). Subway 1, 2, 3 to 96th Street. **Rates** $50-$200 double. **Credit** AmEx, Disc, MC, V. **Map** p406 C16 ⑥⑤

For those who have outgrown the no-frills backpacker experience but haven't quite graduated to a full-service hotel, the hybrid Broadway Hotel & Hostel, which has been given a 'boutique-style' makeover, fills the gap. On the ground floor, exposed brick, leather sofas and three large flatscreen TVs give the sprawling communal spaces a slick, urban veneer, but they still follow the traditional youth-hostel blueprint: TV room, shared kitchen, plus a computer area with eight credit card-operated terminals (if you have your own gadget, Wi-Fi is free). You won't find six-bed set-ups here, though: the cheapest option, the small, basic 'dormitory-style' rooms, jazzed up with striking colour schemes, mass-produced art and ceiling fans (there's AC in the summer too), accommodate a maximum of two in bunk beds. The good-value 'semi-private' rooms offer a queen bed or two doubles/twins, with luxuries such as down comforters and flatscreen TVs, but you'll have to use the (well-scrubbed) shared bathrooms. En suite quarters are also available. The Broadway provides free linens and towels, daily housekeeping service and 24-hour reception.
Concierge. Internet (wireless, free). No smoking. TV.

CONSUME

Hostels

Hostelling International New York

891 Amsterdam Avenue, at 103rd Street,
New York, NY 10025 (1-212 932 2300,
www.hinewyork.org). Subway 1 to 103rd Street.
Rates $35-$49/person in dorm rooms; $145-
$165 private room. **Rooms** 624 beds in dorms;
6 private rooms. **Credit** AmEx, DC, Disc, MC, V.
Map p406 C16 ⑥⑥

This budget lodging is actually the city's only 'real'
hostel (a non-profit accommodation that belongs to
the International Youth Hostel Federation). The
gabled, Gothic-inspired brick and stone building
spans the length of an entire city block, and is much
admired by locals as well as those staying there. The
interior is somewhat institutional and the immaculate rooms are spare, but they're air-conditioned, and
facilities include a shared kitchen and large backyard. Linens and towels are free.
Business centre. Disabled-adapted rooms. Internet
(wireless, free). No smoking.

HARLEM

Moderate

Aloft Harlem

2296 Frederick Douglass Boulevard (Eighth
Avenue), between 123rd & 124th Streets, New
York, NY 10027 (1-212 749 4000, www.aloft
hotels.com). Subway A, B, C, D, 2, 3 to 125th
Street. **Rates** $169-$400 double. **Rooms** 124.
Credit AmEx, DC, Disc, MC, V. **Map** p407 D13 ⑥⑦

Starwood Hotels' fast-expanding Aloft brand pitches
to a young, design-conscious traveller whose budget
might not stretch to a room at one of the company's
W properties. Launched in December 2010, Aloft
Harlem was the first hotel to open in the area since
the early 1960s. The public spaces combine high-
tech amenities (a pair of iMacs, in addition to free
hotel-wide Wi-Fi) with colourful, contemporary
decor (a scrolling news ticker above the elevators, a
pool table in the lobby-lounge). The industrial-edged
w xyz bar hosts DJs, karaoke and jazz nights, while

No Sleep Till Brooklyn

New York's hottest hotel debut is across the East River.

As *Time Out New York*'s weekly listings for
unmissable gigs and hot new bars and
restaurants attest, Williamsburg, Brooklyn,
is one of the most popular neighbourhoods
in New York for a night out on the town.
Although Brooklyn's growing attractions
have been luring visitors for years, until
more recently it hasn't been seen as a
base for tourists. But now that the borough
is synonymous with a particular brand of
unconventional cool, visitors in search of
New York's bohemian spirit may prefer to
stay off-island. Supply is keeping up with

demand: over the past half-dozen years,
more than 40 per cent of new hotel
development has been outside
Manhattan – 18 per cent in Brooklyn.

While the arrival of luxury hotels is a
telltale sign that an area has reached the
tipping point from creative enclave to
commercial playground, Williamsburg's
newest boutique hotel is more in keeping
with the neighbourhood's pre-condo vibe.
The **Wythe Hotel** (*see p248*) may not be
the first hotel in the hipster 'hood – its
forerunners were the unremarkable yet

a slick, open-plan convenience store, re:fuel, dispenses coffee, sandwiches and snacks around the clock. A minimalist approach mitigates tight space in the bedrooms – despite 275sq ft dimensions, standard quarters are outfitted with king-size beds (dressed with deluxe cotton sheets and recycled-cork headboards) and 42in flatscreen TVs, while bathrooms feature oversize rainfall showerheads and products created by W collaborator Bliss Spa.
Bar. Business centre. Disabled-adapted rooms. Gym. Internet (wireless, free). No smoking. TV.
Other locations 216 Duffield Street, between Fulton Mall & Willoughby Street, Downtown Brooklyn (1-718 256 3833).

Budget

★ Harlem Flophouse
*242 W 123rd Street, between Adam Clayton Powell Jr Boulevard (Seventh Avenue) & Frederick Douglass Boulevard (Eighth Avenue), New York, NY 10027 (1-347 632 1960,
www.harlemflophouse.com). Subway A, B, C, D to 125th Street.* **Rates** $125-$170. **Rooms** 4. **Credit** DC, MC, V. **Map** p407 D14 ⑱
The dark-wood interior, moody lighting and lilting jazz make musician Rene Calvo's Harlem inn feel more like a 1930s speakeasy than a 21st-century B&B. The airy suites, named for Harlem Renaissance figures such as Chester Himes and Cozy Cole, have restored tin ceilings, a quirky mix of junk-store furnishings and period knick-knacks, and working sinks in antique cabinets. There are just two suites per floor; each pair shares a bathroom.
Internet (wireless, free). No smoking.

102Brownstone
102 W 118th Street, between Malcolm X Boulevard (Lenox Avenue) & Adam Clayton Powell Jr Boulevard (Seventh Avenue), New York, NY 10026 (1-212 662 4223, www. 102brownstone.com). Subway 2, 3 to 116th Street. **Rates** $125-$200 suite. **Rooms** 6. **Credit** AmEx, MC, V. **Map** p407 D14 ⑲

serviceable Hotel Le Jolie (*see p248*) and the slick party crash-pad Hotel Williamsburg, currently being transformed into King & Grove Williamsburg – but it's the first to capture the neighborhood's elusive hip factor. Since the launch team includes Andrew Tarlow, the restaurateur behind popular local eateries Diner and Marlow & Sons (*see p175*), it's not surprising that the sprawling ground-floor seasonal restaurant, Reynards, was an instant hit. Like Tarlow's restaurants, the hotel has a subtle vintage feel without

going down the full-blown retro route.
A 1901 cooperage near the waterfront has been topped with a three-story glass-and-aluminium addition; on its facade, a 50-foot-tall 'hotel' sign, created from salvaged tin signage by artist Tom Fruin (who created Dumbo's *Watertower* installation, *see p116*), becomes a neon-lit beacon at night. In many of the guest rooms, floor-to-ceiling windows offer a panorama of the Manhattan skyline or face a cool Steve Powers graffiti mural that re-creates vintage Brooklyn advertising. Heated concrete floors, exposed brick, reclaimed-timber beds and witty custom wallpaper (including the Wythe Toile, inspired by local street scenes) create a rustic-industrial vibe, offset by fully plugged-in technology: a cable by the bed turns your iPhone into a surround-sound music system. The utilitarian subway-tiled bathrooms are stocked with luxurious Turkish towels and eco-conscious Goldies products created by a former Diner staffer.
DJ'd parties in the sixth-floor bar aside, the Wythe literally rocks: the hotel accommodates the 'Burg's many touring bands in special quarters that sleep four to six. For other non-couple travelling companions, compact bunk rooms are equipped with individual TVs, and some even have cute terraces.

CONSUME

Located near Marcus Garvey Park on a landmark, tree-lined street, 102Brownstone features half a dozen substantial suites, all renovated and individually themed by lively proprietor Lizette Lanoue, who owns and lives in the 1892 Greek Revival row house with her husband. The couple aims to be unobtrusive and to make guests feel like they are in their own apartment. Quarters include the tranquil Zen and dreamy Luna, both of which have Jacuzzi bathtubs. *Concierge. Internet (wireless, free). No smoking. TV: DVD.*

Brooklyn

BOERUM HILL, CARROLL GARDENS & COBBLE HILL

Moderate

★ Nu Hotel

85 Smith Street, between Atlantic Avenue & State Street, Brooklyn, NY 11201 (1-718 852 8585, www.nuhotelbrooklyn.com). Subway A, C, F to Jay Street-Borough Hall; F, G to Bergen Street; R to Court Street; 2, 3, 4, 5 to Borough Hall. **Rates** $149-$349 double. **Rooms** 93. **Credit** AmEx, DC, Disc, MC, V. **Map** p410 T10 **70**

Conveniently placed for the shops and restaurants of BoCoCa, Nu Hotel has bundled quirky niceties into a classy, eco-friendly package. Cork flooring, organic linens and recycled teak furniture mix it up with 32in flatscreen TVs and Sangean audio systems, free Wi-Fi and AV docks for multimedia devices. The minimalist standard rooms are comfortably sized, but Friends Suites have bunk beds, and the lofty Urban Suites are outfitted with hammocks and a padded-leather sleeping alcove. Cyclists can borrow one of the hotel's loaner bikes to pedal around Brooklyn, and iPads are available for guest use. The lobby bar, which has outside tables in the warmer months, offers a tapas menu designed by *Next Iron Chef* runner-up Jehangir Mehta. *Bar. Business centre. Concierge. Disabled-adapted rooms. Gym. Internet (wireless, free). No smoking. Parking ($25/day). TV: DVD (on request).*

PARK SLOPE

Moderate

Hotel Le Bleu

370 Fourth Avenue, between 3rd & 5th Streets, Brooklyn, NY 11215 (1-718 625 1500, www.hotellebleu.com). Subway F, R to Fourth Avenue-9th Street; R to Union Street. **Rates** $199-$399 double. **Rooms** 48. **Credit** AmEx, Disc, MC, V. **Map** p410 T10 **71**

The Manhattanisation of Park Slope hit new heights in late 2007, when Andres Escobar's steel and glass hotel popped up on industrial Fourth Avenue.

Couples will find the open shower design a plus; more conventional draws include 42in plasma TVs with Bose system DVD/CD players, goose-down comforters, iPod docking stations and free Wi-Fi in every room. *Bar. Business centre. Concierge. Disabled-adapted rooms. Internet (wireless, free). No smoking. Parking (free, limited availability). Restaurant. TV: DVD.*

WILLIAMSBURG & BUSHWICK

Moderate

Hotel Le Jolie

235 Meeker Avenue, at Jackson Street, Brooklyn, NY 11211 (1-718 625 2100, www.hotellejolie.com). Subway G to Metropolitan Avenue; L to Lorimer Street. **Rates** $159-$289 double. **Rooms** 54. **Credit** AmEx, DC, Disc, MC, V. **Map** p411 V8 **72**

This contemporary hotel is a reasonably priced option in Williamsburg – too bad it's right on top of the Brooklyn-Queens Expressway. Inside, though, 54 well-maintained rooms offer king-size beds (fitted with allergen-free goose-down comforters and Egyptian cotton sheets), ergonomic Aeron desk chairs and 42in flatscreen TVs. *Business centre. Concierge. Disabled-adapted rooms. Internet (wireless, free). No smoking. Parking (free). TV.*

★ Wythe Hotel

80 Wythe Avenue, at North 11th Street, Williamsburg, Brooklyn, NY 11249 (1-718 460 8000, www.wythehotel.com). Subway L to Bedford Avenue. **Rates** $179-$399 double. **Rooms** 72. **Credit** AmEx, DC, Disc, MC, V. **Map** p411 U7 **73** *See p246* **No Sleep Till Brooklyn.** *Bar. Concierge. Disabled-adapted rooms. Gym. Internet (wireless, free; high-speed $5/day). No smoking. Restaurant.*

Hostels

★ New York Loft Hostel

249 Varet Street, at Bogart Street, Brooklyn, NY 11206 (1-718 366 1351, www.nylofthostel.com). Subway L to Morgan Avenue. **Rates** $35-$60/person in 3-bed dorm room; $80-$110 private room. **Rooms** 50 beds in dorms; 30 private rooms. **Credit** AmEx, Disc, MC, V. **Map** p411 W9 **74**

Situated in arty Bushwick, this budget lodging fuses the traditional youth hostel set-up (dorm-style rooms with single beds and lockers, communal lounging areas) with a fashionable loft aesthetic. In the former clothing warehouse, linen curtains billow in front of huge windows, and there's plenty of industrial-chic exposed brick and piping. Above the big shared kitchen is a mezzanine equipped with a large flatscreen TV (DVDs can be rented at the front desk). The spacious patio is the site of frequent summer

CONSUME

Z NYC Hotel.

CONSUME

barbecues. Unlike old-school hostels, there's no cur-few; an electronically encoded room-key card opens the front door after hours.

Disabled-adapted rooms. Internet (wireless, free; shared terminal, $2/20mins). No smoking. TV: DVD (shared).

Queens

LONG ISLAND CITY

Moderate

Ravel

8-08 Queens Plaza South, at Vernon Boulevard, Queens, NY 11101 (1-718 289 6101, www.ravel hotel.com). Subway E, M, R to Queens Plaza; F to 21st Street-Queensbridge; N, Q, 7 to Queensboro Plaza. **Rates** $159-$350 double. **Credit** AmEx, DC, Disc, MC, V. **Map** p412 V4 ⓱
Perhaps in keeping with the Ravel's former incarnation as a motel, owner Ravi Patel gave Long Island City's first independent boutique hotel a vaguely 1960s feel; the lobby has cream leatherette seating, silver-bubble ceiling lights and paintings sourced in South America that recall those doe-eyed Spanish girl portraits. Appealing to a young party set, Ravel is also equipped with a 'virtual' wine bar: buy a card at the front desk and use it at a self-serve bank of more than 18 wines. An 8,000sq ft rooftop restaurant-bar has dazzling views of Midtown and hosts film screenings, DJ nights and other events. Rooms are much larger than in similarly priced hotels in Manhattan,

and the majority (many with private balconies) face the river – although a Con-Edison training facility directly below is less than picturesque.
Bars (2). Business centre. Disabled-adapted rooms. Internet (wireless, $10/day, free in lobby). No smoking. Parking (free). Restaurant. Room service. TV: pay movies.

Z NYC Hotel

11-01 43rd Avenue, at 11th Street, Queens, NY 11101 (1-212 319 7000, www.zhotelny.com). Subway E, M to Court Square-23rd Street; F to 21st Street-Queensbridge; N, Q, 7 to Queensboro Plaza. **Rates** $189-$425 double. **Rooms** 100.
Credit AmEx, DC, Disc, MC, V. **Map** p412 V5 ⓰
The Z shares a gritty industrial side street with tool suppliers and flooring wholesalers, but the Queensboro Bridge-side setting and largely low-rise neighbours facilitate its most stunning feature: knock-your-socks-off midtown views through floor-to-ceiling windows. Offbeat details, such as lightbulbs encased in mason jars dangling over the bed, wall stencils of iconic New York images and black flip-flops instead of the standard white slippers, enliven the stock boutique luxury of the accommodation. The public spaces are more dramatic: in the lobby, the check-in desk is built from vintage travel trunks, and an old-school train-station-style 'departure board' above the elevators spells out welcome in 18 languages. In addition to a vintage-styled 'cellar' lounge, there's a roof terrace offering 360-degree panoramas. The hotel bus ferries guests to and from midtown every hour.
Bar. Concierge. Disabled-adapted rooms. Internet (wireless, free). No smoking.

Arts & Entertainment

Children

The Big Apple, for little ones.

The crowded and fast-paced metropolis may not seem like the most kid-friendly place at first glance, but its 21st-century baby boom has given rise to myriad cultural, culinary and just plain fun offerings for families. Icons such as the Ellis Island Immigration Museum and the American Museum of Natural History are not to be missed, but they are just the beginning. Among the most frequented corners of the city are its green spaces and playgrounds – seek one out when you're in need of a breather from the city's constant buzz. And for the latest child-centric events, pick up a copy of the monthly magazine *Time Out New York Kids*, or visit the website www.timeout.com/newyorkkids.

ARTS & ENTERTAINMENT

SIGHTSEEING & ENTERTAINMENT
Animals & nature

See also p256 **Central Park**.

★ Bronx Zoo
For listings, see p135.
Step aboard the Wild Asia Monorail (open May-Oct, admission $4), which tours 38 acres of exhibits housing elephants, Indo-Chinese tigers, antelope, Mongolian wild horses and more. Madagascar! is a permanent home to exotic animals from the lush island nation off the eastern coast of Africa. Among its residents are lemurs, giant crocodiles, lovebirds, radiated tortoises and, coolest (and grossest) of all, hissing cockroaches. Five lemurs were born in the exhibit in its first year.
► *There are also zoos in Central Park (see p95), Brooklyn (see p121) and Queens (see p130).*

New York Aquarium
610 Surf Avenue, at West 8th Street, Coney Island, Brooklyn (1-718 265 3474, www.nya quarium.com). Subway D, N, Q to Coney Island-Stillwell Avenue; F, Q to W 8th Street-NY Aquarium. **Open** *Nov-Mar* 10am-4.30pm daily. *Apr, May* 10am-5pm Mon-Fri; 10am-5.30pm Sat, Sun. *June-Aug* 10am-6pm Mon-Fri; 10am-7pm Sat, Sun. *Sept, Oct* 10am-5pm Mon-Fri; 10am-5.30pm Sat, Sun. **Admission** $14.95; $10.95-$11.95 reductions; free under-3s. Pay what you wish from 3pm Fri. **Credit** AmEx, DC, Disc, MC, V.

Just weeks after announcing the construction of a 57,000-square-foot building that will house a new 'Ocean Wonders: Sharks!' exhibition, slated to open in 2015, the seaside Aquarium was hit hard by Hurricane Sandy, which unleashed its fury on the New York area in late 2012. Some of its inhabitants have been transferred to other aquariums, and at press time it is not clear when the Coney Island mainstay will reopen, so check the website for updates.

★ FREE Prospect Park Audubon Center
Prospect Park, enter from Ocean Avenue, at Lincoln Road, Brooklyn (1-718 287 3400, www.prospectpark.org/audubon). Subway B, Q to Prospect Park. **Open** *Feb, March, Nov, Dec* noon-4pm Sat, Sun. *Apr, June, Sept, Oct* noon-4pm Thur-Sun. *July, Aug* noon-5pm Thur-Sun. Closed *Jan.* **Admission** free. **Map** p410 U12.
Overlooking Prospect Lake, the child-oriented Audubon Center is dedicated to nature education and wildlife preservation. Start at the visitor centre, featuring a giant interactive microscope and live animal presentations, and stick around for woodland tours, storytelling and (seasonal) birdwatching boat tours.

Museums

Defying the stuffy cliché, many of Manhattan's most venerable institutions are extremely child-friendly. The new **DiMenna Children's History Museum** inside the **New-York Historical Society** (*see p104*) engages kids with New York's past by looking at the childhoods of various residents, some famous

(Alexander Hamilton), others anonymous (child newspaper sellers in the early 20th century). For years, the **Museum of Modern Art** (*see p88*) the **Metropolitan Museum of Art** (*see p99*) and the **Rubin Museum** (*see p77*) have offered workshops for kids of all ages; check their websites for schedules. The Met, with its mummies and Temple of Dendur, a real ancient Egyptian temple, is a particular hit with children, as long as you don't try to tackle too much of the massive collection.

Even very young kids will love exploring the **American Museum of Natural History** (*see p104*). The museum's Fossil Halls are home to its huge, beloved dinosaurs – most reconstructed from actual fossils – and the myriad wildlife dioramas are a fascinating (and astonishingly life-like) peek at the world's fauna. The excellent core exhibition 'Behind the Screen' at the **Museum of the Moving Image** (*see p129*), outfitted with state-of-the-art movie-making stations, makes it worth the trek to Astoria, Queens.

Elsewhere, children and adults will be fascinated by the amazing scale-model Panorama of the City of New York at the **Queens Museum of Art** (*see p130*). Youngsters can pretend to drive a real bus and board vintage subway cars at the **New York Transit Museum** (*see p118*), while the highlight at the aircraft carrier-turned-attraction **Intrepid Sea, Air & Space Museum** (*see p84*) is the new Space Shuttle Pavilion, housing the *Enterprise*, an original prototype. Law-abiding types will love the Junior Officers Discovery Zone at the **New York City Police Museum** (*see p54*); younger kids can hop into a police car and the older set can participate in crime-scene investigation activities.

★ Brooklyn Children's Museum

145 Brooklyn Avenue, at St Marks Avenue, Crown Heights, Brooklyn (1-718 735 4400, www.brooklynkids.org). Subway A, C to Nostrand Avenue; C to Kingston-Throop Avenues; 3 to Kingston Avenue. **Open** 10am-5pm Tue-Sun. **Admission** $9; free under-1s; free every 3rd Thur 4-7pm, 1st full wknd of the mth 2-5pm. **Credit** AmEx, Disc, MC, V. **Map** p410 V11.
The city's oldest museum for kids is also one of its best after a major renovation that wrapped up in 2008. The star attraction, 'World Brooklyn', is an interactive maze of small mom-and-pop shops based on real-world Brooklyn businesses. 'Neighborhood Nature' puts the spotlight on the borough's diverse ecosystems with a collection of pond critters in terrariums and a tide-pool touch tank. Under-fives will delight in 'Totally Tots', a sun-drenched play space with a water station, a sand zone, and a special hub for babies aged 18 months and under.

Children's Museum of Manhattan

212 W 83rd Street, between Amsterdam Avenue & Broadway, Upper West Side (1-212 721 1234, www.cmom.org). Subway B, C to 81st Street-Museum of Natural History; 1 to 86th Street. **Open** 10am-5pm Tue-Fri, Sun; 10am-7pm Sat. **Admission** $11; $7 reductions; free under-1s. **Credit** AmEx, DC, MC, V. **Map** p405 C19.
An essential stop on every Upper West Side child's social agenda, this museum customises its themed exhibits by age group. 'PlayWorks', an imaginative play environment, is for babies and toddlers up to four; 'Adventures with Dora and Diego', a bilingual playspace that transports visitors to some of the Nickelodeon TV show's settings, is for ages two to six. 'EatSleepPlay: Building Health Every Day', for all ages, is an interactive exhibit that gives families strategies for taking up a more healthy lifestyle.

★ Children's Museum of the Arts

103 Charlton Street, between Greenwich & Hudson Streets, Soho (1-212 274 0986, www.cmany.org). Subway A, B, C, D, E, F, M to W 4th Street; C, E to Spring Street; 1 to Houston Street. **Open** noon-5pm Mon, Wed; noon-6pm Thur, Fri; 10am-6pm Sat, Sun. **Admission** $11; free under-1s; pay what you wish 4-6pm Thur. **Credit** AmEx, DC, Disc, MC, V. **Map** p403 E30.
The creativity-inspiring Soho mainstay, whose focus is on teaching, creating, collecting and exhibiting kids' artwork, moved into a new, 10,000sq ft space in late 2011. Engaging temporary exhibits are juxtaposed with works from the museum's collection of more than 2,000 pieces of children's art. For kids, the most exciting aspects of the museum are its hands-on art workshops, clay lab and interactive media lab, plus the ball pit for letting off steam. *Photos pp254-255.*

★ New York Hall of Science

47-01 111th Street, at 47th Avenue, Flushing Meadows-Corona Park (1-718 699 0005, www.nysci.org). Subway 7 to 111th Street. **Open** *Sept-Mar* 9.30am-2pm Tue-Thur; 9.30am-5pm Fri; 10am-6pm Sat, Sun. *Apr-June* 9.30am-2pm Mon-Thur; 9.30am-5pm Fri; 10am-6pm Sat, Sun. *July, Aug* 9.30am-5pm Mon-Fri; 10am-6pm Sat, Sun. **Admission** $11; $8 reductions. *Sept-June* free 2-5pm Fri; 10-11am Sun. *Science playground* (open Mar-Dec) extra $4. *Rocket Park Mini Golf* extra $6; $5 reductions. **Credit** AmEx, DC, Disc, MC, V.
Known for the 1964 World's Fair pavilion in which it is housed and the rockets from the US space programme that flank it, this museum has always been worth a trek for its discovery-based interactive exhibits. A massive expansion in 2005 added a new building that houses such permanent exhibits as 'Hidden Kingdoms', where children can get their hands on microscopes, and 'Search for Life Beyond Earth', which investigates the solar system and the

ARTS & ENTERTAINMENT

ARTS & ENTERTAINMENT

different planetary environments. From April through December, the 30,000sq ft outdoor Science Playground teaches children the principles of balance, gravity and energy, while a mini-golf course in Rocket Park lets families play outdoors surrounded by refurbished rockets from the 1960s space race.

Performing arts

Broadway is packed with excellent, if pricey, family fare, from Disney offerings like *The Lion King* and *Mary Poppins* to more offbeat spectacles like *Wicked*, which imagines a prequel to *The Wizard of Oz*. *The Nutcracker* (see *p308* **David H Koch Theater**) is an annual Christmas family tradition. In summer, **Madison Square Park** (*see p78*) hosts regular children's concerts, and warm-weather events such as the **River to River Festival** and **SummerStage** (for both, *see p302* **Everything Under the Sun**) always include music and theatre tailored to little ones.

INSIDE TRACK TALL TIPS

If you want a bird's-eye panorama of the city, try Rockefeller Center's **Top of the Rock** (*see p89*) rather than the Empire State Building. The ride up is like an amusement park adventure, and the tall, railing-less glass panels separating you from the city make the views all the more visceral – and breathtaking.

Big Apple Circus
Damrosch Park, Lincoln Center, 62nd Street, between Columbus & Amsterdam Avenues, Upper West Side (1-212 268 2500, www.big applecircus.org). Subway 1 to 66th Street-Lincoln Center. **Shows** Oct-Jan, times vary. **Tickets** $25-$175. **Credit** AmEx, DC, Disc, MC, V. **Map** p405 C21.
This travelling circus was founded in 1977 as an intimate answer to the scale of the Ringling Bros operation; it typically runs from October to mid January. The non-profit organisation's clowns are among the most creative in the country. If you always wanted to run away to the circus, attend the special late show on New Year's Eve, at the end of which the entire audience joins the performers in the ring.

Carnegie Hall Family Concerts
For listings, see p301. **Tickets** $9.
Even children who solemnly profess to hate classical music are usually impressed by a visit to Carnegie Hall. The Family Concert series builds on that, featuring first-rate classical, world music and jazz performers, plus a pre-concert workshop an hour before the show. It runs roughly monthly from November to May (recommended for ages five to 12).

Galli Theater
347 W 36th Street, between Eighth & Ninth Avenues, Hell's Kitchen (1-212 731 0668, www.gallitheaterny.com). Subway A, C, E to 34th Street-Penn Station. **Shows** 2pm Sat, Sun (see website for additional shows). **Tickets** $20; $15 under-18s. **Credit** Disc, MC, V. **Map** p404 C25.
Classic fairy tales such as *Rapunzel*, *Snow White* and *Hansel and Gretel* come to life through kid-oriented,

Children's Museum of the Arts.
See p253.

often musical adaptations written by playwright and theatre founder Johannes Galli. A hallmark of each show is audience participation: children are frequently invited on stage during the performance.

★ Just Kidding at Symphony Space

For listings, see p304. **Shows** *Oct-early May* Sat (times vary). **Tickets** $15-$35; $13-$25 reductions.
Tell your munchkins to forgo their weekly dose of cartoons. In Manhattan, children can spend Saturday mornings grooving to live concerts or watching theatre, dance or a puppet show. Symphony Space's Just Kidding series features both local and nationally recognised talent, from kid rockers and bluegrass bands to hip hop storytellers and NYC star Gustaver Yellowgold.

★ New Victory Theater

For listings, see p323.
As New York's only full-scale young people's theatre, the New Victory presents international theatre and dance companies at junior prices. Recent shows have included Black Violin, a genre-mashing group that plays a fusion of classical, jazz, bebop, hip hop and R&B, and Circus Oz, an Aussie troupe of high-energy acrobats, jugglers, trapeze artists and clowns, accompanied by a rock band. Shows often sell out well in advance, so reserve seats early.

Puppetworks

338 Sixth Avenue, at 4th Street, Park Slope, Brooklyn (1-718 965 3391, www.puppetworks.org). Subway F to Seventh Avenue. **Shows** 12.30pm, 2.30pm Sat, Sun. **Tickets** $9; $8 under-12s.
No credit cards. Map p410 T11.

The Brooklyn company puts on musicals adapted from fairy tales and children's stories that feature a cast of marionettes operated by two puppeteers (the voice and music track is pre-recorded). The company also demonstrates how the puppets work at the beginning of each performance.

Vital Theatre Company

McGinn/Cazale Theatre, 4th floor, 2162 Broadway, at 76th Street, Upper West Side (1-212 579 0528, www.vitaltheatre.org). Subway 1 to 79th Street; 2, 3 to 72nd Street. **Shows** vary. **Tickets** $29.50-$49.50. **Credit** AmEx, DC, MC, V. **Map** p405 C19.
Founded in 1999, Vital has produced a series of original theatrical hits for kids, the biggest of which it reprises often – including *Angelina Ballerina* and *Fancy Nancy the Musical* – at its Upper West Side home. Its most popular creation, the ongoing *Pinkalicious*, about a girl who comes down with a case of 'Pinkititis', has its own venue: downtown's Culture Project, at 45 Bleecker Street, between Lafayette and Mott Streets.

PARKS & PLAY SPACES

Most New Yorkers don't have their own garden – instead, they run around and let off steam in parks. The most popular of all is **Central Park** (*see p92*), which has places and programmes just for kids.

Battery Park City Parks

Hudson River, between Chambers Street & Battery Place, Financial District (1-212 267 9700, www.bpcparks.org). Subway A, C, 1, 2,

3 to Chambers Street; 1 to Rector Street. **Open** 6am-1am daily. **Admission** free. **Map** p402 D32.
Besides watching the boats along the Hudson, kids can enjoy Teardrop Park, a hidden urban oasis with an enormous slide; Nelson A Rockefeller Park, with an open field for Frisbee and lazing, plus a playground with a unique pedal carousel and a charming duck pond. Don't miss Pier 25, just north of BPC: a top-to-bottom renovation added an excellent new playground, a mini-golf course and snack bar, an Astroturf area and a skate park.

Chelsea Piers
For listings, see p330.
This vast and hugely bustling complex on the Hudson River is ideal in the colder months, thanks to its bowling alley, roller rink, pool, toddler gym, ice-skating rink and climbing walls.

Central Park

For more information and a calendar of events, visit www.centralparknyc.org. Don't miss the antique **Friedsam Memorial Carousel** (open Apr-Oct; $2.50 per ride). There are 21 playgrounds in the park; the large **Heckscher Playground**, in the south-west corner (between Seventh Avenue & Central Park West, from 61st to 63rd Streets), sprawls over more than three acres and has an up-to-date adventure area and handy restrooms.

Belvedere Castle
Midpark, off the 79th Street Transverse Road (1-212 772 0210, www.centralparknyc.org). Subway B, C to 81st Street-Museum of Natural History. **Open** 10am-5pm Tue-Sun. **Admission** free. **Map** p405 D19.
Central Park designer Frederick Law Olmsted planned this fanciful structure to lend his masterful creation a pastoral, fairy tale-like quality. Three viewing platforms give little visitors a stunning view of Turtle Pond below and, in the distance, the expansive, tree-lined Great Lawn (the two higher terraces are accessed from within the castle's turret). During opening hours, budding naturalists can borrow nature kits equipped with binoculars and field guides with which to explore the castle's dominion.

Central Park Zoo
For listings, see p95.
The stars here are the penguins and the polar bear, which live in glass-enclosed habitats so you can watch their underwater antics. The creation of a snow leopard environment a few years ago added a breathtaking endangered animal to the zoo's menagerie and even changed the zoo's topography. Among the zoo's most engaging offerings for kids are the sea lion and penguin feedings and the mist-filled Tropic Zone: The Rainforest, with free-flying birds, plus lots of tropical vegetation, monkeys and

lemurs. The Tisch Children's Zoo, a stone's throw away, houses species that enjoy being petted – and fed – among them llamas, sheep and goats.

Conservatory Water
Central Park, entrance on Fifth Avenue, at 72nd Street. Subway 6 to 68th Street-Hunter College. **Map** p405 E20.
Nicknamed Stuart Little Pond after EB White's story-book mouse, Conservatory Water is a mecca for model-yacht racers. When the boatmaster is around (daily from April through October, weather permitting), you can rent a remote-controlled vessel ($11/30mins; see www.centralparknyc.org forhours). Kids are drawn to two statues near the pond: the bronze rendering of Lewis Carroll's Alice, the Mad Hatter and the White Rabbit is an irresistible climbing spot, while the Hans Christian Andersen statue is a gathering point for free storytelling sessions (early June-late Sept 11am-noon Sat, www.hcastorycenter.org).

Swedish Cottage Marionette Theater
Central Park West, at 81st Street (1-212 988 9093). Subway B, C to 81st Street-Museum of Natural History. **Shows** *Oct-June* 10.30am, noon Tue, Thur, Fri; 10.30am, noon, 2.30pm Wed; 1pm Sat, Sun. *July, Aug* 10.30am, noon Mon-Fri. **Tickets** $8; $5 reductions. **No credit cards**. **Map** p405 D19.
Tucked just inside the western boundary of Central Park is a curiously incongruous old wooden structure. Designed as a schoolhouse, the building was Sweden's entry in the 1876 Centennial Exposition in Philadelphia (it was moved to NYC a year later). Inside is one of the best-kept secrets (and deals) in town: a tiny marionette theatre with regular shows. Reservations are recommended.

Trump Wollman Rink & Victorian Gardens
Trump Wollman Rink *For listings, see p334.* **Victorian Gardens** *1-212 982 2229, www. victoriangardensnyc.com. Subway N, Q, R to Fifth Avenue-59th Street.* **Open** *Mid May-mid Sept* 11am-7pm Mon-Thur; 11am-8pm Fri; 10am-9pm Sat; 10am-8pm Sun. **Admission** $6.50 Mon-Fri; $7.50 Sat, Sun; free children under 36in tall. Games & rides cost extra. **Credit** AmEx, DC, Disc, MC, V. **Map** p405 D21.
Skating in Central Park amid snowy trees, with grand apartment buildings towering in the distance, is a New York tradition. This popular (read: crowded) skating rink offers lessons and skate rentals, plus a snack bar where you can warm up with hot chocolate. In summer, the site hosts Victorian Gardens, a quaint amusement park for younger children. It's hardly white-knuckle stuff, but the mini-teacup carousel and Rio Grande train will satisfy little thrill-seekers.
▶ *For more skating rinks, see p333.*

Horsing Around

Take a spin on one of the prize ponies of Brooklyn's beautifully restored carousel.

Imagine a tiny, antique toy carousel in an elegant glass music box. Now blow it up to life-size proportions, set it down amid several new, vivid green lawns along the East River, and you'll have a good idea of what Jane's Carousel is like. The elegant spinner is, in fact, vintage; it was crafted in 1922 by the Philadelphia Toboggan Company for Idora Park, an amusement park in the steel-manufacturing town of Youngstown, Pennsylvania. In 1975, it had the distinction of becoming the first carousel to be added to the National Register of Historic Places. When a devastating fire destroyed much of Idora in 1984, the park closed for good and put those attractions that survived up for sale at auction. No one expected a buyer to purchase the carousel whole, but Brooklyn residents Jane and David Walentas, an artist and real-estate developer, respectively, had been looking for a quality vintage carousel to restore, in hopes of eventually giving it a home in Brooklyn Bridge Park.

Together with a team of artists, Jane Walentas set about the painstaking refurbishment in her Dumbo studio, removing layers of paint from the 48 hand-carved horses, repainting and releafing them as well as the scenery panels,

reglazing mirrors and rewiring the carousel with 1,200 lights. When her husband's waterfront development project was nixed by city planners, the couple put the carousel on show in a local gallery in 2006, in hopes of sparking interest in seeing it become fully operational in a permanent space.

Once the couple got the go-ahead from the City of New York (with some opposition from neighbours), they commissioned a pavilion from modernist French architect Jean Nouvel. The square transparent box – made of Plexiglas and steel – was completed in August 2011. The structure opens on the side, shuttering at night for a shadowbox-like show each evening. It's designed to withstand any kind of weather (it managed to survive even Hurricane Sandy, in late 2012), so not only is the carousel protected from the elements, but it's also open year-round. Before long, it will be a new generation's nostalgic touchstone.

Jane's Carousel
Empire-Fulton Ferry section of the Brooklyn Bridge Park, Dumbo; enter at Main Street (718-222-2502, www.janescarousel.org). **Open** *May-mid Oct* 11am-7pm Mon, Wed-Sun. *Mid Oct-Apr* 11am-6pm Thur-Sun. **Cost** $2, free under-3s.

ARTS & ENTERTAINMENT

RESTAURANTS & CAFÉS

Alice's Teacup
102 W 73rd Street, at Columbus Avenue, Upper West Side (1-212 799 3006, www.alices teacup.com). Subway B, C to 72nd Street. **Open** 8am-8pm daily. **Credit** AmEx, DC, Disc, MC, V. **Map** p405 C20.

Beloved by Disney-adoring children, this magical spot offers much more than tea (though the three-tiered version, comprising an assortment of sandwiches, scones and desserts, truly is a treat). The brunch menu is fit for royalty, with Alice's Curious French Toast (it's drenched in fruit coulis, crème anglaise and syrup) and scones in scrumptious flavours like blueberry and pumpkin. In the afternoon, the special after-school snack menu features house-made graham crackers and honey, and banana bread topped with jam. At a little shop in the front of the eaterie, you can outfit your fairy princess in training with a pair of glittery wings. **Other locations** 156 E 64th Street, at Lexington Avenue, Upper East Side (1-212 486 9200); 220 E 81st Street, between Second & Third Avenues, Upper East Side (1-212 734 4832).

Cowgirl
519 Hudson Street, at 10th Street, West Village (1-212 633 1133, www.cowgirlnyc.com). Subway 1 to Christopher Street-Sheridan Square. **Open** 11am-11pm Mon-Thur; 11am-midnight Fri; 10am-3.45pm, 4.15pm-midnight Sat; 10am-3.45pm, 4.15-11pm Sun. **Credit** AmEx, MC, V. **Map** p403 D28.

This neighbourhood favourite is one of those rare spots that appeals to both adults and children. Unwind with a pitcher of potent margaritas amid the charming 1950s-era ranch decor. The whimsical setting, along with a small old-time candy shop and plenty of crayons, means the whole crowd will remain buoyant while waiting for rib-sticking fare such as quesadillas, pulled-pork sandwiches and gooey mac and cheese. Finish your meal with the unbelievable ice-cream sundae disguised as a mashed potato. **Other locations** Cowgirl Sea-Horse, 259 Front Street, at Dover Street, Financial District (1-212 608 7873, www.cowgirlseahorse.com).

Crema
111 W 17th Street, between Sixth & Seventh Avenues, Chelsea (1-212 691 4477, www.crema restaurante.com). Subway F, M, 1, 2, 3 to 14th Street; L to Sixth Avenue. **Open** noon-10.30pm Mon-Wed; noon-11pm Thur; noon-midnight Fri; 11.30am-midnight Sat; 11.30am-10pm Sun. **Credit** AmEx, Disc, MC, V. **Map** p403 D27.

Among the many kid-friendly offerings at Julieta Ballesteros's upscale Mexican restaurant are quesadillas. Here they're grilled flour tortillas laced with chihuahua cheese and accented with black beans, shrimp, grilled chicken breast or steak. Other options include a *taco de carne asada* entrée and

sides like seasonal rice or *granielote* (corn kernels with cream). Tropical-flavored lemonade, ice cream and sorbet round out the à la carte offerings.

★ Ditch Plains
29 Bedford Street, at Downing Street, Greenwich Village (1-212 633 0202, www.ditch-plains.com). Subway A, B, C, D, E, F, M to W 4th Street; 1 to Houston Street. **Open** 11am-2am daily. **Credit** AmEx, Disc, MC, V. **Map** p403 D29.

This New England-style fish shack, named for chef-owner Marc Murphy's favourite surfing spot in Montauk, Long Island, is sophisticated and sleek: no seaside knick-knacks here. It's perfect for families at all times of day, as it excels at simple but upscale fare, such as a lobster roll (a mound of luscious chopped meat mixed with scallions, tarragon and aïoli, served on a soft roll with a side of sweet-potato chips), ceviche and soft tacos. The place offers kids a stellar menu of their own, packed with an array of hot dogs and health-conscious treats like wholewheat quesadillas. **Other locations** 100 W 82nd Street, at Columbus Avenue, Upper West Side (1-212 362 4815).

S'MAC
345 E 12th Street, between First & Second Avenues, East Village (1-212 358 7912, www. smacnyc.com). Subway L to First Avenue. **Open** 11am-11pm Mon-Thur, Sun; 11am-1am Fri, Sat. **Credit** AmEx, DC, Disc, MC, V. **Map** p28.

A dozen varieties of mac and cheese range from simple all-American (mild enough for picky types) to a more complex dish with brie, roasted figs and shiitake mushrooms, or mac and manchego with fennel and shallots. There's a size for everyone: 'nosh' (great for kids), 'major munch' (a hearty adult serving), 'mongo' (if you want leftovers to take with you) and 'partay' (which serves eight to 12). Children are offered a regular bowl in lieu of the sizzling skillet in which meals are typically served. **Other locations** 157 E 33rd Street, between Lexington & Third Avenues, Midtown East (1-212 383 3900).

BABYSITTING

Baby Sitters' Guild
1-212 682 0227, www.babysittersguild.com. **Bookings** 9am-9pm daily. **No credit cards** (except when paying through hotel).

Babysitters cost from $30 an hour and up (four-hour minimum), plus transportation ($5, or $10 after midnight). Sitters are available around the clock, and between them speak 17 languages.

Pinch Sitters
1-212 260 6005, www.nypinchsitters.com. **Bookings** 8am-5pm Mon-Fri. **No credit cards**. Charges are $20/hr (four-hour minimum), plus a $10 travel charge after 9pm. A $35 fee is levied for cancellations given with less than 24 hours' notice.

Film & TV

There's a lot to see at the centre of the action.

Woody, Marty, Spike: by now the whole world is on first-name terms with New York's canonical legends. Even if this is your first visit to NYC, the cityscape will feel familiar; every corner has been immortalised on celluloid. It's easy to feel as if you've walked on to a massive movie set, especially when photogenic landmarks such as the Empire State Building pan into view. And you might even stumble upon an actual shoot – the thriving local film industry is based in Queens. Many high-profile TV shows are also produced here and, if you're organised (and lucky), you could snag tickets to a studio taping.

ARTS & ENTERTAINMENT

FILM

Few cities offer the film lover as many options as New York. If you insist, you can check out the blockbusters at the multiplexes on 42nd Street. But Gotham's gems are its arthouses, museums and other film institutions. For listings, see *Time Out New York* magazine or www.timeout.com/newyork.

Art & revival houses

Angelika Film Center
18 W Houston Street, at Mercer Street, Soho (1-212 995 2570, www.angelikafilmcenter.com). Subway B, D, F, M to Broadway-Lafayette Street; N, R to Prince Street; 6 to Bleecker Street. **Tickets** $13.50; $10 reductions. **Credit** AmEx, MC, V. **Map** p403 E29.
When it opened in 1989, the Angelika immediately became a player in the then-booming Amerindie scene, and the six-screen cinema still puts the emphasis on edgier fare, both domestic and foreign. The complex is packed at weekends, so come extra early or visit the website to buy advance tickets.

Anthology Film Archives
32 Second Avenue, at 2nd Street, East Village (1-212 505 5181, www.anthologyfilmarchives.org). Subway F to Lower East Side-Second Avenue; 6 to Bleecker Street. **Tickets** $10; $8 reductions. **Credit** AmEx, Disc, MC, V. **Map** p403 F29.
This red-brick building feels a bit like a fortress – and, in a sense, it is one, protecting the legacy of NYC's fiercest experimenters. Anthology is committed to

screening the world's most adventurous films, from 16mm found-footage works to digital video dreams. Dedicated to the preservation, study and exhibition of independent and avant-garde film, it houses a gallery and film museum and two screens.

★ BAM Rose Cinemas
Brooklyn Academy of Music, 30 Lafayette Avenue, between Ashland Place & St Felix Street, Fort Greene, Brooklyn (1-718 636 4100, www.bam.org). Subway B, Q, 2, 3, 4, 5 to Atlantic Avenue; C to Lafayette Avenue; D, M, N, R to Pacific Street; G to Fulton Street. **Tickets** $12; $9 reductions. **Credit** AmEx, Disc, MC, V. **Map** p410 T10.
Brooklyn's premier art-film venue does double duty as a rep house for well-programmed classics on

---

INSIDE TRACK
OUTDOOR MOVIES

With summer arrives the wonderful New York tradition of free outdoor movie festivals. Look out for the **Bryant Park Summer Film Festival** in Midtown (1-212 512 5700, www.bryantpark.org); **Central Park Conservancy Film Festival** (1-212 310 6600, centralparknyc.org); **Movies with a View** in Brooklyn Bridge Park (1-718 802 0603, www.brooklyn bridgepark.org); the **River to River Festival** (*see p32*) across Lower Manhattan; and **Summer on the Hudson** in Riverside Park South (1-212 408 0219).

35mm and as a first-run multiplex for indie films. It's recently started to host an annual best-of-Sundance programme – far more convenient than going to Utah.

Cinema Village
22 E 12th Street, between Fifth Avenue & University Place, Greenwich Village (1-212 924 3363, www.cinemavillage.com). Subway L, N, Q, R, 4, 5, 6 to 14th Street-Union Square. **Tickets** $11; $6-$8 reductions. **Credit** Disc, MC, V. **Map** p403 E28.
A classic marquee that charmed Noah Baumbach long before he made *The Squid and the Whale*, this three-screener specialises in indie flicks, cutting-edge documentaries and foreign films.

★ Film Forum
209 W Houston Street, between Sixth Avenue & Varick Street, West Village (1-212 727 8110, www.filmforum.org). Subway 1 to Houston Street. **Tickets** $12.50; $7 reductions. **Credit** (online purchases only) AmEx, Disc, MC, V. **Map** p403 D29.
The city's leading tastemaking venue for independent new releases and classic movies, Film Forum is programmed by a fest-scouring staff that takes its duties as seriously as a Kurosawa samurai. A recent renovation included comfy new seats.

★ IFC Center
323 Sixth Avenue, at W 3rd Street, Greenwich Village (1-212 924 7771, www.ifccenter.com). Subway A, B, C, D, E, F, M to W 4th Street. **Tickets** $13; $9 reductions. **Credit** AmEx, Disc, MC, V. **Map** p403 D29.
The long-darkened 1930s Waverly was once again illuminated in 2005 when it was reborn as a modern three-screen arthouse, showing the latest indie hits, choice midnight cult items and occasional foreign classics. You may rub elbows with the directors or the actors on the screen, as many introduce their work on opening night.

Landmark Sunshine Cinema
141-143 E Houston Street, between First & Second Avenues, East Village (1-212 260 7289, www.landmarktheatres.com). Subway F to Lower East Side-Second Avenue. **Tickets** $13; $9 reductions. **Credit** AmEx, MC, V. **Map** p403 F29.
Once a renowned Yiddish theatre, this comfortable, date-friendly venue has snazz and chutzpah to spare. Intimate cinemas and excellent sound are a beautiful complement to the indie films; here too is New York's most consistently excellent midnight series on Fridays and Saturdays.

Leonard Nimoy Thalia
Symphony Space, 2537 Broadway, at 95th Street, entrance on 95th Street, Upper West Side (1-212 864 5400, www.symphonyspace.org).

Subway 1, 2, 3 to 96th Street. **Tickets** $14; $12 reductions. **Credit** AmEx, MC, V. **Map** p406 C17.
The famed Thalia arthouse, which featured in *Annie Hall* (when it was screening *The Sorrow and the Pity*), has since been upgraded. The fare is an eclectic mix of international, arthouse and classic films.

Maysles Cinema
343 Malcolm X Boulevard (Lenox Avenue), between 127th & 128th Streets, Harlem (1-212 582 6050, www.mayslesinstitute.org). Subway A, B, C, D, 2, 3 to 125th Street. **Tickets** *Suggested donation* $10. **No credit cards**. **Map** p407 D13.
Hidden behind a Harlem storefront, this 55-seat neighbourhood film hub serves up an eclectic stew. You might catch rousing hip hop and reggae films, a panel discussion about Times Square starring a zonked-out sex performer from Gotham's sleazy days, or rarities such as *Demon Lover Diary* and *The Police Tapes*.

Paris Theatre
4 W 58th Street, between Fifth & Sixth Avenues, Midtown (1-212 688 3800, www.theparis theatre.com). Subway N, Q, R to Fifth Avenue-59th Street. **Tickets** $14; $10.50 reductions. **Credit** AmEx, MC, V. **Map** p405 E22.
The elegant, single-screen Paris is one of the oldest continually operating movie houses in the country (it was founded in 1948). Its plush carpets and seats, tiny lobby and lack of any on-screen advertising set it apart even from the city's indie houses. It screens new and revival French films whenever possible.

Quad Cinema
34 W 13th Street, between Fifth & Sixth Avenues, Greenwich Village (1-212 255 8800, www.quad cinema.com). Subway F, M to 14th Street; L to Sixth Avenue. **Tickets** $11; $8 reductions. **Credit** AmEx, MC, V. **Map** p403 E28.
The Quad's four small screens show a wide range of foreign and American indie films. However, the real standouts at this Greenwich Village operation are the latest offerings related to gay sexuality and politics.
▶ *Another popular spot for gay-oriented cinema, the Clearview Chelsea, offers drag queen-hosted classic films; see p267 Inside Track.*

Other institutions

★ Film Society of Lincoln Center
70 Lincoln Center Plaza, between Broadway & Amsterdam Avenue, Upper West Side (1-212 875 5600, www.filmlinc.com). Subway 1 to 66th Street-Lincoln Center. **Tickets** $13; $9 reductions. **Credit** AmEx, Disc, MC, V. **Map** p405 C21.
Founded in 1969 to promote contemporary film, the FSLC now also hosts the prestigious New York Film Festival, among other annual fests. Programmes are usually thematic, with an international perspective. The new $40-million Elinor Bunin Munroe Film

Essential New York Films

Six celluloid visions of the great metropolis.

DOG DAY AFTERNOON
dir Sidney Lumet, 1975
Al Pacino heads a stellar ensemble cast in this tense, moving tale of a first-time crook whose plan to rob a Brooklyn bank goes spectacularly awry. The film brims with distinctly New York characters: John Cazale as a spaced-out partner in crime; Chris Sarandon as a fragile transsexual; and Charles Durning as a frazzled detective.

MANHATTAN
dir Woody Allen, 1979
Allen's love sonnet to his home city frames an edgy social comedy. The movie reminds you what a gorgeous, grand sight the island really is from the moment the Gershwin-scored opening montage kicks in: the fish markets and basketball courts; the Fifth Avenue boutiques and Broadway theatres; the high-rise dwellers and lowlifes.

SWEET SMELL OF SUCCESS
dir Alexander Mackendrick, 1957
This adaptation of a novella about a megalomaniacal gossip columnist (Burt Lancaster) – based on newspaperman Walter Winchell – and a parasitic press agent (Tony Curtis) encapsulates what once went down in the booths of the '21' Club and the upper floors of the Brill Building.

DO THE RIGHT THING
dir Spike Lee, 1989
Outraged over the 1986 Howard Beach incident, Lee responded with a 360-degree look at what can happen when New York's melting pot boils over. The film doubles as a vivid portrait of his native Brooklyn, in which every stoop philosopher, nosy matriarch and beat-box-loving B-boy gets his or her moment in the spotlight.

ROSEMARY'S BABY
dir Roman Polanski, 1968
This realistic supernatural drama was a transfusion of thick, urbane blood to the dated horror genre, and much of its revolutionary impact should be credited to the city of New York itself. A young couple, played by Mia Farrow and John Cassavetes, moves into the Dakota Building – every bit the Gothic pile as any Transylvanian vampire's mansion.

TAXI DRIVER
dir Martin Scorsese, 1976
'You talking to me?' Cracked hero Travis Bickle (Robert De Niro) cruises through Greenwich Village and Hell's Kitchen in his taxi. The story may be all in his head: a deranged man's dream of vanilla romance with Cybill Shepherd, unchecked fury at political impotence and the compulsive urge to right every wrong, no matter how slight.

ARTS & ENTERTAINMENT

Center houses two plush cinemas; there are frequent post-screening Q&As. Between these state-of-the-art screens and the operational Walter Reade Theater across the street, a small multiplex has been born. The Bunin also houses a café and bookstore.

★ Museum of Modern Art

For listings, see p88. **Tickets** free with museum admission, or $12; $8-$10 reductions; free under-16s. **Credit** AmEx, Disc, MC, V.

Renowned for its superb programming of art films and experimental work, MoMA draws from a vast vault. You have to buy tickets in person at the museum at the lobby desk or the film desk (see www.moma.org or call 1-212 708 9480 for more information). Note that while museum admission includes the day's film programme, a film ticket doesn't include admission to the museum galleries – although it can be applied towards the cost within 30 days.

Museum of the Moving Image

For listings, see p128. **Tickets** $12; $6-$9 reductions. **Credit** MC, V.

Dinner at the Movies

Gastro-cinemas are breaking free of the popcorn box.

After the Film Society of Lincoln Center (*see p260*) opened its stunning new **Elinor Bunin Munroe Film Center**, restaurateur Jason Denton ('ino, 'inoteca) premiered his smart and casual on-site street-level café attached to the cinema: Indie Food & Wine (144 W 65th Street, between Broadway & Amsterdam Avenue, 1-212 875 5456, www.indiefoodandwine.com). Movie-goers can stop in for Mediterranean-inflected fare such as salads and a milk-braised pork belly sandwich or pick up upgraded concession-stand snacks like organic hot dogs and parmesan-truffle popcorn – it's a far cry from the old spartan arthouse image.

The **Nitehawk Cinema** (136 Metropolitan Avenue, between Berry Street & Wythe Avenue, 1-718 384 3980, www.nitehawk cinema.com) in Williamsburg, Brooklyn, goes one better by serving food in the cinema itself. Seats are arranged in pairs with sturdy tables, and viewers order from a menu created by Michelin-starred chef Saul Bolton. Just write down your order at any point during the movie on a piece of paper for a server to pick up and ferry to the kitchen. The comfort-food grub includes meaty fish tacos and a tasty burger, but the real highlights are the chef's variations on concession-stand staples, such as popcorn tossed with parmesan, black pepper and garlic butter. Two café-bars keep movie-goers loose.

Amid these shiny competitors, trailblazer **reRun Gastropub Theater** (147 Front Street, between Jay & Pearl Streets, Dumbo, Brooklyn, 1-718 766 9110, www.reruntheater.com) still feels original – both food and booze are served from a bar inside the theatre, and guests sit in repurposed minivan seats surrounded by a gritty mural of the city. The bar closes when the lights go down, but food orders placed beforehand – creative riffs on junk food such as mashed potato-stuffed pretzels and duck fat- and herb-tossed popcorn – will be delivered to your seat, and you can load up on discounted buckets of beer or carafes of wine and cocktails to tide you over through the show.

Nitehawk Cinema

ARTS & ENTERTAINMENT

Like the rest of the museum, MMI's theatre has received a magnificent renovation, resulting in a state-of-the-art 264-seat cinema. Expect excellent prints and screenings of the classics.

Foreign-language specialists

You can catch the latest foreign-language flicks at art and revival houses, but there is a wealth of specialist venues as well, including the **French Institute Alliance Française** (22 E 60th Street, 1-212 355 6100, www.fiaf.org), the **Japan Society** (*see p91*) and **Scandinavia House** (*see p81*). The **Asia Society & Museum** (*see p98*) screens works from Asian countries plus Asian-American productions.

Film festivals

From late September to early October, the Film Society of Lincoln Center hosts the **New York Film Festival** (1-212 875 5050, www.filmlinc.com), a showcase packed with premières, features and short flicks from around the globe. Together with Lincoln Center's Film Comment magazine, the FSLC also offers the popular **Film Comment Selects**, showcasing films that have yet to be distributed in the US.

January brings the annual **New York Jewish Film Festival** (1-212 875 5600, www.thejewishmuseum.org) to Lincoln Center's Walter Reade Theater. In early March, the **New York International Children's Film Festival** (1-212 349 0330, www.gkids.com) kicks off two weeks of anime, shorts and features made for kids and teens. Each spring, the Museum of Modern Art and the Film Society of Lincoln Center sponsor the highly regarded **New Directors/New Films** series, presenting works by on-the-cusp filmmakers. And in late April/early May, Robert De Niro's **Tribeca Film Festival** (1-212 941 2400, www.tribecafilmfestival.org) draws around 400,000 fans to screenings of independent movies. It's followed by the **New York Lesbian & Gay Film Festival** (1-646 290 8136, www.newfest.org) in summer. The season also brings several outdoor film festivals (*see p259* **Inside Track**).

TV STUDIO TAPINGS

Colbert Report

513 W 54th Street, between Tenth & Eleventh Avenues, Hell's Kitchen (www.colbertnation. com/tickets). Subway C, E to 50th Street. **Tapings** 6pm Mon-Thur. **Map** p405 C22.
In his cult parody of Bill O'Reilly's right-wing political talk-show, sarcastic correspondent Stephen Colbert tells viewers why everyone else's opinions

are 'just plain wrong'. Reserve tickets online at least six months ahead, or try your luck getting standby tickets on the day at 4pm. You must be 18 and have photo ID.

The Daily Show with Jon Stewart

733 Eleventh Avenue, between 51st & 52nd Streets, Hell's Kitchen (www.thedailyshow.com/tickets). Subway C, E to 50th Street. **Tapings** 5.45pm Mon-Thur. **Map** p405 C22.
Many viewers believe they get a fairer view of current affairs from Stewart's irreverent take than they do from the network news. Reserve tickets online at least three months ahead; as ticket distribution may be in excess of studio capacity, admission is not guaranteed. You must be over 18 and have photo ID.

Late Night with Jimmy Fallon

30 Rockefeller Plaza, between 49th & 50th Streets (1-212 664 3056, www.latenightwithjimmyfallon. com). Subway B, D, F, M to 47th-50th Streets-Rockefeller Center. **Tapings** 5.30pm Mon-Fri. **Map** p405 D22.
Whether you're a fan of Jimmy Fallon from his *SNL* days or you just want to see his house band, the Roots, perform, here's your chance to catch them live. Call at least a month ahead to request advance tickets, or try hanging out under the NBC Studios marquee before 9am to score a same-day standby seat. Fallon's crew announce last-minute ticket openings on Twitter (@LateNightJimmy) and offer special band benches (www.fallonbandbench.com), where fans can sit stageside for performances by their favorite musical guests. You must be 16 or older and have photo ID.

Late Show with David Letterman

1697 Broadway, between 53rd & 54th Streets, Midtown (www.cbs.com/late_show/late_show/ tickets). Subway B, D, E to Seventh Avenue. **Tapings** 4.30pm Mon-Wed; 3.30pm, 6pm Thur. **Map** p405 D22.
Letterman's sardonic humour has been a defining feature of the late-night landscape for decades. Seats are hard to get: fill out a request form online, or try to get a standby ticket by calling 1-212 247 6497 at 11am on the day. You must be 18 with photo ID.

Saturday Night Live

30 Rockefeller Plaza, Sixth Avenue, between 49th & 50th Streets, Midtown (1-212 664 3056, www.nbc.com/snl). Subway B, D, F, M to 47th-50th Streets-Rockefeller Center. **Tapings** *Dress rehearsal* 8pm. *Live show* 11.30pm. **Map** p405 D22.
Tickets to this long-running comedy sketch show are assigned by lottery every autumn. Send an email to snltickets@nbcuni.com in August, or try the standby lottery on the day. Line up by 7am (but get there much earlier) under the NBC Studio marquee (49th Street side of 30 Rockefeller Plaza). You must be over 16 with photo ID.

ARTS & ENTERTAINMENT

Gay & Lesbian

Welcome to America's LGBT capital.

In summer 2011, same-sex marriage became legal in New York State – during Pride week, no less – marking a major civil rights victory in the birthplace of the modern gay rights movement, and cementing New York City's status as the LGBT capital of the US (sorry, San Francisco, you people go to bed too early). But even as gayness becomes middle-of-the-road in New York, the city's queer scene is constantly finding ways to reinvent itself.

Offering much more than drag and piano bars (though, delightfully, they still thrive), today's LGBT New York has popular venues devoted to rock and country music and an abundance of arty, pan-queer parties and events. Downtown cultural institutions such as Joe's Pub and Dixon Place stage performances by iconic artists like Sandra Bernhard and more recent pioneers, including Justin Vivian Bond. Brooklyn – Williamsburg, in particular – is a home base for many young queers, resulting in a thriving scene outside of the traditional Manhattan strongholds of the Village, Chelsea and Hell's Kitchen.

GAY NEIGHBOURHOODS

From a historical point of view, the gayest spot in New York City is Sheridan Square, in the heart of the charming West Village. The tiny triangular park served as a battlefield in June 1969, when fed-up patrons of the Stonewall Inn across the street rose up against the police, who used to routinely raid homosexual establishments and arrest their customers. The Stonewall riots sparked the modern gay rights movement, and Sheridan Square became the epicentre of a neighbourhood 'liberated' by gay activists, with Christopher Street as its main drag. The strip still offers a hotchpotch of gay bars and stores selling rainbow-covered knick-knacks, but the West Village no longer reigns as queen of gay New York (except during LGBT Pride; *see right* **The Queer Calendar**).

Beginning in the mid 1990s, much of the scene shifted north to **Chelsea**, with Eighth Avenue between 14th and 23rd Streets serving as a runway for buffed Chelsea boys eager to show off their biceps, triceps and pecs – an aesthetic that went out of vogue some time in the last decade, along with the Chelsea scene itself. You'll still find a number of homo watering holes, cute shops and cheap, trendy restaurants, but the real action has once again shifted north. Former slum **Hell's Kitchen** began gaining traction as a 'gaybourhood' in the early noughties – its proximity to the Theater District and rising rents in Chelsea were two points in its favour. Over the past decade, a thriving bar scene has evolved: at time of writing there were more than a dozen gay watering holes in the area, mostly on and around Ninth Avenue between 45th and 53nd Streets, and several more in the works. But the affluent, manicured Hell's Kitchen set isn't for everyone. The **East Village** has a more creative, casual gay vibe, and, although Brooklyn doesn't have a queer strip to call its own, several enclaves (**Williamsburg** and **Park Slope**, among others) have large gay and lesbian populations, so you'll find a variety of events and venues throughout Kings County. The city's most diverse borough, Queens, has several gay bars located along Roosevelt Avenue in Jackson Heights, which tend to attract a largely Latino crowd, and the vibe throughout the neighbourhood is friendly and welcoming.

THE QUEER CALENDAR

NYC Pride, New York's biggest queer event, takes place in June (26-30 June in 2013), bringing with it a whirl of parties and performances. The weekend-capping event is the **NYC LGBT Pride March** (*see p33*), which takes five hours to wind down Fifth Avenue from midtown to the West Village and draws millions of spectators and participants. During the summer, New York's gay social scene extends to scenic **Fire Island**, home to the neighbouring beach resorts of Cherry Grove and the Pines, which are about a 90-minute train and ferry ride from Manhattan. In recent years, **Asbury Park** (*see p340*) in New Jersey, just under two hours from Manhattan, has also become something of a gay summer mecca. In the autumn, **Hallowe'en** is a major to-do, with bars and clubs packed with costumed revellers. Annual events that draw many locals and visitors include the notorious **Black Party** (March), the **Folsom Street East** leather-and-fetish street fair (June) and the **Dyke March** (June). Culture buffs can check out summer's annual **Hot!** festival of lesbian and gay arts at Dixon Place (*see p310*), offering a wide variety of queer art, theatre, dance and comedy events. Film fans might like the offerings at the **NewFest** (www.newfest.org) in July.

INFORMATION, MEDIA & CULTURE

In what may be a sign of the times, there are no specifically gay bookstores left in New York. The last one in existence, Oscar Wilde, closed in 2009 after 41 years in business. **Bluestockings** has a good selection of queer and feminist works, while **Rainbows & Triangles** sells plenty of gay titles.

To find out what's going on, refer to the Gay & Lesbian section of *Time Out New York* or www.timeout.com/newyork. Also popular is the gay entertainment magazine *Next* (www.nextmagazine.com), which offers extensive boy-centric information on bars, clubs, restaurants and events; *Odyssey* (www.odysseymagazine.net) also has basic listings for men's parties, as well as columns by local drag queens. The monthly *Go!* (www.gomag.com), 'a cultural road map for the city girl', gives the lowdown on the lesbian nightlife and travel scene. *Gay City News* (www.gaycitynews.com) provides feisty political coverage with an activist slant. All four are free and widely available in street boxes, gay and lesbian bars and stores.

Bluestockings

172 Allen Street, between Rivington & Stanton Streets, Lower East Side (1-212 777 6028, www.bluestockings.com). Subway F to Lower East Side-Second Avenue. **Open** 11am-11pm daily. **Credit** AmEx, MC, V. **Map** p403 F29. This radical bookstore, Fairtrade café and activist resource centre stocks LGBT literature and regularly hosts queer events (often with a feminist slant), including dyke knitting circles, trans-politics forums and women's open-mic nights.

★ Lesbian, Gay, Bisexual & Transgender Community Center

208 W 13th Street, between Seventh & Eighth Avenues, West Village (1-212 620 7310, www.gaycenter.org). Subway A, C, E, 1, 2, 3 to 14th Street; L to Eighth Avenue. **Open** 9am-10pm Mon-Fri; 9am-10pm Sat; 9am-9pm Sun. **Map** p403 D27.

ARTS & ENTERTAINMENT

Black Party.

ARTS & ENTERTAINMENT

XL Nightclub, Cabaret & Lounge.
See p268.

Founded in 1983, the Center provides information and a gay support network. As well as being a friendly resource that offers guidance to gay tourists, it is used as a venue for more than 300 groups. Public programming here includes everything from book signings to monthly Dance 208 DJ parties. The National Archive of Lesbian, Gay, Bisexual and Transgender History (open to the public 6-8pm Thur) and the Pat Parker/Vito Russo Library (6-9pm Mon-Fri; 1-4pm Sat) are housed here, as is an art gallery and a CyberCenter that offers internet access for $3 an hour (11am-9pm Mon-Fri; noon-9pm Sat, Sun).

Lesbian Herstory Archives

484 14th Street, between Eighth Avenue & Prospect Park West, Park Slope, Brooklyn (1-718 768 3953, www.lesbianherstoryarchives.org). Subway F to 15th Street-Prospect Park. **Open** varies; see website calendar. **Map** p410 T12.
The Herstory Archives contain more than 20,000 books (cultural theory, fiction, poetry, plays), 1,600 periodicals, 600 films and videos and assorted memorabilia. The cosy brownstone also hosts screenings, readings and social gatherings, plus an open house in June (during Brooklyn Pride) and December.

★ Leslie-Lohman Museum of Gay & Lesbian Art

26 Wooster Street, between Canal & Grand Streets, Soho (1-212 431 2609, www.leslielohman.org). Subway A, C, E to Canal Street. **Open** noon-6pm Tue-Sat. **Admission** free. **Map** p403 E30.
Formerly the Leslie-Lohman Gay Art Foundation, this institution was granted museum status by the state of New York in 2011. Founded in 1990 by Fritz Lohman and Charles Leslie, the museum seeks to preserve and highlight the contributions of LGBTQ artists throughout history up to the present. In addition to changing exhibitions, it has a large permanent collection and library, and hosts regular book signings, panel discussions and low-key parties.

Rainbows & Triangles

192 Eighth Avenue, between 19th & 20th Streets, Chelsea (1-212 627 2166, www. rainbowsandtriangles.com). Subway C, E to 23rd Street. **Open** 11am-10pm Mon-Sat; noon-9pm Sun. **Credit** AmEx, DC, Disc, MC, V. **Map** p403 D27.
This friendly Chelsea store packs a lot of gayness into a small space. In addition to books and magazines, you'll find novelties like merman Christmas ornaments and naked-hunk calendars, and clothing ranging from goofy tees ('Pitcher' and 'Catcher' shirts, for example) to jock straps. A discreet back room sells porn and other accoutrements for those who are feeling frisky but don't want to be seen going in or out of one of the area's many sex shops.

WHERE TO STAY

While you'd be hard-pressed to find a gay-unfriendly hotel in New York, the following guesthouses and B&Bs are either exclusively gay or geared towards a queer clientele.

Chelsea Mews Guest House

344 W 15th Street, between Eighth & Ninth Avenues, Chelsea (1-212 255 9174, www. chelseamewsguesthouse.com). Subway A,

C, E to 14th Street; L to Eighth Avenue. **Rates**
$150-$175 double. **Rooms** 9. **No credit cards**.
Map p403 C27.

Built in 1840, this clothing-optional guesthouse
caters to gay men. The rooms are comfortable and
well furnished and, in most cases, share a bathroom.
Bicycle tours and coffee are complimentary – as is
access to a songbird aviary! An on-site massage
therapist and soothing Tempur-Pedic beds in every
room help ensure a relaxing stay.
Internet (wireless, free). No smoking.

★ Chelsea Pines Inn

*317 W 14th Street, between Eighth & Ninth
Avenues, Chelsea (1-212 929 1023, 1-888
546 2700, www.chelseapinesinn.com). Subway
A, C, E to 14th Street; L to Eighth Avenue.*
Rates (incl breakfast) $189-$319 double.
Rooms 23. **Credit** AmEx, DC, Disc, MC, V.
Map p403 C27.

On the border of Chelsea and the West Village,
Chelsea Pines welcomes gay guests of all persua-
sions. The rooms are clean and comfortable, with
classic-film themes; all have private bathrooms, and
are equipped with a radio, a TV with satellite channels, a refrigerator and free Wi-Fi.
Concierge. Internet (wireless, free). No smoking. TV.

Colonial House Inn

*318 W 22nd Street, between Eighth & Ninth
Avenues, Chelsea (1-212 243 9669, 1-800
689 3779, www.colonialhouseinn.com). Subway
C, E to 23rd Street.* **Rates** (incl breakfast) $130-
$180 double. **Rooms** 22. **Credit** DC, MC, V.
Map p404 C26.

This beautifully renovated 1850s townhouse sits on
a quiet street in Chelsea. The hotel was founded by
late dance-music legend Mel Cheren, and is still run
by (and primarily for) gay men; it's a great place to
stay, even if some of the cheaper rooms are a bit

INSIDE TRACK MOVIE NIGHT

Once a week, the ever-bubbly green-topped
drag queen Hedda Lettuce takes over the
Clearview Chelsea (260 W 23rd Street,
between Seventh & Eighth Avenues,
1-212 691 5519, www.clearview
cinemas.com/classics) to provide a
comedic fluffing before a (typically) campy
flick. Past screenings have included Zsa
Zsa Gabor vehicle *Queen of Outer Space*,
horror classic *Carrie* and goofy '80s
comedy *Elvira, Mistress of the Dark*.
After the show, head to **XES Lounge**
(157 W 24th Street, between Sixth &
Seventh Avenues, 1-212 604 0212,
www.xesnyc.com) and present your
ticket for a free drink.

---

snug. Bonuses include fireplaces in three of the
deluxe rooms and a rooftop deck (nude sunbathing
is allowed).
*Concierge. Internet (wireless, $3/day; shared
terminal, $12/hr). No smoking (except on roof). TV.*

Incentra Village House

*32 Eighth Avenue, between Jane & 12th Streets,
West Village (1-212 206 0007, www.incentra
village.com). Subway A, C, E to 14th Street; L to
Eighth Avenue.* **Rates** $219-$249 double. **Rooms**
11. **Credit** AmEx, MC, V. **Map** p403 D28.

Two cute 1841 townhouses in the Village make up
this nicely restored and gay-run guesthouse. The
spacious rooms have private bathrooms and kitchenettes; some also have fireplaces. A 1939 Steinway
baby grand graces the parlour and sets a tone of
easy sophistication.
Internet (wireless, free). No smoking. TV.

The Out NYC

*510 W 42nd Street, between Tenth & Eleventh
Avenues (1-212 947 2999, www.theoutnyc.com).
Subway A, C, E to 42nd Street-Port Authority.*
Rates $179-$379 double. **Rooms** 103. **Credit**
AmEx, DC, Disc, MC, V. **Map** p404 C24.
See p268 **Staying in the Out.**
*Bar. Business center. Concierge. Disabled-adapted
rooms. Gym. Internet (wireless, free). Restaurant.
Room service. No smoking. Spa. TV.*

RESTAURANTS & CAFES

The sight of same-sex couples holding hands
across a candlelit table is a pretty commonplace
one in New York City. But if you want to
increase the chances of being part of the
majority when you dine, check out the following
gay-friendly places.

Bamboo 52

*344 W 52nd Street, between Eighth & Ninth
Avenues, Hell's Kitchen (1-212 315 2777,
www.bamboo52nyc.com). Subway C, E to 50th
Street.* **Open** noon-2am Mon; noon-4am Tue-Fri;
4pm-4am Sat; 4pm-2am Sun. **Main courses** $20.
Credit AmEx, Disc, MC, V. **Map** p404 C23.

This Hell's Kitchen sushi restaurant (with a bamboo
garden to boot) feels more like a gay bar with an
extended raw fish menu. There's loungey seating
(patrons nestle on low banquettes and nibble off
knee-high tables), a DJ and free-flowing drinks. The
fun menu features such unorthodox combinations
as buffalo chicken speciality rolls and a spicy sushi
sandwich – a tasty triangle of seasoned rice layered
with spicy tuna, avocado, eel and American cheese.

Elmo

*156 Seventh Avenue, between 19th & 20th
Streets, Chelsea (1-212 337 8000, www.elmo
restaurant.com). Subway 1 to 18th Street.*

Open 11am-midnight Mon-Thur; 11am-1am Fri, Sat; 10am-midnight Sun. **Main courses** $15. **Credit** AmEx, MC, V. **Map** p403 D27.
The attraction at this spacious, brightly decorated eaterie is the good, reasonably priced American comfort food. Then there's the bar, which provides a view of the dining room jammed with guys in clingy tank tops.

★ Empanada Mama
763 Ninth Avenue, between 51st & 52nd Streets, Hell's Kitchen (1-212 698 9008, www.empmamanyc.com). Subway C, E to 50th

Street. **Open** 24hrs daily. **Empanadas** $3. **Credit** AmEx, Disc, MC, V. **Map** p404 C23.
Massive flavours are crammed into tiny packages at this cute Hell's Kitchen spot, right in the middle of the boy-bar crawl. Savoury and sweet empanadas (both flour or corn varieties) make great on-the-go snacks, or combine several for a full meal. The joint tends to be packed from dinner time until the wee hours.

Manatus
340 Bleecker Street, between Christopher & 10th Streets, West Village (1-212 989 7042, www.manatusnyc.com). Subway 1 to Christopher

Staying in the Out

Check in to NYC's first luxury gay hotel.

Sealing its status as the city's current homo hotspot, Hell's Kitchen is the location of New York's first gay-specific (but 'straight-friendly') full-service hotel, **The Out NYC** (*see p267*). Built in the husk of a 1960s motel, it offers more than mere accommodation. The sprawling all-in-one playground also houses **XL Nightclub, Cabaret & Lounge** (*photo p266*), a 14,000-square-foot club operated by nightlife bigwigs John Blair and Beto Sutter, and Tony Fornabaio and Brandon Voss of FV Events. The spot offers separate lounge and cabaret spaces with such flashy features as the city's largest LED wall, and waterfalls in the bathrooms. XL obviously caters to hotel guests, but parties and performances draw gays from all over the city – so that cute guy at the bar might be able to give you an insider's tour in the morning.

The complex is designed around three courtyards, including the faux-ivy-lined sundeck, which leads to a glass-ceilinged area with two hot tubs. In addition to the party space, it has a restaurant, **KTCHN** (www.ktchnnyc.com) and a 5,000-square-foot spa (www.theoutnycspa.com) offering everything from the requisite pedicures and facials to hair removal and yoga classes. Despite a few style statements, the monochrome room decor is on the spare side. The quad rooms ($99-$129 per person), with four curtained cubby-bunks reminiscent of sleeper compartments – upgraded with double beds and TVs – are a budget option for those who are travelling with a crowd or want to make new friends.

With its kitschy-chic aesthetic and moderate rates for midtown, the Out is a worthwhile destination even without the queer distinction – but with the advantage that the hot bear you spot at the check-in desk won't be a straight Midwestern dad in town for a conference.

Off Broadway's *Naked Boys* at **The Out NYC**.

Street-Sheridan Square. **Open** 24hrs daily. **Main courses** $12. **Credit** AmEx, DC, Disc, MC, V. **Map** p403 D28.

Manatus both is and isn't your typical greasy-spoon diner. There are the standard plastic-coated menus listing dozens of fried food items, but distinguishing the place is a full bar, flattering lighting and a flaming gay clientele, especially late at night when tipsy bar-goers pile in.

Rocking Horse Café

182 Eighth Avenue, between 19th & 20th Streets, Chelsea (1-212 463 9511, www.rockinghorse cafe.com). Subway C, E to 23rd Street. **Open** noon-11pm Mon-Thur; noon-midnight Fri; 11am-midnight Sat; 11am-11pm Sun. **Main courses** $16. **Credit** AmEx, MC, V. **Map** p403 D27.

Eclectic Mexican cuisine is what originally established the Rocking Horse Café as a unique place to eat in Chelsea, but the bar now holds a distinguished reputation for its tongue-numbingly stiff frozen margaritas. Decked out in bright colours, it's also still good for ogling beautiful boys doing the Eighth Avenue strut.

Superfine

126 Front Street, between Jay & Pearl Streets, Dumbo, Brooklyn (1-718 243 9005). Subway A, C to High Street; F to York Street. **Open** 11.30am-3pm, 6-11pm Tue-Fri; 12.30-3.30pm, 6-11pm Sat; 11am-3pm, 6-10pm Sun. **Main courses** $18. **Credit** AmEx, DC, Disc, MC, V. **Map** p411 T9.

Owned by a couple of super-cool lesbians, this eatery, bar and gallery serves Mediterranean cuisine in a massive, hip space. The mellow vibe and pool table draw a mixed local crowd. The South-western themed Sunday bluegrass brunch is justifiably popular.

Vynl

754 Ninth Avenue, between 50th & 51st Streets, Hell's Kitchen (1-212 974 2003, www.vynl-nyc.com). Subway C, E to 50th Street. **Open** 11am-11pm Mon, Tue; 11am-midnight Wed, Thur; 11am-1am Fri; 10am-1am Sat; 10am-11pm Sun. **Main courses** $14. **Credit** AmEx, MC, V. **Map** p404 C23.

The boys love this pop music-themed eatery, where old albums adorn the walls above the cosy booths and mirrorballs are shoved into every available space. Menu items are an odd mishmash of comfort food (burgers, turkey meatloaf, spaghetti and meatballs) and Asian cuisine (massaman curry, veggie-basil stir-fry). Cocktails are named after pop icons – Prince, Lady Gaga – and the vibe is all-around fun.

BARS & CLUBS

'It ain't what it used to be,' grumble veterans of New York's gay nightlife. And they're right. The after-hours scene is continually morphing – sometimes for the better, sometimes not. Although gay megaclubs are more or less a thing of the past, **XL Nightclub, Cabaret & Lounge**, within 'urban resort' the Out NYC (*see p268*), opened in 2012. Midsize club nights such as Friday's **F*Word** at **Splash** (*see p271*) draw crowds of hot guys looking to dance to tunes from big-name DJs and even the occasional slumming pop star. But for serious dance music fans, the real action is at smaller venues. The basement disco at the **Monster** (*see p270*) features top-notch parties most nights, and MEN's JD Samson hosts **Scissor Sundays** at the **Rusty Knot** (425 West Street, West Village, 1-212 645 5668), a top-notch tea dance that assembles an eclectic crowd.

Whatever your nightlife pleasure – sleek cocktail lounge, a kinky leather cave, dive bar or kitschy neighbourhood hangout – you'll find it somewhere in New York. Many watering holes offer happy hours, drink specials, live shows, go-go dancers and rotating theme nights, such as bingo parties or talent contests. All bars, gay or straight, enforce the state-wide drinking age of 21; always carry picture ID as you might be asked to show it, even if your 21st birthday is a distant memory.

East Village

The Cock

29 Second Avenue, between 2nd & 3rd Streets (no phone, www.thecockbar.com). Subway F to Lower East Side-Second Avenue. **Open** 11pm-4am daily. **Admission** free-$10. **No credit cards**. **Map** p403 F29.

This grungy hole-in-the-wall still holds the title of New York's sleaziest gay hangout, but nowadays it's hit-and-miss. At weekends, it's a packed grind-fest, but on other nights the place can often be depressingly under-populated. It's best to go very late when the cruising is at its peak.

> ### INSIDE TRACK
> ### NOT-SO-SQUARE DANCING
>
> If throbbing house music isn't your style, one alternative to a club is the **Big Apple Ranch**, a lively gay and lesbian country and western bash held every Saturday night at a Flatiron District dance studio (5th Floor, 39 W 19th Street, between Fifth & Sixth Avenues, 1-212 358 5752, www.bigappleranch.com). Admission is $10 and an 8pm lesson is followed by the party at 9pm – offering a chance to don your chaps and do-si-do.

The Monster.

Eastern Bloc

505 E 6th Street, between Avenues A & B (1-212 777 2555, www.easternblocnyc.com). Subway F to Lower East-Side-Second Avenue. **Open** 7pm-4am daily. **No credit cards. Map** p403 G28.

This cool little space has mostly shed its commie revolutionary decor for a funky living-room feel. The bartenders are cuties, and there are nightly themes, DJs and happy hours to get the ball rolling.

★ Nowhere

322 E 14th Street, at First Avenue (1-212 477 4744, www.nowherebarnyc.com). Subway L to First Avenue. **Open** 3pm-4am daily. **No credit cards. Map** p403 F27.

Low ceilings and dim lighting help to create a speakeasy vibe at this subterranean bar. The place attracts everyone from young lesbians to bears, thanks to an entertaining line-up of theme nights. Tuesdays are especially fun, when DJ Damian's long-running Buddies party takes over. The pool table is another big draw.

INSIDE TRACK SEEKING SEX

While gay men in New York tend to organise encounters online or on mobile apps such as **Grindr** (www.grindr.com) and **Scruff** (www.scruffapp.com), those who favour an old-school approach can try the **West Side Club** (2nd floor, 27 W 20th Street, between Fifth & Sixth Avenues, 1-212 691 2700, www.westsideclub nyc.com) or the **East Side Club** (227 E 56th Street, between Second & Third Avenues, 1-212 753 2222). For between $17 and $40 (plus a $15 temporary membership), each of these clubs gives you four hours of cruising dark hallways lined with nooks and private rooms.

West Village

★ Cubbyhole

281 W 12th Street, between 4th Street & Greenwich Avenue (1-212 243 9041, www.cubby holebar.com). Subway A, C, E to 14th Street; L to Eighth Avenue. **Open** 4pm-4am Mon-Fri; 2pm-4am Sat, Sun. **No credit cards. Map** p403 E28.

This minuscule spot is filled with flirtatious girls (and their dyke-friendly boy pals), with the standard set of Melissa Etheridge or kd lang blaring. Chinese lanterns, tissue-paper fish and old holiday decorations emphasise the festive, homespun charm.

Henrietta Hudson

438 Hudson Street, between Morton & Hudson Streets (1-212 924 3347, www.henrietta hudson.com). Subway 1 to Houston Street. **Open** 5pm-2am Mon, Tue; 4pm-4am Wed-Fri; 2pm-4am Sat; 2pm-2am Sun. **Admission** free-$10. **Credit** (bar only) AmEx, Disc, MC, V. **Map** p409 D29.

A much-loved lesbian hangout, this glam lounge attracts hottie girls from all over the New York area. Every night is different, with hip hop, pop, rock and live shows among the musical offerings.

The Monster

80 Grove Street, at Sheridan Square (1-212 924 3558, www.manhattan-monster.com). Subway 1 to Christopher Street-Sheridan Square. **Open** 4pm-4am Mon-Fri; 2pm-4am Sat, Sun. **Admission** free-$8. **No credit cards. Map** p403 D28.

Upstairs, locals gather to sing showtunes in the piano lounge, adorned with strings of lights and rainbow paraphernalia. The downstairs dancefloor has seen something of a renaissance lately, hosting top-notch house and disco events.

Rockbar

185 Christopher Street, at Weehawken Street (1-212 675 1864, www.rockbarnyc.com). Subway 1 to Christopher Street-Sheridan Square. **Open**

4pm-2am Mon-Thur; 4pm-4am Fri; 2pm-4am Sat; 2pm-2am Sun. **Credit** AmEx, Disc, MC, V. **Map** p403 C29.

A burly, bearish crowd tends to congregate at this far-west dive with a rock 'n' roll theme. Various events include dance parties, game nights, comedy showcases and musical performances.

Stonewall Inn

53 Christopher Street, at Waverly Place (1-212 488 2705, www.thestonewallinnnyc.com). Subway 1 to Christopher Street-Sheridan Square. **Open** 2pm-4am daily. **Credit** AmEx, Disc, MC, V. **Map** p403 D28.

This gay landmark is the site of the 1969 gay rebellion against police harassment (though back then it also included the building next door). Special nights range from dance soirées and drag shows to burlesque performances and bingo gatherings.

▶ *While you're here, check out George Segal's sculptures in nearby Christopher Park; see p73.*

Chelsea & Flatiron District

★ Eagle

554 W 28th Street, at Eleventh Avenue (1-646 473 1866, www.eaglenyc.com). Subway C, E to 23rd Street. **Open** 10pm-4am Tue-Sat; 5pm-4am Sun. **No credit cards. Map** p404 C26.

You don't have to be a kinky leather daddy to enjoy this manly spot, but it definitely doesn't hurt. The fetish bar is home to an array of beer blasts, foot-worship fêtes and leather soirées, plus simple pool playing and cruising nights. Thursdays are gear night, so be sure to dress the part or you might not get past the doorman. In summer, the rooftop is a surprising oasis.

G Lounge

225 W 19th Street, at Seventh Avenue (1-212 929 1085, www.glounge.com). Subway 1 to 18th Street. **Open** 4pm-4am daily. **No credit cards. Map** p403 D27.

The neighbourhood's original slick boy lounge – a moodily lit cave with a cool brick-and-glass arched entrance – wouldn't look out of place in a boutique hotel. It's a favourite after-work cocktail spot, where a roster of DJs stays on top of the mood. *Photo p272.*

Gym Sports Bar

167 Eighth Avenue, between 18th & 19th Streets (1-212 337 2439, www.gymsportsbar.com). Subway A, C, E to 14th Street; L to Eighth Avenue. **Open** 4pm-2am Mon-Thur; 4pm-4am Fri; 1pm-4am Sat; 1pm-2am Sun. **Credit** AmEx, DC, Disc, MC, V. **Map** p403 D27.

This popular spot is all about games – of the actual sporting variety. Catch theme parties that revolve around gay sports leagues, play at the pool tables and video games, or watch the pro events from rodeo competitions to figure skating shown on big-screen TVs.

Splash

50 W 17th Street, between Fifth & Sixth Avenues (1-212 691 0073, www.splashbar.com). Subway F, M to 14th Street; L to Sixth Avenue. **Open** 4pm-4am daily. **Admission** $5-$25. **No credit cards. Map** p403 E27.

This queer institution has 10,000sq ft of dance and lounge space, staffed by super-muscular (and shirtless) bartenders. DJs still rock the house, while local drag celebs give good face, and in-house VJs flash snippets of classic musicals spliced with video visuals.

Eagle.

ARTS & ENTERTAINMENT

ARTS & ENTERTAINMENT

Hell's Kitchen & Theater District

Escuelita

301 W 39th Street, at Eighth Avenue (1-212 631 0588, www.enyclub.com). Subway A, C, E to 42nd Street-Port Authority. **Open** 10pm-4am Mon, Tue, Thur-Sat; 8pm-4am Sun. **Admission** $5-$20. **Credit** MC, V. **Map** p404 D24.

This basement dance club is a hub for New York's vast and varied gay Latin community (embracing Puerto Ricans, Dominicans and Colombians, among others). The main attraction on Fridays and Saturdays is an extravagant and dramatic drag show (in English and Spanish) at 2am. Throughout the week there are also go-go boy contests, karaoke and DJs spinning house, hip hop and salsa.

★ FairyTail Lounge

500 W 48th Street, at Tenth Avenue (1-646 684 3897, www.facebook.com/fairytaillounge). Subway C, E to 50th Street. **Open** 5pm-2am Mon, Tue; 5pm-3am Thur-Sun. **Credit** AmEx, Disc, MC, V. **Map** p404 B23.

An easy-to-miss entrance belies the psychedelic, pseudo-Victorian enchanted forest waiting inside this friendly watering hole. Whether you find a mellow happy-hour crowd or a hyper dance party, the vibe is more East Village arty than midtown pretty-boy scene.

Flaming Saddles

793 Ninth Avenue, at 53rd Street (1-212 713 0481, www.flamingsaddles.com). Subway C, E to 50th Street. **Open** 4pm-2am Mon-Thur, Sun; 2pm-4am Fri, Sat. **No credit cards. Map** p405 C23.

City boys can party honky-tonk-style at this country and western gay bar. It's outfitted to look like a Wild West bordello, with red velvet drapes, antler sconces and rococo wallpaper. Performances by bartenders dancing in cowboy boots add to the raucous vibe.

Industry

355 W 52nd Street, between Eighth & Ninth Avenues (1-646 476 2747, www.industrybar.com). Subway C, E to 50th Street. **Open** 4pm-4am daily. **No credit cards. Map** p405 C23.

Pretty boys flock to this appropriately named garage-like industrial-chic boite, which features a stage for regular drag shows and other performances, a pool table, and couches for lounging. DJs spin nightly to a sexy, fashionable crowd.

Therapy

348 W 52nd Street, between Eighth & Ninth Avenues (1-212 397 1700, www.therapy-nyc.com). Subway C, E to 50th Street. **Open** 5pm-2am Mon-Wed, Sun; 5pm-4am Thur-Sat. **Credit** AmEx, DC, MC, V. **Map** p404 C23.

Therapy is just what your analyst ordered. The dramatic two-level space offers comedy and musical performances, some clever cocktails (including the Freudian Sip) and a crowd of well-scrubbed boys. You'll find good food and a cosy fireplace to boot.

Vlada Lounge

331 W 51st Street, between Eighth & Ninth Avenues (1-212 974 8030, www.vladabar.com). Subway C, E to 50th Street. **Open** 4pm-4am daily. **Credit** AmEx, MC, V. **Map** p404 C23.

This vodka-focused drinkery has more than a dozen infused versions of the spirit. Drag shows take over the space Sunday through Wednesday nights, and tend to skew more towards quirky and scary than campy.

G Lounge. *See p271.*

Party People

Nightlife names you need to know.

To keep up with NYC's after-dark scene, just follow its top promoters. Upscale pretty boys tag along with **Josh Wood** (www.joshwoodproductions.com), the circuit crowd flocks to the legendary **Saint** soirées (www.saintatlarge.com) and the art-boy contingent is loyal to **Spank** dance parties (www.spankartmag.com). **Daniel Nardicio** (www.danielnardicio.com) can be counted on for sleazy, frisky bashes, and **Tony Fornabaio** and **Brandon Voss** of **FV Events** (www.fvevents.com) run some of the most popular parties in town.

The guys behind the trans zine **Original Plumbing** (www.originalplumbing.com) throw parties that tend to draw an arty queer crowd, as does **Sarah Jenny** and **Avory Agony**'s monthly **Hey Queen!** fête (www.heyqueen.org). Lesbians looking to dance and flirt should visit DJ **Whitney Day**'s website to check out her schedule (www.whitneyday.com).

Whitney Day.

Uptown

No Parking
4168 Broadway, between 176th & 177th Streets (1-212 923 8700). Subway A, C, 1 to 168th Street-Washington Heights. **Open** 6pm-3am Mon-Thur; 7pm-4am Fri-Sun. **Credit** AmEx, Disc, MC, V. **Map** p409 B6.
Hang out with cute Harlem and Washington Heights guys at this far-uptown drinkery, which frequently offers shows featuring hunky go-go men.

Brooklyn

Excelsior
390 Fifth Avenue, between 6th & 7th Streets, Park Slope (1-718 832 1599, www.excelsior brooklyn.com). Subway F, R to Fourth Avenue-9th Street. **Open** 6pm-4am Mon-Fri; 2pm-4am Sat, Sun. **No credit cards. Map** p410 T11.
Homey Excelsior has a friendly neighbourhood crowd, an eclectic jukebox and plenty of beers on tap. This straight-friendly spot attracts gay men, lesbians and their hetero pals looking to catch up without the fuss found in trendy lounge bars.

Ginger's Bar
363 Fifth Avenue, between 5th & 6th Streets, Park Slope (1-718 788 0924, www.gingersbar bklyn.com). Subway F, R to Fourth Avenue-9th Street. **Open** 5pm-4am Mon-Fri; 2pm-4am Sat, Sun. **No credit cards. Map** p410 T11.

The front room of Ginger's, with its dark-wood bar, looks out on to a bustling street. The back, with an always-busy pool table, evokes a rec room, while the patio feels like a friend's yard. This local hangout is full of all sorts of dykes, many with their dogs – or favourite gay boys – in tow.

Metropolitan
559 Lorimer Street, at Metropolitan Avenue, Williamsburg (1-718 599 4444, www.my space.com/metropolitan11211). Subway G to Metropolitan Avenue; L to Lorimer Street. **Open** 3pm-4am daily. **No credit cards. Map** p411 V8.
Some Williamsburg spots are a little pretentious, but not this refreshingly unfancy bar, which resembles a 1960s ski lodge, complete with a brick fireplace. Guys dominate, but there's always a female contingent, and even some straight folks. There are weekend barbecues on the patio in summer.

★ This n' That (TNT)
108 North 6th Street, between Berry Street & Wythe Avenue, Williamsburg (1-718 599 5959, www.thisnthatbrooklyn.com). Subway L to Bedford Avenue. **Open** 4pm-4am daily. **Credit** ($15 minimum) AmEx, MC, V. **Map** p411 U7.
The latest addition to the Brooklyn queer-bar scene is parked in the middle of the most hipstery block of the city's most hipstery neighbourhood. Still, most nights you'll find a surprisingly unpretentious crowd here, enjoying various parties (trivia, movie nights, sweaty dance fests)

Nightlife

It's time to stay up late.

Ever wonder how New York earned the right to be called the 'city that never sleeps'? Hint: it's not because of the late-night rubbish collections, chorus of car alarms or even the vats of coffee that Gothamites guzzle daily. No, the town was given that sobriquet for one thing only – its nightlife legacy. This is where David Mancuso transformed DJing into storytelling at the Loft, where Area turned clubbing into an art experience in the 1980s, and where Jackie 60 rode that experience into a freaky-deaky sunset. And we're happy to report that it's still easy to slip into a sleep-deprived stupor carousing after dark – despite a long list of potential party-killers, including club-loathing mayors.

Gotham's comedy scene is undeniably enjoying a moment. New clubs are opening, theatres are thriving, locals are cranking out great Web series and tons of tweets, and the whole world agrees on the greatness of the city's favourite son, Louis CK.

The newest major music venue, the Barclays Center in Brooklyn, is already attracting some of the word's biggest stars, including borough natives Jay-Z and Barbra Streisand. For smaller rock gigs, hit the Lower East Side or Williamsburg in Brooklyn, which is now the epicentre of the indie rock scene.

Classic cabaret took a hit in 2012 with the closure of the iconic Oak Room, but new stage 54 Below quickly stepped into the spotlight, and a boundary-pushing generation of performers is reinvigorating the genre.

Clubs

Even clubland's old-timers – those who like to begin sentences with 'Back when I was a kid' – agree: the current state of NYC nightlife is strong. Granted, there haven't been many essential new clubs opening their doors lately, but a bad economy can be good for clubland, fostering a more vibrant, underground (and, frankly, cheaper) side of the scene. Over the past few years, there's been a burst of 'secret-location' shindigs, which are generally held in out-of-the-way warehouses and lofts. By the nature of the event, these parties can be a bitch to find out about for those not in the loop, but if you keep your eye on underground clubbing websites, such as www.rhythmism.com and www.resident advisor.net – and, of course, your indispensable *Time Out New York* weekly clubs listings – you'll be led in the right direction.

Even the old-guard dance clubs, such as **Sullivan Room** and **Cielo**, have stepped up their games, attracting the world's top DJs to spin everything from hip hop and electro to cutting-edge dubstep and techno. Dinosaur venues such as **Webster Hall** and glammed-up superclubs such as **Pacha**

> ### INSIDE TRACK
> ### WALLET ESSENTIALS
>
> Most clubs operate an over-21 policy, and even if you're in the running for the World's Oldest Clubber award, you'll need a government-issued ID (such as a passport or driving licence) to gain admission. It's also worth carrying cash, as most clubs won't accept credit cards at the door.

have got in on the act, with the former hosting the happening Girls & Boys gala every Friday, and the latter catering to the international-superstar-DJ crowd.

DANCE CLUBS

★ Cielo

18 Little W 12th Street, at Ninth Avenue, Meatpacking District (1-212 645 5700, www.cieloclub.com). Subway A, C, E to 14th Street; L to Eighth Avenue. **Open** 10pm-4am Mon, Wed-Sat. **Admission** $12-$25. **Credit** AmEx, DC, MC, V. **Map** p403 C28.

You'd never guess from the Heidi Montag wannabes hanging out in the neighbourhood that the attitude at this ten-year-old club is close to zero – at least once you get past the bouncers guarding the door. On the sunken dancefloor, hip-to-hip crowds gyrate to deep beats from top DJs, including NYC old-schoolers François K, Tedd Patterson and Louie Vega. Cielo, which features a crystal-clear sound system (by the legendary Funktion One), has won a bevy of 'best club' awards.

Le Bain

The Standard, 444 W 13th Street, at Washington Street, Meatpacking District (1-212 645 4646, www.standardhotels.com). Subway A, C, E to 14th Street; L to Eighth Avenue. **Open** 11pm-4am Wed-Sun. **Admission** free. **Credit** AmEx, Disc, MC, V. **Map** p403 C27.

Although an EDM-driven club scene is filling bigger and bigger venues, for a more intimate night out, head to this penthouse club and terrace atop the Standard hotel. In the swanky space, which offers spectacular Hudson River views from floor-to-ceiling windows, you can get within hugging distance of underground superstars that have included disco daddy Dimitri from Paris, deep-house kingpin Marques Wyatt and the aurally anarchic DJ Harvey.

Pacha

618 W 46th Street, between Eleventh & Twelfth Avenues, Hell's Kitchen (1-212 209 7500, www.pachanyc.com). Subway C, E to 50th Street. **Open** 10pm-6am Fri; 10pm-8am Sat. **Admission** $10-$40. **Credit** (bar only) AmEx, Disc, MC, V. **Map** p404 B23.

The worldwide glam-club chain Pacha, with outposts in nightlife capitals such as Ibiza, London and Buenos Aires, hit the US market back in 2005 with this swanky joint helmed by superstar spinner Erick Morillo. The spot attracts heavyweights ranging from local hero Danny Tenaglia to international crowd-pleasers such as Fedde Le Grande and Benny Benassi. Like most big clubs, it pays to check the line-up in advance if you're into underground (as opposed to lowest-common-denominator) beats.

Cielo.

ARTS & ENTERTAINMENT

Santos Party House.

ARTS & ENTERTAINMENT

★ Santos Party House
96 Lafayette Street, between Walker & White Streets, Tribeca (1-212 584 5492, www.santos partyhouse.com). Subway J, N, Q, R, Z, 6 to Canal Street. **Open** varies Mon-Thur; 6.30pm-4am Fri-Sun. **Admission** $10-$25. **Credit** (bar only) AmEx, Disc, MC, V. **Map** p402 E31.
Launched by a team that includes rocker Andrew WK, Santos Party House – two black, square rooms done out in a bare-bones, generic club style – was initially hailed as a scene game-changer. While those too-high expectations didn't exactly pan out, it's still a rock-solid choice, with nights featuring everything from top-shelf hip hop to underground house.

Sapphire
249 Eldridge Street, between Houston & Stanton Streets, Lower East Side (1-212 777 5153, www.sapphirenyc.com). Subway F to Lower East Side-Second Avenue. **Admission** free-$10. **Credit** (bar only) AmEx, Disc, MC, V. **Map** p403 F29.
Sapphire's bare walls and minimal decor are as raw as it gets, yet the energetic, unpretentious clientele is oblivious to the (lack of) aesthetic. A dance crowd packs the place all week – various nights feature house, hip hop, reggae and disco.

Sullivan Room
218 Sullivan Street, between Bleecker & W 3rd Streets, Greenwich Village (1-212 252 2151, www.sullivanroom.com). Subway A, B, C, D, E, F, M to W 4th Street. **Open** 10pm-5am

Tue-Sun. **Admission** $5-$20. **Credit** (bar only) AmEx, Disc, DC, MC, V. **Map** p403 E29.
Where's the party? It's right here in this unmarked subterranean space, which hosts some of the best deep house, tech-house and breaks bashes the city has to offer. It's an unpretentious place, but all you really need are thumpin' beats and a place to move your feet, right? Keep a lookout for the nights hosted by local stalwarts Sleepy & Boo, featuring top house music stars like Derrick Carter and Mark Farina.

Webster Hall
125 E 11th Street, at Third Avenue, East Village (1-212 353 1600, www.websterhall.com). Subway L to Third Avenue; L, N, Q, R, 4, 5, 6 to 14th Street-Union Square. **Open** 10pm-4am Thur-Sat. **Admission** free-$30. **Credit** AmEx, Disc, MC, V. **Map** p403 F28.
The grand Webster Hall isn't exactly on clubland's A-list, due to a populist DJ policy and a crowd that favours muscle shirts and gelled hair. But hey, it's been open, on and off, since 1866, so it must be doing something right. Friday night's Girls & Boys bash attracts music makers of the stature of Grandmaster Flash and dubstep duo Nero.

BURLESQUE CLUBS

New York's burlesque scene is a winking throwback to the days when the tease was as important as the strip. While it tends to revolve around specific revues rather than dedicated venues, good bets include the monthly

Gotham Burlesque, produced by Gary Beeber, the filmmaker behind the documentary *Dirty Martini and the New Burlesque*, at **Stage 72** (158 W 72nd Street, between Broadway & Columbus Avenue, Upper West Side, 1-212 362 2590, www.gothamburlesque.com), and the Saturday-night **Floating Kabarette** at **Galapagos Art Space** (*see p286*) in Dumbo, Brooklyn. Some of the best producers and performers – they often cross over – are Doc Wasabassco (www.wasabassco.com), Shien Lee (www.dancesofvice.com), Jen Gapay's Thirsty Girl Productions (www.thirstygirlproductions. com), Angie Pontani of the World Famous Pontani Sisters (www.angiepontani.com) and Calamity Chang, 'the Asian Sexation' (www.calamitychang.com).

Nurse Bettie
106 Norfolk Street, between Delancey & Rivington Streets, Lower East Side (1-212 477 7515, www.nursebettie.com). Subway F to Delancey Street; J, Z to Delancey-Essex Streets. **Open** 6pm-4am daily. **Admission** free. **Credit** AmEx, Disc, MC, V. **Map** p403 G30.
The '50s-pinup-inspired venue Nurse Bettie (named after Bettie Page, one of the 20th century's premier hotsy-totsies) is a natural setting for burlesque performers. Weekly shows include Spanking of the Lower East Side, produced by Calamity Chang, which usually includes six or seven acts, as well as preshow go-go dancers. Prepare to get up close and personal in the intimate space.

The Slipper Room
167 Orchard Street, at Stanton Street, Lower East Side (1-212 253 7246, www.slipperroom.com). Subway F to Lower East Side-Second Avenue. **Open** varies Mon; 8.30pm-12.30am Tue; 9pm-3am Wed, Thur; 9pm-4am Fri-Sun. **Admission** varies. **Credit** (bar only) AmEx, MC, V. **Map** p403 F29.
This downtown venue was the epicentre of the neoburlesque and vaudeville scenes, and helped launch the careers of many a burly-Q star (Dirty Martini, Julie Atlas Muz, Murray Hill and boylesquer Tigger!, to name a few). After 11 years of debauchery, co-owner and creative director James Habacker – better known as his borscht belt alter ego, Mel Frye – shuttered the space in 2010 to rebuild it from the ground up. The refurbished club now has state-of-the-art lighting and sound systems, plus a fly-rig for aerial acts. While the eclectic lineup of entertainment now includes theatre, literary events, parties and variety, the Friday-night burlesque shows attract the cream of the city's scene for a night of bump 'n' grind fun.

DANCE PARTIES

New York has a number of regular, peripatetic and season-specific bashes. Nights, locations and prices may vary, so call or check the websites listed.

Blkmarket Membership
www.blkmarketmembership.com.
Competing with the Bunker (*see below*) for the unofficial title of NYC's best techno party, the Blkmarket crew hosts bashes in the city's established clubs as well as out-of-the-way warehouse spaces.

★ The Bunker
Public Assembly (back room), 70 North 6th Street, between Kent & Wythe Avenues, Williamsburg, Brooklyn (1-718 384 4586, www.beyondbooking. com/thebunker). Subway L to Bedford Avenue. **Open** 10pm-6am, usually 1st Fri of mth. **Admission** $15-$30. **Credit** (bar only) AmEx, DC, MC, V. **Map** p411 U7.
Gotham's electronic music fans were in a tizzy when Tonic, the longtime home of the Bunker, closed in 2007, but the shindig is now happily ensconced in Williamsburg's Public Assembly. And, as befits the party that helped to kick off the current craze for all things techno in NYC, Bunker main man DJ Spinoza is still scoring at his (usually) monthly Friday-night get-together. Big guns from labels such as Spectral Sound and Kompakt regularly pack the bunker-like space, and the bash is busier than ever.

★ Body & Soul
www.bodyandsoul-nyc.com.
Some people call the long-running spiritual-house hoedown Body & Soul the best party ever to fill a dancefloor in NYC. The Sunday-night tea dance, helmed by the holy DJ trinity of Danny Krivit, Joe

Claussell and François K, is certainly in the top ten. It's no longer a weekly affair – three editions a year will have to do – but it's still a spectacle, with a few thousand sweaty revellers dancing their hearts out.

Mister Saturday Night/Mister Sunday
www.mistersaturdaynight.com. **Tickets** $10-$20. Two of clubland's stalwart DJs, Justin Carter and Eamon Harkin, have pooled their years of experience to throw the friendliest of parties in venues ranging from intimate loft spaces and raw warehouses to tree-shaded meadows along the Gowanus Canal. The music runs the gamut too – deep disco, jacking house, and outer-fringes dubstep and techno – with some of the underground's top names stopping by for a date on the decks. *See also p279* **Q&A**.

Turntables on the Hudson
www.turntablesonthehudson.com. This ultra-funky affair lost its longtime home at the Lightship Frying Pan when the city put the kibosh on the vessel's parties, but resident Nickodemus and his crew still pop up at clubs and loft spaces all over the city (though rarely on the Hudson itself).

★ Warm Up
MoMA PS1 (for listings, *see p126*). **Open** July, Aug noon-9pm Sat. **Admission** (incl museum admission) $15. **No credit cards. Map** p412 V5. Since 1997, PS1's courtyard has played host to one of the most anticipated, resolutely underground clubbing events in the city. Thousands of dance-music fanatics and alt-rock enthusiasts make the pilgrimage to Long Island City on summer Saturdays to drink and dance. The sounds range from spiritually inclined soul to full-bore techno, spun by local and international stars.

Comedy

Beyond the dedicated venues, you'll find many worthwhile shows in the back rooms of pubs and other venues. Look out for Liam McEneaney's long-running monthly **Tell Your Friends!** (www.tyfcomedy.com) at the Bell House (www.thebellhouseny.com) in Gowanus, Brooklyn, and **Big Terrific**, from Gabe Liedman and Max Silvestri at Williamsburg's Cameo (www.cameony.com); **Comedy at KFBK with Hannibal Buress** at the Knitting Factory (*see p288*); and Eugene Mirman's weekly **Pretty Good Friends** at Union Hall (*see p290*).

COMEDY VENUES

★ 92YTribeca
200 Hudson Street, at Canal Street, Tribeca (1-212 601 1000, www.92ytribeca.org). Subway A, C, E, 1 to Canal Street. **Shows** vary. **Admission** free-$15. **Credit** (tickets only) AmEx, Disc, MC, V. **Map** p403 D30.

As a venue responsible for all sorts of cultural programming, it's amazing that 92YTribeca has time to concoct such an energising slate of comedic events. With regular evenings of stand-up and conversations with comedy legends, plus storytelling and singalong musical film screenings, there's something for everyone. Keep an eye out for Comedy Below Canal, a series that often includes popular performers from HBO or Comedy Central.

Broadway Comedy Club
318 W 53rd Street, between Eighth & Ninth Avenues, Theater District (1-212 757 2323, www.broadwaycomedyclub.com). Subway C, E to 50th Street. **Shows** daily, times vary. **Admission** $15-$20 (2-drink min). **Credit** AmEx, Disc, MC, V. **Map** p404 D23. BCC features TV faces and club circuit regulars. On Friday and Saturday, it's home to Chicago City Limits (1-212 888 5233, www.chicagocitylimits.com); the group's format of topical sketches, songs and audience-inspired improv can seem a little dated.

★ Carolines on Broadway
1626 Broadway, between 49th & 50th Streets, Theater District (1-212 757 4100, www.carolines.com). Subway N, Q, R to 49th Street; 1 to 50th Street. **Shows** vary. **Admission** $20-$50 (2-drink min). **Credit** AmEx, MC, V. **Map** p404 D23. Carolines is a New York City institution. It's attained that status in part because of its long-term relationships with national headliners, sitcom stars and cable-special pros, which ensures that its stage always features marquee names. Although the majority of bookings skew towards mainstream appetites, the club also makes time for undisputedly darker and edgier fare, such as Paul Mooney and Louis CK.

Comedy Cellar
117 MacDougal Street, between Bleecker & 3rd Streets, Greenwich Village (1-212 254 3480, www.comedycellar.com). Subway A, B, C, D, E, F, M to W 4th Street. **Shows** 8pm, 10pm Mon-Wed, Sun; 8pm, 10pm, midnight Thur; 7pm, 8.45pm; 10.39pm, 12.15am Fri; 7.30pm, 9.15pm, 11pm, 12.45am Sat. **Admission** $12-$24 (2-item min). **Credit** AmEx, MC, V. **Map** p403 E29. Despite being dubbed one of the best stand-up clubs in the city year after year, the Comedy Cellar has maintained a hip, underground feel. It gets incredibly crowded, but the bookings, which typically include no-nonsense comics Dave Chapelle, Jim Norton and Marina Franklin, are enough to distract you from your bachelorette party neighbours.

Comic Strip Live
1568 Second Avenue, between 81st & 82nd Streets, Upper East Side (1-212 861 9386, www.comicstriplive.com). Subway 4, 5, 6 to 86th Street. **Shows** 8.30pm Mon-Thur, Sun;

Q&A: Justin Carter and Eamon Harkin

Nightlife editor Bruce Tantum catches up with the Mister Saturday Night duo.

When was the first Mister Saturday Night party?

Justin Carter: It was January 17, 2009. We had both been doing parties where we were parts of these larger crews, playing at this venue and that venue. Everything felt very nebulous. Eamon and I had been talking for a while, and we both realised that we wanted to do something that would focus our energy on one thing, instead of focusing on one party one night and then another party the next night. It felt like the right thing to do.

Eamon Harkin: We really put all of our efforts into this party; we don't really play anywhere else in New York very often. That's by design, and we think that it helps to make each party as special as it can be.

I've always wondered how much of a thought process went into the spelling out of Mister, rather than the more common abbreviation.

Carter: Believe it or not, we talk a lot about things like that! I actually don't remember the specifics of how we decided to spell it out, but it probably had something to do with us looking at different versions of flyers and seeing what we liked better. I think we just decided it looked better that way

It's definitely more memorable.

Harkin: That's exactly what we were going for. And when people abbreviate Mister when they write about it, it bugs the hell out of us.

How do you choose your guests? It's such a wide range, from the Horse Meat Disco guys to more esoteric artists like Four Tet, a lot of Detroit guys like Omar-S and Kyle Hall...

Carter: We even had DJ Premier at one of the first parties. It's really as simple as the way we think about what we would play in our DJ sets. It's who we're inspired by, and what music we're listening to. It's just whatever or whoever we like.

Harkin: The way the party has progressed over its three years, we've actually been making a conscious move toward having fewer guests. For us, the best parties – the ones that we've been inspired by – have been much more than just a bunch of DJ bookings. They've had their own scene and community, and that comes from resident DJs.

Carter: As we've had more parties with no guests, one thing I've realised is that most people play very differently than how we play. And when we do have guests, it's actually really great when they play a totally different sound in the middle of a party. Like when we had [house-meets-R&B-meets-bass-music artist] Jacques Greene on, it was very different than the way we play; but the crowd that's developed around the party is pretty broad-minded, so it totally worked. And hearing different people – Jacques Greene one week, Pearson Sound the next, Omar-S the next – do different things than what we do both broadens the scope of the party and is a great way for us to get inspired.

ARTS & ENTERTAINMENT

8pm, 10.30pm, 12.15am Fri, Sat. **Admission** $20-$35 (2-drink min). **Credit** AmEx, Disc, MC, V. **Map** p405 F19.

The Upper East Side isn't exactly a breeding ground for edgy entertainment, so you'll be grateful to find this fabled, long-running showcase. Established in 1975, CSL launched the careers of Eddie Murphy and Chris Rock. The fare is more standard these days, but the club does attract a lot of stand-ups from the late-night talk-show circuit.

The Creek & the Cave

10-93 Jackson Avenue, at 11th Street, Long Island City, Queens (1-718 706 8783, www.creeklic.com). Subway 7 to Vernon Boulevard-Jackson Avenue. **Shows** daily, times vary. **Admission** free-$5. **Credit** AmEx, Disc, MC, V. **Map** p412 V5.

This hardworking Long Island City venue offers all the things comedians and their fans need to survive: multiple performance venues, convivial environs, a fully stocked bar, cheap Mexican food and a patio on which to rant and laugh late into the night. As if this weren't enough, owner Rebecca Trent also shows her appreciation for all who make the trek to Queens by making nearly every show free.

Dangerfield's

1118 First Avenue, between 61st & 62nd Streets, Upper East Side (1-212 593 1650, www.dangerfields.com). Subway N, Q, R to Lexington Avenue-59th Street; 4, 5, 6 to 59th Street. **Shows** 8.45pm Mon-Thur, Sun; 8.30pm, 10.30pm, 12.30am Fri; 8pm, 10.30pm, 12.30am Sat. **Admission** free-$20 (2-item min). **Credit** AmEx, DC, Disc, MC, V. **Map** p405 F22.

The decor and gentility of New York City's oldest comedy club are throwbacks to the era of its founder, the late great Rodney Dangerfield, who established it in 1969. And instead of putting eight to ten comics in a showcase, Dangerfield's gives three or four stand-ups the opportunity to settle into longer acts.

Gotham Comedy Club

208 W 23rd Street, between Seventh & Eighth Avenues, Chelsea (1-212 367 9000, www.gotham comedyclub.com). Subway F, M, N, R to 23rd Street. **Shows** vary Mon-Thur; 8.30pm, 10.30pm Fri; 8pm, 10pm, 11.45pm Sat; 8.30pm Sun. **Admission** $10-$25 (2-drink min). **Credit** AmEx, MC, V. **Map** p404 D26.

Chris Mazzilli's vision for his club involves elegant surroundings, professional behaviour and mutual respect. That's why the talents he fosters, such as

Greenwich Village Comedy Club.

Tribeca Comedy Lounge. *See p283.*

Jim Gaffigan, Tom Papa and Ted Alexandro, keep coming back here after they've found national fame.

Greenwich Village Comedy Club

99 MacDougal Street, between Bleecker Street & Minetta Lane, Greenwich Village (1-212 777 5233, www.greenwichvillagecomedyclub.com). Subway A, B, C, D, E, F, M to W 4th Street. **Shows** 9.30pm Mon-Thur, Sun; 9pm, 11.30pm Fri; 8.15pm, 10.30pm, 12.30am Sat. **Admission** $15-$20 (2-drink min). **Credit** AmEx, MC, V. **Map** p403 E29.

Al Martin, the longtime owner of both the New York Comedy Club and Broadway Comedy Club, follows the same basic tenets in his new room – an intimate basement space below an Indian restaurant – as in his other ventures. Although a few pillars in the 60-seat room interfere with sight lines, the pub grub, extensive cocktail selection and long list of stars who just might do a spot while passing through town are drawing crowds every night. Regulars include staples Christian Finnegan, Marina Franklin and Tom Shillue.

Magnet Theater

254 W 29th Street, between Seventh & Eighth Avenues, Chelsea (1-212 244 8824, www. magnettheater.com). Subway A, C, E to 34th Street-Penn Station; 1 to 28th Street. **Shows** vary. **Admission** free-$10. **Credit** AmEx, Disc, MC, V. **Map** p404 D25.

This dedicated comedy theatre exudes a distinctly Chicago vibe, from its DIY aesthetic to its performers, many of whom are former denizens of the Windy City. Even the local players here prefer theatrical to premise-based improvisation, and their shows give the impression they're not just seeking fame or commercial exposure, but pursue the craft simply for the joy of being on stage.

Peoples Improv Theater

123 E 24th Street, between Park & Lexington Avenues, Flatiron District (1-212 563 7488, www.thepit-nyc.com). Subway 6 to 23rd Street. **Shows** daily, times vary. **Admission** free-$25. **Credit** (online purchases only) AmEx, Disc, MC, V. **Map** p404 E26.

After inhabiting a black box in Chelsea for eight years, the PIT leapt across town into the former Algonquin Theatre space, where the improv and sketch venue has upgraded to a beautiful proscenium stage, an additional basement space for experimental shows or stand-up, and an elegant (if cluttered) full-service bar and coffee shop. The move helps legitimise the PIT's growing roster of classes and performers as well as the community values it espouses.

The Stand

239 Third Avenue, between 19th & 20th Streets, Gramercy Park (1-212 677 2600, www.thestand nyc.com). Subway L, N, Q, R, 4, 5, 6 to 14th Street-Union Square. **Open** 5.30pm-midnight Mon, Tue, Sun; 5.30pm-2am Wed-Sat. **Shows** 8.30pm Mon-Thur; 8.30pm, 10.30pm Fri, Sat; varies Sun. **Admission** $5-$40. **Credit** AmEx, MC, V. **Map** p403 F27.

Smackdown: MSG vs Barclays Center

After 45 years, there's a challenger to the title of the city's top arena.

The **Barclays Center** (*see p327*) opened its doors in autumn 2012, and its debut could not have been more dazzling. For the first time, Manhattan's legendary music and sports hub **Madison Square Garden** (*see p327*) has some serious competition. So which venue wins the crown as New York's greatest stadium? The heavyweights slug it out.

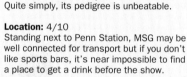

BARCLAYS CENTER

Star power: 6/10
Jay-Z (who has a share in the venue's basketball team) blessed Barclays with coolness with an unprecedented weeklong run. The Stones made it the first US stop on their '50 and Counting' tour, and Rihanna is booked for May 2013. Very dope. But as for history? Nope.

Location: 9/10
The Barclays Center is in the fashionable heart of Brooklyn, blocks away from BAM and the grooviness of Fort Greene. Excellent MTA connections, too.

Comfort: 8/10
Because it's a brand new venue, Barclays takes care of your creature comforts. The food is good (there are veggie options as well as local snacks like Nathan's hot dogs and Blue Marble ice-cream), and there are shiny sportswear shops aplenty.

Sports: 5/10
Can Barclays pick up some bonus points for sporting action? The fact that its basketball team, the Nets, have brought sports back to Brooklyn for the first time since 1957 says yes. The fact the Nets aren't actually very good says nu-uh.

FINAL SCORE 28

MADISON SQUARE GARDEN

Star power: 10/10
If you are a rock 'n' roll, hip hop, pop or soul act and you are amazing, you have played the Garden. The Stones filmed most of *Gimme Shelter* there; Elvis and Elton have recorded live albums at MSG, and it hosted LCD Soundsystem's last show. Quite simply, its pedigree is unbeatable.

Location: 4/10
Standing next to Penn Station, MSG may be well connected for transport but if you don't like sports bars, it's near impossible to find a place to get a drink before the show.

Comfort: 6/10
With so much history, it's small wonder MSG became somewhat shabby. The venue is undergoing a major revamp, which has brought new seating and food. Whether it can address the labyrinthine, *Spinal Tap*-style walkways remains to be seen.

Sports: 8/10
If you're a basketball fan, and a New Yorker, chances are you've seen the New York Knicks or women's team the Liberty play at the Garden. The arena is also home to hockey's Rangers. A classic American sports venue.

FINAL SCORE 28

SUMMARY
It's a draw! What the Garden lacks in sophistication it makes up for in history; and the hip Barclays Center now has to establish itself as a truly enduring force.

After producing popular stand-up shows for years, the four partners behind Cringe Humor (cringehumor.net) founded a venue in which to promote their favourite comics – think bawdy, raw and dark acts like Jim Norton and Dave Attell. The new bi-level Gramercy spot offers cocktails and embellished comfort food upstairs while shows take place seven nights a week in its long, narrow basement. The snug 75-seat room places the audience of frat guys and young professionals in close proximity to the performers, and they get pumped when one of their idols (Dane Cook, for instance) drops by.

Stand-up New York

236 W 78th Street, at Broadway, Upper West Side (1-212 595 0850, www.standupny.com). Subway 1 to 79th Street. **Shows** 8pm, 10.15pm Mon-Thur, Sun; 7pm, 9pm, 11pm Fri, Sat. **Admission** $15-$20 (2-drink min). **Credit** AmEx, DC, Disc, MC, V. **Map** p405 C19.

After some managerial shifts, this musty uptown spot has begun to garner attention again. The line-ups (including stalwart club denizens such as Jay Oakerson and Godfrey) keep things pretty simple, but there's almost always one performer on the bill that makes it worth the trip.

Tribeca Comedy Lounge

22 Warren Street, between Broadway & Church Street, Tribeca (1-646 504 5653, www.tribecacomedylounge.com). Subway A, C, 1, 2, 3 to Chambers Street; N, R to City Hall. **Shows** 8pm Tue, Wed, Thur; 8pm, 10pm Fri, Sat. **Admission** $20 (2-item min). **Credit** AmEx, MC, V. **Map** p402 E32.

The atmosphere in this spot – not to be confused with the space's previous occupant, the Tribeca Comedy Club – is a congenial one. Its brick walls and makeshift stage remind you that you're in a basement, but the doting waitstaff, haute Italian menu from Brick NYC upstairs and roomy layout will please fans of creature comforts, or those too claustrophobic for the likes of the Comedy Cellar. Adam Strauss, the owner-booker and a burgeoning comic himself, makes sure that his programming is packed with next-wave talent (young, funny stars such as Sara Schaefer, Dan St Germain and Kevin Barnett) while also saving stage time for himself. *Photo p281.*

★ Upright Citizens Brigade Theatre

307 W 26th Street, at Eighth Avenue, Chelsea (1-212 366 9176, www.ucbtheatre.com). Subway C, E to 23rd Street; 1 to 28th Street. **Shows** daily, times vary. **Admission** free-$10. **No credit cards. Map** p404 D26.

The UCB has been the most visible catalyst in New York's current alternative comedy boom. The improv troupes and sketch groups anchored here are some of the best in the city. Stars of *Saturday Night Live* and writers for late-night talk-shows gather on Sunday nights to wow crowds in the long-running ASSSSCAT 3000. Other premier teams include the Stepfathers (Friday) and Death by Roo Roo (Saturday). Arrive early and choose a good seat – the venue has challenging sightlines.

UCBEast, which opened in autumn 2011, gives the enormous community another space – and a bar. The warm lighting and low, rounded ceiling of the ex-art-house cinema create immediate intimacy, whether the

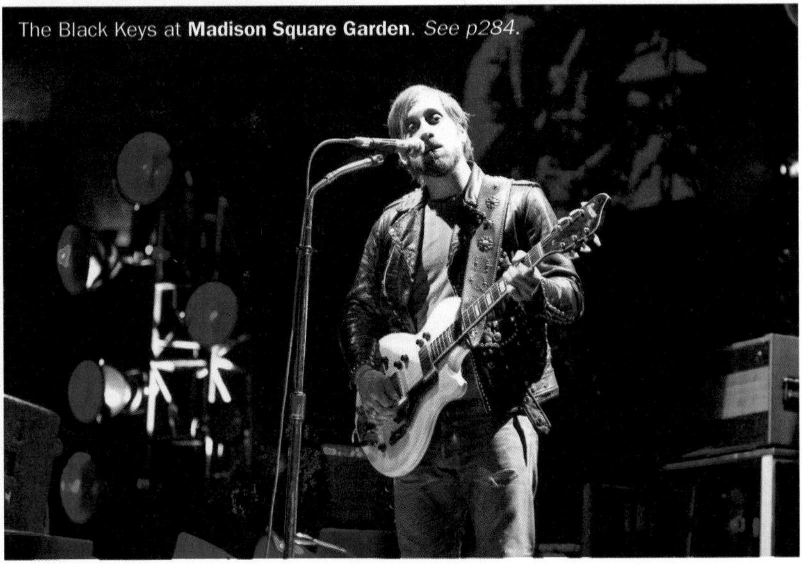

The Black Keys at **Madison Square Garden**. *See p284.*

ARTS & ENTERTAINMENT

fare is improv or stand-up, and the venue has already snapped up some of the fledgling comedy variety shows scattered in East Side venues.
Other locations UCBEast, 153 E Third Street, between Avenues A & B, East Village (1-212 366 9231).

Music

ROCK, POP & SOUL

Not only are venues offering increasingly eclectic fare, but gigs are busting out of their usual club and concert hall confines: the **City Winery** (*see p286*) crushes and ferments grapes as well as staging shows, while **Brooklyn Bowl** (*see p332*) has a 600-capacity music space that features small acts for tiny cover charges, as well as a smattering of larger concerts (Art Brut, Sharon Jones & the Dap-Kings). Questlove of the Roots has a weekly DJ residency, Soul Train, which frequently features surprise high-profile guests.

Information & tickets

Tickets are usually available from clubs in advance and at the door, though a few small and medium-size venues also sell tickets through local record stores. For larger events, buy online through the venue's website or through **Ticketmaster** or **TicketWeb** (for both, *see p221*). Remember to phone ahead for information and show times, which often change without notice.

Major arenas & stadiums

★ Barclays Center
For listings, *see p327*.
See *p282* **MSG vs Barclays Center**.

Izod Center
For listings, *see p327* Meadowlands Sports Complex. New Jersey's answer to Madison Square Garden has played host to the likes of Beyoncé, Foo Fighters and, of course, Bruce Springsteen and the E-Street Band. Sometimes, shows that sell out at the Garden may be available here, a sizeable bus ride away.

★ Madison Square Garden
For listings, *see p327*.
Some of music's biggest acts – Jay-Z, Lady Gaga, Rush – come out to play at the world's most famous basketball arena. Whether you'll actually be able to get a look at them depends on your seat number or the quality of your binoculars. The arena is too vast for a rich concert experience, ugly and musty – though it's undergoing a major refurbishment, which has brought improved seating and food from top NYC

ARTS & ENTERTAINMENT

Apollo Theater.

chefs like Andrew Carmellini. The striking circular ceiling will be restored before the revamp wraps up in autumn 2013. Regardless, it is part of the fabric of New York and begrudgingly beloved. There's also a smaller theatre within the complex. *See also p282* **MSG vs Barclays Center.** *Photo p283.*

Nassau Veterans Memorial Coliseum

For listings, *see p327.*
Long Island's arena hosts mainstream acts such as Lil Wayne and Metallica, punctuated by teen shows (Taylor Swift, Rihanna) and occasional over-the-top Bollywood showcases.

Venues

92YTribeca

200 Hudson Street, between Canal & Desbrosses Streets, Tribeca (1-212 601 1000, www.92 ytribeca.org). Subway A, C, E, 1 to Canal Street. **Box office** noon-7pm Wed; noon-7pm, 9-11pm Thur; noon-5pm Fri; 5pm-midnight Sat; 10am-3pm Sun. **Tickets** free-$15. **Credit** AmEx, DC, MC, V. **Map** p402 D30.
The downtown outpost of the 92nd Street Y, 92YTribeca is ostensibly a cultural centre for hip young Jews. Yet the club – which houses a performance space, screening room, art gallery and café – is by no means restricted to Jewish events or artists. In fact, since it opened in 2008, it has quickly become one of the most daring venues in Manhattan. The club's breadth is impressive, featuring obscure indie rock, world music, country and mixed-media shows.

★ Apollo Theater

253 W 125th Street, between Adam Clayton Powell Jr Boulevard (Seventh Avenue) & Frederick Douglass Boulevard (Eighth Avenue), Harlem (1-212 531 5300, www.apollotheater.org). Subway A, B, C, D, 1 to 125th Street. **Box office** 10am-6pm Mon-Fri; noon-5pm Sat. **Tickets** $20-$40. **Credit** AmEx, DC, Disc, MC, V. **Map** p407 D13.
Visitors may think they know this venerable theatre from TV's *Showtime at the Apollo.* But as the saying goes, the small screen adds about ten pounds: the city's home of R&B and soul music is actually quite cosy. Known for launching the careers of Ella Fitzgerald and D'Angelo, among many others, the Apollo continues to mix veteran talents such as Dianne Reeves with younger artists such as John Legend. For a taste of classic New York, check out the Apollo's now-legendary Amateur Night showcase, which has been running since 1934.

Barbès

376 9th Street, between Sixth & Seventh Avenues, Park Slope, Brooklyn (1-347 422 0248, www.barbesbrooklyn.com). Subway F to Seventh Avenue. **Open** 5pm-2am Mon-Thur; 2pm-4am Fri, Sat; 2pm-2am Sun. **Tickets** free-$10. **Credit** MC, V. **Map** p410 T11.

Show up early if you want to get into Park Slope's global-bohemian club – it's tiny. Run by musically inclined French expats, this boîte brings in traditional swing and jazz of more daring stripes – depending on the night, you could catch African, French, Brazilian or Colombian music or acts that often defy categorisation (One Ring Zero). Chicha Libre, a Brooklyn band reviving psychedelic Peruvian music, holds down Mondays.

Beacon Theatre

2124 Broadway, between 74th & 75th Streets, Upper West Side (1-212 465 6500, www.beacon theatrenyc.com). Subway 1, 2, 3 to 72nd Street. **Box office** 11am-6pm Tue-Sat. **Tickets** $15-$175. **Credit** AmEx, Disc, MC, V. **Map** p405 C20.
This spacious former vaudeville theatre, resplendent after a recent renovation, hosts a variety of popular acts, from Aziz Ansari to ZZ Top; once a year, the Allman Brothers take over for a lengthy residency. While the vastness can be daunting to performers and audience alike, the baroque, gilded interior and uptown location make you feel as though you're having a real night out on the town.

Best Buy Theater

1515 Broadway, at 44th Street, Theater District (1-212 930 1950, www.bestbuytheater.com). Subway N, Q, R, S, 1, 2, 3, 7 to 42nd Street-Times Square. **Box office** noon-6pm Mon-Sat. **Tickets** $20-$70. **Credit** AmEx, Disc, MC, V. **Map** p404 D24.
This large, corporate club begs for character but finds redemption in its creature comforts. The sound and sightlines are both good, and there's even edible food. Those who wish to look into a musician's eyes can stand in the ample front section; foot-weary fans can sit in the cinema-like section at the back. It's a comfortable place to see a well-known band that hasn't (yet) reached stadium-filling fame.

★ Bowery Ballroom

6 Delancey Street, between Bowery & Chrystie Street, Lower East Side (1-212 533 2111, www.boweryballroom.com). Subway B, D to Grand Street; J, Z to Bowery; 6 to Spring Street. **Box office** at Mercury Lounge (*see p289*). **Tickets** $12-$35. **Credit** (bar only) AmEx, Disc, MC, V. **Map** p403 F30.

ARTS & ENTERTAINMENT

The Bowery Ballroom is probably the best venue in the city for seeing indie bands, either on the way up or holding their own. However, the Ballroom also brings in a diverse range of artists from home and abroad, and you can expect a clear view and bright sound from any spot in the venue. The spacious downstairs lounge is a great place to hang out between sets.

★ Cake Shop

152 Ludlow Street, between Rivington & Stanton Streets, Lower East Side (1-212 253 0036, www.cake-shop.com). Subway F to Lower East Side-Second Avenue. **Open** 5pm-2am Mon-Thur, Sun; 5pm-4am Fri, Sat. **Tickets** $6-$12. **No credit cards.** **Map** p403 G29.

It can be difficult to see the stage in this narrow, stuffy basement space, but Cake Shop gets big points for its keen indie and underground-rock bookings, among the best and most adventurous in the city. The venue lives up to its name, selling vegan pastries and coffee upstairs, while the back room at street level sells record-store ephemera.

City Winery

155 Varick Street, at Vandam Street, Tribeca (1-212 608 0555, www.citywinery.com). Subway 1 to Houston Street. **Open** 11.30am-3pm, 5.30pm-midnight Mon-Fri; 5pm-midnight Sat; 10am-3pm, 5.30pm-midnight Sun. **Box office** 11am-6pm Mon-Fri. **Tickets** $10-$85. **Credit** AmEx, DC, Disc, MC, V. **Map** p403 D30.

Unabashedly grown-up and yuppie-friendly, this slick, spacious club launched by oenophile Michael Dorf is New York's only fully functioning winery – as well as a 300-seat concert space. Acts tend to be on the quiet side – this is, after all, a wine bar – but that doesn't mean the shows lack bite. Younger singer-songwriters such as Laura Marling and Keren Ann have appeared, but the place is dominated by older artists (Steve Earle, Los Lobos).
▶ *Michael Dorf was also the founder of the Knitting Factory; see p288.*

Galapagos Art Space

16 Main Street, at Water Street, Dumbo, Brooklyn (1-718 222 8500, www.galapagosartspace.com). Subway A, C to High Street; F to York Street. **Shows** vary. **Tickets** free-$25. **Credit** AmEx, MC, V. **Map** p411 S9.

Galapagos established itself in Williamsburg years before the neighbourhood's renaissance – and, like many colonisers, eventually got squeezed out of the scene it had helped to create. The much larger space in Dumbo offers a grander mix of the cultural offerings for which Galapagos is known and loved: music, performance art, burlesque, drag queens and other weird stuff. Just be careful not to fall into the pools of water strategically placed throughout the club.

Glasslands Gallery

289 Kent Avenue, between South 1st & 2nd Streets, Williamsburg, Brooklyn (no phone, http://glasslands. blogspot.com). Subway L to Bedford Avenue. **Shows** vary (usually 8.30pm daily). **Tickets** free-$10. **No credit cards.** **Map** p411 U8.

If you're looking to catch a Brooklyn buzz band before it breaks, look here. Marvel at the cool DIY decor (we're partial to the cloud-like creations adorning the ceiling above the stage) while nodding to sets from local indie faves such as Ducktails and Cults. The music/burlesque/party destination spotlights less-hyped acts; metal band Liturgy has rocked the house, and Canadian electro-rock crew Suuns have played here.

Goodbye Blue Monday

1087 Broadway, at Dodworth Street, Bushwick, Brooklyn (1-718 453 6343, www.goodbye-blue-monday.com). Subway J to Kosciuszko Street. **Open** 11am-2am Mon-Thur, Sun; 11am-3am Fri, Sat. **Tickets** free-$7. **Credit** ($10 min, bar & food only) AmEx, Disc, MC, V. **Map** p411 W9.

Relax while taking in this cult Bushwick drinkery's distinct junkyard aesthetic (the walls are lined with old books, random lamps and retro radios). The acts that play here are pretty eclectic, ranging from anti-folk to experimental jazz, and, best of all, gigs are almost always free. If you can, check out the popular Bushwick Book Club series, where bands play new tunes based on that month's reading assignment.

Cake Shop.

Gramercy Theatre

127 E 23rd Street, between Park & Lexington Avenues, Gramercy Park (1-212 614 6932, www.thegramercytheatre.com). Subway N, R, 6 to 23rd Street. **Box office** at Irving Plaza (*see below*). **Tickets** $10-$100. **Credit** AmEx, MC, V. **Map** p404 E26.

The Gramercy Theatre looks exactly like what it is, a run-down former movie theatre; yet it has a decent sound system and good sightlines. Concert-goers can lounge in raised seats on the top level or get closer to the stage. Bookings have included such Baby Boom underdogs as Loudon Wainwright III and Todd Rundgren, and the occasional hip hop show (Kool Keith, Pusha T), but tilt towards niche metal and emo.

Hammerstein Ballroom

Manhattan Center, 311 W 34th Street, between Eighth & Ninth Avenues, Garment District (1-212 279 7740, Ticketmaster 1-800 745 3000, www.mcstudios.com). Subway A, C, E to 34th Street-Penn Station. **Tickets** $10-$150. **Credit** AmEx, MC, V. **Map** p404 C25.

Queues can wind across the block, drinks prices are high, and those seated in the balcony should bring binoculars if they want a clear view of the band. Still, this cavernous space regularly draws big performers in the limbo between club and arena shows, and it's ideal for theatrical blow-outs; Kylie, the Pet Shop Boys and Grace Jones have all wowed here.

Highline Ballroom

431 W 16th Street, between Ninth & Tenth Avenues, Chelsea (1-212 414 5994, www.highlineballroom.com). Subway A, C, E to 14th Street; L to Eighth Avenue. **Box office** 11am-end of show. **Tickets** free-$100 ($10 food/drink min at tables). **Credit** AmEx, Disc, MC, V. **Map** p403 C27.

This West Side club, situated next to a Western Beef grocer, is LA-slick and bland, in a corporate sense. But despite this, it has a lot to recommend it: the sound is top-of-the-heap and sightlines are pretty good. The bookings are also impressive, ranging from hip hop heatseekers such as Yelawolf and Wiz Khalifa, to singer-songwriter pop, world music and burlesque. *Photo p288.*

Irving Plaza

17 Irving Place, at 15th Street, Union Square (1-212 777 6800, www.irvingplaza.com). Subway L, N, Q, R, 4, 5, 6 to 14th Street-Union Square. **Box office** noon-6.30pm Mon-Fri; 1-4pm Sat. **Tickets** $10-$65. **Credit** AmEx, MC, V. **Map** p403 E27.

Lying just east of Union Square, this midsize rock venue has served as a Democratic Party lecture hall (in the 19th century), a Yiddish theatre and a burlesque house (Gypsy Rose Lee made an appearance). Most importantly, it's a great place to see big stars keeping a low profile (Jeff Beck, Jane's Addiction and Lenny Kravitz) and medium heavies on their way up.

ARTS & ENTERTAINMENT

★ Joe's Pub

Public Theater, 425 Lafayette Street, between Astor Place & E 4th Street, East Village (1-212 967 7555, www.joespub.com). Subway N, R to 8th Street-NYU; 6 to Astor Place. **Box office** 1-6pm Mon, Sun; 1-7.30pm Tue-Sat. **Tickets** ($12 food or 2-drink minimum) $12-$30. **Credit** AmEx, DC, MC, V. **Map** p403 E28.

One of the city's premier small spots for sit-down audiences, the recently refurbished Joe's Pub brings in impeccable talent of all genres and origins. While some well-established names play here (Steve Martin's bluegrass crew, the Steep Canyon Rangers, to give an example), Joe's also lends its stage to up-and-comers (this is where Amy Winehouse made her debut in the United States), drag acts and cabaret performers (Justin Vivian Bond is a mainstay). A small but solid menu and deep bar selections seal the deal – just be sure to keep an eye on the drinks prices.

Knitting Factory Brooklyn

361 Metropolitan Avenue, at Havemeyer Street, Williamsburg, Brooklyn (1-347 529 6696, www.knittingfactory.com). Subway L to Lorimer Street; G to Metropolitan Avenue. **Open** 5pm-3am daily. **Tickets** free-$25. **Credit** AmEx, Disc, MC, V. **Map** p411 U8.

Once a downtown Manhattan incubator of experimental music – both of the jazz and indie-rock variety – Knitting Factory now has outposts across the country, and has moved its New York base to music hub Williamsburg. It's a professional, well-managed

club, with a happening front-room bar, and solid indie-rock and hip hop bills (Zola Jesus, Black Milk) designed to suit its hipster clientele.
► *For Knitting Factory founder Michael Dorf's latest venture, see p286 City Winery.*

Living Room

154 Ludlow Street, between Rivington & Stanton Streets, Lower East Side (1-212 533 7237, www.livingroomny.com). Subway F to Lower East Side-Second Avenue; J, Z to Delancey-Essex Streets. **Open** 5pm-2am Mon-Thur, Sun; 5pm-4am Fri, Sat. **Admission** free-$15 (1-drink min). **No credit cards. Map** p403 G29.

Many local clubs claim to be the place where Norah Jones got her start, but the Living Room is the real McCoy – she even donated a piano as a way of saying thanks to the place. Mind you, that was in the venue's older (and rather drabber) location, a former fried-chicken establishment; since it moved to the Lower East Side's version of Main Street, the stream of singer-songwriters has taken on a bit more gleam, and the warmly lit environs always seem to be bustling. Upstairs is Googie's Lounge, an even more intimate space.

Maxwell's

1039 Washington Street, at 11th Street, Hoboken, NJ (1-201 798 0406, www.maxwellsnj.com). PATH train to Hoboken, then taxi, Red Apple bus or NJ Transit 126 bus to 11th Street. **Open** 5pm-2am Mon-Thur, Sun; 5pm-3am Fri, Sat. **Tickets** $7-$25. **Credit** AmEx, Disc, MC, V.

Highline Ballroom. *See p287.*

The trip to Maxwell's, across the Hudson River in New Jersey, can be a hassle, but the 15-minute walk once you're finally off the PATH train can make you feel like you're in small-town America. The restaurant in front is big and friendly; for dessert you can feast on musical fare from popular indie rock acts (the Fiery Furnaces, Big Pink) and garage favourites (King Khan & BBQ Show). Hometown heroes Yo La Tengo stage their more or less annual Hanukkah shows here.

Mercury Lounge

217 E Houston Street, between Essex & Ludlow Streets, Lower East Side (1-212 260 4700, www.mercuryloungenyc.com). Subway F to Lower East Side-Second Avenue. **Box office** noon-7pm Mon-Sat. **Tickets** $8-$20. **Credit** (bar only) AmEx, Disc, MC, V. **Map** p403 G29.

The unassuming, boxy Mercury Lounge is an old standby, with solid sound and sightlines (and a cramped bar in the front room). There are four-band bills most nights, although they can seem stylistically haphazard and set times are often later than advertised. (It's a good rule of thumb to show up half an hour later than you think you should.) Some of the bigger shows sell out in advance, and the club thrives during fall's CMJ Music Marathon; young hopefuls from years gone by include Mumford & Sons. *Photo p291.*

Music Hall of Williamsburg

66 North 6th Street, between Kent & Wythe Avenues, Williamsburg, Brooklyn (1-718 486 5400, www.musichallofwilliamsburg.com). Subway L to Bedford Avenue. **Box office** 11am-6pm Sat. **Tickets** $12-$35. **Credit** (online purchases only) AmEx, Disc, MC, V. **Map** p411 U7.

When, in 2007, the local promoter Bowery Presents found itself in need of a Williamsburg outpost, it gave the former Northsix a facelift and took over the bookings. It's basically a Bowery Ballroom in Brooklyn – and bands such as Sonic Youth, Hot Chip and Real Estate headline, often on the day after they've played Bowery Ballroom or Terminal 5.

★ Pete's Candy Store

709 Lorimer Street, between Frost & Richardson Streets, Williamsburg, Brooklyn (1-718 302 3770, www.petescandystore.com). Subway L to Lorimer Street. **Open** 5pm-2am Mon-Wed; 5pm-4am Thur; 4pm-4am Fri, Sat; 4pm-2am Sun. **Admission** free. **Credit** AmEx, Disc, MC, V. **Map** p411 V7.

An overlooked gem tucked away in an old candy shop, Pete's is beautifully ramshackle, tiny and almost always free. The performers are generally unknown and crowds can be thin, but it can be a charming place to catch a singer-songwriter. Worthy underdogs may stop by for casual sets.

Pianos

158 Ludlow Street, between Rivington & Stanton Streets, Lower East Side (1-212 505 3733, www.pianosnyc.com). Subway F to Delancey Street; J, Z to Delancey-Essex Streets. **Open** 2pm-4am daily. **Admission** free-$12. **Credit** AmEx, Disc, MC, V. **Map** p403 G29.

In recent years, a lot of the cooler bookings have moved down the block to venues such as Cake Shop or to Brooklyn. But while the sound is often lousy and the room can get uncomfortably mobbed, there are always good reasons to go back to Pianos – very often the under-the-radar, emerging rock bands that make local music scenes tick.

★ Le Poisson Rouge

158 Bleecker Street, at Thompson Street, Greenwich Village (1-212 505 3474, www.le poissonrouge.com). Subway A, B, C, D, E, F, M to W 4th Street. **Open** 5pm-2am Mon-Wed, Sun; 5pm-4am Thur-Sat. **Box office** 5pm-close daily. **Tickets** free-$30. **Credit** AmEx (bar only), DC, Disc, MC, V. **Map** p403 E29.

Tucked into the basement of the long-gone Village Gate – a legendary performance space that hosted everyone from Miles Davis to Jimi Hendrix – Le Poisson Rouge was opened in 2008 by a group of young music enthusiasts with ties to both the classical and indie rock worlds. The cabaret space's booking policy reflects both camps, often on a single bill. No other joint in town books such a wide range of great music, whether from a feverish Malian band (Toumani Diabaté's Symmetric Orchestra), rising indie stars (Zola Jesus) or young classical stars (pianist Simone Dinnerstein).

★ Radio City Music Hall

1260 Sixth Avenue, at 50th Street, Midtown (1-212 247 4777, www.radiocity.com). Subway B, D, F, M to 47th-50th Streets-Rockefeller Center. **Box office** *Jan-Sept* 11.30am-6pm Mon-Sat. *Oct-Dec* 10am-8pm daily. **Tickets** vary. **Credit** AmEx, Disc, MC, V. **Map** p404 D23.

Few rooms scream 'New York City!' more than this gilded hall, which has recently drawn Leonard Cohen, Drake and Bon Iver as headliners. The greatest challenge for any performer is not to be upstaged by the awe-inspiring art deco surroundings, although those same surroundings lend historic heft to even the flimsiest showing. Bookings are all over the map; expect everything from seasonal staples like the Rockettes to lectures with the Dalai Lama. *Photos pp292-293.*

Roseland Ballroom

239 W 52nd Street, between Broadway & Eighth Avenue, Theater District (1-212 247 0200, www.roselandballroom.com). Subway B, D, E to Seventh Avenue; C, E to 50th Street; N, Q, R to 49th Street. **Box office** (*see p287*). **Tickets** $17-$75. **Credit** (advance purchases only) AmEx, MC, V. **Map** p404 D23.

ARTS & ENTERTAINMENT

This dreary Times Square club is bigger than Irving Plaza and smaller than the Hammerstein Ballroom. As such, it draws big talent (Yo La Tengo, Them Crooked Vultures) but remains a vaguely depressing place to spend a night, recalling a dank, slightly neglected rec room.

Sidewalk Café
94 Avenue A, at 6th Street, East Village (1-212 473 7373, www.sidewalkny.com). Subway 6 to Astor Place. **Open** 11am-4am daily. **Shows** usually 7pm daily. **Admission** free (1-drink min). **Credit** AmEx, MC, V. **Map** p403 G28.
Despite its cramped, awkward layout, the Sidewalk Café is the focal point of the city's anti-folk scene – although that category means just about anything from piano pop to wry folk. Nellie McKay, Regina Spektor and the Moldy Peaches all started here.

SOB's
204 Varick Street, at Houston Street, Tribeca (1-212 243 4940, www.sobs.com). Subway 1 to Houston Street. **Box office** 11am-6pm Mon-Fri. **Tickets** $5-$40. **Credit** (food & bar only) Disc, MC, V. **Map** p403 D29.
The titular Sounds of Brazil (SOB, geddit?) are just some of the many global genres that keep this venue hopping. Soul, hip hop, reggae and Latin beats figure in the mix, with Raphael Saadiq, Maceo Parker and Eddie Palmieri each appearing of late. The drinks are expensive, but the sharp-looking clientele doesn't seem to mind.

Terminal 5
610 W 56th Street, between 11th & 12th Avenues, Hell's Kitchen (1-212 260 4700, www.terminal5nyc.com). Subway A, B, C, D, 1 to 59th Street-Columbus Circle. **Box office** at Mercury Lounge (*see p289*). **Tickets** $15-$90. **Credit** (online purchases & bar only) AmEx, Disc, MC, V. **Map** p405 C22.
Opened by Bowery Presents, this three-floor, 3,000-capacity place is the largest midtown venue to set up shop in more than a decade. Bookings include bands that only a short time ago were playing in the smaller Bowery confines (Odd Future), plus bigger stars (Florence and the Machine) and veterans with their loyal fan bases (Morrissey, Jane's Addiction). It's great for dancey acts (Chromeo, Matt & Kim), but be warned: sightlines from the T5 balconies are among the worst in the city.

★ Town Hall
123 W 43rd Street, between Sixth Avenue & Broadway, Theater District (1-212 840 2824, www.the-townhall-nyc.org). Subway B, D, F, M to 42nd Street-Bryant Park; N, Q, R, S, 1, 2, 3, 7 to 42nd Street-Times Square; 7 to Fifth Avenue. **Box office** noon-6pm Mon-Sat. **Tickets** $10-$120. **Credit** AmEx, MC, V. **Map** p404 D24.

Acoustics at the 1921 'people's auditorium' are superb, and there's no doubting the gravitas of the Town Hall's surroundings – the building was designed by illustrious architects McKim, Mead & White as a meeting house for a suffragist organisation. George Benson, Grizzly Bear and Lindsey Buckingham have performed here in recent times, and smart indie songwriters such as the Magnetic Fields have set up shop for a number of nights.

Union Hall
702 Union Street, between Fifth & Sixth Avenues, Park Slope, Brooklyn (1-718 638 4400, www.unionhallny.com). Subway R to Union Street. **Open** 4pm-4am Mon-Fri; noon-4am Sat, Sun. **Tickets** $5-$20. **Credit** AmEx, MC, V. **Map** p410 T11.
The spacious main floor of this Brooklyn bar (*see p188*) has a garden, food service and a bocce ball court. Tucked in the basement is a comfortable space dominated by the more delicate side of indie rock, with infrequent sets by indie comics such as Daniel Kitson and Eugene Mirman.

Union Pool
484 Union Avenue, at Meeker Avenue, Williamsburg, Brooklyn (1-718 609 0484, www.union-pool.com). Subway L to Lorimer Street; G to Metropolitan Avenue. **Open** 5pm-4am Mon-Fri; 1pm-4am Sat, Sun. **Tickets** free-$12. **Credit** (bar only) AmEx, Disc, MC, V. **Map** p411 V8.
Wind through the kitschy backyard space of this modest but super-cool Williamsburg bar (which featured in the movie *Nick and Norah's Infinite Playlist*) and you'll find yourself back indoors, facing a small stage. Local stars check in from time to time (members of Yeah Yeah Yeahs have showed off their side projects here), but it's dominated by well-plucked smaller indie acts. For a rowdy, amusing Monday night, check out Reverend Vince Anderson and his Love Choir.

United Palace Theatre
4140 Broadway, at 175th Street, Washington Heights (Ticketmaster 1-800 745 3000, www.ticketmaster.com). Subway A to 175th Street. **Tickets** $50-$150. **Credit** AmEx, DC, Disc, MC, V. **Map** p409 B7.
This renovated movie house, which was once a vaudeville theatre, dates from the 1930s. And it really does feel as if you've entered a palace here, with its shimmering chandeliers, ornate detailed ceiling and gold-drenched corridors. The venue's solid booking has ranged, over the past few years, from popular young acts such as Adele, Vampire Weekend and Bon Iver, to stalwarts of the music world such as Bob Dylan and the Allman Brothers Band. Located in upper Manhattan, far beyond the traditional nightlife or tourist zone, the theatre is nevertheless easily accessible by subway.

Mercury Lounge. *See p289.*

Webster Hall

125 E 11th Street, between Third & Fourth Avenues, East Village (1-212 353 1600, www. websterhall.com). Subway L to Third Avenue; L, N, Q, R, 4, 5, 6 to 14th Street-Union Square. **Box office** at Mercury Lounge (*see p289*). **Tickets** $15-$50. **Credit** (bar only) AmEx, Disc, MC, V. **Map** p403 F28.

A great-sounding alternative for bands (and fans) who've had their fill of the comparably sized Irving Plaza, Webster Hall is booked by Bowery Presents, the folks who run Bowery Ballroom and Mercury Lounge. Expect to find high-calibre indie acts (Animal Collective, Battles, Gossip), but be sure to arrive early if you want a decent view. A smaller space downstairs, the Studio at Webster Hall, hosts cheaper shows, mainly by local bands.

WORLD, COUNTRY & ROOTS

Among the cornucopia of live entertainment programmes at the **Brooklyn Academy of Music** (*see p299*), the **BAMcafé** above the lobby comes to life on weekend nights with country, world music and other genres. *See also p290* **SOB's**, *p285* **Barbès** and *p292* **BB King Blues Club & Grill**.

Nublu

151 Avenue C, between East Ninth Street & East 10th Street, East Village (1-646 546 5206, www.nublu.net). **Open** call for information. **Admission** $5-$10. **No credit cards.** **Map** p403 G28.

Nublu's prominence on the local globalist club scene has been inversely proportional to its size. A pressure-cooker of creativity, it gave rise to the Brazilian Girls, who started jamming at one late-night session and haven't stopped yet, and started NYC's romance with the northern Brazilian style *forró*. However, at time of writing, the East Village club was looking for a new venue – call or see website for updates.

Rodeo Bar & Grill

375 Third Avenue, at 27th Street, Gramercy Park (1-212 683 6500, www.rodeobar.com). Subway 6 to 28th Street. **Shows** 9pm-midnight Mon-Wed, Sun; 9.30pm-12.30am Thur; 11pm-2am Fri, Sat. **Admission** free. **Credit** AmEx, Disc, MC, V. **Map** p404 F26.

The unpretentious, if sometimes raucous crowd, roadhouse atmosphere and absence of a cover charge help make the Rodeo the city's best roots club, with a steady stream of rockabilly, country and related sounds. Kick back with a beer from the bar – a funked-up trailer in the middle of the room.

JAZZ, BLUES & EXPERIMENTAL

Ever since Duke Ellington urged folks to take the A train up to Harlem, New York has been a hotbed of improvisational talent. While Harlem is no longer the centre of the jazz scene, in the Village, you can soak up the vibe at clubs that once provided a platform for the virtuoso experimentations of Miles Davis, John Coltrane and Thelonious Monk. Boundaries are still being pushed in eclectic avant-garde venues like **Roulette Brooklyn**, **Spectrum** (for both, *see p304*) and the **Stone**. For well-known jazz joints such as the **Village Vanguard** and **Birdland**, booking ahead is recommended.

55 Bar

55 Christopher Street, between Seventh Avenue South & Waverly Place, West Village (1-212 929 9883, www.55bar.com). Subway 1 to Christopher Street-Sheridan Square. **Open** 3pm-4am daily. **Tickets** free-$15. **No credit cards. Map** p403 D28.

This tiny Prohibition-era dive is one of New York's most artist-friendly rooms, thanks to its knowledgeable, appreciative audience. You can catch emerging talent almost every night at the free-of-charge early shows; late sets regularly feature established artists such as David Binney and Leni Stern.

92nd Street Y

For listings, *see p298*.

Best known for the series Jazz in July and spring's Lyrics & Lyricists, this multidisciplinary cultural centre also offers gospel, mainstream jazz and singer-songwriters. The small, handsome theatre provides a fine setting for the sophisticated fare.

BB King Blues Club & Grill

237 W 42nd Street, between Seventh & Eighth Avenues, Theater District (1-212 997 4144, www.bbkingblues.com). Subway A, C, E to 42nd Street-Port Authority; N, Q, R, S, 1, 2, 3, 7 to 42nd Street-Times Square. **Box office** 11am-midnight daily. **Tickets** $12-$150. **Credit** AmEx, DC, Disc, MC, V. **Map** p404 D24.

BB's Times Square joint hosts one of the most varied music schedules in town. Cover bands and tributes fill the gaps between big-name bookings such as George Clinton and Buddy Guy, but the venue also regularly hosts hip hop and the odd extreme-metal blowout. The best seats are often at the dinner tables in front, but the menu prices are steep (and watch out for drink minimums). The Harlem Gospel Choir's buffet brunch ($42.50, $40 booked in advance, 12.30pm Sun) raises the roof.

Birdland

315 W 44th Street, between Eighth & Ninth Avenues, Theater District (1-212 581 3080, www.birdlandjazz.com). Subway A, C, E to 42nd Street-Port Authority. **Open** 5pm-1am daily. **Tickets** $20-$50 ($10 food/drink min). **Credit** AmEx, MC, V. **Map** p404 C24.

Its name is synonymous with jazz (Jim Hall, Greg Osby), but Birdland is also a prime cabaret destination (Christine Ebersole, various up-and-coming songwriters). Arturo O'Farrill's Afro Latin Jazz Orchestra owns Sundays, and David Ostwald's Louis Armstrong Centennial Band hits on Wednesdays; Mondays see cabaret's waggish Jim Caruso and his Cast Party.

Blue Note

131 W 3rd Street, between MacDougal Street & Sixth Avenue, Greenwich Village (1-212 475 8592, www.bluenote.net). Subway A, B, C, D,

Radio City Music Hall. *See p289.*

E, F, M to W 4th Street. **Shows** 8pm, 10.30pm
Mon-Thur, Sun; 8pm, 10.30pm, 12.30am Fri, Sat.
Tickets $10-$75 ($5 food/drink min). **Credit**
AmEx, MC, V. **Map** p403 E29.
The Blue Note prides itself on being 'the jazz capital
of the world'. Bona fide musical titans (Jimmy Heath,
Lee Konitz) rub against contemporary heavyweights
(the Bad Plus), while the close-set tables in the club
get patrons rubbing up against each other. The edgy
Friday Late Night Groove series and the Sunday
brunches (11.30am-4pm; $29.50 including show) are
the best bargain bets.

Carnegie Hall

For listings, *see p301.*
Carnegie Hall means the big time. In recent years,
though, the 599-seat, state-of-the-art Zankel Hall
has greatly augmented the venue's pop, jazz and
world music offerings. Between both halls, the
complex has welcomed Keith Jarrett, Randy
Newman and Bobby McFerrin, among other high-
wattage names.

Cornelia Street Café

*29 Cornelia Street, between Bleecker & 4th
Streets, Greenwich Village (1-212 989 9319,
www.corneliastreetcafe.com). Subway A, B,
C, D, E, F, M to W 4th Street.* **Open** 10am-
midnight Mon-Thur, Sun; 10am-1am Fri, Sat.
Shows 6pm, 9pm Mon-Thur, Sun; 6pm, 9pm,
10.30pm Fri, Sat. **Tickets** $10-$15 ($7-$10
drink min). **Credit** (food & bar only) AmEx,
Disc, MC, V. **Map** p403 D29.

Upstairs at the Cornelia Street Café is a cosy little
eaterie. Downstairs is an even cosier music space hosting adventurous jazz, poetry, world music and folk.
Regular mini-festivals spotlight blues and songwriters. It's a good idea to arrive when the doors open for
shows (5.45pm, 8.30pm or 10.15pm) because reservations aren't held once the set starts.

★ Iridium

*1650 Broadway, at 51st Street, Theater District
(1-212 582 2121, www.iridiumjazzclub.com).
Subway 1 to 50th Street; N, R to 49th Street.*
Shows 8pm, 10pm daily. **Tickets** $25-$40 ($15
food/drink min). **Credit** AmEx, Disc, MC, V.
Map p404 D23.
One of the nicer places to dine while being hit with
top-shelf jazz, Iridium is located bang in the middle
of Broadway's bright lights. Recent guests have
included Nicholas Payton and Bucky Pizzarelli.
Increasingly, the club has been straying from traditional jazz bookings, spotlighting rockers ranging
from the Doors' Robby Krieger to former King
Crimson-ite Adrien Belew.

Jazz Gallery

*5th floor, 1158-60 Broadway, at 27th Street,
Flatiron District (no phone, www.jazzgallery.
org). Subway N, R to 23rd Street; 4, 6 to 28th
Street.* **Shows** vary. **Tickets** $10-$35. **Credit**
(online purchases only) AmEx, Disc, MC, V.
Map p404 E26.
Displaced from its West Village digs, at the time of
writing the Jazz Gallery was preparing to move into

a new 1,800sq ft loft-style space near the Flatiron Building. It still promises to be a place to witness true works of art from the sometimes obscure but always interesting jazzers who play the club (Henry Threadgill and Vijay Iyer, to name a couple).

★ Jazz at Lincoln Center

Frederick P Rose Hall, Broadway, at 60th Street, Upper West Side (1-212 258 9800, www.jalc.org). Subway A, B, C, D, 1 to 59th Street-Columbus Circle.
Rose Theater & the Allen Room *CenterCharge* 1-212 721 6500. **Shows** vary. **Box office** 10am-6pm Mon-Sat; noon-6pm Sun. **Tickets** *Rose Theater* $30-$120. *The Allen Room* $55-$65.
Dizzy's Club Coca-Cola *1-212 258 9595.*
Shows 7.30pm, 9.30pm Mon-Thur, Sun; 7.30pm, 9.30pm, 11.30pm Fri, Sat. **Tickets** $10-$35 ($5-$10 food/drink min). **Credit** AmEx, DC, MC, V. **Map** p405 D22.
The jazz arm of Lincoln Center is located several blocks away from the main campus, high atop the Time Warner Center. It includes three rooms: the Rose Theater is a traditional midsize space, but the crown jewels are the Allen Room and the smaller Dizzy's Club Coca-Cola, with stages that are framed by enormous windows looking on to Columbus Circle and Central Park. The venues feel like a Hollywood cinematographer's vision of a Manhattan jazz club. Some of the best players in the business regularly grace the spot; among them is Wynton Marsalis, Jazz at Lincoln Center's famed artistic director.

Jazz Standard

116 E 27th Street, between Park Avenue South & Lexington Avenue, Flatiron District (1-212 576 2232, www.jazzstandard.com). Subway 6 to 28th Street. **Shows** 7.30pm, 9.30pm Mon-Thur; 7.30pm, 9.30pm, 11.30pm Fri, Sat. **Tickets** $20-$35. **Credit** AmEx, DC, Disc, MC, V. **Map** p404 E26.
Jazz Standard's airy, multi-tiered floor plan makes for splendid sightlines to match the sterling sound. In keeping with the rib-sticking chow upstairs at Danny Meyer's Blue Smoke barbecue joint, the jazz is often of the groovy, hard-swinging variety, with musicians such as saxist George Coleman and vocalist José James. The mighty Mingus Orchestra, long-time local favourites, hold down Monday nights.

Merkin Concert Hall

For listings, *see p303*.
Just north of Lincoln Center, the Merkin provides a polished platform for classical and jazz composers, with chamber music, jazz, folk, cabaret and experimental and experimental music performers taking the stage at the intimate venue. Popular annual series include the New York Guitar Festival, WNYC's New Sounds Live (part of the Ecstatic Music Festival) and Broadway Close Up.

★ Smalls

183 W 10th Street, between Seventh Avenue South & W 4th Street, West Village (1-212 252 5091, www.smallsjazzclub.com). Subway 1 to Christopher Street-Sheridan Square. **Open** 4pm-4am daily. **Admission** free (1-drink min)-$20.
No credit cards. Map p403 D28.
Sometimes you want old-school jazz sans the shtick you've come to expect at a dinner-club gig. Luckily, this cosy basement venue is still kicking. Inside, it feels like one of those hole-in-the-wall NYC jazz haunts of yore over which fans routinely obsess. The line-up is solid, with a fun late-night jam session starting after midnight each evening (when admission drops to $10 at 12.30am). If you arrive before 7.30pm, admission is free with a one-drink minimum – there's a fully stocked bar. It's a great place to catch the best and brightest up-and-comers as well as the occasional moonlighting star.

Smoke

2751 Broadway, between 105th & 106th Streets, Upper West Side (1-212 864 6662, www.smoke jazz.com). Subway 1 to 103rd Street. **Shows** 7pm, 9pm, 10.30pm, 11pm Mon-Thur, Sun; 8pm, 10pm, 11.30pm, 12.45am Fri, Sat. **Admission** free ($20 food/drink min) Mon-Thur, Sun; $35 Fri, Sat.
Credit AmEx, Disc, MC, V. **Map** p406 C16.
Not unlike a swanky living room, Smoke is a classy little joint that acts as a haven for local jazz legends and touring artists looking to play an intimate space. Early in the week, evenings are themed: on Monday, catch a big band; Tuesday, organ jazz; and, on Wednesday, jazz-soul. On weekends, renowned jazzers hit the stage, relishing the opportunity to play informal gigs uptown.

★ The Stone

Avenue C, at 2nd Street, East Village (no phone, www.thestonenyc.com). Subway F to Lower East Side-Second Avenue. **Shows** 8pm, 10pm Tue-Sun. Admission $10. **No credit cards. Map** p403 G29.
Don't call sax star John Zorn's not-for-profit venture a 'club'. You'll find no food or drinks here, and no nonsense, either: the Stone is an art space dedicated to 'the experimental and the avant-garde'. If you're down for some rigorously adventurous sounds (intense improvisers like Tim Berne and Okkyung Lee, or moonlighting rock mavericks such as Thurston Moore), Zorn has made it easy: no advance sales, and all ages admitted (under-19s get discounts, under-12s free). The bookings are left to a different artist-curator each month.

★ Village Vanguard

178 Seventh Avenue South, at Perry Street, West Village (1-212 255 4037, www.village vanguard.com). Subway A, C, E, 1, 2, 3 to 14th Street; L to Eighth Avenue. **Shows** 9pm, 11pm daily. **Tickets** $25 (1-drink min). **Credit** MC, V. **Map** p403 D28.

Come Back to the Cabaret

The quintessentially New York style is being rejuvenated, says Adam Feldman.

Cabaret is dead! Long live cabaret! And while we're on the subject, please remind me: what exactly is cabaret, again? This last question has always been tricky. Cabaret is defined by where it takes place: in small rooms that permit a sense of intimate exchange. It is less a genre than, literally, an approach – a risky closeness to the material and the audience. In its early European years, cabaret was tied to what we now call burlesque; in New York, it reached its apex in the swinging nightclubs of the 1950s. Now, after a period of sleepy gentility, it is roaring back to its old life in multiple places and forms.

For every phoenix, however, there must be ashes, and 2012 was a crematorium. In January, the Oak Room announced that it was closing for good after 32 years; in July, another of the city's three ritziest cabaret venues, Feinstein's, revealed that it would shutter forever in December. But in some ways, the era of classic cabaret had already ended. The preservationist attitude that dominated the industry for decades had a taxidermic air – a whiff not just of formality but of formaldehyde. Tethered to the music of an increasingly distant past and supported by an ageing audience, cabaret lost the lifeblood that distinguished it as an art form in the first place.

Now that blood is starting to course again, and its most prominent artery is **54 Below** (*see p296*). Located in the Theater

District beneath the former Studio 54, this gorgeous new venue draws on New York nightclub history – but the style it evokes is that of the deluxe anything-goes speakeasy, not the ritzy jacket-and-tie supper club. 54 Below's sound, lighting and sight lines are first-rate, but what marks it as New York's prime destination for cabaret is the remarkable diversity of its programming. The venue has a distinct theatrical bent; it opened in June 2012 with a smashing set by überdiva Patti LuPone, and its schedule is anchored by major musical-theatre stars. But in addition to such marquee names, 54 Below also offers shows, at lower prices, by outstanding performers from the emerging alt-cabaret scene: Bridget Everett, Justin Vivian Bond, Cole Escola and others.

This is significant because it is in that downtown scene that the real revolution in cabaret, untelevised and largely untelevisable, has been taking place in a variety of venues, from jazz joints to gay bars. Alt-cabaret blurs the lines between music, comedy and performance art into a fabulous mess; it thrives on sex, danger, originality and impolite laughter, and feels thrillingly present tense. This is not merely because it often draws on modern material, but because it does so with a modern attitude. Cabaret, in other words, is not dying; it is evolving. The Great American Songbook shares a widening shelf in an art form that remains, at its core and at its best, a small world after all.

Going strong for more than three-quarters of a century, the Village Vanguard is one of New York's legendary jazz centres. History surrounds you: the likes of John Coltrane, Miles Davis and Bill Evans have all grooved in this hallowed basement haunt. Big names – both old and new – continue to fill the schedule here, and the Grammy Award-winning Vanguard Jazz Orchestra has been the Monday-night regular here for more than 45 years. Reservations are recommended.

CABARET

In an age of globalism, cabaret is a fundamentally local art: a private party in a cosy club, where music gets stripped down to its bare essence. The intense intimacy of the experience can make it transformative if you're lucky, or mortifying if you're not. Expect consistently high-grade entertainment at Manhattan's fanciest venues, the **Café Carlyle** and the more theatre-oriented **54 Below**. Local clubs such as **Don't Tell Mama** and the **Duplex** are cheaper and more casual, but the talent is sometimes entry-level. The **Metropolitan Room** and the **Laurie Beechman Theatre** fall between these two poles.

★ 54 Below

254 W 54th Street, between Broadway & Eighth Avenue, Theater District (1-646 476 3551, Ticketweb 1-866 468 7619, www.54below.com). Subway B, D, E to Seventh Avenue; C, E, 1 to 50th Street; R to 57th Street. **Shows** vary; 1-2 shows per night. **Admission** $15-$95 ($25 food/drink min). **Credit** AmEx, Disc, MC, V. **Map** p405 D22.

A team of Broadway producers is behind the city's premier cabaret destination: a swank new speakeasy-style supper club located in the bowels of the legendary Studio 54 space. The schedule is dominated by big Broadway talent – such as Patti LuPone, Ben Vereen and Sherie Rene Scott – but there is also room for edgier talents such as Justin Vivian Bond and Jackie Hoffman. *See also p295* **Come Back to the Cabaret**.

Café Carlyle

Carlyle, 35 E 76th Street, at Madison Avenue, Upper East Side (1-212 744 1600, 1-800 227 5737 reservations, www.thecarlyle.com). Subway 6 to 77th Street. **Shows** vary. **Admission** $65-$185 (dinner required). **Credit** AmEx, DC, Disc, MC, V. **Map** p405 E20.

With its airy murals by Marcel Vertes, this elegant boîte in the Carlyle hotel remains the epitome of New York class, attracting such top-level singers as folk legend Judy Collins and soul queen Bettye LaVette. Woody Allen often plays clarinet with Eddie Davis and his New Orleans Jazz Band on Monday nights.

▶ *Bemelmans Bar, across the hall, has an excellent pianist for those who want to drink in the atmosphere at a lower price; see p186.*

Don't Tell Mama

343 W 46th Street, between Eighth & Ninth Avenues, Theater District (1-212 757 0788, www.donttellmamanyc.com). Subway A, C, E to 42nd Street-Port Authority. **Open** *Piano bar* 9pm-2.30am Mon-Thur, Sun; 9pm-3.30am Fri, Sat. **Shows** vary; 2-4 shows per night. **Admission** $10-$25 (2-drink min). *Piano bar* free (2-drink min). **No credit cards. Map** p404 C23.

Showbiz pros and piano-bar buffs adore this dank but homey Theater District stalwart, where acts range from the strictly amateur to potential stars of tomorrow. The line-up may include pop, jazz and musical-theatre singers, as well as comedians and drag artists (including veteran Judy Garland impersonator Tommy Femia).

The Duplex

61 Christopher Street, at Seventh Avenue South, West Village (1-212 255 5438, www.theduplex.com). Subway 1 to Christopher Street-Sheridan Square. **Open** *Piano bar* 9pm-4am daily. **Shows** vary; 1-2 shows per night. **Admission** free-$20 (2-drink min). **Credit** AmEx, DC, MC, V. **Map** p403 D28.

This cosy, brick-lined room, located in the heart of the West Village, is a good-natured testing ground for new talent. The eclectic offerings often come served with a generous dollop of good, old-fashioned camp. The downstairs piano bar provides an open microphone for patrons until the wee hours of the morning.

Laurie Beechman Theatre

407 W 42nd Street, at Ninth Avenue, Theater District (1-212 695 6909, www.westbank cafe.com). Subway A, C, E to 42nd Street-Port Authority. **Shows** vary; 1-2 shows per night. **Admission** free-$40 ($15 food/drink min). **Credit** AmEx, MC, V. **Map** p404 C24.

Tucked away beneath the West Bank Café on 42nd Street, the Beechman provides a stage for singers from the worlds of musical theatre and cabaret, including some of the city's most popular drag entertainers. It also hosts occasional comedy shows.

★ Metropolitan Room

34 W 22nd Street, between Fifth & Sixth Avenues, Flatiron District (1-212 206 0440, www.metropolitanroom.com). Subway F, M, N, R to 23rd Street. **Shows** vary; 1-2 shows per night. **Admission** $15-$35 (2-drink min). **Credit** AmEx, MC, V. **Map** p404 E26.

The Met Room often features high-level nightclub singing that won't bust your wallet. Regular performers range from rising musical-theatre stars to established cabaret acts (including Baby Jane Dexter and English songstress Barb Jungr), plus legends such as Tammy Grimes and Annie Ross.

Performing Arts

From poetry slams to Broadway blockbusters, the shows just go on.

As the centre of publishing in the US, New York offers a full programme of author readings and literary events – some of which combine words and music. In fact, mixing art forms is becoming increasingly common practice on the cultural scene.

The city is continuing to enjoy a classical music renaissance, with visionary impresarios and enthusiastic young performers casting aside the genre's fusty, curmudgeonly reputation in favour of unbridled creativity. Small genre-crossing venues such as the recently opened Spectrum on the Lower East Side are laboratories for exciting new sounds.

Dance is also stepping beyond traditional boundaries; in addition to the classic stages at Lincoln Center and numerous small dance venues downtown and in the outer boroughs, art institutions, including the Museum of Modern Art and the Whitney Museum of American Art, are proving that movement-based performance is a vital part of the creative landscape by staging on-site performances.

For many, visiting New York without seeing a Broadway show would be like going to Las Vegas without hitting a casino, but Gotham is also becoming a great place to catch excellent, inexpensive productions. An Off-Broadway boom has resulted in several lower-priced offshoots of established theatres, including Lincoln Center's newly built Claire Tow Theater and Brooklyn Academy of Music's Richard B Fisher Building, a seven-storey performing-arts centre, which provides a space not only for theatre, but also dance, music and performance art.

Check out the weekly *Time Out New York* magazine or www.timeout.com/newyork for current cultural listings.

Books & Poetry

Almost every touring literary luminary stops in New York City to read. Venues include theatres, bookshops, libraries and even bars. **Barnes & Noble**'s Union Square flagship (33 E 17th Street, between Broadway & Park Avenue South, 1-212 253 0810, www.barnesandnoble.com) offers the vibrant and well-curated series, Upstairs at the Square, which pairs authors with musical performers. Music venue **Cake Shop** (*see p286*) hosts Mixer, which also showcases writers – often with a pop-cultural bent – and musical guests. Amanda Stern's long-running, convivial **Happy Ending Series** (www.amandastern.com), which requires participants to take some sort of risk on-stage, returns in September 2013. For independent bookshops that regularly host events, such as **Housing Works Bookstore Café**, **McNally Jackson Bookstore** and **192 Books**, *see pp195-196*.

LITERARY VENUES

KGB Bar

2nd Floor, 85 E 4th Street, between Second & Third Avenues, East Village (1-212 505 3360, www.kgbbar.com). Subway F to Lower East Side-Second Avenue; 6 to Astor Place. **Admission** free. **Map** p403 F29.

This dimly lit East Village hangout with an old-school communist theme runs several top-notch weekly series featuring NYC writers, poets, fantasy authors, travel writers and others.

The New School

66 W 12th Street, between Fifth & Sixth Avenues, Greenwich Village (1-212 229 5353, 1-212 229 5488 tickets, www.newschool.edu). Subway F, M to 14th Street; L to Sixth Avenue. **Admission** free-$15. **Credit** AmEx, Disc, MC, V. **Map** p403 E28.

A great place to hear award-winning authors; contributors to the *Best American Poetry* anthology and National Book Award finalists read here annually.

New York Public Library

Stephen A Schwarzman Building, Celeste Bartos Forum, 42nd Street, at Fifth Avenue, Midtown (1-212 930 0855, www.nypl.org/events). Subway B, D, F, M to 42nd Street-Bryant Park; 7 to Fifth Avenue. **Admission** $25; $15 reductions. **Credit** (online purchases only) AmEx, Disc, MC, V. **Map** p404 E24.

The 'Live from the NYPL' series is ambitious and well curated, a magnet for the smart set. All the programming is superb, but the stand-out events are the Robert Silvers lectures, in which thinkers – Mary Beard or Darryl Pinckney, for example – tackle complex intellectual issues.

► *For tours of the library itself, see p88.*

92nd Street Y

1395 Lexington Avenue, at 92nd Street, Upper East Side (1-212 415 5500, www.92y.org). Subway 6 to 96th Street. **Admission** $10-$50. **Credit** AmEx, MC, V. **Map** p406 F17.

Big-name novelists, essayists, journalists and poets preside over some grand intellectual feasts here, with talks by critic James Wood, as well as a worthwhile reading series featuring the likes of Ian McEwan, Salman Rushdie, Toni Morrison and Jonathan Franzen. The 'Books and Bagels' events are also popular, allowing participants to munch on breakfast goods while authors such as Joyce Carol Oates chat about their work.

► *For the Y's classical music offerings, see p304.*

★ NYU's Lillian Vernon Creative Writers House

58 W 10th Street, between Fifth & Sixth Avenues, Greenwich Village (1-212 998 8816, http://cwp.fas.nyu.edu/page/readingseries). Subway A, B, C, D, E, F, M to W 4th Street. **Admission** free. **Map** p403 E28.

A major destination for literary authors with devout followings, this space – part of NYU – has recently showcased Jonathan Safran Foer, Zadie Smith, Rick Moody and Jennifer Egan.

Powerhouse Arena

37 Main Street, between Front & Water Streets, Dumbo, Brooklyn (1-718 666 3049, www. powerhousearena.com). Subway A, C to High Street; F to York Street. **Admission** varies. **Map** p411 S9.

Powerhouse publishes excellent photo books on everything from graffiti art to Darfur. Its cavernous, industrial-style space serves as a gallery and hosts some great literary events – readings by TC Boyle, Daniel Menaker and Paul Auster, to name a few. Check the website for happenings and pricing.

POETRY VENUES & SPOKEN WORD EVENTS

Most events begin with a featured poet or two, then move on to an open mic. To take part, show up early and ask for the sign-up sheet.

Moth StorySLAM

Various venues (1-212 742 0551, www.themoth. org). **Admission** $8. **No credit cards.**

Known for its big-name monthly storytelling shows, the Moth also sponsors four open slams in various venues every month. Ten raconteurs get five minutes each to tell a story (no notes are allowed) to a panel of judges randomly selected from the audience.

Nuyorican Poets Café

236 E 3rd Street, between Avenues B & C, East Village (1-212 505 8183, www.nuyorican.org). Subway F to Lower East Side-Second Avenue. **Admission** $7-$20. **Credit** AmEx, DC, Disc, MC, V. **Map** p403 G29.

This arts centre is known for its raucous slams, jam sessions and anything-goes open mics.

Poets House

10 River Terrace, between Murray Street & Park Place West, Financial District (1-212 431 7920, www.poetshouse.org). Subway 1, 2, 3 to Chambers Street. **Open** 11am-7pm Tue-Fri; 11am-6pm Sat. **Admission** *Library* free. *Events* $10-$15; $7-$13.50 reductions. **Credit** AmEx, Disc, MC, V. **Map** p402 D32.

Founded in 1985 by poet Stanley Kunitz and arts administrator Elizabeth Kray, Poets House has long been a gathering place for anyone who writes or reads verse. In 2009, it moved from its Soho location to a new 'green' space near the Hudson River in Battery Park City, where it continues to offer classes, workshops and author events. You might hear a discussion with such award-winning writers as Rae Armantrout, Yusef Komunyakaa and John D'Agata; the library, open to all and free of charge, houses more than 50,000 volumes that you can peruse at your leisure.

Poetry Project

St Mark's Church in-the-Bowery, 131 E 10th Street, at Second Avenue, East Village (1-212 674 0910, www.poetryproject.org). Subway L to First Avenue; 6 to Astor Place. **Admission** $8; $7 reductions. **No credit cards. Map** p403 F28.

The Project, housed in a lovely old church in the East Village, has hosted an amazing roster of poets since its inception in 1966.

Classical Music & Opera

At the big institutions such as the New York and Brooklyn Philharmonics, the Metropolitan and New York City Operas and Carnegie Hall, confident artistic leaders such as Alan Gilbert, Alan Pierson, Peter Gelb, George Steel and Clive Gillinson are embracing new productions, living composers and innovative approaches to programming.

Meanwhile, some of the most exciting work is happening outside of Lincoln Center and Carnegie Hall. New-music groups like the International Contemporary Ensemble, Alarm Will Sound, Brooklyn Rider and So Percussion have grown from promising upstarts to become influential pillars of the artistic community. Genre-blind venues, including **Le Poisson Rouge** (*see p289*), the **Stone** (*see p294*) and **Spectrum** (*see p304*), are happy to give them space to do their thing. These days it's not rare for a Baroque opera to be followed by a DJ set or for an orchestra to interpret music by Mos Def or Sufjan Stevens. This is the postmodern aesthetic in full bloom and there's no better place to experience it right now than New York.

The standard New York concert season lasts from September to June, but there are plenty of summer events and performances (*see p202* **Everything Under the Sun**). Box office hours may change in summer, so phone ahead or check websites for times.

Information & tickets

You can buy tickets directly from most venues, whether by phone, online or at the box office. However, a surcharge is generally added to tickets not bought in person. For more on tickets, *see p221*.

MAJOR CONCERT HALLS

★ Brooklyn Academy of Music
Peter Jay Sharp Building *30 Lafayette Avenue, between Ashland Place & St Felix Street, Fort Greene, Brooklyn. Subway B, Q, 2, 3, 4, 5 to Atlantic Avenue; C to Lafayette Avenue; D, N, R to Pacific Street; G to Fulton Street.*
BAM Harvey Theater *651 Fulton Street at Rockwell Place, Fort Greene, Brooklyn. Subway B, Q, R to DeKalb Avenue; C to Lafayette Avenue; G to Fulton Street; 2, 3, 4, 5 to Nevins Street.*
BAM Richard B Fisher Building
321 Ashland Place between Ashland Place & Lafayette Avenue, Fort Greene, Brooklyn.

ARTS & ENTERTAINMENT

John Irving at **92nd Street Y**.

Carnegie Hall.

Subway B, Q, 2, 3, 4, 5 to Atlantic Avenue; C to Lafayette Avenue; D, N, R to Pacific Street; G to Fulton Street.
All *1-718 636 4100, www.bam.org.* **Box office** noon-6pm Mon-Sat. *Phone bookings* 10am-6pm Mon-Fri; noon-6pm Sat; noon-4pm Sun (show days). **Tickets** $20-$225. **Credit** AmEx, MC, V. **Map** p410 T10.
America's oldest performing-arts academy continues to present some of the freshest programming in the city. Every year in autumn and winter, the Next Wave Festival provides avant-garde music, dance and theatre. The nearby BAM Harvey Theater offers a smaller and more atmospheric setting for multimedia creations by composers and performers such as Tan Dun, So Percussion and Meredith Monk, as well as innovative stagings of Baroque opera. And the newest facility, BAM Fisher, houses an intimate performance space and studios.

★ Carnegie Hall

154 W 57th Street, at Seventh Avenue, Midtown (1-212 247 7800, www.carnegiehall.org). Subway N, Q, R to 57th Street. **Box office** 11am-6pm Mon-Sat; noon-6pm Sun. *Phone bookings* 8am-8pm daily. **Tickets** $15-$220. **Credit** AmEx, DC, Disc, MC, V. **Map** p405 D22.
Artistic director Clive Gillinson continues to put his stamp on Carnegie Hall. The stars – both soloists and orchestras – still shine brightly inside this renowned concert hall in the Isaac Stern Auditorium. But it's the spunky upstart Zankel Hall that has generated the most buzz, offering an eclectic mix of classical, contemporary, jazz, pop and world music. Next door, the Weill Recital Hall hosts intimate concerts and chamber music programmes. Look out for Ensemble ACJW, which comprises some of the city's most exciting young musicians and also performs at the Juilliard School of music, and, in May 2013, Spring for Music, which features eclectic programmes from North America's most innovative regional orchestras.

Lincoln Center

Columbus Avenue, between 62nd & 65th Streets, Upper West Side (1-212 546 2656, www.lincolncenter.org). Subway 1 to 66th Street-Lincoln Center. **Map** p405 C21.
Built in the early 1960s, this massive complex is the nexus of Manhattan's – in fact, probably the whole country's – performing arts scene. The campus has undergone a major revamp, providing new performance facilities as well as more inviting public gathering spaces and restaurants. Lincoln Center hosts lectures and symposia in the **Rose Building**, Sunday recitals and Rob Kapilow's 'What Makes it Great?' series at the **Walter Reade Theater** and events in its main concert halls (*see p303*), and its **Vivian Beaumont Theater** and

Mitzi E Newhouse Theater (for both, *see p322*). Also here are the **Juilliard School** (*see p306*) and the **Fiorello H La Guardia High School of Music & Art and Performing Arts** (100 Amsterdam Avenue, between 64th & 65th Streets, www.laguardiahs.org), which frequently hosts performances by professional ensembles as well as students who may go on to be the stars of tomorrow.
Big stars such as Valery Gergiev, Sir Colin Davis and Emanuel Ax are Lincoln Center's meat and potatoes. Lately, though, the divide between the flagship Great Performers season and the more audacious, multidisciplinary **Lincoln Center Out of Doors festival** (*see p33*) continues to narrow. The **Mostly Mozart Festival** (late July-Aug), a formerly moribund four-week summer staple, has been thoroughly reinvented as a showcase of up-and-coming conductors and innovative performers such as the world-class International Contemporary Ensemble, which began a three-year stint as the festival's ensemble-in-residence in 2011. In autumn, the recently inaugurated White Light Festival blends high-quality classical performers with world and popular musicians, all of whom angle to tap into the spiritually transcendent qualities of music.
The main entry point for Lincoln Center is from Columbus Avenue, at 65th Street, but the venues that follow are spread out across the square of blocks from 62nd to 66th Streets, between Amsterdam and Columbus Avenues. Tickets to most performances at Lincoln Center are sold through **Centercharge** (1-212 721 6500, 10am-9pm daily). There is now a central box office selling discounted tickets to same-day performances at the **David Rubenstein Atrium** (between W 62nd & W 63rd Streets, Broadway & Columbus Avenues).

INSIDE TRACK
LUNCH WITH THE ORCHESTRA

A variety of cheap or free lunchtime concerts is held around New York by some of the city's brightest up-and-comers. The free early music series **Midtown Concerts** presides over Midtown East's Saint Peter's Church (619 Lexington Avenue, at 54th Street, www.midtownconcerts.org) every Thursday at 1.15pm. Downtown, stately sanctuary Trinity Church (*see p54*) offers free Thursday afternoon recitals in its **Concerts at One** series, though it takes a break in summer; its satellite St Paul's Chapel also hosts weekly music.

ARTS & ENTERTAINMENT

Everything Under the Sun

When summer arrives, New York's music scene goes outside.

The main fixture on the summer calendar is **SummerStage** (*see p31*), a New York institution that has an ear for every sound under the sun, and also includes theatre, dance and spoken-word performances. Although the mainstage is in Central Park, the series brings great world music to parks throughout the five boroughs. Many of the shows are free, with a handful of rock-centred benefits (TV on the Radio, the reunited Pavement) covering for them.

If your tastes are more classical, the **Metropolitan Opera** (www.metopera family.org) and the **New York Philharmonic** (www.nyphil.org) both stage free concerts in Central Park and other large green spaces during the summer months.

Not far from Central Park is **Lincoln Center** (*see p301*), where the multi-tiered floorplan allows for several outdoor stages to be set up. The most popular venues are the North Plaza, which rolls out the red carpet for the likes of Sonny Rollins, and the Damrosch Park Bandshell, which houses the **Midsummer Night Swing** concerts (*see p32*).

There's also a great deal of action downtown. During the **River to River**

River To River Festival.

Festival (1-212 219 9401, www.rivertoriver nyc.com; *see also p32*), indie bands take to the stage at the South Street Seaport (last year's Veronica Falls and the Philip Glass Ensemble, for example), while the historic fort of Castle Clinton in Battery Park welcomes roots artists where the US Army once set up shop. (Tickets must be picked up in person on the day of a show, and they always go fast.)

New York Philharmonic.

Alice Tully Hall

1-212 875 5050. **Box office** 10am-6pm Mon-Sat; noon-6pm Sun. **Tickets** vary. **Credit** AmEx, DC, Disc, MC, V.

An 18-month renovation turned the cosy home of the Chamber Music Society of Lincoln Center (www.chambermusicsociety.org) into a world-class, 1,096-seat theatre. A new contemporary foyer with an elegant (if a bit pricey) café is immediately striking, but, more importantly, the revamp also brought dramatic acoustical improvements.

Avery Fisher Hall

1-212 875 5030. **Box office** 10am-6pm Mon-Sat; noon-6pm Sun. **Tickets** vary. **Credit** AmEx, DC, Disc, MC, V.

This handsome, comfortable, 2,700-seat hall is the headquarters of the New York Philharmonic (1-212 875 5656, www.nyphil.org), the country's oldest symphony orchestra (founded in 1842) – and one of its finest. Depending on who you ask, the sound ranges from good to atrocious (an overhaul is planned for 2017). Inexpensive, early evening 'rush hour' concerts and open rehearsals are presented on a regular basis. The ongoing Great Performers series features top international soloists and ensembles.

Metropolitan Opera House

1-212 362 6000, www.metoperafamily.org. **Box office** 10am-8pm Mon-Sat; noon-6pm Sun. **Tickets** $25-$400. **Credit** AmEx, DC, Disc, MC, V.

The grandest of the - Center buildings, the Met is a spectacular place to see and hear opera. It hosts the Metropolitan Opera from September to May, with major visiting companies appearing in summer. Audiences are knowledgeable and fiercely devoted, with subscriptions remaining in families for generations. Opera's biggest stars appear here regularly, and artistic director James Levine has turned the orchestra into a true symphonic force.

The Met had already started becoming more inclusive before current impresario Peter Gelb took the reins in 2006. Now, the company is placing a priority on creating novel theatrical experiences with visionary directors (Robert Lepage, Bartlett Sher, Michael Grandage, David McVicar) and assembling a new company of physically graceful, telegenic stars (Anna Netrebko, Danielle de Niese, Jonas Kaufmann, Erwin Schrott). Its high-definition movie-theatre broadcasts continue to reign supreme outside the opera house. Although most tickets are expensive, 200 prime seats (50 of which are reserved for over-65s) for all are sold for a mere $20 apiece on weekdays and $25 on weekends, two hours before the curtain. *Photo p305.*

OTHER VENUES

★ Bargemusic

Fulton Ferry Landing, between Old Fulton & Water Streets, Dumbo, Brooklyn (1-718 624 2083, www.bargemusic.org). Subway A, C to High Street; F to York Street; 2, 3 to Clark Street. **Tickets** $35-$45; $15-$40 reductions. **No credit cards. Map** p411 S9.

This former coffee bean barge usually presents four chamber concerts a week set against a panoramic view of lower Manhattan. It's a magical experience (and the programming has recently grown more ambitious), but be sure to dress warmly in the winter. In less chilly months, enjoy a drink on the upper deck during the interval.

Frick Collection

For listings, *see p98.* **Tickets** $35.

Concerts in the Frick Collection's elegantly appointed concert hall are a rare treat, generally featuring both promising debutants and lesser-known but world-class performers. Concerts are broadcast live in the Garden Court, where tickets aren't required.

Gilder Lehrman Hall

Morgan Library & Museum, 225 Madison Avenue, at 36th Street, Murray Hill (1-212 685 0008, www.themorgan.org). Subway 6 to 33rd Street. **Tickets** vary. **Credit** AmEx, MC, V. **Map** p404 E25.

This elegant, 280-seat gem of a concert hall is a perfect venue for song recitals and chamber groups. The St Luke's Chamber Ensemble and Glimmerglass Opera were quick to establish a presence here.

Merkin Concert Hall

Kaufman Center, 129 W 67th Street, between Amsterdam Avenue & Broadway, Upper West Side (1-212 501 3330, www.kaufman-center.org). Subway 1 to 66th Street-Lincoln Center. **Box office** noon-7pm Mon-Thur, Sun; noon-4pm (until 3pm Nov-Jan) Fri. **Tickets** $15-$60. **Credit** AmEx, Disc, MC, V. **Map** p405 C21.

On a side street in the shadow of Lincoln Center, this renovated 449-seat gem offers a robust mix of early music and avant-garde programming, plus a healthy amount of jazz, folk and some more eclectic fare. The Ecstatic Music Festival, featuring the latest generation of composers and performers, heats up the space each January, and the New York Festival of Song regularly presents outstanding singers in appealingly quirky thematic programmes.

Metropolitan Museum of Art

For listings, *see p99.* **Tickets** $15-$65.

When it comes to established virtuosos and revered chamber ensembles, the Met's year-round programming is rich and full (and ticket prices can be correspondingly high). Under the leadership of Limor Tomer, the museum's programming has recently taken a sharp turn towards genre-flouting performers and intriguing artistic juxtapositions. Lately, performances by Chanticleer and the Wordless Music Orchestra have transformed the museum's famous Temple of Dendur into an atmospheric spot to hear some mystical music.

▶ *At Christmas and Easter, early music concerts are held in the Fuentidueña Chapel at the Cloisters; see p112.*

★ Miller Theatre at Columbia University

2960 Broadway, at 116th Street, Morningside Heights (1-212 854 7799, www.millertheatre.com). Subway 1 to 116th Street-Columbia University. **Box office** noon-6pm Mon-Fri (also 2hrs before performance on show days). **Tickets** $25-$40. **Credit** AmEx, MC, V. **Map** p407 C14.

Columbia University's Miller Theatre is at the forefront of making contemporary classical music sexy in New York City. The credit belongs to former executive director George Steel, who has proved that presenting challenging fare in a casual, unaffected setting could attract young audiences – and hang on to them. With Steel now at City Opera, director Melissa Smey seems to be continuing the tradition with programmes ranging from early music to contemporary, highlighted by musical upstarts such as Ensemble Signal and violinist Jennifer Koh.

92nd Street Y

1395 Lexington Avenue, at 92nd Street, Upper East Side (1-212 415 5500, www. 92y.org). Subway 6 to 96th Street. **Box office** noon-8pm Mon-Thur, Sun; noon-5pm Fri. **Tickets** $25-$62. **Credit** AmEx, DC, MC, V. **Map** p406 F17.

The Y has always stood for solidly traditional orchestral, solo and chamber masterpieces. But the organisation also fosters the careers of young musicians and explores European and Jewish-American music traditions, with innovative results. In addition to showcasing several master classes (such as guitarist Eliot Fisk), the Y has recently lent its stage to the Takács Quartet and pianist Paul Lewis. And in an effort to make its concerts more affordable, $25 tickets to premium programmes are available to everyone age 35 and younger.

INSIDE TRACK
BACKSTAGE PASSES

It's possible to go behind the scenes at several of the city's major concert venues. **Backstage at the Met** (1-212 769 7028, $20, $10 reductions) shows you around the famous opera house from October to mid May. A tour of **Carnegie Hall** (1-212 903 9765, $10, $4-$8 reductions, Oct-May) ushers you through what is perhaps the world's most famous concert hall. For $18, you may also watch an open rehearsal of the **New York Philharmonic** (1-212 875 5656, Sept-June,

---

Roulette Brooklyn

509 Atlantic Avenue, at Third Avenue, Boerum Hill, Brooklyn (1-917 267 0363, www.roulette.org). Subway B, Q, 2, 3, 4, 5 to Atlantic Avenue; D, N, R to Pacific Street. **Box office** 1-4pm Mon-Fri (also during performances). **Tickets** vary. **Credit** MC, V. **Map** p410 T10.

This legendary experimental music institution recently packed its bags and moved from its dingy Soho digs to a spectacularly redesigned art deco theatre in Brooklyn. The setting may have changed, but Roulette continues to offer a gold mine of far-out programming that could include anything from a John Cage Musicircus, where the audience is invited to wander through a forest of musical acts all playing at once, to a four-day festival of genre-defying fare from Anthony Braxton.

Spectrum

2nd Floor, 121 Ludlow Street, between Delancey & Rivington Streets, Lower East Side (no phone, www.spectrumnyc.com). Subway F to Lower East Side-Second Ave or Delancey Street; J, Z to Delancey-Essex Streets. **Tickets** vary. **No credit cards. Map** p403 G30.

New York's newest contemporary-classical laboratory harkens back to the days when the city's most innovative work was done in private lofts and similar spaces. Housed in a cosy Lower East Side walk-up, this busy venue largely relies on word of mouth and social media to publicise its ambitious chamber music, progressive jazz and avant-garde rock events.

Symphony Space

2537 Broadway, between 94th & 95th Streets, Upper West Side (1-212 864 5400, www. symphonyspace.org). Subway 1, 2, 3 to 96th Street. **Box office** Mon (times vary, show days only); 1-6pm Tue-Sun. **Tickets** vary. **Credit** AmEx, MC, V. **Map** p406 C17.

Despite the name, programming at Symphony Space is anything but orchestra-centric: recent seasons have featured sax quartets, Indian classical music, a cappella ensembles and HD opera simulcasts from Europe. The annual Wall to Wall marathons (usually held in spring) provide a full day of music free of charge, all focused on a particular composer.

Churches

From sacred to secular, a thrilling variety of music is performed in New York's churches. Superb acoustics, out-of-this-world choirs and serene surroundings make these houses of worship particularly attractive venues. A bonus is that some concerts are free or very cheap.

Church of the Ascension

12 W 11th Street, between Fifth & Sixth Avenues, Greenwich Village (1-212 358 1469, tickets 1-212 358 7060, www.voicesofascension.org). Subway N,

ARTS & ENTERTAINMENT

Metropolitan Opera House. See p303.

ARTS & ENTERTAINMENT

R to 8th Street-NYU. **Tickets** $10-$65. **Credit** (advance purchases only) MC, V. **Map** p403 E28.
There's a first-rate professional choir, the Voices of Ascension, at this little Village church. You can catch the choir at Lincoln Center on occasion, but home turf is the best place to hear it.

Church of St Ignatius Loyola

980 Park Avenue, between 83rd & 84th Streets, Upper East Side (1-212 288 2520, www.smssconcerts.org). Subway, 4, 5, 6 to 86th Street. **Tickets** $5-$60. **Credit** AmEx, Disc, MC, V. **Map** p406 E18.
The 'Sacred Music in a Sacred Space' series is a high point of Upper East Side music culture. Lincoln Center also holds concerts here, capitalising on the church's fine acoustics and prime location.

Corpus Christi Church

529 W 121st Street, between Amsterdam Avenue & Broadway, Morningside Heights (1-212 666 9266, www.mb1800.org). Subway 1 to 116th Street-Columbia Unversity. **Tickets** $10-$45. **Credit** AmEx, MC, V. **Map** p407 C14.
Fans of early music can get their fix from 'Music Before 1800', a series that regularly imports the world's leading antiquarian artists and ensembles.

Holy Trinity Lutheran Church

3 W 65th Street, at Central Park West, Upper West Side (1-212 877 6815, www.bachvespersnyc.org).

Subway 1 to 66th Street-Lincoln Center. **Tickets** vary. **Credit** AmEx, Disc, MC, V. **Map** p405 D21.
The choir, organist and period-instrument chamber orchestra of this church, located in the shadow of Lincoln Center, perform free concerts of Baroque music every Sunday from October through Easter as part of the venerable Bach Vespers series.

St Bartholomew's Church

325 Park Avenue, at 51st Street, Midtown East (1-212 378 0248, www.stbarts.org). Subway E, M to Lexington Avenue-53rd Street; 6 to 51st Street. **Tickets** $15-$40. **Credit** AmEx, MC, V. **Map** p404 E23.
This magnificent church hosts the Summer Festival of Sacred Music, one of the city's most ambitious choral music series. It fills the rest of the year with performances by resident ensembles and guests.

St Thomas Church Fifth Avenue

1 W 53rd Street, at Fifth Avenue, Midtown East (1-212 757 7013, www.saintthomas church.org). Subway E, M to Fifth Avenue-53rd Street. **Tickets** free-$95. **Credit** (online purchases only) AmEx, Disc, MC, V. **Map** p405 E22.
The country's only fully accredited choir school for boys keeps the great Anglican choral tradition alive in Gotham. St Thomas's annual performance of Handel's *Messiah* is a must-hear that's worth the rather steep ticket price.

Trinity Wall Street

89 Broadway, at Wall Street, Financial District (1-212 602 0800, www.trinitywallstreet.org). Subway R, 1 to Rector Street; 4, 5 to Wall Street. **Tickets** vary. (online purchases only) **Credit** AmEx, Disc, MC, V. **Map** p405 E22.

This historic Financial District church has an ambitious music series and is home to one of the city's finest choirs, which regularly performs here and sometimes visits Carnegie Hall and Lincoln Center. Several times a week, Trinity hosts free lunchtime concerts in both the church and the nearby St Paul's Chapel (209 Broadway, between Fulton and Vesey Streets).

Schools

The **Juilliard School** and the **Manhattan School of Music** are renowned for their talented students, faculty and artists-in-residence, all of whom regularly perform for free or at low cost. Lately, **Mannes College of Music** has made great strides.

Juilliard School

60 Lincoln Center Plaza, Broadway, at 65th Street, Upper West Side (1-212 769 7406, www.juilliard.edu). Subway 1 to 66th Street-Lincoln Center. **Box office** 11am-6pm Mon-Fri. **Tickets** free-$30. **Credit** AmEx, Disc, MC, V. **Map** p405 C21.

New York City's premier conservatory stages weekly concerts by student soloists, orchestras and chamber ensembles, as well as elaborate opera performances that can rival many professional productions. It's likely the singers you see here will be making their Met or City Opera debuts within the next few years.

Manhattan School of Music

120 Claremont Avenue, at 122nd Street, Morningside Heights (1-917 493 4428, www.msmnyc.edu). Subway 1 to 125th Street. **Box office** 10am-5pm Mon-Fri. **Tickets** free-$20. **Credit** AmEx, Disc, MC, V. **Map** p407 B14.

The Manhattan School offers master classes, recitals and off-site concerts by its students and faculty as well as visiting professionals. The American String Quartet has been in residence here since 1984 and gives concerts regularly, while the Augustine Guitar Series includes recitals by top soloists. Recently, MSM has also become known for performing opera rarities, such as John Corigliano's *The Ghosts of Versailles* and Schubert's *Die Verschworenen*.

Mannes College of Music

150 W 85th Street, between Columbus & Amsterdam Avenues, Upper West Side (1-212 580 0210 ext 4817, www.mannes.edu). Subway B, C, 1 to 86th Street. **Tickets** usually free. **Map** p406 C18.

In addition to student concerts and faculty recitals, Mannes also mounts its own ambitious, historically themed concert series; the summer is given over to festivals and workshops for instrumentalists. Productions by the Mannes Opera, whose fresh-faced members are drilled by seasoned opera professionals, are a perennial treat.

Opera companies

The **Metropolitan Opera** (*see p303*) and the **New York City Opera** (*see p307*) may be the leaders of the pack, but they're hardly the only game in town. Call the organisations or check online for information and prices, schedules and venues.

American Opera Projects

South Oxford Space, 138 S Oxford Street, between Atlantic Avenue & Hanson Place, Fort Greene, Brooklyn (1-718 398 4024, www.operaprojects.org). Subway B, Q, 2, 3, 4, 5 to Atlantic Avenue; C to Lafayette Avenue; D, N, R to Pacific Street; G to Fulton Street. **Tickets** vary (average $20). **Credit** AmEx, Disc, MC, V. **Map** p410 T10.

AOP is not so much an opera company as a living, breathing workshop that lets you follow a new work from gestation to completion. Shows, which can be anything from a table reading of a libretto to a complete orchestral production, are staged around the city and beyond.

Amore Opera Company

Connelly Theatre, 220 E 4th Street, between Avenues A & B, Lower East Side (OvationTix 1-866 811 4111, www.amoreopera.org). Subway F to Lower East Side-Second Avenue. **Tickets** $15-$40. **Credit** AmEx, Disc, MC, V. **Map** p403 G29.

One of two successors to the late, great Amato Opera Company, the Amore has literally inherited the beloved former company's sets and costumes. Many of the cast members have migrated as well to keep the feisty Amato spirit alive. In 2011 they presented the US première of Mercadante's forgotten 1835 opera *I due Figaro* in combination with two more famous Figaro incarnations – Mozart's *The Marriage of Figaro* and Rossini's *The Barber of Seville* – and in 2012 produced another première, Donizetti's *Olivo e Pasquale*.

Dicapo Opera Theatre

184 E 76th Street, between Lexington & Third Avenues, Upper East Side (1-212 288 9438, SmartTix 1-212 868 4444, www.dicapo.com). Subway 6 to 77th Street. **Box office** 11am-4pm Mon-Fri. **Tickets** $50. **Credit** AmEx, MC, V. **Map** p405 F20.

This top-notch chamber opera troupe benefits from the participation of City Opera-quality singers performing in a delightfully intimate setting in the basement of St Jean Baptiste Church. Dicapo has recently augmented its diet of standard classics with a healthy dose of offbeat works and even premières, thanks in part to composer Tobias Picker's arrival as artistic adviser.

★ Gotham Chamber Opera

1-212 868 4460, Ticket Central 1-212 279 4200, www.gothamchamberopera.org. **Tickets** $30-$175. **Credit** AmEx, MC, V. **Map** p403 G30.
Though they perform in a variety of venues in the city – such as the Hayden Planetarium for a highly imaginative production of Haydn's *Il Mondo della Luna* – this fine young company often appears at John Jay College's Gerald W Lynch Theater on the Upper West Side. Expect a treasure trove of rarely staged shows (directed by the likes of Mark Morris and Tony-winner Diane Paulus) and new fare, such as, from June 2013, *Rappaccini's Daughter* by Daniel Catán, a modern opera on power and corruption with a libretto by Nobel Prize winner Octavio Paz.

New York City Opera

20 Lincoln Center, Upper West Side (1-212 870 5600, www.nycopera.com). Subway 1 to 66th Street-Lincoln Center. **Tickets** $25-$250. **Credit** AmEx, MC, V. **Map** p405 F20.
New York's top alternative to the Met abandoned its home at the David H Koch Theater in Lincoln Center and truncated its season to only four productions for 2012, to be performed at various venues in the city. While its future is uncertain, all hope lies with artistic director George Steel, who is infusing the company with innovative productions and new works by unlikely opera composers such as Stephen Schwartz (*Wicked, Pippin*) and Rufus Wainwright.

Dance

In the New York scene, there is what's known as uptown and downtown dance. While Lincoln Center remains the hotspot for traditional balletic offerings, with annual seasons by American Ballet Theatre and New York City Ballet, the deeper downtown you travel, the more you will encounter more subversive, modern voices – and it's not limited to Manhattan. In Brooklyn, Williamsburg, Bushwick and Bedford-Stuyvesant have sparked a new generation of dancers and choreographers, and Long Island City, Queens, is also pulsing with movement.

NOTABLE NAMES & EVENTS

The companies of modern dance icons such as Martha Graham, Alvin Ailey, Trisha Brown, Paul Taylor and Mark Morris are still based in the city, alongside a wealth of contemporary choreographers who create works outside the traditional company structure. (There is one notable loss: in December 2011, the Merce Cunningham Dance Company disbanded.) Even in financially perilous times, the downtown performance world is full of singular voices, including Sarah Michelson, Trajal Harrell, Ralph Lemon, Maria Hassabi, Beth Gill and Ann Liv Young, as well as collectives such as AUNTS, a group of young artists who present performances in unlikely places.

Dance isn't relegated to devoted venues. Increasingly, the art form is making an appearance in museums and galleries. **Roulette Brooklyn** (*see p304*), a space for experimental music, now has its share of dance offerings, and multidisciplinary festivals such as **Crossing the Line** in autumn, presented by the French Institute Alliance Française (22 E 60th Street, between Madison & Park Avenues, 1-212 355 6100, www.fiaf.org), and **Performa** (1-212 366 5700, www.performa-arts.org), a November biennial, showcase the latest developments in dance and performance.

Autumn is especially vibrant: other festivals include **DanceNow/NYC**, held mainly at New York Live Arts, and **Fall for Dance** at City Center, which focuses on eclectic mixed bills. In January, during the Association of Performing Arts Presenters' annual winter conference, there is an abundance of mini-festivals, including American Realness, held at Abrons Arts Center, and Coil, presented by Performance Space 122. In the spring, **La MaMa Moves** takes place at La MaMa Downtown. The scene is quietest in summer, when outdoor (usually free) performances rule the land at Central Park's **SummerStage**, **Lincoln Center Out of Doors** and the **River to River Festival** in lower Manhattan. In July, Lincoln Center Festival showcases international companies.

MAJOR VENUES

Baryshnikov Arts Center

450 W 37th Street, between Ninth & Tenth Avenues, Hell's Kitchen (1-646 731 3200,

Arts & Entertainment

New York City Ballet.

www.bacnyc.org). Subway A, C, E to 34th Street-Penn Station. **Tickets** *free-$25.* **Credit** *AmEx, MC, V.* **Map** *p404 C25.*
Mikhail Baryshnikov, former artistic director of American Ballet Theatre, is something of an impresario. His home base, on a stark overpass near the Lincoln Tunnel, includes several studios, the Howard Gilman Performance Space – a 136-seat theatre – and superb facilities for rehearsals and workshops. With 238 seats, the recently renovated Jerome Robbins Theatre is both intimate and refined. The multidisciplinary Wooster Group is the resident company.

Brooklyn Academy of Music
For listings, *see p299.*
The 2,100-seat Howard Gilman Opera House, with its Federal-style columns and carved marble, remains the Brooklyn Academy of Music's most regal dance venue, where the Mark Morris Dance Group regularly performs (along with out-of-towners such as Ohad Naharin and William Forsythe). The 1904 Harvey Theater hosts contemporary choreographers – past artists have included Wally Cardona, John Jasperse and Sarah Michelson. Annual events include the Dance Africa Festival, held each Memorial Day weekend (late May), and the Next Wave Festival, which showcases established groups from New York and abroad in autumn. You can get your *Nutcracker* fix here, too: each December, American Ballet Theatre presents Alexei Ratmansky's witty and romantic version of the classical ballet.

★ David H Koch Theater
Lincoln Center, 64th Street, at Columbus Avenue, Upper West Side (1-212 870 5570, www.davidkochtheater.com). Subway 1 to 66th Street-Lincoln Center. **Tickets** *$10-$200.* **Credit** *AmEx, DC, Disc, MC, V.* **Map** *p405 C21.*
The neoclassical New York City Ballet headlines at this opulent theatre, which Philip Johnson designed to resemble a jewellery box. Ballets by George Balanchine are performed by a wonderful crop of young dancers; there are also plenty by Jerome Robbins, Peter Martins (the company's ballet master in chief) and former resident choreographer Christopher Wheeldon. In the early spring, look for performances by the revered Paul Taylor Dance Company. The company offers its popular *Nutcracker* at the very end of November, carrying just into the new year, followed by a winter repertory season. The spring season begins in April. In the autumn, American Ballet Theatre, abandoning New York City Center, will also host a season.

Joyce Theater
175 Eighth Avenue, at 19th Street, Chelsea (1-212 242 0800, www.joyce.org). Subway A, C, E to 14th Street; 1 to 18th Street; L to Eighth Avenue. **Tickets** *$10-$59.* **Credit** *AmEx, Disc, MC, V.* **Map** *p403 D27.*
This intimate space houses one of the finest theatres – we're talking about sightlines – in town. Companies and choreographers that present work here, among them Ballet Hispanico, Pilobolus Dance Theater and Doug Varone, tend to be somewhat

ARTS & ENTERTAINMENT

traditional. Regional ballet troupes, such as the Houston Ballet or Pacific Northwest Ballet, appear here too. The Joyce also hosts dance throughout much of the year – Pilobolus is a summer staple.

Metropolitan Opera House

For listings, *see p303.*

A range of international companies, from the Paris Opera Ballet to the Kirov, performs at the Met. In spring, the majestic space is home to American Ballet Theatre, which presents full-length traditional story ballets, contemporary classics by Frederick Ashton and Antony Tudor, and the occasional world première by the likes of Twyla Tharp. The acoustics are wonderful, but the theatre is immense: get as close to the stage as you can afford.

New York City Center

131 W 55th Street, between Sixth & Seventh Avenues, Midtown (1-212 581 7907, www. nycitycenter.org). Subway B, D, E to Seventh Avenue; F, N, Q, R to 57th Street. **Tickets** $10-$150. **Credit** AmEx, DC, MC, V. **Map** p405 D22.

Before Lincoln Center changed the city's cultural geography, this was the home of the American Ballet Theatre, the Joffrey Ballet and the New York City Ballet. City Center's lavish decor is golden – the theatre has recently been renovated – as are the companies that pass through here. Regular events include Alvin Ailey American Dance Theater in December and the popular Fall for Dance Festival, in autumn, which features mixed bills for just $15. Understandably, they sell out fast.

OTHER VENUES

★ Abrons Arts Center

466 Grand Street, at Pitt Street, Lower East Side (1-212 598 0400, www.henrystreet.org/arts). Subway B, D to Grand Street; F to Delancey Street; J, Z to Delancey-Essex Streets. **Tickets** $15-$25. **Credit** AmEx, MC, V. **Map** p403 G30.

This venue, which features a beautiful proscenium theatre, focuses on a wealth of contemporary dance, courtesy of artistic director Jay Wegman; past artists have included Miguel Gutierrez, Jonah Bokaer, Ann Liv Young and Fitzgerald & Stapleton.

Ailey Citigroup Theater

Joan Weill Center for Dance, 405 W 55th Street, at Ninth Avenue, Hell's Kitchen (1-212 405 9000, www.alvinailey.org). Subway A, B, C, D, 1 to 59th Street-Columbus Circle; N, Q, R to 57th Street. **Tickets** $10-$50. **Credit** AmEx, Disc, MC, V. **Map** p405 C22.

The elegant home of Alvin Ailey American Theater contains this flexible downstairs venue; when not in use as rehearsal space by the company or for the home seasons of Ailey II, its junior ensemble, it is rented out to a range of groups of varying quality.

Brooklyn Arts Exchange

421 Fifth Avenue, between 7th & 8th Streets, Park Slope, Brooklyn (1-718 832 0018, www. bax.org). Subway F, G, R to Fourth Avenue-9th Street. **Tickets** $5-$20. **Credit** AmEx, Disc, MC, V. **Map** p410 T11.

ARTS & ENTERTAINMENT

David H Koch Theater

Brooklyn Arts Exchange holds classes and performances in its intimate theatre; the space hosts more than 50 performance evenings each season. Artists in residence have included choreographers Yasuko Yokoshi, Dean Moss and Jillian Peña; it's a great place to witness the creative process up close.

Center for Performance Research

Greenbelt, Unit 1, 361 Manhattan Avenue, at Jackson Street, Williamsburg, Brooklyn (1-718 349 1210, www.cprnyc.org). Subway L to Graham Avenue. **Tickets** $10-$15. **Credit** (online purchases only) MC, V. **Map** p411 V8.

CPR, founded and curated by choreographers Jonah Bokaer and John Jasperse, represents a new trend of artists taking control of the means of production. It's based in an LEED-certified eco-conscious building with a performance space of approximately 40ft by 40ft. Presentations are sporadic.

★ Chocolate Factory Theater

5-49 49th Avenue, at Vernon Boulevard, Queens (1-718 482 7069, www.chocolatefactorytheater.org). Subway G to 21st Street; 7 to Vernon Boulevard-Jackson Avenue. **Tickets** $15. **Credit** AmEx, Disc, MC. **Map** p412 V5.

Brian Rogers and Sheila Lewandowski founded this 5,000sq ft performance venue in Long Island City in 2005, converting a one-time hardware store into two spaces: a low-ceilinged downstairs room and a loftier, brighter upstairs white box that caters to the interdisciplinary and the avant-garde. Past choreographers include Beth Gill, Jillian Peña, Big Dance Theater and Tere O'Connor. Rogers, an artist in his own right, also presents work here.

★ Danspace Project

St Mark's Church in-the-Bowery, 131 E 10th Street, at Second Avenue, East Village (1-212 674 8112 information, 1-866 811 4111 reservations, www.danspaceproject.org). Subway L to Third Avenue; 6 to Astor Place. **Tickets** free-$18. **Credit** (online or phone booking only) AmEx, Disc, MC, V. **Map** p403 F28.

A space is only as good as its producer, and executive director Judy Hussie-Taylor has injected new life into Danspace's programming by creating the Platform series, in which artists curate seasons based on a particular idea. Moreover, the space itself – a high-ceilinged sanctuary – is very handsome. Ticket prices are reasonable, making it easy to take a chance on unknown work. In autumn 2013, Danspace Project will take an in-depth look at the idea of a retrospective, focusing on the work of DD Dorvillier.

Dance New Amsterdam (DNA)

280 Broadway, at Chambers Street, Financial District (1-212 625 8369, www.dnadance.org). Subway R to City Hall; 4, 5, 6 to Brooklyn Bridge-City Hall. **Tickets** $12-$17. **Credit** AmEx, Disc, MC, V. **Map** p402 E31.

Housed in the historic Sun Building, DNA has a 135-seat theatre that hosts about 50 performances a year. Past performers have included Urban Bush Women, Julie Bour and Foofwa d'Imobilité.

Dixon Place

161 Chrystie Street, at Delancey Street, Lower East Side (1-212 219 0736, www.dixonplace.org). Subway F to Lower East Side-Second Avenue; J, Z to Bowery. **Tickets** free-$20. **Credit** AmEx, Disc, MC, V. **Map** p403 F30.

Ellie Covan started hosting experimental performances in her living room in the mid 1980s; two decades later, this plucky organisation finally opened a state-of-the-art space on the Lower East Side. Along with a mainstage theatre, there is a pub – perfect for post-show discussions. Dixon Place supports emerging artists and works in progress; summer events include the annual Hot! festival of lesbian and gay arts.

The Flea

41 White Street, between Church Street & Broadway, Tribeca (1-212 352 3101, www.theflea.org). Subway A, C, E, N, Q, R, 6 to Canal Street; 1 to Franklin Street. **Tickets** free-$40. **Credit** AmEx, DC, Disc, MC, V. **Map** p402 E31.

Two stages here host a variety of offerings including the free annual festival, Dance Conversations, which will resume in June 2013, with more than 30 performance pieces from both established and emerging choreographers.

Harlem Stage at the Gatehouse
150 Convent Avenue, at W 135th Street, Harlem (1-212 281 9240, www.harlemstage.org). Subway 1 to 137th Street-City College. **Tickets** free-$45. **Credit** AmEx, Disc, MC, V. **Map** p407 C12.
Performances at this theatre, formerly an operations centre for the Croton Aqueduct water system, celebrate African-American life and culture. Companies that have graced this flexible space, designed by Frederick S Cook and now designated a New York City landmark, include the Bill T Jones/Arnie Zane Dance Company and Kyle Abraham. Each spring, the space hosts the E-Moves Festival.

★ The Kitchen
512 W 19th Street, between Tenth & Eleventh Avenues, Chelsea (1-212 255 5793, www.thekitchen.org). Subway A, C, E to 14th Street; L to Eighth Avenue. **Tickets** free-$25. **Credit** AmEx, MC, V. **Map** p403 C27.

Movement Research at the Judson Church.

The Kitchen, led by Tim Griffin, offers some of the best experimental dance around: inventive, provocative and rigorous. Some of the artists who have presented work here are the finest in New York, such as Sarah Michelson (who also curates artists), Dean Moss, Ann Liv Young and Jodi Melnick.

La MaMa ETC
74A E 4th Street, between Bowery & Second Avenue, East Village (1-212 475 7710, www.lamama.org). Subway F to Lower East Side-Second Avenue; 6 to Astor Place. **Tickets** $10-$25. **Credit** AmEx, MC, V. **Map** p403 F29.
This experimental theatre hosts the La MaMa Moves dance festival every spring, featuring a variety of up-and-coming artists, and presents international troupes throughout the year. While shows here can be worthwhile, some programming is marginal.

Movement Research at the Judson Church
55 Washington Square South, at Thompson Street, Greenwich Village (1-212 598 0551, www.movementresearch.org). Subway A, B, C, D, E, F, M to W 4th Street. **Tickets** free. **Map** p403 E28.
This free performance series is a great place to check out experimental works and up-and-coming artists. Performances are held roughly every Monday evening, from September to June, but it's best to check the website. The group's autumn and spring festivals, which take place in December and June, feature a week-long series of performances held in venues across the city. Movement Research also offers a variety of classes and other events around town.

New York Live Arts
219 W 19th Street, between Seventh & Eighth Avenues, Chelsea (1-212 924 0077, www.newyorklivearts.org). Subway 1 to 18th Street. **Tickets** $15-$40. **Credit** AmEx, MC, V. **Map** p403 D27.
At the end of 2010, the Dance Theater Workshop and the Bill T Jones/Arnie Zane Dance Company merged to form New York Live Arts, which is dedicated to contemporary dance under Mr Jones and Carla Peterson. The company performs here regularly, in addition to local and European choreographers. This year, Kyle Abraham succeeds Yasuko Yokoshi as the New York Live Arts Resident Commissioned Artist through 2014.

Performance Space 122
1-212 477 5829, www.ps122.org.
This venue – the public school where *Fame* was shot – is under renovation through 2015 but is making do by presenting work at other spaces (see website for updates). Ronald K Brown and Doug Varone started out here; more recent artists include Maria Hassabi and Ishmael Houston-Jones.

ARTS & ENTERTAINMENT

Symphony Space

2537 Broadway, at 95th Street, Upper West Side (1-212 864 5400, www.symphonyspace.org). Subway 1, 2, 3 to 96th Street. **Box office** (3pm-30min before performance, show days only) Mon; 1-6pm Tue-Sun. **Tickets** $12.50-$45. **Credit** AmEx, MC, V. **Map** p406 C17.

The World Music Institute hosts traditional dancers from around the globe at this multidisciplinary performing arts centre, but Symphony Space also stages works by contemporary choreographers, especially with its spring Thalia dance season.

▶ *See p260 for details of the Thalia cinema.*

Triskelion Arts

3rd Floor, 118 North 11th Street, between Berry Street & Wythe Avenue (1-718 599 3577, www.triskelionarts.org). Subwaye G to Nassau Avenue; L to Bedford Avenue. **Tickets** $15-$25. **No credit cards. Map** p411 U7.

Triskelion features two black-box performance spaces, as well as studios, and is the home of resident companies Abby Bender Schmantze Theatre and Andrew Dickerson's Cirque This. Curated festivals and individual seasons spotlight the work of choreographer and clown groups.

Theatre

Al Pacino, Scarlett Johansson, Jessica Chastain, Paul Rudd and Vanessa Redgrave are among the many boldface names that have shone on Broadway marquees lately. Major musicals tend not to have big names above the title, but favour the familiar in a different way. In recent years, many of them have been adapted from famous pop-culture sources (such as *Spider-Man: Turn Off the Dark*) or have been built around existing catalogues of popular songs (such as *Jersey Boys* and *Rock of Ages*).

Tickets and information

Nearly all Broadway and Off Broadway shows are served by one of the city's 24-hour ticketing agencies (we've provided them in our listings where relevant). For cheap seats, your best bet is one of the Theatre Development Fund's **TKTS** discount booths. If you're interested in seeing more than one Off-Off Broadway show or dance event, you might consider purchasing a set of four vouchers ($36) from the TDF, either online or at their offices.

For more ticket tips, *see* **Inside Track** *p313* and *p317*.

TKTS

Father Duffy Square, Broadway & 47th Street, Theater District (www.tdf.org). Subway N, Q, R, S, 1, 2, 3, 7 to 42nd Street-Times Square.

TKTS.

Open *For evening tickets* 3-8pm Mon, Wed-Sun; 2-8pm Tue. *For same-day matinée tickets* 10am-2pm Wed, Sat; 11am-3pm Sun. **Credit** AmEx, DC, Disc, MC, V. **Map** p404 D24.

At the architecturally striking TKTS base, you can get tickets on the day of the performance (or the evening before, in the case of matinées) for as much as 50% off face value. Although there is often a queue when it opens for business, this has usually dispersed one to two hours later, so it's worth trying your luck an hour or two before the show. The Downtown and Brooklyn branches, which are much less busy and open earlier (so you can secure your tickets on the morning of the show), also sell matinée tickets the day before a show (see website for hours). Never buy tickets from anyone who approaches you in the queue as they may have been obtained illegally.

Other locations 1 Metrotech Center, corner of Jay Street & Myrtle Avenue Promenade, Downtown Brooklyn.

BROADWAY

Technically speaking, 'Broadway' is the theatre district that surrounds Times Square on either side of Broadway (the actual avenue), between 41st and 54th Streets (plus the Vivian Beaumont Theater, uptown at Lincoln Center). This is where you'll find the grandest theatres in town: wood-panelled, frescoed jewel boxes, mostly built between 1900 and 1930. Officially, 39 of them – those with more than 500 seats – are designated as being part of Broadway. Full-price tickets can easily set you back more than $100;

the very best (so-called 'premium') seats can sell for almost $500 at the most popular shows.

The big musicals are still there, and hard to miss. At any given point, however, there are also a handful of new plays, as well as serious revivals of classic dramas by the likes of Tennessee Williams, Arthur Miller and David Mamet. Each season also usually includes several small, artistically adventurous musicals to balance out the rafter-rattlers.

Long-running shows

Straight plays can provide some of Broadway's most stirring experiences, but they're less likely than musicals to enjoy long runs. Check *Time Out New York* magazine for current listings and reviews. (The playing schedules listed below are subject to change.)

Annie
Palace Theatre, 1564 Broadway, at 47th Street, Theater District (Ticketmaster 1-877 250 2929, www.anniethemusical.com). Subway C, E to 50th Street; N, Q, R, S, 1, 2, 3, 7 to 42nd Street-Times Square; N, R to 49th Street. **Box office** 10am-8pm Mon-Sat. **Tickets** $59-$199. **Credit** AmEx, MC, V. **Map** p404 D23.
James Lapine's revival of this beloved rags-to-riches musical, about a spunky orphan rescued from Great Depression penury by a gruff billionaire, is grimmer in tone than the 1977 original. But darned if Annie doesn't still recharge Broadway like a copper-topped battery of hope. Stick up your chin! And grin! 'Tomorrow' never dies. *Photo p315.*

★ The Book of Mormon
Eugene O'Neill Theatre, 230 W 49th Street, between Broadway & Eighth Avenue, Theater District (Telecharge 1-212 239 6200, www. bookofmormonbroadway.com). Subway C, E to 50th Street; N, Q, R, S, 1, 2, 3, 7 to 42nd Street-Times Square; N, R to 49th Street. **Box office** 10am-8pm Mon-Sat; noon-6pm Sun. **Tickets** $69-$477. **Credit** AmEx, Disc, MC, V. **Map** p404 D23.
This gleefully obscene and subversive satire may be the funniest show to grace the Great White Way since *The Producers* and *Urinetown*. Writers Trey Parker and Matt Stone of *South Park*, along with composer Robert Lopez (*Avenue Q*), find the perfect blend of sweet and nasty for this tale of mismatched Mormon proselytisers in Uganda.

Chicago
Ambassador Theater, 219 W 49th Street, between Broadway and Eighth Avenue, Theater District,

---

INSIDE TRACK HOT TICKETS

Buzzed-about shows, especially those with big stars on the bill, sell out fast. Keep on top of openings by checking sites such as www.playbill.com and www.theatermania.com, as well as the Theater section of www.timeout.com/ newyork. All feature the latest news and interviews; Theatermania also has an online booking service and discounted tickets for some shows.

Annie. *See p313.*

ARTS & ENTERTAINMENT

(Telecharge 1-212 239 6200, www.chicagothe musical.com). Subway C, E, 1 to 50th Street; N, R to 49th Street. **Box office** 10am-8pm Mon-Sat; noon-7pm Sun. **Tickets** $50-$252. **Credit** AmEx, Disc, MC, V. **Map** p404 D23.

This John Kander-Fred Ebb-Bob Fosse favourite – revived by director Walter Bobbie and choreographer Ann Reinking – tells the saga of chorus girl Roxie Hart, who murders her lover and, with the help of a huckster lawyer, becomes a vaudeville star.

Jersey Boys

August Wilson Theatre, 245 W 52nd Street, between Broadway & Eighth Avenue, Theater District (Telecharge 1-212 239 6200, www. jerseyboysinfo.com/broadway). Subway C, E, 1 to 50th Street. **Box office** 10am-8pm Mon-Sat; noon-6pm Sun. **Tickets** $47-$297. **Credit** AmEx, DC, Disc, MC, V. **Map** p404 D23.

The Broadway musical finally does right by the jukebox with this nostalgic behind-the-music tale, presenting the Four Seasons' infectiously energetic 1960s tunes (including 'Walk Like a Man' and 'Big Girls Don't Cry') as they were intended to be performed. Sleek direction by Des McAnuff ensures that Marshall Brickman and Rick Elice's script feels canny instead of canned. *Photo p317.*

★ The Lion King

Minskoff Theatre, 200 W 45th Street, between Broadway & Eighth Avenue, Theater District (TicketMaster 1-866 870 2717, www.lion king.com). Subway A, C, E to 42nd Street-Port Authority; N, Q, R, S, 1, 2, 3, 7 to 42nd Street-Times Square. **Box office** 10am-8pm Mon-Sat; noon-6pm Sun. **Tickets** $80-$290. **Credit** AmEx, MC, V. **Map** p404 D24.

Director-designer Julie Taymor surrounds the Disney movie's mythic plot and Elton John-Tim Rice score with African rhythm and music. Through elegant puppetry, Taymor populates the stage with a menagerie of African beasts; her staging has expanded a simple cub into the pride of Broadway.

Newsies

Nederlander Theatre, 208 W 41st Street, between Broadway & Eighth Avenue (Ticketmaster 1-866 870 2717, www.newsies themusical.com). Subway A, C, E to 42nd Street-Port Authority; N, Q, R, S, 1, 2, 3, 7 to 42nd Street-Times Square. **Box office** 10am-8pm Mon-Sat. **Tickets** $67-$288. **Credit** AmEx, MC, V. **Map** p404 D24.

Not since *Wicked* has there been a big-tent, family-friendly Broadway musical that gets so much so right. Disney's barnstorming, four-alarm delight focuses on the newsboy strike of 1899, in which spunky (and high-kicking) newspaper hawkers stand up to the media magnates of their day. The Alan Menken tunes are pleasing, the book is sharp, and the dances are simply spectacular.

★ Once

Bernard B Jacobs Theatre, 242 W 45th Street, between Broadway & Eighth Avenue (Telecharge 1-212 239 6200, www.oncemusical.com). Subway A, C, E to 42nd Street-Port Authority; N, Q, R, S, 1, 2, 3, 7 to 42nd Street-Times Square. **Box office** 10am-8pm Mon-Sat; noon-6pm Sun. **Tickets** $60-$252. **Credit** AmEx, Disc, MC, V. **Map** p404 D24.

Known for big, splashy spectacles, Broadway also has room for more sincere and understated musicals. This touching hit, adapted from the 2006 indie flick about an Irish songwriter and the Czech immigrant who inspires and enchants him, has a brooding emo-folk score and a bittersweet sense of longing that make it an ideal choice for a romantic evening out. *Photo p319.*

Spider-Man: Turn Off the Dark

Foxwoods Theatre, 213 W 42nd Street, between Seventh & Eighth Avenues, Theater District (Ticketmaster 1-877 250 2929, www.spidermanonbroadway.com). Subway A, C, E to 42nd Street-Port Authority; N, Q, R, S, 1, 2, 3, 7 to 42nd Street-Times Square. **Box office** 10am-8pm Mon-Sat; 10am-7pm Sun. **Tickets** $49-$300. **Credit** AmEx, MC, V. **Map** p404 D24.

The woe-plagued, $75-million musical based on the Marvel superhero ends its long, strange journey (grisly injuries, Julie Taymor fired, 183 previews) as a moderately enjoyable show that is still a hotchpotch of rock, circus and romantic comedy. You do care about Peter Parker and Mary Jane Watson

---

INSIDE TRACK CHEAP SEATS

Some of the cheapest tickets on Broadway are known as 'rush' tickets, purchased on the day of a show at a theatre's box office (not all theatres have them). On average, they cost $25. Some venues reserve them for students, while others use a lottery, which is held two hours before the performance.

---

more, but the show is still dragged down by plot holes and a lumbering, bland score by Bono and the Edge.

★ Wicked

Gershwin Theatre, 222 W 51st Street, between Broadway & Eighth Avenue, Theater District (Ticketmaster 1-800 982 2787, www.wickedthemusical.com). Subway C, E, 1 to 50th Street. **Box office** 10am-8pm Mon-Sat; noon-6pm Sun. **Tickets** $65-$315. **Credit** AmEx, Disc, MC, V. **Map** p404 D23.

Based on novelist Gregory Maguire's 1995 riff on *The Wizard of Oz, Wicked* is a witty prequel to the classic children's book and movie. The show's combination of pop dynamism and sumptuous spectacle has made it the most popular show on Broadway. Teenage girls, especially, have responded to the story of how a green girl named Elphaba comes to be known as the Wicked Witch of the West.

Jersey Boys. *See p315.*

ARTS & ENTERTAINMENT

OFF BROADWAY

As the cost of mounting shows on Broadway continues to soar, many serious playwrights (including major ones such as Edward Albee and Tony Kushner) are opening their shows in the less financially arduous world of Off Broadway, where many of the theatres are not-for-profit enterprises. The venues here have between 100 and 499 seats; tickets usually run from $35 to $80. Here, we've listed some reliable long-running shows, plus some of the best theatres and repertory companies.

Long-running shows

Avenue Q

New World Stages, 340 W 50th Street, between Eighth & Ninth Avenues, Theater District (Telecharge 1-212 239 6200, www.avenueq.com). Subway C, E, 1 to 50th Street. **Box office** 1-8pm Mon, Thur, Fri; 1-7pm Tue; 10am-8pm Wed; 10am-8pm Sat; 10am-7.30pm Sun. **Tickets** $72.50-$150. **Credit** AmEx, DC, Disc, MC, V. **Map** p404 D23.

After many years, which have included a Broadway run followed by a return to its Off Broadway roots, the sassy and clever puppet musical doesn't show its age. Robert Lopez and Jeff Marx's deft *Sesame Street*-esque novelty tunes about porn and racism still earn their laughs, and *Avenue Q* remains a sly and winning piece of metamusical tomfoolery.

Blue Man Group

Astor Place Theatre, 434 Lafayette Street, between Astor Place & 4th Street, East Village (1-800 258 3626, www.blueman.com). Subway N, R to 8th Street-NYU; 6 to Astor Place. **Box office** noon-7.45pm daily. **Tickets** $70-$105. **Credit** AmEx, DC, Disc, MC, V. **Map** p403 F28.

Three deadpan men with extraterrestrial imaginations (and head-to-toe blue body paint) carry this long-time favourite, which may be the world's most accessible piece of multimedia performance art. A weird, exuberant trip through the trappings of modern culture, the show is as smart as it is ridiculous.

★ Sleep No More

McKittrick Hotel, 530 W 27th Street, between Tenth & Eleventh Avenues, Chelsea (Ovationtix 1-866 811 4111, www.sleepnomorenyc.com). Subway 1 to 28th Street; C, E to 23rd Street. **Tickets** $75-$125. **Credit** AmEx, DC, Disc, MC, V. **Map** p404 C26.

A multitude of searing sights awaits at this bedazzling and uncanny installation by the English company Punchdrunk. Your sense of space is blurred as you wend through more than 90 discrete spaces, from a cloistral chapel to a ballroom floor. A Shakespearean can check off allusions to *Macbeth*; others can just revel in the haunted-house vibe. *Photo p321.*

Once. See p317.

ARTS & ENTERTAINMENT

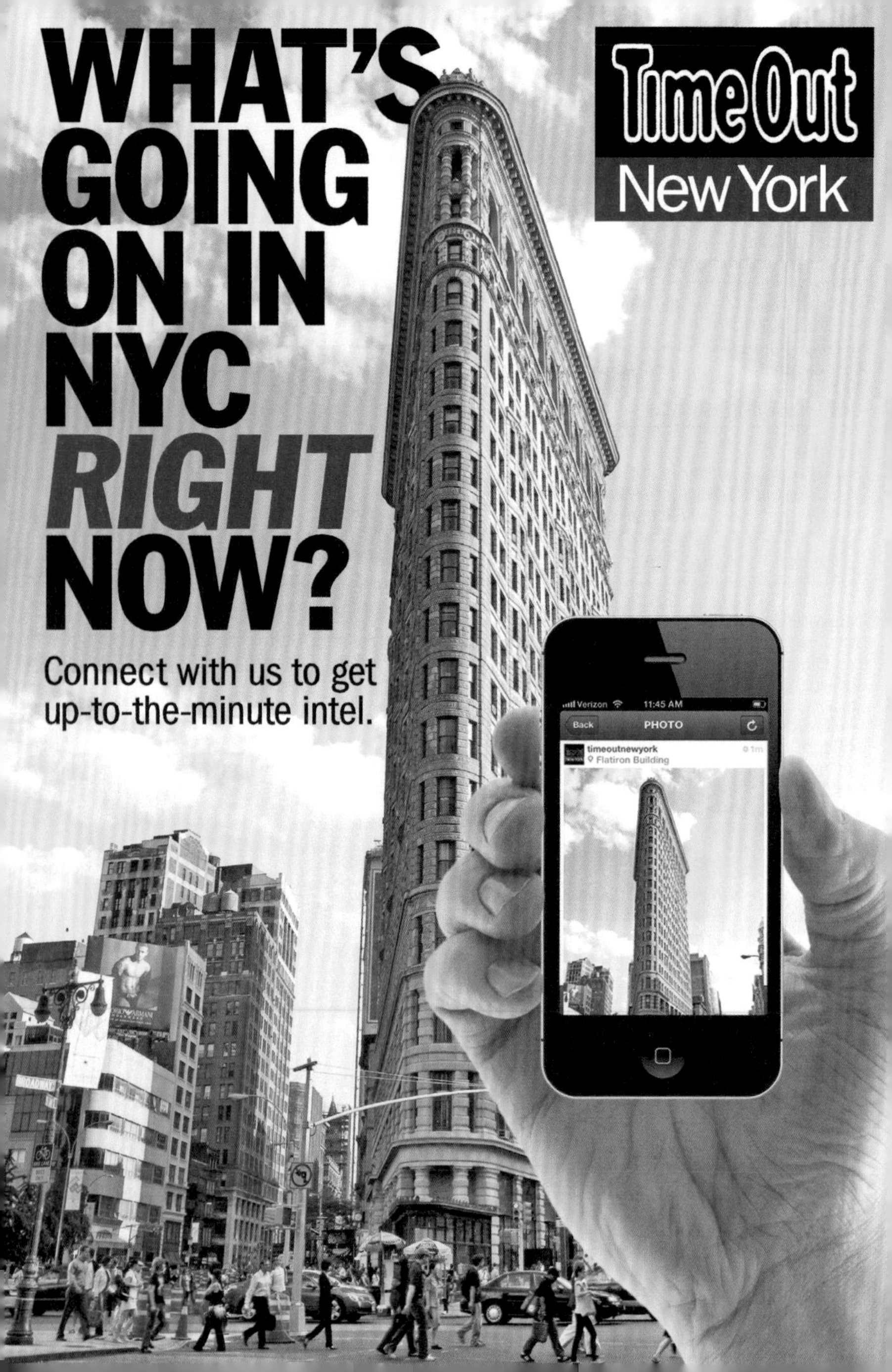
WHAT'S GOING ON IN NYC RIGHT NOW?
Connect with us to get up-to-the-minute intel.
Time Out
New York
Verizon
11:45 AM
Back
PHOTO
timeoutnewyork
Flatiron Building
1m

Repertory companies & venues

Ars Nova

511 W 54th Street, between Tenth & Eleventh Avenues, Hell's Kitchen (1-212 489 9800, Ovationtix 1-866 811 4111, www.arsnova nyc.com). Subway C, E, 1 to 50th Street. **Tickets** $15. **Credit** AmEx, Disc, MC, V. **Map** p405 C22.

Committed to presenting innovative new theatre, music and comedy, this offbeat Hell's Kitchen space has been a boon to developing artists since it opened in 2002. Along with full productions, Ars Nova also presents an eclectic monthly special called Showgasm and the annual ANT Fest for emerging talents. *Photos pp322-323.*

Atlantic Theater Company

336 W 20th Street, between Eighth & Ninth Avenues, Chelsea (1-212 691 5919, Ticket Central 1-212 279 4200, www.atlantictheater.org). Subway C, E to 23rd Street. **Box office** noon-6pm Mon-Friday. **Tickets** $35-$70. **Credit** AmEx, MC, V. **Map** p403 D27.

Created in 1985 as an offshoot of acting workshops led by playwright David Mamet and actor William H Macy, this dynamic company has presented dozens of new works; among them have been Martin McDonagh's *The Lieutenant of Inishmore* and the rock musical *Spring Awakening*. The company also has a smaller second stage deep underground at 330 W 16th Street.

INSIDE TRACK
UNDERSTUDY REFUNDS

If you've come to see a particular performer on Broadway, you may be able to cash in your ticket if that star doesn't show up. As a general rule, you are entitled to a refund if the star's name appears above the title of the show. A card on the wall of the lobby will announce any absences that day – go to the box office if you want your money back.

★ Brooklyn Academy of Music

For listings, *see p299.*

BAM's beautifully distressed Harvey Theater – along with its grand old opera house in the Peter Jay Sharp Building – is the site of the Next Wave Festival (*see p34*) and other international events. The spring season usually features high-profile productions of classics by the likes of Chekov and Shakespeare, often shipped from England with major actors attached.

Classic Stage Company

136 E 13th Street, between Third & Fourth Avenues, East Village (1-212 677 4210, www. classicstage.org). Subway L, N, Q, R, 4, 5, 6 to 14th Street-Union Square. **Box office** noon-6pm Mon-Fri. **Tickets** $55-$75. **Credit** AmEx, Disc, MC, V. **Map** p403 F27.

ARTS & ENTERTAINMENT

Sleep No More. *See p319.*

With a purview that runs from medieval mystery plays and Elizabethan standards to early modern drama and original period pieces, Classic Stage Company is committed to making the old new again. Under artistic director Brian Kulick, the company has a knack for attracting major stars, as recent productions of Chekhov plays with Maggie Gyllenhaal and Dianne Wiest attest.

59E59 Theaters

59 E 59th Street, between Madison & Park Avenues, Upper East Side (1-212 753 5959, Ticket Central 1-212 279 4200, www.59e59.org). Subway N, Q, R to Lexington Avenue-59th Street; 4, 5, 6 to 59th Street. **Box office** noon-6pm Mon; noon-7.30pm Tue-Thur; noon-8.30pm Fri, Sat; noon-3.30pm Sun. **Tickets** $15-$60. **Credit** AmEx, MC, V. **Map** p405 E22.

This chic, state-of-the-art venue, which comprises an Off Broadway space and two smaller theatres, is home to the Primary Stages company. It's also where you'll find the annual Brits Off Broadway festival (www.britsoffbroadway.com), which imports some of the UK's best work for brief runs, and its newer offshoot, Americas Off Broadway.

Flea Theater

41 White Street, between Broadway & Church Street, Tribeca (1-212 226 2407, Ovationtix

1-866 811 4111, www.theflea.org). Subway A, C, E, J, M, N, Q, R, Z, 6 to Canal Street; 1 to Franklin Street. **Box office** noon-6pm Mon-Sat. **Tickets** $15-$60. **Credit** AmEx, Disc, MC, V. **Map** p402 E31.

Founded in 1997, Jim Simpson's versatile and well-appointed venue has presented avant-garde experimentation and politically provocative satires. A second, basement theatre hosts the Flea's resident young acting company, the Bats.

Irish Repertory Theatre

132 W 22nd Street, between Sixth & Seventh Avenues, Chelsea (1-212 727 2737, www.irish rep.org). Subway F, M, 1 to 23rd Street. **Box office** 10am-6pm Mon; 10am-8pm Tue-Fri; 11am-8pm Sat; 11am-6pm Sun. **Tickets** $55-$65. **Credit** AmEx, MC, V. **Map** p404 D26.

Set in a cosily odd, L-shaped venue, this outfit puts on compelling shows by Irish and Irish-American playwrights. Fine revivals of classics by the likes of Oscar Wilde and George Bernard Shaw alternate with plays by lesser-known modern authors.

Lincoln Center Theater

Lincoln Center, 150 W 65th Street, at Broadway, Upper West Side (Telecharge 1-212 239 6200, www.lct.org). Subway 1 to 66th Street-Lincoln Center. **Box office** 10am-8pm Mon-Sat;

Ars Nova. *See p321.*

noon-7pm Sun. **Tickets** $35-$145. **Credit** AmEx, DC, Disc, MC, V. **Map** p405 C21.

The majestic and prestigious Lincoln Center Theater complex has a pair of amphitheatre-style drama venues. The Broadway house, the 1,138-seat Vivian Beaumont Theater is home to star-studded and elegant major productions. Downstairs is the 338-seat Mitzi E Newhouse Theater, an Off Broadway space devoted to new work by the upper layer of American playwrights. In 2008, in an effort to shake off its reputation for stodginess, Lincoln Center launched LCT3, which presents the work of emerging playwrights and directors at the new Claire Tow Theater, perched atop the Beaumont (*see p325* **Second Acts**).

▶ *For music and festivals at Lincoln Center, see* *pp301-303 and p33, respectively.*

Manhattan Theatre Club

Samuel J Friedman Theatre, 261 W 47th Street, between Broadway & Eighth Avenue, Theater District (Telecharge 1-212 239 6200, www. manhattantheatreclub.com). Subway N, Q, R, S, 1, 2, 3, 7 to 42nd Street-Times Square. **Box office** noon-6pm Tue-Sun. **Tickets** $30-$120. **Credit** AmEx, DC, Disc, MC, V. **Map** p404 D24.

One of the city's most important non-profit companies, Manhattan Theatre Club spent decades as an Off Broadway outfit before moving into the 622-seat

Friedman Theatre in 2003. But it still maintains two smaller spaces at New York City Center (*see p309*), where it presents some of its best material – such as Lynn Nottage's 2009 Pulitzer Prize winner, *Ruined*. Twentysomethings and teens can sign up for the 30 Under 30 Club to get tickets at both theatres for $30.

Mint Theater Company

3rd Floor, 311 W 43rd Street, between Eighth & Ninth Avenues, Theater District (1-212 315 0231, Ovationtix 1-866 811 4111, http://mint theater.org). Subway A, C, E to 42nd Street-Port Authority. **Box office** noon-6pm Mon-Fri. **Tickets** $45-$55. **Credit** AmEx, DC, Disc, MC, V. **Map** p404 D24.

The Mint specialises in theatrical archaeology, unearthing obscure but worthy plays for a full airing. Recent productions have included rarities by Hemingway, Tolstoy and DH Lawrence.

New Victory Theater

209 W 42nd Street, between Seventh & Eighth Avenues, Theater District (1-646 223 3010, www.newvictory.org). Subway N, Q, R, S, 1, 2, 3, 7 to 42nd Street-Times Square. **Box office** 11am-5pm Mon, Sun; noon-7pm Tue-Sat. **Tickets** $14-$38. **Credit** AmEx, MC, V. **Map** p404 D24.

The New Victory Theater is a perfect symbol of the transformation that has occurred in Times Square. Built in 1900, Manhattan's oldest surviving theatre became a strip club and adult cinema in the sleazy days of the 1970s and '80s. Renovated by the city in 1995, the building now functions as a kind of kiddie version of the Brooklyn Academy of Music, offering a full season of smart, adventurous, reasonably priced and family-friendly plays (including many international productions).

New World Stages

340 W 50th Street, between Eighth & Ninth Avenues, Theater District (1-646 871 1730, Telecharge 1-212 239 6200, www.newworld stages.com). Subway C, E, 1 to 50th Street. **Box office** 1-8pm Mon, Thur, Fri; 1-7pm Tue; 10am-8pm Wed, Sat; 10am-7.30pm Sun. **Tickets** $40-$150. **Credit** AmEx, DC, Disc, MC, V. **Map** p404 C23.

Formerly a movie multiplex, this centre – one of the last bastions of commercial Off Broadway in New York – boasts a shiny, space-age interior and five stages, presenting everything from campy revues such as *Forever Dusty* to downsized transfers of Broadway musicals *(including Avenue Q)*.

★ New York Theatre Workshop

79 E 4th Street, between Bowery & Second Avenue, East Village (1-212 460 5475, www.nytw.org). Subway F to Lower East Side-Second Avenue; 6 to Astor Place. **Box office** 1-6pm Tue-Sun. **Tickets** $45-$70. **Credit** AmEx, MC, V. **Map** p403 F29.

ARTS & ENTERTAINMENT

Founded in 1979, the New York Theatre Workshop works with emerging directors eager to take on challenging pieces. Besides presenting plays by world-class artists such as Caryl Churchill and Tony Kushner, this company also premièred *Rent*, Jonathan Larson's seminal 1990s musical. The iconoclastic Flemish director Ivo van Hove has made the NYTW his New York pied-à-terre.

Pershing Square Signature Center

480 W 42nd Street, at Tenth Avenue, Hell's Kitchen (1-212 244 7529, www.signature theatre.org). Subway A, C, E to 42nd Street-Port Authority. **Box office** 11am-6pm Tue-Sun. **Tickets** $25-$65. **Credit** AmEx, MC, V. **Map** p404 C24.

The award-winning Signature Theatre Company focuses on the works of a single living playwright each season, with special programmes designed to keep prices low. In past years, it has delved into the oeuvres of August Wilson, John Guare, Horton Foote and many more. In 2012 the troupe expanded hugely into a new theatre complex, designed by Frank Gehry, with three major spaces and ambitious longterm commission programmes, cementing it as one of the city's key cultural institutions.

★ Playwrights Horizons

416 W 42nd Street, between Ninth & Tenth Avenues, Theater District (1-212 279 4200, www.playwrights horizons.org). Subway A, C, E to 42nd Street-Port Authority. **Box office** noon-8pm daily. **Tickets** $50-$90. **Credit** AmEx, DC, MC, V. **Map** p404 C24.

More than 300 important contemporary plays have premièred here, including dramas (*Driving Miss Daisy, The Heidi Chronicles)* and musicals (Stephen Sondheim's *Assassins* and *Sunday in the Park with George).* Recent seasons have included new works by Edward Albee and Craig Lucas, as well as Bruce Norris's Pulitzer Prize-winning *Clybourne Park.*

★ Public Theater

425 Lafayette Street, between Astor Place & 4th Street, East Village (1-212 539 8500, tickets 1-212 967 7555, www.publictheater.org). Subway N, R to 8th Street-NYU; 6 to Astor Place. **Box office** 1-6pm Mon, Sun; 1-7.30pm Tue-Sat. **Tickets** $15-$75. **Credit** AmEx, MC, V. **Map** p403 F28.

Under the guidance of the civic-minded Oskar Eustis, this local institution – dedicated to producing the work of new American playwrights, but also known for its Shakespeare in the Park productions – has regained its place at the forefront of the Off Broadway world. The ambitious, multicultural programming ranges from new works by major playwrights to the annual Under the Radar festival for emerging artists. The company's home building, an Astor Place landmark, has five stages and has recently been extensively renovated.

▶ *The building is also home to Joe's Pub; see p288.*

Roundabout Theatre Company

American Airlines Theatre, 227 W 42rd Street between Seventh & Eighth Avenues, Theater District (1-212 719 1300, www.roundabout theatre.org). Subway N, Q, R, S, 1, 2, 3, 7 to 42nd Street-Times Square. **Box office** 10am-6pm Mon, Sun; 10am-8pm Tue-Sat. **Tickets** $20-$147. **Credit** AmEx, DC, Disc, MC, V. **Map** p404 D24.

Devoted entirely to revivals, the Roundabout often pairs beloved old chestnuts with celebrity casts. In addition to its Broadway flagship, the company also mounts shows at Studio 54 (254 W 54th Street, between Broadway & Eighth Avenue), the Stephen Sondheim Theatre (124 West 43rd Street, between Sixth & Seventh Avenues) and Off Broadway's Laura Pels Theatre (111 W 46th Street, between Sixth & Seventh Avenues).

St Ann's Warehouse

29 Jay Street, between John & Plymouth Streets, Dumbo, Brooklyn (1-718 254 8779, www.stanns warehouse.org). Subway A, C to High Street; F to York Street. **Box office** 1-7pm Tue-Sat. **Tickets** $25-$75. **Credit** AmEx, Disc, MC, V. **Map** p411 T9.

The adventurous theatregoer's alternative to Brooklyn Academy of Music (*see p299*), St Ann's Warehouse offers an eclectic line-up of theatre and music. The company recently left its longtime digs on Water Street for a nearby Dumbo location but will eventually move into a converted space within Brooklyn Bridge Park's 1870s Tobacco Warehouse. Recent shows have included high-level work by the Wooster Group and the National Theatre of Scotland. Spring 2013 brings the first American stagings of Tristan Sturrock's *Mayday Mayday* and Cora Bisset's *Roadkill.*

Second Stage Theatre

307 W 43rd Street, at Eighth Avenue, Theater District (1-212 246 4422, www.2st.com). Subway A, C, E to 42nd Street-Port Authority. **Box office** 10am-6pm Mon-Sat; 10am-3pm Sun. **Tickets** $75-$125. **Credit** AmEx, MC, V. **Map** p404 D24.

Occupying a beautiful Rem Koolhaas-designed space near Times Square, Second Stage Theatre specialises in American playwrights, and hosted the New York première of Edward Albee's *Peter and Jerry.* It also provides a stage for serious new musicals, such as the Pulitzer Prize-winning *Next to Normal.*

Shakespeare in the Park at the Delacorte Theater

Park entrance on Central Park West, at 81st Street, then follow the signs (1-212 539 8750, www.shakespeareinthepark.org). Subway B, C to 81st Street-Museum of Natural History. **Tickets** free. **Map** p405 D19.

Second Acts

Established theatres debut less-expensive stages.

Claire Tow Theater.

The New York theatre community has been wringing its hands for years about the difficulty of attracting new audiences, especially as ticket prices soar. But lately, those same hands have unclenched into applause. In a sustained effort to make theatre more affordable and relevant to younger people, some of the stateliest theatrical trees in New York have sprouted smaller branches. Since 2007, **Roundabout Theatre Company** (*see p324*) has presented shows priced at $20 in the subterranean, 60-seat Roundabout Underground space; in 2008 the **Public Theater** (*see p324*) began its Public Lab programme, which charges $15 for works that are in development or relatively cheap to produce. And in autumn 2012, three major new spaces joined their ranks.

CLAIRE TOW THEATER
Lincoln Center Theater (*see p322*) launched its $20 LCT3 program in 2008, but while a permanent home was being constructed, productions were staged off-site. Now LCT3 has its own gorgeous space: the 131-seat Claire Tow, an elegant box of glass and steel that sits on a field of grass atop Lincoln Center's Vivian Beaumont Theater. For $20, you can see

works by some of the city's most promising emerging writers, then head to the rooftop terrace for a different kind of fresh air.

BAM RICHARD B FISHER BUILDING
The **Brooklyn Academy of Music** (*see p299*) operates two imposing old-school performance venues, but now it has a space appropriate for more intimate local theatre, performance art, music and dance. The centrepiece of the newly built seven-storey Fisher Building is the 250-seat Fishman Space, whose flexible structure is intended to respond to the creative needs of individual artists; a series of $20 shows broke in the space as part of the 2012 Next Wave Festival.

STUDIO AT STAGE II
Manhattan Theatre Club (*see p323*) used to occupy both downstairs spaces at City Center (*see p309*), but abandoned the smaller of the two in 2009. Now it has reclaimed the site, which can accommodate an audience of up to 150 people, and dedicated it to works by up-and-coming writers. The initiative's inaugural production, the musical *Murder Ballad*, charged $30 and rearranged the venue completely for interactive cabaret-style seating.

The Delacorte Theater in Central Park is the fair-weather sister of the Public Theater (*see p324*). When not producing Shakespeare in the East Village, the Public offers the best of the Bard outdoors during Shakespeare in the Park (June-Sept). Free tickets (two per person) are distributed at the Delacorte at 1pm on the day of the performance. Around 8am is usually a good time to begin waiting, although the queue can start forming as early as 6am when big-name stars are on the bill. There is also an online lottery for tickets.

▶ *See pp92-95 for other Central Park attractions.*

★ Soho Rep

46 Walker Street, between Broadway & Church Street, Tribeca (1-212 352 3101, www.soho rep.org). Subway A, C, E, N, R, 6 to Canal Street; 1 to Franklin Street. **Box office** 9am-9pm Mon-Fri; 10am-9pm Sat, Sun. **Tickets** 99¢-$30. **Credit** AmEx, MC, V. **Map** p402 E31.

A couple of years ago, this Off-Off mainstay moved to an Off Broadway contract, but tickets for most shows have remained cheap for Off Broadway. Artistic director Sarah Benson's programming is diverse and audacious: recent productions include works by Young Jean Lee, Sarah Kane and the Nature Theater of Oklahoma.

Theatre Row

410 W 42nd Street, between Ninth & Tenth Avenues, Theater District (1-212 714 2442, Telecharge 1-212 239 6200, www.theatrerow.org). Subway A, C, E to 42nd Street-Port Authority. **Box office** noon-6pm daily. **Tickets** $18-$60. **Credit** AmEx, DC, Disc, MC, V. **Map** p404 C24.

Comprising five main venues of various sizes, Theatre Row hosts new plays and revivals by the trendy and celebrity-friendly New Group (Ethan Hawke and Matthew Broderick are among the recent stars), as well as scores of other productions by assorted theatre companies.

Vineyard Theatre

108 E 15th Street, at Union Square East, Union Square (1-212 353 0303, www.vineyard theatre.org). Subway L, N, Q, R, 4, 5, 6 to 14th Street-Union Square. **Box office** 1-6pm Mon-Fri. **Tickets** $45-$100. **Credit** AmEx, MC, V. **Map** p403 E27.

The Vineyard Theatre produces some excellent new plays and musicals, including *The North Pool Boys*, the wittily named *[title of show]* and the Tony Award-winning *Avenue Q*, all of which transferred to Broadway.

OFF-OFF BROADWAY

Technically, Off-Off Broadway denotes a show that is presented at a theatre with fewer than 100 seats, usually for less than $25. It's where some of the most daring writers and performers – who aren't necessarily card-carrying union professionals – create their edgiest work: **Radiohole** (www.radiohole.com), the **Debate Society** (www.thedebatesociety.org) and **Banana Bag & Bodice** (www.banana bagandbodice.org) are among many troupes that offer inspired theatre. The **New York International Fringe Festival** (1-212 279 4488, www.fringenyc.org), held every August, provides a wide opportunity to see the wacky side of the stage, and the **New York Musical Theatre Festival** (www.nymf.org) in autumn has become an important testing ground for composers and lyricists.

Repertory companies & venues

For the multidisciplinary **Dixon Place**, *see p310.*

The Brick

575 Metropolitan Avenue, between Lorimer Street & Union Avenue, Williamsburg, Brooklyn (1-718 907 6189, Ovationtix 1-866-811-4111, www.bricktheater.com). Subway G to Metropolitan Avenue; L to Lorimer Street. **Box office** opens 15mins before curtain. **Tickets** $15-$20. **No credit cards. Map** p411 V8.

This spunky, brick-lined venue presents a variety of experimental work. Its tongue-in-cheek themed summer series have included Moral Values, Pretentious and, most recently, Antidepressant Festivals.

HERE

145 Sixth Avenue, between Broome & Spring Streets, Soho (1-212 647 0202, tickets 1-212 352 3101, http://here.org). Subway C, E to Spring Street. **Box office** 5-10pm daily. **Tickets** $20-$50. **Credit** AmEx, Disc, MC, V. **Map** p403 E30.

This Soho arts complex, dedicated to non-profit arts enterprises, has been the launching pad for such shows as Eve Ensler's *The Vagina Monologues*. More recently, HERE has showcased the talents of the brilliantly freaky playwright-performer Taylor Mac.

La MaMa ETC

74A E Fourth Street, between Bowery & Second Avenue, East Village (1-212 475 7710, www. lamama.org). Subway 6 to Bleecker Street. **Box office** noon-6pm Mon-Sun. **Tickets** $10-$25. **Credit** AmEx, MC, V. **Map** p403 F29.

Founded by the late Ellen Stewart, La MaMa recently celebrated its 50th anniversary as a bastion of the Off-Off scene. Over the years, the complex has helped nurture such innovators as Sam Shepard, Charles Ludlam, Lanford Wilson and Ping Chong; it continues to be an important rung in many rising artists' ladders.

Sport & Fitness

Whether you're a player or a fan, NYC is always on the move.

As anyone who's ever witnessed one of the Yankees' many World Series victory parades down the 'Canyon of Heroes' (a spot reserved for ticker-tape parades on Broadway) can attest, New Yorkers are wild about their professional sports teams. Even baseball's lowly Mets command rapt attention from locals, though it generally turns to scorn as each succeeding dismal year takes them further from their heyday.

Though teams' successes wax and wane, watching a live game has never been more comfortable. The Yankees, Mets, and football's Giants and Jets have all moved into new flashy stadiums in the past few years. Brooklyn has its first professional team since 1957 as the Nets moved into the new Barclays Center. But even if you loathe everything New York teams represent (big payrolls, bigger egos), there are plenty of worthwhile off-field activities.

ARTS & ENTERTAINMENT

SPECTATOR SPORTS

Major venues

Advance tickets for events at the major venues listed below are sold through **Ticketmaster** (1-800 745 3000, www.ticketmaster.com).

Barclays Center

620 Atlantic Avenue, at Flatbush Avenue, Prospect Heights, Brooklyn (1-917 618 6700, www.barclayscenter.com) Subway B, D, N, Q, R, 2, 3, 4, 5 to Atlantic Avenue-Barclays Center. **Box office** 10am-6pm Mon-Fri; varies Sat, Sun depending on event. **Tickets** vary. **Credit** AmEx, DC, Disc, MC, V. **Map** p410 T10.

The city's newest arena opened in September 2012. Although controversy over the construction still causes tensions among locals, the venue has already secured a slate of splashy shows – such as the opening series of concerts by native son and Nets investor Jay-Z – and sporting events.

Madison Square Garden

Seventh Avenue, between 31st & 33rd Streets, Garment District (1-212 465 6741, www.the garden.com). Subway A, C, E, 1, 2, 3 to 34th Street-Penn Station. **Box office** 9am-6pm Mon-Fri; 10am-6pm Sat. **Tickets** vary. **Credit** AmEx, Disc, MC, V. **Map** p404 D25.

Manhattan's major arena is undergoing a renovation slated for completion in autumn 2013, but because the work is scheduled outside the seasons of resident teams New York Rangers (hockey; *see p329*) and New York Knicks (basketball; *see p329*), it won't affect games.

▶ *For more on the arena's history, see p81.*

Meadowlands Sports Complex

East Rutherford, NJ (1-201 935 3900, www.mead owlands.com). NJ Transit train from Penn Station to Secaucus Junction, then Meadowlands Line to Meadowlands Station. **Box office** 11am-6pm Mon-Fri; varies Sat, Sun depending on event. **Tickets** vary. **Credit** AmEx, MC, V.

The Izod Center (which is now used primarily for mega music concerts by Bruce Springsteen and others), the Meadowlands Racetrack and MetLife Stadium are all part of this massive multi-venue complex situated across the Hudson River.

Nassau Veterans Memorial Coliseum

1255 Hempstead Turnpike, Uniondale, Long Island (1-516 794 9303, www.nassaucoliseum.com). LIRR train from Penn Station to Hempstead, then N70, N71 or N72 bus. **Box office** 9.30am-4.45pm Mon-Fri. **Tickets** vary. **Credit** AmEx, Disc, MC, V.

This is where the New York Islanders hockey team (*see p329*) keep pro sports in Long Island alive –

Yankee Stadium

until the team's planned move to the Barclays Center in 2015 – and where you can also catch the occasional monster truck rally alongside a cavalcade of sell-out concerts.

Prudential Center

165 Mulberry Street, between Edison Place & Lafayette Street, Newark, NJ (1-973 757 6000, 1-800 745 3000 Ticketmaster, www.prucenter. com). PATH train to Newark. **Box office** 11am-6pm Mon-Fri. **Tickets** vary. **Credit** AmEx, MC, V.

The home of the New Jersey Devils hockey team and the Liberty women's basketball team, (for both, *see p329*) through 2013, until they move back to Madison Square Garden (*see p327*).

Baseball

New York lays claim to the most storied baseball history of any city. Perennial contenders the **New York Yankees** have won 27 World Series championships in their 100-plus year history, including an impressive romp through the 2009 play-offs, culminating in a World Series victory. The **New York Mets**, who have not won the Series since 1986, are in less awesome shape; among their most recent sub-.500 campaign's lowlights was the fallout from owners' implication in the Bernie Madoff financial scandal.

After some initial scepticism, New Yorkers are warming up to the new stadiums, especially the improved food selections. The pulled pork sandwiches at Citi Field's Blue Smoke restaurant are aces for the Mets, and the Yanks now offer meatball subs from nouveau Nolita Italian-American favourite Parm. The Major League Baseball season runs from April to September, with play-offs in October.

NYC also has two minor-league clubs: the **Brooklyn Cyclones**, in Coney Island, and the **Staten Island Yankees**. While both may lack the star power of the big leagues, the price and surrounding stadium scenery can't be beat.

Brooklyn Cyclones *MCU Park, 1904 Surf Avenue, between 17th & 19th Streets, Coney Island, Brooklyn (1-718 449 8497, www.brooklyncyclones.com). Subway D, F, N, Q to Coney Island-Stillwell Avenue.* **Box office** 9am-5pm Mon-Fri; 10am-4pm Sat (during game season only). **Tickets** $8-$17. **Credit** AmEx, Disc, MC, V.

★ **New York Mets** *Citi Field, Roosevelt Avenue, near 126th Street, Flushing, Queens (1-718 507 8499, newyork.mets.mlb.com). Subway 7 to Mets-Willets Point.* **Box office** 9am-5.30pm Mon-Fri; 9am-3pm Sat. **Tickets** $12-$455. **Credit** AmEx, Disc, MC, V.

★ **New York Yankees** *Yankee Stadium, River Avenue, at 161st Street, Bronx (1-718 293 6000, newyork.yankees.mlb.com). Subway B, D, 4 to 161st Street-Yankee Stadium.* **Box office** 9am-5pm Mon-Sat; 10am-4pm Sun; also during games. **Tickets** $5-$325. **Credit** AmEx, Disc, MC, V.

Staten Island Yankees *Richmond County Bank Ballpark, 75 Richmond Terrace, at Bay Street, Staten Island (1-718 720 9265, www.siyanks.com). Staten Island Ferry to St George Terminal.* **Box office** 10am-5pm Mon-Fri; also during games. **Tickets** $10-$18. **Credit** AmEx, Disc, MC, V.

Basketball

After being an NBA force in the 1990s, the **New York Knicks** have spent much of the last decade in the wilderness, but back-to-back playoff appearances in 2011 and '12 – the first appearances in the post-season since 2004 – inspire optimism for diehard fans, even if the team ownership let go of crowd favourite Jeremy Lin. Many of this year's hopes centre on the addition of Rasheed Wallace and JR Smith to the superstar duo Amar'e Stoudemire and Carmelo Anthony. Now that the stalled Atlantic Yards development project is forging ahead, the New Jersey Nets decamped in fall 2012 for their new home, the Barclays Center, and have become the **Brooklyn Nets**.

The NBA season begins at the tail end of October and runs into the middle of April (the play-offs run into June), and it is then followed by the WNBA season in May, featuring the **New York Liberty** women's basketball team.

Brooklyn Nets *Barclays Center* (for listings, *see p327*). *1-917 618 6700, www.nba.com/nets*. **Tickets** $10-$525.
New York Knicks *Madison Square Garden* (for listings, *see p327*). *www.nba.com/knicks*. **Tickets** $10-$900.
New York Liberty *Prudential Center, Newark, NJ* (for listings, *see p328*). *www.wnba.com/liberty*. **Tickets** $10-$250.

Boxing

Church Street Boxing Gym

25 Park Place, between Broadway & Church Street, Financial District (1-212 571 1333, www.nyboxinggym.com). Subway 2, 3 to Park Place; 4, 5, 6 to Brooklyn Bridge-City Hall. **Open** 7am-9.30pm Mon-Fri; 10am-4pm Sat. **Fights** 7.30pm Fri, roughly once a month. **Tickets** $40-$125. **Credit** (online purchases only) AmEx, MC, V. **Map** p402 E32.

Thanks to pound-for-pound superstars Floyd Mayweather and Manny Pacquiao, boxing has been enjoying a bit of a resurgence of late. This workout gym and amateur boxing venue launched

---

INSIDE TRACK GASTRO-GAMES

As venues devise ways to lure fans away from their HD TVs, the fame of some of the chefs powering the concessions stands at sporting events rivals that of star athletes. **Citi Field** raised the stakes with a partnership with prolific NYC restaurateur Danny Meyer. Not to be outdone, the **Yankees** collaborated on sandwich shops with upscale butcher Lobel's and downtown favourite Torrisi Italian Specialties (*see p148*). **Madison Square Garden**'s renovation includes new menus conceived by gastro-guru Jean-Georges Vongerichten and Andrew Carmellini, the chef behind the Dutch (*see p145*) and Locanda Verde (*see p147*), among others. Most recently, the **Barclays Center** has incorporated more than 30 borough-based eateries into its food offerings from neighbourhood standbys like Nathans and Junior's.

---

the popular off-site Friday Night Fights series (www.fridaynightfights.com).

Madison Square Garden

For listings, *see p327*. **Tickets** $25-$1,200.
The Garden still hosts some great pro fights, plus the annual Golden Gloves amateur championships.

Football

The **New York Giants** have become one of the league's elite teams after winning the 2012 Super Bowl, behind the star combination of quarterback Eli Manning and coach Tom Coughlin. After years of mediocrity, the **New York Jets** have become perennial contenders behind young quarterback Mark Sanchez, but the recent addition of fan favourite Tim Tebow has fuelled a competition for the starting position. Tickets can be difficult to get (games sell out well ahead), but there are usually stray tickets floating around the internet in the lead-up to a gridiron clash. The season starts in September; play-offs are in January.

New York Giants *MetLife Stadium, Meadowlands Sports Complex* (for listings, *see p327*). *1-201 935 8222, www.giants.com.* **Tickets** $110-$525.
New York Jets *MetLife Stadium, Meadowlands Sports Complex* (for listings, *see p327*). *1-800 469 5387, www.newyorkjets.com.* **Tickets** $50-$700.

Hockey

Hockey doesn't have quite the following it used to in New York, but marquee talents in the league (Alex Ovechkin, Sidney Crosby, Steven Stamkos) ensure that there are reasons to tune in, when the owners haven't locked out the players due to labour disputes. The **New Jersey Devils** continue to play at a consistently high level at their digs in Newark, and the **New York Rangers** and debonair Swedish goalie Henrik Lundqvist are still a draw. As for the **Islanders**, despite high hopes for John Tavares, the No. 1 overall pick of the 2009 draft, he hasn't turned the team around; the Isles have finished last place in their division for five straight years. The regular season runs from early October until April.

New Jersey Devils *Prudential Center* (for listings, *see p328*). *http://devils.nhl.com.* **Tickets** $20-$375.
New York Islanders *Nassau Veterans Memorial Coliseum* (for listings, *see p327*). *http://islanders. nhl.com.* **Tickets** $24-$225.
New York Rangers *Madison Square Garden* (for listings, *see p327*). *http://rangers.nhl.com.* **Tickets** $39-$120.

ARTS & ENTERTAINMENT

ARTS & ENTERTAINMENT

INSIDE TRACK
PLAY WITH THE PROS

The **USTA Billie Jean King National Tennis Center** (1-718 760 6200, www.usta.com) may host the US Open (*see below*), but scrubs looking to experience the high life are welcome at its 46 courts the rest of the year (reservations are required two days in advance, $22-$66/hr). You might even spot Roger Federer or a Williams sister, if you time it right.

Soccer

In 2010, the **New York Red Bulls** moved into a new home – the 25,000-seat Red Bull Arena (about 45 minutes outside the city in Harrison, New Jersey), acquired their first true superstar, Thierry Henry, and finished at the top of the Eastern Conference. They remain one of the more successful teams in the MLS, but have not had much success outside the regular season.

New York Red Bulls *Red Bull Arena, 600 Cape May Street, Harrison, NJ (1-877 727 6223, www.newyorkredbulls.com, www.redbullarena.us).* PATH *train from World Trade Center to Harrison Station.* **Tickets** $25-$250. **Credit** AmEx, Disc, MC, V.

Tennis

★ US Open

USTA Billie Jean King National Tennis Center, Flushing Meadows-Corona Park, Queens (1-866 673 6849, www.usopen.org). Subway 7 to Mets-Willets Point. **Tickets** $24-$86. **Credit** AmEx, Disc, MC, V.

For two weeks starting at the end of August every year, hordes of fans descend on Queens to watch the world's finest players compete for the US Open Championship in this Grand Slam tournament. Tickets go on sale in June.

ACTIVE SPORTS
Gyms & sports centres

The fitness centres below offer single-day membership. If you can schedule a workout during off-peak hours, there'll probably be less competition for machines. Call for class details.

★ Chelsea Piers

Piers 59-62, W 17th to 23rd Streets, at Eleventh Avenue, Chelsea (1-212 336 6666, www.chelseapiers. com). Subway C, E to 23rd Street. **Open** varies.

Cost varies; Sports Center Health Club $50 day pass. **Credit** AmEx, Disc, MC, V. **Map** p403 C27.

Chelsea Piers is still the most impressive all-in-one athletic facility in New York. Between the Sky Rink (Pier 61, 1-212 336 6100), the bowling alley (between Piers 59 & 60, 1-212 835 2695), the driving range (Pier 59, 1-212 336 6400) and scads of other choices, there's definitely something for everyone here. But wait, there's more. The Field House (between Piers 61 & 62, 1-212 336 6500) has a climbing wall, a gymnastics training centre, batting cages and basketball courts. At the Sports Center Health Club (Pier 60, 1-212 336 6000), you'll find an expansive gym, complete with comprehensive weight deck and 100 cardio machines, plus classes covering everything from boxing to triathlon training in the 75ft pool.

Crunch

404 Lafayette Street, between Astor Place & 4th Street, East Village (1-212 614 0120, www.crunch.com). Subway N, R to 8th Street-NYU; 6 to Astor Place. **Open** 24hrs from 5.30pm Mon-9pm Sat; 8am-9pm Sun. **Admission** $35 day pass. **Credit** AmEx, Disc, MC, V. **Map** p403 F28.

With ten branches in Manhattan and two in Brooklyn, Crunch works hard to take the tedium out of a gym session; this East Village location features a boxing ring, Pilates sessions and a weekly evening DJ spot to amp up your workout. Crunch is known for its roster of imaginative classes – for example, 'Surfboarding' using a BOSU Balance Trainer and gliding discs; 'Celebrity Body' modelled on stars' workouts; and dance based on choreography in current Broadway shows.

Other locations throughout the city.

New York Sports Club

151 E 86th Street, between Lexington & Third Avenues, Upper East Side (1-212 860 8630, club directory 1-800 301 1231, www.mysportsclubs.com). Subway 4, 5, 6 to 86th Street. **Open** 5am-11pm Mon-Thur; 5am-10pm Fri; 7am-9pm Sat, Sun. **Admission** $30 day pass. **Credit** AmEx, Disc, MC, V. **Map** p406 F18.

Day membership at New York Sports Club includes aerobics classes and access to the weights room, cardio machines and sauna. The 62nd and 86th Street branches feature squash courts, and several locations have pools (the website allows you to search for specific features).

Other locations throughout the city.

Bowling

See also p331 **Life in the Gutter**.

Bowlmor Lanes

110 University Place, between 12th & 13th Streets, Greenwich Village (1-212 255 8188, www.bowlmor.com). Subway L, N, Q, R, 4, 5, 6 to 14th Street-Union Square. **Open** (over-21s only

Life in the Gutter

A louche new breed of bowling alley has more than balls.

Blame it on *The Big Lebowski*, the Coens' 1998 cult film that spawned a nationwide screening-and-bowling festival, but the preserve of ageing, chain-smoking, overweight white dudes has experienced a serious shift in demographic.

Located inside Port Authority, **Frames** (*see p332*) used to be your typically run-down, nicotine-stained alley. But after a slick revamp, it now enforces a dress code: no hats, baggy jeans or construction boots, and guys must wear shirts with sleeves (what would the Dude say?).

But it's not just about style; the latest spots go beyond the Bud-and-burger formula. Sweeping in on the ironically retro tide, the **Gutter** (200 North 14th Street, between Wythe Avenue & Berry Street, Williamsburg, Brooklyn, 1-718 387 3585, www.thegutterbrooklyn.com) looks straight out of early 1980s Milwaukee. At the eight-lane bowling alley, locals toss frames, then retreat to the lounge, decorated with trophies and ancient beer signs, to drown their seven-ten-split sorrows. A dozen killer microbrews on tap include local suds like Chelsea Checker Cab.

Hot on its rubber-soled heels, the much larger **Brooklyn Bowl** (*see p332*) upped the ante with a menu from popular local eatery Blue Ribbon (crispy pork rinds doused in cilantro and peppers, fatty brisket) and a full-size concert venue. Built in the 19th century, the block-long, former ironworks foundry takes its design cues from the Coney Island of the 1930s and '40s, with reproductions of old freak-show posters and carnival-game relics. All the beer – by Sixpoint, Kelso and next-door Brooklyn Brewery – is made in the borough.

Not to be outdone, Greenwich Village's **Bowlmor Lanes** (*see p330*) recently opened a country club-style nightclub (www.gvcc nyc.com) on its top floor: a kitschy mix of AstroTurf flooring, flannel walls, and retro fibreglass animals. The space includes the DJ'd Clubhouse, mini golf, shuffleboard and a menu created by celeb chef David Burke. Bowlmor also opened a sprawling Times Square location in 2011; spread over two floors, the tastefully appointed pleasure zone features 50 lanes, an upscale sports bar with food from Burke and a loft-style nightclub. Seven Gotham-themed alleys include the pagoda-sheltered Chinatown, the elegant Prohibition, and Pop New York, channelling the vibe of Andy Warhol's Factory.

ARTS & ENTERTAINMENT

Bowlmor Lanes.

after 8pm Mon; after 7pm Fri-Sun) 4pm-1am Mon; 4pm-midnight Tue-Thur; noon-4am Fri; 11am-4am Sat; 11am-1am Sun. **Cost** $9-$12 per person per game. *Shoe rental* $6. **Credit** AmEx, MC, V. **Map** p403 E28.
With 42 lanes, Bowlmor is the fanciest of New York City's bowling alleys. You can request drink service, and there's a nightclub and lounge, the Greenwich Village Country Club, on the top floor. For the budget-conscious, every Monday is 'Night Strike': unlimited bowling after 8pm for $24.
Other location 222 W 44th Street, between Seventh & Eighth Avenues, Theater District (1-212 680 0012).

★ Brooklyn Bowl
61 Wythe Avenue, between North 11th & 12th Streets, Williamsburg, Brooklyn (1-718 963 3369, www.brooklynbowl.com). Subway L to Bedford Avenue. **Open** (over-21s only except noon-6pm Sat) 6pm-midnight Mon-Wed; 6pm-2am Thur, Fri; noon-2am Sat; noon-midnight Sun. **Cost** $20 per lane per 30mins Mon-Thur; $25 per lane per 30mins Fri-Sun. *Shoe rental* $4.95. **Credit** AmEx, DC, MC, V. **Map** p411 U7.
Brooklyn's bowling alley-music venue hybrid is a sprawling homage to good food, local beer and casual bowlers. We say 'casual' because the pins seem to be strung together with fishing wire for easy resetting. It slightly affects the game, but not the fun.

Frames
550 Ninth Avenue, between 40th & 41st Streets, Hell's Kitchen (1-212 268 6909, www.frames nyc.com). Subway A, C, E to 42nd Street-Port Authority. **Open** (over-21s only after 8pm) noon-midnight Mon-Wed; noon-3am Thur; 10am-3am Fri; 11am-3am Sat; 11am-11pm Sun. **Cost** $7-$10.50 per game. *Shoe rental* $6. **Credit** AmEx, Disc, MC, V. **Map** p404 C24.
This 26-lane alley in the Port Authority has eschewed bare-bones bowling for a more clubby atmosphere (there's even a dress code); it recently opened a billiards court and an arcade area.

Cycling

Cycling is a divisive topic in New York. The cyclists hate the motorists for driving in their bike lanes and running them off the road, but the pedestrians hate the bikers for much the same reasons. Still, cycling is a great way to see the city – on two wheels you can cover more distance than by walking, without going underground or boarding a bus. In recent years the mayor's office has been making an effort to create space for all commuters, installing bike lanes and launching a citywide bike-sharing programme in March 2013.
The **Manhattan Waterfront Greenway**, a 32-mile route that circumnavigates the island

of Manhattan, is a fantastic asset: you can now ride, uninterrupted, along the Hudson River from Battery Park up to the George Washington Bridge, at 178th Street. The free NYC Cycling Map, covering cycle lanes in all five boroughs, is available from the **Department of City Planning Bookstore** (22 Reade Street, between Broadway & Elk Street, Civic Center, open noon-4pm Mon, 10am-1pm Tue-Fri, 1-212 720 3667), or you can download it from www.nyc.gov/planning.
You can also get free maps at **Transportation Alternatives** (Suite 1002, 10th Floor, 127 W 26th Street, between Sixth & Seventh Avenues, Chelsea, 1-212 629 8080, www.transalt.org, 9.30am-5.30pm Mon-Fri; closed Sat, Sun), a non-profit group that lobbies for more bike-friendly streets, or download them from its website.
Organised bike rides are available from a number of outfits. The 'queer and queer-friendly' group **Fast & Fabulous** (1-212 567 7160, www.fastnfab.org) leads tours that usually meet in Central Park and head out of the city. **Five Borough Bicycle Club** (1-347 688 2925, www.5bbc.org) offers a full slate of leisurely rides around the city, as well as jaunts that head further afield; most trips are free. **Time's Up!** (1-212 802 8222, www.times-up.org), an alternative-transportation advocacy group, organises many of the city's most innovative cycling events, including the monthly Critical Mass and other group rides. For other bike tours, *see p40*; for the annual **TD Five Boro Bike Tour**, *see p30*.
Cycle hire is available from the following:

Bike & Roll *Pier 84, 557 Twelfth Avenue, at 43rd Street, Midtown (1-212 260 0400, www.bike-newyorkcity.com). Subway A, C, E to 42nd Street-Port Authority.* **Open** (weather permitting) *Mid Mar-mid May, Sept-mid Nov* 9am-6pm daily. *Mid May-Aug* 8am-8pm daily. **Rates** (incl helmet) $14-

---

INSIDE TRACK CITY CYCLING

Following urban examples in Portland, London and Paris, New York will launch a city-wide bike sharing programme in March 2013, bringing 10,000 bikers and 600 stations to the streets. Initially planned for summer 2012, the fleet's installation was delayed due to bugs in the operating software. The pricing system favours short rides and one-way commutes, as pedallers who sign up for a temporary pass or annual membership can take up to 30- or 45-minute rides, respectively, for no additional cost.

Citi Pond at Bryant Park.

$20/hr; $40-$69/day. Rent at one branch and drop off at another for an extra $5. **Credit** AmEx, Disc, MC, V (credit card & ID required for rental). **Map** p404 B24.
Other locations throughout the city.
Gotham Bikes *112 W Broadway, between Duane & Reade Streets, Tribeca (1-212 732 2453, www.togabikes.com). Subway A, C, 1, 2, 3 to Chambers Street.* **Open** 10am-6.30pm Mon, Wed, Fri, Sat; 10am-7.30pm Thur; 10.30am-5pm Sun. **Rates** (full-day rental only, incl helmet) $35/24hrs. **Credit** AmEx, Disc, MC, V (credit card & ID required for rental). **Map** p402 E31.
Loeb Boathouse *Central Park, entrance on Fifth Avenue, at 72nd Street (1-212 517 2233, www.centralparknyc.org). Subway 6 to 68th Street-Hunter College.* **Open** *Apr-Nov* 10am-6pm daily, weather permitting. **Rates** (incl helmet) $6-$15/hr; $45-$50/day. **Credit** (for required $200 deposit only) AmEx, MC, V. **Map** p405 E20.
Metro Bicycles *1311 Lexington Avenue, at 88th Street, Upper East Side (1-212 427 4450, www.metrobicycles.com). Subway 4, 5, 6 to 86th Street.* **Open** usually 10am-6.30pm Mon-Fri; 10am-6pm Sat, Sun. **Rates** ($200 deposit required) $9/hr; $45/day. **Credit** AmEx, Disc, MC, V. **Map** p406 E18.
Other locations throughout the city.

Horse riding

Kensington Stables
51 Caton Place, between Coney Island Avenue & 8th Street, Kensington, Brooklyn (1-718 972 4588, www.kensingtonstables.com). Subway F to Fort Hamilton Parkway. **Open** 10am-dusk daily.

Rates *Guided trail ride* $37/hr. *Private lessons* (reservations required) $57/hr. **Credit** AmEx, Disc, MC, V. **Map** p410 U13.
Designed in the pre-automotive age, Brooklyn's beautiful Prospect Park was meant to be explored on horseback. Guided rides can be tailored to rider experience, but none is really necessary.

Ice skating

Citi Pond at Bryant Park
Bryant Park, Sixth Avenue, between 40th & 42nd Streets, Midtown (1-212 768 4242, www.citipond atbryantpark.com). Subway B, D, F, M to 42nd Street-Bryant Park; 7 to Fifth Avenue. **Open** *Late Oct-early Mar* 8am-10pm Mon-Thur, Sun; 8am-midnight Fri, Sat. **Rates** free. *Skate rental* $14. **Credit** AmEx, Disc, MC, V. **Map** p404 E24.
Access to Bryant Park's 17,000sq ft rink is free if you have your own skates. Until early January, the surrounding holiday crafts fair adds to the festive atmosphere.

Ice Rink at Rockefeller Center
1 Rockefeller Plaza, from 49th to 50th Streets, between Fifth & Sixth Avenues, Midtown (1-212 332 7654, www.rockefellercenter.com). Subway B, D, F, M to 47-50th Streets-Rockefeller Center. **Open** *Mid Oct-early Nov* 8.30am-midnight daily; *Nov-Apr* 7am-midnight daily. **Rates** $20-$25; $12-$15 reductions. *Skate rental* $10. **Credit** AmEx, DC, Disc, MC, V. **Map** p404 E23.
The most famous New York rink returns for its 77th season in 2013 – and it's bound to be as cramped as ever. Go early in the morning; otherwise, you can expect a one- to two-hour wait.

McCarren Park Pool.

Trump Wollman Rink
Central Park, midpark at 62nd Street (1-212 439 6900, www.wollmanskatingrink.com). Subway N, Q, R to Fifth Avenue-59th Street. **Open** *Late Oct-Apr* 10am-2.30pm Mon, Tue; 10am-10pm Wed, Thur; 10am-11pm Fri, Sat; 10am-9pm Sun. **Rates** $11-$17; $5-$9 reductions. *Skate rental* $7. **No credit cards.** **Map** p405 E21.
Glide along beneath the trees of Central Park at this picturesque rink, which tends to be less crowded than Rockefeller Center's.

In-line skating

Many in-line skaters congregate in **Central Park**, in and around the Mall (east of the Sheep Meadow, between 66th & 72nd Streets). The gear shop **Blades** (156 W 72nd Street, between Broadway & Columbus Avenue, 1-212 787 3911, www.blades.com) is convenient for the park, and also rents out skates by the day (cost is $25, including helmet and other accoutrements).

Empire Skate Club of New York
1-212 774 1774, www.empireskate.org.
This club organises in-line and rollerskating events, including island-hopping tours and the Tuesday Night Skate (weather permitting): meet outside Blades (*see above*) at 8pm.

INSIDE TRACK
RESERVOIR JOGS

Follow in the fitness footsteps of Jackie Kennedy Onassis, who used to jog around the **Central Park reservoir** that carries her name. The path commands spectacular views of the skyscrapers surrounding the park, especially when you reach the northern bank and look southwards.

Kayaking

Downtown Boathouse
Pier 96, Clinton Cove Park, 56th Street & West Side Highway, Hell's Kitchen (no phone, www.downtownboathouse.org). Subway A, C, 1 to 59th St-Columbus Circle. **Open** *Mid May-June, Sept-mid Oct* 9am-6pm Sat, Sun. *July, Aug* 5-7pm Mon-Fri; 9am-6pm Sat, Sun. *Classes* 6pm Wed (see online calendar for details). **Rates** free. **Map** p405 B22.
Weather permitting, this volunteer-run organisation offers free, no-reservations kayaking in front of the boathouses, at three locations. Twenty-minute paddles are offered on a first come, first served basis. You must be able to swim. Trips are also offered for experienced kayakers, and classes are available for beginners.
Other locations Pier 40, West Side Highway, at W Houston Street, West Village; Riverside Park promenade, at 72nd Street, Upper West Side.

Running

Battery Park City's promenade, Riverside Park, Central Park and Brooklyn's Prospect Park all feature excellent running terrain.

New York Road Runners
9 E 89th Street, between Fifth & Madison Avenues, Upper East Side (1-212 860 4455, www.nyrr.org). Subway 4, 5, 6 to 86th Street. **Open** 10am-8pm Mon-Fri; 10am-5pm Sat; 10am-3pm Sun. **Rates** vary. **Credit** AmEx, MC, V. **Map** p406 E18.
Hardly a weekend passes without some sort of run or race sponsored by the NYRR, which is behind the New York City Marathon (*see p36*). Most races take place in Central Park and are open to the public. Sign up in advance to secure your spot. The club also offers classes and clinics.

NYC Hash House Harriers
1-212 427 4692, www.hashnyc.com. **Rates** $20 (covers food & beer after the run).

Hashing is a fantastic mix of exercise and debauchery. This group has been running around New York for over two decades. A designated 'hare' plots a trail and is followed by the group. Afterwards, beer and bawdy songs are an integral part of the experience.

Skateboarding

New York City presents numerous obstacles for skaters, but, over the last decade, the city parks department has been constructing skate parks within all boroughs for these road warriors. The 16,000-square foot **Maloof Skate Plaza** in Flushing Meadows-Corona Park (Grand Central Parkway, at Van Wyck Expressway, Flushing, Queens) has been an annual stop for the professional Maloof Money Cup since 2010. Other recently opened options include **Astoria Park** (Hoyt Avenue, at 21st Street, Astoria, Queens) and, in Manhattan, two additions along **Hudson River Park** at Piers 25 and 62 (Hudson River at Harrison Street & 22nd Street, respectively; www.hudsonriverpark.org). For more, visit www.nycgovparks.org/facilities/skateparks.

Swimming

The Harlem, Vanderbilt and West Side **YMCA**s (www.ymcanyc.org) have pools, as do some private gyms and many hotels. The city of New York also maintains several facilities, including recently reopened **McCarren Park** (475 Lorimer Street, between Bayard Street & Driggs Avenue, Greenpoint, 1-718 218-2380); **Hamilton Fish** (Pitt Street, between Houston & Stanton Streets, Lower East Side, 1-212 387 7687); **Asser Levy Pool** (23rd Street, between First Avenue & FDR Drive, Gramercy Park, 1-212 447 2020); **Tony Dapolito Recreation Center** (Clarkson Street, at Seventh Avenue South, West Village,

INSIDE TRACK HIP DIP

McCarren Park Pool opened in 1936, one of 11 huge swimming facilities built by the Works Progress Administration. After a $50 million renovation, it reopened in summer 2012, drawing capacity crowds of Brooklyn scenesters and sweltering city residents. Although the Olympic-size pool accommodates 1,500 bathers at a time, the waters fill up quickly. Get to the park early to avoid the queues.

1-212 242 5228); **Recreation Center 54** (348 54th Street, between First & Second Avenues, Midtown East, 1-212 754 5411), which has an indoor pool only; and the **Floating Pool Lady** (Barretto Point Park, 1-718 430 4601) – a seven-lane pool facility set on a barge in Hunts Point, Bronx. Public outdoor pools are free and open from late June to Labor Day (the first Monday in September). For a complete list, visit www.nycgovparks.org/facilities/pools.

Tennis

The city maintains excellent municipal courts throughout the five boroughs, open from April until November. **Central Park** has 30 pristine courts (enter at 96th Street and Central Park West), while the ten red clay courts in **Riverside Park** (96th Street, at Hudson River, Upper West Side) are a hidden treasure within the parks system. Single-play (one-hour) tickets cost $15 and both locations offer lessons and clinics, as well as sign-up boards for players looking for a partner. For a list of courts, visit www.nycgovparks.org/facilities/tennis.

ARTS & ENTERTAINMENT

Tennis in **Central Park**.

Escapes & Excursions

Escapes & Excursions

Swap the urban scene for open spaces or sea and sand.

Need a break from the city? You're in luck. New York is well situated for both coastal and countryside getaways, and there are plenty of worthwhile destinations within reach of the five boroughs. Bucolic areas such as New York State's Hudson Valley, north of Manhattan, are little more than an hour away; and although New Jersey is the butt of some unkind jokes, even hardened urbanites concede it has some lovely beaches that can be reached in little more time than it takes to get across town on a bus. What's more, many getaway spots are accessible by public transport, allowing you to avoid the often exorbitant car-rental rates and the heavy summer traffic in and out of town.

Hit the Trails

The city's parks are great for a little casual relaxation. But if you're hankering after a real fresh-air escape, set off on one of these day hikes, between one and three hours away. Bring water and snacks: refuelling options are scarce.

BREAKNECK RIDGE

The trek at Breakneck Ridge, in Hudson Highlands State Park, is a favourite of hikers for its accessibility, variety of trails and views of the Hudson Valley and the Catskill Mountains. The trail head is a half-mile walk along the highway from the Cold Spring stop on Metro-North's Hudson line (at weekends, the train stops closer to the trail, at the Breakneck Ridge stop).

You can spend anywhere from two hours to a full day hiking Breakneck, so plan your route in advance. The start of the trail is on the river's eastern bank, atop a tunnel that was drilled

out for Route 9D: it's marked with small white paint splotches (called 'blazes' in hiking parlance) on nearby trees. Be warned, though, that Breakneck got its name for a reason. The initial trail ascends 500 feet in just a mile and a half, and gains another 500 feet via a series of dips and rises over the next few miles. If you're not in good shape, you might want to think about an alternative hike. But if you do choose this path, there are plenty of dramatic overlooks where you can stretch out on a rock and take in the majestic Hudson River below.

After the difficult initial climb, Breakneck Ridge offers options for all levels of hikers, and several crossings in the first few miles provide alternative routes back down the slope. Trail information and maps of all the paths, which are clearly marked with different coloured blazes, are available from the New York-New Jersey Trail Conference; it's strongly recommended that you carry them with you.

Tourist information

Hudson Highlands State Park
1-845 225 7207, www.nysparks.state.ny.us.
New York-New Jersey Trail Conference
1-201 512 9348, www.nynjtc.org.

Getting there

By train Take the Metro-North Hudson train from Grand Central to the Cold Spring stop, or catch the early train to the Breakneck Ridge stop (Sat & Sun

---

INSIDE TRACK
SLEEPY HOLLOW

South of Cold Spring is the small town of **Sleepy Hollow**. It's most famous as the putative location for Washington Irving's short story *The Legend of Sleepy Hollow*, later adapted into a movie by Tim Burton. Irving is buried in the village cemetery.

---

only). Journey time 1hr 15mins; round-trip ticket $24.50-$32.50 ($12.50-$16 reductions). Contact the MTA (www.mta.info/mnr) for schedules.

HARRIMAN STATE PARK

Across the Hudson River and south-west of the sprawling campus of West Point lies Harriman State Park, containing more than 200 miles of trails and 31 lakes. It's accessible from stops on the Metro-North Port Jervis line. Of the various trails, our favourite is the **Triangle Trail**. Part of the White Bar Trail, this is an eight-mile jaunt that begins just past the parking lot at Tuxedo station (which is a little over an hour's journey from Penn Station). The route climbs steadily more than 1,000 feet towards the summit of Parker Cabin Mountain before turning south to offer lovely views of two lakes, Skenonto and Sebago. From there, it heads down steadily, although steeply at times, before ending after roughly five miles at a path marked with red dashes on white. It's a long distance to cover, but the terrain is varied and there are shortcuts. On a hot day, however, the best detour is to take a dip in one of the lakes followed by a nap in the sun.

Tourist information

Palisades Interstate Park Commission
1-201 768 1360, www.nysparks.state.ny.us.
New York-New Jersey Trail Conference
1-201 512 9348, www.nynjtc.org.

Getting there

By train Take the Metro-North/NJ Transit Port Jervis train from Penn Station to the Tuxedo stop (with a train switch in Secaucus, NJ). The journey takes 1hr 15mins, and an off-peak round-trip ticket costs $19.75. Contact the MTA (www.mta.info/mnr) for schedules.

OTIS PIKE WILDERNESS

If you're looking for ocean views and a less aggressive hike, consider Fire Island's Otis Pike Wilderness Area. The journey takes 90 minutes on the LIRR from Penn Station to Patchogue, on Long Island, followed by a 45-minute ferry ride south to the Watch Hill Visitor Center, but the pristine beaches and wildlife are worth the effort. The stretch of preserved wilderness from Watch Hill to Smith Point is home to deer, rabbits, foxes and numerous types of seabirds, including the piping plover, which nests during the summer. Just be sure you stay out of the plovers' nesting grounds, which are marked with signs, and don't feed any wildlife you see along the way.

Apart from a few sand dunes, Fire Island is completely flat; even so, walking on the beaches and sandy paths can be slow-going. After traversing the boardwalk leading from the Watch Hill Center, hike along Burma Road, a path that runs across the entire island, and in seven miles you'll arrive at the Wilderness Visitor Center (1-631 281 3010, hours vary by season, check www.nps.gov/fiis) at Smith Point.

Tourist information

Fire Island National Seashore
1-631 687 4750, www.nps.gov/fiis.

Getting there

By train/ferry Take the LIRR Montauk train from Penn Station to Patchogue; a one-way ticket costs $11.75-$16.25. Contact the MTA (www.mta.info/lirr) for schedules. The Davis Park Ferry (1-631 475 1665, www.davisparkferry.com) from Patchogue to Watch Hill operates mid Mar-Nov, with reduced crossings in spring and autumn, and costs $16 round trip ($10.50-$15 reductions). The journey should take about 2hrs 30mins in total.

ESCAPES & EXCURSIONS

Breakneck Ridge.

The ferry to **Sandy Hook**.

Head for the Ocean

CITY ISLAND

It may look like a New England fishing village, but City Island, on the north-west edge of Long Island Sound, is part of the Bronx and accessible from anywhere in the city by public transport. With a population of fewer than 5,000, it formed the slightly gritty backdrop for films such as *Margot at the Wedding* and *A Bronx Tale*. Yet in its heyday, around World War II, it was home to no fewer than 17 shipyards. Seven America's Cup-winning yachts were built on the island – and, residents add, the Cup was lost in 1983, the very same year they stopped building the boats here. You'll find a room devoted to the island's nautical past at the free **City Island Historical Society & Nautical Museum** (190 Fordham Street, between Minnieford & King Avenues, 1-718 885 0008, www.cityislandmuseum.org, open 1-5pm Sat, Sun). Housed in a quaint former schoolhouse, it's stocked with model ships, Revolutionary War artefacts and tributes to such local heroes as Ruby Price Dill, the island's first kindergarten teacher.

With seafood spots on practically every corner and boats bobbing in the background, the small community exudes maritime charm. There are still a few sailmakers in the phone book, but City Islanders are far more likely to head into Manhattan for work nowadays.

If you're here at night, don't miss the eerie views of nearby Hart Island. The former site of an insane asylum, a missile base and a narcotics rehab centre, Hart is also home to NYC's public cemetery, where you can sometimes spot Rikers Island inmates burying the unnamed dead. How's that for a fishy tale?

Eating & drinking

Over on Belden Point are **Johnny's Reef** (2 City Island Avenue, 1-718 885 2086, www. johnnysreefrestaurant.com, open Mar-Nov) and **Tony's Pier Restaurant** (1 City Island Avenue, 1-718 885 1424); both have outdoor seating. Grab a couple of beers and a basket of fried clams, sit at one of the picnic tables and watch the boats sail by.

Getting there

By subway/bus Take the 6 line to Pelham Bay Park and transfer to the Bx29 bus to City Island.

LONG BRANCH

Although it's not the high-society retreat it was in 1869, when President Ulysses S Grant made it his summer base, this Jersey Shore enclave is in the midst of a revival that has nothing to do with girls with poufed hair or guys with overdeveloped abs. Years after a 1987 fire reduced its amusement pier to a charred skeleton, Jersey boys David and Michael Barry took over the decrepit boardwalk to create Pier Village, comprising apartments, restaurants, shops and a boutique hotel. Nearby, Asbury Park, with its rich rock 'n' roll legacy, is also poised for a comeback.

A day badge to access the pristine **Long Branch beach** costs just $5-$7 for adults (free-$3 reductions), available from the seasonal office at Ocean Boulevard and Melrose Terrace. But, for $25 per day, guests at the Bungalow hotel (*see p341*) can luxuriate at **Le Club** – an exclusive stretch open from the end of May until early September. Lounge under imported palm trees and sip cocktails from the hotel's upscale eaterie Avenue (*see p341*). Atop the restaurant is a private pool deck and bar, which morphs into a slick nightclub.

For a grittier seaside vibe, catch the 837 bus from Long Branch Station to **Asbury Park**. Here, continuing redevelopment is bringing indie businesses to the boardwalk opposite the Boss's old stomping ground, **The Stone Pony** (913 Ocean Avenue, at Second Avenue, 1-732 502 0600, www.stoneponyonline.com). Across the street, you can join the pinheads at **Silverball Museum Arcade** (1000 Ocean Avenue, 1-732 774 4994, www.silverballmuseum.com), where collector Rob Ilvento lets the public play on 200 of his prize pinball machines, dating from 1932 to 2005 ($15/2hours or $20/day). From the seafront, stroll along Cookman Avenue and browse the strip's vintage and interiors shops.

Eating & drinking

Order the spicy, orange-spiked lobster roll in a brioche bun ($18) at the David Collins-designed beachfront brasserie, **Avenue** (23 Ocean Avenue, at Pier Village, 1-732 759 2900, www. lelubavenue.com), which offers lovely ocean vistas and an outdoor deck. In Asbury Park, get a taste of exotic destinations at **Langosta Lounge** (1000 Ocean Avenue, at Second Avenue, 1-732 455 3275, www.langostalounge.com), where surfer-chef Marilyn Schlossbach's menu is inspired by 'vacation cuisine'.

Hotels

The design of **Bungalow** (50 Laird Street, at Landmark Place, Pier Village, 1-732 229 3700,

INSIDE TRACK
JERSEY CITY ART JAUNT

A mere ten-minute ride away on the PATH train (www.panynj.gov/path) from the World Trade Center to Grove Street, **Jersey City** offers a down-to-earth art scene. Check out the East Coast's largest public mural (143 Christopher Columbus Drive, between Barrow & Grove Streets), a 15,000-square foot rendering of the Colgate clock, Pulaski Skyway and other area landmarks, before hitting local galleries such as **Curious Matter** (272 Fifth Street, between Coles Street & Jersey Avenue, 1-201 659 5771, www. curiousmatter.org, open noon-3pm Sun or by appt), which shows works by local and international artists in the parlour of an 1860s row house, and **Fish with Braids Gallery** (190 Christopher Columbus Drive, between Coles Street & Jersey Avenue, 1-646 573 7164, www.fishwithbraids. blogspot.com, open 2-8pm Mon-Wed, by appt noon-6pm Sat, Sun), a space for all kinds of creative expression, especially urban, new media and performance art. Afterwards, hang out with the creative crowd at bar-gallery **LITM** (140 Newark Avenue, between Grove & Erie Streets, 1-202 536 5557, www.litm.com).

www.bungalowhotel.net, $159-$629 double) may have been chronicled in a reality-TV show – *9 by Design*, about Robert and Cortney Novogratz, who juggle work and a large brood – but that doesn't dilute its cool factor. A hand-crafted wood bar by upstate New York artist John Houshmand, a vintage pool table, old board games and a 1960s foosball table encourage hanging out in the lobby. In the 24 guest rooms, whitewashed wood floors and mixed-media works by British artist Ann Carrington evoke the feel of a private beach house.

Getting there

By train Take the North Jersey Coast train from Penn Station to Long Branch. The journey takes 40mins and the fare is $15 one way ($6.75 reductions). Contact New Jersey Transit (1-973 275 5555, www.njtransit.com) for schedules. From the station, it's about a 10mins walk to Pier Village and the boardwalk, or you can catch a cab.

SANDY HOOK

The first thing you should know about Sandy Hook, New Jersey, is that there's a nude beach at its north end (Gunnison Beach, at parking lot G). The sights it affords compel boaters with binoculars to anchor close to shore, and there's also a cruisy gay scene – but there's much more to this 1,665-acre natural wonderland than sunbathers in the buff. With all that the expansive Hook has to offer, it's a little like an island getaway on the city's doorstep.

Along with seven miles of dune-backed ocean beach, the **Gateway National Recreation Area** is home to the nation's oldest lighthouse (which you can tour), as well as extensive fortifications from the days when Sandy Hook formed the outer line of defence for New York Harbor. You can explore the area's past at the **Fort Hancock Museum**, in the old post guardhouse, and at **History House**, located in one of the elegant century-old officer's houses that form an arc facing Sandy Hook Bay. The abandoned forts are worth a look as well.

Elsewhere, natural areas such as the **Maritime Holly Forest** attract an astounding variety of birds. In fact, large stretches of beach are closed in summer to allow the endangered piping plover a quiet place to mate. In winter the Audubon Society offers bird walks through the forest.

There's even a cool way to get there: hop on the ferry from Manhattan and turn an excursion to the beach into a scenic mini-cruise. Once you dock at Fort Hancock, shuttle buses transport you to beaches along the peninsula.

Hyatt Regency

Liberty House
by Amessé
Photography

The Westin
courtesy of The
Westin Jersey City
Newport Hotel

BIG APPLE FUN, JERSEY PRICE TAG

Jersey City gives you the excitement of Manhattan—at a fraction of the cost. With the Statue of Liberty at our doorstep, world-class hotels, restaurants and shops, and easy access to Manhattan, Jersey City is an unbeatable bargain.

New Jersey
visitnj.org

Supported by a grant from New Jersey
Department of State, Division of Travel and Tourism

SHOPPER'S PARADISE

With luxury malls and quirky shops, Jersey City has no sales tax on clothing and minimal tax at Urban Enterprise Zone locations.

WORLD-CLASS RESTAURANTS

A true American melting pot, Jersey City offers great international cuisine, waterfront dining, hip nightspots and gourmet delights.

SAY HEY TO THE STATUE

The Statue of Liberty is right at our doorstep! Just board the ferry in Liberty State Park and see Lady Liberty up close.

HAVE A NEED FOR SPEED?

Get action-packed excitement at the state-of-the-art indoor Pole Position, with the fastest electric cars in the U.S. Travel at 45 mph on tracks developed by NASCAR racers.

LEARNING IS FUN

Find hundreds of things to do and see at the interactive, high-tech Liberty Science Center. Catch a movie at the nation's largest IMAX theater while you're here.

ON PATH TRAIN LINE
★

Only a mile from lower Manhattan and an easy train or ferry ride away, Jersey City hotels average 25 to 30 percent less than in New York City.

PATH ROUTES

EXCHANGE PLACE

Candlewood Suites
21 Second St.
201-659-2500
ichotelsgroup.com

NEWPORT

Courtyard by Marriott
540 Washington Blvd.
201-626-6600
marriott.com

NEWPORT

Doubletree Hotel
455 Washington Blvd.
201-499-2400
jerseycity.doubletree.com

NEWPORT

Holland Motor Lodge
175 12th Street
201-963-6200
hollandmotorlodge.com

EXCHANGE PLACE

Hyatt Regency
2 Exchange Pl.
201-469-1234
jerseycity.hyatt.com

JOURNAL SQUARE

Ramada Limited
65 Tonnele Ave.
201-432-6100
www.ramada.com

NEWPORT

The Westin
479 Washington Blvd.
201-626-2900
Westin.com/JerseyCity

DESTINATION
★
JERSEY CITY

★ GO HERE TO LEARN MORE AND BOOK ONLINE! ★

destinationjerseycity.com/timeout

Boardwalk Empires

Atlantic City is gradually regaining its glamour, thanks to glitzy new resorts.

Take a walk (or a ride in one of the iconic rolling chairs) along the famous four-mile-long seaside promenade in Atlantic City, New Jersey, and you'll be partaking in a tradition that goes back to 1870, when America's first boardwalk was a mere eight-foot-wide strip that was dismantled at the end of each season. Since then, the Boardwalk has been the subject of songs, starred in movies, lent a stage to showbiz legends, beauty queens, high-diving horses and boxing cats, and houses the most expensive property on the Monopoly board.

Revel

After the Camden and Atlantic Railroad was built in the mid-19th century and grand hotels sprang up along the seafront, hordes of visitors arrived in 'America's Playground' for its beach, sophisticated entertainment, quirky attractions and undercurrent of sin. Though AC has suffered a few turns of fortune over the past century and a half, the old excitement is back. A new generation of casino-hotels offer not just gaming, but a dizzying range of diversions, from early-morning yoga to late-night burlesque.

It's all about the agua at AC's newest player. **Revel** (500 Boardwalk between Metropolitan & New Jersey Avenues, 1-855 348 0500, www.revelresorts.com; rooms from $179) offers 1,898 ocean-view rooms on 20 acres of prime beach frontage. If you actually want to get wet, take a dip in the year-round InOut Pool – perched more than 100 feet above sea level – which begins indoors and stretches out into the open air. The centrepiece of the sprawling health and relaxation complex, Bask, is a 3,000-square-foot contemporary take on a classical bathhouse, equipped with hydrotherapy pools and a healing salt room. If the body-blitzing Core Fusion and yoga classes sound like too much effort, book the signature Flow Massage ($165). The resort's theatrical casino, conceived by performing-arts design firm Scéno Plus, features more than 2,000 slot machines, nearly 100 game tables and a high-stakes poker room. Among the $2.4 billion playground's many amenities are 14 eclectic eateries plus an entertainment lineup that includes Ivan Kane's Royal Jelly Burlesque Nightclub and the 5,500-seat Ovation Hall, which hosts megastars of the calibre of Beyoncé and Kanye West.

From its custom-made mattresses, topped with 300-thread-count Egyptian cotton sheets, to its glass-enclosed marble showers for two, every detail of the 2,000-plus rooms and suites at **Borgata** (1 Borgata Way, at Huron Avenue, 1-609 317 1000, www.theborgata. com; rooms from $89) has been designed with luxury in mind. There are a dozen dining options bearing the names of top chefs, including Bobby Flay Steak and Wolfgang Puck American Grille, plus two spas – Spa Toccare and Immersion Spa in the non-gaming annex, the Water Club and five distinct drinkeries. While the casino has 3,475 slot machines and 180-plus game tables, serious players come here with one thing on their minds: the 85-table poker room is the biggest in Atlantic City.

If gambling isn't your thing, make like a lost – and much, much younger – member of the Rat Pack at the **Chelsea** (111 S Chelsea Avenue, between Boardwalk & Pacific Avenue, 1-800 548 3030, www.thechelsea-ac.com, rooms from $99), a nongaming hotel, which aims to recapture the resort town's heyday with cosy spaces such as fireplace lounges and poolside cabanas. Developer Curtis Bashaw converted two chain lodgings (a Howard Johnson and a Holiday Inn) into one destination with a spa, saltwater pool and two restaurants: the Chelsea Prime steakhouse and upscale diner Teplitzky's.

Traditionally known for Italian food, Atlantic City now offers wildly eclectic dining options in the big hotels, from well-known chain eateries to celebrity-chef destinations. But it's worth leaving the complex to have lunch at **White House Sub Shop** (2301 Arctic Avenue, at Mississippi Avenue, 1-609 345 1564, www.whitehousesubshop.net, no credit cards). The iconic sandwich shop was opened in 1946 by returning World War II vet Anthony Basile and midday queues can stretch around the block. Order the massive White House Special, laden with Italian cold cuts – Genoa salami, capocollo and cotechino and provolone. Another old-school spot, the 100-year-old **Knife and Fork Inn** (3600 Atlantic Avenue, between Albany & Pacific Avenues, 1-609 344 1133, www. knifeandforkinn.com) was originally a private club frequented by the likes of Enoch 'Nucky' Johnson, the real-life prohibition boss who inspired Boardwalk Empire's Nucky Thompson. It's owned by the same clan behind **Dock's Oyster House** (2405 Atlantic Avenue, between Florida & Georgia Avenues, 1-609 345 0092, www.docksoysterhouse. com), which has been family-owned and -operated since it opened in 1897. Ask your hotel concierge to secure you a table at **Chef Vola's** (111 S Albion Place, between Boardwalk & Pacific Avenues, 1-609 345 2022, no credit cards), a hidden dining room in a private home that requires a referral. Be prepared for long waits and tight quarters, but the fish, pastas and luminous sauces render these inconveniences trivial.

Although the all-inclusive complexes have more than enough diversions to keep you occupied, venture out to take in the expansive ocean views and offbeat sights. Located on the recently restored 1913 Garden Pier, the free **Atlantic City Historical Museum** (Boardwalk, at S New Jersey Avenue, 1-609 347 5839, www.atlanticcityexperience.org) reopened in August 2012 under the auspices of the Atlantic City Free Public Library. Displays are devoted to 'Nucky', Monopoly and the Miss America pageant, which made its debut as a local beauty contest in 1921,

and a 35-minute film charts the rise, fall and resurrection of AC, from wholesome seaside retreat through its 20th-century entertainment heyday, subsequent decline and revitalisation thanks to the legalisation of gaming and casino development.

A major public-art project, **ARTLANTIC: wonder**, is making good use of spaces left by stalled developments along the Boardwalk. Over the next five years, curator Lance Fung and a team of local and international artists and landscape designers will transform empty lots into green, art-filled spaces. While already visible, the first two installations officially open in May 2013. A seven-acre site bordered by Indiana and Pacific Avenues, Dr Martin Luther King Jr Boulevard and the Boardwalk features an infinity shape formed by grassy banks – a nod to Steel Pier's rollercoasters – that will contain and be surrounded by pieces by Robert Barry, Ilya and Emilia Kabakov and Kiki Smith. A second, smaller graphic work designed by John Roloff, incorporating trees and seating, is on the Boardwalk at California Avenue.

GETTING THERE

There is no longer a direct train connecting NYC to Atlantic City. Bus services are run by **Academy Bus** (1-800 442 7272, www. academybus.com, $36 round trip), **Greyhound** (1-800 231 2222, www.lucky streakbus.com, $37-$40 round trip) and the more upscale **Hampton Luxury Liner** (1-631 537 5800, www.hamptonluxuryliner.com, $45-$60 round trip). The trip takes about two hours. Once in AC, the **Jitney** ($2.25; www.jitneyac.com) is the best way to get around town.

Steel Pier.

Eating & drinking

Hot dogs and other typical waterside snacks are available from concession stands at the beach areas. But for more ambitious grub – caesar salad with grilled tuna, for instance – head to the **Sea Gull's Nest** (1-732 872 0025, www.seagullsnest.info), the park's sole restaurant; it's located at Area D, about three miles south of the ferry dock, but since it suffered badly in 2012's hurricane, it may still be temporarily closed, so call before setting out.

Alternatively, picnics are permitted on the beach, so you can bring along goodies for dining alfresco. Guardian Park, at the south end of Fort Hancock, has tables and barbecue grills.

Tourist information

Sandy Hook Gateway National Recreation Area 1-732 872 5970, www.nps.gov/gate.

Getting there

By boat The ferry operates from late May through September from E 35th Street and the East River or at Pier 11 in the Financial District (at the eastern end of Wall Street). Fares are $45 round trip (free-$5 reductions). Contact Sea Streak (1-800 262 8743, www.seastreak.com) for schedules. The ride takes 45 minutes.

Museum Escapes
DIA:BEACON

Take a model example of early 20th-century industrial architecture. Combine it with some of the most ambitious and uncompromising art of the past 50 years. What do you get? One of the finest aesthetic experiences on earth. Indeed, for the 24 artists whose work is on view, and for the visiting public, Dia Art Foundation's outpost in the Hudson Valley is truly a blessing.

The Dia Art Foundation's founders, Heiner Friedrich and his wife Philippa de Menil (an heir to the Schlumberger oil fortune), acquired many of their holdings in the 1960s and '70s. The pair had a taste for the minimal, the conceptual and the monumental, and supported artists with radical ideas about what art was, what it could do and where it should happen. Together with others of their generation, the Dia circle (Robert Smithson, Michael Heizer, Walter De Maria, Donald Judd and Dan Flavin) made it difficult to consider a work of art apart from its context – be it visual, philosophical or historical – ever again. Since 2003, that context has been the Riggio Galleries, a huge museum on a 31-acre tract of land overlooking the Hudson River, as

INSIDE TRACK CASTLE COUP

On the train to Beacon, which runs alongside the Hudson River, keep an eye out for the atmospheric ruins of **Bannerman Castle**, a re-creation of a medieval Scottish pile built on tiny Pollepel Island in the early 1900s by an army surplus heir. Tours are also available via kayak or passenger boat between April and October from Beacon and several other Hudson River locations (see www.bannermancastle.org for details).

Dia's hugely scaled collection had outgrown even its cavernous former galleries in Chelsea.

An 80-minute train ride from Grand Central Station, the 300,000-square foot complex of three brick buildings was erected in 1929 as a box-printing factory for Nabisco. No less than 34,000 square feet of north-facing skylights provide almost all the illumination within. The permanent collection also includes works by such 20th-century luminaries as Louise Bourgeois, Andy Warhol, Sol LeWitt and Joseph Beuys. But what really sets Dia:Beacon apart from other museums is its confounding intimacy. The design of the galleries and gardens by California light-and-space artist Robert Irwin, in collaboration with the Manhattan architectural collective OpenOffice, not only makes this enormous museum feel more like a private house, it also allows the gallery's curators to draw correspondences between artworks into an elegant and intriguing narrative of connoisseurship.

If you're travelling by car, consider stopping at **Storm King Art Center**, about 14 miles south-west of Beacon on the other side of the Hudson. The gorgeous, at times surreal, sculpture park, open April through mid November, features monumental works by Maya Lin, Alexander Calder and Richard Serra, among others.

Further information

Dia:Beacon Riggio Galleries 3 Beekman Street, Beacon, NY (1-845 440 0100, www.diaart.org). **Open** Jan-Mar 11am-4pm Mon, Fri-Sun. Apr-Oct 11am-6pm Mon, Thur-Sun (until 8pm Sat June-Aug). Nov, Dec 11am-4pm Mon, Thur-Sun. **Admission** $12; $8-$10 reductions; free under-12s. **Credit** AmEx, MC, V.
Storm King Art Center Old Pleasant Hill Road, Mountainville, NY (1-845 534 3115, www.stormking.org). **Open** Apr-Oct 10am-5.30pm Wed-Sun. Early-mid Nov 10am-5pm Wed-Sun. **Admission** $12; $8-$10 reductions; free under-5s. **Credit** AmEx, DC, Disc, MC, V.

Getting there

By train Take the Metro-North train from Grand Central Terminal to Beacon station. The journey takes 1hr 20mins, and the round-trip fare is $28-$37.50 (reductions $14-$18.50). Discount rail and admission packages are available; for details, see 'Deals & Getaways' at www.mta.info/mnr.

COOPERSTOWN

A mecca for baseball devotees, Cooperstown, north of Manhattan, isn't known for much besides its famous hall of rawhide ephemera, old pine tar-stained lumber and October memories. Happily for those who don't care a lick about America's national pastime, there's more than Major League history to be found at this single-stoplight village (population 2,000) on the shores of Lake Otsego.

The **National Baseball Hall of Fame & Museum** draws around 300,000 visitors a year. The actual hall is exactly what it claims to be: a corridor full of plaques. And as such, it's the museum that's the real diamond here. You'll see everything from Babe Ruth's locker to racist hate mail sent to Jackie Robinson, and the glove worn by Willie Mays when he made his over-the-shoulder catch in the 1954 World Series.

Local shopping is devoted primarily to baseball, so if you're looking for memorabilia or limited-edition collectibles, the **Cooperstown Bat Company** (118 Main Street, at Chestnut Street, 1-607 547 2415, closed Sun Jan-Mar) is worth checking out. For a dose of non-sport history, take a walk through the **Christ Episcopal Churchyard Cemetery** (46 River Street, at Church Street, 1-607 547 9555), where the Cooper family is buried. A three-minute drive north along Route 80 brings you to the **Fenimore Art Museum**, which displays its fine collection of American art – including folk art and Native American works – in a 1930s mansion on Lake Otsego. Temporary shows have focused on such crowd-pleasing subjects as Modernism and Edward Hopper.

Heading south out of town, the nearby **Brewery Ommegang** (656 County Highway 33, 1-800 544 1800, www.ommegang.com), set in a 136-acre farmstead, brews five award-winning Belgian-style ales. You can see how the whole brewing process works on one of the hourly tours, which include a tasting of the product.

Eating & drinking

On Cooperstown's Main Street, the **Doubleday Café** (no.93, at Pioneer Street, 1-607 547 5468) provides good American grub, while at **Alex & Ika** (no.149, at Chestnut Street, www.alex andika.com, 1-607 547 4070), hostess Ika Fognell

and chef Alex Webster serve creative dishes such as sesame-crusted salmon with sesame noodle, rocket and cucumber salad. The local dive, **Cooley's Stone House Tavern** (49 Pioneer Street, at Main Street, 1-607 544 1311), is a beautifully restored tavern that dates from before the Civil War – it's a good spot for a nightcap.

Hotels

Check in to the **Inn at Cooperstown** (16 Chestnut Street, at Main Street, 1-607 547 5756, www.innatcooperstown.com, $110-$225 double). Four-poster beds, afternoon tea and a fireplace provide a cosy backdrop for the boardgames.

If you're looking for something a little more swanky, stay at the grand lakeside **Otesaga Hotel** (60 Lake Street, at Pine Boulevard, 1-800 348 6222, www.otesaga.com, $425-$680) and play a round on the par-72 golf course.

Further information

National Baseball Hall of Fame & Museum *25 Main Street, at Fair Street (1-888 425 5633, www.baseballhall.org).* **Open** *June-Aug* 9am-9pm daily. *Sept-May* 9am-5pm daily. **Admission** $19.50; $7-$12 reductions. **Credit** AmEx, Disc, MC, V.
Fenimore Art Museum *5798 Lake Road (State Highway 80) (1-607 547 1400, www.fenimoreart museum.org).* **Open** *Apr-mid May, early Oct-Dec* 10am-4pm Tue-Sun. *Mid May-early Oct* 10am-5pm daily. Closed Jan-March. **Admission** $12; $10.50 reductions; free under-13s. **Credit** AmEx, Disc, MC, V.

Tourist information

Cooperstown/Otsego County Tourism *1-607 643 0059, www.thisiscooperstown.com.*

Getting there

By car Take I-87N to I-90 to exit 25A. Take I-88W to exit 24. Follow Route 7 to Route 20W to Route 80S to Cooperstown. The journey takes about 4hrs.

GETTING THERE

Although the railway was key to the resort town's early development, there is no longer a direct train connecting NYC to Atlantic City. Bus services are run by **Academy Bus** (1-800 442 7272, academybus.com, $36 round trip), **Greyhound** (1-800 231 2222, www.lucky streakbus.com, $37-$40 round trip) and the more upscale **Hampton Luxury Liner** (1-631 537 5800, www.hamptonluxuryliner.com, $45-$60 round trip). The trip takes about two hours. Once in AC, the **Jitney** ($2.25; www.jitneyac.com) is the best way to get around town.

In Context

History

The seeds of the Big Apple.

TEXT: KATHLEEN SQUIRES & RICHARD KOSS

More than 400 years ago, Henry Hudson, an English explorer in the service of the Dutch East India Company, sailed into New York Harbor, triggering events that would lead to the creation of the most dynamic and ethnically diverse city in the world. A steady flow of settlers, immigrants and fortune-seekers has seen New York evolve with the energy and aspirations of each successive wave of new arrivals. Intertwining cultural legacies have produced the densely layered character of the metropolis, from the wealthy and powerful Anglos who helped build the city's riches to the fabled tired, poor huddled masses who arrived from far-off lands and faced a tougher struggle. From its beginnings, this forward-looking town has been shaped by a cast of hard-working, ambitious characters, and continues to be so today.

NATIVE NEW YORKERS

The area's first residents were the indigenous Lenape tribe. They lived among the forests, meadows and farms of the land they called Lenapehoking, pretty much undisturbed by outsiders – until the 16th century, when their idyll was interrupted by European visitors. The first to cast his eyes upon this land was Giovanni da Verrazano in 1524. An Italian explorer commissioned by the French to find a shortcut to the Orient, he found Staten Island instead. Recognising that he was on the wrong track, Verrazano hauled anchor nearly as quickly as he had dropped it, never setting foot on dry land.

Eighty-five years later, Henry Hudson, an Englishman in the service of the Dutch East India Company, happened on New York Harbor in the same way. After trading with the Lenape, he ventured up the river that now bears his name, thinking it offered a north-west passage to Asia, but halted just south of present-day Albany when the river's shallowness convinced him it didn't lead to the Pacific. Hudson turned back, and his tales of the lush, river-crossed countryside captured the Dutch imagination. In 1624, the Dutch West India Company sent 110 settlers to establish a trading post here, planting themselves at the southern tip of the island called Mannahata and christening the colony Nieuw Amsterdam (New Amsterdam). In many bloody battles against the local Lenape, they did their best to drive the natives away from the little company town. But the tribe were immovable.

In 1626, Peter Minuit, New Amsterdam's first governor, thought he had solved the Lenape problem by pulling off the city's very first real-estate rip-off. He made them an offer they couldn't refuse: he 'bought' the island of Manhattan – all 14,000 acres of it – from the Lenape for 60 guilders' worth of goods. Legend famously values the purchase price at $24, but modern historians set the amount closer to $500. (These days, that would only cover a fraction of a month's rent for a closet-size studio apartment in Manhattan.) It was a slick trick, and one that set a

precedent for countless future self-serving business transactions.

The Dutch quickly made the port of New Amsterdam a centre for fur trading. The population didn't grow as fast as the business, however, and the Dutch West India Company had a hard time finding recruits to move to this unknown island an ocean away. The company instead gathered servants, orphans and slaves, and other more unsavoury outcasts such as thieves, drunkards and prostitutes. The population grew to 400 within ten years, but drunkenness, crime and squalor prevailed. If the colony was to thrive, it needed a strong leader. Enter Dutch West India Company director Peter Stuyvesant.

PEG-LEG PETE

A one-legged, puritanical bully with a quick temper, Stuyvesant – or Peg-leg Pete, as he was known – may have been less than popular, but he was the colony's first effective governor. He made peace with the Lenape, formed the first policing force (consisting of nine men), cracked down on debauchery by shutting taverns and outlawing drinking on Sunday, and established the first school, post office, hospital, prison and poorhouse. Within a decade, the population had quadrupled, and the settlement had become an important trading port.

Lined with canals and windmills, and dotted with gabled farmhouses, New Amsterdam slowly began to resemble its namesake. Newcomers arrived to work in the fur and slave trades, or to farm. Soon, a dozen and a half languages could be heard in the streets – a fact that made Stuyvesant nervous. In 1654, he attempted to quash immigration by turning away Sephardic Jews who were fleeing the Spanish Inquisition. But, surprisingly for the time, the corporate honchos at the Dutch West India Company reprimanded him for his intolerance and overturned his decision, leading to the establishment of the earliest Jewish community in the New World. It was the first time that the inflexible Stuyvesant was forced to mend his ways. The second time put an end to the 40-year Dutch rule for good.

IN CONTEXT

BRITISH INVASION

In late August 1664, English warships sailed into the harbour, set on taking over the now prosperous colony. To avoid bloodshed and destruction, Stuyvesant surrendered quickly. Soon after, New Amsterdam was renamed New York (after the Duke of York, brother of King Charles II) and Stuyvesant quietly retired to his farm. Unlike Stuyvesant, the English battled with the Lenape; by 1695, those members of the tribe who hadn't been killed off were sent packing upstate, and New York's European population shot up to 3,000. Over the next 35 years, Dutch-style farmhouses and windmills gave way to stately townhouses and monuments to English royals. By 1740, the slave trade had made New York the third-busiest port in the British Empire. The city, now home to more than 11,000 residents, continued to prosper for a quarter-century. But resentment was beginning to build in the colony, fuelled by the ever-heavier burden of British taxation.

One very angry young man was Alexander Hamilton (see p353 **Profile**). A fierce intellectual, Hamilton enrolled in King's College (now Columbia University) in 1773 and became politically active writing anti-British pamphlets, eventually serving as a lieutenant colonel in General George Washington's army.

Fearing revolution, New York's citizenry fled the city in droves in 1775, causing the population to plummet from 25,000 to just 5,000. The following year, 100 British warships sailed into the harbour of this virtual ghost town, carrying with them an intimidating army of 32,000 men – nearly four times the size of Washington's militia. Despite the British presence, Washington organised a reading of the Declaration of Independence, and American patriots tore the statue of King George III from its pedestal. Revolution was inevitable.

The battle for New York officially began on 26 August 1776, and Washington's army sustained heavy losses; nearly a quarter of his men were slaughtered in two-day period. As Washington retreated, a fire – thought to have been started by patriots – destroyed 493 buildings, including Trinity Church, the city's tallest structure. The British found a scorched city, and a populace living in tents.

The city continued to suffer for seven years. Eventually, of course, Washington's luck turned. As the British forces left, he and his troops marched triumphantly down Broadway to reclaim the city as a part of the newly established United States of America. A week and a half later, on 4 December 1783, the general bade farewell to his dispersing troops at Fraunces Tavern (see p49).

For his part, Hamilton got busy in the rebuilding effort, laying the groundwork for New York City institutions that remain vital to this day. He started by establishing the Bank of New York, the city's first bank, in 1784. When Washington was inaugurated as the nation's first president in 1789, at Federal Hall on Wall Street, he brought Hamilton on board as the first secretary of the treasury. Thanks to Hamilton's business savvy, trade in stocks and bonds flourished, leading to the establishment in 1792 of what would eventually be known as the New York Stock Exchange.

THE CITY TAKES SHAPE...

New York continued to grow and prosper for the next three decades. Maritime commerce soared, and Robert Fulton's innovative steamboat made its maiden voyage on the Hudson River in 1807. Eleven years later, a group of merchants introduced regularly scheduled shipping (a novel concept at the time) between New York and Liverpool on the Black Ball Line. A boom in the maritime trades lured hundreds of European labourers, and the city, which was still entirely crammed in below Houston Street, grew more and more congested. Where Dutch farms and English estates once stood, taller, far more efficient structures took hold. Manhattan real estate became the most expensive in the world.

The first man to tackle the city's congestion problem was Mayor DeWitt Clinton, a brilliant politician and a protégé of Hamilton. Clinton's dream was to organise the entire island of Manhattan in such a way that it could cope with the

Profile Alexander Hamilton

The founding father had a remarkable life – and a violent death.

The ultimate self-made man, Alexander Hamilton was born on the Caribbean island of Nevis in 1755, the illegitimate son of a Scottish nobleman. Left to fend for himself after the death of his mother, he became an apprentice to a counting house before he'd entered his teens. In 1773, he moved to New York to attend King's College, now Columbia University. His studies were interrupted by the Revolutionary War, for which he volunteered a year later, rising through the ranks to be promoted to lieutenant colonel at the age of 21 by George Washington.

After the war, Hamilton represented New York at the Continental Congress in Philadelphia, but soon returned to the city to found the Bank of New York. He attended the Constitutional Convention in Philadelphia in 1787 as one of New York's delegates, was the only person from the state to sign the Constitution, and served as America's first Secretary of the Treasury from 1789 to 1795. A federalist who believed in strong central government, Hamilton was instrumental in founding the US Mint and the First National Bank.

After an attempted blackmail over an adulterous affair led to his resignation, Hamilton returned to New York and, in 1801, he established the *Evening Post*, (now the *New York Post)*. He continued to be involved in national politics, working to defeat John Adams in the presidential election of 1800, but he is best remembered today for the tragic outcome of his longstanding feud with Vice President Aaron Burr.

Ostensibly political (Hamilton had backed Thomas Jefferson in the 1800 fight for the presidency), their rivalry grew personal, resulting in a duel that was held on 11 July 1804, in Weehawken, New Jersey. Burr shot Hamilton (Hamilton missed) and Hamilton died the next day. He is buried in the graveyard of Trinity Church (*see p54)*, not far from the centres of the financial world he helped to create. His 1802 estate, Hamilton Grange (*see p110)*, reopened to the public after a lengthy renovation (and relocation around the corner from its original site) in autumn 2011.

IN CONTEXT

eventual population creep northwards. In 1807, he created a commission to map out the foreseeable sprawl. It presented its work four years later, and the destiny of this new city was made manifest: it would be a regular grid of crossing thoroughfares, 12 avenues wide and 155 streets long. Then Clinton simply overstepped the city's boundaries. In 1811, he presented a plan to build a 363-mile canal linking the Hudson River with Lake Erie. Many of his contemporaries thought it was simply an impossible task: at the time, the longest canal in the world ran a mere 27 miles. But the silver-tongued politician pressed on and raised a staggering $6 million for the project.

Work on the Erie Canal began in 1817 and was completed in 1825 – three years ahead of schedule. It shortened the journey between New York City and Buffalo from three weeks to one, and cut the shipping cost per ton from about $100 to $4. Goods, people and money poured into New York, fostering a merchant elite that moved northwards in Manhattan to escape the urban crush. Estates multiplied above Houston Street – all grander and more imposing than their modest colonial forerunners. Once slavery was abolished in New York in 1827, free blacks became an essential part of the workforce. In 1831, the first public transport system began operating, pulling passengers in horse-drawn omnibuses to the city's far reaches. With the inrush of people and money, there was only one thing New York could do: grow.

...AND SO DO THE SLUMS
As the population multiplied (swelling to 240,000 by 1830 and 700,000 by 1850), so did the city's problems. Tensions bubbled between immigrant newcomers and those who could trace their American lineage back a generation or two. Crime rose and lurid tales filled the 'penny press', the city's proto-tabloids. While wealthy New Yorkers were moving as far 'uptown' as Greenwich Village, the infamous Five Points neighbourhood – the city's first slum – festered in the area now occupied by City Hall, the courthouses and Chinatown. Built on a fetid drained

pond, Five Points became the ramshackle home of poor immigrants and blacks. Brutal gangs with colourful names such as the Forty Thieves, Plug Uglies and Dead Rabbits often met in bloody clashes in the streets, but what finally sent a mass of 100,000 people scurrying from lower Manhattan was an outbreak of cholera in 1832. In just six weeks, 3,513 New Yorkers died.

In 1837, a financial panic left hundreds of Wall Street businesses crumbling. Commerce stagnated at the docks, the real-estate market collapsed, and all but three city banks closed. Some 50,000 New Yorkers lost their jobs, while 200,000 teetered on the edge of poverty. The panic sparked civil unrest and violence. In 1849, a xenophobic mob of 8,000 protesting the performance of an English actor at the Astor Place Opera House was met by a militia that opened fire, killing 22. But the Draft Riots of 1863, 'the bloodiest riots in American history', were much worse. After a law was passed exempting men from the draft for a $300 fee, the (mostly Irish) poor rose up, forming a 15,000-strong force that rampaged through the city. Fuelled by anger about the Civil War (for which they blamed blacks), the rioters set fire to the Colored Orphan Asylum and vandalised black homes. Blacks were beaten in the streets, and some were lynched. A federal force of 6,000 men was sent to subdue the violence. After four days and at least 100 deaths, peace was finally restored.

ON THE MOVE
Amid the chaos of the mid 19th century, the pace of progress continued unabated. Compared to the major Southern cities, New York emerged nearly unscathed from the Civil War. The population ballooned to two million in the 1880s, and new technologies revolutionised daily life. The elevated railway helped New Yorkers to move into what are now the Upper East and Upper West Sides, while other trains connected the city with upstate New York, New England and the Midwest. By 1871, regional train traffic had grown so much that rail tycoon Cornelius Vanderbilt built the original Grand Central Depot, which

IN CONTEXT

Federal Hall. *See p352.*

could accommodate no fewer than 15,000 passengers at a time. (It was replaced in 1913 by the current Grand Central Terminal.)

One ambitious project was inspired by the harsh winter of 1867. The East River froze over, halting ferry traffic between Brooklyn and Manhattan for weeks. Brooklyn, by then, had become the nation's third most populous city, and its politicians, businessmen and community leaders realised that the boroughs had to be linked.

The New York Bridge Company's goal was to build the world's longest bridge, spanning the East River between downtown Manhattan and south-western Brooklyn. Over 16 years (four times longer than projected), 14,000 miles of steel cable were stretched across the 1,595-foot span, while the towers rose a staggering 276 feet above the river. Worker deaths and corruption dogged the project, but the Brooklyn Bridge opened in triumph on 24 May 1883.

THE GREED OF TWEED

As New York recovered from the turmoil of the mid 1800s, William M 'Boss' Tweed began pulling the strings. Using his ample charm, the six-foot-tall, 300-pound bookkeeper, chair-maker and volunteer firefighter became one of the city's most powerful politicians. He had been an alderman and district leader; he had served in the US House of Representatives and as a state senator; and he was a chairman of the Democratic General Committee and leader of

Tammany Hall, a political organisation formed by local craftsmen ostensibly to keep the wealthy classes' political clout in check. But even though Tweed opened orphanages, poorhouses and hospitals, his good deeds were overshadowed by his and his cohorts' gross embezzlement of city funds. By 1870, members of the 'Tweed Ring' had created a new city charter, granting themselves control of the City Treasury. Using fake leases and wildly inflated bills for city supplies and services, Tweed and his cronies may ultimately have pocketed as much as $200 million.

Tweed was eventually sued by the city for $6 million, and charged with forgery and larceny. He escaped from debtors' prison in 1875, but was captured in Spain a year later and died in 1878. But his greed hurt many. As he was emptying the city's coffers, poverty spread. Then the stock market took a nosedive, factories closed and railroads went bankrupt. By 1874, New York estimated its homeless population at 90,000. That winter, *Harper's Weekly* reported, 900 New Yorkers starved to death.

IMMIGRANT DREAMS

In September 1882, a new era dawned brightly when Thomas Alva Edison lit up half a square mile of lower Manhattan with 3,000 electric lamps. One of the newly illuminated offices belonged to financier JP Morgan, who played an essential part in bringing New York's, and America's, economy back to life. By bailing out a number of failing railroads,

IN CONTEXT

then merging and restructuring them, Morgan jump-started commerce in New York once again. Goods, jobs and businesses returned to the city, and very soon such aggressive businessmen as John D Rockefeller, Andrew Carnegie and Henry Frick wanted a piece of the action. They made New York the HQ of Standard Oil and US Steel, corporations that went on to shape America's economic future.

A shining symbol for less fortunate immigrants also made New York its home around that time. To commemorate the centennial of the Declaration of Independence, the French gave the United States the Statue of Liberty, which was dedicated in 1886. Between 1892 and 1954, the statue ushered more than 12 million immigrants into New York Harbor, and Ellis Island processed many of them. The island had opened as an immigration centre in 1892 with expectations of accommodating 500,000 people annually, but the number peaked at more than a million in 1907. In the 34-building complex, crowds of would-be Americans were herded through examinations, inspections and interrogations. About 98 per cent got through, turning New York into what British playwright Israel Zangwill optimistically called 'the great melting pot where all the races of Europe are melting and reforming'.

Many of these new immigrants crowded into dark, squalid tenements on the Lower East Side, while millionaires such as Vanderbilt and Frick constructed huge French-style mansions along Fifth Avenue. Jacob A Riis, a Danish immigrant and police reporter for the *New York Tribune*, made it his business to expose this dichotomy, scouring filthy alleys and overcrowded tenements to research and photograph his 1890 book, *How the Other Half Lives*. Largely as a result of Riis's work, the state passed the Tenement House Act of 1901, which called for drastic housing reforms.

SOARING ASPIRATIONS

By the close of the 19th century, 40 fragmented governments had been formed in and around Manhattan, creating a state of wholesale political confusion.

Construction of the **Empire State Building**.

So, on 1 January 1898, the boroughs of Manhattan, Brooklyn, Queens, Staten Island and the Bronx consolidated to form New York City, the largest metropolis in America with over three million residents. More and more companies started to move their headquarters to this new city, increasing the demand for office space. With little land left to develop in lower Manhattan, New York embraced the steel revolution and grew steadily skywards (*see p367* **Race to the Top**).

By 1920, New York boasted more than 60 skyscrapers, including the 20-storey Fuller Building (now known as the Flatiron Building) at Fifth Avenue and 23rd Street, and the 25-storey New York Times Tower in Longacre (now Times) Square. Within four years, these two buildings would be completely dwarfed by the 47-storey Singer Building on lower Broadway, which enjoyed the status of tallest building in the world – but only for 18 months. The 700-foot Metropolitan Life Tower in Madison Square claimed the title from the Singer Building in 1909, but the 793-foot Woolworth Building on Broadway and Park Place topped it in 1913 – and held the distinction for nearly two decades.

If that weren't enough to demonstrate New Yorkers' unending ambition, the city burrowed below the streets at the same time, starting work on its underground transit system in 1900. The $35-million project took nearly four and a half years to complete. Less than a decade after opening, it was the most heavily travelled subway system in the world, carrying almost a billion passengers on its trains every year.

CHANGING TIMES

By 1909, 30,000 factories were operating in the city, churning out everything from heavy machinery to artificial flowers. Mistrusted, abused and underpaid, factory workers faced impossible quotas, had their pay docked for minor mistakes and were often locked in during working hours. In the end, it took the inevitable tragedy, in the form of the Triangle Shirtwaist Company fire (*see p358* **Sweatshop Inferno**), to bring about real changes in employment laws.

Another sort of rights movement was taking hold during this time. Between 1910 and 1913, New York City was the site of the largest women's suffrage rallies in the United States. Harriet Stanton Blatch (the daughter of famed suffragette Elizabeth Cady Stanton, and founder of the Equality League of Self-Supporting Women) and Carrie Chapman Catt (the organiser of the New York City Women's Suffrage Party) arranged attention-grabbing demonstrations intended to pressure the state into authorising a referendum on a woman's right to vote. The measure's defeat in 1915 only steeled the suffragettes' resolve. Finally, with the support of Tammany Hall, the law was passed in 1919, challenging the male stranglehold on voting throughout the country. With New York leading the nation, the 19th Amendment was ratified in 1920.

In 1919, as New York welcomed troops home from World War I with a parade, the city also celebrated its emergence on the global stage. It had supplanted London as the investment capital of the world, and had become the centre of publishing, thanks to two men: Joseph Pulitzer and William Randolph Hearst. *The New York Times* had become the country's most

respected newspaper; Broadway was the focal point of American theatre; and Greenwich Village had become an international bohemian nexus, where flamboyant artists, writers and political revolutionaries gathered in galleries and coffeehouses.

The more personal side of the women's movement also found a home in New York City. A nurse and midwife who grew up in a family of 11 children, Margaret Sanger was a fierce advocate of birth control and family planning. She opened the first ever birth-control clinic in Brooklyn on 16 October 1916. Finding this unseemly, the police closed the clinic soon after and imprisoned Sanger for 30 days. She was not deterred, however, and, in 1921, formed the American Birth Control League – the forerunner of the organisation Planned Parenthood – which researched birth control methods and provided gynaecological services.

ALL THAT JAZZ

Forward-thinking women such as Sanger set the tone for an era when women, now a voting political force, were moving beyond the moral conventions of the 19th century. The country ushered in the Jazz Age in 1919 by ratifying the 18th Amendment, which outlawed the distribution and sale of alcoholic beverages. Prohibition turned the city into the epicentre of bootlegging, speakeasies and organised crime. By the early 1920s, New York boasted 32,000 illegal watering holes – twice the number of legal bars before Prohibition.

In 1925, New Yorkers elected the magnetic James J Walker as mayor. A charming ex-songwriter (as well as a speakeasy patron and skirt-chaser), Walker was the perfect match for his city's flashy style, hunger for publicity and consequences-be-damned attitude. Fame flowed in the city's veins: home-run hero Babe Ruth drew a million fans each season to baseball games at the newly built Yankee Stadium, and sharp-tongued Walter Winchell filled his newspaper columns with celebrity titbits and scandals. Alexander Woollcott, Dorothy Parker, Robert Benchley and other writers

IN CONTEXT

IN CONTEXT

Sweatshop Inferno

A reform movement rises from the ashes of tragedy.

As 25 March 1911 fell on a Saturday, the roughly 500 garment workers – many of them teenage girls – at the Triangle Shirtwaist Company were putting in only a seven-hour shift, as opposed to the nine demanded of them on weekdays. At 4.45pm, they were only 15 minutes from their brief weekend, when fire broke out on the eighth floor of the ten-storey building on the corner of Greene Street and Washington Place in Greenwich Village, where Triangle owned the top three floors. Fed by the fabrics, the flames spread rapidly up the building, engulfing the sewing room on the ninth floor. As workers rushed to escape, they found many of the exits locked, and the single flimsy fire escape melted in the heat and fell uselessly away from the building. Roughly 350 made it out on to the adjoining rooftops before the inferno closed off all the exits. New Yorkers spending a leisurely Saturday in Washington Square Park a block away rushed to the scene, only to watch in horror as 54 workers jumped or fell to their deaths from the windows. A total of 146 perished.

The Triangle Shirtwaist Fire was one of the worst industrial disasters in New York City history. More than 100,000 people attended the funeral procession. The two factory owners who were tried for manslaughter were acquitted, but the fire did at least spur labour and union organisations into seeking and winning major reforms. The Factory Commission of 1911 was established by the State Legislature, headed by Senator Robert F Wagner, Alfred E Smith and Samuel Gompers, president of the American Federation of Labour. It spawned the Fire Prevention division of the Fire Department, which enforced the creation and maintenance of fire escape routes in the workplace. The fire also garnered much-needed support for the Ladies Garment Workers Union – a major force in the 1920s and '30s.

met up daily to trade witticisms around a table at the Algonquin Hotel; the result, in February 1925, was *The New Yorker*.

The Harlem Renaissance blossomed at the same time. Writers Langston Hughes, Zora Neale Hurston and James Weldon Johnson transformed the African-American experience into lyrical literary works, and white society flocked to the Cotton Club to see genre-defining musicians such as Bessie Smith, Cab Calloway, Louis Armstrong and Duke Ellington. (Blacks were only allowed into the club if they were performing on the stage, they could not be part of the audience.)

Downtown, Broadway houses were packed out with fans of George and Ira Gershwin, Irving Berlin, Cole Porter, Lorenz Hart, Richard Rodgers and Oscar Hammerstein II. Towards the end of the 1920s, New York-born Al Jolson wowed audiences in *The Jazz Singer*, the first talking picture.

AFTER THE CRASH

The dizzying excitement ended on 29 October 1929, when the stock market crashed. Corruption eroded Mayor Walker's hold on the city: despite a tenure that saw the opening of the Holland Tunnel, the completion of the George Washington Bridge and the construction of the Chrysler and Empire State Buildings, Walker's lustre faded in the growing shadow of graft accusations. He resigned in 1932, as New York, in the depths of the Great Depression, had one million unemployed inhabitants.

In 1934, an unstoppable force named Fiorello La Guardia took office as mayor, rolling up his sleeves to crack down on mobsters, gambling, smut and government corruption. The son of an Italian father and a Jewish mother, La Guardia was a tough-talking politician who was known for nearly coming to blows with other city officials; he described himself as 'inconsiderate, arbitrary, authoritative, difficult, complicated, intolerant and somewhat theatrical'. La Guardia's act played well: he ushered New York into an era of unparalleled prosperity over the course of his three terms. The 'Little Flower', as La Guardia was known,

streamlined city government, paid down the debt and updated the transportation, hospital, reservoir and sewer systems. New highways made the city more accessible, and North Beach (now La Guardia) Airport became the city's first commercial landing field.

Helping La Guardia to modernise the city was Robert Moses, a hard-nosed visionary who would do much to shape – and in some cases, destroy – New York's landscape. Moses spent 44 years stepping on toes to build expressways, parks, beaches, public housing, bridges and tunnels, creating such landmarks as Lincoln Center, the United Nations complex and the Verrazano-Narrows Bridge, which connected Staten Island to Brooklyn in 1964.

PROTEST AND REFORM

Despite La Guardia's belt-tightening and Moses's renovations, New York began to fall apart financially. When World War II ended, 800,000 industrial jobs disappeared from the city. Factories in need of more space moved to the suburbs, along with nearly five million residents. But more crowding occurred as rural African-Americans and Latinos (primarily Puerto Ricans) flocked to the metropolis in the 1950s and '60s, only to meet with ruthless discrimination and a dearth of jobs. Moses's Slum Clearance Committee reduced many neighbourhoods to rubble, forcing out residents in order to build huge, isolating housing projects that became magnets for crime. In 1963, the city also lost Pennsylvania Station, when the Pennsylvania Railroad Company demolished the site over the protests of picketers in order to make way for a modern station and the new sports and entertainment venue Madison Square Garden. It was a wake-up call for New York: architectural changes were hurtling out of control.

But Moses and his wrecking ball couldn't knock over one steadfast West Village woman. Architectural writer and urban-planning critic Jane Jacobs organised local residents when the city unveiled its plan to clear a 14-block tract of her neighbourhood to make space for

IN CONTEXT

yet more public housing. Her obstinacy was applauded by many, including an influential councilman named Ed Koch (who would become mayor in 1978). The group fought the plan and won, causing Mayor Robert F Wagner to back down. As a result of Jacobs's efforts in the wake of Pennsylvania Station's demolition, the Landmarks Preservation Commission – the first such group in the US – was established in 1965.

At the dawning of the Age of Aquarius, the city harboured its share of innovative creators. Allen Ginsberg, Jack Kerouac and others gathered in Village coffeehouses to create a new voice for poetry. A folk music scene brewed in tiny clubs around Bleecker Street, showcasing musicians such as Bob Dylan. A former advertising illustrator named Andy Warhol turned images of mass consumerism into deadpan, ironic art statements. And in 1969, the city's long-closeted gay communities came out into the streets, as patrons at the Stonewall Inn on Christopher Street demonstrated against a police raid. The protests, known as the Stonewall riots, gave birth to the modern gay rights movement.

MEAN STREETS

By the early 1970s, deficits had forced heavy cutbacks in city services. The streets were dirty, and subway cars and buildings were scrawled with graffiti; crime skyrocketed as the city's debt deepened to $6 billion. Despite the huge downturn, construction commenced on the World Trade Center; when completed, in 1973, its twin 110-storey towers were the world's tallest buildings. Even as the WTC rose, the city became so desperately overdrawn that Mayor Abraham Beame appealed to the federal government for financial assistance in 1975. Yet President Gerald Ford refused to bail out the city, a decision summed up by the immortal *Daily News* headline: 'Ford to City: Drop Dead'.

Times Square had degenerated into a morass of sex shops and porn theatres, drug use rose and subway use hit an all-time low due to a fear of crime. In 1977, serial killer Son of Sam terrorised the city

with six killings, and a blackout one hot August night that same year led to widespread looting and arson. The angst of the time fuelled the punk culture that rose in downtown clubs such as CBGB. At the same time, celebrities, designers and models converged on Midtown to disco their nights away at Studio 54.

The Wall Street boom of the 1980s and fiscal petitioning by Mayor Ed Koch brought money flooding back into New York. Gentrification glamorised neighbourhoods such as Soho, Tribeca and the East Village, but deeper societal ills lurked. In 1988, a protest against the city's efforts to impose a strict curfew and displace the homeless from Tompkins Square Park erupted into a violent clash with the police. Crack use became endemic in the ghettos, homelessness rose and AIDS emerged as a new scourge.

By 1989, citizens were restless for change. They turned to David N Dinkins, electing him as the city's first African-American mayor. A distinguished, softly spoken man, Dinkins held office for only a single term, marked by a record murder rate, flaring racial tensions in Manhattan's Washington Heights and Brooklyn's Crown Heights and Flatbush neighbourhoods, and the explosion of a bomb in the basement parking garage of the World Trade Center in 1993 that killed six, injured 1,000 and foreshadowed the attacks of 2001.

Deeming the polite Dinkins ineffective, New Yorkers voted in former federal prosecutor Rudolph Giuliani. An abrasive leader, Giuliani used bullying tactics to get things done, as his 'quality of life' campaign cracked down on everything from drug dealing and pornography to unsolicited windshield washing. As cases of severe police brutality grabbed the headlines and racial polarisation was palpable, crime plummeted, tourism soared and New York became cleaner and safer than it had been in decades. Times Square was transformed into a family-friendly tourist destination, and the dot-com explosion brought young wannabes to the Flatiron District's Silicon Alley. Giuliani's second term as mayor would close, however, on a devastating tragedy.

9/11 AND BEYOND

On 11 September 2001, terrorists flew two hijacked passenger jets into the Twin Towers of the World Trade Center, collapsing the entire complex and killing nearly 3,000 people. Amid the trauma, the attack triggered a citywide sense of unity, as New Yorkers did what they could to help their fellow citizens – from feeding emergency crews to cheering on rescue workers en route to Ground Zero.

Two months later, billionaire Michael Bloomberg was elected mayor and took on the daunting task of repairing not only the city's skyline but also its battered economy and shattered psyche. He proved adept at steering New York back on the road to health as the stock market revived, downtown businesses re-emerged and plans for rebuilding the World Trade Center were drawn. True to form, however, New Yorkers debated the future of the site for more than a year until architect Daniel Libeskind was awarded the redevelopment job in 2003; the 9/11 Memorial opened on 11 September 2011 (*see p55* **Rebuilding Ground Zero**).

Yet despite Bloomberg's many efforts to make New York a more civil place – imposing a citywide smoking ban in bars and restaurants and a strict noise ordinance – New Yorkers continued to uphold their hard-edged image. In 2007, the mayor announced plans to 'green up' NYC, aiming to reduce carbon emissions by 30 per cent and to fight traffic jams by making motorists pay driving fees in parts of Manhattan. His congestion pricing plan

was so opposed it didn't even make it to the State assembly. However, other initiatives, such as green building regulations, have since come into effect.

As Bloomberg's second term neared its end, he became increasingly frustrated that some of his pet proposals hadn't been realised. In the midst of 2008's deepening financial crisis, he proposed a controversial bill to extend the tenure of elected officials from two four-year terms to three. Although it was narrowly passed by the New York City Council in October 2008, many politicos (and citizens) opposed the law change. The incumbent poured a record sum of money into his campaign the following year, beating Comptroller William Thompson Jr with just 51 per cent of the vote to become the fourth mayor in New York's history to serve a third term. In October 2010, in a remarkable display of chutzpah, Bloomberg reversed himself and voted to restore the two-term limitation.

In June 2011, New York celebrated yet another civil rights milestone when it became the largest state in the US to legalise same-sex marriage. A few months later, a group of protesters set up camp in the Financial District's Zuccotti Park, demanding jobs and denouncing the financial industry. Occupy Wall Street demonstrators managed to hold their ground for almost two months until they were forced out by police in November. But the group had already inspired similar movements around the world, spreading the message of the '99 per cent'.

IN CONTEXT

Key Events

New York in brief.

1524 Giovanni da Verrazano sails into New York Harbor.
1624 First Dutch settlers establish Nieuw Amsterdam.
1626 Peter Minuit purchases Manhattan for goods worth 60 guilders.
1639 The Broncks settle north of Manhattan.
1646 Village of Breuckelen founded.
1664 Dutch rule ends; Nieuw Amsterdam renamed New York.
1754 King's College (now Columbia University) founded.
1776 Battle for New York begins; fire ravages city.
1783 George Washington's troops march triumphantly down Broadway.
1784 Alexander Hamilton founds the Bank of New York.
1785 City becomes nation's capital.
1789 President Washington inaugurated at Federal Hall.
1792 New York Stock Exchange opens.
1804 New York becomes country's most populous city, with 80,000 inhabitants.
1811 Mayor DeWitt Clinton's grid plan for Manhattan introduced.
1827 Slavery officially abolished in New York State.
1851 *The New-York Daily Times* (now *The New York Times*) launched.
1880 Metropolitan Museum of Art opens to the public.
1883 Brooklyn Bridge opens.
1886 Statue of Liberty unveiled.
1891 Carnegie Hall opens.
1892 Ellis Island opens.
1898 The five boroughs are consolidated into the city of New York.
1900 Electric lights replace gas along lower Broadway.
1902 The Fuller (Flatiron) Building becomes the world's first skyscraper.
1904 New York's first subway line opens.
1908 First ball dropped to celebrate the new year in Times Square.

1911 Fire in the Triangle Shirtwaist Company kills 146.
1913 Woolworth Building completed; Grand Central Terminal opens.
1923 The first Yankee Stadium opens.
1929 Stock market crashes; Museum of Modern Art opens.
1931 George Washington Bridge completed; Empire State Building completed; Whitney Museum opens.
1934 Fiorello La Guardia elected mayor.
1939 New York hosts the World's Fair.
1950 United Nations complex finished.
1953 Robert Moses spearheads building of the Cross Bronx Expressway.
1957 Brooklyn Dodgers baseball team move to Los Angeles; New York Giants move to San Francisco.
1962 New York Mets debut at the Polo Grounds; Philharmonic Hall, first building in Lincoln Center, opens.
1964 Verrazano-Narrows Bridge completed; World's Fair held in Flushing Meadows-Corona Park in Queens.
1970 First New York City Marathon.
1973 World Trade Center completed.
1975 On verge of bankruptcy, city is snubbed by federal government.
1977 Studio 54 opens; 4,000 arrested during citywide blackout.
1989 David N Dinkins elected city's first black mayor.
1993 Bomb explodes in World Trade Center, killing six and injuring 1,000.
2001 Hijackers fly two jets into World Trade Center, killing nearly 3,000.
2004 Statue of Liberty reopens for first time since 9/11.
2009 Yankees and Mets move into new state-of-the-art stadiums.
2010 Mayor Bloomberg is inaugurated as the fourth mayor in New York's history to serve a third term.
2011 Gay marriage is legalised in New York State; the 9/11 Memorial debuts.
2012 The Barclays Center, home to Brooklyn's first pro sports team since 1957, opens.

Architecture

The ups and downs of the world's most famous skyline.

TEXT: ERIC P NASH

Manhattan, of course, is synonymous with skyscrapers. Following advances in iron and steel technology in the middle of the 19th century, and the pressing need for space on an already overcrowded island, New York's architects realised that the only way was up. The race to reach the heavens in the early 20th century was supplanted by the minimalist post-war International Style, which saw a rash of towering glass boxes spread across midtown. Even now, despite less than favourable economic conditions, a surprising number of new high-rises are soaring skyward.

However, those with an architectural interest and an observant eye will be rewarded by the fascinating mix of styles and unexpected details closer to the ground in virtually every corner of the metropolis, from gargoyles crouching on the façade of an early 20th-century apartment building to extravagant cast-iron decoration adorning a humble warehouse. And it's worth remembering that under New York's gleaming exoskeleton of steel and glass lies the heart of a 17th-century Dutch city.

IN CONTEXT

LOWLAND LEGACY

The Dutch influence is still traceable in the downtown web of narrow, winding lanes, reminiscent of the streets of medieval European cities. Because the Cartesian grid that rules the city was laid out by the Commissioners' Plan in 1811, only a few examples of Dutch architecture remain, mostly off the beaten path. One is the 1785 **Dyckman Farmhouse Museum** (4881 Broadway, at 204th Street, 1-212 304 9422, www.dyckmanfarmhouse.org; closed Mon-Thur) in Inwood, Manhattan's northernmost neighbourhood. Its decorative brickwork and gambrel roof reflect the fashion of the late 18th century. The oldest house still standing in the five boroughs, however, is the **Wyckoff Farmhouse Museum** (5816 Clarendon Road, at Ralph Avenue, Flatbush, Brooklyn, 1-718 629 5400, www.wyckoffassociation. org; closed Mon Apr-Oct, Mon & Sun Nov-Mar). Erected around 1652, it's a typical Dutch farmhouse with deep eaves and roughly shingled walls.

In Manhattan, the only building left from pre-Revolutionary times is the stately columned and quoined **St Paul's Chapel** (*see p54*), completed in 1766 (a spire was added in 1796). George Washington, a parishioner here, was officially received in the chapel after his 1789 presidential inauguration. The Enlightenment ideals upon which the nation was founded influenced the church's highly democratic, non-hierarchical layout. **Trinity Church** (*see p54*) of 1846, one of the first and finest Gothic Revival churches in the country, was designed by Richard Upjohn. It's difficult to imagine now that its crocketed, finialed 281-foot spire held sway for decades as the tallest structure in Manhattan.

Holdouts remain from each epoch of the city's architectural history. An outstanding example of Greek Revival from the first half of the 19th century is the 1842 **Federal Hall National Memorial** (*see p52*), the mighty marble colonnaded structure on the site where George Washington took his oath of office. A larger-than-life statue of Washington by the sculptor John Quincy Adams Ward stands in front. The city's most celebrated blocks of Greek Revival townhouses, built in the 1830s, are known

simply as the **Row** (1-13 Washington Square North, between Fifth Avenue & Washington Square West); they're exemplars of the more genteel metropolis of Henry James and Edith Wharton.

Greek Revival gave way to Renaissance-inspired Beaux Arts architecture, which itself reflected the imperial ambitions of a wealthy young nation during the Gilded Age of the late 19th century. Like Emperor Augustus, who boasted that he had found Rome a city of brick and left it a city of marble, the firm of McKim, Mead & White built noble civic monuments and palazzi for the rich. The best-known buildings of the classicist Charles Follen McKim include the main campus of **Columbia University** (*see p106*), begun in the 1890s, and the austere 1906 **Morgan Library** (*see p80*), which underwent an interior renovation completed in 2010. His partner, socialite and bon vivant Stanford White (scandalously murdered by his mistress's husband in 1906 on the roof of the original Madison Square Garden, which he himself designed), conceived more festive spaces, such as the **Metropolitan Club** (1 E 60th Street, at Fifth Avenue) and the luxe Villard Houses of 1882, now part of the **New York Palace Hotel** (*see p243*).

Downtown, the old **Alexander Hamilton US Custom House**, which now houses the National Museum of the American Indian (*see p49*), was built by Cass Gilbert in 1907 and is a symbol of New York Harbor's significance in Manhattan's growth (before 1913, the city's chief source of revenue was customs duties). Gilbert's domed marble edifice is suitably monumental – its carved figures of the Four Continents are by Daniel Chester French, the sculptor of the Lincoln Memorial in Washington, DC. Another Beaux Arts treasure from the city's grand metropolitan era is Carrère & Hastings' sumptuous white marble **New York Public Library** of 1911 (*see p88*), built on the site of a former Revolutionary War battleground. The 1913 travertine-lined **Grand Central Terminal** (*see p91*) remains an elegant transportation hub, thanks to preservationists (including Jacqueline Kennedy Onassis) who saved it from the wrecking ball.

VERTICAL REALITY

Cast-iron architecture peaked in the latter half of the 19th century, coinciding with the Civil War. Iron and steel components freed architects from the bulk, weight and cost of stone, and allowed them to build taller structures. Cast-iron columns – cheap to mass-produce – could support enormous weight. The façades of many Soho buildings, with their intricate details of Italianate columns, were manufactured on assembly lines and could be ordered in pieces from catalogues. This led to an aesthetic of uniform building façades, which had a direct impact on later steel skyscrapers and continues to inform the skyline today. To enjoy one of the most telling vistas of skyscraper history, gaze north from the 1859 **Cooper Union** building (*see p69*) in the East Village, the oldest steel-beam-framed building in America.

The most visible effect of the move towards cast-iron construction was the way it opened up solid-stone façades to expanses of glass. In fact, window-shopping came into vogue in the 1860s. Mrs Lincoln bought the White House china at the **Haughwout Store** (488-492 Broadway, at Broome Street). The 1857 building's Palladian-style façade recalls Renaissance Venice, but its regular, open fenestration was also a portent of the future. (Look carefully: the cast-iron elevator sign is a relic of the world's first working safety passenger elevator, designed by Elisha Graves Otis in 1852.)

Once engineers perfected steel, which is stronger and lighter than iron, and created the interlocking steel-cage construction that distributed the weight of a building over its entire frame, the sky was the limit. New York has one structure by the great Chicago-based innovator Louis Sullivan: the 1898 **Bayard-Condict Building** (65-69 Bleecker Street, between Broadway & Lafayette Street). Though only 13 storeys tall, Sullivan's building, covered with richly decorative terracotta, was one of the earliest to have a purely vertical design rather than one that imitated the horizontal styles of the past. Sullivan wrote that a skyscraper 'must be tall, every inch of it tall… From bottom to top, it is a unit without a single dissenting line.'

The 21-storey **Flatiron Building** (*see p78*), designed by fellow Chicagoan Daniel H Burnham and completed in 1902, is another standout of the era. Its height and modern design combined with traditional masonry decoration – breathtaking even today – was made possible only by its steel-cage construction.

The new century saw a frenzy of skyward construction, resulting in buildings of record-breaking height. When it was built in 1899, the 30-storey, 391-foot **Park Row Building** (15 Park Row, between Ann & Beekman Streets) was the tallest building in the world; by 1931, though, Shreve, Lamb & Harmon's 1,250-foot **Empire State Building** (*see p87*) had more than tripled its record. (For more on the battle for the city's tallest building, *see p367* **Race to the Top**.) Although they were retroactively labelled art deco (such buildings were then simply called 'modern'), the Empire State's setbacks were actually a response to the zoning code of 1916, which required a building's upper storeys to be tapered in order not to block out sunlight and air circulation to the streets. The code engendered some of the city's most fanciful architectural designs, such as the ziggurat-crowned 1926 **Paramount Building** (1501 Broadway, between 43rd & 44th Streets) and the romantically slender spire of the former **Cities Service Building** (70 Pine Street, at Pearl Street), illuminated from within like an enormous rare gem.

OUTSIDE THE BOX

The post-World War II period saw the rise of the International Style, pioneered by such giants as Le Corbusier and Ludwig Mies van der Rohe. The International Style relied on a new set of aesthetics: minimal decoration, clear expression of construction, an honest use of materials and a near-Platonic harmony of proportions. The style's most visible symbol was the all-glass façade, similar to that found on the sleek slab of the **United Nations Headquarters' Secretariat Building** (*see p91*).

Designed by Gordon Bunshaft of Skidmore, Owings & Merrill, **Lever House** (390 Park Avenue, between 53rd & 54th

IN CONTEXT

Streets) became the city's first all-steel-and-glass structure when it was built in 1952. It's almost impossible to imagine the radical vision this glass construction represented on the all-masonry corridor of Park Avenue, because nearly every building since has followed suit. Mies van der Rohe's celebrated bronze-skinned **Seagram Building** (375 Park Avenue, between 52nd & 53rd Streets), which reigns in isolation in its own plaza, is the epitome of the architect's cryptic dicta that 'Less is more' and 'God is in the details'. The detailing on the building is exquisite – the custom-made bolts securing the miniature bronze piers that run the length of the façade must be polished by hand every year to keep them from oxidising and turning green. With this heady combination of grandeur and attention to detail, it's the Rolls-Royce of skyscrapers.

High modernism began to show cracks in its façade during the mid 1960s. By then, New York had built too many such structures in midtown and below. The public had never fully warmed to the undecorated style, and the International Style's sheer arrogance in trying to supplant the traditional city structure didn't endear the movement to anyone. The **MetLife Building** (200 Park Avenue, at 45th Street), originally the Pan Am Building of 1963, was the prime culprit, not so much because of its design (by Walter Gropius of the Bauhaus) but because of its presumptuous location, straddling Park Avenue and looming over Grand Central. There was even a plan to raze Grand Central and construct a twin Pan Am in its place. The International Style had obviously reached its end when Philip Johnson, instrumental in defining the movement with his book *The International Style* (co-written with Henry-Russell Hitchcock), began disparaging the aesthetic as 'glass-boxitis'.

New blood was needed. A glimmer on the horizon was provided by Boston architect Hugh Stubbins' triangle-topped **Citigroup Center** (Lexington Avenue, between 53rd & 54th Streets), which utilised contemporary engineering (the building cantilevers almost magically on high stilts above street level) while harking

back to the decorative tops of yesteryear. Sly old Johnson turned the tables on everyone with the heretical Chippendale crown on his **Sony Building**, originally the AT&T Building (350 Madison Avenue, between 55th & 56th Streets), a bold throwback to decoration for its own sake.

Postmodernism provided a theoretical basis for a new wave of buildings that mixed past and present, often taking cues from the environs. Some notable examples include Helmut Jahn's **425 Lexington Avenue** (between 43rd & 44th Streets) of 1988; David Childs's retro diamond-tipped **Worldwide Plaza** (825 Eighth Avenue, between 49th & 50th Streets) of 1989; and the honky-tonk agglomeration of Skidmore, Owings & Merrill's **Bertelsmann Building** (1540 Broadway, between 45th & 46th Streets) of 1990. But even postmodernism became old hat after a while: too many architects relied on fussy fenestration and passive commentary on other styles, and too few were creating vital new building façades.

The electronic spectacle of **Times Square** (*see p82*) provided one possible direction for architects. Upon seeing the myriad electric lights of Times Square in 1922, British wit GK Chesterton remarked: 'What a glorious garden of wonder this would be, to anyone who was lucky enough to be unable to read.' The Crossroads of the World continues to be at the cybernetic cutting edge, with the 120-foot-tall, quarter-acre-in-area NASDAQ sign; the real-time stock tickers and jumbo TV screens; and the news ticker wrapping around the original 1904 New York Times HQ, **1 Times Square** (between Broadway & Seventh Avenue). The public's appetite for new images seems so insatiable that a building's fixed profile no longer suffices here – only an ever-shifting electronic skin will do.

CONTEMPORARY VISION

Early 21st-century architecture is moving beyond applied symbolism to radical new forms, facilitated by computer-based design methods. A stellar example is Kohn Pedersen Fox's stainless steel and glass 'vertical campus', the **Baruch College Academic Complex** (55 Lexington Avenue,

Race to the Top

How NYC's architects egged each other onwards and upwards.

For nearly half a century after its 1846 completion, the 281-foot steeple of Richard Upjohn's Gothic Revival **Trinity Church** (*see p54*) reigned in lonely serenity at the foot of Wall Street as the tallest structure in Manhattan. The church was finally topped in 1890 by the since-demolished, 348-foot **New York World Building**. But it wasn't until the turn of the century that New York's architects started to reach for the skies. So began a mad rush to the top, with building after building capturing the title of the world's tallest.

When it was completed in 1899, the 30-storey, 391-foot **Park Row Building** (15 Park Row, between Ann & Beekman Streets) became the tallest building in the world. However, its record was shattered by the 612-foot **Singer Building** in 1908 (which, in 1968, became the tallest building ever to be demolished); the 52-storey, 700-foot **Metropolitan Life Tower** (*see p78*) of 1909; and the 793-foot **Woolworth Building** (*see p56*), Cass Gilbert's Gothic 1913 masterpiece.

The Woolworth stood in solitary splendour until skyscraper construction reached a crescendo in the late 1920s, with a famed three-way race. The now largely forgotten **Bank of Manhattan Building** (now known as the Trump Building) at 40 Wall Street was briefly the record-holder, at 71 storeys and 927 feet in 1930. Soon after, William Van Alen, the architect of the **Chrysler Building** (*see p91*), unveiled his secret weapon: a 'vertex', a spire of chrome nickel steel put together inside the dome and raised from within, which brought the building's height to 1,046 feet. But then, 13 months later, Van Alen's homage to the Automobile Age was itself outstripped by Shreve, Lamb & Harmon's 1,250-foot **Empire State Building** (*see p87*). With its broad base, narrow shaft and needled crown, it

Chrysler Building.

remains the quintessential skyscraper, and one of the most famous buildings in the world.

Incredibly, there were no challengers for the distinction of New York's – and the world's – tallest building for more than 40 years, until the 110-storey, 1,362- and 1,368-foot **Twin Towers** of Minoru Yamasaki's World Trade Center were completed in 1973. They were trumped by Chicago's Sears Tower a year later, but reigned as the city's tallest buildings until 11 September 2001, when the New York crown reverted to the Empire State Building. However, the World Trade Center has since regained the title. In spring 2012, **1 World Trade Center** (formerly known as the Freedom Tower), designed by David Childs of Skidmore, Owings & Merrill to replace the Twin Towers, overtook the ESB. By early 2013, it will surpass the original towers at a height of 1,776 feet. Don't look down...

IN CONTEXT

between 24th & 25th Streets). The phantasmagoric designs that curve and dart in sculptural space are so beyond the timid window-dressing of postmodernism that they deserve a new label.

Frank Gehry's ten-storey, white-glass mirage of a building in Chelsea, completed in 2007, is emblematic of the radical reworking of the New York cityscape. Gehry's first office building in New York, the headquarters for Barry Diller's **InterActiveCorp** (555 W 18th Street, at West Side Highway) comprises tilting glass volumes that resemble a fully rigged tall ship. Change is quite literally in the air in this area. Once an ugly-duckling neighbourhood of warehouses and industrial buildings, it is being transformed by the **High Line**, a former elevated railroad viaduct that has been reconceived as a cutting-edge urban park (*see p82* **Profile**). Renzo Piano broke ground on the downtown satellite of the **Whitney Museum of American Art** (*see p100*) at the southern end in May 2011. The museum, which will have double the floor space of the existing museum uptown, is expected to be finished in 2015. Down south, the **Urban Glass House** (330 Spring Street, at Washington Street), one of the late Philip Johnson's last designs, sprang up in 2006 amid Tribeca's hulking industrial edifices. The mini-skyscraper is a multiplication of his iconic Glass House in New Canaan, Connecticut.

Midtown West has recently become an unlikely hotbed of new construction, with its architectural attractions enhanced in 2006 by Norman Foster's elegant, 46-storey, 597-foot crystalline addition to the art deco base of the **Hearst Magazine Building** (300 W 57th Street, at Eighth Avenue). The structure is a breathtaking combination of old and new, with the massive triangular struts of the tower penetrating the façade of the base and opening up great airy spaces within. Even as the age of superblock modernism seems to be coming to a close, a new era of green, eco-conscious architecture is emerging. Cook + Fox's **Bank of America Tower** at 1 Bryant Park (Sixth Avenue, between 42nd & 43rd Streets) bills itself as the greenest skyscraper in the city, with

torqued, glass facets reaching 54 storeys. The structure has a thermal storage system, daylight dimmers, green roofs and double-wall construction to reduce heat build-up. Renzo Piano's 2007 tower for the *New York Times* at **620 Eighth Avenue** (between 40th & 41st Streets) also offers such green amenities as automatic shades that respond to the heat of the sun and recycled air. The glass-walled design is a literal representation of the paper's desire for transparency in reporting; the lobby moss garden with birch trees is also an interesting metaphor for an old-fashioned, paper-based industry in the computer age.

Further north, and among the more controversial facelifts of recent years, is Brad Cloepfil's renovation of Edward Durell Stone's 1964 modernism meets Venetian palazzo, **2 Columbus Circle**, originally the home of A&P heir Huntington Hartford's Gallery of Modern Art. In the same way that the gallery's collection of mostly figurative painting was seen as reactionary in the face of the abstract art movement, Stone's quotation of a historicist style was laughed into apostasy. However, Stone's work is being re-evaluated as a precursor to postmodernism, and many 20th-century architecture enthusiasts lamented the loss of the original façade after a lengthy, unsuccessful battle by the Landmarks Preservation Commission. The building is now the home of the Museum of Arts & Design (*see p104*).

BEST-LAID PLANS

Some of New York's more ambitious architectural projects have been significantly scaled back in the face of new economic realities. The World Trade Center site, conceived by Daniel Libeskind, saw frustratingly little progress in the years after the tragedy of 9/11. The 16-acre site's overseers, the Port Authority of New York and New Jersey, reported in 2008 that construction of the 26 interrelated projects was years behind schedule and billions of dollars over its $16 billion budget. However, it seems to be back on track: the steel structure of David Childs's centrepiece 1,776-foot tower, **1 World Trade Center** (formerly known as the Freedom Tower), with a revised completion date of early 2014, had reached 105 storeys by autumn 2012, and the **9/11 Memorial Plaza** opened in time for the tenth anniversary of the Twin Towers' fall. Santiago Calatrava's spectacular plans for a shimmering, subterranean World Trade Center Transportation Hub, linking the suburban PATH trains to the subway, no longer features retractable roof wings, but the ribbed ceiling will still let in the sun with a skylight. The station is expected to be completed in 2015. *See also p55* **Rebuilding Ground Zero**.

Scaling back seems to be a key phrase in the second decade of the 21st century, and grandiose schemes have settled earthward. The transformation of Brooklyn's **Atlantic Yards** (*see p121*) into a mega-development started boldly as an architectural site for Frank Gehry and Enrique Norten, but Gehry's design for the Nets' arena was rejected as too expensive. Realised by SHoP Architects, the 19,000-seat **Barclays Center** (*see p284, p327*), featuring a rust-coloured steel-panelled façade, was officially unveiled in autumn 2012, but the developer had yet to break ground on the planned residential buildings. The proposed $1.5 billion renovation of **Lincoln Center** was also kept in check, leaving a team of top-notch architects to work with what was already there. Diller Scofidio + Renfro, one of the most creative teams on the scene, turned the travertine marble façade of Alice Tully Hall into a show window, integrating inside and out with glass walls; elsewhere, Billie Tsien and Tod Williams transformed a public atrium across from Lincoln Center, between Broadway and Columbus, and 62nd and 63rd Streets, into a sky-lit 'theatrical garden', lined with ferns, moss and flowering vines, for buying tickets and sipping refreshments.

Seeing no end in sight to growth and profits, developers tend to overbuild commercial space until there's a bust – plans for the World Trade Center site alone call for new office space that equates to five times the amount in downtown Atlanta, but there have been difficulties attracting tenants. Setbacks have also met Pritzker Prize-winner Jean Nouvel's exciting plan for the sloped, crystalline **Tower Verre**, with an exoskeleton of irregularly crossing beams, that is planned to rise next door to the Museum of Modern Art. Initially proposed to reach 1,250 feet (the same height as the Empire State Building), the tower was opposed by activists who feared its shadow would loom over Central Park and it was rejected by the city's Planning Commission. After 200 feet were snipped off the top, the plan received the green light and should be a glamorous presence on the city skyline.

In a reversal of the city's historical pattern of development, much of the money is migrating downtown. The **Blue Building**, Bernard Tschumi's multifaceted, blue glass-walled condominium, is a startling breakaway from the low-rise brick buildings that make up the Lower East Side. Also noteworthy is the Japanese firm SANAA's **New Museum of Contemporary Art** (*see p66*); its asymmetrically staggered boxy volumes covered in aluminum mesh shake up the traditional streetfront of the Bowery. A block north, at **257 Bowery** (between Stanton & Houston Streets), Norman Foster's slender gallery building for Sperone Westwater art dealers – complete with a 12- by 20-foot lift that doubles as a moving exhibition space – has taken shape in a narrow gap. Meanwhile, Frank Gehry's boldly named 76-storey **New York by Gehry** (formerly known as the Beekman Tower), just south of City Hall, is now the tallest residential tower in the western hemisphere; at 870 feet, its curled and warped stainless-steel façade has the unmistakable stamp of its creator. However, it will soon be topped by French architect Christian de Portzamparc's glassy midtown titan **One57** (157 W 57th Street, between Sixth & Seventh Avenues), which will reach more than 1,000 feet.

To keep up with what's going up in New York, visit the **AIA Center for Architecture** (*see p72*), the **Skyscraper Museum** (*see p52*) and the **Storefront for Art & Architecture** (97 Kenmare Street, between Mulberry Street & Cleveland Place, 1-212 431 5795, www.storefrontnews.org, closed Mon & Sun), a non-profit organisation that hosts a programme of exhibitions, talks, screenings and more.

IN CONTEXT

Essential Information

Getting Around

ARRIVING & LEAVING

By air

Three major airports serve the New York City area, but none of them is particularly close or convenient. For a list of transport services between New York City and its major airports, call 1-800 247 7433. **Public transport** is the cheapest method of travelling between the city and the airports, but it can be frustrating and time-consuming – especially during rush hour.

Private bus or van services are usually the best bargains, but you need to allow extra time as vans will be picking up other passengers. As well as the choices for each airport below, blue **SuperShuttle** (1-800 258 3826, www.supershuttle.com) vans offer door-to-door service between NYC and the major airports.

Yellow cabs can be flagged on the street or picked up from designated locations at airports. You may also reserve a car service in advance to pick you up or drop you off (*see p374*). Avoid car-service drivers and unlicensed 'gypsy cabs' at the baggage-claim areas, outside the terminal or on city streets – it's illegal to solicit customers.

Airports

John F Kennedy International Airport *1-718 244 4444, www.panynj.gov/airports/jfk.html.* The subway is the cheapest option, but, depending on your destination, it can be time-consuming. The **AirTrain** ($5) from JFK links to the A train at Howard Beach or the E, J and Z trains at Sutphin Boulevard-Archer Avenue ($2.50). For further information, visit www.airtrainjfk.com. Private bus and van services are a good compromise between value and convenience – for **SuperShuttle**, *see above*. **New York Airport Service** buses (1-212 875 8200, www.nyairportservice.com) run frequently between Manhattan and JFK (one way $15, round trip $25) from early morning to late night, with stops near Grand Central Terminal (Park Avenue, between 41st & 42nd Streets), near Penn Station (33rd Street, at Seventh

Avenue), inside the Port Authority Bus Terminal (*see below*) and outside a number of Midtown hotels (for an extra charge). A **yellow cab** to Manhattan will charge a flat $52.50 fare, plus toll (usually $5) and tip (15 per cent is the norm). The fare to JFK from Manhattan is not a set fare, but is usually roughly the same. For taxi rates, *see p374*.

La Guardia Airport *1-718 533 3400, www.panynj.gov/airports/laguardia.html.* Seasoned New Yorkers take the **M60 bus** ($2.50), which runs between the airport and 106th Street at Broadway. The ride takes 40-60mins (depending on traffic) and runs 24/7. The route crosses Manhattan at 125th Street in Harlem. Get off at Lexington Avenue for the 4, 5 and 6 trains; at Malcolm X Boulevard (Lenox Avenue) for the 2 and 3; or at St Nicholas Avenue for the A, B, C and D trains. You can also disembark on Broadway at 116th or 110th Street for the 1 train. Less time-consuming options include **SuperShuttle** (*see left*) and **New York Airport Service** buses (1-212 875 8200, www.nyairport service.com), which run frequently between Manhattan and La Guardia (one way $12, round trip $21). **Taxis and car services** charge about $30, plus toll and tip.

Newark Liberty International Airport *1-973 961 6000, www.panynj.gov/airports/newark-liberty.html.* Newark has good mass transit access to NYC. The best bet is the 30min, $12.50 trip by **New Jersey Transit** to or from Penn Station. The airport's monorail, **AirTrain Newark** (www.air trainnewark.com), is linked to . the NJ Transit and Amtrak train systems. Bus services operated by **Coach USA** (1-877 894 9155, www.coachusa.com) run between Newark and Manhattan, stopping outside Grand Central Station (41st Street, between Park & Lexington Avenues), and inside the Port Authority Bus Terminal (one way $16, round trip $28); buses leave every 15-30mins. A **car or taxi** runs at $60-$75, plus toll and tip.

By bus

Buses aren't very quick and can be uncomfortable, but you probably won't need to book. **Greyhound** (1-800 231 2222, www.greyhound. com) offers long-distance bus travel to destinations across North America. The company has recently responded to the growth of cheaper independent bus companies with its **BoltBus** (1-877 265 8287, www.boltbus.com), which is booked online, serves several East Coast cities and departs from central locations. As well as a fleet of new coaches and free Wi-Fi, it offers low fares. **New Jersey Transit** (1-973 275 5555, www.njtransit.com) runs a bus service to nearly everywhere in the Garden State and parts of New York State. Finally, **Peter Pan** (1-800 343 9999, www.peter panbus.com) runs extensive services to cities across the North-east; its tickets are also valid on Greyhound buses. Most out-of-town buses come and go from the Port Authority Bus Terminal (*see below*).

George Washington Bridge Bus Station *4211 Broadway, between 178th & 179th Streets, Washington Heights (1-212 564 8484, www.panynj.gov/bus-terminals/george-washington-bridge-bus-station.html). Subway A, 1 to 181st Street.* **Map** p409 B6. A few bus lines serving New Jersey and Rockland County are based here.

Port Authority Bus Terminal *625 Eighth Avenue, between 40th & 42nd Streets, Garment District (1-212 564 8484, www.panynj.gov/bus-terminals/port-authority-bus-terminal.html). Subway A, C, E to 42nd Street-Port Authority.* **Map** p410 S13. This terminus is the hub for many commuter and long-distance services. Though it's perfectly safe, watch out for the occasional pickpocket, especially at night, and note that the food concessions don't open until around 7am.

By car

If you drive into the city, you may face delays, from 15 minutes to two hours, at bridge and tunnel crossings (check www.nyc.gov and

ESSENTIAL INFORMATION

www.panynj.gov). Tune in to **WINS** (1010 AM) for traffic reports. Tolls range from $5.33 to $15. Try to time your arrival and departure against the commuter flow. If you drive to NYC, consider leaving your car in a garage. Street parking is problematic and car theft not unheard of. Garages are expensive but plentiful. If you want to park for less than $15 a day, try a garage outside Manhattan and take public transport into the city.

By rail

America's national rail service is run by **Amtrak** (1-800 872 7245, www.amtrak.com). Nationwide routes are slow and infrequent (yet full of character), but there are some good fast services linking the eastern seaboard cities. (For commuter rail services, *see below* **Public transport: Rail**.)

Grand Central Terminal *42nd to 44th Streets, between Vanderbilt & Lexington Avenues, Midtown East. Subway S, 4, 5, 6, 7 to 42nd Street-Grand Central.* **Map** p404 E24.
Grand Central is home to Metro-North, which runs trains to more than 100 stations in New York State and Connecticut.
Penn Station *31st to 33rd Streets, between Seventh & Eighth Avenues, Garment District. Subway A, C, E, 1, 2, 3 to 34th Street-Penn Station.* **Map** p404 D25.
Amtrak, Long Island Rail Road and New Jersey Transit trains depart from this terminal.

PUBLIC TRANSPORT

Changes to schedules can occur at short notice, especially at weekends – check the MTA's website before travelling and pay attention to the posters on subway station walls and announcements you may hear in trains and on subway platforms.

Metropolitan Transportation Authority (MTA) *511 local, 1-877 690 5116 outside New York State, 1-212 878 7000 international, www.mta.info.*
The MTA runs the subway and bus lines, as well as services to points outside Manhattan. News of service interruptions and MTA maps are on its website. Be warned: since 9/11, backpacks, handbags and large containers may be subject to random searches.

Fares & tickets

Although you can pay with coins (no dollar bills) on the buses, you'll need a **MetroCard** to enter the subway system. You can buy them from booths or vending machines in the stations; from the Official NYC Information Center; from the New York Transit Museum in Brooklyn or Grand Central Terminal; and from many hotels. The standard fare across the subway and bus network on a MetroCard is $2.50 (though if you buy a $5 MetroCard, you'll receive a five per cent bonus, *see below*). Free transfers between the subway and buses are available only with a MetroCard (for bus-to-bus transfers on cash fares, *see right*). Up to four people can use a **pay-per-ride MetroCard**, sold in denominations from $5 to $80.
If you put $5 or more on the card, you'll receive a five per cent bonus – or 25 cents for every $5 – thus reducing the cost of each ride. However, if you're planning to use the subway or buses often, an **Unlimited Ride MetroCard** is great value. These cards are offered in two denominations, available at station vending machines but not at booths: a seven-day pass ($30) and a 30-day pass ($112). All are good for unlimited rides within those periods, but you can't share a card with your travel companions.

Subway

Cleaner and safer than it has been for decades, the city's subway system is one of the world's largest and cheapest, with a flat fare of $2.50. Trains run around the clock. If you are travelling late at night, board the train from the designated off-peak waiting area, usually near the middle of the platform; this is more secure than the ends of the platform, which are often less populated in the wee hours.
Use the same common-sense safety precautions on the subway that you would in any urban environment. Hold your bag with the opening facing you, keep your wallet in a front pocket and keep valuables and electronic gadgets out of sight. Petty crime levels increase during the holidays.
Stations are most often named after the street on which they're located. Entrances are marked with a green and white globe (open 24 hours) or a red and white globe (limited hours). Many stations have separate entrances for the uptown and downtown platforms

– look before you pay. Trains are identified by letters or numbers, colour-coded according to the line on which they run. Local trains stop at every station on the line; express trains stop at major stations only.
The most current subway map is reprinted at the back of this guide (*see pp414-416*); you can also ask MTA workers in service booths for a free copy, or refer to enlarged subway maps displayed in each subway station.

City buses

White and blue MTA buses are usually the best way to travel crosstown and a pleasant way to travel up- or downtown, as long as you're not in a hurry. They have a digital destination sign on the front, along with a route number preceded by a letter (M for Manhattan, B for Brooklyn, Bx for the Bronx, Q for Queens and S for Staten Island). Maps are posted on most buses and at all subway stops; they're also available from the **Official NYC Information Center** (*see p382*). The Manhattan bus map is also reprinted in this guide; *see p413*. All local buses are equipped with wheelchair lifts.
The $2.50 fare is payable with a MetroCard (*see above*) or exact change (coins only; no pennies or dollar bills). MetroCards allow for an automatic transfer from bus to bus, and between bus and subway. If you pay cash, and you're travelling uptown or downtown and want to go crosstown (or vice versa), ask the driver for a transfer when you get on – you'll be given a ticket for use on the second leg of your journey, valid for two hours. MTA's express buses usually head to the outer boroughs ($6 fare).

Rail

The following commuter trains serve NY's hinterland.

Long Island Rail Road *511 local, 1-718 217 5477 outside New York State, www.mta.info/lirr.*
Provides rail services from Penn Station, Brooklyn and Queens to towns throughout Long Island.
Metro-North Railroad *511 local, 1-212 532 4900 outside New York State, www.mta.info/mnr.*
Commuter trains serve towns north of Manhattan and leave from Grand Central Terminal.
New Jersey Transit *1-973 275 5555, www.njtransit.com.*
Service from Penn Station reaches

Service from Penn Station reaches most of New Jersey, some points in New York State and Philadelphia.
PATH Trains 1-800 234 7284, www.panynj.gov/path.
PATH (Port Authority Trans-Hudson) trains run from six stations in Manhattan to various places across the Hudson in New Jersey, including Hoboken, Jersey City and Newark. The 24-hour service costs $2.25 (pay by MetroCard or single-fare ticket available from PATH station vending machines).

Boat

NY Waterway (1-800 533 3779, www.nywaterway.com) operates a water-transportation service that connects Manhattan to Queens, Brooklyn and some New Jersey cities. The **East River Ferry** runs between Midtown East at 34th Street and Downtown Manhattan at Pier 11 via Long Island City in Queens and Greenpoint, Williamsburg and Dumbo in Brooklyn (6.45am-9pm Mon-Fri; 9am-9pm Sat, Sun; tickets from $4 one way). The line extends to Governors Island (see p49) on weekends in the summer. On the West Side, **Hudson River Ferries** link Manhattan at 39th Street, 14th Street and Wall Street to destinations in New Jersey, including Hoboken and Jersey City (5.45am-10pm Mon-Fri; times vary on weekends; tickets from $21.50 one-way). A surcharge applies if you are travelling with your bike.

In addition to its hop-on hop-off service and tours (see p43), **New York Water Taxi** (1-212 742 1969, www.nywatertaxi.com) offers a popular shuttle service connecting Pier 11 in Manhattan and IKEA in Red Hook, Brooklyn (2-8pm Mon-Fri; 11.20am-9.20pm Sat, Sun). The $5 fare is waived on weekends and for children under 12.

TAXIS

Yellow cabs are rarely in short supply in New York, except at rush hour and during unpleasant weather. If the centre light atop the taxi is lit, the cab is available and should stop if you flag it down. Get in and then tell the driver where you're going (New Yorkers generally give cross-streets rather than addresses). By law, taxis cannot refuse to take you anywhere inside the five boroughs or to New York airports. Use only yellow medallion (licensed) cabs; avoid unregulated 'gypsy cabs'.

Taxis will carry up to four passengers for the same price: $2.50 plus 50¢ per fifth of a mile or per minute idling, with an extra 50¢ charge (a new state tax), another 50¢ from 8pm to 6am and a $1 surcharge during rush hour (4-8pm Mon-Fri). The average fare for a three-mile ride is about $14, depending on the time and traffic.

Not all drivers know their way around the city, so it helps if you know where you're going. If you have a problem, take down the medallion and driver's numbers, posted on the partition. Always ask for a receipt – there's a meter number on it. To complain or to trace lost property, call the **Taxi & Limousine Commission** (1-212 227 0700, 8am-4pm Mon-Fri) or visit www.nyc.gov/taxi. Tip 15-20 per cent. All taxis are now required to accept major credit cards.

Late at night, cabs tend to stick to fast-flowing routes. Try the avenues and key streets (Canal, Houston, 14th, 23rd, 34th, 42nd, 57th, 72nd and 86th). Bridge and tunnel exits are good for a steady flow of taxis returning from airports.

Car services

Car services are regulated by the **Taxi & Limousine Commission** (see above) and make only pre-arranged pick-ups. Don't try to hail one, and be wary of those that offer you a ride. The following companies will pick you up anywhere in the city, at any time, for a set fare.

Carmel 1-212 666 6666.
Dial 7 1-212 777 7777.
GroundLink 1-877 227 7260.

DRIVING

Car hire

You need a credit card to rent a car in the US, and usually must be at least 25 years old. Car hire is cheaper in the city's outskirts, and in New Jersey and Connecticut, than in Manhattan. Companies outside New York State exclude loss/damage waiver insurance from their rates. Rental companies in New York State are required by law to insure their own cars (the renter pays the first $100 in damage to the vehicle). UK residents may find cheaper rental insurance at www.insurance4car hire.com. In NYC, car hire companies add 19.875 per cent in taxes.

If you just want a car for a couple of hours, **Zipcar** (US: 1-866 494 7227, www.zipcar.com; UK: 0333 240

9000, www.zipcar.co.uk) is a cost-effective option, especially if you already have a membership.
Aamcar 1-888 500 8460, www.aamcar.com.
Alamo US: 1-877 222 9075, www.alamo.com. UK: 0871 384 1086, www.alamo.co.uk.
Avis US: 1-800 230 4898, www.avis.com. UK: 0844 581 0147, www.avis.co.uk.
Budget US: 1-800 527 0700, www.budget.com. UK: 0844 581 2231, www.budget.co.uk.
Dollar US: 1-800 800 4000, www.dollar.com. UK: 0800 252 897, www.dollar.co.uk.
Enterprise US: 1-800 261 7331, www.enterprise.com. UK: 020 3468 7685, www.enterprise.co.uk.
Hertz US: 1-800 654 3131, www.hertz.com. UK: 0843 309 3099, www.hertz.co.uk.
National US: 1-877 222 9058, www.nationalcar.com. UK: 0845 120 2071, www.nationalcar.co.uk.
Thrifty US: 1-800 847 4389, www.thrifty.com. UK: 01494 751500, www.thrifty.co.uk.

Parking

Make sure you read parking signs and never park within 15 feet of a fire hydrant (to avoid a $115 ticket and/or having your car towed). Parking is off-limits on most streets for at least a few hours daily. The **Department of Transportation** provides information on daily changes to regulations (dial 311). If precautions fail, call 1-212 971 0771 or 1-212 971 0772 for Manhattan towing and impoundment information; go to www.nyc.gov for phone numbers in other boroughs.

CYCLING

Aside from Central Park, and along the wide bike paths around the perimeter of Manhattan, biking in the city is only recommended for seasoned urban riders. But zipping through bumper-to-bumper traffic holds allure for those with the requisite skills and gear. For maps, cycling organisations and bike rental, see p332.

WALKING

One of the best ways to take in NYC is on foot. Most of the streets are laid out in a grid pattern and are relatively easy to navigate.

GUIDED TOURS

See pp40-45 **Tour New York**.

Resources A-Z

ADDRESSES

Addresses follow the standard US format. The room, apartment or suite number usually appears after the street address, followed on the next line by the name of the city and the zip code.

AGE RESTRICTIONS

Buying/drinking alcohol 21
Driving 16
Sex 17
Smoking 18

ATTITUDE & ETIQUETTE

New Yorkers have a reputation for being rude, but 'outspoken' is more apt: they are unlikely to hold their tongues in the face of injustice or inconvenience, but they can also be very welcoming and will often go out of their way to offer advice or help.

Some old-fashioned restaurants and swanky clubs operate dress codes (jacket and tie for men, for example, or no baseball caps or ripped jeans – phone to check). However, on the whole, anything goes sartorially.

BUSINESS

Courier services

DHL *1-800 225 5345, www.dhl.com.*
FedEx *1-800 463 3339, www.fedex.com.*
UPS *1-800 742 5877, www.ups.com.*

Messenger services

A to Z Couriers *1-212 253 6500, www.atozcouriers.com.*

Breakaway *1-212 947 7777, www.breakawaycourier.com.*

Office services

All-Language Translation Services *77 W 55th Street, between Fifth & Sixth Avenues, Midtown (1-212 986 1688, www.all-language.com). Subway F to 57th Street.* **Open** 24hrs daily, by appt only. **Credit** AmEx, Disc, MC, V. **Map** p405 E22.
Copy Specialist *44 E 21st Street, at Park Avenue South, Gramercy Park (1-212 533 7560, www.thecopyspecialist.com). Subway N, R, 6 to 23rd Street.* **Open** 8.30am-7pm Mon-Fri; Sat by appt. **Credit** AmEx, DC, MC, V. **Map** p404 E26. **Other locations** 71 W 23rd Street between Fifth & Sixth Avenues, Flatiron District (1-646 336 6999).
FedEx Office *1-800 463 3339, www.fedex.com.* There are outposts of this efficient computer and copy centre all over the city; many are open 24 hours.

CONSUMER

New York City Department of Consumer Affairs *Consumer Services Division, 9th Floor, 42 Broadway, New York, NY 10004 (311 local, 1-212 639 9675 outside New York State, www.nyc.gov/dca).* File complaints on consumer-related matters by mail or phone. The non-emergency, 24-hour three-digit number, 311, can also be used to get answers and register complaints about city issues, from parking regulations to real-estate auctions and consumer tips.

CUSTOMS

US Customs allows foreigners to bring in $100 worth of gifts (the limit is $800 for returning Americans) without paying duty. One carton of 200 cigarettes (or 50 cigars) and one litre of liquor (spirits) are allowed. Plants, meat and fresh produce of any kind cannot be brought into the country. You will have to fill out a form if you carry more than $10,000 in currency. You will be handed a white form on your inbound flight to fill in, confirming that you haven't exceeded any of these allowances.

If you need to bring prescription drugs into the US, make sure the container is clearly marked, and bring your doctor's statement or a prescription. Marijuana, cocaine and most opiate derivatives, along with a number of other drugs and chemicals, are not permitted: the possession is punishable by a stiff fine and/or imprisonment. Check in with the US Customs and Border Protection Service (www.cbp.gov) before you arrive if you're unsure.

HM Revenue & Customs allows returning visitors to the UK to bring £390 worth of 'gifts, souvenirs and other goods' into the country duty-free, along with the usual duty-free goods.

DISABLED

Under New York City law, all facilities constructed after 1987 must provide complete access for the disabled, including entrances and restrooms. In 1990, the Americans with Disabilities Act made the same requirement federal law. In the wake of this legislation, many older buildings have added

ESSENTIAL INFORMATION

disabled-access features. There has been widespread (though imperfect) compliance with the law; call ahead to check facilities. New York City can still be very challenging for disabled visitors. For information on accessible cultural institutions, contact the **Mayor's Office for People with Disabilities** (*see below*). All Broadway theatres are equipped with devices for the hearing-impaired; call **Sound Associates** (1-888 772 7686, www.soundassociates.com) for more information. For the visually impaired, **HAI** (1-212 575 7676, www.hainyc.org) offers live audio descriptions of selected theatre performances. You can find a list of audio-described, open-captioned and sign-interpreted shows on the website of the **Theatre Development Fund** (1-212 912 9770, www.tdf.org). **Hands On** (1-212 740 3087, www.handson.org) also provides interpreter services for the deaf and hard of hearing. **Telecharge** (1-212 239 6200, www.telecharge.com) reserves tickets for wheelchair seating in Broadway and Off Broadway venues.

Lighthouse International
111 E 59th Street, between Park & Lexington Avenues, Upper East Side (1-212 821 9200, 1-212 821 9384 store, www.lighthouse.org). Subway N, R to Lexington Avenue-59th Street; 4, 5, 6 to 59th Street. **Open** *9am-5pm Mon-Fri. Store 10am-6pm Mon-Fri.* **Map** *p405 E29.*
In addition to running a store that sells handy items for the vision-impaired, Lighthouse provides helpful information for blind people (residents and visitors).
Mayor's Office for People with Disabilities
2nd Floor, 100 Gold Street, between Frankfort & Spruce Streets, Financial District (1-212 788 2830). Subway J, Z to Chambers Street; 4, 5, 6 to Brooklyn Bridge-City Hall. **Open** *9am-5pm Mon-Fri.* **Map** *p402 F32.*
This city office provides a broad range of services for the disabled.
New York Society for the Deaf
315 Hudson Street, between Vandam & Spring Streets, Soho (1-212 366 0066, www.fegs.org). Subway C, E to Spring Street; 1 to Houston Street. **Open** *8.30am-7pm Mon-Thur; 8.30am-5pm Fri.* **Map** *p403 D30.*
Information and a range of services for the deaf and hearing-impaired.
Society for Accessible Travel & Hospitality
1-212 447 7284, www.sath.org.

This non-profit group educates the public about travel facilities for people with disabilities, and promotes travel for the disabled. Membership ($49/yr; $29 reductions) includes access to an information service and a quarterly newsletter.

DRUGS

Possession of marijuana can result in anything from a $100 fine and a warning (for a first offence, 25g or less) to felony charges and prison time (for greater amounts and/or repeat offenders). Penalties, ranging from class B misdemeanours to class C felonies, are greater for the sale and cultivation of marijuana.

Possession of 'controlled substances' (cocaine, ecstasy, heroin, etc) is not taken lightly, and charges come with stiff penalties – especially if you are convicted of possession with intent to sell. Convictions carry anything from a mandatory one- to three-year prison sentence to a maximum of 25 years.

ELECTRICITY

The US uses 110-120V, 60-cycle alternating current rather than the 220-240V, 50-cycle AC used in Europe. The transformers that power or recharge newer electronic devices such as laptops are designed to handle either current and may need nothing more than an adaptor for the wall outlet. Other appliances may also require a power converter. Adaptors and converters can be purchased at airport shops, pharmacies, department stores and at branches of electronics chain Radio Shack (www.radioshack.com).

EMBASSIES & CONSULATES

Check the phone book for a list of consulates and embassies. *See also p375* **Travel Advice.**

Australia *1-212 351 6500.*
Canada *1-212 596 1628.*
Great Britain *1-212 745 0200.*
Ireland *1-212 319 2555.*
New Zealand *1-212 832 4038.*

EMERGENCIES

In an emergency only, dial **911** for an ambulance, the police or the fire department, or call the operator (dial 0). For hospitals, *see right*; for helplines, *see right*; for the police, *see p380.*

GAY & LESBIAN

For more gay and lesbian resources, including the Lesbian, Gay, Bisexual & Transgender Community Center, *see pp264-273.*

Gay, Lesbian, Bisexual & Transgender National Hotline
1-888 843 4564, www.glbtnational helpcenter.org. **Open** *4pm-midnight Mon-Fri; noon-5pm Sat.*
This phone service offers excellent peer counselling, legal referrals, details of gay and lesbian organisations, and information on bars, restaurants and hotels. Younger callers can contact the toll-free GLBT National Youth Talk Line (1-800 246 7743, 4pm-midnight Mon-Fri; noon-5pm Sat).

HEALTH

Public health care is virtually nonexistent in the US, and private health care is very expensive. Make sure you have comprehensive medical insurance before you leave. For HIV testing and HIV/AIDS counselling, *see right* **Helplines.** For a list of hospitals, *see below.*
For other hospitals, consult the *Yellow Pages* directory.

Accident & emergency

You will be billed for any emergency treatment. Call your travel insurance company before seeking treatment to find out which hospitals accept your insurance. The following hospitals have emergency rooms:

Downtown Hospital
83 Gold Street, between Spruce & Beekman Streets, Financial District (1-212 312 5000). Subway 4, 5, 6 to Brooklyn Bridge-City Hall. **Map** *p402 F32.*
Mount Sinai Hospital *Madison Avenue, at 100th Street, Upper East Side (1-212 241 6500). Subway 6 to 103rd Street.* **Map** *p406 E16.*
New York-Presbyterian Hospital/Weill Cornell Medical Center *525 E 68th Street, at York Avenue, Upper East Side (1-212 746 5454). Subway 6 to 68th Street.* **Map** *p405 G21.*
Roosevelt Hospital *1000 Tenth Avenue, at 59th Street, Upper West Side (1-212 523 4000). Subway A, B, C, D, 1 to 59th Street-Columbus Circle.* **Map** *p405 C22.*

Clinics

Walk-in clinics offer treatment for minor ailments. Most clinics will require immediate payment for treatments and consultations, though some will send their bill directly to your insurance company if you're a US resident. You will have to file a claim to recover the cost of any prescription medication that is required.

Beth Israel Medical Group
55 E 34th Street, between Madison & Park Avenues, Murray Hill (1-212 252 6000, www.wehealny. org/services/bimg). Subway 6 to 33rd Street. **Open** walk-in 8am-8pm daily; also by appt. **Cost** from $125. **Credit** AmEx, DC, Disc, MC, V. **Map** p404 E25.
Primary-care facilities offering by-appointment and walk-in services. **Other locations** 202 W 23rd Street, at Seventh Avenue (1-212 352 2600).

NY Hotel Urgent Medical Services
Suite 1D, 952 Fifth Avenue, between 76th & 77th Streets, Upper East Side (1-212 737 1212, www.travelmd.com). Subway 6 to 77th Street. **Open** 24hrs by appt only. **Cost** from $200. **Credit** MC, V. **Map** p405 E19.
Specialist medical attention, from a simple prescription to urgent medical care. House calls are available.

Dentists

New York County Dental Society
1-212 573 8500, www.nycdentalsociety.org. **Open** 9am-5pm Mon-Fri.
Can provide local referrals. An emergency line at the number above runs outside office hours; alternatively, use the search facility on the society's website.

Opticians

See p215.

Pharmacies

For a list of pharmacies (including 24-hour locations), *see p215.* Note that pharmacies in New York will not refill foreign prescriptions and may not sell the same products you use at home.

STDs, HIV & AIDS

For the National STD & AIDS Hotline, *see right* **Helplines.**

NYC Department of Health Chelsea Health Center
303 Ninth Avenue, at 28th Street, Chelsea (no phone). Subway C, E to 23rd Street. **Open** walk-in 8.30am-3pm Mon-Fri; 8.30am-noon Sat. Extended hours for rapid HIV testing only 5-7pm Tue-Thur. **Map** p404 B26.
Call 311 or visit www.nyc.gov for other free clinics.

Gay Men's Health Crisis
446 W 33rd Street, at Tenth Avenue, Hell's Kitchen (1-212 367 1000, 1-800 243 7692 HIV/AIDS helpline, www.gmhc.org). Subway A, C, E, 1, 2, 3 to 34th Street-Penn Station. **Open** *Centre* walk-in 9.30am-4pm Mon-Wed; 12.30-7pm Fri; by appt 9.30am-4pm Thur. *Hotline* 2-6pm Mon, Fri; 10am-2pm Wed; recorded information at other times. **Map** p404 C25.
GMHC was the world's first organisation dedicated to helping people with AIDS, and offers testing, counselling and other services on a walk-in and appointment basis, regardless of sexual orientation. The Testing Center is now located within the new Center for HIV Prevention (224 W 29th Street, between Seventh & Eighth Avenues, Chelsea, 1-212 367 1100). See website for separate walk-in and appointment-only hours.

Contraception & abortion

Parkmed Physicians Center
7th Floor, 800 Second Avenue, between 42nd & 43rd Streets, Midtown East (1-212 686 6066, www.parkmed.com). Subway S, 4, 5, 6, 7 to 42nd Street-Grand Central. **Open** by appt only 7am-8pm Mon-Fri; 7am-6pm Sat; 9am-5pm Sun. **Credit** AmEx, DC, Disc, MC, V. **Map** p404 F24.
Urine pregnancy tests are free. Counselling, contraception services and non-surgical abortions are also available at the centre.

Planned Parenthood of New York City *Margaret Sanger Center, 26 Bleecker Street, at Mott Street, Greenwich Village (1-212 965 7000, 1-800 230 7526, www.ppnyc.org). Subway B, D, F, M to Broadway-Lafayette Street; N, R to Prince Street; 6 to Bleecker Street.* **Open** 8am-4.30pm Mon, Tue; 8am-6.30pm Wed-Fri; 7.30am-4pm Sat. **Credit** AmEx, DC, MC, V. **Map** p403 F29.
The best-known network of family-planning clinics in the US. Counselling and treatment are available for a full range of needs,

including abortion, contraception, HIV testing and treatment of STDs. **Other locations** 44 Court Street, between Joralemon & Remsen Streets, Brooklyn Heights, Brooklyn (1-212 965 7000).

All numbers are open 24 hours unless otherwise stated.

Addictions Hotline
1-800 522 5353.
Alcoholics Anonymous
1-212 647 1680.
Open 9am-2am daily.
Childhelp USA's National Child Abuse Hotline
1-800 422 4453.
Cocaine Anonymous
1-212 262 2463.
National STD & AIDS Hotline
1-800 232 4636.
Pills Anonymous
1-212 874 0700 recorded information.
Safe Horizon Crisis Hotline
1-212 227 3000, www.safehorizon.org.
Counselling for victims of domestic violence, rape or other crimes.
Samaritans
1-212 673 3000.
Counselling for suicide prevention.
Special Victims Liaison Unit of the NYPD Rape Hotline
1-212 267 7273.

ID

Always carry picture ID: even people well over 18 or 21 may be carded when buying tobacco or alcohol, ordering drinks in bars, or entering clubs.

INSURANCE

Non-nationals and US citizens should have travel and medical insurance before travelling. For a list of New York urgent-care facilities, *see left.*

INTERNET

Cyber Café *250 W 49th Street, between Broadway & Eighth Avenue, Theater District (1-212 333 4109). Subway C, E, 1 to 50th Street; N, Q, R to 49th Street.* **Open** 8am-9pm daily. **Cost** $12.50/hr; 50¢/printed page. **Credit** AmEx, DC, MC, V. **Map** p404 D23.
This is a standard internet access café that also happens to serve great coffee and snacks.
FedEx Office *1-800 463 3339, www.fedex.com.*

ESSENTIAL INFORMATION

Outposts of this ubiquitous and very efficient computer and copy centre are peppered throughout the city; many are open 24 hours a day.

New York Public Library
1-212 592 7000, www.nypl.org.
Branches of the NYPL are great places to get online for free, offering both Wi-Fi and computers for public use. (Ask for an out-of-state card, for which you need proof of residence, or a guest pass.)

The Science, Industry & Business Library (188 Madison Avenue, at 34th Street) and the Mid-Manhattan Library (455 Fifth Avenue, at 40th Street) have about 50 computers apiece. All libraries have a computer limit of 45 minutes per day.

NYCWireless *www.nycwireless.net.*
This group has established dozens of hotspots in the city for free Wi-Fi access. (For example, most parks below 59th Street are covered.) Visit the website information and a map.

Starbucks *www.starbucks.com.*
Many branches offer free Wi-Fi; the website has a search facility.

LEFT LUGGAGE

There are luggage-storage facilities at arrivals halls in JFK Airport (Terminal 1: 7am-11pm, $4-$16 per bag per day; call 1-718 751 2947); (Terminal 4: 24hrs, $4-$16 per bag per day; call 1-718 751 4001). At Penn Station, Amtrak offers checked baggage services for a small fee for some of its ticketed passengers. Due to heightened security, luggage storage is not available at the Port Authority Bus Terminal, Grand Central, or LaGuardia or Newark airports.

One Midtown alternative is to leave bags with the private firm, located between Penn Station and Port Authority, listed below. Some hotels may allow you to leave suitcases with the front desk before check-in or after check-out; if so, be sure to tip the concierge.

Schwartz Travel Services
355 W 36th Street, between Eighth & Ninth Avenues (1-212 290 2626, www.schwartztravel.com). **Open** 8am-11pm daily. **Rates** $7-$10 per bag per day. **No credit cards.**
Other locations 34 W 46th Street, between Fifth & Sixth Avenues (same phone).

LEGAL HELP

If you need a lawyer in NYC, contact the **New York City BarAssociation** (1-212 626 7373, www.abcny.org), which can provide referrals to attorneys practising in almost every area of the law, from personal injury to criminal defence. Outside the city, contact the **New York State Bar Association Lawyer Referral & Information Service** (1-800 342 3661, www.nysba.org). If you're arrested and held in custody, call your insurer's emergency number or contact your embassy or consulate (*see p376*).

Legal Aid Society *1-212 577 3300, www.legal-aid.org.* **Open** 9am-5pm Mon-Fri.
This non-profit organisation provides legal representation for low-income residents.

LIBRARIES

See left **New York Public Library**.

LOST PROPERTY

For lost credit cards or travellers' cheques, *see p380*.

Grand Central Terminal *Lower level, near Track 110. 1-212 532 4900.* **Open** 7am-6pm Mon-Fri.
You can call 24 hrs a day to file a claim if you've left something on a Metro-North train.
JFK Airport *1-718 244 4225,* or contact your airline.
La Guardia Airport *1-718 533 3988,* or contact your airline.
Newark Liberty International Airport *1-973 961 6243,* or contact your airline.
Penn Station: Amtrak *1-212 630 7389.* **Open** 7.30am-4pm Mon-Fri.
Penn Station: Long Island Rail Road *1-718 217 5477.* **Open** 7.20am-7.20pm Mon-Fri.
Penn Station: New Jersey Transit *1-973 275 5555.*
Open 7am-7pm daily.
Subway & Buses *New York City Metropolitan Transit Authority, 34th Street-Penn Station, near the A-train platform, Garment District (call 511).* **Open** 8am-3.30pm Mon, Tue, Fri; 11am-6.30pm Wed, Thur. **Map** p404 D25.
Call if you've left something on a subway train or a bus.
Taxis *1-212 639 9675, www.nyc.gov/taxi.*
Call for items left in a cab.

MEDIA

Daily newspapers

Founded in 1801 by Alexander Hamilton, the **New York Post** is the nation's oldest continuously published daily newspaper. It has swerved sharply to the right under current owner Rupert Murdoch, includes more gossip than any other local paper, and its headlines are often sassy and sensational.

The **Daily News** has drifted politically from the Neanderthal right to a more moderate but always tough-minded stance under the ownership of noted real-estate mogul Mort Zuckerman.

Despite recent financial woes, **The New York Times** remains the city's, and the nation's, paper of record. Founded as the *New-York Daily Times* in 1851, it has the broadest and deepest coverage of world and national events and, as the masthead proclaims, it delivers 'All the News That's Fit to Print'. The hefty Sunday edition includes a very well-regarded magazine, as well as arts, book review, travel, real-estate and various other sections.

The **New York Amsterdam News**, one of the nation's longest-running black newspapers, offers a trenchant African-American viewpoint. New York also supports a Spanish-language daily: **El Diario La Prensa**. **Newsday** is a Long Island-based daily with a tabloid format but a sober tone. Free tabloids **AM New York** and **New York Metro** offer locally slanted news, arts and entertainment listings.

Weekly newspapers

Downtown journalism is a battlefield, with the **New York Press** pitted against the **Village Voice**. The *Press* is full of irreverence, as well as cynicism and self-absorption. The *Voice* is at turns passionate and ironic, but just as often strident and predictable. Both are free.

Most neighbourhoods boast free publications featuring local news, reviews and gossip, such as **Our Town East Side**, **West Side Spirit**, the **Westsider** and **Chelsea Clinton News**.

Magazines

New York magazine is part news weekly, part lifestyle reporting and part listings. Since the 1920s, the **New Yorker** has been known for its fine wit, elegant prose and sophisticated cartoons. It has also evolved into a respected forum for serious long-form journalism.

Based on the tried and trusted format of its London parent magazine, **Time Out New York** is an intelligent, irreverent, indispensable weekly guide to what's going on in the city: arts, restaurants, bars, shops and more.

Since its launch in 1996, the bimonthly **BlackBook Magazine** has covered New York's high fashion and culture with intelligent bravado. **Gotham**, a monthly from the publisher of glossy gab-rags *Hamptons* and *Aspen Peak*, unveiled its larger-than-life celeb-filled pages in 2001. And for more than two decades, **Paper** has offered buzz on bars, clubs, downtown boutiques and more.

Commercial radio

American commercial radio is rigidly formatted, which makes most pop stations extremely tedious and repetitive during the day. Tune in on evenings and weekends for more interesting programming. Always popular, **WQHT-FM 97.1**, 'Hot 97', is a commercial hip hop station with all-day rap and R&B. **WKTU-FM 103.5** is the premier dance music station. **WWPR-FM 105.1**, 'Power 105', plays top hip hop and a few old-school hits. **WBLS-FM 107.5** showcases classic and new funk, soul and R&B. **WBGO-FM 88.3** is strictly jazz. **WAXQ-FM 104.3** offers classic rock. Pop station **WXRK-FM 92.3** attracts and appals listeners with its 6-10am weekday gossip fest.

WQEW-AM 1560, 'Radio Disney', has kids' programming. **WNYC-FM 93.9** (*see also below*) and **WQXR-FM 105.9** serve up a range of new and classical music. **WXNY-FM 96.3** and **WQBU-FM 92.7** spin Spanish and Latin sounds.

Public & college radio

The city's excellent NPR-affiliated public radio station, **WNYC-AM 820/FM 93.9**, provides news and current-affairs commentary and broadcasts the BBC World Service. **WBAI-FM 99.5** is a left-leaning community radio station. **WWRL-AM 1600**, the former flagship of defunct Air America, is a more liberal answer to right-wing talk radio.

College radio is innovative and commercial-free, but reception is often compromised by Manhattan's high-rise topography. **WNYU-FM 89.1** and **WKCR-FM 89.9** are,

respectively, the stations of New York University and Columbia. **WFUV-FM 90.7**, Fordham University's station, airs a variety of shows, including Beale Street Caravan, the world's most widely distributed blues programme.

Talk radio & sports

WABC-AM 770, **WCBS-AM 880** and **WINS-AM 1010** offer news, plus traffic and weather reports. **WFAN-AM 660** airs Giants, Nets, Mets and Devils games, while **WCBS-AM 880** covers the Yankees. **WEPN-AM 1050** is devoted to news and sports talk and is the home of the Jets, Knicks and Rangers.

Television

Six major networks broadcast nationwide. All offer ratings-driven variations on a theme.

CBS (Channel 2 in NYC) has the top-rated investigative show, *60 Minutes*, on Sundays at 7pm; overall, programming is geared to a middle-aged demographic, but CBS also screens shows such as *CSI* and the reality series *Survivor*. **NBC** (4) is the home of *Law & Order*, the long-running sketch-comedy series *Saturday Night Live* (11.30pm Sat), and popular prime-time shows that include *The Office* and *30 Rock*. **Fox-WNYW** (5) is popular with younger audiences for shows such as *Glee*, *Family Guy*, *The Simpsons*

and *The X Factor*. **ABC** (7) is the king of daytime soaps, family-friendly sitcoms and hits like *Modern Family*, *Grey's Anatomy* and *Dancing With the Stars*.

Public TV is on channels 13, 21 and 25. Documentaries, arts shows and science series alternate with *Masterpiece* (Anglo costume and contemporary dramas packaged for a US audience) and reruns of British sitcoms.

For channel numbers for cable TV providers, such as **Time Warner Cable**, **Cablevision** and **RCN**, check a local newspaper or the Web. **FSN (Fox Sports Network)**, **MSG (Madison Square Garden)**, **ESPN** and **ESPN2** are all-sports stations. **Comedy Central** is all comedy, airing *South Park*, *The Daily Show with Jon Stewart* and its hugely popular spin-off *The Colbert Report*. **Cinemax**, the **Disney Channel**, the **Movie Channel**, **HBO** and **Showtime** are often available in hotels. They show uninterrupted feature films and exclusive specials; the latter two offer popular series such as *Boardwalk Empire*, *Girls*, *Homeland* and *Nurse Jackie*.

MONEY

Over the past few years, much of American currency has undergone a subtle facelift, partly to deter increasingly adept counterfeiters; all denominations except the $1 bill have recently been updated by the

ESSENTIAL INFORMATION

SIZE CHARTS

WOMEN'S CLOTHES

British	French	US
4	32	2
6	34	4
8	36	6
10	38	8
12	40	10
14	42	12
16	44	14
18	46	16
20	48	18

WOMEN'S SHOES

British	French	US
3	36	5
4	37	6
5	38	7
6	39	8
7	40	9
8	41	10
9	42	11

MEN'S CLOTHES

British	French	US
34	44	34
36	46	36
38	48	38
40	50	40
42	52	42
44	54	44
46	56	46
48	58	48

MEN'S SHOES

British	French	US
6	39	7
7.5	40	7.5
8	41	8
8	42	8.5
9	43	9.5
10	44	10.5
11	45	11
12	46	11.5

US Treasury. (However, 'old' money still remains in circulation.) Coins include copper pennies (1¢) and silver-coloured nickels (5¢), dimes (10¢) and quarters (25¢). Half-dollar coins (50¢) and the gold-coloured dollar coins are less common.

All paper money is the same size, so make sure you fork over the right bill. It comes in denominations of $1, $2, $5, $10, $20, $50 and $100 (and higher, but you'll never see those bills). The $2 bills are quite rare. Try to keep some low notes on you because getting change may be a problem with anything bigger than a $20 bill.

ATMs

The city is full of ATMs, located in bank branches, delis and many small shops. Most accept Visa, MasterCard and major bank cards. Some UK banks charge up to £4 per transaction plus a variable payment to cover themselves against any exchange rate fluctuations. Most ATM cards now double as debit cards, if they bear Maestro or Cirrus logos.

Banks & bureaux de change

Banks are generally open from 9am to 6pm Monday to Friday, though some stay open longer and/or on Saturdays. You need photo ID, such as a passport, to cash travellers' cheques. Many banks will not exchange foreign currency; many bureaux de change, limited to tourist-trap areas, close at around 6pm or 7pm. In emergencies, most large hotels offer 24-hour exchange facilities, but the rates won't be great.

Chase Bank
1-800 935 9935, www.chase.com. Chase's website gives information on foreign currency exchange, branch locations and credit cards. For foreign currency delivered in a hurry, call the number listed above.
TD Bank
1-888 751 9000, www.tdbank.com. All Manhattan branches (there are nearly 40) of the Canadian-owned bank are open seven days a week.
People's Foreign Exchange
60 E 42nd Street, between Madison & Park Avenues, Midtown East (1-212 883 0550, www.peoplesfx.com). Subway S, 4, 5, 6, 7 to 42nd Street-Grand Central. **Open** *9am-5.30pm Mon-Fri; 10.30am-3pm Sat, Sun.* **Map** p404 E23.

People's Foreign Exchange offers foreign currency exchange on travellers' cheques for one per cent commission or bank notes of any denomination for a flat fee of $5.
Other locations 3rd Floor, 575 Fifth Avenue, at 47th Street, Midtown East (same phone).
Travelex
1578 Broadway, at 47th Street, Theater District (1-212 265 6063, www.travelex.com). Subway N, Q, R to 49th Street. **Open** *9am-10pm daily.* **Map** p404 D23.
Travelex offers a complete range of foreign-exchange services. The Times Square outpost stays open late; see website for other locations.
Other locations throughout the city.

Credit cards & travellers' cheques

Credit cards are essential for renting cars and booking hotels, and handy for buying tickets over the phone and the internet. The five major cards accepted in the US are **American Express** (abbreviated as AmEx throughout this book), **Diners Club** (DC), **Discover** (Disc), **MasterCard** (MC) and **Visa** (V). MasterCard and Visa are the most popular; American Express is also widely accepted. Thanks to a 2004 deal between MasterCard and Diners Club, all businesses that accept the former can now in theory accept the latter, though in practice many business are unaware of this and may not comply.

If your cards or travellers' cheques are lost or stolen, call the following numbers:

American Express *1-800 528 2122, 1-800 221 7282 travellers' cheques.*
Diners Club *1-800 234 6377.*
Discover *1-800 347 2683.*
Mastercard/Maestro *1-800 826 2181, 1-800 223 9920 travellers' cheques.*
Visa/Cirrus *1-800 336 8472, 1-800 336 8472 travellers' cheques.*

Tax

Sales tax is 8.875 per cent in New York City, and is applicable to restaurant bills, services and the purchase of just about anything, except most store-bought foods, clothing and shoes. The latter two are subject only to the four per cent state tax if an item costs under $110, and exempt if it costs $55 or less.

In the US, sales tax is almost never included in the price of the item, but added on to the final bill at the till. There is no tax refund option for foreign visitors.

Wire services

Funds can be wired from home through the following companies:

Moneygram *1-800 666 3947, www.moneygram.com.*
Western Union *1-800 325 6000, www.westernunion.com.*

OPENING HOURS

Banks and government offices, including post offices, close on federal holidays. Retail in the city shuts down on Christmas Day and New Year's Day, although movie theatres and some restaurants remain open. Most museums are closed on Mondays, but may open when a public holiday falls on a Monday. New York's subway runs 24 hours a day, 365 days a year, but always check station signs for track or schedule changes, especially during weekends and holidays.

Banks 9am-6pm Mon-Fri; generally also Sat mornings.
Businesses 9am or 10am to 5pm or 6pm Mon-Fri.
Post offices 9am-5pm Mon-Fri (a few open as early as 7.30am and close as late as 8.30pm); some are open Sat until 3pm or 4pm. The James A Farley Post Office (*see right*) has extended hours.
Pubs & bars 4pm-2am Mon-Thur, Sun; noon-4am Fri, Sat (but hours vary widely).
Shops 9am, 10am or 11am to 7pm or 8pm Mon-Sat (some open at noon and/or close at 9pm). Many are also open on Sun, usually from 11am or noon to 6pm.

POLICE

In an emergency only, dial **911**. The NYPD stations below are in central, tourist-heavy areas of Manhattan. For the location of your nearest police precinct or information about police services, call 1-646 610 5000 or visit www.nyc.gov.

Sixth Precinct
233 West 10th Street, between Bleecker & Hudson Streets, West Village (1-212 741 4811).
Seventh Precinct
19½ Pitt Street, at Broome Street, Lower East Side (1-212 477 7311).

Midtown South Precinct
357 W 35th Street, between Eighth & Ninth Avenues, Garment District (1-212 239 9811).
Midtown North Precinct
306 W 54th Street, between Eighth & Ninth Avenues, Hell's Kitchen (1-212 760 8300).
17th Precinct
167 E 51st Street, between Third & Lexington Avenues, Midtown East (1-212 826 3211).
Central Park Precinct
86th Street & Transverse Road, Central Park (1-212 570 4820).

POSTAL SERVICES

Stamps are available at all US post offices, from drugstore vending machines and at most newsstands. It costs 45¢ to send a 1oz letter within the US. Each additional ounce costs 20¢. Postcards mailed within the US cost 35¢. Airmailed letters or postcards to Canada and Mexico cost 85¢ for the first ounce; to all other countries it's $1.05 for the first ounce. The cost of additional ounces varies by country.

For faster **Express Mail**, you must fill out a form, either at a post office or by arranging a pick-up; 24-hour delivery to major US cities is guaranteed. International delivery takes two to three days, with no guarantee. Call 1-800 275 8777 for more information. For couriers and messengers, *see p375*.

James A Farley Post Office
421 Eighth Avenue, between 31st & 33rd Streets, Garment District (1-212 330 3296, 1-800 275 8777 24hr information, www.usps.com). Subway A, C, E to 34th Street-Penn Station. **Open** 24 hrs daily. *Counter service* 7am-10pm Mon-Fri; 9am-9pm Sat; 11am-7pm Sun. **Credit** DC, MC, V. **Map** p404 D25.
In addition to counter service, NYC's general post office has automated self-service machines for buying stamps and posting packages.
General Delivery
390 Ninth Avenue, between 31st & 33rd Streets, Garment District (1-212 330 3099). Subway A, C, E to 34th Street-Penn Station. **Open** 10am-1pm Mon-Fri; 10am-noon Sat. **Map** p404 C25.
US residents without local addresses and foreign visitors can receive their post here; it should be addressed to the recipient, General Delivery, 390 Ninth Avenue, New York, NY 10001. You will need to show a passport or ID card when picking up letters.

RELIGION

Here are just a few of New York's many places of worship. Check the telephone book for more listings.

Abyssinian Baptist Church
For listings, *see p109*.
Cathedral Church of St John the Divine For listings, *see p106*.
Church of St Paul & St Andrew, United Methodist
263 W 86th Street, between Broadway & West End Avenue, Upper West Side (1-212 362 3179, www.stpaulandstandrew.org). Subway 1 to 86th Street. **Map** p406 C18.
Islamic Cultural Center of New York *1711 Third Avenue, between 96th & 97th Streets, Upper East Side (1-212 722 5234, www.islamicculturalcenter-ny.org). Subway 6 to 96th Street.* **Map** p406 F17.
Madison Avenue Presbyterian Church *921 Madison Avenue, between 73rd & 74th Streets, Upper East Side (1-212 288 8920, www.mapc.com). Subway 6 to 72nd Street.* **Map** p405 E20.
New York Buddhist Church
331-332 Riverside Drive, between 105th & 106th Streets, Upper West Side (1-212 678 0305, www.newyorkbuddhistchurch.org). Subway 1 to 103rd Street. **Map** p406 B16.
St Patrick's Cathedral
For listings, *see p89*.
UJA-Federation of New York Resource Line *1-877 852 6951, www.ujafedny.org*. **Open** 9am-5pm Mon-Thur; 9am-4pm Fri.
This hotline provides referrals to temples, synagogues, other Jewish organisations and groups.

SAFETY & SECURITY

New York's crime rate, particularly for violent crime, has waned during the past two decades. Most crime occurs late at night and in low-income neighbourhoods. Don't arrive in NYC thinking your safety is at risk wherever you go; it is unlikely that you will ever be bothered.

Still, a bit of common sense won't hurt. Don't flaunt your money and valuables, keep phones and other electronic gadgets out of sight, and try not to look obviously lost. Avoid deserted and poorly lit streets; walk facing oncoming traffic so no one can drive up alongside you undetected, and close to or on the street; muggers prefer to hang back in doorways and shadows. If you

are threatened, hand over your valuables at once, then dial 911.

Be extra alert to pickpockets and street hustlers – especially in crowded areas like Times Square.

SMOKING

The 1995 NYC Smoke-Free Air Act makes it illegal to smoke in virtually all indoor public places, including the subway and cinemas; for a few exceptions, *see p179* **Inside Track**. As of May 2011, smoking is also prohibited in New York City parks, pedestrian plazas (such as the ones in Times Square and Herald Square) and on beaches. Violators could face a $50 fine.

STUDY

Those who study in NYC have access to an endless extracurricular education, as well as a non-stop playground. Foreign students should get hold of an International Student Identity Card (ISIC) in order to secure discounts. These cards can be purchased from your local student-travel agent (go to www.isic.org or ask at your student union or an STA Travel office).

Manhattan's main universities include: the **City University of New York**'s 23 colleges (1-212 794 5555, www.cuny.edu); **Columbia University** (2960 Broadway, at 116th Street, Morningside Heights, 1-212 854 1754, www.columbia.edu); the **Cooper Union** (30 Cooper Square, between 5th & 6th Streets, East Village, 1-212 353 4100, www.cooper.edu); **Fordham University**, which has campuses in the Bronx and on the Upper East Side (1-718 817 1000, 1-212 636 6000, www.fordham.edu); the **New School** (55 W 13th Street, between Fifth & Sixth Avenues, Greenwich Village, 1-212 229 5600, www.newschool.edu); **New York University** (70 Washington Square South, Greenwich Village, 1-212 998 1212, www.nyu.edu); and performing arts school **Juilliard** (60 Lincoln Center Plaza, at Broadway, Upper West Side, 1-212 799 5000, www.juilliard.edu).

TELEPHONES
Dialling & codes

As a rule, you must dial 1 + the area code before a number, even if the place you are calling is in the same area code. The area codes for Manhattan are **212** and **646**; Brooklyn, Queens, Staten Island

ESSENTIAL INFORMATION

and the Bronx are **718** and **347**; **917** is now reserved mostly for mobile phones and pagers. Long Island area codes are 516 and 631; codes for New Jersey are 201, 551, 609, 732, 848, 856, 862, 908 and 973. Numbers preceded by **800**, **877** and **888** are free of charge when dialled from within the US.

In an **emergency**, dial 911. All calls are free (including those from pay and mobile phones).

For the **operator**, dial 0. If you're not used to US phones, then note that the ringing tone is long; the engaged tone, or 'busy signal', consists of much shorter, higher pitched beeps.

Collect calls are also known as reverse-charge calls. To make one, dial 0 followed by the number, or dial AT&T's 1-800 225 5288, MCI's 1-800 265 5328 or Sprint's 1-800 663 3463.

For **directory assistance**, dial 411 or 1 + area code + 555 1212. Doing so may cost nothing, depending on the pay phone you are using; carrier fees may apply. Long-distance directory assistance may also incur long-distance charges. For a directory of toll-free numbers, dial 1-800 555 1212.

For **international calls**, dial 011 + country code (Australia 61; New Zealand 64; UK 44), then the number (omitting any initial zero).

Mobile phones

Most US mobile phones will work in NYC, but since the US doesn't have a standard national network, visitors should check with their provider that their phone will work here, and whether they need to unlock a roaming option. Visitors from other countries will need a tri-band handset and a roaming agreement, and may find charges so high that rental (*see p197*) or, depending on the length of their stay, purchase of a US phone (or SIM card) will make better economic sense.

If you carry a mobile phone, make sure you turn it off in museums and restaurants, and at plays, movies and concerts. New Yorkers are quick to show their annoyance at an ill-timed ring. Some establishments now even post signs designating a cellular-free zone.

Public phones

Functioning public pay phones are becoming increasingly hard to find. Phones take any combination of silver coins: local calls usually

cost 50¢ for three minutes. To call long-distance or to make an international call from a pay phone, you need to go through a long-distance company. Most of the pay phones in New York automatically use AT&T, but phones in and around transportation hubs usually contract other long-distance carriers, and charges can be outrageous. MCI and Sprint (*see left*) are respected brand names.

Make the call by either dialling 0 for an operator or dialling direct, which is cheaper. To find out how much it will cost, dial the number, and a computerised voice will tell you how much money to deposit. You can pay for calls with your credit card. The best way to make long-distance calls is with a phone card, available from any post office branch, many newsagents and delis, or from chain stores such as Duane Reade and Rite Aid (*see p215* **Pharmacies**).

TIME & DATES

New York is on Eastern Standard Time, which extends from the Atlantic coast to the eastern shore of Lake Michigan and south to the Gulf of Mexico. This is five hours behind Greenwich Mean Time. Clocks are set forward one hour in early March for Daylight Saving Time (Eastern Daylight Time) and back one hour at the beginning of November. Going from east to west, Eastern Time is one hour ahead of Central Time, two hours ahead of Mountain Time and three hours ahead of Pacific Time.

In the United States, the date is written as month, day and year; so 3/8/13 is 8 March 2013.

Forms that foreigners may need to fill in, however, are often the other way round.

TIPPING

In restaurants, it's customary to tip at least 15 per cent, and since NYC tax is 8.875 per cent, a quick way to calculate the tip is to double the tax. In many restaurants, when you are with a group of six or more, the tip will be included in the bill. For tipping on taxi fares, *see p374*.

TOILETS

The media had a field day when the first pay toilet to open in the city since 1975 received its 'first flush' by officials in a special ceremony in 2008. 'Public Toilet No.1', as the *New York Post*

christened it, is in Madison Square Park (Madison Avenue, between 23rd & 24th Streets, Flatiron District) and was due to be followed by around 20 across the city within the following couple of years; progress, however, has been stalled. It costs 25¢ to enter the large stainless steel and tempered glass box (dawdlers and OCD sufferers, beware: the door opens after 15 minutes). Below is a list of other convenient rest stops.

Downtown

Battery Park Castle Clinton
Subway 1 to South Ferry; 4, 5 to Bowling Green.
Tompkins Square Park *Avenue A, at 9th Street. Subway L to First Avenue; 6 to Astor Place.*
Washington Square Park
Thompson Street, at Washington Square South. Subway A, B, C, D, E, F, M to W 4th Street.

Midtown

Bryant Park *42nd Street, between Fifth & Sixth Avenues. Subway B, D, F, M to 42nd Street-Bryant Park; 7 to Fifth Avenue.*
Grand Central Terminal *42nd Street, at Park Avenue, Lower Concourse. Subway S, 4, 5, 6, 7 to 42nd Street-Grand Central.*
Penn Station *Seventh Avenue, between 31st & 33rd Streets, Subway A, C, E, 1, 2, 3 to 34th Street-Penn Station.*

Uptown

Avery Fisher Hall *Broadway, at 65th Street. Subway 1 to 66th Street-Lincoln Center.*
Charles A Dana Discovery Center *Central Park, north side of Harlem Meer, 110th Street at Malcolm X Boulevard (Lenox Avenue). Subway 2, 3 to 110th Street-Central Park North.*
Delacorte Theater *Central Park, midpark, at 81st Street. Subway B, C to 81st Street-Museum of Natural History.*

TOURIST INFORMATION

Official NYC Information Center
810 Seventh Avenue, between 52nd & 53rd Streets, Theater District (1-212 484 1222, www.nycgo.com). Subway B, D, E to Seventh Avenue. **Open** 8.30am-6pm Mon-Fri; 9am-5pm Sat, Sun. **Map** p404 D23.

The city's official (private, non-profit) visitors' information centre recently got a high-tech renovation, complete with interactive map tables that allow you to navigate the city's attractions, hotels and restaurants, and send your itineraries to your email address or mobile device. The centre also doles out maps, leaflets, coupons and advice; and sells MetroCards and tickets to attractions such as Top of the Rock, the Statue of Liberty and the Empire State Building, potentially saving you time waiting in line. For other locations and information kiosks around the city, go to www.nycgo.com/articles/official-nyc-information-centers. **Other locations** throughout the city.

Times Square Museum & Visitor Center *Seventh Avenue, between 46th & 47th Streets, Theater District (1-212 452 5283, www.timessquarenyc.org). Subway N, Q, R, S, 1, 2, 3, 7 to 42nd Street-Times Square.* **Open** 8am-8pm daily. **Map** p404 D24.
This centre offers an official information desk, a Broadway ticket concierge, free maps and other useful goods and services, predominantly for the Theater District. There are also restrooms, a photo booth, a gift shop and a mini Times Square museum.

Brooklyn Tourism & Visitors Center *Brooklyn Borough Hall, 209 Joralemon Street, between Court & Adams Streets (1-718 802 3846, www.visitbrooklyn.org). Subway A, C, F to Jay Street-Borough Hall; R to Court Street; 2, 3, 4, 5, to Borough Hall.* **Open** 10am-6pm Mon-Fri.
A wealth of information on attractions, sites and events in the city's largest borough, plus local-interest books and gifts.

VISAS & IMMIGRATION

Visas

Currently, 36 countries participate in the **Visa Waiver Program** (VWP; www.cbp.gov/esta), including Australia, Ireland, New Zealand, and the UK. Citizens of these countries do not need a visa for stays in the US shorter than 90 days (business or pleasure) as long as they have a machine-readable passport (e-passport) valid for the full 90-day period, a return ticket, and authorisation to travel through the ESTA (Electronic System for Travel Authorization) scheme.

Visitors must fill in the ESTA form at least 24 hours before travelling (72 hours is recommended) and pay a $14 fee; the form can be found at www.cbp.gov/xp/cgov/travel/id_visa/esta/).

If you do not qualify for entry under the VWP, you will need a visa; leave plenty of time to obtain one before travelling.

For information about visas, see www.travel.state.gov or call 1-603 334 0700 (7am-midnight Mon-Fri; recorded information at other times). UK citizens can find information at www.usembassy.org.uk, or by calling the embassy's Visa Information Hotline (09042 450100; calls cost £1.23 per minute from a land line).

Immigration

Your airline will give all visitors an immigration form to be presented to an official when you land. Fill it in clearly and be prepared to give an address at which you are staying (a hotel is fine).

Upon arrival in the US, you may have to wait an hour or, if you're unlucky, considerably longer, in Immigration, where, owing to tightened security, you can expect slow-moving queues. You may be prepared to explain your visit; be polite and prepared. Note that all visitors to the US are now photographed and electronically fingerprinted on arrival on every trip.

WEIGHTS & MEASURES

Despite attempts to bring in metric measurements, you'll find imperial used in almost all contexts in New York and throughout the US. People think in ounces, inches, gallons and miles.

WHEN TO GO

There is no bad time to visit New York, and visitor numbers are fairly steady year-round. However, the weather can be unpleasantly hot and humid in summer (especially August) and, although winter snow (usually heaviest in January and February) is picturesque before it gets dirty and slushy, these months are often brutally cold. Late spring and early autumn bring pleasantly moderate temperatures that are perfect for walking and exploring.

Public holidays

New Year's Day 1 Jan
Martin Luther King, Jr Day 3rd Mon in Jan
Presidents Day 3rd Mon in Feb
Memorial Day last Mon in May
Independence Day 4 July
Labor Day 1st Mon in Sept
Columbus Day 2nd Mon in Oct
Veterans Day 11 Nov
Thanksgiving Day 4th Thur in Nov
Christmas Day 25 Dec

WORK

Non-nationals cannot work in the United States without the appropriate visa; these are hard to get and generally require you to prove that your job could not be done by a US citizen. Contact your local embassy for further details. Some student visas allow part-time work after the first academic year.

UK students who want to spend a summer vacation working in the US should contact the **British Universities North America Club** (BUNAC) for help in securing a temporary job and also the requisite visa (16 Bowling Green Lane, London EC1R 0QH, 020 7251 3472, www.bunac.org/uk).

THE LOCAL CLIMATE

Average temperatures and monthly rainfall in New York.

	High (°C/°F)	Low (°C/°F)	Rainfall (mm/in)
Jan	2 / 36	-5 / 23	94 / 3.7
Feb	4 / 40	-4 / 24	75 / 3.0
Mar	9 / 48	0 / 32	104 / 4.1
Apr	14 / 58	6 / 42	103 / 4.1
May	20 / 68	12 / 53	114 / 4.5
June	25 / 77	17 / 63	88 / 3.5
July	28 / 83	20 / 68	106 / 4.2
Aug	27 / 81	19 / 66	103 / 4.1
Sep	23 / 74	14 / 58	103 / 4.1
Oct	17 / 63	8 / 47	89 / 3.5
Nov	11 / 52	3 / 38	102 / 4.0
Dec	6 / 42	-2 / 28	98 / 3.9

Further Reference

BOOKS

Architecture

Richard Berenholtz
New York, New York
Miniature panoramic images
of the city through the seasons.
Stanley Greenberg
Invisible New York
A photographic account of hidden
architectural triumphs.
**New York City Landmarks
Preservation Commission**
Guide to New York City Landmarks
Karl Sabbagh *Skyscraper*
How the tall ones are built.
Kevin Walsh *Forgotten New York*
Discover overlooked architectural
gems and anachronistic remnants.
**Norval White & Elliot
Willensky** *The AIA Guide
to New York City*
A comprehensive directory
of important buildings.

Culture & recollections

Irving Lewis Allen
The City in Slang
NYC-bred words and phrases.
Joseph Berger
The World in a City
The *New York Times* columnist
explores the communities located
within the five boroughs.
Andrew Blauner (ed)
Central Park: An Anthology
Writers reflect on the city's most
celebrated green space.
Anatole Broyard
*Kafka Was the Rage:
A Greenwich Village Memoir*
Vivid account of 1940s Village
bohemia and its characters.
George Chauncey *Gay New York*
The evolution of gay culture
from 1890 to 1940.
**Martha Cooper & Henry
Chalfant** *Subway Art*
A definitive survey of city graffiti.
Naomi Fertitta & Paul Aresu
*New York: The Big City and
its Little Neighborhoods*
This photojournalism/guidebook
hybrid illuminates New York's
immigrant populations.
Josh Alan Friedman
Tales of Times Square
Sleaze and decay in the old days.
Nelson George *Hip Hop America*
The real history of hip hop, from
Grandmaster Flash to Puff Daddy.

Jane Jacobs *The Death and
Life of Great American Cities*
A hugely influential critique
of modern urban planning.
Chuck Katz
Manhattan on Film 1 & 2
On-location walking tours.
Gillian McCain & Legs McNeil
Please Kill Me
An oral history of the punk scene.
Joseph Mitchell
Up in the Old Hotel
Quirky recollections of New
York from the 1930s to the 1960s.
**Thurston Moore &
Byron Coley** *No Wave*
Musicians reminisce about the
downtown post-punk underground
scene in this nostalgia trip co-edited
by the Sonic Youth frontman.
Adrienne Onofri
Walking Brooklyn
Thirty tours illuminate the culture
and history of the borough.
Sam Stephenson *The Jazz Loft
Project: Photographs and Tapes
of W Eugene Smith from 821
Sixth Avenue, 1957-1965*
Images and transcripts of
conversations from the jazz-
obsessed photographer's loft, which
became a rehearsal space for some
of the era's greatest musicians.
Judith Stonehill *New York's
Unique & Unexpected Places*
Fifty special yet less-visited spots.
Time Out
1000 Things To Do in New York
Original and inspirational ideas
to appeal to jaded residents and
newly arrived visitors.
EB White *Here is New York*
A clear-eyed love letter to Gotham.

History

Herbert Asbury *The Gangs
of New York: An Informal History
of the Underworld*
A racy journalistic portrait of the
city at the turn of the 19th century.
Robert A Caro *The Power Broker*
A biography of Robert Moses, New
York's mid 20th-century master
builder, and his chequered legacy.
Federal Writers' Project
The WPA Guide to New York City
A wonderful evocation of the
1930s by writers who were
employed under FDR's New Deal.
Sanna Feirstein
Naming New York
How Manhattan places got named.

Tom Folsom
*The Mad Ones: Crazy Joe Gallo
and the Revolution at the Edge
of the Underworld*
Engaging ride though the world
of the Mafia during the 1960s.
Eric Homberger *The Historical
Atlas of New York City*
Through maps, photographs,
illustrations and essays,
this hefty volume charts the
metropolis's 400-year heritage.
Clifton Hood *722 Miles: The
Building of the Subways and How
They Transformed New York*
The birth of the world's longest
rapid transit system.
Kenneth T Jackson (ed)
The Encyclopedia of New York City
An ambitious and useful
reference guide.
David Levering Lewis
When Harlem Was in Vogue
A study of the Harlem Renaissance.
Jonathan Mahler *Ladies and
Gentlemen, the Bronx is Burning*
A gritty snapshot of NYC in 1977.
Mitchell Pacelle *Empire*
The story of the fight to build
the Empire State Building.
Clayton Patterson (ed)
Resistance
This collection of essays reflects
on the Lower East Side's history
as a radical hotbed.
Luc Sante *Low Life*
Opium dens and brothels in New
York from the 1840s to the 1920s.
Russell Shorto *The Island
at the Center of the World*
How the Dutch colony shaped
Manhattan – and America.
**Mike Wallace & Edwin G
Burrows** *Gotham: A History
of New York City to 1898*
The first volume in a planned
mammoth history of NYC.

Fiction & poetry

Kurt Andersen
Turn of the Century
Millennial Manhattan as seen
through the eyes of media players.
Paul Auster
*The New York Trilogy:
City of Glass, Ghosts* and
The Locked Room
A search for the madness behind
the method of Manhattan's grid.
Kevin Baker *Dreamland*
A poetic novel about Coney
Island's glory days.

James A Baldwin
Another Country
Racism under the bohemian
veneer of the 1960s.
Michael Chabon *The Amazing
Adventures of Kavalier and Clay*
Jewish comic-book artists battling
with crises of identity in the 1940s.
Ralph Ellison *Invisible Man*
Epic examination of race
and racism in 1950s Harlem.
Jack Finney *Time and Again*
An illustrator travels back to
19th-century New York City.
Larry Kramer *Faggots*
A devastating satire of gay NYC.
Jonathan Lethem *Chronic City*
The author of *The Fortress of
Solitude* packs his latest novel
with pop-culture references.
Phillip Lopate (ed)
Writing New York
An excellent anthology of short
stories, essays and poems.
Colum McCann
Let the Great World Spin
Interconnected stories set
in 1970s New York.
Patrick McGrath *Trauma*
A first-person account of psychic
decay that floats a critique of post-
9/11 social and political amnesia.
Tim McLoughlin (ed)
Brooklyn Noir 1, 2 & 3
Second-borough crime tales.
Frank O'Hara *The Collected
Poems of Frank O'Hara*
The great NYC poet found
inspiration in his hometown.
Richard Price *Lush Life*
A contemporary murder story
set on the Lower East Side.
David Schickler
Kissing in Manhattan
The lives of quirky tenants in
a teeming Manhattan block.
Hubert Selby Jr
Last Exit to Brooklyn
Dockland degradation, circa 1950s.
Edith Wharton *Old New York*
Four novellas of 19th-century NYC.
Colson Whitehead *The Colossus
of New York: A City in 13 Parts*
A lyrical tribute to city life.
Tom Wolfe
The Bonfire of the Vanities
Rich/poor, black/white – an
unmatched slice of 1980s NYC.

FILM

Annie Hall (1977)
Woody Allen and Diane Keaton
in this valentine to Manhattan.
Breakfast at Tiffany's (1961)
Audrey Hepburn as the cash-poor,
time-rich socialite Holly Golightly.
Dog Day Afternoon (1975)
Al Pacino is a Brooklyn bank robber
in Sidney Lumet's classic.

Do the Right Thing (1989)
Racial strife in Brooklyn's Bedford-
Stuyvesant in Spike Lee's drama.
The French Connection (1971)
As detective Jimmy 'Popeye' Doyle,
Gene Hackman chases down drug
traffickers in William Friedkin's
much-imitated thriller.
The Godfather (1972), **The
Godfather: Part II** (1974)
Francis Ford Coppola's brilliant
commentary on capitalism in
America is told through the
violent saga of Italian gangsters.
Mean Streets (1973)
Robert De Niro and Harvey Keitel
shine as small-time Little Italy
hoods in Martin Scorsese's
breakthrough film.
Midnight Cowboy (1969)
Street creatures 'Ratso' Rizzo
and Joe Buck face an unforgiving
Times Square in John Schlesinger's
darkly amusing classic.
Spider-Man (2002)
The comic book web-slinger from
Forest Hills comes to life in Sam
Raimi's pitch-perfect crowd-pleaser.
Superfly (1972)
Blaxploitation classic, propelled
by legendary Curtis Mayfield
soundtrack.
The Taking of Pelham 1 2 3
(2009)
The plot premise may be flawed –
in this Denzel Washington/John
Travolta remake, as well as in
the 1974 original – but it stirs
up strap-hangers' darkest fears.
Taxi Driver (1976)
Robert De Niro is a crazed cabbie
who sees all of New York as a den
of iniquity in Scorsese's drama.

MUSIC

Beastie Boys
'No Sleep Till Brooklyn'
The hip-hop troupe's on-the-road
anthem exudes local pride
Leonard Cohen
'Chelsea Hotel #2'
Of all the songs inspired by
the Chelsea, this bleak vision of
doomed love is on a level of its own.
Jay-Z with Alicia Keys
"Empire State of Mind"
The Brooklyn rapper's ode to NYC
is a 21st-century rival to Sinatra's
classic anthem.
Billy Joel
'New York State of Mind'
This heartfelt ballad exemplifies
the city's effect on the souls of its
visitors and residents.
Charles Mingus *Mingus Ah Um*
Mingus brought the gospel to jazz
and created an NYC masterpiece.
Public Enemy *It Takes a Nation
of Millions to Hold Us Back*

A ferociously political tour de force
from the Long Island hip hop group
whose own Chuck D once called
rap 'the CNN for black America'.
The Ramones *Ramones*
Four Queens roughnecks, a few
buzzsaw chords, and clipped
musings on turning tricks and
sniffing glue – it transformed
rock 'n' roll.
Frank Sinatra 'Theme
from *New York, New York*'
Trite and true, Ol' Blue Eyes'
bombastic love letter melts
those little-town blues.
Bruce Springsteen
'My City of Ruins'
The Boss praises the city's
resilience post-September 11
with this track from *The Rising*.
The Strokes *Is This It*
The effortlessly hip debut of
this hometown band garnered
praise and worldwide attention.
The Velvet Underground
The Velvet Underground & Nico
Their first album is still the gold
standard of downtown cool.
Wu Tang Clan
Few artists embodied '90s hip hop
like the Wu, its members – RZA,
GZA and the late ODB among them
– coining a cinematic rap aesthetic
that influences artists to this day.

WEBSITES

www.timeout.com/newyork
The recently relaunched *Time Out
New York* website covers all the
city has to offer, from upcoming
museum exhibitions, shows and
events to the latest shop openings,
plus thousands of restaurant and
bar reviews written by our critics.
www.clubplanet.com
Follow the city's nocturnal scene
and buy tickets to big events.
www.forgotten-ny.com
Discover old New York here.
www.hopstop.com
Works out door-to-door directions
on public transportation.
www.manhattanusersguide.com
An insiders' guide to what's
going on around town.
www.mta.info
Subway and bus service news.
www.nyc.gov
City Hall's official New York City
website has lots of useful links.
www.nycgo.com
The official New York City tourism
organisation provides information
on sights, attractions, hotels,
restaurants, shops and more.
www.nytimes.com
'All the News That's Fit to Print'
from *The New York Times* (limited
access for non-subscribers).

ESSENTIAL INFORMATION

Index

★ indicates a critic's choice

INDEX

INDEX

Central Park.

INDEX

George Washington Bridge.

INDEX

INDEX

INDEX

Advertisers' Index

Maps

Street Index

STREET INDEX

STREET INDEX

STREET INDEX

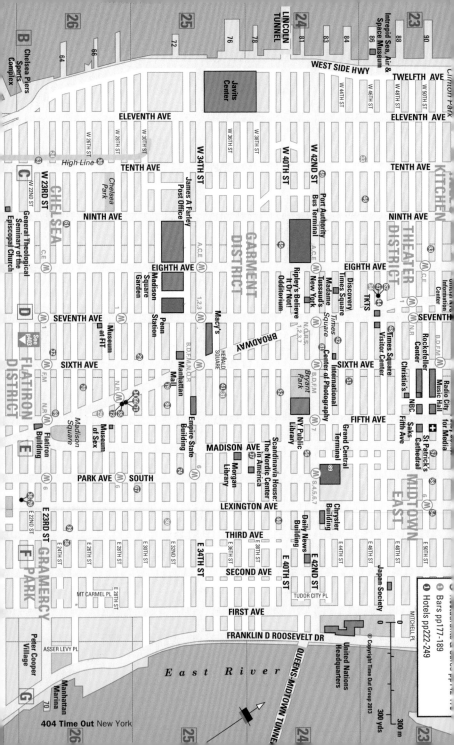

404 Time Out New York

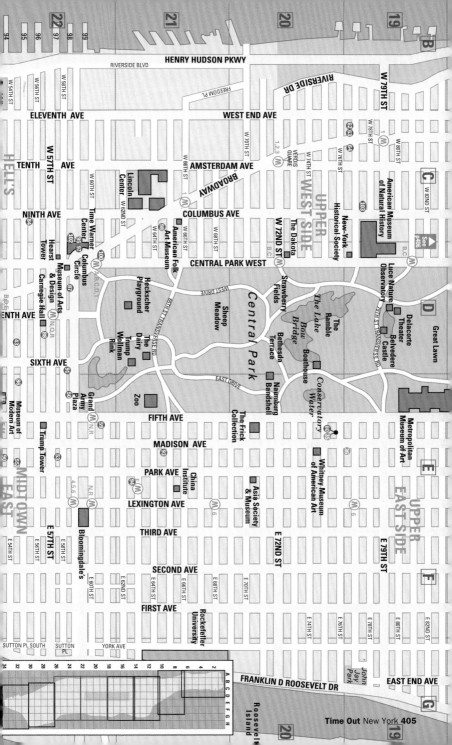

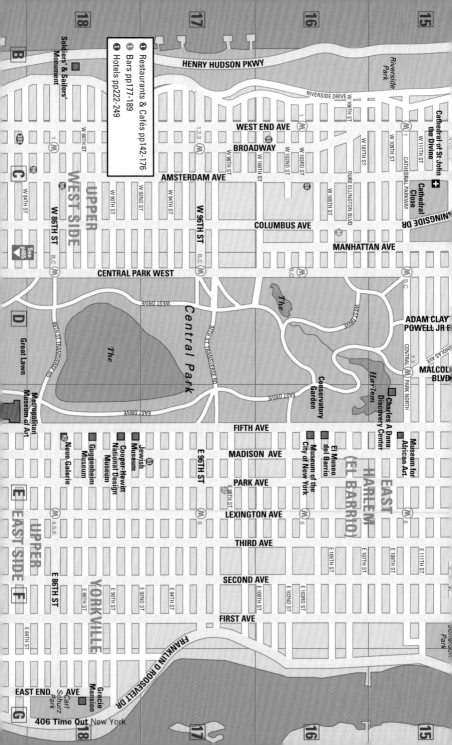

1 Restaurants & Cafés pp142-176

2 Bars pp177-189

3 Hotels pp222-249

Soldiers' & Sailors' Monument

Cathedral of St John the Divine

Cathedral Close

HENRY HUDSON PKWY

RIVERSIDE DRIVE

Riverside Park

WEST END AVE

BROADWAY

AMSTERDAM AVE

COLUMBUS AVE

MANHATTAN AVE

CENTRAL PARK WEST

CATHEDRAL PARKWAY

DUKE ELLINGTON BLVD

UPPER WEST SIDE

W 88TH ST
W 90TH ST
W 92ND ST
W 94TH ST

W 96TH ST

W 86TH ST

W 84TH ST

W 98TH ST
W 100TH ST
W 102ND ST
W 103RD ST

W 105TH ST

W 106TH ST
W 107TH ST
W 109TH ST
W 111TH ST

MORNINGSIDE DR

ADAM CLAY POWELL JR F

MALCOL BLVD

Museum for African Art,

EAST HARLEM (EL BARRIO)

E 105TH ST
E 107TH ST
E 109TH ST
E 111TH ST

E 100TH ST
E 102ND ST
E 103RD ST

Central Park

The

The

West Drive

Harlem Meer

Conservatory Garden

Charles A Dana Discovery Center

Great Lawn

Metropolitan Museum of Art

Neue Galerie

Guggenheim Museum

Cooper-Hewitt National Design Museum

Jewish Museum

El Museo del Barrio

Museum of the City of New York

FIFTH AVE

MADISON AVE

PARK AVE

LEXINGTON AVE

THIRD AVE

SECOND AVE

FIRST AVE

E 96TH ST

E 86TH ST

UPPER EAST SIDE

YORKVILLE

E 88TH ST
E 90TH ST
E 92ND ST
E 94TH ST

E 84TH ST

E 89TH ST

FRANKLIN ROOSEVELT DR

EAST END AVE

Carl Schurz Park

Gracie Mansion

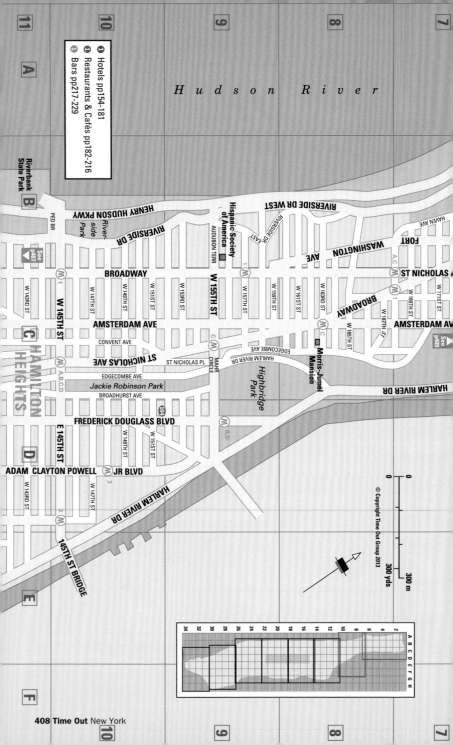

Hudson River

Riverbank State Park

HENRY HUDSON PKWY

RIVERSIDE DR

RIVERSIDE DR WEST

Riverside Park

PED BR

See p407

Hispanic Society of America

AUDUBON TERR

BROADWAY

W 143RD ST

W 147TH ST

W 149TH ST

W 151ST ST

W 153RD ST

W 155TH ST

W 157TH ST

W 159TH ST

W 161ST ST

W 163RD ST

BROADWAY

ST NICHOLAS

W 169TH ST

W 171ST ST

FORT WASHINGTON AVE

HAVEN AVE

AMSTERDAM AVE

AMSTERDAM AV

W 165TH ST

W 167TH ST

See p409

W 145TH ST

CONVENT AVE

ST NICHOLAS AVE

ST NICHOLAS PL

EDGECOMBE AVE

Jackie Robinson Park

BROADHURST AVE

MAHR CIRCLE

HARLEM RIVER DR

EDGECOMBE AVE

Morris-Jumel Mansion

Highbridge Park

HARLEM RIVER DR

FREDERICK DOUGLASS BLVD

W 149TH ST

W 151ST ST

HAMILTON HEIGHTS

E 145TH ST

W 143RD ST

W 147TH ST

ADAM CLAYTON POWELL JR BLVD

HARLEM RIVER DR

145TH ST BRIDGE

0 300 m
0 300 yds

© Copyright Time Out Group 2013

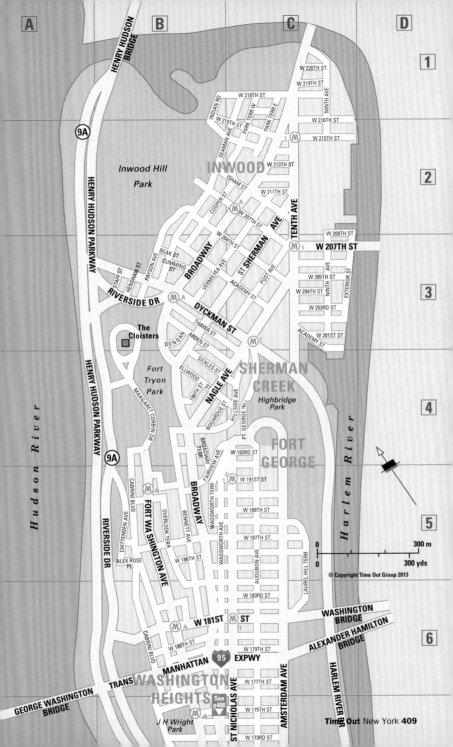

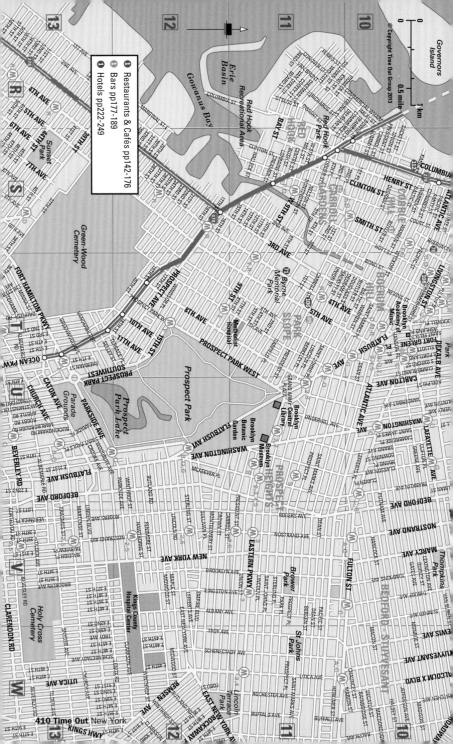

Queens

❶ Restaurants & Cafés pp142-176
❶ Bars pp177-189
❶ Hotels pp222-249

0   1 km
0   0.5 mile

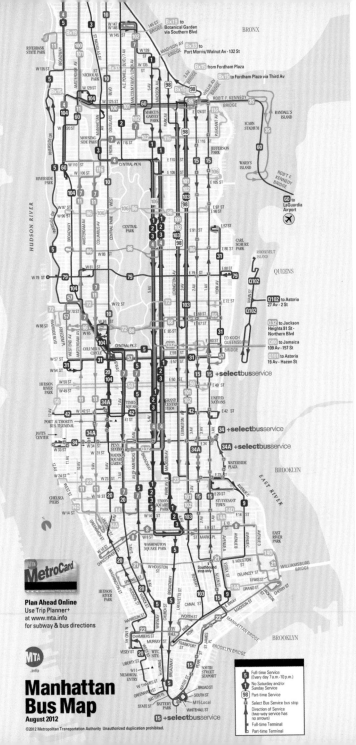

Manhattan Bus Map

August 2012

©2012 Metropolitan Transportation Authority Unauthorized duplication prohibited.

MetroCard

Plan Ahead Online
Use Trip Planner+
at www.mta.info
for subway & bus directions

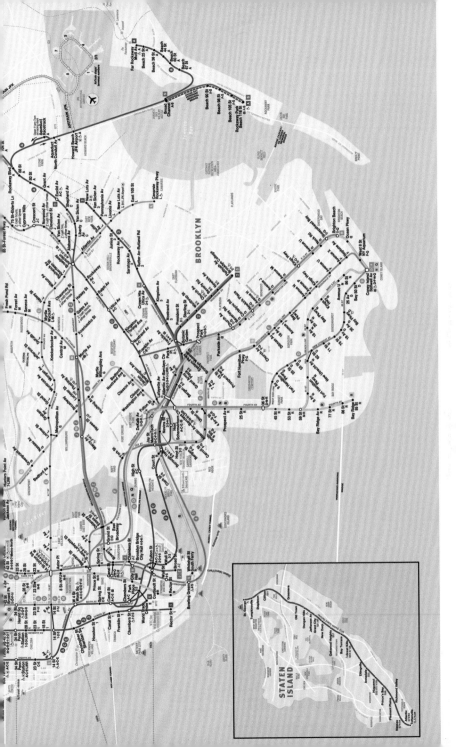

Manhattan
Subway Map

August 2012

©2012 Metropolitan Transportation Authority. Unauthorized duplication prohibited.